MORE THAN MERE SPECTACLE

Austrian and Habsburg Studies

General Editor: Howard Louthan, Center for Austrian Studies, University of Minnesota

Before 1918, Austria and the Habsburg lands constituted an expansive multinational and multiethnic empire, the second largest state in Europe and a key site for cultural and intellectual developments across the continent. At the turn of the twentieth century, the region gave birth to modern psychology, philosophy, economics, and music, and since then has played an important mediating role between Western and Eastern Europe, today participating as a critical member of the European Union. The volumes in this series address specific themes and questions around the history, culture, politics, social, and economic experience of Austria, the Habsburg Empire, and its successor states in Central and Eastern Europe.

Recent volumes:

Volume 31
More Than Mere Spectacle: Coronations and Inaugurations in the Habsburg Monarchy during the Eighteenth and Nineteenth Centuries
Edited by Klaas Van Gelder

Volume 30
Estates and Constitution: The Parliament in Eighteenth-Century Hungary
István Szijártó

Volume 29
Antisemitism in Galicia: Agitation, Politics, and Violence against Jews in the Late Habsburg Monarchy
Tim Buchen

Volume 28
Revisiting Austria: Tourism, Space, and National Identity, 1945 to the Present
Gundolf Graml

Volume 27
Empty Signs, Historical Imaginaries: The Entangled Nationalization of Names and Naming in a Late Habsburg Borderland
Ágoston Berecz

Volume 26
Men under Fire: Motivation, Morale, and Masculinity among Czech Soldiers in the Great War, 1914–1918
Jiří Hutečka

Volume 25
Nationalism Revisited: Austrian Social Closure from Romanticism to the Digital Age
Christian Karner

Volume 24
Entangled Entertainers: Jews and Popular Culture in Fin-de-Siècle Vienna
Klaus Hödl

Volume 23
Comical Modernity: Popular Humour and the Transformation of Urban Space in Late Nineteenth-Century Vienna
Heidi Hakkarainen

Volume 22
Embers of Empire: Continuity and Rupture in the Habsburg Successor States after 1918
Edited by Paul Miller and Claire Morelon

For a full volume listing, please see the series page on our website: http://berghahnbooks.com/series/austrian-habsburg-studies.

MORE THAN MERE SPECTACLE

Coronations and Inaugurations
in the Habsburg Monarchy during
the Eighteenth and Nineteenth Centuries

Edited by Klaas Van Gelder

berghahn
NEW YORK • OXFORD
www.berghahnbooks.com

First published in 2021 by
Berghahn Books
www.berghahnbooks.com

© 2021, 2026 Klaas Van Gelder
First paperback edition published in 2026

Except for the quotation of short passages
for the purposes of criticism and review, no part of this book
may be reproduced in any form or by any means, electronic or
mechanical, including photocopying, recording, or any information
storage and retrieval system now known or to be invented,
without written permission of the publisher.

Library of Congress Cataloging-in-Publication Data

Names: Gelder, Klaas Van, editor.
Title: More than mere spectacle : coronations and inaugurations in the Habsburg monarchy during the eighteenth and nineteenth centuries / edited by Klaas Van Gelder.
Description: New York : Berghahn Books, 2020. | Series: Austrian and Habsburg studies ; volume 31 | Includes bibliographical references and index.
Identifiers: LCCN 2020017484 (print) | LCCN 2020017485 (ebook) | ISBN 9781789208771 (hardback) | ISBN 9781789208788 (ebook)
Subjects: LCSH: Coronations—Austria—History—18th century. | Coronations—Austria—History—19th century. | Habsburg, House of. | Austria—Kings and rulers. | Austria—History—1789–1900.
Classification: LCC DB36.1 .M59 2020 (print) | LCC DB36.1 (ebook) | DDC 943.6/032—dc23
LC record available at https://lccn.loc.gov/2020017484
LC ebook record available at https://lccn.loc.gov/2020017485

British Library Cataloguing in Publication Data

A catalogue record for this book is available from the British Library

EU GPSR Authorized Representative

LOGOS EUROPE, 9 rue Nicolas Poussin, 17000, LA ROCHELLE, France
Email: Contact@logoseurope.eu

ISBN 978-1-78920-877-1 hardback
ISBN 978-1-83695-365-4 paperback
ISBN 978-1-83695-364-7 epub
ISBN 978-1-78920-878-8 web pdf

https://doi.org/10.3167/9781789208771

Contents

List of Illustrations		vii
Acknowledgments		ix
List of Abbreviations		x
Note on Place Names		xii
Introduction.	Eighteenth- and Nineteenth-Century Coronations and Inaugurations in the Habsburg Monarchy: Why Do They Matter? *Klaas Van Gelder*	1
Chapter 1.	The Care of Thrones: A Plethora of Investitures in the Habsburg Composite Monarchy and Beyond from the Sixteenth to the Eighteenth Century *Petr Maťa*	29
Chapter 2.	Meaningless Spectacles? Eighteenth-Century Imperial Coronations in the Holy Roman Empire Reconsidered *Harriet Rudolph*	67
Chapter 3.	The Hungarian Coronations of Charles VI and Leopold II and the Representation of Political Compromise *Fanni Hende*	99
Chapter 4.	Maria Theresa, the Habsburgs, and the Hungarian Coronations in the Light of the Coronation Medals, 1687–1741 *Werner Telesko*	119
Chapter 5.	The Bohemian Coronation of Charles VI and Its Hidden Message *Petra Vokáčová*	143

Chapter 6.	Inaugurations in the Austrian Netherlands: Flexible Formats at the Interface between Constitution, Political Negotiation, and Representation *Klaas Van Gelder*	168
Chapter 7.	Conditioning Sovereignty in the Austrian Netherlands: The Joyous Entry Charter and the Inauguration of Maria Theresa in Brabant *Thomas Cambrelin*	198
Chapter 8.	Shaping a New Habsburg Territory: The 1773 Lemberg Act of Homage and the Galician Polish Nobility *Miloš Řezník*	223
Chapter 9.	Pageantry in the Revolutionary Age: Inaugural Rites in the Habsburg Monarchy, 1790–1848 *William D. Godsey*	247
Chapter 10.	After 1848: The Heightened Constitutional Importance of the Habsburg Coronation in Hungary *Judit Beke-Martos*	283
Afterword.	The Last Habsburg Coronation and What It Means to Be Anointed *Helen Watanabe-O'Kelly*	303
Index		313

Illustrations

Figures

Figure 0.1. The Estates of Bohemia pledging obedience to Maria Theresa in Prague in 1743. Engraving by Johann Josef Dietzler and Michael Heinrich Rentz.   5

Figure 1.1. The key moment of the Lower Austrian homage ceremony in Vienna in 1705: the Lower Austrian Estates—prelates, nobles, and townsmen—gathered in the Hofburg to pledge fealty to Emperor Joseph I surrounded by the holders of the hereditary offices presenting the archducal hat and other regalia and symbols. Engraving embellishing the printed volume published by the Estates to commemorate Joseph I's inauguration.   31

Figure 1.2. Emperor Charles VI swearing to uphold the provincial laws, privileges, and habits before the committee of the Estates during his Styrian inauguration in Graz in 1728.   48

Figure 2.1. Copper engraving of the coronation of Emperor Leopold II in 1790.   72

Figure 2.2. Allegorical copper engraving for the coronation of Leopold II by J. C. Berndt.   80

Figure 3.1. King Leopold II swearing to uphold the rights and liberties of the Hungarian Estates during his coronation in Pressburg in 1790.   109

Figure 4.1. Coronation medal for the Bohemian coronation of Maria Theresa, created by Anton Franz Widemann, reverse, 1743.   123

Figure 4.2. Coronation coin for the Hungarian coronation of Maria Theresa, reverse, 1741.   125

Figure 4.3. Coronation medal for the Hungarian coronation of Maria Theresa created by Anton Franz Widemann, reverse, 1745.   125

Figure 4.4. Numismatic explanatory print by Johann Carl Edler Neuen von Neuenstein, 1741. 127

Figure 4.5. Coronation medal for the Hungarian coronation of Maria Theresa, created by Andreas Vestner of Nuremberg, reverse, 1745. 129

Figure 4.6. Coronation medal for the Hungarian coronation of Emperor Joseph I created by Georg Hautsch and Lazar Gottlieb Lauffer, reverse, 1687. 129

Figure 5.1. Silver commemorative medal for the Bohemian coronation of Charles VI and Elisabeth Christine and the founding millennium of Prague, designed by Carl Gustav Heraeus and created by Benedikt Richter and Daniel Warou, obverse and reverse, 1723. 153

Figure 5.2. Allegorical copper engraving for the Bohemian coronation of Charles VI and Elisabeth Christine by Conrad Adolph von Albrecht, 1723. 154

Figure 6.1. Stage on the Friday Market in Ghent for the inauguration of Joseph II as count of Flanders, 1781. Watercolor presumably by P. J. Goetghebuer based on a painting by Engelbert Lieven van Siclers. 170

Figure 9.1. Silver commemorative coin from the Lower Austrian act of homage of Leopold II, 1790. 256

Figure 9.2. Emperor Francis being hailed in Innsbruck by local people following the Tyrolian act of homage, 1816. Lithograph by Johann Nepomuk Hoechle, 1835. 264

Tables

Table 6.1. List of inaugurations in the Austrian Netherlands. 182

Table 6.2. Printed inauguration books in the Austrian Netherlands. 185

Table 9.1. Inaugural rites personally undergone by Habsburg rulers or their consorts, 1790–1848. 249

Acknowledgments

This themed volume is the result of several brainstorming sessions, searches in libraries and archives all over Europe, analyses of newly discovered data, and reconsiderations of well-known facts. Some of the contributors to this volume participated in a panel dedicated to eighteenth-century inaugurations and coronations at the Fourteenth International Congress for Eighteenth-Century Studies (ISECS) in Rotterdam in July 2015, as well as at a conference with the same topic held at Ghent University in September 2016. Both expert gatherings led to lively discussions on the changing meanings of such inaugural rites and the conviction that these oft-neglected ritual performances during the eighteenth and nineteenth centuries deserve more attention. Thus, the seeds of this volume were sown.

As the editor of this collection of essays, I was fortunate to be able to collaborate with very competent historians, art historians, and legal historians that helped to sharpen my own ideas over time. I thank all of them for their confidence, their efforts for this volume, and their reliability. William Godsey and Petr Maťa guided me through the editing process with practical help and suggestions concerning content and language. I am tremendously grateful for their invaluable advice and support. I am also most grateful to the three anonymous reviewers who gave valuable feedback on an earlier version of the volume. Thomas Winkelbauer and the *Institut für Österreichische Geschichtsforschung* at the University of Vienna provided the financial means to have the original manuscript proofread. Stephan Stockinger assumed the proofreading task and did so very skillfully. His approachability and flexibility helped to solve linguistic problems encountered along the way quickly and satisfactorily. All these persons and institutions were indispensable for the success of this undertaking, but, naturally, I am responsible for any remaining errors.

Klaas Van Gelder
Jette, 8 July 2020

ABBREVIATIONS

ACA	Archives et Centre Culturel d'Arenberg/Archief en Cultureel Centrum van Arenberg (Enghien/Edingen)
APH	Archiv Pražského hradu (Prague)
AR–AGR	Algemeen Rijksarchief/Archives générales du Royaume (Brussels)
ASMi	Archivio di Stato di Milano (Milan)
AVA	Allgemeines Verwaltungsarchiv (Vienna)
ÄZA	Ältere Zeremonialakten
Belgien–Depeschen	Belgien DD A—Kaiserliche Depeschen, rote Nummer
BNL	Bibliothèque nationale du Luxembourg/Nationalbibliothéik (Luxembourg)
ČDK	Česká dvorská kancelář
CIH	*Corpus Iuris Hungarici—Magyar Törvénytár 1000–1895*, ed. Dezső Márkus (Budapest, 1896–1901)
Corr. L. P.	Correspondence of Leopold Philip, Duke of Arenberg
DN/DPB	Departement van de Nederlanden van de Hof- en Staatskanselarij te Wenen/Département des Pays-Bas de la Chancellerie de la Cour et d'État à Vienne
fasc.	Fascicle(s)
FHKA	Finanz- und Hofkammerarchiv (Vienna)
fol.	Folio(s)
Fol. Lat.	Folium latinum

GR/CP	Geheime Raad—Oostenrijkse Periode/Conseil privé—Période autrichienne
HF/FH	Heraldisch Fonds/Fonds héraldique
HHStA	Haus-, Hof- und Staatsarchiv (Vienna)
LAA	Landschaftliches Archiv Antiquum
MIÖG	*Mitteilungen des Instituts für Österreichische Geschichtsforschung*
MNL OL	National Hungarian Archives (Budapest)
MÖStA	*Mitteilungen des Österreichischen Staatsarchivs*
NA	Národní archiv (Prague)
n.d.	no date
no(s)	Number(s)
NÖLA	Niederösterreichisches Landesarchiv (St. Pölten)
n.p.	no place/no publisher
NZA	Neuere Zeremonialakten
OKäA	Oberstkämmereramt
OMeA	Obersthofmeisteramt
ÖStA	Österreichisches Staatsarchiv (Vienna)
OSZKK	Országos Széchényi Könyvtár, Kézirattár (Budapest)
r	recto
SEG/SSO	Secrétairerie d'État et de Guerre/Secretarie van State en Oorlog
SLUB	Sächsische Landesbibliothek—Staats- und Universitätsbibliothek (Dresden)
SM	Stará manipulace
StAN	Staatsarchiv Nürnberg (Nuremberg)
StLA	Steiermärkisches Landesarchiv (Graz)
UB Gent	Universiteitsbibliotheek Gent/University Library Ghent
v	verso
ZA Prot	Zeremonialprotokolle

NOTE ON PLACE NAMES

The nomenclature of territories, cities, and towns in the multilingual Habsburg Monarchy is notoriously complex. In fact, this composite political entity ruled by the Austrian branch of the Habsburg dynasty did not even have a proper name in itself, but "Habsburg Monarchy" is the commonly used term denominating it. Many places had distinct names in the different regional languages—and linguistic frontiers shifted over time, sometimes resulting in new place names. The most famous example is Bratislava, today the capital of Slovakia with a primarily Slovak-speaking population. Prior to 1919, the majority of the city's inhabitants were German-speaking, and it was known as Pressburg (Preßburg); this is therefore also the name the authors of this volume have used. "Pozsony" was the Hungarian name for the city, while Slovaks called it "Prešporok." "Bratislava" became the official name only in 1919 in the wake of World War I and the independence of Czechoslovakia.

In order to solve these toponymic challenges and be consistent throughout the volume, the authors have applied a three-tier rule to the names of cities and towns. First, names with a common English equivalent are mentioned in English (i.e., we speak of Vienna, Prague, Brussels, and Milan). Second, if no common English name is available, names are given in their current official language if such usage is not anachronistic for the eighteenth and nineteenth centuries (e.g., readers will encounter Brno, Olomouc, Ljubljana, Székesfehérvár, and Dendermonde in this book). Third, if the current official name appears anachronistic, contemporary German names are used, such as Pressburg, Breslau (and not Wrocław) or Lemberg (instead of Lviv). Some debatable cases cannot be completely excluded, however. These rules only apply to the body of the chapters in this volume; in references in the endnotes and the bibliographies, the authors use English names when possible, and otherwise toponyms in the present-day official language.

Introduction

EIGHTEENTH- AND NINETEENTH-CENTURY CORONATIONS AND INAUGURATIONS IN THE HABSBURG MONARCHY
Why Do They Matter?

Klaas Van Gelder

Royal rites and ceremonies appeal very strongly to the imagination of people worldwide. Millions of tourists gaze at the St. Edward's Crown, the Imperial State Crown, and the other regalia in the London Tower each year. Many people know the scenes of Elizabeth II's coronation in 1953, which are frequently shown in the media. Documentary films such as *The Coronation* by BBC One, broadcast in May 2018 on the occasion of the sixty-fifth jubilee of the crowning and featuring the Queen reminiscing about her father's and her own coronation, only add to the appeal of these rare events. The same allure can be observed in the case of the imperial crowns in Vienna's *Schatzkammer* and the St. Stephen's Crown of Hungary in the parliament building in Budapest—the latter referred to as the embodiment of "the constitutional continuity of Hungary's statehood and the unity of the nation" in the country's "fundamental law" dating from 2011.[1]

Analogously to popular fascination, scholarly interest in rituals accompanying and substantiating the start of a new reign—and more generally in symbolic communication—has increased steadily over the past three to four decades. New insights into the significance of ritual and ceremony for power relations have induced new generations of historians and art historians to reconsider coronations and inaugurations. They have realized that these performances were not merely dazzling trivialities; they carried constitutional, political, and social meaning. In the premodern society, where power was effective only when it was visible, these inaugural rites helped to end the risky interregnum following the death of a ruler and stabilize the position of his or her successor. Edward Muir classifies coronations among those rites that enacted kingship as opposed to representing it. In his view, they were among the most important rites of passage—together with royal funerals—that made princely succession possible. Nevertheless, Muir also indicates that coronations were part of a string of rituals during the interregnum period, such as joyous entries, the dressing of the new prince in regal attire, and anointing.[2] As we will see in the different chapters in this volume, this ritual complex actually fused rites of enactment and representation. In the modern era, coronations then acquired new functions like uniting the nation around its dynasty or sanctioning the transition toward parliamentary monarchy.

Despite the recent upsurge in historical interest, significant gaps remain. This holds true first and foremost from a geographical perspective. Long-term analyses examining the actual meaning of specific early modern and modern coronations and the transformations they underwent have appeared for several countries. Richard Jackson was a pioneer with his monograph on the French coronations from Charles V to Charles X.[3] Equally ambitious are Roy Strong's magnificently illustrated book on English coronations[4] and Richard Wortman's analysis of Russian royal ritual and ceremony from Peter the Great to Nicholas II, including the czarist coronations.[5] A research project on the Hungarian coronations under supervision of Géza Pálffy has been running at the Hungarian Academy of Sciences since 2012.[6] When we look at inaugurations, casuistic inquiries are the norm, though exceptions exist for the German and Swiss area and the Burgundian and Spanish Habsburg Netherlands.[7] Nevertheless, historians seem to have largely neglected most of the lands of the sprawling Habsburg Monarchy,[8] an entity that during the eighteenth and nineteenth centuries at least temporarily covered all or almost all of present-day Austria, Hungary, the Czech Republic, Slovakia, Slovenia, Croatia, Belgium, and Luxembourg, as well as significant parts of Germany, Romania, Ukraine, Serbia, Italy, and Poland, and even parts of the Netherlands and Switzerland.[9] This neglect is all the more regrettable because the rulers of this composite monarchy—more than any other princes—participated in countless inaugural rites personally or through representatives; a rough estimation yields some one hundred of them between 1700 and 1848.[10]

Historical interest has been unevenly divided not just geographically but also chronologically. Even a superficial glance at the existing body of literature on princely investitures shows a bias toward the Late Middle Ages and the first half of the early modern period, roughly spanning the mid-fifteenth to the mid-seventeenth century. Several works that do examine a longer time frame end with the turn to the eighteenth century, despite evident continuities beyond it.[11] The rare long-term analyses covering the eighteenth and nineteenth centuries, such as Matthias Schwengelbeck's book on inaugurations in Germany, confirm this impression.[12]

This book therefore proposes to bring to the fore both the eighteenth and nineteenth centuries and the Habsburg realm. It argues firstly that the countless inaugurations and coronations constituted and remained an integral part of the Habsburg conception of rule until the dissolution of the Estates in 1848, and to a lesser degree even beyond. It was precisely the existence of these Estates and their vital role in the state apparatus that necessitated special rites of investiture establishing mutual rights and duties between the Estates and the prince and warranting the continuation of their collaboration. These rites both mirrored ("represented") and helped perpetuate ("enacted") the composite character of the monarchy and the contractual nature of its administration, as Petr Maťa explains in the first chapter of this volume. He presents a broad chronological overview that includes the entire early modern period and supplies the background for the ensuing chapters dealing with one or more specific eighteenth- and nineteenth-century inaugurations or coronations. Maťa demonstrates the uniqueness of the unparalleled number of enthronements that the Austrian Habsburgs participated in. The only other monarchy coming close to their prolificacy was Spain, though the number of inaugural rites on the Iberian Peninsula did not match that in which the Central European Habsburgs were involved. Of course, numbers do not explain everything. The significance of individual investitures could change over time and differed from one territory to another. Moreover, the exact time at which an inauguration or coronation took place is often very telling. They could occur quickly after a new ruler assumed power, or at a later stage when he or she needed support from the Estates or local administrations for specific policies.

Secondly, this volume asserts that inaugural rites in the Habsburg Monarchy more often than not retained their constitutional, political, and social significance and did not degenerate into mere spectacles glorifying new princes. In the late twentieth century, several historians took such a putative loss of meaning for granted,[13] whereas twenty-first-century scholarship usually emphasizes the continued relevance of rites and ceremonies in the eighteenth and nineteenth centuries. What the chapters in this volume aim to highlight, however, is what specific roles coronations and inaugurations played in the different lands of the Habsburg Monarchy.

It cannot be denied that starting with Leopold I, the Habsburgs interrupted the tradition of some inaugurations—and even some coronations, most notably under Joseph II. This demonstrates that by the late seventeenth century, Habsburg rule was sufficiently strong and considered legitimate enough that neglecting some investitures no longer posed any problems. It is almost certainly no coincidence that this happened primarily in some of the central territories of the monarchy such as Moravia, Styria, and Upper Austria—and not in Hungary, where royal power was less secure, or in the faraway Netherlands with their self-confident and financially very potent Estates. However, the fact that the Habsburgs retained many rites of investiture is telling as well, for it proves that these events held advantages for both the ruler and the representative bodies of specific territories. Even Joseph II's refusal to participate in many investiture rituals shows how important they still were—he avoided them precisely because he understood their binding character very well. Even if his successors Leopold II and Francis II had wished to do so, they could not have followed in his footsteps. Joseph's policies had caused so much discontent that organizing the contractual rites of investiture became an essential element of his successors' appeasement policy, as I argue in my chapter on the Austrian Netherlands. Just as revealing is the fact that in 1790, Tyrol hosted an inauguration for the first time since 1711.

Foregoing such rites once, therefore, did not necessarily mean eliminating them forever. The political turmoil in the late eighteenth century—the French Revolution and the Napoleonic Wars in the first place, but also political and social unrest in various Habsburg lands—even led to a genuine revival of coronations and inaugurations attended by members of the House of Austria, as William D. Godsey argues in Chapter 9. This revival included performing rites that had existed for many generations, but also staging redesigned versions of previously abandoned rites such as the Lombardo-Venetian coronation in 1838. Moreover, the meaning of these rites changed considerably in the early nineteenth century. A rather different affair was the puzzling Galician inauguration of 1772, which had no precursor whatsoever: it was an invention necessary to integrate a newly acquired territory into the Austrian state system, as Miloš Řezník's contribution demonstrates. The continued organization of coronations and inaugurations implies that they were not meaningless for contemporaries. Rather, their survival suggests that centuries-old ritual could successfully be adapted to new political circumstances, as all authors in this volume agree.

Before turning to the reasons for the aforementioned historiographical neglect and some considerations as to why these rites should be taken seriously, it seems requisite to briefly explain what the authors in this volume mean when they write about "coronations" and "inaugurations" (also called "acts of homage" or "acclamations"; German: *Huldigungen*). Both types of inaugural or investiture rites were functional equivalents that ritually enacted the assumption of power by a new ruler. Coronations implied a royal or imperial title and usually also the anointing of the protagonist and the placement of a crown on the head, all of which were mostly absent in the case of inaugurations. In Bohemia, acts of homage had been part of the coronation festivities since 1627 (see figure 0.1). This meant that the Bohemian coronation also involved a contractual aspect, for a key element of many late medieval and early modern homages was an exchange of oaths between the new ruler and his or her subjects—oaths to protect the country's privileges and liberties versus oaths of allegiance to the new prince.

Figure 0.1. The Estates of Bohemia pledging obedience to Maria Theresa in Prague in 1743. Engraving by Johann Josef Dietzler and Michael Heinrich Rentz (Vienna, Österreichische Nationalbibliothek, Bildarchiv und Graphiksammlung, 107199 C).

It is hazardous to assess coronations as more important than inaugurations by definition. For sure, in the hierarchy of titles, the Roman emperor ranked highest on the European continent, followed by kings.[14] The imperial coronation was even more important politically due to the fact that the Empire was an elective monarchy. Nevertheless, as has been mentioned before, Habsburg coronations sometimes implied an accompanying inauguration, like in Bohemia. The inauguration guaranteed the contractual bond between ruler and subjects. In many territories, inaugurations were independent events—and in those cases, the rulers did not necessarily deem them inferior or less important. One specific inauguration should be counted among the investitures standing out for their importance: the inauguration in Lower Austria, the archduchy surrounding Vienna. As William D. Godsey argued in a 2005 essay, it was—together with the Hungarian coronation—the only investiture that always took place after 1700 with the exception of Joseph II. Moreover, from 1700 onward it was the first investiture any new Habsburg ruler underwent, and it took place in Vienna, the capital of the Habsburg Monarchy since the early seventeenth century. It was therefore the only enthronement directly linked to their accession. Together with the coronations in Hungary and Bohemia, these Lower Austrian acts of homage served as stabilizing events for the new Habsburg ruler and were consequently upgraded during the eighteenth and nineteenth centuries. Due to the gradual abolishment of ever more investitures in the other Austrian territories, such as Styria, Carinthia, or Upper Austria, the inauguration in Vienna even acquired supraregional significance.[15]

The terms "coronation" and "inauguration" both commonly refer to a series of rites that together lifted the new ruler to full power. A wide range of regional variations existed, but some components are almost always encountered: a ceremonial entrance into the city, artillery salvos and bell ringing, high masses and *Te Deums*, and the handing over of the regalia. Consecrations—the most famous being the French *sacre* or anointing with holy oil that gave the French kings thaumaturgic power—also constituted key elements of various European coronations since the Middle Ages.[16] They granted the prince a quasi-sacred aura. Pivotal for the Habsburgs in this context were the consecrations of the emperor and the king of Hungary. Celebrations involving all groups of society followed the official parts of the enthronements and comprised wine fountains, fireworks, illuminations, the throwing of coins and medals to the crowds, and of course banquets, balls, concerts, and theater.

After 1700, the members of the House of Austria, residing in Vienna and ruling a gamut of lands with different constitutions and dissimilar relations to the center of power, apparently still deemed it appropriate or even important to organize inaugural rites or participate in them. How can we relate this to the remarkable neglect of eighteenth- and nineteenth-century coronations and inaugurations in historiography? To a considerable degree, sneering contemporary observations may have accounted for later misinterpretation. See, for example, the scathing assessment by Frederick II of the 1701 coronation of his grandfather, who crowned himself Frederick I, king in Prussia:

> He [Frederick I] mistook vanities for true greatness. He was more concerned with appearances than with useful things that are soundly made. He sacrificed thirty thousand subjects in different wars of the emperor and allies in order to provide himself with the royal crown. He only desired the crown so fervently because he needed a superficial pretext to justify his weakness for ceremony and his wasteful extravagance.[17]

Even though Frederick II modified his judgment by acknowledging the importance of the royal dignity for the Prussian state in the long run, the tone was set. Similarly disdainful statements were made by others elsewhere as well. In 1758, the cameralist thinker and lawyer Johann Heinrich Gottlob von Justi called coronations and inaugurations *"bloß äußerliche Ceremonien"* ("mere outward ceremonies"). In his opinion, they had been invented to underline the subjects' obligation of loyalty toward their rulers, but were dispensable for the establishment of the new reign.[18] In 1774, the philosopher Marquis of Condorcet wrote to the equally skeptical French controller-general of finances, Anne Robert Jacques Turgot:

[It would be timely] to destroy the prejudice which fixes the destiny of the fate of the city of Reims, ensures that an oil considered to work miracles (according to a fable rejected by every critic) is used there, adds to the false opinion of a virtue no less fabulous, and could also contribute to the impression that this ceremony, which adds nothing to the rights of the monarch, is necessary.[19]

This quotation illustrates the raging debate about the miraculous powers of the French kings as a result of their anointing, the aforementioned *sacre*—miraculous powers that were used to heal those suffering from scrofula by royal touch and became the target of increasing ridicule during the eighteenth century. Voltaire bluntly stated that he lost his belief in these royal healing powers on learning that one of the sun king's mistresses had died of scrofula despite having been copiously touched by the king.[20] Perhaps the best embodiment of the growing tendency toward contempt for ritual and ceremony was Emperor Joseph II, who was notorious for his aversion for ceremony. He dropped the traditional court dress and reduced the amount of everyday ceremony at court;[21] and after being crowned king of the Romans in Frankfurt in 1764, he never participated in another coronation or inauguration. To be sure, such repudiation of ritual had already occurred before: as early as the sixteenth century, Erasmus of Rotterdam and Thomas Cranmer expressed doubts concerning the efficacy of the coronation ritual and the healing powers bestowed upon kings by anointing with holy oil. Ritual-opposing stances seem to have become much more common in the eighteenth century, however.[22]

These and other observations led historians to believe that coronations and inaugurations in the eighteenth century developed into hollow pageantry—if they were not abolished altogether. These statements, however, are in sharp contrast to the efforts and amounts of money dedicated to these investitures. In fact, huge sums were invested into dozens of coronations and inaugurations held throughout eighteenth- and nineteenth-century Europe. One account of the aforementioned Prussian coronation in 1701 states that thirty thousand horses were needed to transport the king, his family, and his entire court from Berlin to Königsberg and back. The retinue of Frederick I and his wife Sophia Charlotte of Hanover alone required three hundred carriages and carts, and the crown for the queen cost three hundred thousand *Taler*. Estimations of the total cost of all ceremonies and festivities surrounding the coronation amount to six million *Taler*—twice the annual revenues of the Hohenzollern administration.[23] The *sacre* of Louis XVI in Reims in 1774 was less extravagant, with a cost ceiling of nine hundred thousand *livres*. Rumor had it, however, that the actual costs ran as high as a stunning seven million *livres*, which contributed to discrediting the monarchy given the financial instability and staggering debt of the French state.[24] The cost of the five months' progress and coronation of Charles VI in Bohemia in 1723 amounted to slightly more than one million Rhenish guilders. After subtracting the usual costs and salaries of the court, a little more than 625,000 guilders remain as extraordinary costs for the coronation. Contemporaries apparently considered this sum reasonable.[25] Entirely different were the British reactions to the extravagance of George IV's coronation in 1821. The king wished to outdo the magnificence of Napoleon's coronation in 1804, and expenditure rose as high as £238,000. His predecessor George III had even ordered diamonds worth £375,000 to refurbish the St. Edward's Crown.[26] Russian coronations in the nineteenth century were equally expensive, and a single number shall suffice to evoke the gigantic scale of these celebrations: for the coronation of Czar Alexander III in 1883, a feast for four hundred thousand people was prepared. It is presumed, however, that six hundred thousand ultimately attended. Unfortunately, Richard Wortman provides no information on the expenses for the coronation festivities.[27]

If nothing else, these figures prove that many eighteenth- and nineteenth-century princes and their entourage, but also the host cities and the Estates, did not deem such high costs superfluous. Moreover, despite his fierce criticism of his grandfather's spending on ritual, Frederick II of Prussia exploited the benefits of inaugural rites himself, albeit in a less exorbitant fashion. After his assumption of power, he gave orders for more than ten inaugurations in the various territories of his composite monarchy, since he was aware of their legal importance. He personally assisted in Königsberg and Berlin, although—just like his father—he refused to be crowned.[28] Having seized Silesia in 1741, he participated in a series of inaugurations in the Silesian territories between July 1741 and March 1743, thereby acknowledging their value for consolidating his takeover of these regions.[29] This confirms the above observation of increasing doubts as to the supernatural powers coronations bestowed upon the crowned heads, but also that even the most enlightened rulers acknowledged the value of acts of homage for lending legitimacy to their rule and establishing legal bonds with their subjects. In short, there were good reasons to invest a good deal of time and money into coronations and inaugurations even after 1700.

As has been mentioned before, older literature advanced the thesis that in the eighteenth century, inaugural rites turned into pure spectacle in exaltation of princely glory. In part, of course, this notion holds true, for coronations and inaugurations *did* serve the purposes of propaganda, princely representation, and the glorification of rulers to different degrees. Christopher Clark emphasizes the instrumentality of the Prussian coronation of 1701, aimed at inculcating the new royal status on the spectators and the readers of the pamphlets and propagandistic reports printed for the occasion. Frederick and his entourage assembled the self-coronation from ceremonial concepts borrowed from across Europe. Political meaning permeated the highly artificial amalgam they created. For example, it broadcast the independence of the king from the Estates with respect to his coronation and the self-made character of his royal status. Clark calls the 1701 coronation an assembly of traditions from elsewhere rather than an invention of tradition.[30] The situation was different in Milan in 1805, however, when Napoleon was crowned king of Italy. This remarkably complex ritual sought to accommodate Italian history and French empire, stressing partnership with the Italian elites and aimed at establishing affinities with and within that group.[31]

The Habsburgs were no exception to the general rule, attempting to instrumentalize their coronations and inaugurations as much as their fellow rulers did. Seventeenth- and eighteenth-century *Zeremonialwissenschaft* (ceremonial science) stressed the didactic-educational function of baroque ceremonies for commoners, thereby underscoring the instrumentalist approach to the enthronement ritual.[32] This applies very well to Petra Vokáčová's chapter on Charles VI's Bohemian coronation in 1723. A leitmotiv in the staging of the emblems, panegyric, and rhetoric surrounding Charles's crowning seems to have been the message of the unbreakable bond between the hereditary Kingdom of Bohemia and the Habsburg dynasty. This was the immediate response to Saxon and Bavarian claims to parts of Charles's heritage. In the same vein, the coronation medals for Maria Theresa in Hungary visualized historical continuity, as Werner Telesko argues in Chapter 4. The medals also emphasized the importance of the Kingdom of Hungary for the young ruler facing invasions by an international coalition including Prussia and Bavaria. Adam Wandruszka previously pointed out the cleverness of Leopold II on the occasion of his election as king of the Romans and his coronation as emperor in 1790: due to the mistrust raised by Joseph II's radical policies, Leopold acted carefully. He was a champion of less costly ritual, yet he understood and skillfully used its power to engender trust in the Holy Roman Empire. Among other things, he participated in popular feasts, which gave him a flair of naturalness.[33] In Chapter 2 on the imperial coronations, Harriet Rudolph confirms the importance of Leopold's approachability, which formed part of a new style of government in which the crowning developed into a protonational constitutional celebration. Ritual thus was and remained a means of self-stylizing and propaganda.

Nevertheless, propaganda is only one part of the story and threatens to conceal the many actors that participated in the feverish organization and performance of many Habsburg public spectacles. Indeed, recent historiography on dynastic ritual tends to drift away from long-established top-down approaches and examines the agency of the wide range of co-organizers. These include princely commissioners, the Estates of the different regions, the magistrates of the host cities, urban militias, princely soldiers, the secular and regular clergy, confraternities, craftsmen, artists, and so on. Their interest in collaborating relates to the fact that early modern Europe was still largely a society of princes lacking written constitutions in the modern sense. The death of a prince and the subsequent assumption of power by his or her successor remained critical moments. In these transition phases, the aforementioned actors therefore communicated, negotiated, and compromised or clashed with regard to the nature of princely power and its range of action. Enthronements thus offered opportunities for (privileged) subjects as well: they could display their own traditions, stress their free consent to being ruled by the new prince, and visibly act as stakeholders in the monarchical enterprise. The prince in turn had to recognize certain rights and privileges. The cultural approach to politics goes one step further yet, emphasizing the aspect of communication and thus including not only the co-organizers but also all participants in the ceremonies, even the onlookers, as relevant actors. By participating or attending, they implicitly accepted the new ruler.

The extent to which groups of subjects had a say in the organization varied considerably from one region to another. The court in Vienna arranged some coronations and inaugurations on a top-down basis, while others included lengthy negotiations with the Estates and depended on the latter's goodwill and Vienna's willingness to accommodate. The preparations for Charles VI's Bohemian coronation in 1723 exemplify the first pattern, as Petra Vokáčová documents in Chapter 5. It may have been one of the most magnificent coronations in eighteenth-century Europe, but the Bohemian Estates could only marginally influence its design, let alone wrest additional guarantees to safeguard their constitution from the central government. The opposite was true for the Austrian Netherlands: in these regions, the Estates swore the oath of homage after lengthy negotiations, as the chapters by Klaas Van Gelder and Thomas Cambrelin show. The Estates did not hesitate to exact concessions by refusing taxes and postponing the inaugurations, or at least threatening to do so. By employing both tactics, the Estates of Flanders and Brabant even succeeded in extorting an imperial promise to renegotiate the Barrier Treaty of 1715 with Great Britain and the Dutch Republic as a precondition for their oath of homage to Charles VI.[34]

The Austrian lands seem to have taken a middle ground. In 1728, at the last Carinthian *Huldigung*, the Estates negotiated with the imperial entourage only after the emperor had already arrived in Klagenfurt. This considerably curtailed their bargaining position. The main points on the agenda concerned ceremonial issues and the exact procedure of the inauguration.[35] The fate of the Lower Austrian Estates seems not to have been structurally different, although perhaps they had a bit more room for maneuver. In the weeks and months preceding the act of homage in Lower Austria, meetings took place with delegates from both sides to discuss ritual and legal matters connected to the accession and the investiture. Until the end of the eighteenth century at least, the Lower Austrian inauguration provided the opportunity to hand in petitions (*gravamina*) to the new archduke. A clear solution for the problems mentioned in these petitions rarely followed quickly, but William D. Godsey nevertheless relates them to the positioning of the Estates vis-à-vis the new prince. In his view, the inauguration first and foremost expressed the search for a consensus between the ruler and the Estates and their will to collaborate and tackle the task of government jointly.[36] Still, these negotiations can hardly be compared to the long bargaining processes in the Netherlands. The same holds true for the Hungarian Estates, as Chapter 3 by

Fanni Hende shows. With the coronations in 1712 and 1790 following substantial internal turmoil, the Viennese courts of Charles VI and his grandson Leopold II managed to impose versions of the *diploma inaugurale* on the Hungarians that were beneficial to the dynasty, even though they compromised on other points so as not to offend the Hungarian Diet too strongly. The critical point seems to have been whether or not the organization of the inaugural rites and bargaining over taxes were intertwined. Where this was the case, as in the Netherlands, the Estates were in a much more powerful position to impose their will.

The fact that most inaugural rites included reciprocal oaths shows that they remained very meaningful in a constitutional sense, albeit to a different extent in the various lands of the monarchy. The term "constitution" obtained its current meaning—a written basic law containing the rules of the government and outlining the government's relationship with the citizens within a particular state—only during the second half of the eighteenth century. Previously, constitutions consisted of an amalgam of privileges, laws, and traditions, partly passed down orally through the ages and partly written down. This compound helped create political unity and social order and was confirmed during the inaugural rites, whose markedly festive character evoked and renewed the social and legal order and made it tangible.[37] The relationship between the ruler and his or her subjects was therefore central to these ritual acts: it all came down to finding (or restoring) and expressing (a fiction of) consensus between the constituents of the body politic—dissent was omnipresent but could be integrated ritually into the celebration.[38] Andreas Gestrich thus refers to acts of homage as "reciprocal communicative acts."[39] And even if the reciprocal character was stronger in some regions than in others—depending on the unique constitutional features of each region and of political events that had altered its relationship with Vienna—reciprocity remained a key feature of almost all Habsburg inaugural rites. The coronations and inaugurations discussed in this volume demonstrate the contractual and consensual nature of Habsburg rule as well as the engagement of many interacting groups in the Habsburg project, evidenced not least in the fact that the members of the House of Austria never resorted to self-coronation.[40] The few exceptions to the rule of reciprocity—the so-called Retroceded Lands surrounding Ieper and Veurne in the Austrian Netherlands, the Military Frontier securing Habsburg's borders with the Ottoman Empire, perhaps also Galicia—do not contradict the general trend.

It was not only the outcome of the interactions between the involved stakeholders that was important, however. These interactions usually took place within well-established political, administrative, and symbolic-ritual frameworks; and in doing so, they helped to stabilize the body politic. But communication did not occur exclusively between the prince and his or her government apparatus on the one hand and the subjects and their representatives on the other. Rather, the organization of inaugural rites vibrated a web of material and nonmaterial interests, goals, and tactics between many groups of actors who interacted partly in competition, partly in co-operation with each other. For the Estates and host cities, enthronements offered the opportunity to bargain and obtain royal confirmation of age-old as well as recent (and even of completely new) privileges. Moreover, coronations and inaugurations underlined their privileged position in the state machinery or their ascendency over rivals. The Holy Roman Empire and the imperial coronations illustrate this perfectly. Contrary to many other polities, the empire had no undisputed capital, and many cities, including Aachen, Frankfurt, Vienna, Nuremberg, and Regensburg, played a role in its constitution and administration. In 1759, Aachen brought before the Aulic Council (*Reichshofrat*) its petition for the return of the imperial insignia it had lost to Nuremberg in the first quarter of the fifteenth century, but was unsuccessful. By the sixteenth century, Aachen had also definitively lost its status as coronation city to Frankfurt, but its status as coronation site—a privilege contained in the Golden Bull of 1356—continued to be confirmed time and again until the end of the eighteenth century.[41] A similar dispute and ceremonial solution existed in the Duchy of Brabant between the original capital city of Leuven and the later capital, Brussels.

Not only cities bickered over privileges. In neighboring Flanders, where the nobility had no separate seat in the Estates' assembly, the nobles made sure to be well represented during each inauguration, which was practically the only event allowing them to present themselves as a corporate group.[42] During the Bohemian coronations of 1791 and 1792, Prince Lobkowitz and Prince Schwarzenberg respectively asserted claims of precedence for themselves or their equipage.[43] In the mid-seventeenth century, a dispute arose between the archbishops of Mainz and Cologne as to which prelate had the right to crown the newly elected emperor. By means of compromise, they arranged to alternate in those coronations that took place outside their respective dioceses. The subsequent *Wahlkapitulationen* even mentioned this agreement, which seems to have been respected until the end of the Holy Roman Empire.[44] What all these examples show is that the symbolic stakes were high, that quarrels were frequent, and that solutions could be of a ceremonial as well as a material nature.

Enthronements thus offered a stage for corporations and individual participants to display their rank in society. Over the past two decades, a new generation of historians, with Barbara Stollberg-Rilinger as one of its pioneers, has stressed that premodern political actions were always symbolic in nature. This applies not only to performative public rites and ceremonies, however, as had long been assumed—symbolic actions also shaped the gatherings and discussions that nineteenth- and twentieth-century historians considered to be solely for the purpose of policy-making, such as diets, Estates' assemblies, and council meetings. To sit or not to sit, to sit or stand closer to the ruler, to sit or stand at his or her right or left side, to sit on an individual chair—with or without cushion and/or armrests—or simply on a bench were meaningful indicators of social status.

Simultaneously, these indicators helped establish and circumscribe status. And in the same manner, the spot occupied in a procession or during an inauguration or coronation, as well as the acts one was entitled to perform and the dress one was allowed to wear at these occasions, were by no means trivial. During the early modern period, the significance of hierarchy, rank, and precedence increased due to the growing amount of handwritten and printed documents communicating order of rank to an audience—contemporary and future—much larger than the number of actual spectators at a given event. This increased the pressure to claim positions, as even the slightest omission could become a precedent for the disadvantage of later generations. Every seat or spot in a public ritual had legal and social relevance. Or, in the terminology of David M. Luebke, public spectacles such as coronations and inaugurations were a unique opportunity to "theatricalize social order."[45] Thanks to the ever more widespread coverage of public celebrations in prints and newspapers, this remained true—and possibly even became more compelling—in the eighteenth and nineteenth centuries. Several authors in this book refer to this reality, including Fanni Hende, who describes the change in precedence at the Hungarian coronation banquet after Archduke Leopold Alexander was elected as the new palatine in 1790 (Chapter 3), and Klaas Van Gelder, who mentions the discussion on the numbers of delegates in the Flemish inaugurations (Chapter 6).

The importance of the medial outreach of public ceremonies thus increased. Printed and often illustrated official and unofficial coronation or inauguration books, commemorative medals, engravings, newspapers, and panegyric leaflets spread the news of the celebrations and the multitude of messages of the ritual gestures, decorations, and musical-theatrical performances. As a result, the total audience was much larger than the group of immediate participants and onlookers, allowing inaugural rites to achieve international resonance.[46] Of course, many sources (most of them written on behalf of the organizers) must be evaluated critically, since they invariably stress the magnitude of the attending crowd to lend increased legitimacy to the respective act. Numerous thanksgivings, artillery salvos, *Te Deums*, and sermons across the respective country similarly served as multipliers.[47] Furthermore, the progress of the new ruler and his or her court to the site of the investiture and back home often became a triumphal and celebratory journey, an extension of the act of enthronement itself. This was not unimportant for the Habsburgs in particular, who had to travel large distances to the many capital cities in their multiterritorial monarchy.[48]

Given the large number of bystanders that the enthronements attracted and the growing circle of inhabitants and foreigners eager to learn more about them, commercial incentives played an increasing role for certain actors participating in or observing them as well. Grandiose public celebrations, which the coronations and inaugurations as well as liturgical processions, jubilees and commemorations, solemn entries of prelates and governors, and celebrations of peace treaties or royal marriages and births doubtlessly were, attracted thousands of spectators to the hosting city. In the course of the eighteenth century, a genuine form of tourism developed around these celebrations—a process that was both demand- and supply-driven. Precise and reliable numbers of spectators are rare. Nevertheless, given the enormous publicity that many host cities generated for upcoming investitures in the eighteenth and early nineteenth century, it is safe to assume that these events were well-attended and lucrative. Estimations of the crowd at Leopold II's coronation in Frankfurt in 1790 run as high as eighty thousand.[49] The people's celebrations (*Volksfeste*) at Francis II's and Ferdinand I's Bohemian coronations in 1792 and 1836 are said to have attracted forty and sixty thousand spectators respectively.[50] At the same time, printed souvenirs ranging from cheap leaflets to luxuriously bound treatises and festival books flooded the market, as Harriet Rudolph exemplifies for Leopold's imperial coronation (Chapter 2). The agency of the ruler in this development was limited, while the agency of commercial actors not associated with the official organizers became ever more real.[51]

Besides being—or rather remaining—a vehicle for propaganda, a focal point of political bargaining processes at different levels, and a means of visualizing order of rank, investiture ritual also reflected political developments and transformations in society. There was, in the words of David Cannadine, a "dynamic dialogue between ritual and society."[52] In the early eighteenth century, baroque princely representation of monarchical authority was an essential attribute of Austrian rule and underlined the *Gottesgnadentum*—the divinely mandated character of kings—of the Habsburg dynasty. The display of pompous ritual and visual arts laden with historical, mythological, and antique allegories reached its climax in what has been called the *Kaiserstil* displayed during the reign of Charles VI.[53] The sophisticated iconographic messages sent out during Charles's Bohemian coronation in 1723 (chapter by Petra Vokáčová) or the coronation medals for Maria Theresa in the 1740s (chapter by Werner Telesko) illustrate the many overlapping layers of meaning that allowed for different readings. Nevertheless, a public sphere emerged and matured alongside court culture in eighteenth-century Europe, and this public gradually supplanted the courts as the driving force of European culture. Essential characteristics of the public sphere were the exchange of information, ideas, and criticism through newspapers, novels, public concerts, art exhibitions, coffee houses, and public libraries.[54] At the same time, supported by cameralist and Enlightenment thinkers, the concepts of the social contract and popular sovereignty gained increasing influence, and the notion of "the state" or even "the nation" came to replace "the prince" as the sole source of law and legitimate power within a specific territorial circumscription. As the eighteenth century drew to a close, princes were primarily regarded as servants of the state— and in several states, they had to integrate the rise of national identity into their own agenda and purpose.[55] This also influenced the function of coronations, as Harriet Rudolph and William D. Godsey explain in Chapters 2 and 9.[56]

Modern political ideas and social tensions shook the foundations of Europe during the last quarter of the eighteenth century. Revolutions in Britain's North American colonies, France, the Austrian Netherlands, the Prince-Bishopric of Liège, and elsewhere, spurred by an ever more lively, fearless, and less controllable public sphere, attacked the very idea of a God-given monarchy. They led to Europe's first modern constitutions, to territorial rearrangements, and to democratic experiments on a supralocal level. The Habsburg Monarchy was not untouched by these developments. Joseph II's anticeremonial stance and his far-reaching reforms, followed by the ensuing revolution in the Austrian Netherlands and the loss of these rich territories, struck the monarchy hard. But despite the revolutionary upheavals, Napoleon's military ventures across the continent, Francis II's assumption of the title of Austrian Emperor in 1804, and the dissolution of the Holy Roman Empire in 1806, the Habsburg Monarchy would retain its estates-based structure until 1848. With the exception of the last chapter on the Hungarian coronation of 1867, all authors in this volume deal with inaugural rites within this estates-based framework, which sets the discussed investitures apart from the coronations in France after 1789 or the inaugurations in the new parliamentary monarchies that came into being in the nineteenth century, such as the Netherlands and Belgium.

The question remains, however, how the aforementioned developments affected the different investitures in the Habsburg Monarchy. William D. Godsey provides a concise answer in his chapter using the example—among others—of Tyrol: this Alpine princely county obtained a constitutional patent in 1816 in the wake of the Napoleonic upheavals. Francis I's subsequent inauguration in May 1816 was the first Habsburg inaugural rite to take place within this new and henceforth no longer unwritten constitutional framework. The emperor did not swear an oath, and the celebration no longer enacted a constitution. Godsey calls this Tyrolean inauguration "the first thoroughly modern Habsburg inaugural ceremony."

Another new feature of several inaugural rites during the revolutionary era was the emphasis on national identity and patriotic pride. Hugh LeCaine Agnew masterfully demonstrates how both the Bohemian Estates and the Czech "awakeners," a group of intellectual patriots, used the Prague coronations in 1791, 1792, and 1836 to express Bohemia's unique status in the monarchy. They certainly had diverging interests and political goals, but the coronations served both groups of people who understood themselves as legitimate bearers of Czech identity in completely different ways. Elements that underlined that identity were the ritual use of the Czech language in greetings and welcome speeches during the coronation, and even more so in the preceding swearing of the oath of fealty, the appearance of the traditional officers of the Bohemian crown lands, the creation of new knights of the Order of St. Wenceslas, and perhaps most of all the display of the so-called St. Wenceslas's Crown that was returned from Vienna to Prague in 1791. Completely new forms of entertainment alongside the coronations highlighted the achievements and cultural heritage of the Kingdom of Bohemia, such as industrial exhibitions, sessions of the Royal Bohemian Society of Sciences, and people's celebrations in which peasants from all parts of the country participated in traditional costumes.[57] Similarly, Harriet Rudolph underlines in Chapter 2 that the festivities surrounding the last two imperial coronations featured nationalistic characteristics relating to Germany as an imagined nation. William D. Godsey also argues in Chapter 9 that several Habsburg inaugural rites after 1790 served to boost popular patriotic support beyond territorial identities, not least to support Austria's war efforts against Napoleonic France.

The argument that inaugural rites in the Habsburg Monarchy did not fall victim to modernity but instead adapted to changing circumstances in the revolutionary era is in line with findings for other monarchies. Matthias Schwengelbeck speaks of a "ceremonial renaissance" in the nineteenth century, which was a response to the growing pressure to legitimize monarchy in postrevolutionary Europe. The organizers of dynastic ritual still largely drew on traditional elements, but these often lost their legal and constitutional meanings. The turning point, according to Schwengelbeck, was the introduction of written constitutions, as a result of which inaugural acts as constitutions *in actu* became dispensable.[58] Focusing on several German states such as Prussia and Baden, he shows how the inaugural acts gradually developed into performances devoid of legal consequences. Investitures such as William I's coronation in Königsberg in 1861 no longer entailed a change of status. Nevertheless, they lent legitimacy to governments that were undergoing radical changes in the transition from estates-based to parliamentary monarchies. Newspapers played a major role in this process, which explains the heightened importance of censorship while at the same time exposing the dwindling chances to monopolize the readings of ritual performances.[59]

The transition Schwengelbeck perceives in nineteenth-century Germany can be observed in other monarchies as well, but it was by no means universal. The Kingdom of Hungary provides an interesting counterexample, as Judit Beke-Martos argues in the last chapter of this volume. Hungary lacked a proper written constitution until 1949, as a result of which the coronation with the St. Stephen's Crown did not lose its constitutional significance. Even though Francis Joseph was the actual reigning king of Hungary from 1848 onward, he was the *de jure* king only after his crowning in Buda and Pest in 1867. The act was necessary to bestow upon him the entirety of the royal authority and sovereignty. His coronation and the issuing of a *diploma inaugurale* were central parts of the Compromise that established the dual Austro-Hungarian Monarchy and put an end to almost two decades of constitutional crisis.[60]

In light of these observations, several concluding remarks can be made. Behind the seeming outward invariability of the main components of coronations and inaugurations, their format was easily adaptable to changes in society. They survived antiritualistic attacks—and contrary to previously held notions, these attacks may even emphasize their importance: Joseph II's decision to forego most inaugural rites signals his eagerness not to be bound by them. Investiture rites were reinterpreted during revolutionary turmoil, the rise of nationalist ideologies, and the promulgation of written constitutions. It is difficult to detect distinct ruptures in the eighteenth- and nineteenth-century Habsburg inaugural rites other than the end of the estates-based society in 1848.[61] Maurer's claim that the French Revolution constituted a clear break in the history of festivities in Europe cannot be applied to the coronations and inaugurations in the Habsburg Monarchy, as this volume clearly shows.[62] Enlightenment thinking obviously helped to sharpen criticism of ritual and desacralize monarchic rule, even in the Habsburg territories. But the inaugural rites performed by the House of Austria in the late eighteenth and nineteenth centuries nevertheless testify to the remaining validity of contractual rulership and the continued importance of the link between the dynasty and the Church. The historian can thus derive several benefits from the study of these coronations and inaugurations. On a general level, they are illustrative for the role and images of royalty in a modernizing society. They reveal changing political identities and shifting power relations between the dynasty and the privileged partners in the body politic. Specifically for the Habsburgs, they also clarify the extent to which contractual rule and the composite character of the monarchy remained essential features not only before 1848, but also thereafter—and this despite the connecting Austrian emperorship.

This volume has the ambition to give the neglected enthronement ritual in the eighteenth- and nineteenth-century Habsburg Monarchy the scholarly attention it deserves. However, in no way does it claim to be exhaustive. The essays in this book, as well as the Afterword by Helen Watanabe-O'Kelly, are new steps in shifting historical attention to coronations and inaugurations during the final decades of the early modern period and the turn to contemporary history. The attentive reader will notice that some important Habsburg lands have no separate chapter in this book, among them Upper and Lower Austria, the Inner Austrian lands, and the Italian possessions. Dozens of inaugural rites in territories such as Bukovina, Transylvania, and the *Innviertel* also need to be examined to obtain a full picture of the functionality and developments of Habsburg's investitures. Another item on the historical agenda should be the wider reception of these celebrations and the different meanings contemporaries ascribed to them. For this, scholars need to look beyond the official reports. What tensions did these performances hide, and how did different groups of spectators interpret them? Perhaps Edward Muir's contention that ritual was not primarily about transferring meaning, but about touching the emotions should be borne in mind when tackling these questions.[63] The authors in this volume formulate some initial answers in hopes that their contributions will incite new research into the splendid world of Habsburg's inaugural rites that, even after 1700, were much more than mere spectacle.

Klaas Van Gelder is a postdoctoral researcher at the State Archives in Ghent and at Ghent University, Belgium. Until August 2020, he was a postdoctoral fellow of the Research Foundation—Flanders (FWO). From November 2016 until October 2018, he was a Lise Meitner-Fellow of the Austrian *Wissenschaftsfonds* (FWF) at the *Institut für Österreichische Geschichtsforschung* (Institute for Austrian Historical Research) at the University of Vienna. His research interests include early modern political culture, elites and nobilities, the Habsburg Monarchy and its links to the Austrian Netherlands, and dynastic ritual and ceremony. He is the author of *Regime Change at a Distance: Austria and the Southern Netherlands Following the War of the Spanish Succession (1716–1725)* (Leuven, 2016) as well as articles in several peer-reviewed journals, including *Zeitschrift für historische Forschung, European Review of History/Revue européenne d'histoire, Revue d'Histoire moderne et contemporaine*, and *Tijdschrift voor Geschiedenis*.

Notes

I am deeply indebted to Ellinor Forster and Petr Maťa for their helpful suggestions and comments on the first version of this introductory chapter.

1. Ministry of Justice, Hungary. "The Fundamental Law of Hungary," accessed 26 October 2019, https://www.kormany.hu/download/f/3e/61000/TheFundamentalLawofHungary_20180629_FIN.pdf. I wish to thank Ellinor Forster and Judit Beke-Martos for this information.
2. Edward Muir, *Ritual in Early Modern Europe*, 2nd ed. (Cambridge, UK, 2005), 271–73.
3. Richard A. Jackson, *Vive le roi! A History of the French Coronation from Charles V to Charles X: Vivat Rex* (Chapel Hill, 1984).
4. Roy Strong, *Coronation from the 8th to the 21st Century* (London, 2005).
5. Richard S. Wortman, *Scenarios of Power: Myth and Ceremony in Russian Monarchy from Peter the Great to the Abdication of Nicholas II* (Princeton, 2006).
6. Research project "Az MTA BTK TTI 'Lendület' Szent Korona Kutatócsoport" ["Holy Crown of Hungary Research Project"] under supervision of Géza Pálffy at the Institute of History, Research Centre for the Humanities at the Hungarian Academy of Sciences, accessed 10 October 2019, https://www.btk.mta.hu/aktualis-main/76-az-mta-btk-tti-lendulet-szent-korona-kutatocsoportja.
7. André Holenstein, *Die Huldigung der Untertanen: Rechtskultur und Herrschaftsordnung (800–1800)* (Stuttgart, 1991); Matthias Schwengelbeck, *Die Politik des Zeremoniells: Huldigungsfeiern im langen 19. Jahrhundert* (Frankfurt, 2007); Hugo Soly, "Plechtige intochten in de steden van de Zuidelijke Nederlanden tijdens de overgang van Middeleeuwen naar Nieuwe Tijd: communicatie, propaganda, spektakel," *Tijdschrift voor Geschiedenis* 97 (1984): 341–60.
8. Coronations of royal consorts received even less attention. Katrin Keller offers a fresh approach in her article on the crowning of the early modern Roman empresses, in which she pleads for a gendered perspective on ritual: Katrin Keller, "Gender and Ritual: Crowning Empresses in the Holy Roman Empire," *German History* 37, no. 2 (2019): 172–85.

9. For example, the Dutch city of Roermond was Austrian until 1794. The Fricktal, with Laufenburg and Rheinfelden as its main urban centers and nowadays part of the Swiss Confederation, belonged to *Vorderösterreich* until the Treaty of Campo Formio in 1797. The case of Bosnia and Herzegovina is different: it was an Austrian protectorate since 1878 and was formally annexed to the Habsburg Monarchy only in 1908.
10. On the composite nature of many states in early modern Europe, in which the Central European Habsburg Monarchy stands out, see Helmut G. Koenigsberger, "Composite States, Representative Institutions and the American Revolution," *Historical Research: The Bulletin of the Institute of Historical Research* 62, no. 148 (1989): 135–53; J. H. Elliott, "A Europe of Composite Monarchies," *Past & Present* 137 (1992): 48–71. These seminal articles remain valuable even though later historians have criticized parts of their views. John Morrill, for example stresses the volatile nature of many early modern territorial conglomerates and the role of dynastic glory as a catalyst for their formation. He therefore prefers the term "dynastic agglomeration." Recently, a group of scholars studying the Spanish and Portuguese empires proposed the term "polycentric monarchies." They wish to replace the top-down view of a policy-making center and a receptive, passive periphery with an approach that examines the links between multiple centers within territorial conglomerates. These different centers all contributed to the formation of policy: John Morrill, "Thinking about the New British History," in *British Political Thought in History, Literature and Theory, 1500–1800*, ed. David Armitage (Cambridge, UK, 2006), 23–46; Pedro Cardim, Tamar Herzog, José Javier Ruiz Ibáñez, and Gaetano Sabatini, eds., *Polycentric Monarchies: How Did Early Modern Spain and Portugal Achieve and Maintain a Global Hegemony?* (Eastbourne, 2012).
11. Illustrative are the volumes in Routledge's European Festival Studies series, which covers the period between 1450 and 1700. See, for example, J. R. Mulryne, Maria Ines Aliverti, and Anna Maria Testaverde, eds., *Ceremonial Entries in Early Modern Europe: The Iconography of Power* (Aldershot, 2015). Another example is the aforementioned article by Hugo Soly, which disregards the decades after 1685: Soly, "Plechtige intochten."
12. Schwengelbeck, *Die Politik des Zeremoniells*.
13. André Holenstein, "Huldigung und Herrschaftszeremoniell im Zeitalter des Absolutismus und der Aufklärung," in *Zum Wandel von Zeremoniell und Gesellschaftsritualen in der Zeit der Aufklärung*, ed. Klaus Gerteis (Hamburg, 1992), 21–46; Soly, "Plechtige intochten." Stijn Bussels and Bram van Oostveldt endorsed Soly's thesis from an art historian's perspective: Stijn Bussels and Bram van Oostveldt, "De traditie van de tableaux vivants bij de plechtige intochten in de Zuidelijke Nederlanden (1496–1635)," *Tijdschrift voor Geschiedenis* 115, no. 2 (2002): 166–80.
14. Indeed, at the close of the seventeenth century, a series of princes intensively lobbied for the so-called royal treatment or for royal titles. Since 1697 the elector of Saxony was also king of Poland, and the elector of Brandenburg became king in Prussia in 1701. Their colleague from Hanover became king of Great Britain in 1713, and Victor Amadeus II of Savoy obtained Sicily and its royal status in the same year (in 1720, Sicily was exchanged for Sardinia, as a result of which Victor Amadeus became king of Sardinia). Christopher Clark speaks of a "wave of regalisation": Christopher Clark, "When Culture Meets Power: The Prussian Coronation of 1701," in *Cultures of Power in Europe during the Long Eighteenth Century*, ed. Hamish Scott and Brendan Simms (Cambridge, UK, 2007), 27.
15. William D. Godsey, "Herrschaft und politische Kultur im Habsburgerreich: Die niederösterreichische Erbhuldigung (ca. 1648–1848)," in *Aufbrüche in die Moderne: Früh-*

parlamentarismus zwischen altständischer Ordnung und monarchischem Konstitutionalismus 1750–1850. Schlesien—Deutschland—Mitteleuropa, ed. Ronald Gehrke (Cologne, 2005), 145–51.
16. For a concise summary of the origins of the consecration in European coronation rites, see Jackson, *Vive le roi*, 3–19.
17. Quoted in German in Peter Baumgart, "Die preußische Königskrönung von 1701, das Reich und die europäische Politik," in *Preußen, Europa und das Reich*, ed. Oswald Hauser (Cologne, 1987), 65–66. Other publications on the Prussian coronation of 1701: Iselin Gundermann, "Ob die Salbung einem Könige nothwendig sey," in *Dreihundert Jahre Preußische Königskrönung: Eine Tagungsdokumentation*, ed. Johannes Kunisch (Berlin, 2002), 115–33; Clark, "When Culture Meets Power," 14–35.
18. Quoted in Holenstein, "Huldigung und Herrschaftszeremoniell," 42–43.
19. Quoted in Chantal Grell, "The *sacre* of Louis XVI: The End of a Myth," in *Monarchy and Religion: The Transformation of Royal Culture in Eighteenth-Century Europe*, ed. Michael Schaich (London, 2007), 347–48. On the *sacre* of Louis XVI, see also Hermann Weber, "Le sacre de Louis XVI le 11 juin 1775 et la crise de l'Ancien Régime," in *Le sacre des rois: Actes du Colloque international d'histoire sur les sacres et couronnements royaux (Reims 1975)* (Paris, 1985), 255–72. Page 257 contains the original French quotation.
20. Marc Bloch, *Les rois thaumaturges. Études sur le caractère surnaturel attribué à la puissance royale particulièrement en France et en Angleterre* (Paris, 1961), 398.
21. Philip Mansel, *Dressed to Rule: Royal and Court Costume from Louis XIV to Elizabeth II* (New Haven, 2005), 26–27; Anna Mader-Kratky, "Das Zeremoniell unter Maria Theresia und Franz I. Stephan," in *Die Wiener Hofburg 1705–1835: Die kaiserliche Residenz vom Barock bis zum Klassizismus*, ed. Hellmut Lorenz and Anna Mader-Kratky (Vienna, 2016), 325–31; Marina Beck, *Macht-Räume Maria Theresias: Funktion und Zeremoniell in ihren Residenzen, Jagd- und Lustschlössern* (Munich, 2017), 48.
22. Peter Burke, *The Historical Anthropology of Early Modern Italy: Essays on Perception and Communication*, 2nd ed. (Cambridge, UK, 1994), 223–38; Barbara Stollberg-Rilinger, "Verfassung und Fest: Überlegungen zur festlichen Inszenierung vormoderner und moderner Verfassungen," in *Interdependenzen zwischen Verfassung und Kultur*, ed. Hans-Jürgen Becker (Berlin, 2003), 26–30. Symptomatic are State Chancellor Kaunitz's calls to economize in regard to the imperial election and coronation of Francis II in 1792. Although the instigation to economize was almost universal in early modern coronations and inaugurations, Kaunitz's specific propositions—for example excluding ladies from the coronation—and antiritualistic arguments were definitely new: Christian Hattenhauer, *Wahl und Krönung Franz II. AD 1792: Das Heilige Reich krönt seinen letzten Kaiser—Das Tagebuch des Reichsquartiermeisters Hieronymus Gottfried von Müller und Anlagen* (Frankfurt am Main, 1995), 380–84.
23. Baumgart, "Die preußische Königskrönung," 75–76; Clark, "When Culture Meets Power," 17.
24. Grell, "The *sacre* of Louis XVI," 347. Between 1768 and 1788, revenues rose from 317 million to 450 million *livres*. In the 1770s, debt service consumed about a third of these resources: James B. Collins, *The State in Early Modern France*, 2nd ed. (Cambridge, UK, 2009), 308–22.
25. The Estates of the Bohemian lands contributed two hundred thousand as *subsidii itinerarii*: Ottocar Weber, "Eine Kaiserreise nach Böhmen im Jahre 1723," *Mittheilungen des Vereines für Geschichte der Deutschen in Böhmen* 36, no. 2 (1897): 142–43 and 199–204.

Interesting as comparison is the humbler inauguration of Maria Theresa in the County of Flanders during the War of the Austrian Succession in 1744. It cost the Flemish Estates and the city of Ghent 157,868 Brabant guilders *courant*, approximately 8.5 percent of the annual Flemish taxes to the government: Klaas Van Gelder and Bert Van Cauter, "Een publieke ceremonie in een turbulent tijdvak: De inauguratie van Maria Theresia als gravin van Vlaanderen (1744)," *Handelingen der Maatschappij voor Geschiedenis en Oudheidkunde te Gent* 67 (2013): 126–27. Taking into account the exchange rates in the eighteenth century, two hundred thousand Rhenish guilders (paid by the Estates of the Bohemian lands) equaled around two hundred eighty thousand Brabant guilders *courant*.

26. Strong, *Coronation*, 372–34. Nevertheless, David Cannadine stresses that the early nineteenth-century British royal ceremonies, including the extravagant coronations, failed to appeal. Instead of conveying the impression of grandeur, they turned into farce and were food for ridicule—among other things because of the unpopularity of the royal family itself: David Cannadine, "The Context, Performance and Meaning of Ritual: The British Monarchy and the 'Invention of Tradition,' c. 1820–1977," in *The Invention of Tradition*, ed. Eric Hobsbawm and Terence Ranger (Cambridge, UK, 1983), 115–120.
27. Wortman, *Scenarios of Power*, 270–81.
28. Walther Hubatsch, *Friedrich der Große und die preußische Verwaltung* (Cologne, 1973), 39–53.
29. Hubatsch, *Friedrich der Große*, 72–73; Peter Baumgart, "Schlesien als eigenständige Provinz im altpreußischen Staat (1740–1808)," in *Schlesien*, ed. Norbert Conrads (Berlin, 1994), 355.
30. Clark, "When Culture Meets Power," 17–22.
31. Ambrogio A. Caiani, "Ornamentalism in a European Context? Napoleon's Italian Coronation, 26 May 1805," *The English Historical Review* 132, no. 554 (2017): 41–72.
32. Holenstein, "Huldigung und Herrschaftszeremoniell," 22.
33. Adam Wandruszka, *Leopold II.: Erzherzog von Österreich, Grossherzog von Toskana, König von Ungarn und Böhmen, Römischer Kaiser*, 2 vols. (Vienna, 1965), 2: 302–11.
34. Klaas Van Gelder, "The Investiture of Emperor Charles VI in Brabant and Flanders: A Test Case for the Authority of the New Austrian Government," *European Review of History/Revue européenne d'histoire* 18, no. 4 (2011): 450–53.
35. Stefan Seitschek, "Die Erbhuldigung 1728 in Kärnten, ihre Organisation und Durchführung anhand ausgewählter Quellen," *Carinthia: Zeitschrift für Geschichtliche Landeskunde von Kärnten* 202 (2012): 145–48.
36. Godsey, "Herrschaft und politische Kultur," 156–77.
37. This festive character, most visible in the banquets and balls for the dignitaries and wine fountains for the crowds, did not preclude human drama. The traditional distribution of beef, wine and other dishes to the masses of spectators at the *Römerplatz* in Frankfurt after the imperial coronations repeatedly escalated and led to fights and injuries. This violence was restricted in time and place and therefore tolerated, however. Moreover, it served as an inversion ritual during the coronation festivities: Harriet Rudolph, "Die Herrschererhebung als Fest: Krönungsfeste im Vergleich," in *Festkulturen im Vergleich: Inszenierungen des Religiösen und Politischen*, ed. Michael Maurer (Cologne, 2010), 34–37. In 1781, the fireworks on Brussels's central market square for the inauguration of Joseph II exploded and killed twenty-seven onlookers: Guy van Dievoet, "L'empereur Joseph II et la Joyeuse Entrée de Brabant: Les dernières années de la constitution brabançonne," *Anciens Pays et Assemblées d'États/Standen en Landen* 16 (1958): 100.

38. Stollberg-Rilinger, "Verfassung und Fest"; Stollberg-Rilinger, "Symbolische Kommunikation in der Vormoderne: Begriffe—Thesen—Forschungsperspektiven," *Zeitschrift für Historische Forschung* 31 (2004): 505–11 and 518–20; Muir, *Ritual*, 252–55.
39. Andreas Gestrich, *Absolutismus und Öffentlichkeit: Politische Kommunikation in Deutschland zu Beginn des 18. Jahrhunderts* (Göttingen, 1994), 118–20; Michael Maurer, "Feste und Feiern als historischer Forschungsgegenstand," *Historische Zeitschrift* 253 (1991): 118.
40. Famous examples of self-coronations are the ones by Charles XII of Sweden in 1697, Frederick I of Prussia in 1701, Napoleon Bonaparte in 1804, and the Russian imperial coronations during the eighteenth and nineteenth centuries: Gundermann, "Ob die Salbung einem König nothwendig sey," 120; Wortman, *Scenarios of Power*, passim. On Napoleon's imperial coronation, see David Chanteranne, *Le Sacre de Napoléon* (Paris, 2004); Laurence Chatel de Brancion, *Le sacre de Napoléon: Le rêve de changer le monde* (Paris, 2004); Thierry Lentz, ed., *Le sacre de Napoléon* (Ligugé, 2003).
41. Karl Härter, "Aachen—Frankfurt—Nürnberg—Regensburg: Politische Zentren des Reiches zwischen 1356 und 1806," in *Wahl und Krönung*, ed. Bernd Heidenreich and Frank-Lothar Kroll (Frankfurt am Main, 2006), 175–88.
42. Van Gelder and Van Cauter, "Een publieke ceremonie," 114–15.
43. Hugh LeCaine Agnew, "Ambiguities of Ritual: Dynastic Loyalty, Territorial Patriotism and Nationalism in the Last Three Royal Coronations in Bohemia, 1791–1836," *Bohemia* 41, no. 1 (2000): 4.
44. Wolfgang Sellert, "Zur rechtshistorischen Bedeutung der Krönung und des Streites um das Krönungsrecht zwischen Mainz und Köln," in *Herrscherweihe und Königskrönung im frühneuzeitlichen Europa*, ed. Heinz Duchhardt (Wiesbaden, 1983), 21–25.
45. With respect to the Imperial Diet, see Barbara Stollberg-Rilinger, "Zeremoniell als politisches Verfahren: Rangordnung und Rangstreit als Strukturmerkmale des frühneuzeitlichen Reichstags," in *Neue Studien zur frühneuzeitlichen Reichsgeschichte*, ed. Johannes Kunisch (Berlin, 1997), 91–132. On the many conflicts about precedence and order of rank, which were frequently subject to lawsuits between circa 1650 and 1750, see Barbara Stollberg-Rilinger, "Rang vor Gericht: Zur Verrechtlichung sozialer Rangkonflikte in der frühen Neuzeit," *Zeitschrift für historische Forschung* 28, no. 3 (2001): 385–418. On the role of precedence and order of rank in Estates' assemblies, see Tim Neu, "Zeremonielle Verfahren: Zur Funktionalität vormoderner politisch-administrativer Prozesse am Beispiel des Landtags im Fürstbistum Münster," in *Im Schatten der Macht: Kommunikationskulturen in Politik und Verwaltung 1600–1950*, ed. Stefan Haas and Mark Hengerer (Frankfurt, 2008), 23–50; David M. Luebke, "Ceremony and Dissent: Religion, Procedural Conflicts, and the 'Fiction of Consensus' in Seventeenth-Century Germany," in *The Holy Roman Empire, Reconsidered*, ed. Jason Philip Coy, Benjamin Marschke, and David Warren Sabean (New York, 2010), 145–61; Petr Maťa, "Der steirische Landtag in Raum und Bild um 1730: Symbolische Ordnung und visuelle Darstellung," *Zeitschrift des historischen Vereins für Steiermark* 104 (2013): 163–218.
46. In German historiography, the terms *Präsenzöffentlichkeit* and *Medienöffentlichkeit* have been coined to underline this difference. See Harriet Rudolph, *Das Reich als Ereignis: Formen und Funktionen der Herrschaftsinszenierung bei Kaisereinzügen (1558–1618)* (Cologne, 2011), in particular Chapter V. For the semiofficial election and coronation books in the eighteenth-century Holy Roman Empire, see Barbara Dölemeyer, "Wahl und

Krönung im Spiegel der Diarien des 18. Jahrhunderts," in *Wahl und Krönung*, ed. Bernd Heidenreich and Frank-Lothar Kroll (Frankfurt am Main, 2006), 79–98.
47. Rudolph, "Die Herrschererhebung als Fest," 20–22; Klaas Van Gelder, "Dynastic Communication, Urban Rites and Ceremonies, and the Representation of Maria Theresa in the Austrian Netherlands," in *Die Repräsentation Maria Theresias: Herrschaft und Bildpolitik im Zeitalter der Aufklärung*, ed. Werner Telesko, Sandra Hertel, and Stefanie Linsboth (Vienna, 2020), 369–79.
48. For a detailed description of the coronation journey of Charles VI to Prague and back to Vienna, which aimed to maximize the propagandistic impact on his competitors in the empire, see Štěpán Vácha, Irena Veselá, Vít Vlnas, and Petra Vokáčová, *Karel VI. & Alžběta Kristýna: Česká korunovace 1723* (Prague, 2009), 90–114.
49. Rudolph, "Die Herrschererhebung als Fest," 24.
50. Agnew, "Ambiguities of Ritual," 19–20.
51. For more information on the media coverage and the purposes and strategies of its producers in the mid-eighteenth-century Holy Roman Empire, see Werner Telesko, Sandra Hertel, and Stefanie Linsboth, "Zwischen Panegyrik und Tatsachenbericht: Zu Struktur und Zielsetzung von Medienereignissen zur Zeit Maria Theresias," *Zeitschrift für historische Forschung* 44, no. 3 (2017): 441–86.
52. Cannadine, "The Context, Performance and Meaning of Ritual," 161.
53. Franz Matsche, *Die Kunst im Dienst der Staatsidee Kaiser Karls VI. Ikonographie, Ikonologie und Programmatik des 'Kaiserstils'* (Berlin, 1981); Elisabeth Kovács, "Die Apotheose des Hauses Österreich: Repräsentation und politischer Anspruch" and Friedrich Polleroß, "Zur Repräsentation der Habsburger in der bildenden Kunst," both in *Welt des Barock*, ed. Rupert Feuchtmüller and Elisabeth Kovács (Vienna, 1986), 53–86 and 87–104; Huberta Weigl, "Stift Klosterneuburg—Der 'Österreichische Escorial,'" in *Die Krone des Landes*, ed. Karl Holubar and Wolfgang Christian Huber (Klosterneuburg, 1996), 75–98.
54. T. C. W. Blanning, *The Culture of Power and the Power of Culture: Old Regime Europe 1660–1789* (Oxford, 2002), passim.
55. Robert von Friedeburg, "Review of The Culture of Power and the Power of Culture: Old Regime Europe 1660–1789," *European Journal of Political Theory* 4, no. 3 (2005): 309–18.
56. See also Schwengelbeck, *Die Politik des Zeremoniells*, 107–51.
57. Agnew, "Ambiguities of Ritual." The link between nationalism and imperial celebrations is also a central element in Daniel Unowsky's monograph *The Pomp and Politics of Patriotism*. Unowsky focuses on the imperial visits to the various lands of the monarchy, on processions and jubilees, but not on crownings or inaugurations, which were virtually absent during the reign of Francis Joseph: Daniel L. Unowsky, *The Pomp and Politics of Patriotism: Imperial Celebrations in Habsburg Austria, 1848–1916* (West Lafayette, 2005).
58. For criticism of the constitutional necessity of French coronations from the fifteenth to the seventeenth century, mainly evoking the arguments of Ralph E. Giesey, see Muir, *Ritual*, 276–79.
59. Schwengelbeck, *Die Politik des Zeremoniells*, passim; Schwengelbeck, "Monarchische Herrschaftsrepräsentationen zwischen Konsens und Konflikt: Zum Wandel des Huldigungs- und Inthronisationszeremoniells im 19. Jahrhundert," in *Die Sinnlichkeit der Macht: Herrschaft und Repräsentation seit der Frühen Neuzeit*, ed. Jan Andres, Alexa Geisthövel, and Matthias Schwengelbeck (Frankfurt, 2005), 123–62.

60. Despite taking place in a modern constitutional framework, to this day, the new Belgian king (and in the future, perhaps also the queen) officially becomes "king of the Belgians" only after swearing the inaugural oath before the assembled chambers of parliament. In the period of time between the death or abdication of a ruler and the swearing in of his successor, the government performs the constitutional duties of the king: Articles 90 and 91 of the Belgian constitution, "De Belgische Grondwet," accessed 19 July 2019, https://www.senate.be/doc/const_nl.html.
61. After 1848, the number of inaugural rites in the Habsburg Monarchy decreased dramatically, with the Hungarian coronation probably being the only one to remain. There was never a coronation for the Austrian emperor. On the abortive attempt to crown Francis Joseph king of Bohemia, see Hugh LeCaine Agnew, "The Flyspecks on Palivec's Portrait: Franz Joseph, the Symbols of Monarchy, and Czech Popular Loyalty," in *The Limits of Loyalty: Imperial Symbolism, Popular Allegiances, and State Patriotism in the Late Habsburg Monarchy*, ed. Laurence Cole and Daniel Unowsky (New York, 2007), 48–61. For the ritual and ceremony centered on the emperor Francis Joseph that substituted for the loss of coronations, see Unowsky, *The Pomp and Politics*, passim. On the absence of a coronation for the emperor of Austria and the decline in coronations in general within the context of the many continuities between the Holy Roman Empire and the Austrian emperorship and the political relevance of the former for the latter, see Brigitte Mazohl and Karin Schneider, "'Translatio Imperii'? Reichsidee und Kaisermythos in der Habsburgermonarchie," in *Was vom Alten Reiche blieb: Deutungen, Institutionen und Bilder des frühneuzeitlichen Heiligen Römischen Reiches deutscher Nation im 19. und 20. Jahrhundert*, ed. Matthias Asche (Munich, 2011), 101–28, especially 118–20.
62. Maurer, "Feste und Feiern," 115–20.
63. Muir, *Ritual*, 299. For references to the emotional appeal of royal ritual in this volume, see the chapters by Harriet Rudolph and William Godsey.

Bibliography

Agnew, Hugh LeCaine. "Ambiguities of Ritual: Dynastic Loyalty, Territorial Patriotism and Nationalism in the Last Three Royal Coronations in Bohemia, 1791–1836." *Bohemia* 41, no. 1 (2000): 3–22.

———. "The Flyspecks on Palivec's Portrait: Franz Joseph, the Symbols of Monarchy, and Czech Popular Loyalty." In *The Limits of Loyalty: Imperial Symbolism, Popular Allegiances, and State Patriotism in the Late Habsburg Monarchy*, edited by Laurence Cole and Daniel Unowsky, 48–61. New York: Berghahn Books, 2007.

"Az MTA BTK TTI 'Lendület' Szent Korona Kutatócsoportja." Accessed 10 October 2019. https://www.btk.mta.hu/aktualis-main/76-az-mta-btk-tti-lendulet-szent-korona-kutatocsoportja.

Baumgart, Peter. "Die preußische Königskrönung von 1701, das Reich und die europäische Politik." In *Preußen, Europa und das Reich*, edited by Oswald Hauser, 65–86. Cologne: Böhlau Verlag, 1987.

———. "Schlesien als eigenständige Provinz im altpreußischen Staat (1740–1808)." In *Schlesien*, edited by Norbert Conrads, 345–464. Berlin: Siedler Verlag, 1994.

Beck, Marina. *Macht-Räume Maria Theresias: Funktion und Zeremoniell in ihren Residenzen, Jagd- und Lustschlössern*. Munich: Deutscher Kunstverlag, 2017.

Blanning, T. C. W. *The Culture of Power and the Power of Culture: Old Regime Europe 1660–1789*. Oxford: Oxford University Press, 2002.
Bloch, Marc. *Les rois thaumaturges: Études sur le caractère surnaturel attribué à la puissance royale particulièrement en France et en Angleterre*. Paris: Colin, 1961.
Burke, Peter. *The Historical Anthropology of Early Modern Italy: Essays on Perception and Communication*, 2nd ed. Cambridge, UK: Cambridge University Press, 1994.
Bussels, Stijn, and Bram van Oostveldt. "De traditie van de tableaux vivants bij de plechtige intochten in de Zuidelijke Nederlanden (1496–1635)." *Tijdschrift voor Geschiedenis* 115, no. 2 (2002): 166–80.
Caiani, Ambrogio A. "Ornamentalism in a European Context? Napoleon's Italian Coronation, 26 May 1805." *English Historical Review* 132, no. 554 (2017): 41–72.
Cannadine, David. "The Context, Performance and Meaning of Ritual: The British Monarchy and the 'Invention of Tradition,' c. 1820–1977." In *The Invention of Tradition*, edited by Eric Hobsbawm and Terence Ranger, 101–64. Cambridge, UK: Cambridge University Press, 1983.
Cardim, Pedro, Tamar Herzog, José Javier Ruiz Ibáñez, and Gaetano Sabatini, eds. *Polycentric Monarchies: How Did Early Modern Spain and Portugal Achieve and Maintain a Global Hegemony?* Eastbourne: Sussex Academic Press, 2012.
Chanteranne, David. *Le Sacre de Napoléon*. Paris: Tallandier, 2004.
Chatel de Brancion, Laurence. *Le sacre de Napoléon: Le rêve de changer le monde*. Paris: Perrin, 2004.
Clark, Christopher. "When Culture Meets Power: The Prussian Coronation of 1701." In *Cultures of Power in Europe during the Long Eighteenth Century*, edited by Hamish Scott and Brendan Simms, 14–35. Cambridge, UK: Cambridge University Press, 2007.
Collins, James B. *The State in Early Modern France*, 2nd ed. Cambridge, UK: Cambridge University Press, 2009.
"De Belgische Grondwet." Accessed 19 July 2019. https://www.senate.be/doc/const_nl.html.
Dölemeyer, Barbara. "Wahl und Krönung im Spiegel der Diarien des 18. Jahrhunderts." In *Wahl und Krönung*, edited by Frank-Lothar Kroll and Bernd Heidenreich, 79–98. Frankfurt am Main: Societätsverlag, 2006.
Elliott, J. H. "A Europe of Composite Monarchies." *Past & Present* 137 (1992): 48–71.
Friedeburg, Robert von. "Review of the Culture of Power and the Power of Culture: Old Regime Europe 1660–1789." *European Journal of Political Theory* 4, no. 3 (2005): 309–18.
Gestrich, Andreas. *Absolutismus und Öffentlichkeit: Politische Kommunikation in Deutschland zu Beginn des 18. Jahrhunderts*. Göttingen: Vandenhoeck & Ruprecht, 1994.
Godsey, William D. "Herrschaft und politische Kultur im Habsburgerreich: Die niederösterreichische Erbhuldigung (ca. 1648–1848)." In *Aufbrüche in die Moderne: Frühparlamentarismus zwischen altständischer Ordnung und monarchischem Konstitutionalismus 1750–1850. Schlesien—Deutschland—Mitteleuropa*, edited by Roland Gehrke, 141–77. Cologne: Böhlau Verlag, 2005.
Grell, Chantal. "The *sacre* of Louis XVI: The End of a Myth." In *Monarchy and Religion: The Transformation of Royal Culture in Eighteenth-Century Europe*, edited by Michael Schaich, 345–66. London: German Historical Institute/Oxford University Press, 2007.
Gundermann, Iselin. "Ob die Salbung einem Könige nothwendig sey." In *Dreihundert Jahre Preußische Königskrönung: Eine Tagungsdokumentation*, edited by Johannes Kunisch, 115–33. Berlin: Duncker & Humblot, 2002.

Härter, Karl. "Aachen—Frankfurt—Nürnberg—Regensburg: Politische Zentren des Reiches zwischen 1356 und 1806." In *Wahl und Krönung*, edited by Bernd Heidenreich and Frank-Lothar Kroll, 175–88. Frankfurt am Main: Societätsverlag, 2006.

Hattenhauer, Christian. *Wahl und Krönung Franz II. AD 1792: Das Heilige Reich krönt seinen letzten Kaiser—Das Tagebuch des Reichsquartiermeisters Hieronymus Gottfried von Müller und Anlagen*. Frankfurt am Main: Peter Lang, 1995.

Holenstein, André. *Die Huldigung der Untertanen: Rechtskultur und Herrschaftsordnung (800–1800)*. Stuttgart: Gustav Fischer Verlag, 1991.

———. "Huldigung und Herrschaftszeremoniell im Zeitalter des Absolutismus und der Aufklärung." In *Zum Wandel von Zeremoniell und Gesellschaftsritualen in der Zeit der Aufklärung*, edited by Klaus Gerteis, 21–46. Hamburg: Felix Meiner Verlag, 1992.

Hubatsch, Walther. *Friedrich der Große und die preußische Verwaltung*. Cologne: Grote, 1973.

Jackson, Richard A. *Vive le roi! A History of the French Coronation from Charles V to Charles X: Vivat Rex*. Chapel Hill: University of North Carolina Press, 1984. [English translation of the French original: *Vivat Rex! Histoire des sacres et couronnements en France, 1364–1825*. Strasbourg: Presses universitaires de Strasbourg, 1984.]

Keller, Katrin. "Gender and Ritual: Crowning Empresses in the Holy Roman Empire." *German History* 37, no. 2 (2019): 172–85.

Koenigsberger, Helmut G. "Composite States, Representative Institutions and the American Revolution." *Historical Research: The Bulletin of the Institute of Historical Research* 62, no. 148 (1989): 135–53.

Kovács, Elisabeth. "Die Apotheose des Hauses Österreich: Repräsentation und politischer Anspruch." In *Welt des Barock*, edited by Rupert Feuchtmüller and Elisabeth Kovács, 53–86. Vienna: Herder, 1986.

Lentz, Thierry, ed. *Le sacre de Napoléon*. Ligugé: Nouveau Monde Éditions, 2003.

Luebke, David M. "Ceremony and Dissent: Religion, Procedural Conflicts, and the 'Fiction of Consensus' in Seventeenth-Century Germany." In *The Holy Roman Empire, Reconsidered*, edited by Jason Philip Coy, Benjamin Marschke, and David Warren Sabean, 145–61. New York: Berghahn Books, 2010.

Mader-Kratky, Anna. "Das Zeremoniell unter Maria Theresia und Franz I. Stephan." In *Die Wiener Hofburg 1705–1835: Die kaiserliche Residenz vom Barock bis zum Klassizismus*, edited by Hellmut Lorenz and Anna Mader-Kratky, 325–31. Vienna: Verlag der Österreichischen Akademie der Wissenschaften, 2016.

Mansel, Philip. *Dressed to Rule: Royal and Court Costume from Louis XIV to Elizabeth II*. New Haven: Yale University Press, 2005.

Mat'a, Petr. "Der steierische Landtag in Raum und Bild um 1730: Symbolische Ordnung und visuelle Darstellung." *Zeitschrift des Historische Vereines für Steiermark* 104 (2013): 163–218.

Matsche, Franz. *Die Kunst im Dienst der Staatsidee Kaiser Karls VI. Ikonographie, Ikonologie und Programmatik des "Kaiserstils."* 2 vols. Berlin: Walter de Gruyter, 1981.

Maurer, Michael. "Feste und Feiern als historischer Forschungsgegenstand." *Historische Zeitschrift* 253 (1991): 101–30.

Mazohl, Brigitte, and Karin Schneider. "'Translatio Imperii'? Reichsidee und Kaisermythos in der Habsburgermonarchie." In *Was vom Alten Reiche blieb: Deutungen, Institutionen und Bilder des frühneuzeitlichen Heiligen Römischen Reiches deutscher Nation im 19. und 20. Jahrhundert*, edited by Matthias Asche, 101–28. Munich: Bayerische Landeszentrale für politische Bildungsarbeit, 2011.

Morrill, John. "Thinking about the New British History." In *British Political Thought in History, Literature and Theory, 1500–1800*, edited by David Armitage, 23–46. Cambridge, UK: Cambridge University Press, 2006.

Muir, Edward. *Ritual in Early Modern Europe*. Cambridge, UK: Cambridge University Press, 1997 (2nd ed. 2005).

Mulryne, J. R., Maria Ines Aliverti, and Anna Maria Testaverde, eds. *Ceremonial Entries in Early Modern Europe: The Iconography of Power*. Aldershot: Ashgate, 2015.

Neu, Tim. "Zeremonielle Verfahren: Zur Funktionalität vormoderner politisch-administrativer Prozesse am Beispiel des Landtags im Fürstbistum Münster." In *Im Schatten der Macht: Kommunikationskulturen in Politik und Verwaltung 1600–1950*, edited by Stefan Haas and Mark Hengerer, 23–50. Frankfurt: Campus Verlag, 2008.

Polleroß, Friedrich. "Zur Repräsentation der Habsburger in der bildenden Kunst." In *Welt des Barock*, edited by Rupert Feuchtmüller and Elisabeth Kovács, 87–104. Vienna: Herder, 1986.

Rudolph, Harriet. *Das Reich als Ereignis: Formen und Funktionen der Herrschaftsinszenierung bei Kaisereinzügen (1558–1618)*. Cologne: Böhlau, 2011.

———. "Die Herrschererhebung als Fest: Krönungsfeste im Vergleich." In *Festkulturen im Vergleich: Inszenierungen des Religiösen und Politischen*, edited by Michael Maurer, 13–42. Cologne: Böhlau, 2010.

Schwengelbeck, Matthias. *Die Politik des Zeremoniells: Huldigungsfeiern im langen 19. Jahrhundert*. Frankfurt: Campus, 2007.

———. "Monarchische Herrschaftsrepräsentationen zwischen Konsens und Konflikt: Zum Wandel des Huldigungs- und Inthronisationszeremoniells im 19. Jahrhundert." In *Die Sinnlichkeit der Macht: Herrschaft und Repräsentation seit der Frühen Neuzeit*, edited by Jan Andres, Alexa Geisthövel, and Matthias Schwengelbeck, 123–62. Frankfurt: Campus, 2005.

Seitschek, Stefan. "Die Erbhuldigung 1728 in Kärnten, ihre Organisation und Durchführung anhand ausgewählter Quellen." *Carinthia: Zeitschrift für geschichtliche Landeskunde von Kärnten* 202 (2012): 125–78.

Sellert, Wolfgang. "Zur rechtshistorischen Bedeutung der Krönung und des Streites um das Krönungsrecht zwischen Mainz und Köln." In *Herrscherweihe und Königskrönung im frühneuzeitlichen Europa*, edited by Heinz Duchhardt, 21–32. Wiesbaden: Franz Steiner, 1983.

Soly, Hugo. "Plechtige intochten in de steden van de Zuidelijke Nederlanden tijdens de overgang van Middeleeuwen naar Nieuwe Tijd: communicatie, propaganda, spektakel." *Tijdschrift voor Geschiedenis* 97 (1984): 341–60.

Stollberg-Rilinger, Barbara. "Rang vor Gericht: Zur Verrechtlichung sozialer Rangkonflikte in der frühen Neuzeit." *Zeitschrift für historische Forschung* 28, no. 3 (2001): 385–418.

———. "Symbolische Kommunikation in der Vormoderne: Begriffe—Thesen—Forschungsperspektiven." *Zeitschrift für Historische Forschung* 31 (2004): 489–527.

———. "Verfassung und Fest: Überlegungen zur festlichen Inszenierung vormoderner und moderner Verfassungen." In *Interdependenzen zwischen Verfassung und Kultur*, edited by Hans-Jürgen Becker, 7–37. Berlin: Duncker & Humblot, 2003.

———. "Zeremoniell als politisches Verfahren: Rangordnung und Rangstreit als Strukturmerkmale des frühneuzeitlichen Reichstags." In *Neue Studien zur frühneuzeitlichen Reichsgeschichte*, edited by Johannes Kunisch, 91–132. Berlin: Duncker & Humblot, 1997.

Strong, Roy. *Coronation from the 8th to the 21st Century*. London: Harper Perennial, 2005.

Telesko, Werner, Sandra Hertel, and Stefanie Linsboth. "Zwischen Panegyrik und Tatsachenbericht: Zu Struktur und Zielsetzung von Medienereignissen zur Zeit Maria Theresias." *Zeitschrift für historische Forschung* 44, no. 3 (2017): 441–86.

"The Fundamental Law of Hungary." Accessed 26 October 2019. https://www.kormany.hu/download/f/3e/61000/TheFundamentalLawofHungary_20180629_FIN.pdf.

Unowsky, Daniel L. *The Pomp and Politics of Patriotism: Imperial Celebrations in Habsburg Austria, 1848–1916*. West Lafayette: Purdue University Press, 2005.

Vácha, Štěpán, Irena Veselá, Vít Vlnas, and Petra Vokáčová. *Karel VI. & Alžběta Kristýna: Česká korunovace 1723*. Prague: Národní galerie v Praze, 2009.

van Dievoet, Guido [Guy]. "L'empereur Joseph II et la Joyeuse Entrée de Brabant: Les dernières années de la constitution brabançonne." *Anciens Pays et Assemblées d'États/Standen en Landen* 16 (1958): 87–140.

Van Gelder, Klaas. "Dynastic Communication, Urban Rites and Ceremonies, and the Representation of Maria Theresa in the Austrian Netherlands." In *Die Repräsentation Maria Theresias: Herrschaft und Bildpolitik im Zeitalter der Aufklärung*, edited by Werner Telesko, Sandra Hertel, and Stefanie Linsboth, 369–79. Vienna: Böhlau, 2020.

———. "The Investiture of Emperor Charles VI in Brabant and Flanders: A Test Case for the Authority of the New Austrian Government." *European Review of History/Revue européenne d'histoire* 18, no. 4 (2011): 443–63.

Van Gelder, Klaas, and Bert Van Cauter. "Een publieke ceremonie in een turbulent tijdvak: De inauguratie van Maria Theresia als gravin van Vlaanderen (1744)." *Handelingen der Maatschappij voor Geschiedenis en Oudheidkunde te Gent* 67 (2013): 101–30.

Wandruszka Adam. *Leopold II.: Erzherzog von Österreich, Grossherzog von Toskana, König von Ungarn und Böhmen, Römischer Kaiser*. 2 vols. Vienna: Herold Verlag, 1963–65.

Weber, Hermann. "Le sacre de Louis XVI le 11 juin 1775 et la crise de l'Ancien Régime." In *Le sacre des rois: Actes du Colloque international d'histoire sur les sacres et couronnements royaux (Reims 1975)*, 255–72. Paris: Les belles Lettres, 1985.

Weber, Ottocar. "Eine Kaiserreise nach Böhmen im Jahre 1723." *Mitteilungen des Vereines für Geschichte der Deutschen in Böhmen* 36, no. 2 (1897): 137–204.

Weigl, Huberta. "Stift Klosterneuburg—Der 'Österreichische Escorial.'" In *Die Krone des Landes*, edited by Karl Holubar and Wolfgang Christian Huber, 75–98. Klosterneuburg: Mayer & Comp. Verlag, 1996.

Wortman, Richard S. *Scenarios of Power: Myth and Ceremony in Russian Monarchy from Peter the Great to the Abdication of Nicholas II*. Princeton: Princeton University Press, 2006.

Chapter 1

THE CARE OF THRONES
A Plethora of Investitures in the Habsburg Composite Monarchy and Beyond from the Sixteenth to the Eighteenth Century

Petr Maťa

In recent decades, a rich strand of research has developed from the concept of the composite monarchy, enabling historians to analyze early modern polities on their own terms from a comparative perspective. One aspect has rarely been addressed in this context, however, despite seeming to suggest itself: the interplay between the composite structure of monarchies and the inaugural rites of their rulers. In some cases, analyzing this connection makes little sense. A good example is early modern France, though it was "a state that was still essentially composite in character."[1] Here, the act of assuming the royal powers consisted of various rituals—most notably the coronation and the *lit de justice*—whose relevance changed over time but which were singular and binding for the entire kingdom.[2] But how did monarchs and dynasties that held sway over multiple kingdoms and much more fragmented conglomerates handle the ascension to rule in their diverse domains with distinct traditions and constitutions? Despite the vast literature on coronations and rites of power, their political relevance and symbolic meaning, we lack studies that effectively link these findings to the reality of composite polities and systematically examine the relationship between an individual reign and multiple inaugural rites.

What fails to make much sense in the French case is in fact crucial with regard to the Habsburg Monarchy. Here, a plethora of investitures and their continuing—albeit noticeably changing—political relevance remained a defining feature well into the nineteenth century. Historians have paid increasing attention to the inaugural rites in individual kingdoms and provinces, and a growing tendency toward comparisons can be observed.[3] Nevertheless, we still lack a broader picture of Habsburg investitures that does justice to their manifoldness.

This chapter attempts to shed light on the variety of Habsburg inaugural rituals and outline the dynasty's changing strategy toward them from the emergence of the Habsburg Monarchy in the 1520s until the end of the eighteenth century. Besides asking how individual Habsburgs dealt with multiple investitures and under which political and dynastic circumstances these were staged, it will also consider to what extent the Habsburg case was exceptional in a European context.[4]

Coronations and Homages: Constitutional Analogy and Ceremonial Variety

A remark on terminology seems necessary at the very beginning. I use the term "inaugural rite" as an umbrella for both coronations and acts of hereditary homage, with the latter usually called *Huldigung* or *Erbhuldigung* in German sources and literature. This helps to treat coronation rites and homage ceremonies in the Habsburg lands as functional analogies and thus to focus on the main feature they originally had in common: the authorization and legitimation of a new sovereign to exercise full princely jurisdiction over a particular political unit—be it a kingdom, a duchy, or an autonomous municipality.

There were no doubt significant ceremonial differences between coronations and *Huldigungen* of which we need to remain aware. The centerpieces of a coronation were the placing of a crown upon the king's (or emperor's) head, the investiture with insignias, and the enthronement, all framed by liturgy. But early modern coronation ceremonies contained elements of homage as well, namely the mutual commitment made by oath or pledge by both the sovereign and the political community, typically the Estates.[5] Similarly, homage ceremonies more often than not comprised a sacral dimension in that they regularly began with a mass of the Holy Spirit and ended with a *Te Deum laudamus*. In Moravia—to name a less familiar case I will be referring to frequently—the homage itself took place in the church. A subsequent banquet held in profane space was another component that coronations and homages had in common.

The Lower Austrian inaugural ceremony even featured distinct insignias, including the archducal hat (*Erzherzogshut*) fabricated in 1616, which was nevertheless subject to a different ceremonial handling than the Hungarian, Bohemian, and imperial crowns (see figure 1.1). Since the Habsburg dominion over

Figure 1.1. The key moment of the Lower Austrian homage ceremony in Vienna in 1705: the Lower Austrian Estates—prelates, nobles, and townsmen—gathered in the Hofburg to pledge fealty to Emperor Joseph I surrounded by the holders of the hereditary offices presenting the archducal hat and other regalia and symbols. Engraving embellishing the printed volume published by the Estates to commemorate Joseph I's inauguration (Munich, Bayerische Staatsbibliothek, shelfmark Res/2 Austr. 69: http://daten.digitale-sammlungen.de/~db/0007/bsb00077459/images/; CC license, Art. 25 para. 1 clause 2 ABOB).

the archduchy was hereditary and all members of the house shared the title of archduke or archduchess, there was no need to place this fancy hat on the head of the new sovereign. Instead, it was simply carried and presented during the ceremony. But the way in which the hat was stored is reminiscent of the practice in Bohemia until the 1620s (where the crown was kept in the royal castle at Karlštejn, which was in the control of the Estates) and in Hungary since 1608 (where the crown was stored in a locked chest in Pressburg Castle). The Lower Austrian archducal hat was kept in Klosterneuburg Abbey and solemnly brought to Vienna by a committee of the Lower Austrian Estates on the occasion of the inauguration.[6]

Coronations and homage ceremonies in the Habsburg Monarchy shared many other elements: from acoustic signals such as bell ringing, drums, and gunshots to customary manifestations of generosity by way of distributing commemorative medals and coins or making bread, meat, and a wine fountain available to the crowd. The newly invented *Huldigung* of Galicia and Lodomeria, staged in Lemberg in 1773 (see Chapter 8 in this volume), also made use of this standard repertoire: gunshots were fired, coins were thrown to the populace, bread was handed out, oxen were roasted—like in Frankfurt on the occasion of an imperial coronation[7]—and alcoholic beverages were available, with the characteristic difference that the crowd received beer and spirits instead of wine.[8]

Each inaugural rite also had distinct elements, of course. The king dismounting a horse before the welcoming committee of the Estates, and subsequently the provincial captain leading the horse with the king by bridle through the streets of one of the provincial capital towns, be it Olomouc or Brno, were crucial components of the inaugural ceremony in Moravia.[9] In the Austrian Netherlands, the oath taking occurred in the open on sophisticated, ephemeral constructions[10] for which hardly any parallels can be found in Central European Habsburg provinces (see figure 6.1). Triumphal arches were designed for many investitures, but few were as magnificent as those erected by the Silesian "princes and Estates" in Breslau between 1563 and 1620.[11] In Carinthia, archaic medieval rituals initially performed in the open outside of Klagenfurt were significantly reduced and eventually abandoned entirely in 1660, but they remained associated with the inauguration, and Habsburg rulers continued to issue charters confirming the right of the Estates to require the performance from their successors.[12]

Similarly, coronations differed from each other in essential aspects. Bohemian coronations were performed exclusively at the St. Vitus Cathedral in Prague; only the banquet took place at the nearby royal palace.[13] By contrast, five different locations inside and outside the city walls were needed for a Hungarian coronation, regardless of whether it took place in Székesfehérvár, Pressburg, Sopron, or Buda: two churches (for the coronation proper and for the subsequent accolade), a wooden stage on which the king took his oath, and an artificial hill to the top of which he galloped on his horse, waving his sword in four directions; the banquet eventually took place at the royal castle.[14] All these ceremonies thus combined common and individual components—but they were all inaugural rites, their function being to transform a new ruler into a rightful and legitimate sovereign.

Numbers

Statistics may help us to comprehend the scope of this subject.[15] Between 1526 and 1800, twenty-one different rulers from the German branch of the House of Austria—both Habsburg and Habsburg-Lorraine—participated in person in no less than 108 investitures.[16] This number encompasses imperial coronations as well as inaugural rites at the provincial level, including those that pertained to Habsburg cadet branches residing in Graz and Innsbruck. I am excluding inaugurations in autonomous municipalities in hereditary possession (Trieste and Fiume) and homages in Habsburg petty lordships in Upper Germany, which deserve a separate focus.[17] Likewise excluded are unilateral oaths of loyalty provided by various subjects of the Holy Roman Empire, such as the *Lokalhuldigungen* by imperial cities systematically enforced since 1660[18] and the *Kaiserhuldigungen* of the Jewry of Frankfurt introduced in 1711.[19] These did not fully adopt the character of investitures despite being related to imperial elections and coronations. For the purpose of this statistic, election and coronation count as one act,[20] and the same applies to "composite" inaugural ceremonies where different corporations of a province took oaths of loyalty in different ways and at separate occasions. If these were counted separately, the numbers would be even higher.

These 108 early modern personal inaugural rites relate to fifteen political units of differing scope and relevance. Over a period of almost three hundred years, there were fourteen personal investitures in the Holy Roman Empire; thirteen in Hungary; twelve each in Bohemia and Lower Austria; ten in Tyrol; eight in Upper Austria; six in Moravia; five in Silesia (with this number being a simplification, as will be explained later); another five in certain Silesian duchies; four each in Styria, Carinthia, Carniola, Upper Lusatia, and Lower Lusatia; two in Gorizia, and one for Brabant and Limburg combined. In addition to these 108 personal investitures, there were twenty-two coronations of Habsburg rulers' consorts during the same period: eleven in Hungary, eight in Bohemia, and five in the Holy Roman Empire.[21] Maria Theresa, crowned in Hungary and Bohemia as *rex*, not *regina*, is not included in this category. Furthermore, the personal investitures of two unsuccessful "usurpers"—Frederick of the Palatinate and Charles Albert of Bavaria—could likewise be examined in the context of Habsburg inaugural rites, since they were provided more or less deliberately by the Estates of various Habsburg provinces.[22]

It should be stressed that all the above figures refer to personal enthronements. In addition, there were homage ceremonies during which a commissioner acted in place of the new ruler. Some of these events were inconspicuous and thus often neglected by historians, while others like those in Brussels and Ghent during the eighteenth century were quite splendid. If we take account of these as well, we have at least ninety or presumably even more additional ceremonies: around half of them in the eighteenth-century Austrian Netherlands, the rest in Styria, Carinthia, Carniola, Gorizia, Silesia, Croatia, Transylvania, Milan, Mantua, Parma and Piacenza, Galicia, Bukovina—and probably in other provinces as well. Altogether, there were around two hundred inaugural rituals of some importance that could and should be examined together if we intend to grasp the entire landscape of early modern Habsburg investitures.

The Habsburg Inaugural Process

The number of ceremonies—surprisingly large compared to other European monarchies—reflects an essential feature of the Habsburg concept of kingship in a state that was utterly composite. Admittedly, early modern Europe was a continent of composite monarchies, each of them structured in its own distinct fashion. It is through the lens of inaugural rites, however, that we can uncover the essential peculiarity of the Habsburg case. Although the Habsburg agglomeration in Central Europe largely consisted of contiguous territorial blocks and quickly developed into a viable financial and military union of growing effectiveness, a full incorporative union never developed. The Habsburg *Königreiche und Länder*, as they were routinely labeled, remained intrinsically juxtaposed, and their essential constitutional independence survived even the progressive institutional and juridical merger of the Austrian and Bohemian provinces in the mid-eighteenth century.

In terms of succession and legitimation, this certainly posed major problems. The Habsburg rulers did not ascend a single throne but, instead, many, with each one requiring an investiture ceremony that until the seventeenth century had to be performed in the respective province and (with few exceptions) in the ruler's presence.

Ferdinand I as the "constructor" of this union, combining the Austrian hereditary provinces, the Bohemian composite state, Hungary with its dependencies, and the Holy Roman Empire, underwent at least nine investitures in person. Having been initially sworn in, together with his older brother and only *per procurationem*, by the Estates of the hereditary provinces in 1520, he was invested anew as exclusive ruler in both parts of the Archduchy of Austria as well as in Styria the following year. Another year later, he was inaugurated in Carniola and Gorizia (by proxy), while his personal investiture in Tyrol had to wait until 1529 when the partition agreement between him and Charles V was made public. In 1521, the Carinthians refused to swear him in due to an unsettled dispute over territory with Tyrol, and there is no indication that a Carinthian inauguration ever took place.[23] In the meantime, Ferdinand succeeded his brother-in-law in Hungary and the Bohemian lands and had to arrange himself with the assertive Estates of those territories. This involved much negotiation and even humiliation: in April 1527, outside the city walls of Brno, Ferdinand was forced to haggle in the rain until sundown about whether he was obliged to dismount his horse before the welcome committee of the Moravian Estates. Eventually, he had to accept that the Estates would not swear but only pledge obedience; whereas he would have to swear to respect the laws and confirm the Estates' liberties first.[24] One month later, he was invested as supreme duke of Silesia in Breslau and underwent a special inauguration in the twin Duchy of Schweidnitz-Jauer. In Hungary, only part of the nobility elected Ferdinand, while the Estates of Croatia (where only commissioners had been sent) accepted him as sovereign in a peculiar and never-repeated inaugural act whose substance would later become controversial between Croatian and Hungarian nationalist historians.[25] The Hungarian coronation took place in November 1527. Ferdinand was elected and crowned king of the Romans in January 1531 and eventually proclaimed emperor as late as March 1558 following his brother's abdication.[26]

This series of inaugural rites through which Ferdinand established his new domain was by no means unique. His successors had to reiterate the same process of legitimation in all kingdoms and provinces, albeit with modifications. Even visits to Upper and Lower Lusatia and to Carniola and Carinthia, where Ferdinand had been inaugurated in absence, became obligatory Maximilian II was first crowned king of Bohemia in Prague (September 1562) and king of the Romans in Frankfurt (November 1562), then king of Hungary in Pressburg (September 1563), from where he immediately proceeded to Olomouc, Breslau, Lübben, and Bautzen to be inaugurated as margrave of Moravia, supreme duke of Silesia and margrave of Lower and Upper Lusatia respectively. On the way, he took the oath of fealty from the Estates of the petty principality of Sagan. The Viennese inauguration for Lower Austria in March 1564 was followed by Ferdinand I's death in July, and the Upper Austrian inauguration in Linz was subsequently postponed until December 1565. Two decades later, Rudolf II faced a similarly long and winding road to fully secured accession with only slight modifications of sequence. This time, the process was begun in Hungary, the homages in the Bohemian and Austrian lands were postponed until after Maximilian's death, and Rudolf eventually toured the Bohemian lands in opposite order to his father.

Maximilian II, Rudolf II, and Matthias took part in ten inaugural rites each, slightly more than Ferdinand I and exactly as many as Leopold I and Charles VI in the mid-seventeenth and eighteenth centuries (Trieste and Fiume not included). Ferdinand II was the record holder with twelve personal investitures. We can see that a Habsburg sovereign's ascension to rule consisted of a series of inaugural rites to be held in different places and with different participants, some of them typically being clustered into a tour of sorts (*Huldigungsreise*). Although no binding sequence developed, the arduous accessions in Bohemia, Hungary, and the Holy Roman Empire were typically undertaken first. The inaugural process was usually initiated during the predecessor's reign but rarely completed before his death.

There are two interrelated reasons why Habsburg authority remained dependent on inaugural rites and why the dynasty could not risk avoiding these rites— or even reducing their number—until the mid-seventeenth century. First, the investitures had constitutive importance for the royal succession and thus for the integrity of the newly formed union of disparate domains. To be sure, the conditions of succession in different Habsburg realms varied greatly, and this circumstance significantly complicated the transfer of power from one ruler to another. The imperial throne was elective and remained so until the end of the Holy Roman Empire, making the election a crucial concern of Habsburg international policy.[27] Contrary to a widespread textbook interpretation, Bohemia and Hungary were not unquestionably elective under Habsburg rule. Despite having been freely elected in both kingdoms, Ferdinand I skillfully sought to circumscribe the Estates' right to participate in the selection of his successor, exploiting the fact that Bohemian and Hungarian dependencies such as Moravia and Croatia acknowledged the hereditary right of his wife Anna Jagiello. But the Bohemian and Hungarian Estates still exerted considerable influence on the succession process, and their claims to the right of royal election could be reasserted should the dynasty's authority decline, as was the case during the late years of Rudolf II. The Habsburg succession thus remained fragile until unequivocal hereditary succession was established in Bohemia in 1627 and in Hungary in 1687.[28] In the *Erblande*, hereditary succession was not controversial, but Habsburg rulers faced another problem there: the lack of the primogeniture principle complicated the transfer of power, causing divisions and disputes over succession and giving the Estates opportunities to exploit the uncertainties. Here, too, investitures were essential for ensuring the ascension to power, and there was virtually no way of avoiding them until Ferdinand II altered the pattern of succession and proclaimed primogeniture in his last will (1621). It was not until the Pragmatic Sanction that the succession rules of the various Habsburg domains became fully synchronized.[29]

Second, inaugural rites had essential implications for the highly contractual relationship between Habsburg rulers and the Estates of the individual provinces. Far from being acts of unilateral submission, they served the purpose of mutual recognition and obligation through reciprocal oath taking. The Estates acknowledged their ruler and promised loyalty, and in return, the ruler confirmed the Estates' rights and liberties. Avoiding an inaugural rite or altering its ceremonial would have threatened to undermine the established distribution of power. Not just the *Reichsstände* and the Estates of Bohemia and Hungary, but even junior provinces with little chance of influencing the succession proved to be resolute guardians of their constitutions, insisting on proper inaugurations before conceding full authority to the new sovereign. Arno Strohmeyer has demonstrated that the religious divide greatly reinforced the political relevance of enthronement ceremonies and contributed to transforming them into the most important arena of struggle between the predominantly Protestant Estates and the Catholic rulers until the crucial confrontation during the first quarter of the seventeenth century would reconfigure their mutual relationship.[30]

It speaks for itself that not a single inaugural rite was omitted in the seven Austrian provinces, the five Bohemian lands, and in Hungary until the Thirty Years' War.[31] Moreover, the process of legitimation by way of personal investitures was always completed no later than two years after the death of the predecessor or after attaining majority.[32] An example from Moravia may illuminate why this was so: in March 1577, only five months after the death of Maximilian II, the Estates flatly refused to negotiate any further tax grant until Rudolf II came to legitimize his rule over the margraviate in a personal inauguration.[33] Even in a province that defined itself as hereditary, the obedience of the Estates thus remained conditional until sealed by mutual recognition in a formal investiture. This explains why the Habsburgs, who were dependent on provincial tax grants, made efforts to conclude their processes of legitimation as quickly as possible. Even the possibility of sending commissioners to perform inaugurations was discontinued except for the County of Gorizia, which belonged to the Habsburg cadet branch between 1564 and 1619, and a few Silesian principalities where inauguration by commissioner was the rule.

The latter case deserves a digression. Unlike other Habsburg provinces, the Duchy of Lower and Upper Silesia (as per the official nomenclature) was not a unit, but a bewildering conglomerate of principalities and minor lordships ruled either directly by the Habsburgs or by local princely dynasties, and in one case by the bishop of Breslau. Therefore, the Silesian inauguration itself was also quite literally composite. It consisted of a series of oaths that particular subjects and corporations—the bishop, princes, feudal lords, both chapters of Breslau, abbots of prominent monasteries, Estates of the principalities under direct Habsburg rule, the municipal council of Breslau, and the community of burghers—swore one after another with varying wording, differing gestures, and even in different locations in the city.[34] This usually lasted several days and was thus very dissimilar to the inaugural rites in other Habsburg provinces, where the ceremony was mostly a single act during which different corporations swore together.[35] Moreover, local Estates in some *Erbfürstentümer* (principalities under direct Habsburg rule such as Schweidnitz-Jauer, Oppeln-Ratibor, Glogau, and Troppau) demanded to take their oaths within the borders of their particular territories. The Habsburg rulers could not visit all these principalities in person during their inaugural tours. Instead, they preferred to obtain as much recognition as they could in Breslau and during their journey through Silesia, and sent commissioners elsewhere.[36]

European Parallels

It is worth considering the broader European context to fully grasp the uniqueness of the Habsburg enthronement practices. In his examination of French coronations, Richard A. Jackson was able to scrutinize only ten early modern ceremonies. The number remains unimpressive even if we add the coronations of seven queens, the last of which took place in 1610.[37] Admittedly, there were other inaugural rituals in France as well, but they were of a different nature than the ones outlined in this chapter. Neither French nor English monarchs were obliged to tour their realms to be sworn in.

There were certain analogies, however, that help to underline the singularity of Habsburg inaugurations. In the multiple kingdoms in the British Isles, despite a certain tradition of peripatetic kingship,[38] only three early modern monarchs underwent more than one coronation. The first was James VI/I, the founder of the Union of Crowns, who was anointed king of Scotland in 1567 as a one-year-old baby and crowned king of England in 1603. His direct successors, Charles I and Charles II, however, were invested under very specific political circumstances that prevented the development of any tradition resembling the Habsburg case.[39]

The sixteenth- and seventeenth-century French monarchy had a tradition of royal entries into cities. These important political rituals, extensively researched over the past few decades, were primarily encounters with municipal elites. They were instrumental in pacifying revolts and publicly reestablishing royal authority following civil wars and military campaigns. Constitutional elements such as an oath confirming municipal rights and liberties disappeared after the mid-sixteenth century. At times, a royal progress to major cities and provinces of France was organized that included several entries but no formal inaugural ceremonies resembling those in the Habsburg lands.[40] The most famous—if also exceptional—journey of this kind was the grand tour of France organized by the queen mother Catherine de' Medici for her son Charles IX between 1564 and 1566. During this trip, which began three years after Charles's coronation and lasted more than two years, the teenage king made 108 entries and held *lits de justice* in the *parlements* of Dijon, Toulouse, and Bordeaux. Despite certain analogies, however, this extraordinary journey was not a constitutional obligation the way the Habsburg inaugural trips were.[41]

Besides the coronation, the mutual swearing of oaths between the French kings and the États of the peripheral petty Principality of Béarn resembled Habsburg inaugural practices most closely from a constitutional point of view. But Louis XIII, annexing the province to France in 1620, was the only French king to swear the oath to respect the local liberties on the spot. Louis XIV still did so in the vicinity, though only as a by-product of his journey to meet the Spanish infanta he was to marry in 1659–60. Later on, the inaugural oath ceremony took place in Versailles with Béarnais delegates in attendance.[42]

The closest analogies to the inaugural process of the Central European Habsburgs can be identified within the family, namely in the Spanish monarchy—itself the paradigm of a conglomerate state. Coronations disappeared from the kingdoms on the Iberian Peninsula during the Middle Ages, but there were inaugural oaths (*juramentos*) in Castile, Navarre, Aragon, Valencia, and Catalonia, and additional ceremonies in the Low Countries and the Italian holdings. To submit to all of these rites in person was impossible—although Philip II made an effort as crown prince, visiting even Milan and the Low Countries in the mid-sixteenth century. His successors were much less active, authorizing delegates to act on their behalf outside the peninsula. In Spain proper, personal swearing-in remained the custom, with a viceroy sometimes standing in for the absent king or prince only in Navarre.[43]

It is difficult to obtain a clear picture of these inaugural oaths because their modalities varied greatly. One reason for this—and one of the distinctions between the *juramentos* and the Central European *Huldigungen*—is the customary temporal, spatial, and legal separation of the oath taken by the ruler (*juramento de los fueros*) from the one sworn to him by a community (*juramento de fidelidad*). Instead of one ceremony, there were often two. Unilateral oaths to underage princes represent another peculiarity. From a dynastic point of view, such *juramentos* served the purpose of ensuring an undisputed succession, and they were therefore often performed when the respective successor was very young. In Castile, which held a special position in this respect, members of the dynasty swore a unilateral oath of fealty to the *principe heredero* together with the Cortes in a ceremony that took place at the Church of San Jerónimo el Real in Madrid from 1573 onward. With the exception of Don Carlos, all six crown princes who received this oath of allegiance between 1528 and 1632 were children between ten months and six years of age.[44] Those who eventually ascended the throne swore in response before the Cortes of Castile upon their succession.[45]

United with the Spanish monarchy for three generations, Portugal followed this Castilian custom. Under Habsburg rule, six *juramentos* took place in four distinct ceremonies. Philip II took and reciprocally received an oath in Tomar in 1581. He immediately let the Cortes swear loyalty to the five-year-old prince Diego Félix. After Diego died, the Cortes repeated this unilateral ceremony in Lisbon in 1583 for Philip's second son, the later Philip III (Philip II in Portugal), who by then was almost five.[46] Only in 1619, after having ruled Portugal for twenty-one years, did Philip take an oath in return on the occasion of his only journey to Portugal. The Cortes swore fealty to his fourteen-year-old son during the very same ceremony.[47]

For the Crown of Aragon, the situation was more complex. Here, the dynasty only once made a child the subject of a unilateral *juramento de fidelidad*. The eastern kingdoms, however, required an oath by the heir apparent to respect their *fueros* once he reached the age of fourteen, and a ruler could be forced to swear again when ascending the throne. Hence, Philip III first received the *juramento de fidelidad* as a child at the Cortes of Monzón in 1585. He then swore his primogenitary oath first at the Cortes of Taracona in 1592 before repeating it in Zaragoza in 1599, legitimizing his ascendancy to power as king of Aragon.[48] In Barcelona, the king or prince swore twice: upon his solemn entry, he took the unilateral oath *de la ciudad y por las islas* in the open air, swearing to sustain the eternal union of Catalonia with the Balearic Islands and other dependencies. A few days later, a mutual oath between the king and the Catalonian political community followed in the royal palace.[49] In Valencia and Navarre, the *juramentos* were staged only as a reciprocal obligation, usually during the Cortes.[50] It was here, in the Crown of Aragon and in Navarre, that the inaugural process most closely resembled the one in the Central European Habsburg domains, with successors regularly touring the composite realm to be installed onto different thrones by different communities. The timing of these ceremonies was contingent upon the fortunes of the dynasty and its authority at the respective time, but progresses with at least three personal inaugurations took place in every generation: in 1542, 1563–64, 1585, 1599, 1626, and 1645–46.

It was the royal minority starting in 1665 that would radically change this situation and paralyze this form of legitimation. Upon reaching adulthood, Charles II seems to have undertaken only an inaugural trip to Zaragoza (1677), and the viceroy of Navarre took the oath in Pamplona during the same year.[51] Once the Bourbon dynasty took over the Spanish kingdoms, Philip V initially revived the *juramentos* to legitimize his rule before breaking with the tradition. The only inaugural oath his successors performed in person was the unilateral ceremony of allegiance to the heirs duly staged in San Jerónimo el Real in Madrid.[52]

From Philip II to Charles II, between 1528 and 1677, around thirty-four inaugural oaths took place in Spain in the presence of a king or crown prince, almost a third of them in Castile. This is a significant number compared to other monarchies in Western Europe, but still amounts to only half as many personal enthronements as undergone by the cousins of the Spanish rulers in Central Europe during the same period. This suggests that the inaugural process customary in the Habsburg Monarchy, despite having certain analogies elsewhere, was exceptional in its complexity as well as its longevity. Central European Habsburgs did not need to revisit certain destinations to repeat their inaugural oath as did their Spanish cousins, and their inaugural tours were never as extensive as Charles IX's voyage through France. Nevertheless, their inaugural process required a great deal of time, travel, financial backing, and co-ordination, and on occasions, it also involved hard bargaining with the Estates of the political units involved.

Making Habsburg Inaugural Rites Facultative

In the seventeenth century, however, a fundamental change occurred in the Habsburg Monarchy: Habsburg rulers, who had hitherto painstakingly attended all inaugural rites, began to discontinue some of them. This transformation—evidently a process, not a radical break—has never been described in detail. It is even harder to explain because historians are often faced with difficulties in deciding whether any given foregoing of an inauguration was the result of contingencies and exigencies of the moment or whether it followed a conscious master plan. In absence of articulated statements, researchers are forced to deduce the dynasty's attitude toward the inaugurations indirectly, and the picture thus obtained is rather ambivalent: it reveals a trend toward reducing the number of investitures, but—surprisingly—no straightforward and consistent policy.

First, the division of the Austrian hereditary possessions in 1564 eased the inaugural process significantly. Attendance of the inaugurations in Styria, Carinthia, Carniola, Gorizia, and Tyrol (with its dependencies in Upper Germany) was yielded to the cadet lines, while the less than a dozen remaining inaugurations continued to be the business of the imperial branch. Second, the discontinuation of inaugural rites was certainly facilitated by the disastrous defeat of the confederated Protestant Estates in 1620. The subsequent political change greatly advanced the power of the monarchy in both the Bohemian and Austrian provinces. But the forbearance of investitures was by no means an immediate result of the political upheaval, but rather its long-term outcome. Ferdinand II, himself personally inaugurated in all provinces under his sway,[53] still attempted to legitimize his son born in 1608 as his successor as early as possible. The inaugural process was begun in 1625 with the Hungarian coronation in Sopron. In 1627, Ferdinand III was crowned king of Bohemia, with the kingdom being proclaimed hereditary, the ceremony modified, and an additional homage introduced on the day before the coronation proper.[54] In 1628, on his journey back from Prague, he received an unspectacular oath of fealty from the Moravian Estates in Znojmo,[55] and the inaugurations in Lower and Upper Austria took place in 1629 and 1630. Crowned king of the Romans in Regensburg in December 1636, Ferdinand III became the only Habsburg ruler whose entire process of legitimation predated the death of his predecessor, if only by seven weeks.

The new political climate helped to expedite the inaugural process and simultaneously reduce its complexity. Undergoing the Moravian inauguration on his way back to Vienna, Ferdinand III was the first king who did not embark on the customary tour through the Bohemian lands (whose number declined when both Lusatias were ceded to the elector of Saxony). At the same time, he skipped three personal investitures in Inner Austria, sending a princely commissioner to Styria, Carinthia, Carniola, and Gorizia in 1631. Even more remarkable was the situation in Silesia, where the composite character of the inauguration allowed a radical modification: against all custom and privilege, the crown prince received the oaths of allegiance from his subjects separately, and he did so either by sending commissioners to individual duchies or receiving dukes and deputies in Vienna instead of visiting the province himself. The entire procedure took six years from 1625 to 1631.[56] New strategies were thus developed to make the inaugural process more practicable for the dynasty without dispensing with investitures altogether. The absolute priority remained the same, however: to obtain legitimation from every province. Even though many investitures were altered considerably, none were actually foregone.

This began to change only during the next generation, albeit quite ambivalently. Ferdinand IV died prematurely in 1654, having been invested personally in Bohemia (1646), Hungary (1647), Lower Austria (1651), Upper Austria (1652), and the Holy Roman Empire (1654), and by proxy in the Inner Austrian provinces (1651). In doing so, he followed the pattern his father had established twenty years earlier. Ferdinand IV was never invested in Moravia and Silesia, however, and we will likely never know whether these inaugurations had been scheduled or were intentionally avoided.[57]

Leopold I was the first Habsburg to entirely avoid an inauguration during his almost fifty-year reign. Surprisingly, it was not peripheral and labyrinthine Silesia, but consolidated and easily accessible Moravia that became the first among many Habsburg provinces to have its inaugural rites permanently cancelled. This seems an interesting turning point in the history of Habsburg enthronements that historians have hitherto overlooked entirely. It likewise remains puzzling why Moravia was the only province Leopold ignored. Indeed, Leopold appears to have been a monarch who cared much about his thrones. He was inclined to perform, revive, and even introduce personal inaugurations in other provinces, and he invested much time and effort into these ceremonies: having been invested in Lower Austria (1655) and crowned in Hungary (1655) and Bohemia (1656), he deputed commissioners in 1657, a few months after his father's death, to receive the oath of fealty from his Silesian subjects in what would become the last Habsburg inauguration in Breslau. On the way back from the imperial coronation in Frankfurt (1658), he received the *Erbhuldigung* in Upper Austria. He also set out for Innsbruck to take the homage from the Tyroleans immediately after inheriting the province in 1665.

The most striking circumstance here is the discrepancy between Leopold's inaugural strategies toward Moravia and the Inner Austrian provinces. Twice deprived of royal presence in 1631 and 1651, these Alpine duchies may seem to have had little hope of reviving "their" personal investitures, the last of which had taken place in 1596–97. Nevertheless, as opposed to the Moravians, the Inner Austrian Estates actively clamored for an inauguration soon after Ferdinand III died. The Styrians claimed—as had the Moravians in 1577, but now in a much humbler manner—that the *Erbhuldigung* was a condition for opening a new diet.⁵⁸ Surprisingly, the response from the court was benevolent: Leopold neither contradicted the petition, nor did he send another commissioner. Instead, he declared that he would personally appear in Graz.⁵⁹ Even more surprising was that he kept his promise. In 1660, he embarked on a long journey to Inner Austria. He not only visited Graz, Klagenfurt, and Ljubljana, becoming the first Habsburg to receive the homages as emperor, but proceeded to Gorizia and even to Trieste, thereby introducing personal inaugurations where they had never been customary.⁶⁰

This not only reveals that the process of abandoning inaugural rites was far from being straightforward: even a repeated previous avoidance of certain personal investitures could be reversed. It also sheds light on a strikingly inconsequent attitude toward inaugurations. While Leopold willingly complied with the requests from the Alpine principalities, no inauguration was held in Moravia, and not even a commissioner was sent there. Why did Leopold ignore Moravia when he was prepared to trudge all the way to Gorizia and Trieste? Was it the pressure of the Styrian Estates (which on the whole does not seem to have been excessive or insuperable)? Was it the curiosity of the still teenage sovereign to whom the ambassador of Venice attested "il genio particolare . . . di viaggiare e cambiar stanza" and "gusto . . . di mutar spesso soggiorno"⁶¹ in 1659?⁶² Or did influential ministers from Inner Austria encourage him to set out for what would become a long and uncomfortable journey? Whatever the reason, for all who cared, Moravia could easily be viewed as a test case: it was the first Habsburg province to lose its inaugural rite forever—and without any public outcry.⁶³ It demonstrated that legitimation through inauguration was no longer indispensable for exerting authority, at least in a situation of undisputed succession.

Joseph I's Avoided Investitures

A major break in the Habsburg dynasty's handling of investitures occurred during the last decades of Leopold's long reign. Whereas his ancestors had struggled to enthrone their successors in as many provinces as possible during their own lifetime, Leopold's approach was radically different. His heir Joseph I was crowned in Hungary in 1687 as a nine-year-old boy and in the Holy Roman Empire in 1690 at the age of eleven. At this point, however, the inaugural process stopped, and it was not continued during the last fifteen years of the emperor's life. Joseph continued this policy following his father's death in 1705: no *Erbhuldigungen* were announced, no commissioners were sent. The only exception was the homage in Lower Austria, which the new emperor celebrated in person five months after Leopold's death. This too was an innovation that would provide a pattern for the future: as demonstrated by William Godsey, from 1705 onward, the Lower Austrian ceremony was usually staged shortly after the predecessor's death,⁶⁴ and we may consider it a distant equivalent of the *lit de justice* that displaced the traditional inaugural program of the French kings in the seventeenth century.[65]

While the Lower Austrian inauguration adopted a new meaning, other inaugural rites were neglected. In Bohemia, it was the first time since 1526 that no successor had been crowned before the predecessor's death—and the first time ever that a royal coronation was avoided altogether. By 1690, contemporaries seem to have expected that the legitimation process would continue as usual with a third coronation in Bohemia,[66] but it did not. It has been suggested that Joseph I's premature death in 1711, after a reign that lasted only six years, prevented his coronation.[67] This interpretation, isolating the Bohemian case, appears unconvincing, however, when examining the customary pattern of Habsburg investitures. Joseph I lived for more than two decades after his imperial coronation in January 1690, and the decision to avoid a coronation in Bohemia was thus already made during Leopold's reign. In fact, a ministerial conference in June 1689 discussed whether Joseph needed to be crowned king of Bohemia before he could be elected king of the Romans. The conclusion was negative,[68] even though Leopold I continued to assure his aristocratic pen friends that a visit to Prague was still on the table.

What actually impeded the Bohemian coronation as well as other inaugural rites was not a lack of time, but more likely a desperate lack of money owing to a series of wars that reached an unprecedented scale precisely around 1690.[69] At the same time, the increase in ceremonial requirements since the mid-seventeenth century made it difficult to organize a ceremony of this kind in a respectable manner at short notice and low cost. That the Viennese court became more sedentary than ever before under Leopold I may have played a role as well.[70] It is difficult to tell which of these circumstances was decisive; perhaps it was simply the Habsburg dynasty's overstretching after 1700 that helped to sidetrack the issue of investitures, at least in provinces where the succession was considered consolidated.

Exhausted by a long and costly period of warfare, the Habsburg provinces themselves seem to have readily accepted the new policy, remaining remarkably silent after Joseph came to power in 1705. Unlike half a century earlier, the Styrians opened a new diet without even seeking an inauguration. The Carinthians remonstrated, but the reaction was neither a promise nor a delegated commissioner, only a letter of indemnity (*Schadlosbrief*)—a standard measure for undermining a privilege while claiming the opposite.[71] Likewise abortive was the request made on 21 September 1705 by the Silesian "princes and Estates" who, admitting that "der gegenwärtige zustand des universi" [the current state of the universe] would hardly allow a progress to Silesia, asked Joseph I to delegate the homage.[72]

Hence, it was at the beginning of the eighteenth century that Bohemia, Silesia, and the Austrian hereditary lands with the remarkable exception of Lower

Austria were for the first time—and in several cases permanently—deprived of their inaugural ceremonies. What began as an exception in Moravia with Leopold I developed into standard practice, although it remains difficult to determine whether the abandonment of investiture rites was a dynastic program at this stage or merely the result of contingencies and financial shortcomings. Apparently, Habsburg policy in this regard caused confusion even in the Viennese corridors of power. A well-informed man as Christian Julius Schierl von Schierendorff, the secretary of the Aulic Chamber who designed a series of bold reform proposals to Joseph I (and later also to Charles VI), still counted on a near Bohemian coronation once Leopold I had died in 1705.[73]

Eighteenth-Century Habsburg Investitures: Suspended, Invented, Revived

The eighteenth century brought another major change. Until Leopold I, successors had regularly been inaugurated during their predecessor's lifetime. Of all the seventeenth-century personal investitures, thirty were realized in this way and only twelve took place after the predecessor's death—though never more than four years after it. In the eighteenth century, however, successors were *not* inaugurated during their predecessor's lifetime, with Joseph II's coronation as king of the Romans in 1764 being the only (and very specific) exception. A closer look reveals that the elimination of inaugural rites *vivente praedecessore* often resulted from contingencies and succession crises that were symptomatic for dynastic rule in general and for the eighteenth-century Habsburg Monarchy in particular. Charles VI and Leopold II were catapulted to the throne unexpectedly. Moreover, the latter died so early and so suddenly that he had virtually no chance to prepare the succession of his son Francis.

Ironically (and rarely acknowledged), Maria Theresa—whose succession turned out to be the most precarious of all—was not inaugurated in any province before 1740 either. The last Habsburg emperor may have believed that the Pragmatic Sanction demoted inaugural rites to secondary importance. But from the perspective of what occurred after his death, his failure to see to his daughter's enthronements appears particularly misconceived. Had Maria Theresa been crowned *rex* of Hungary and Bohemia and solemnly inaugurated as ruler in Austria before 1740, it would certainly have been more difficult for the elector of Bavaria to stage his investitures in Upper Austria and Bohemia in 1741 as ascensions to vacant thrones rather than usurpations.[74] Regarding his daughter's investitures, Charles VI was trapped within the established succession law and his own amendments: any enthronement of an heiress during his lifetime would prejudice a possible male heir yet to be born. This may support Charles Ingrao's argument that the Pragmatic Sanction was "more a millstone than a milestone" in Charles VI's efforts to secure an undivided succession.[75] At any rate, the eighteenth century witnessed a striking discontinuation of the practice of anticipative investitures that had been customary until Leopold I.

From what has been said above, it may appear that inaugural rites were gradually declining in the eighteenth-century Habsburg Monarchy, but the actual situation was more complex. To be sure, some of the rites disappeared, and the contractual and reciprocal character of many others was diminishing, albeit at a different pace in different political units. Nevertheless, 26 of the 108 early modern personal investitures (i.e., roughly a quarter) took place in the eighteenth century, ten of them for Charles VI alone. The remaining sixteen were mostly the imperial, Hungarian, and Bohemian coronations, as well as the homage ceremonies in Lower Austria.[76] In addition, the territorial expansion of the Habsburg Monarchy brought new inaugurations into play in Transylvania, Italy, and the Netherlands. Admittedly, with the remarkable exception of Francis II's appearance in Brussels in 1794, these inaugurations were investitures by proxy. Sending commissioners to perform the inaugurations had always been an option for the Habsburgs in regard to minor territories or during irregular situations. In the seventeenth century, delegates were typically employed to avoid an inaugural trip without discontinuing the investiture ritual as such. But for the newly acquired peripheral provinces, this practice can hardly be viewed as derogatory. In the former Spanish Netherlands, the Austrian Habsburgs continued the local investiture traditions of notable constitutional importance throughout the entire eighteenth century,[77] just as they continued the inaugurations in Lombardy[78] and Transylvania.[79] Even under Joseph II, who avoided personal investitures except for the imperial coronation, a dozen inaugurations were staged in these peripheral provinces from mid-July to early October 1781. The three oaths of fealty in Milan, Brussels, and Ghent, as well as the final one in Mantua, were taken by governors-general—one of which was Joseph's brother Ferdinand; the other his brother-in-law, Albert of Saxony-Teschen.[80]

On the opposite end of the spectrum from Joseph II, who was notorious for his disdain for ceremonial, we find his grandfather Charles VI. With at least ten personal investitures (Catalonia 1705, Valencia 1706, and Trieste and Fiume 1728 not included), a number that would never be reached again, Charles ostensibly appears to have simply revived the pattern that had been customary before his father's reign. But there was a crucial difference: while Leopold I spent only five years completing the inaugural process, Charles took an unparalleled twenty-one years. Of his ten investitures, four were undertaken swiftly within one year of his succeeding his brother (1711–12): the homage in Tyrol on the way from Spain to Frankfurt, where he was crowned emperor, then the Hungarian coronation, and finally the inauguration in Lower Austria. The remaining ceremonies were celebrated with unprecedented delay on the respective occasions of progresses to

Bohemia (1723), Inner Austria (1728), and Upper Austria (1732) during a rare decade of peace.[81] These belated investitures were obviously considered facultative by then, but Charles was ready to stage them as great spectacles—not as a means of legitimizing his ascension to power, but as a vehicle for propagating his broader political goals such as the Pragmatic Sanction.[82]

An accidentally recorded episode reveals the subtlety of the negotiations preceding the decision whether and how a belated inaugural rite should be performed. The Moravian *Landeshauptmann* Maximilian Ulrich von Kaunitz informed the provincial diet in May 1726 about his informal talk with the influential and well-informed court counselor Johann Christoph von Freyenfels, who was responsible for Moravian affairs in the Bohemian Chancellery. Surprisingly, Freyenfels had asked whether the Estates were interested in having the Emperor for the inaugural rite, stating that a commissioner would otherwise be sent to Moravia. The Estates authorized Kaunitz to continue the talks, which eventually led nowhere, however.[83] The reason why is unclear, but the episode as a whole evidences that even in Moravia, the possibility of performing the inaugural ceremony was still on the table.

Despite being conceived as a concession rather than a constitutional obligation, these inaugural rites remained "multivocal performances"[84]; the Estates could use them for their own benefit as well. A good example is the splendid volume with text and engravings produced by the Styrian Estates to commemorate Charles's inauguration in Graz in 1728, imitating the practice customary in Lower Austria. Besides common scenes like the reception of the emperor at the frontier or the procession of the Estates in the church, the Styrians included in their book—apparently without asking for permission—an engraving depicting Charles VI swearing to uphold Styrian laws, privileges, and habits (see figure 1.2).[85] This fascinating image has received scarce attention in historiography despite the fact that it may be one of only two representations of an eighteenth-century emperor swearing an oath—a rare event at any rate.[86] The argument that this represented nothing but a humiliation for the Estates since the oath was taken before a small committee and not the entire diet seems to miss the point spectacularly.[87] In fact, the message was aimed in the opposite direction, stressing the contractual character and constitutional relevance of the ritual. Did Charles's openness to inaugural rites go so far as to let him enjoy this reminder of Styria's long-standing liberties and limitations of his power?

His daughter Maria Theresa, who radically intervened in the self-government of the Inner Austrian lands, very probably did not. Had someone reminded her on the occasion of her trip through Graz and Klagenfurt to Innsbruck in 1765[88] of the opportunity to summon the Estates and renew the mutual obligation, this depiction alone would certainly have sufficed to dampen her enthusiasm. In fact, she avoided most personal enthronements during her long rule. At the

Figure 1.2. Emperor Charles VI swearing to uphold the provincial laws, privileges, and habits before the committee of the Estates during his Styrian inauguration in Graz in 1728. A series of engravings was produced to embellish a commemorative volume published by the Estates in 1740, but this particular engraving, reminding the dynasty of the contractual nature of their rule over the Duchy of Styria, was eventually included only in selected copies (Graz, Steiermärkisches Landesarchiv).

same time, however, her four personal inaugurations in Lower Austria, Hungary, Bohemia, and Upper Austria between November 1740 and June 1743, framing the serious succession crisis that nearly destroyed the monarchy,[89] reveal the importance these rituals assumed as soon as the legitimacy of Habsburg rule was at stake. In January 1743, while preparing her coronation trip to Bohemia, Maria Theresa was apparently still considering the revival of a personal *Huldigung* in Moravia.[90] A decade later, she would choose inaugural ceremonies—her Hungarian and Bohemian coronations together with the inaugural entries of her husband in Florence in 1739 and in Frankfurt in 1745—as motifs for the reliefs decorating the sides of their magnificent double sarcophagus in Vienna's imperial crypt, the *Kapuzinergruft*.[91]

A similar reactivation of inaugural ceremonies was employed once more for the sake of power consolidation in the early 1790s. Leopold II skillfully used his personal enthronements in Lower Austria, Hungary, and Bohemia to calm the political turmoil and discontent his brother's reforms had occasioned (see figure 3.1). This included a revival of the homage in Tyrol, staged for the first time since 1711 and now accepted by Leopold's sister Maria Elisabeth, the abbess of the

Damenstift in Innsbruck.[92] With regard to other provinces that demanded the resumption of their respective inaugural rites in their grievances, Leopold at least signaled his readiness to reinstate the investitures in the future[93] or provided a surrogate. Thus, the Moravian and Silesian Estates dispatched delegations to Prague in 1791 to swear the oath of fealty together with the Bohemian Estates on the day before the coronation.[94] Although this intriguing innovation with serious implications did not help to reactivate the Moravian homage, it established the pattern for the ensuing Bohemian coronations in 1792 and 1836. The restitution of the inaugural symbols that Joseph II had collected in the *Schatzkammer* relates to Leopold II's cautious and appeasing policy toward his provinces as well.[95] Would Maria Theresa have submitted to an inauguration in Silesia had she succeeded in reconquering the province during the Seven Years' War? In the opinions of experts on how Silesia should be governed in such a fortuitous case, regaining the loyalty of the Silesians was a topic—but no mention of an inaugural rite as a tool for this purpose was made.[96] Perhaps Maria Theresa would just have delegated a commissioner—as she did in Galicia and Bukovina, where *Huldigungen* were held in 1773 and 1777 to ensure the loyalty of the local elites of these newly annexed provinces,[97] though the empress considered this act little more than "une cérémonie, car il sera toujours forcé et arraché à ces pauvres gens."[98]

Looking more closely at eighteenth-century inaugurations performed by proxy, we observe a remarkable constitutional hierarchy. The inaugurations in the Netherlands were decidedly mutual commitments and remained so until the end of the Austrian regime. On 23 April 1794, Emperor Francis II still swore the *Blijde Inkomst/Joyeuse Entrée* publicly and in person in Brussels.[99] By contrast, the *giuramenti* staged in Milan since 1707, in Mantua since 1708, and in Parma and Piacenza in 1738 and 1741 consisted of unilateral oaths. In Transylvania, a transformation can be observed: there, the Estates originally swore unilaterally to the commissioner, usually a military diplomat, after having received the written confirmation of the *Diploma Leopoldinum* guaranteeing their constitution. In 1790, however, the ceremony was altered to have the royal commissioner swearing to the Estates as well.[100] Nevertheless, all these ceremonies were restaged every time power passed to a new monarch, thereby giving the government and the local elites the opportunity to symbolically reaffirm their mutual relationship. The same was not the case in Galicia and Bukovina, however, where the *Huldigungen* of 1773 and 1777 remained ad-hoc rituals marking the submission of these newly constituted provinces to Habsburg rule and seem not to have been restaged thereafter.[101] Hence, they appear to have less in common with the inaugurations in the Netherlands than with the homage act celebrated in Braunau in June 1779. In this ceremony, the Bavarian prelates, nobility, and towns of the annexed *Innviertel* entered into Habsburg vassalage and, as a significant difference to the Galician and Bukovinian acquisitions, were incorporated into the existing province of Upper Austria.[102]

Taken as a whole, the picture of eighteenth-century Habsburg inaugural rites is ambiguous and by no means reveals a linear decline. Instead, we observe a peculiar mix of continuity, interruption, and resumption of inauguration rituals. Some traditional ceremonies, mostly in the Austrian lands, were abandoned forever. At the same time, a limited number of inaugural rites continued until the nineteenth century—for various reasons meriting further examination. The Lower Austrian inauguration adopted a new function as the first major ceremonial performance a ruler would stage after his or her assumption of power. In the outlying territories—the Netherlands, Lombardy, and Transylvania—inaugurations in the presence of a commissioner (often a member of the dynasty) were staged for every new sovereign. New homage ceremonies were performed in the newly acquired provinces. And most importantly, almost every Habsburg generation displayed a unique approach to investiture ceremonies.

This makes it difficult to say whether the eighteenth century was a period of abandonment or rather one of revival, reemployment, and reinterpretation of Habsburg inaugural rites. Three things seem beyond doubt, however: First, although it was modified, the essentially composite character of Habsburg rulership did not disappear—the many rites of investiture and their different terms testify to this. Second, inaugural rites mattered and were employed as a means of legitimation and power consolidation on various occasions, even if their legitimizing effects differed from the time when Ferdinand I had to argue with the Moravian Estates about whether they were obliged to swear or pledge. And third, the ways in which the inaugural rites mattered can best be considered if we take them seriously, as the authors of this volume attempt to do.

Petr Maťa received his PhD from Charles University in Prague. He has been based in Vienna since 2006 and was employed as a nontenured assistant professor (*Universitätsassistent*) at the Institute of History and the Institute of Austrian Historical Research at the University of Vienna from 2008 to 2018. In March 2018, he joined the Institute for Habsburg and Balkan Studies at the Austrian Academy of Sciences. He was a EURIAS fellow at the Institute for Advanced Study at Central European University (CEU) in Budapest from 2012 to 2013 and worked as visiting professor at CEU in the winter trimester of 2017 as well. His research has focused on various aspects of the early modern Habsburg Monarchy, especially its social elites. He is coeditor of the compendium project *Verwaltungsgeschichte der Habsburgermonarchie in der Frühen Neuzeit* and has recently submitted a postdoctoral thesis analyzing the provincial diets and political culture of the Estates in the Bohemian and Austrian lands in the early modern era.

Notes

1. J. H. Elliott, "A Europe of Composite Monarchies," *Past and Present* 137 (1992): 51.
2. Sarah Hanley, *The Lit de Justice of the Kings of France: Constitutional Ideology in Legend, Ritual, and Discourse* (Princeton, 1983), 198–204; Richard A. Jackson, *Vive le Roi! A History of the French Coronation from Charles V to Charles X* (Chapel Hill, 1984). See also Hanley's review of Jackson's monograph in Speculum: A Journal of Medieval Studies 61, no. 4 (1986): 940–42. See below on the exception regarding Béarn.
3. Karl Vocelka and Lynne Heller, *Die Lebenswelten der Habsburger: Kultur- und Mentalitätsgeschichte einer Familie* (Graz, 1997), 179–204—a useful overview that nevertheless omits inaugural ceremonies in the dependencies of Bohemia as well as inaugurations by proxy. A fresh approach to the topic that challenges the traditional narrative of decline has been taken by William D. Godsey, "Herrschaft und politische Kultur im Habsburgerreich: Die niederösterreichische Erbhuldigung (ca. 1648–1848)," in *Aufbrüche in die Moderne: Frühparlamentarismus zwischen altständischer Ordnung und monarchischem Konstitutionalismus 1750–1850. Schlesien—Deutschland—Mitteleuropa*, ed. Roland Gehrke (Cologne, 2005), 141–77.
4. This chapter is based on an extended and still ongoing examination of Habsburg inauguration rites undertaken by the author in the margins of other projects. Only the most relevant works out of a considerable but fragmented and often antiquated bibliography are referred to in endnotes, whereas most other references to individual sources are excluded.
5. André Holenstein, *Die Huldigung der Untertanen: Rechtskultur und Herrschaftsordnung (800–1800)* (Stuttgart, 1991).
6. Petr Čornej, "Klíče ke Karlštejnu," *Studia mediaevalia Bohemica* 1 (2009): 37–73; Anton Radvánszky, "Das Amt des Kronhüters im Staatsrecht und in der Geschichte Ungarns," *Ungarn-Jahrbuch* 11 (1980–81): 1–62; Anna Hedwig Berna, "Hut oder Krone? Ein Beitrag zur Ikonographie des Erzherzogshutes," *MÖStA* 24 (1971): 87–139; Georg Johannes Kugler, "Der österreichische Erzherzogshut und die Erbhuldigung," in *Der heilige Leopold: Landesfürst und Staatssymbol* (Vienna, 1985), 84–91.
7. Bernd Herbert Wanger, *Kaiserwahl und Krönung im Frankfurt des 17. Jahrhunderts: Darstellung anhand der zeitgenössischen Bild- und Schriftquellen und unter besonderer Berücksichtigung der Erhebung des Jahres 1612* (Frankfurt am Main, 1994).
8. *Wienerisches Diarium*, 19 January 1774, 4–5.
9. On the largely unknown Moravian inaugurations, see František Kameníček, *Zemské sněmy a sjezdy moravské: Jejich složení, obor působnosti a význam. Od nastoupení na trůn krále Ferdinanda I. až po vydání obnoveného zřízení zemského (1526–1628)*, 3 vols. (Brno, 1900–1905); Jaroslav Dřímal, *Zemský dům v Brně* (Brno, 1947), 26–38.
10. Louis Lebeer, "Les estampes relatives aux inaugurations de Philippe V et de Charles VI à Bruxelles," *Anciens Pays et Assemblées d'États/Standen en Landen* 16 (1958): 35–63; Klaas Van Gelder, "The Investiture of Emperor Charles VI in Brabant and Flanders: A Test Case for the Authority of the New Austrian Government," *European Review of History/Revue européenne d'histoire* 18, no. 4 (2011): 443–63.
11. Anna Śliwowska, *Uroczyste wjazdy monarsze do Wrocławia w latach 1527–1620* (Wrocław, 2008); Mlada Holá, *Holdovací cesty českých panovníků do Vratislavi v pozdním středověku a raném novověku (1437–1617)* (Prague, 2012).
12. Paul Puntschart, *Herzogseinsetzung und Huldigung in Kärnten: Ein verfassungs- und kulturgeschichtlicher Beitrag* (Leipzig, 1899); Anette Kehnel, "Toren spiel und Geltungsmacht:

Die Geschichte der Symbole der Kärntner Herzogeinsetzung," in *Institutionalität und Symbolisierung: Verstetigungen kultureller Ordnungsmuster in Vergangenheit und Gegenwart*, ed. Gert Melville (Cologne, 2001), 477–91; Christof Paulus, "Ein seltzamme gewonheit: . . . Die Zeremonien an Fürstenstein und Herzogstuhl in der Sicht des Spätmittelalters und der Frühen Neuzeit," *MIÖG* 112 (2014): 22–39; Stefan Seitschek, "Die Erbhuldigung 1728 in Kärnten, ihre Organisation und Durchführung anhand ausgewählter Quellen," *Carinthia: Zeitschrift für Geschichtliche Landeskunde von Kärnten* 202 (2012): 125–78.

13. Benita Berning, *"Nach alltem löblichen Gebrauch": Die böhmischen Königskrönungen der Frühen Neuzeit (1526–1743)* (Cologne, 2008); Jiří Hrbek, *České barokní korunovace* (Prague, 2010).
14. Štefan Holčík, *Krönungsfeierlichkeiten in Preßburg/Bratislava 1563–1830* (Bratislava, 1992); Géza Pálffy, "Krönungsmähler in Ungarn im Spätmittelalter und in der Frühen Neuzeit: Weiterleben des Tafelzeremoniells des selbständigen ungarischen Königshofes und Machtrepräsentation der ungarischen politischen Elite," *MIÖG* 115 (2007): 85–111; 116 (2008): 60–91; Friedrich Polleroß, *"Austriacus Hungariae Rex*: Zur Darstellung der Habsburger als ungarische Könige in der frühneuzeitlichen Graphik," in *"Ez világ, mint egy kert . . . " Tanulmányok Galavics Géza tiszteletére*, ed. Orsolya Bubryák (Budapest, 2010), 63–78; Tünde Lengyelová and Géza Pálffy, eds., *Korunovácie a pohreby: Mocenské rituály a ceremónie v ranom novoveku* (Budapest, 2016).
15. The following numbers, presented here for the first time, are based on extensive research of both primary sources and secondary literature. It is impossible to provide even only partial references here.
16. Included in this number is the imperial coronation of Francis Stephen of Lorraine in 1745. Excluded are the inaugural oaths that Charles VI (as Charles III) took in Barcelona in 1705 and in Valencia in 1706, as well as the inaugural rites in eighteenth-century Tuscany, which never shared a common ruler with the Habsburg Monarchy.
17. For some useful remarks, see Franz Quarthal, *Landstände und landständisches Steuerwesen in Schwäbisch Österreich* (Stuttgart, 1980), 98, 118, 138, 151, 169–71, 213, 222, and 226.
18. André Krischer, *Reichsstädte in der Fürstengesellschaft: Politischer Zeichengebrauch in der Frühen Neuzeit* (Darmstadt, 2006), 346–68.
19. Stephan Wendehorst, "Die Kaiserhuldigungen der Frankfurter Juden im 18. Jahrhundert," in *Die Frankfurter Judengasse: Jüdisches Leben in der Frühen Neuzeit*, ed. Fritz Backhaus, Gisela Engel, Robert Liberles, and Margarete Schlüter (Frankfurt, 2006), 213–35.
20. Likewise, not counted is the extraordinary proclamation of Ferdinand I as emperor in 1558.
21. Katrin Keller, "Gender and Ritual: Crowning Empresses in the Holy Roman Empire," *German History* 37, no. 2 (2019): 172–85; Jutta Götzmann, "Zwischen Realität und Idealität: Kaiserinnenkrönungen und ihre künstlerische Rezeption in der Frühen Neuzeit," in *Die Bildlichkeit symbolischer Akte*, ed. Barbara Stollber-Rilinger and Thomas Weißbrich (Münster, 2010), 351–74.
22. Jana Hubková, "Holdovací cesta Fridricha Falckého do Vratislavi," in *Rezidence a správní sídla v zemích České koruny ve 14.–17. století*, ed. Lenka Bobková and Jana Konvičná (Prague, 2007), 319–49; Eila Hassenpflug-Elzholz, *Böhmen und die böhmischen Stände in der Zeit des beginnenden Zentralismus: Eine Strukturanalyse der böhmischen Adelsnation um die Mitte des 18. Jahrhunderts* (Munich, 1982); Gustav Otruba, "Die Erbhuldigungen

der oberösterreichischen Stände 1732–1741–1743: Eine Studie zur Geschichte des Treueverhaltens von Klerus, Adel und Bürgertum gegenüber Karl VI., Karl Albert und Maria Theresia," *Mitteilungen des Oberösterreichischen Landesarchivs* 16 (1990): 135–301. Not included are the Hungarian rival kings John Szápolyai (elected and crowned) and Gabriel Bethlen (only elected) as well as Frederick II of Prussia, since Silesia, where he took the oaths of fealty in 1741, was never restituted to the Habsburgs.

23. Günther R. Burkert, *Landesfürst und Stände: Karl V., Ferdinand I. und die österreichischen Erbländer im Ringen um Gesamtstaat und Landesinteressen* (Graz, 1987), 108, 130.
24. Dřímal, *Zemský dům*, 32–37.
25. Ferdo Šišić (Ferdinand von Šišić), *Die Wahl Ferdinands I. von Österreich zum König von Kroatien* (Zagreb, 1917); Szabolcs Varga, "Az 1527. évi horvát-szlavón kettős 'királyválasztás' története," *Századok* 142 (2008): 1075–134. Ferdinand's delegates nevertheless did not consider this act a free election but an "Erbhuldigung"; see Ferdo Šišić, ed., *Hrvatski saborski spisi*, vol. 1 (Zagreb, 1912), 57–64.
26. Alfred Kohler, *Antihabsburgische Politik in der Epoche Karls V. Die reichsständische Opposition gegen die Wahl Ferdinands I. zum römischen König und gegen die Anerkennung seines Königtums (1524–1534)* (Göttingen, 1982), 33 and 182–83.
27. Helmut Neuhaus, "Die Römische Königswahl vivente imperatore in der Neuzeit: Zum Problem der Kontinuität in einer frühneuzeitlichen Wahlmonarchie," in *Neue Studien zur frühneuzeitlichen Rechtsgeschichte*, ed. Johannes Kunisch (Berlin, 1997), 1–53.
28. Jaroslav Pánek, "Königswahl oder Königsaufnahme? Thronwechsel im Königreich Böhmen an der Schwelle zur Neuzeit," in *Der frühmoderne Staat in Ostzentraleuropa*, ed. Wolfgang J. Weber (Augsburg, 2000), 37–52; Géza Pálffy, *The Kingdom of Hungary and the Habsburg Monarchy in the Sixteenth Century* (New York, 2009), 161–68.
29. Winfried Schulze, "Hausgesetzgebung und Verstaatlichung im Hause Österreich vom Tode Maximilians I. bis zur Pragmatischen Sanktion," in *Der dynastische Fürstenstaat: Zur Bedeutung von Sukzessionsordnungen für die Entstehung des frühmodernen Staates*, ed. Johannes Kunisch (Berlin, 1982), 253–71; Thomas Winkelbauer, 'Dynastische Erbfolgeregelungen und länderspezifisches Thronfolgerecht," in *Verwaltungsgeschichte der Habsburgermonarchie in der Frühen Neuzeit*, vol. 1/1, ed. Michael Hochedlinger, Petr Maťa, and Thomas Winkelbauer (Vienna, 2019), 83–98.
30. Arno Strohmeyer, *Konfessionskonflikt und Herrschaftsordnung: Widerstandsrecht bei den österreichischen Ständen (1550–1650)* (Mainz, 2006).
31. Carinthia under Ferdinand I may be the only exception (see above).
32. Maximilian II's and Rudolf II's last inaugurations, in Upper Austria in 1565 and 1578 respectively, took place seventeen and nineteen months after the death of their respective predecessors. The only exception was Archduke Ferdinand, whose inauguration as count of Tyrol took place in January 1567, while his father had died in July 1564. In this case, the slow departure from Bohemia, where the archduke held the position of *Statthalter*, caused the delay. Michael A. Chisholm, "Hans Ernnstingers Beschreibung des Einzugs Erzherzogs Ferdinands II. in Tirol im Jahre 1567," *Tiroler Heimat* 73 (2009): 71–98.
33. Kameníček, *Zemské sněmy*, vol. 2, 318.
34. Holá, *Holdovací cesty*.
35. Royal towns in Moravia likewise used to swear on another day and in a different place than prelates and nobles.
36. Ferdinand I took an additional oath of loyalty in Schweidnitz in 1527, Maximilian II in Sagan in 1564, Rudolf II in 1577, and Matthias in 1611 in Freudenthal from the Estates

of Troppau. In an unusual exception, Archduke Charles received the homage from the Estates of Oppeln-Ratibor in person in 1624.

37. Jackson, *Vive le Roi*, 221.
38. Jayne Elisabeth Archer, Elizabeth Goldring, and Sarah Knight, eds., *The Progresses, Pageants, and Entertainments of Queen Elizabeth I* (Oxford, 2007).
39. Allan I. Macinnes, "The Multiple Kingdoms of Britain and Ireland: The 'British Problem,'" in *A Companion to Stuart Britain*, ed. Barry Coward (Malden, 2003), 3–25; Kevin Sharp, *Image Wars: Promoting Kings and Commonwealths in England 1603–1660* (New Haven, 2010).
40. Lawrence Bryant, *The King and the City in the Parisian Royal Entry Ceremony* (Geneva, 1986); Marie-France Wagner and Daniel Vaillancourt, eds., *Le Roi dans la ville: Anthologie des entrées royales dans les villes de province (1615–1660)* (Paris, 2001); Daniel Vaillancourt and Marie-France Wagner, eds., "Les entrées royales: urbanité et société au XVIIe siècle," *XVIIe Siècle* 53, no. 3 (2001); Nicolas Russell and Hélène Visentin, eds., *French Ceremonial Entries in the Sixteenth Century: Event, Image, Text* (Toronto, 2007); Marie-France Wagner, ed., *Les Entrées royales et solenelles du règne d'Henri IV dans les villes françaises* (Paris, 2010); Marie-Claude Canova-Green, "Warrior King or King of War? Louis XIII's Entries into his Bonnes Villes (1620–1629)," in *Ceremonial Entries in Early Modern Europe: The Iconography of Power*, ed. J. R. Mulryne, Maria Ines Aliverti, and Anna Maria Testaverde, 2nd ed. (London, 2016), 77–98; Neil Murphy, "The Court on the Move: Ceremonial Entries, Gift-Giving and Access to the Monarch in France, c. 1440–1570," in *The Key to Power? The Culture of Access in Princely Courts, 1400–1750*, ed. Dries Raeymaekers and Sebastian Derks (Leiden, 2016), 40–64.
41. Abel Jouan, *Recueil et Discours du Voyage du Roy Charles IX. De ce nom à present regnant, accompagné des choses dignes de memoire faictes en chacun endroit faisant sondit voyage en ses païs & provinces de Champaigne, Bourgoigne, Daulphiné, Prouence, Languedoc, Gascoigne, Baïonne, & plusieurs autres lieux, suyuant son retour depuis son partement de Paris iusques à son retour audit lieu* (Paris, 1566); Pierre Champion, *Catherine de Médicis présente à Charles IX son royaume (1564–1566)* (Paris, 1937); Jean Boutier, Alain Dewerpe, and Daniel Nordman, *Un tour de France royal: Le voyage de Charles IX (1564–1566)* (Paris, 1984); Victor E. Graham and W. McAllister-Johnson, eds., *The Royal Tour of France by Charles IX and Catherine de' Medici: Festivals and Entries, 1564–66* (Toronto, 1979); Hanley, The Lit de Justice, 198–204.
42. Christian Desplat, "Louis XIII and the Union of Béarn to France," in *Conquest and Coalescence, The Shaping of the State in Early Modern Europe*, ed. Mark Greengrass (London, 1991), 77; J. B. Laborde, "La députación des Etats du Béarn à Saint-Jean-de-Luz en 1660 pour recevoir le serment de Louis XIV," *Revue régionaliste des Pyrénées* 44 (1960): 32–34; Paul Viollet, *Le roi et ses ministres pendant les trois derniers siècles de la monarchie* (Paris, 1912), 9; Hubert Delpont, *Parade pour une infante: Le périple nuptial de Louis XIV à travers le midi de la France (1659–1660)* (Narrosse, 2007). See also the report on the last "Huldigung" in the *Wienerisches Diarium*, 27 January 1776 (no. 8), 3–4.
43. There seems to be no general account of these inaugural rites apart from short but illuminating passages by María José del Río Barredo, *Madrid, Urbs Regia: La capital ceremonial de la Monarquía Católica* (Madrid, 2000), 23–33, and by Teofilo F. Ruiz, *A King Travels: Festive Traditions in Late Medieval and Early Modern Spain* (Princeton, 2012), 146–92 and 316–20. Dates and places can be reconstructed with the help of Don Jenaro Alenda y Mira, *Relaciones de solemnidades y fiestas públicas de España*, vol. 1 (Madrid, 1903), and

Alexander S. Wilkinson, ed., *Iberian Books: Books Published in Spanish or Portuguese or on the Iberian Peninsula before 1601* (Leiden, 2010); Alexander S. Wilkinson and Alejandra Ulla Lorenzo, *Iberian Books (Volumes II & III): Books Published in Spain, Portugal and the New World or elsewhere in Spanish or Portuguese between 1601 and 1650* (Leiden, 2015). Ralph E. Giesey, *If Not, Not: The Oath of the Aragonese and the Legendary Laws of Sobrarbe* (Princeton, 1968), 186–216, helps to comprehend the impressive legal and jurisdictional complexity of these ceremonies.

44. María Cristina Sánchez Alonso, "Juramentos de príncipes herederos en Marid (1561–1598)," *Anales del Instituto de Estudios Madrileños* 6 (1970): 29–41.
45. I. A. A. Thompson, "The End of the Cortes of Castile," *Parliaments, Estates and Representations* 4 (1984): 126, footnote 5.
46. Fernando Bouza, ed., *Cartas de Felipe II a sus hijas* (Madrid, 1998), 35–39 and 101–2.
47. Francisco Ribeiro da Silva, "A viagem de Filipe III a Portugal: itinerários e problemática," *Revista de Ciências Históricas* 2 (1987): 223–60; Pedro Gan Giménez, "La jornada de Felipe III a Portugal (1619)," *Chronica Nova* 19 (1991): 407–31; Jacobo Sanz Hermida, "Un viaje conflictivo: relaciones de sucesos para la jornada del Rey N. S. Don Felipe III deste nombre, al Reyno de Portugal (1619)," *Peninsula: Revista de Estudos Ibéricos* 0 (2003): 289–320. See also the contemporary description by João Baptista Lavanha, *Viagem da Catholica Real Magestade del Rey D. Filipe II. N. S. ao Reyno de Portugal E rellação do solene recebimento que nelle se lhe fez S. Magestade a mandou escrever por João Baptista Lavanha seu Coronista Mayor* (Madrid, 1622), fol. 63r–66v.
48. Eliseo Serrano Martín, "No demandamos sino el modo: Los juramentos reales en Aragón en la Edad Moderna," *Pedralbes* 28 (2008): 435–64.
49. *Dietaris de la Generalitat de Catalunya*, 10 vols. (Barcelona, 1994–2007), vol. 2: 12 and 149–54; vol. 3: 340–45; vol. 5: 127–30; vol. 10: 34–39, 652–54, and 670–71.
50. Pablo M. Orduna Portús, "Visita de Filipe II a Pamplona (1592) narrada por el abad de Olloqui, don Juan de Zozaya," *Príncipe de Viana* 67, no. 239 (2006): 931–42; Alfredo Floristán Imízcoz, "El uso de la imagen como representación jurídica y como profecía política en el siglo XVII," in *La historia imaginada: Construcciones visuales del pasado en la Edad Moderna*, ed. Joan Lluís Palos and Diana Carrió-Invernizzi (Madrid, 2008), 307–26.
51. Alfredo Floristán Imízcoz, "Los juramentos de los fueros de Aragón y de Navarra en 1677," *Príncipe de Viana* 262 (2015): 603–17.
52. José Maria Vallejo García-Hevia, "La última máscara del rey: Las cortes de Castilla de 1789 en la España del antiguo régimen," in *Corte y monarquía en España*, ed. Dolores del Mar Sánchez González (Madrid, 2003), 191–258, here 207–17; Francisco José Portela Sandoval, "A propósito de la jura de los príncipes herederos: Una nueva lectura del cuadro Jura de don Fernando (VII) como príncipe de Asturias, de Luis Paret," *En la España Medieval*, número extraordinario 1 (2006): 337–47.
53. A special case was Upper Austria, whose Estates refused the homage and, having been militarily defeated in 1620, spent eight unhappy years in pawn to Maximilian of Bavaria. The homage ceremony in 1630 thus pertained to both Ferdinand II and Ferdinand III together: Strohmeyer, *Konfessionskonflikt*, 275–90 and 352–68.
54. Berning, "Nach alltem löblichen Gebrauch," 155–64; Hrbek, *České barokní korunovace*, 35–44.
55. In this case, the ceremonial was significantly altered, with elements symbolizing contractual relationship being eliminated. See the opinion presented by the Bohemian Chancellery: Prague, NA, ČDK, carton 710.

56. Rich documentation on this little-known case can be found in: Prague, NA, ČDK, carton 14f.
57. The sequence of inaugural rites routinely considered and often followed immediate precedents. In 1628, the Moravian inauguration took place immediately after the Bohemian coronation. In 1646, when Ferdinand IV was crowned in Prague, this was not an option, since the Swedish army occupied large areas of Moravia. In addition, Ferdinand III hurried to Pressburg with his son to initiate lengthy negotiations, which eventually led to Ferdinand IV's Hungarian coronation in June 1647: Mark Hengerer, *Kaiser Ferdinand III. (1608–1657): Eine Biographie* (Vienna, 2012), 248–56.
58. StLA, LAA III, carton 124, fascicle 457, fol. 86r and 88r (diet session on 26 November 1657). The *Ausschuß* held on 9 January 1658 requested a suspension of the diet, asked the privy counselors from Graz to mediate, and proposed to make common cause with Carinthia and Carniola as usual: StLA, LAA III, carton 315, fascicle 1018, fol. 5r–7v.
59. On 18 February 1658, Leopold I's assurance that he would personally attend the inauguration was presented to the diet: StLA, LAA III, carton 124, fascicle 457, fol. 95r–7r. Reminders by the Estates: 8 May and 11 August 1659: StLA, LAA III, carton 124, fascicle 457, fol. 168r, 178r, and 189v.
60. Lorenzo de Churelichz, *Breve, e succinto Racconto de Viaggio, solenne Entrate, et ossequiosi Vasalaggi, Essibiti alla Gloriosa Maestà dell'Augustissimo Imperator Leopoldo dall'Eccelsi Stati e fedelissimi Vasalli dell'inclite Ducale Provincie di Stiria, Carinthia, Carniola, Goricia, Trieste, etc. Prinicipiato nel Mese di Giugno, e finito d'Ottobre L'Anno 1660.* (Vienna, 1661); Donatella Porcedda, "La visita imperiale di Leopoldo I. a Gorizia nel 1660," *Memorie storiche forogiuliesi* 76 (1996): 89–122; Jakob Löwenthal, *Geschichte der Stadt Triest* (Trieste, 1857), 113–21.
61. "A particular desire to travel and alternate his dwelling" and "an inclination to change often stay."
62. *Venetianische Depeschen vom Kaiserhofe (Dispacci di Germania)*, 2nd section, vol. 1, ed. Alfred Francis Pribram (Vienna, 1901), 245.
63. No protest by the Moravian Estates is detectable. When they addressed the king with extensive grievances on various matters in 1659, the question of homage was not mentioned: Brno, Moravský zemský archiv, G 140: Rodinný archiv Ditrichštejnů, inventory no. 596, carton 193, fol. 73r–74v.
64. Godsey, "Herrschaft," 147–51.
65. Hanley, *The Lit de Justice*.
66. In a letter to Count Christoph Wenzel Nostitz on 12 September 1688 from Prague, Count Karl Maximilian Lažanský pointed to rumors of a future coronation (*den spargirten crönungsfall*): Klášter, Státní oblastní archiv v Plzni, pracoviště Klášter, Rodinný archiv Nostitzů (Planá), carton 54. Grand burggrave Count Adolf Vratislav Sternberg, one of the emperor's confidants, reported to Nostitz on 14 January 1690 that Leopold would not visit Prague on his journey back from Augsburg, "dahingegen sie wenigstens ein gantzes jahr, wann selbdte einstens anhero kommen würden, alhier gern subsistiren möchten": Klášter, Státní oblastní archiv v Plzni, pracoviště Klášter, Rodinný archiv Nostitzů (Planá), carton 78. On 17 December 1692, Sternberg expressed hopes that the Bohemian coronation of Joseph I and Leopold I's third wife would take place within a year. See the report sent by delegates from Kutná Hora to their town council: Kutná Hora, Státní okresní archiv v Kutné Hoře, Archiv města Kutné Hory, Aktová sbírka, 12.858.

67. Hrbek, České barokní korunovace, 34–35. Valentin Urfus, *Císař Josef I. Nekorunovaný Habsburk na českém trůně* (Prague, 2004), 69–72, remains sceptical.
68. Alexander Begert, *Böhmen, die böhmische Kur und das Reich vom Hochmittelalter bis zum Ende des Alten Reiches: Studien zur Kurwürde und zur staatsrechtlichen Stellung Böhmens* (Husum, 2003), 418.
69. Michael Hochedlinger, *Austria's Wars of Emergence: War, State and Society in the Habsburg Monarchy 1683–1797* (London, 2003), 168–93.
70. Rotraut Miller, "Die Hofreisen Kaiser Leopolds I.," *MIÖG* 75 (1967): 66–103.
71. The letter of indemnification for Styria was issued on 27 February 1706 and presented in the diet session on 19 May. The related comment by the *Landeshauptmann* makes it clear that the remonstrance of the Carinthians motivated the privy counselors in Graz to issue the *Schadlosbrief* for Styria as well: StLA, LAA III, carton 142, fascicle 492, fol. 118r and 120r–v.
72. NA, ČDK, carton 15.
73. Alfred Fischel, "Christian Julius Schierendorff, ein Vorläufer des liberalen Zentralismus unter Josef I. und Karl VI.", in *Studien zur Österreichischen Reichsgeschichte*, ed. Alfred Fischel (Vienna, 1906), 137–305, here 165, 181, 259, 278, and 286.
74. See, e.g., the patent issued in Prague on 8 December 1741 by means of which Charles Albert as king of Bohemia forbade his Bohemian and Upper Austrian vassals to serve the "Gross-Herzogin von Toscana": Josef Schwerdfeger, "Der bairisch-französische Einfall in Ober- und Niederösterreich (1741) und die Stände der Erherzogthümer. I. Theil: Karl Albrecht und die Franzosen in Ober-Österreich," *Archiv für österreichische Geschichte* 87 (1899): 444–45.
75. Charles Ingrao, "Pragmatic Sanction and the Theresian Succession: A Reevaluation," *Études Danubiennes* 9, no 1 (1993): 71–87.
76. Five coronations of three Habsburg women could be added, namely the wives of Charles VI, Leopold II, and Francis II.
77. Alphonse de Witte, "Les jetons et les médailles d'inauguration frappés par ordre du gouvernement général aux Pays-Bas autrichiens, 1717–1794," *Revue belge de Numismatique* 53 (1897): 160–74, 263–75, 435–46; 54 (1898), 161–74, 326–34; 56 (1900), 104–13, 205–18, 411–27; 57 (1901), 187–212; Klaas Van Gelder and Bert Van Cauter, "Een publieke ceremonie in een turbulent tijdvak: De inauguratie van Maria Theresia als gravin van Vlaanderen (1744)," *Handelingen der Maatschappij voor Geschiedenis en Oudheidkunde te Gent* 67 (2013): 101–29; Guy van Dievoet, "L'empereur Joseph II et la Joyeuse Entrée de Brabant: Les dernières années de la constitution brabançonne," *Anciens Pays et Assemblées d'États/Standen en Landen* 16 (1958): 87–140. See the chapter by Klaas Van Gelder.
78. There seems to be no specific literature on the topic. See *Storia di Milano*, vol. 12: *L'Età delle riforme (1706–1796)* (Milan, 1959), 98, 204–5, and 207.
79. Rolf Kutschera, *Landtag und Gubernium in Siebenbürgen 1688–1869* (Cologne, 1985), 69, 94–95, 99–100, 224, and 276.
80. On the Netherlands, see footnote 77. On Milan, Mantua, and Transylvania, see *Wiener Zeitung*, 15 August 1781 (no. 65), appendix; 19 September 1781 (no. 75); and 24 October 1781 (no. 85), appendix.
81. The authorities in Vienna collected documents concerning Inner Austrian inaugurations as early as 1717: Seitschek, "Die Erbhuldigung 1728," 135. Like Leopold I, Charles VI avoided personal inaugurations in Moravia and Silesia.

82. The idea that the festivities organized on occasion of the Bohemian coronation in 1723 sought to counteract Bavaria and Saxony's dynastic ambitions was raised for the first time by Andreas Gugler, "Constantia et Fortitudine (Bankette und Schauessen im Zusammenhang der Krönungsfeierlichkeiten in Prag 1723)," *Život na dvorech barokní šlechty (1600–1750)*, ed. Václav Bůžek (České Budějovice, 1996), 267–92. There is a more recent and complex interdisciplinary analysis by Štěpán Vácha, Irena Veselá, Vít Vlnas, and Petra Vokáčová, *Karel VI. & Alžběta Kristýna: Česká korunovace 1723* (Prague, 2009). See also the chapter by Petra Vokáčová in this volume. On Charles's later trips, see Seitschek, "Die Erbhuldigung 1728"; Otruba, "Die Erbhuldigung," 138–61.
83. "His Excellency puts forward that the court counselor von Freyenfels had asked him whether the Estates would like to have His Majesty here for the homage, otherwise a commissioner would be sent here to accept the homage." The decision: "Let it be omitted until more information concerning His Majesty's intention in this regard is available. And His Excellency is asked to maintain further correspondence in this matter." [*Ihro Ex. proponiren, das der herr hofrath von Freyenfels deroselben gesaget hatte, ob nicht die herren stände Ihro May. zur huldigung hiehero wolten, widrigens würde ein commissarius zur abnehmung der huldigung hiehero geschikhet werden. Supersedeatur, bis man ein nähendtere nachricht haben würde, ob und wie Ihro May. disfals eigentlich gesinnet seynt? Und werden Seine Ex. umb die diesfals pflegen-mögendte correspondenz ersuchet.*] Brno, Moravský zemský archiv, A4, carton 27, 6 May 1726, fol. 14v–15r.
84. This term is borrowed from Ruiz, *A King Travels*, 71 and 157.
85. Interestingly, the engraving representing the oath was included only in selected prints, including the one that the Estates dedicated to the emperor: Theodor Graff and Ulrike Müller, eds., *Georg Jakob von Deyerlsperg: Erbhuldigung der steirischen Landstände aus dem Jahre 1728*, 2 vols. (facsimile and introduction) (Graz, 1980), 11–13, 21–22, 33, and 36. For further considerations on the genesis of these images, see Petr Maťa, "Der steierische Landtag in Raum und Bild um 1730: Symbolische Ordnung und visuelle Darstellung," *Zeitschrift des Historische Vereines für Steiermark* 104 (2013): 176–88.
86. Another representation, of which several variations exist, depicts Leopold II swearing the oath in Pressburg in 1790 (see figure 3.1 in this volume): Holčík, *Krönungsfeierlichkeiten*, 46 and 113.
87. Hannes P. Naschenweng, *Die Landeshauptleute der Steiermark 1263–2002* (Graz, 2002), 158.
88. Renate Zedinger, ed., *Innsbruck 1765: Prunkvolle Hochzeit, fröhliche Feste, tragischer Ausklang* (Bochum, 2015).
89. Godsey, "Herrschaft"; Eduard Maur, *12. 5. 1743. Marie Terezie: Korunovace na usmířenou* (Prague, 2003); Otruba, "Die Erbhuldigungen," 231–67.
90. Jaroslav Prokeš, "Marie Terezie a přípravy k české korunovaci roku 1742," in *Sborník prací věnovaný prof. Dru Gustavu Friedrichovi k šedesátým narozeninám* (Prague, 1932), 338.
91. Werner Telesko, "Hier wird einmal gutt ruhen seyn: Balthasar Ferdinand Molls Prunksarkophag für Franz Stephan und Maria Theresia in der Wiener Kapuzinergruft (1754)," *Wiener Jahrbuch für Kunstgeschichte* 59 (2010): 103–26.
92. *Wiener Zeitung* (1790), no. 62 (4 August), 2003f.
93. See Leopold II's reply to the Upper Austrian Estates on 29 July 1791: *Sr. k. k. Majestät Leopold des Zweyten politische Gesetze und Verordnungen für die deutschen, böhmischen und galizischen Erbländer*, vol. 4 (Vienna, 1792), 114.

94. Anna M. Drabek, "Patriotismus und nationale Identität in Böhmen und Mähren," in *Patriotismus und Nationsbildung am Ende des Heiligen Römischen Reiches*, ed. Otto Dann, Miroslav Hroch, and Johannes Koll (Cologne, 2003), 151–70, here 154.
95. Adam Wandruszka, *Leopold II.: Erzherzog von Österreich, Grossherzog von Toskana, König von Ungarn und Böhmen, Römischer Kaiser*, vol. 2 (Vienna, 1965); Ákos Barcsay, *Herrschaftsantritt in Ungarn des 18. Jahrhunderts: Studien zum Verhältnis zwischen Krongewalt und Ständetum im Zeitalter des Absolutismus* (St. Katharinen, 2002); Hugh LeCaine Agnew, "Ambiguities of Ritual: Dynastic Loyalty, Territorial Patriotism and Nationalism in the Last Three Royal Coronations in Bohemia, 1791–1836," *Bohemia* 41, no. 1 (2000): 3–22; Philip Steiner, *Die Landstände in Steiermark, Kärnten und Krain und die josephinische Reformation: Bedrohungskommunikation angesichts konkurrierender Ordnungsvorstellungen (1789–1792)* (Münster, 2017), 251–76.
96. Hans-Wolfgang Bergerhausen, "Die schlesische Landesverfassung vor und nach 1742 im Urteil theresianischer Staatsmänner: Quellenedition und Kommentar," *Jahrbuch der schlesischen Friedrich-Wilhelms-Universität zu Breslau* 49 (2009): 63–128.
97. Miloš Řezník, *Neuorientierung einer Elite: Aristokratie, Ständewesen und Loyalität in Galizien (1772–1795)* (Frankfurt am Main, 2016), 214 and 222–47; Johann Polek, "Die Huldigung der Bukowina am 12. Oktober 1777," *Jahrbuch des Bukowiner Landesmuseums* 10 (1902): 3–36.
98. Translation: "a ceremony because it will always be forced and imposed on these poor people". Alfred von Arneth, ed., *Maria Theresia und Joseph II. Ihre Correspondenz sammt Briefen Joseph's an seinen Bruder Leopold*, vol. 2 (Vienna, 1867), 10.
99. *Wiener Zeitung*, 7 May 1794 (no. 37), 1351–53.
100. Ferdinand von Zieglauer, *Die politische Reformbewegung in Siebenbürgen in der Zeit Joseph's II. und Leopold's II.* (Vienna, 1881), 146–65. The described procedure even took place in 1837 when Archduke Ferdinand Charles d'Este acted in this role: *Vereinigte Ofner Pester Zeitung*, 30 April 1837 (no. 35), 768–69. There seems to be no account on how the ceremonial changed over time.
101. Nevertheless, in October 1791, there was a rumor in Lemberg that Leopold II would receive the *Huldigung* of Galicia either personally or through his son Archduke Francis on 7 May 1792: *Preßburger Zeitung*, 26 October 1791 (no. 86), 890; 5 November 1791 (no. 89), 927–28; and 9 November 1791 (no. 90), 639.
102. Konrad Meindl, *Die Vereinigung des Inviertels mit Österreich in Folge des Friedensschlusses zu Teschen am 13. Mai 1779* (Linz, 1879), 29–34.

Bibliography

Agnew, Hugh LeCaine. "Ambiguities of Ritual: Dynastic Loyalty, Territorial Patriotism and Nationalism in the Last Three Royal Coronations in Bohemia, 1791–1836." *Bohemia* 41, no. 1 (2000): 3–22.
Alenda y Mira, Don Jenaro. *Relaciones de solemnidades y fiestas públicas de España*. Vol. 1. Madrid: Sucesores de Rivadeneyra, 1903.
Archer, Jayne Elisabeth, Elizabeth Goldring, and Sarah Knight, eds. *The Progresses, Pageants, and Entertainments of Queen Elizabeth I*. Oxford: Oxford University Press, 2007.
Arneth, Alfred von, ed. *Maria Theresia und Joseph II. Ihre Correspondenz sammt Briefen Joseph's an seinen Bruder Leopold*. Vol. 2. Vienna: Carl Gerold's Sohn, 1867.

Barcsay, Ákos. *Herrschaftsantritt im Ungarn des 18. Jahrhunderts: Studien zum Verhältnis zwischen Krongewalt und Ständetum im Zeitalter des Absolutismus*. St. Katharinen: Scripta Mercaturae Verlag, 2002.

Begert, Alexander. *Böhmen, die böhmische Kur und das Reich vom Hochmittelalter bis zum Ende des Alten Reiches: Studien zur Kurwürde und zur staatsrechtlichen Stellung Böhmens*. Husum: Matthiesen Verlag, 2003.

Benna, Anna Hedwig. "Hut oder Krone? Ein Beitrag zur Ikonographie des Erzherzogshutes." *MÖStA* 24 (1971): 87–139.

Bergerhausen, Hans-Wolfgang. "Die schlesische Landesverfassung vor und nach 1742 im Urteil theresianischer Staatsmänner: Quellenedition und Kommentar." *Jahrbuch der schlesischen Friedrich-Wilhelms-Universität zu Breslau* 49 (2009): 63–128.

Berning, Benita. *"Nach alltem löblichen Gebrauch": Die böhmischen Königskrönungen der Frühen Neuzeit (1526–1743)*. Cologne: Böhlau Verlag, 2008.

Boutier, Jean, Alain Dewerpe, and Daniel Nordman. *Un tour de France royal: Le voyage de Charles IX (1564–1566)*. Paris: Aubier, 1984.

Bouza, Fernando, ed. *Cartas de Felipe II a sus hijas*. Madrid: Ediciones Akal, 1998.

Bryant, Lawrence. *The King and the City in the Parisian Royal Entry Ceremony*. Geneva: Droz, 1986.

Burkert, Günther R. *Landesfürst und Stände: Karl V., Ferdinand I. und die österreichischen Erbländer im Ringen um Gesamtstaat und Landesinteressen*. Graz: Selbstverlag der Historischen Landeskommission für Steiermark, 1987.

Canova-Green, Marie-Claude. "Warrior King or King of War? Louis XIII's Entries into his Bonnes Villes (1620–1629)." In *Ceremonial Entries in Early Modern Europe: The Iconography of Power*, edited by J. R. Mulryne, Maria Ines Aliverti, and Anna Maria Testaverde, 2nd ed., 77–98. London: Routledge, 2016.

Champion, Pierre. *Catherine de Médicis présente à Charles IX son royaume (1564–1566)*. Paris: Grasset, 1937.

Chisholm, Michael A. "Hans Ernnstingers Beschreibung des Einzugs Erherzogs Ferdinands II. in Tirol im Jahre 1567." *Tiroler Heimat* 73 (2009): 71–98.

de Churelichz, Lorenzo. *Breve, e succinto Racconto de Viaggio, solenne Entrate, et ossequiosi Vasalaggi, Essibiti alla Gloriosa Maestà dell'Augustissimo Imperator Leopoldo dall'Eccelsi Stati e fedelissimi Vasalli dell'inclite Ducale Provincie di Stiria, Carinthia, Carniola, Goricia, Trieste, etc. Prinicipiato nel Mese di Giugno, e finito d'Ottobre L'Anno 1660*. Vienna: Matthaeus Riccius, 1661.

Čornej, Petr. "Klíče ke Karlštejnu." *Studia mediaevalia Bohemica* 1 (2009): 37–73.

Delpont, Hubert. *Parade pour une infante: Le périple nuptial de Louis XIV à travers le midi de la France (1659–1660)*. Narrosse: Édition d'Albret, 2007.

del Río Barredo, María José. *Madrid, Urbs Regia: La capital ceremonial de la Monarquía Católica*. Madrid: Marcial Pons, 2000.

Desplat, Christian. "Louis XIII and the Union of Béarn to France." In *Conquest and Coalescence: The Shaping of the State in Early Modern Europe*, edited by Mark Greengrass, 68–83. London: E. Arnold, 1991.

de Witte, Alphonse. "Les jetons et les médailles d'inauguration frappés par ordre du gouvernement général aux Pays-Bas autrichiens, 1717–1794." *Revue belge de Numismatique* 53 (1897), 160–74, 263–75, 435–46; 54 (1898), 161–74, 326–34; 56 (1900), 104–13, 205–18, 411–27; 57 (1901), 187–212.

Dietaris de la Generalitat de Catalunya. 10 vols. Barcelona: Generalitat de Catalunya, 1994–2007.
Drabek, Anna M. "Patriotismus und nationale Identität in Böhmen und Mähren." In *Patriotismus und Nationsbildung am Ende des Heiligen Römischen Reiches*, edited by Otto Dann, Miroslav Hroch and Johannes Koll, 151–70. Cologne: SH-Verlag, 2003.
Dřímal, Jaroslav. *Zemský dům v Brně*. Brno: ÚNV zemského hlavního města Brna, 1947.
Elliott, J. H. "A Europe of Composite Monarchies." *Past and Present* 137 (1992): 48–71.
Fischel, Alfred, ed. "Christian Julius Schierendorff, ein Vorläufer des liberalen Zentralismus unter Josef I. und Karl VI." In *Studien zur Österreichischen Reichsgeschichte*, edited by Alfred Fischel (Vienna: Alfred Hölder, 1906), 137–305.
Floristán Imízcoz, Alfredo. "El uso de la imagen como representación jurídica y come profecía política en el siglo XVII." In *La historia imaginada: Construcciones visuales del pasado en la Edad Moderna*, edited by Joan Lluís Palos and Diana Carrió-Invernizzi, 307–26. Madrid: Centro de Estudios Europa Hispánica, 2008.
———. "Los juramentos de los fueros de Aragón y de Navarra en 1677." *Príncipe de Viana* 262 (2015): 603–17.
Gan Giménez, Pedro. "La jornada de Felipe III a Portugal (1619)." *Chronica Nova* 19 (1991): 407–31.
Giesey, Ralph E. *If Not, Not: The Oath of the Aragonese and the Legendary Laws of Sobrarbe*. Princeton: Princeton University Press, 1968.
Godsey, William D "Herrschaft und politische Kultur im Habsburgerreich: Die niederösterreichische Erbhuldigung (ca. 1648–1848)." In *Aufbrüche in die Moderne: Frühparlamentarismus zwischen altständischer Ordnung und monarchischem Konstitutionalismus 1750–1850. Schlesien—Deutschland—Mitteleuropa*, edited by Roland Gehrke, 141–77. Cologne: Böhlau Verlag, 2005.
Götzmann, Jutta. "Zwischen Realität und Idealität: Kaiserinnenkrönungen und ihre künstlerische Rezeption in der Frühen Neuzeit." In *Die Bildlichkeit symbolischer Akte*, edited by Barbara Stollber-Rilinger and Thomas Weißbrich, 351–73. Münster: Rhema, 2010.
Graff, Theodor, and Ulrike Müller, eds. *Georg Jakob von Deyerlsperg: Erbhuldigung der steirischen Landstände aus dem Jahre 1728*. 2 vols. Graz: Akademische Druck- und Verlagsanstalt, 1980.
Graham, Victor E., and W. McAllister-Johnson, eds. *The Royal Tour of France by Charles IX and Catherine de Medici: Festivals and Entries, 1564–66*. Toronto: University of Toronto Press, 1979.
Gugler, Andreas. "Constantia et Fortitudine (Bankette und Schauessen im Zusammenhang der Krönungsfeierlichkeiten in Prag 1723)." In *Život na dvorech barokní šlechty (1600–1750)*, edited by Václav Bůžek, 267–92. České Budějovice: Editio Universitatis Bohemiae Meridionalis, 1996.
Hanley, Sarah. *The Lit de Justice of the Kings of France: Constitutional Ideology in Legend, Ritual, and Discourse*. Princeton: Princeton University Press, 1983.
———. "Review of Jackson, Richard A., Vive le Roi! A History of the French Coronation from Charles V to Charles X." *Speculum: A Journal of Medieval Studies* 61, no. 4 (1986): 940–42.
Hassenpflug-Elzholz, Eila. *Böhmen und die böhmischen Stände in der Zeit des beginnenden Zentralismus: Eine Strukturanalyse der böhmischen Adelsnation um die Mitte des 18. Jahrhunderts*. Munich: R. Oldenbourg Verlag, 1982.

Hengerer, Mark. *Kaiser Ferdinand III. (1608–1657): Eine Biographie*. Vienna: Böhlau Verlag, 2012.

Hochedlinger, Michael. *Austria's Wars of Emergence: War, State and Society in the Habsburg Monarchy 1683–1797*. London: Longman, 2003.

Holá, Mlada. *Holdovací cesty českých panovníků do Vratislavi v pozdním středověku a raném novověku (1437–1617)*. Prague: Casablanca, 2012.

Holčík, Štefan. *Krönungsfeierlichkeiten in Preßburg/Bratislava 1563–1830*. Bratislava: Tatran, 1992.

Holenstein, André. *Die Huldigung der Untertanen: Rechtskultur und Herrschaftsordnung (800–1800)*. Stuttgart: Gustav Fischer Verlag, 1991.

Hrbek, Jiří. *České barokní korunovace*. Prague: Nakladatelství Lidové noviny, 2010.

Hubková, Jana. "Holdovací cesta Fridricha Falckého do Vratislavi." In *Rezidence a správní sídla v zemích České koruny ve 14.–17. století*, edited by Lenka Bobková and Jana Konvičná, 319–49. Prague: Univerzita Karlova v Praze, Filozofická fakulta, 2007.

Ingrao, Charles. "Pragmatic Sanction and the Theresian Succession: A Reevaluation." *Études Danubiennes* 9, no. 1 (1993): 71–87.

Jackson, Richard A. *Vive le Roi! A History of the French Coronation from Charles V to Charles X*: Chapel Hill: University of North Carolina Press, 1984.

Jouan, Abel. *Recueil et Discours du Voyage du Roy Charles IX. De ce nom à present regnant, accompagné des choses dignes de memoire faictes en chacun endroit faisant sondit voyage en ses païs & provinces de Champaigne, Bourgoigne, Daulphiné, Prouence, Languedoc, Gascoigne, Baïonne, & plusieurs autres lieux, suyuant son retour depuis son partement de Paris iusques à son retour audit lieu*. Paris: Iean Bonfons Libraire, 1566.

Kameníček, František. *Zemské sněmy a sjezdy moravské: Jejich složení, obor působnosti a význam. Od nastoupení na trůn krále Ferdinanda I. až po vydání obnoveného zřízení zemského (1526–1628)*. 3 vols. Brno: Moravská akciová knihtiskárna, 1900–1905.

Kehnel, Anette. "Toren spiel und Geltungsmacht: Die Geschichte der Symbole der Kärntner Herzogeinsetzung." In *Institutionalität und Symbolisierung: Verstetigungen kultureller Ordnungsmuster in Vergangenheit und Gegenwart*, edited by Gert Melville, 477–91. Cologne: Böhlau Verlag, 2001.

Keller, Katrin. "Gender and Ritual: Crowning Empresses in the Holy Roman Empire." *German History* 37, no. 2 (2019): 172–85.

Kohler, Alfred. *Antihabsburgische Politik in der Epoche Karls V. Die reichsständische Opposition gegen die Wahl Ferdinands I. zum römischen König und gegen die Anerkennung seines Königtums (1524–1534)*. Göttingen: Vandenhoeck & Ruprecht, 1982.

Krischer, André. *Reichsstädte in der Fürstengesellschaft: Politischer Zeichengebrauch in der Frühen Neuzeit*. Darmstadt: Wissenschaftliche Buchgesellschaft, 2006.

Kugler, Georg Johannes. "Der österreichische Erzherzogshut und die Erbhuldigung." In *Der heilige Leopold: Landesfürst und Staatssymbol*, 84–91. Vienna: Amt der NÖ Landesregierung, 1985.

Kutschera, Rolf. *Landtag und Gubernium in Siebenbürgen 1688–1869*. Cologne: Böhlau Verlag, 1985.

Laborde, J. B. "La députación des Etats du Béarn à Saint-Jean-de-Luz en 1660 pour recevoir le serment de Louis XIV." *Revue régionaliste des Pyrénées* 44 (1960): 32–34.

Lavanha, João Baptista. *Viagem da Catholica Real Magestade del Rey D. Filipe II. N. S. ao Reyno de Portugal E rellação do solene recebimento que nelle se lhe fez S. Magestade a mandou escrever por Ioão Baptista Lavanha seu Coronista Mayor*. Madrid: Thomas Iunti, 1622.

Lebeer, Louis. "Les estampes relatives aux inaugurations de Philippe V et de Charles VI à Bruxelles." *Anciens Pays et Assemblées d'États/Standen en Landen* 16 (1958): 35–63.
Lengyelová, Tünde, and Géza Pálffy, eds. *Korunovácie a pohreby: Mocenské rituály a ceremónie v ranom novoveku*. Budapest: Historický ústav Filozofického výzkumného centra Maďarskej akadémie vied. Výzkumný ústav Slovákov v Maďarsku, 2016.
Löwenthal, Jakob. *Geschichte der Stadt Triest*e. Trieste: Literarisch-artist. Abtheilung des österr. Lloyd, 1857.
Macinnes, Allan I. "The Multiple Kingdoms of Britain and Ireland: The 'British Problem.'" In *A Companion to Stuart Britain*, edited by Barry Coward, 3–25. Malden: Blackwell, 2003.
Maťa, Petr. "Der steierische Landtag in Raum und Bild um 1730: Symbolische Ordnung und visuelle Darstellung." *Zeitschrift des Historischen Vereines für Steiermark* 104 (2013): 163–218.
Maur, Eduard. *12. 5. 1743. Marie Terezie: Korunovace na usmířenou*. Prague: Havran, 2003.
Meindl, Konrad. *Die Vereinigung des Inviertels mit Österreich in Folge des Friedensschlusses zu Teschen am 13. Mai 1779*. Linz: Verlag der F. J. Ebenhöch'schen Buchhandlung (Heinrich Korb), 1879.
Miller, Rotraut. "Die Hofreiser Kaiser Leopolds I." *MIÖG* 75 (1967): 66–103.
Murphy, Neil. "The Court on the Move: Ceremonial Entries, Gift-Giving and Access to the Monarch in France, c. 1440–1570." In *The Key to Power? The Culture of Access in Princely Courts, 1400–1750*, edited by Dries Raeymaekers and Sebastian Derks, 40–64. Leiden: Brill, 2016.
Naschenweng, Hannes P. *Die Landeshauptleute der Steiermark 1263–2002*. Graz: Styria, 2002.
Neuhaus, Helmut. "Die Römische Königswahl vivente imperatore in der Neuzeit: Zum Problem der Kontinuität in einer frühneuzeitlichen Wahlmonarchie." In *Neue Studien zur frühneuzeitlichen Rechtsgeschichte*, edited by Johannes Kunisch, 1–53. Berlin: Duncker & Humblot, 1997.
Orduna Portús, Pablo M. "Visita de Filipe II a Pamplona (1592) narrada por el abad de Olloqui, don Juan de Zozaya." *Príncipe de Viana* 67, no. 239 (2006): 931–42.
Otruba, Gustav. "Die Erbhuldigungen der oberösterreichischen Stände 1732–1741–1743: Eine Studie zur Geschichte des Treueverhaltens von Klerus, Adel und Bürgertum gegenüber Karl VI., Karl Albert und Maria Theresia." *Mitteilungen des Oberösterreichischen Landesarchivs* 16 (1990): 135–301.
Pálffy, Géza. *The Kingdom of Hungary and the Habsburg Monarchy in the Sixteenth Century*. New York: Columbia University Press, 2009.
———. "Krönungsmähler in Ungarn im Spätmittelalter und in der Frühen Neuzeit: Weiterleben des Tafelzeremoniells des selbständigen ungarischen Königshofes und Machtrepräsentation der ungarischen politischen Elite." *MIÖG* 115 (2007): 85–111; 116 (2008): 60–91.
Pánek, Jaroslav. "Königswahl oder Königsaufnahme? Thronwechsel im Königreich Böhmen an der Schwelle zur Neuzeit." In *Der frühmoderne Staat in Ostzentraleuropa*, edited by Wolfgang J. Weber, 37–52. Augsburg: Dr. Bernd Wißner Verlag, 2000.
Paulus, Christof. "Ein seltzamme gewonheit: . . . Die Zeremonien an Fürstenstein und Herzogstuhl in der Sicht des Spätmittelalters und der Frühen Neuzeit." *MIÖG* 112 (2014): 22–39.
Polek, Johann. "Die Huldigung der Bukowina am 12. Oktober 1777." *Jahrbuch des Bukowiner Landesmuseums* 10 (1902): 3–36.
Polleroß, Friedrich. "*Austriacus Hungariae Rex*: Zur Darstellung der Habsburger als ungarische Könige in der frühneuzeitlichen Graphik." In *"Ez világ, mint egy kert . . ." Tanulmányok*

Galavics Géza tiszteletére, edited by Orsolya Bubryák, 63–78. Budapest: MTA Müveszet-történeti Kutatóintézet/Gondolat Kiadó, 2010.

Porcedda, Donatella. "La visita imperiale di Leopoldo I. a Gorizia nel 1660." *Memorie storiche forogiuliesi* 76 (1996): 89–122.

Portela Sandoval, Francisco José. "A própósito de la jura de los príncipes herederos: Una nueva lectura del cuadro Jura de don Fernando (VII) como príncipe de Asturias, de Luis Paret." *En la España Medieval*, número extraordinario 1 (2006): 337–47.

Prokeš, Jaroslav. "Marie Terezie a přípravy k české korunovaci roku 1742." In *Sborník prací věnovaný prof. Dru Gustavu Friedrichovi k šedesátým narozeninám*, 331–51. Prague: Historický spolek v Praze, 1932.

Puntschart, Paul. *Herzogseinsetzung und Huldigung in Kärnten: Ein verfassungs- und kulturgeschichtlicher Beitrag*. Leipzig: Veit & Comp., 1899.

Quarthal, Franz. *Landstände und landständisches Steuerwesen in Schwäbisch Österreich*. Stuttgart: Müller & Gräff, 1980.

Radvánszky, Anton. "Das Amt des Kronhüters im Staatsrecht und in der Geschichte Ungarns." *Ungarn-Jahrbuch* 11 (1980–81): 1–62.

Řezník, Miloš. *Neuorientierung einer Elite: Aristokratie, Ständewesen und Loyalität in Galizien (1772–1795)*. Frankfurt am Main: Peter Lang, 2016.

Ribeiro da Silva, Francisco. "A viagem de Filipe III a Portugal: itinerários e problemática." *Revista de Ciências Históricas* 2 (1987): 223–60.

Ruiz, Teofilo F. *A King Travels: Festive Traditions in Late Medieval and Early Modern Spain*. Princeton: Princeton University Press, 2012.

Russell, Nicolas, and Hélène Visentin, eds. *French Ceremonial Entries in the Sixteenth Century: Event, Image, Text*. Toronto: Centre for Reformation and Renaissance Studies, 2007.

Sánchez Alonso, María Cristina. "Juramentos de príncipes herederos en Marid (1561–1598)." *Anales del Instituto de Estudios Madrileños* 6 (1970): 29–41.

Sanz Hermida, Jacobo. "Un viaje conflictivo: relaciones de sucesos para la jornada del Rey N. S. Don Felipe III deste nombre, al Reyno de Portugal (1619)." *Península: Revista de Estudos Ibéricos* 0 (2003): 289–320.

Schulze, Winfried. "Hausgesetzgebung und Verstaatlichung im Hause Österreich vom Tode Maximilians I. bis zur Pragmatischen Sanktion." In *Der dynastische Fürstenstaat: Zur Bedeutung von Sukzessionsordnungen für die Entstehung des frühmodernen Staates*, edited by Johannes Kunisch, 253–71. Berlin: Duncker & Humblot, 1982.

Schwerdfeger, Josef. "Der bairisch-französische Einfall in Ober- und Niederösterreich (1741) und die Stände der Erherzogthümer. I. Theil: Karl Albrecht und die Franzosen in Ober-Österreich." *Archiv für österreichische Geschichte* 87 (1899): 319–446.

Seitschek, Stefan. "Die Erbhuldigung 1728 in Kärnten, ihre Organisation und Durchführung anhand ausgewählter Quellen." *Carinthia: Zeitschrift für geschichtliche Landeskunde von Kärnten* 202 (2012): 125–78.

Serrano Martín, Eliseo. "No demandamos sino el modo: Los juramentos reales en Aragón en la Edad Moderna." *Pedralbes* 28 (2008): 435–64.

Sharp, Kevin. *Image Wars: Promoting Kings and Commonwealths in England 1603–1660*. New Haven: Yale University Press, 2010.

Šišić, Ferdo (Šišić, Ferdinand von). *Die Wahl Ferdinands I. von Österreich zum König von Kroatien*. Zagreb: Verlag der Kgl. Akad. Universitätsbuchhandlung Fr. Suppan (St. Kugli), 1917.

———, ed. *Hrvatski saborski spisi*. Vol. 1. Zagreb: Academia scientiarum et artium Slavorum Meridionalium, 1912.

Śliwowska, Anna. *Uroczyste wjazdy monarsze do Wrocławia w latach 1527–1620.* Wrocław: Oficyna Wydawnicza ATUT, 2008.
Sr. k. k. *Majestät Leopold des Zweyten politische Gesetze und Verordnungen für die deutschen, böhmischen und galizischen Erbländer.* Vol. 4. Vienna: Joseph Edler von Kurzbeck, 1792.
Steiner, Philip. *Die Landstände in Steiermark, Kärnten und Krain und die josephinische Reformation: Bedrohungskommunikation angesichts konkurrierender Ordnungsvorstellungen (1789–1792).* Münster: Aschendorff Verlag, 2017.
Storia di Milano. Vol. 12: *L'Età delle riforme (1706–1796).* Milan: Fondazione Treccani degli Alfieri, 1959.
Strohmeyer, Arno. *Konfessionskonflikt und Herrschaftsordnung: Widerstandsrecht bei den österreichischen Ständen (1550–1650).* Mainz: Verlag Philipp von Zabern, 2006.
Telesko, Werner. "Hier wird einmal gutt ruhen seyn: Balthasar Ferdinand Molls Prunksarkophag für Franz Stephan und Maria Theresia in der Wiener Kapuzinergruft (1754)." *Wiener Jahrbuch für Kunstgeschichte* 59 (2010): 103–26.
Thompson, I. A. A. "The End of the Cortes of Castile." *Parliaments, Estates and Representations* 4 (1984): 125–33.
Urfus, Valentin. *Císař Josef I. Nekorunovaný Habsburk na českém trůně.* Prague: Libri, 2004.
Vácha, Štěpán, Irena Veselá, Vít Vlnas, and Petra Vokáčová. *Karel VI. & Alžběta Kristýna: Česká korunovace 1723.* Prague: Národní galerie v Praze, 2009.
Vaillancourt, Daniel, and Marie-France Wagner, eds. "Les entrées royales: urbanité et société au XVIIe siècle." *XVIIe Siècle* 53, no. 3 (2001).
Vallejo García-Hevia, José María. "La última máscara del rey: Las cortes de Castilla de 1789 en la España del antiguo régimen." In *Corte y monarquía en España*, edited by Dolores del Mar Sánchez González, 191–258. Madrid: Centro de estudios Ramon Aceres, 2003.
van Dievoet, Guy. "L'empereur Joseph II et la Joyeuse Entrée de Brabant: Les dernières années de la constitution brabançonne." *Anciens Pays et Assemblées d'États/Standen en Landen* 16 (1958): 87–140.
Van Gelder, Klaas. "The Investiture of Emperor Charles VI in Brabant and Flanders: A Test Case for Authority of the New Austrian Government." *European Review of History/Revue européenne d'histoire* 18, no. 4 (2011): 443–63.
Van Gelder, Klaas, and Bert Van Cauter. "Een publieke ceremonie in een turbulent tijdvak: De inauguratie van Maria Theresia als gravin van Vlaanderen (1744)." *Handelingen der Maatschappij voor Geschiederis en Oudheidkunde te Gent* 67 (2013): 101–30.
Varga, Szabolcs. "Az 1527. évi horvát-szlavón kettős 'királyválasztás' története." *Századok* 142 (2008): 1075–134.
Venetianische Depeschen vom Kaiserhofe (Dispacci di Germania). 2nd section Vol. 1, edited by Alfred Francis Pribram. Vienna: F. Tempsky, 1901.
Viollet, Paul. *Le roi et ses ministres pendant les trois derniers siècles de la monarchie.* Paris: Larose et Tenin, 1912.
Vocelka, Karl, and Lynne Heller. *Die Lebenswelten der Habsburger: Kultur- und Mentalitätsgeschichte einer Familie.* Graz: Styria, 1997.
Wagner, Marie-France, ed. *Les Entrées royales et solenelles du règne d'Henri IV dans les villes françaises.* Paris: Éditions Classiques Garnier, 2010.
Wagner, Marie-France, and Daniel Vaillancourt, eds. *Le Roi dans la ville: Anthologie des entrées royales dans les villes de province (1615–1660).* Paris: H. Champion, 2001.
Wandruszka, Adam. *Leopold II.: Erzherzog von Österreich, Grossherzog von Toskana, König von Ungarn und Böhmen, Römischer Kaiser.* 2 vols. Vienna: Herold Verlag, 1963–65.

Wanger, Bernd Herbert. *Kaiserwahl und Krönung im Frankfurt des 17. Jahrhunderts: Darstellung anhand der zeitgenössischen Bild- und Schriftquellen und unter besonderer Berücksichtigung der Erhebung des Jahres 1612*. Frankfurt am Main: Verlag Waldemar Kramer, 1994.

Wendehorst, Stephan. "Die Kaiserhuldigungen der Frankfurter Juden im 18. Jahrhundert." In *Die Frankfurter Judengasse: Jüdisches Leben in der Frühen Neuzeit*, edited by Fritz Backhaus, Gisela Engel, Robert Liberles, and Margarete Schlüter, 213–35. Frankfurt: Societätsverlag, 2006.

Winkelbauer, Thomas. "Dynastische Erbfolgeregelungen und länderspezifisches Thronfolgerecht." In *Verwaltungsgechichte der Habsburgermonarchie in der Frühen Neuzeit*. Vol. 1/1, edited by Michael Hochedlinger, Petr Maťa, and Thomas Winkelbauer, 83–98. Vienna: Böhlau Verlag, 2019.

Wilkinson, Alexander S., ed. *Iberian Books: Books Published in Spanish or Portuguese or on the Iberian Peninsula before 1601*. Leiden, Boston: Brill, 2010.

Wilkinson, Alexander S., and Alejandra Ulla Lorenzo. *Iberian Books (Volumes II & III): Books Published in Spain, Portugal and the New World or elsewhere in Spanish or Portuguese between 1601 and 1650*. Leiden: Brill 2015.

Zedinger, Renate, ed. *Innsbruck 1765: Prunkvolle Hochzeit, fröhliche Feste, tragischer Ausklang*. Bochum: Verlag Dr. Dieter Winkler, 2015.

Zieglauer, Ferdinand von. *Die politische Reformbewegung in Siebenbürgen in der Zeit Joseph's II. und Leopold's II*. Vienna: Wilhelm Braumüller, 1881.

Chapter 2

MEANINGLESS SPECTACLES?
Eighteenth-Century Imperial Coronations in the Holy Roman Empire Reconsidered

Harriet Rudolph

The crowning of a Roman emperor in Frankfurt was certainly one of the most august and at the same time magnificent spectacles that the world has ever seen. Everything down to the minutest details spoke to the spirit and the heart, through the power of the tradition as well as through the aggregation of so much splendor.
—Klemens Wenzel Nepomuk Lothar Fürst von Metternich-Winneburg, *Aus Metternich's nachgelassenen Papieren*

The investiture of a king of the Romans represented the most complex ritual of elevation performed in the Holy Roman Empire. Following the election of the future ruler by the electors, the coronation formed the second act of a political ritual institutionalized since the Late Middle Ages through custom and processes of textualization and maintained until the end of the Empire. During the eighteenth century, six coronations took place in the imperial city of Frankfurt. Five of these were coronations of emperors, while one was the crowning of King Joseph II (1764). But what functions did such ceremonies fulfill at the end of the Old Empire in a phase of profound upheaval and increasing internal as well as international conflicts? Did the coronation truly represent a *solemnitas accidentalis*[1] considered nothing more than a "bizarre anachronism"[2] by contemporaries? Had the formerly constitutive ritual of investiture become a changeable ceremony—

perhaps even a "profane act of state"?[3] Did the Enlightenment really bring about an "erosion of sacramental signs," causing the purport of the coronation liturgy to no longer be understood?[4] How did the system of print media and the development of "public opinion" affect the evaluation of such acts? And finally, the question arises: How did the coronations fit into the still prevalent narrative of a continuous decline of the Holy Roman Empire at least since the second half of the eighteenth century?[5]

For Europe, the anointing and coronation of rulers combined within a single ritual of elevation are first documented for the Carolingians, who therefore served as a symbolic point of reference for later coronations in France, England, and the Holy Roman Empire alike.[6] Thus, the coronation ritual in the Empire is older than the election ritual, which developed only during the Late Middle Ages. In contrast to medieval times,[7] there are no recent monographs focusing on the elevation of kings and emperors in the early modern Empire. This is because historians attached significantly less relevance to the topic for understanding the unique nature of the Empire as a far-ranging and multireligious confederation of dominions incorporating various types of rule. In the nineteenth and twentieth centuries, historians commonly held the notion that one should write the history of the early modern Empire as a history of progress in the sense of increasing desymbolization and territorial state building. A further reason was an ahistorical concept of the imperial constitution that reduced it to graspable content in terms of legal positivism while disregarding its essential performative dimension.[8]

In contrast to elections, historians therefore considered early modern coronations to be mere spectacles of courtly representation that increased the publicity of the investiture, bestowed a divine blessing on the new ruler, and promoted the acceptance of his rule by the ordinary people, but remained without significant constitutional relevance. In the perception of older research, maintaining ritual forms that were already historically obsolete by the eighteenth century mirrored the emperorship's loss of political importance, which went hand in hand with— and was reinforced by—an increasing focus of the Habsburg emperors on their hereditary lands.[9] And while historians paid more attention to coronation rituals in the course of the boom in research into ceremonial after 2000, the resulting studies generally focused heavily on ceremonial conflicts. But the significance of an imperial coronation went beyond the staging of a frequently contentious order of precedence by participating ruling elites and office-bearers—even though many of these actors did of course attribute great relevance to their rank within the princely society of the Empire as reflected in certain rights of precedence and participation in the acts of election and coronation.

To be able to understand the continuing relevance of imperial coronations in the early modern Empire, it may be useful to draw on the concept of the diverse bodies of premodern kings. Ernst H. Kantorowicz distinguished between the political-legal (institutional) and the historical-physical (natural) body of the king; more recent research has added the notion of a third, sacral body of the king.[10] During the complex ritual of investiture in the Holy Roman Empire, the institution of emperorship was connected to the natural body of the future emperor not only through legal acts such as the election and signing of the electoral capitulation (*Wahlkapitulation*), but also by ostentatiously staging the emperor's sacral body in the coronation mass.[11] The sacral body of the emperor differed fundamentally from the holy body of the French and English kings created in French and English coronation rituals, however. The German emperors could not lay any claim to thaumaturgic capabilities, and they did not officiate as supreme heads of the Church.[12] On the other hand, they ruled the *Holy* Roman Empire, which had been considered to occupy an exceptional position in God's plan of salvation for several centuries.[13] While their function as supreme defenders of Christianity—affirmed several times by speech acts during the coronation ritual—had gained new topicality during the Ottoman expansion from the 1520s onward, it was simultaneously called into question as a result of the religious division. In the latter part of the eighteenth century, the Ottoman threat was history, and imperial and territorial law regulated confessional diversity. In addition, processes of secularization, rationalization, and disenchantment were, to a certain degree, well under way.

Nevertheless, contemporaries attached great significance to the act of coronation, and this became readily apparent in the terminology they used. When speaking of the *Kaiserkrönung* (coronation of the emperor), they generally meant the election *and* crowning of a new head of the Empire. Had coronations truly lost their constitutive function, it would seem much more logical for people to have used the term *Kaiserwahl* (election of the emperor). And while the former expression could refer to the entire act of coronation, to the coronation mass, or merely to the actual putting on of the crown, it usually stood *pars pro toto* for the entire ritual of elevation. The term *Kaiserwahl*, on the other hand, almost always referred only to the election itself and rarely included the subsequent coronation. In the eyes of most subjects, the elevation of an emperor was apparently only completed through the act of crowning. Due to its significantly greater publicity and display of splendor, but most of all due to its ritual forms aimed at creating transcendence, the majority of people considered the coronation the central element of the investiture of a new emperor.

This interpretation was vehemently disputed by certain groups of stakeholders in the early modern period, however. One of these groups were the secular electors, who beyond possible desires for confessional distinction were clearly subordinate to the spiritual electors during coronations and whose symbolic benefit thus seemed insignificant from the outset. The organization of the coronation ritual fell to the court of the emperor and—as far as the liturgy of the coronation mass was concerned—to the elector of Mainz, who acted as consecrator. The second such group consisted of Protestant publicists in the field of imperial constitutional law and court officials who denied any legal import of the coronation.[14] In their opinion, the new emperor was fully able to govern after signing his *Wahlkapitulation*; coronations consequently appeared dispensable. This theory could have been conclusively proven only in the case of a corresponding conflict of rule, but such a conflict in fact never occurred in political practice since all early modern coronations except that of Emperor Charles V took place very soon after the respective elections. Further factors drawing the constitutive function of coronations into question supervened in the eighteenth century; they will be discussed in the first part of this chapter, while the second part uses the final two coronations of emperors as examples to investigate the potential of such acts for establishing legitimation of rule and generating societal integration.

Hard Times for a Medieval Rite of Passage

There were two phases in the early modern history of the Empire in which the ritual process of elevating an emperor faced specific challenges and had to prove its adaptability to changing historical conditions. The first such phase came after the Peace of Augsburg signed in 1555, when the Protestant electors—backed by imperial law—contested a number of traditional religious elements of the ritual that were now being defined as Catholic. This occurred first in 1558 when the emperorship was transferred to King Ferdinand I, and again in the course of the following two elections and coronations of Roman kings in 1562 and 1575.[15] The good standing of the emperors with the electors, however, allowed a compromise that maintained the traditional Catholic liturgy during the election and coronation masses even in times of a bi- or even tri-confessional Empire. In addition, even the majority of the Protestant electors had no interest in challenging the emperor's legitimation to rule by redesigning elevation rituals regulated by the imperial constitution, and as a result, the achieved compromise under which the Protestant electors temporarily left the *locus ritualis* during certain parts of the mass was eventually discontinued in 1612.

The second and far more problematic phase was the period following the death of Charles VI in 1740, when a multitude of political and cultural factors coincided that threatened to undermine the legitimizing power of the elevation ritual. Although this notion is increasingly being challenged, it is not by chance that research still generally views this period as the one in the history of the Empire in which its own decline and that of its institutions inexorably manifested themselves.[16] This period was preceded by the War of the Spanish Succession (1701–14), a large-scale military conflict already characterized by a number of dynamics that would decisively shape later phases of the century as well. Among these were the intensifying formation process of European great powers, the striving of secular imperial princes for elevation in rank, and an overall cumulation of military conflicts.[17]

These developments affected particularly heavily the periods in which new emperors were elevated. The election and crowning of Charles VI (1711) took place during the War of the Spanish Succession; those of Charles VII (1742) and Francis I (1745) during the War of the Austrian Succession (1740–48). The elevation of Joseph II to king of the Romans (1764) was directly linked to the Seven Years' War (1756–63). Even the coronations of Leopold II (1790) and Francis II (1792) coincided with military conflicts and political unrest in the Habsburg lands.[18] By contrast, at least three (1612, 1653, 1658) of the six imperial coronations during the seventeenth century occurred in periods of peace. Even more striking is the difference from the sixteenth century, in which all elevations had taken place in times of peace despite the constant Ottoman threat, military clashes between the Habsburgs and the French kings, and political as well as confessional conflicts within the Empire. Unsurprisingly, the only elevation of an emperor who was not a member of the Habsburg dynasty took place in the eighteenth century. Charles VII attempted to compensate for his self-perceived legitimation deficit with a splendor during his coronation ceremony unlike any before seen.[19] That he could not compensate his pivotal lack of instrumental resources of power with an accumulation of symbolic capital was evidenced by his three-year rule in Frankfurt, where he resided in less than grand fashion and with his military defeat imminent.

In the eighteenth century, the limited symbolic benefit of participating in the election and coronation ritual was reversed into its opposite for those secular electors who had been able to ascend to royalty (Saxony as king of Poland in 1697, Brandenburg as king in Prussia in 1701, Hanover as king of Great Britain in 1714).[20] They could now have no interest in any form of symbolic submission to the emperor during the coronation—and the same applied to the electors of Bavaria and the Palatinate, even though they had failed to attain royal rank. But the fact that the secular electors no longer took part in election and coronation acts was not only owed to changes in the power-political circumstances and the ranking order within the Empire, it was also brought about by an increasing need for economy of representation. Nevertheless, the presence of all electors—achieved for the last time in 1562—would remain an ideal until the very end of the Empire, as illustrated by a copper engraving of the coronation of Leopold II (see figure 2.1). Of the seven electors shown in the image, only three actually attended the act in 1790.[21]

In addition, the established elevation procedures had to stand the test of certain cultural developments in the Old Empire that fundamentally challenged the ritual forms of the coronation as well as the concepts of imperial rule and the claims to legitimacy communicated by them. For example, scholars in the ceremonial sciences,[22] who were mostly of nonnoble ancestry, tended to be critical of elaborate ceremonial practices, which they considered a waste of time and

Figure 2.1. Copper engraving of the coronation of Emperor Leopold II in 1790 ("Vorstellung der Festlichen Krönung Ihro K. K. Majestät Leopoldi II. zum Römischen Kaiser zu Frankfurt den 9. October 1790." Munich, Leopold Wenger-Institut, Sammlung Karl von Amira, folder 85, no. II.13).

money. At the same time, they facilitated a continually increasing differentiation of ceremonials with their multiplication of ceremonial sources—and thus of the claims to rule and dignity that were attached to the procedures described in them. Especially from this period on, we find an ideational separation between the political elite, allegedly difficult to impress with displays of magnificence, and the "rabble," whose acceptance of rule depended on the pageantry displayed by its authorities. In this interpretation, courtly splendor becomes a concession by rational rulers to their irrational subjects.

This same attitude is encountered in Emperor Francis I and his son Joseph II, who described the observance of the complex baroque ceremonial associated with their reign as an annoying duty, but who were nevertheless apparently deeply impressed by the emotional impact and ritual dynamic of the coronation rites.[23] For such monarchs, their use of criticism of and ironic comments about solemn rituals primarily served to portray themselves as enlightened rulers who stood above ceremonial squabbles—as they were in fact able to do because they stood at the top of the rank hierarchy anyway. Correspondingly, the ceremonial complexity and the display of grandeur during the coronation of Francis I (1745) and Joseph II (1764) barely fell short of the ritual for Charles VII (1742). In 1764, Francis I had even commissioned elaborate copies of the coronation regalia so that he and Joseph II could both wear them on the day of the coronation.[24]

This particular symbol of the institution of the emperorship was thus linked with the dynasty of the Habsburgs as a whole—which was apparently considered especially important after the Wittelsbach intermezzo twenty years before. And although Maria Theresa had remained in Vienna in 1764—and allegedly scoffed at the out-of-time crowning ritual in 1745—she commissioned her court painter Martin van Meytens to create a large-scale, six-part series of coronation paintings. This commission demonstrates the great significance she attached to the act far more convincingly than any spoken or written word.[25]

In the second half of the eighteenth century, the Enlightenment as the putative age of reason and rationality influenced the way in which educated elites perceived coronations. A special role in this regard fell to the notion of a clear separation between a desirable inwardness and an outwardness rejected as being superficial.[26] Toward the end of the empire, this notion even shaped the tenor of coronation diaries. The author of the official diary of 1790, for example, addressed his report explicitly to "the thinking part of the readers" and therefore dispensed with descriptions of sensual impressions, pointing instead to a schematic copper engraving of a coronation scene—which did not compensate the void in terms of splendor in any way, however.[27] The sociopolitical logic of rituals as performative acts rested upon the very idea of congruence between form and content: the system of rule that became visible in the relations between people, spaces, and artifacts during the coronation mass was meant to embody power relations that existed in reality.

The obvious discrepancy between factual relations and the ritually performed ones allowed disputatious contemporaries to malign coronations as political "spectacles."[28] Other authors tried to defend the elaborate ritual with the argument that even those "societies that make the culture of reason and intellectual engagement their main ultimate purpose do not entirely forbear the use of ceremonies."[29] They depicted coronations as desirable rituals involving all parts of the population and symbolically referring to central elements of the imperial constitution. From their point of view, the coronation ritual invited all observers to recollect the times when "the magnanimous Teutons willingly submitted to a ruler because they knew from their own experience that anarchy undermines the fortunes of the state, but elected him themselves and placed unalterable boundaries on his power through certain stipulations."[30] Even Georg Forster argued that the pomp of the imperial coronation "can be justified with good reason as remembrance of the genesis of the German imperial constitution,"[31] thereby evaluating the constitution as positive and still standing on a solid foundation at the time. Rudolph Hommel considered the imperial insignia as "venerable monuments of German character and art"[32] that remained present in the collective consciousness through their ritual use.

While the Catholic coronation liturgy, despite the confessional divide, survived the sixteenth century because tradition as such had been considered to establish legitimacy, this argument had lost most of its persuasiveness for "enlightened" contemporaries in the eighteenth century—especially in regard to medieval traditions. With the Middle Ages bearing a primarily negative connotation, critical observers described the coronation ritual as "barbaric," "gothic," "feudal," "Byzantine," or even "Jewish."[33] The style and material of the coronation robes and the *Reichskleinodien* (imperial regalia) appeared tasteless and cheap to them; their bad state of preservation supposedly mirrored the lamentable state of the Empire itself. Especially on the occasion of the last two coronations, some authors employed criticism of the elevation ritual to distinguish themselves as representatives of a "reasoning" public. Depending on individual positioning, their argumentation exhibited an anti-Catholic, antiaristocratic, antiplebeian, or anti-Jewish thrust. While one can indeed speak of a representative public as defined by Habermas regarding the media coverage of imperial coronations until the middle of the eighteenth century, the same does not hold true for the last two acts—not least due to the influence of the French Revolution.[34]

Even critical authors, such as Wilhelm Ludwig Wekhrlin, remained loyal to the emperor and the electors as the political elite of the Empire, however, and explicitly excluded them from any criticism.[35] Until the end of the Empire, the emperor remained a figure of identification for large parts of the populace irrespective of their membership in a particular social class. The multitude of general studies on the elevation of emperors, treatises about the imperial insignia, and depictions of emperors in the coronation robes published during the last two decades of the Empire even point to an increase in popularity of the rituals of Empire and emperorship during this era.[36] In the last decade of the century, romanticism with its criticism of the demystification of the world caused by Reformation and Enlightenment was gaining influence in regard to the perception of the Holy Roman Empire. For romantic authors, the Middle Ages represented an "age of unity, wholeness and community."[37] Rituals with medieval roots like the coronation of an emperor now served as images of a great German history not yet characterized by confessional conflict and the Enlightenment's adverseness to a sensuality that was considered highly desirable.

Outdated? The Adaptation Potential of Coronations at the End of the Empire

The crowning of two emperors within two years in the early 1790s was an incident never seen before in the history of the Holy Roman Empire with the exception of times of anti-kings.[38] Similarly short interstices had previously only occurred during times of crisis before or during large-scale military conflicts, like the Thirty Years' War (Matthias—1612; Ferdinand II—1619) or the War of the Austrian Succession (Charles VII—1742; Francis I—1745). They negated the exceptional character of such events, the symbolic efficacy of which was normally heightened even further by their infrequence. The great financial expense posed significant challenges for the involved stakeholders as well—especially for the aspirant to the throne. These structural problems affected the coronation of 1792 in particular. An important backdrop for both coronations was provided by the French Revolution, whose internal dynamics influenced to a certain degree the procedures—and in any case the perception and evaluation—of both imperial elevations.[39] After all, the developments in France were being observed closely in the Empire. While some prorevolutionary voices are documented in the context of the elevation of 1790, public opinion had turned around by 1792—provoked by the repeated escalation of violence in France, the capture of the king after his escape to Varennes, and the French declaration of war on Austria on 20 April 1792.

Seven months after the death of Emperor Joseph II, the election of his successor, Leopold II, Grand Duke of Tuscany, took place on 30 September 1790.[40] Leopold, who was more reform-oriented but also strategically more prudent than his brother, could hope to be met with a considerable level of acceptance within the Empire.[41] In the perception of politically informed contemporaries, he represented a diametric counterpole to Louis XVI of France. Supposedly elected "by the most august and powerful princes of Europe as their ruler," he ceremonially paraded into Frankfurt on 4 October 1790 and signed the electoral capitulation in the collegiate church. With him came papal, Russian, and Sardinian legations as well as Ferdinand III/IV of Sicily/Naples and Maria Carolina of Austria as parents of Maria Theresa of Sicily/Naples, who had previously been wed to Archduke Francis of Austria, the eventual emperor Francis II, in Vienna. As early as 9 October 1790, a Saturday, the three-part coronation ritual, consisting of the coronation mass, the solemn procession to the *Römer*, and the coronation banquet including the *Preisgabe* (donation of meat, wine, cloth, etc.) and coin toss, was performed.[42] At the center of the festivities was the coronation mass in which the ruler was ritually instated into his office. The subsequent parts of the procedure, on the other hand, merely expressed the change in hierarchy effected by the coronation while simultaneously presenting it to wider parts of the population and involving them as ritual actors rather than pure spectators.

The liturgical procedure of the coronation mass was defined by the Aachen coronation *ordo* created in the first quarter of the fourteenth century, which incorporated the consecration of the king of the Romans into a service for the Three Kings.[43] This high mass was particularly suited for the act in question because its observers could directly relate the story of the Three Kings submitting to the newborn Christ to the submission of the imperial princes to the new emperor. Profane acts like the congratulation of the emperor by the electors, the *Ritterschlag* (knightly accolade) and the admission of the emperor into the Aachen cathedral canonry were not included in the ordo. To properly perform these, one therefore resorted to the tradition produced by the Mainz archchancellery and the imperial court. In order to avoid ritual mishaps during the mass, the imperial court produced an extensive "Directorium circa Actum consecrationis regis Romanum" detailing the entire sequence of acts.[44] It was presumably this document that Leopold II, who submitted to the complex and time-consuming liturgy as had his predecessors, found beside his prie-dieu in the Church of St. Bartholomew.[45]

The coronation mass represented a complex *rite de passage* that followed the usual dramaturgy of ritual abasement, ritual *communitas*, and ritual elevation—repeated several times. The intended redundancy served to "safeguard" the investiture; it mentally and physically reminded the new emperor of his humility before the Almighty God to whom he was subordinate. During the performance, the new emperor appeared in part as a passive object and in part as an active subject of ritual acts. Through the constant alternation of walking, standing, sitting, prostrating, and kneeling, of enrobing and disrobing, of receiving and yielding the imperial insignia, of silence and sound,[46] the emperor was to internalize his office as ruler of the Empire and protector of the Christian Church—not merely enact it like in a play. The participants could observe all three dimensions of sacral kingship during the coronation mass: the notion of monarchical rule *Dei gratia* combined with the idea that the emperor was chosen by God, that he was to serve as proxy for God, and that he was assigned a priest-like position—though the latter certainly to the least extent.[47] The consecrator and other clerics ostentatiously exemplified these dimensions on the ritual-sacral body of the emperor through the performance of speech acts, hymns, and gestures.

The coronation day began with the solemn procession of the elected emperor, accompanied by the secular princes, to the Church of St. Bartholomew at 11:00 a.m., which was relatively late in comparison to coronations in previous centuries, when the procession had usually been scheduled at 9:00 a.m. When the emperor entered the church at around 11:30 a.m., most spectators had already been waiting there for three to four hours to ensure they had good seats. The roughly three-hour coronation mass consisted of five phases[48]: (1) introductory rites, such as the reception of the emperor outside the church by the clergy, and his solemn entry into the church, with a great silver cross and a silver staff bearing his seals carried ahead; (2) the first part of the Epiphany Mass, with the Penitential Act and then the Litany of the Saints; (3) the by far longest phase with the actual consecration rites: the interrogation of the king (*scrutinium*) followed by his first oath, his acclamation by the people, his anointing, his enrobing in the coronation regalia (which by no means represented "only an 'amusing' costume"[49]) in the sacristy, the bestowal of the imperial insignia,[50] and the coronation oath spoken in a voice loud enough to be heard in the entire church[51]; (4) the second part of the Epiphany Mass, with the profession of faith and incorporating as its most important sequences the sacrifice and communion; and, finally, (5) several declarative acts that were not part of the high mass, such as the enthronement of the emperor, the congratulation by the electors, and the knightly accolade.[52]

Interjected between all these sequences were various benedictions of and prayers for the new emperor; Bible texts such as the *Surge illuminare Jerusalem* (Isa. 60:1) were read, hymns were sung, and instrumental music was played by the imperial chapel complemented by members of the Mainz chapel.[53] The emperor was sprinkled several times with holy water, and he kissed certain holy artifacts such as the paten, the gospel, and the cross to demonstrate his exceptional piety. While reading the mass, the consecrator interacted alternately with the emperor, other clerical protagonists, the imperial chapel, or the entire congregation. Besides the coronation oath, the congratulations by the electors, and the address of gratitude by the emperor, all speech acts and songs were recited in Latin. Because the most important texts had been translated in printed descriptions since the early eighteenth century, even attendants who were not versed in Latin could understand their religious and constitutional substance. Authors such as Johann Philipp Schulin even commented on important paragraphs. Concerning the final question of the *scrutinium*, Schulin describes the subservience to the pope as "a consequence of those dark times" when the Catholic Church was more powerful than the emperors, explaining to his readers that this passage "may today no longer be translated literally, nor even less understood that way."[54] By contrast, he qualifies the "Fiat" of the acclamation as "a remnant of those times not yet obliterated by any law or peace settlement when every freeborn German was entitled to say a word regarding the election of an emperor"—a version of the imperial constitution he obviously considered very desirable.[55]

All of these sequences, serving especially to express the sacradness of the emperor's office, were performed unaltered in 1790. Leopold II even reactivated certain elements that had previously been abandoned: prior to the beginning of the Litany of the Saints, for example, he prostrated himself in the shape of a cross on the floor of the church, which was covered with golden pillows. By contrast, Francis I in 1745 and Joseph I in 1764 had only dropped to their knees.[56] Hommel exuberantly describes this act as a "great scene" during which all electors and clerics kneeled while "the lord of twenty million subjects . . . now lay before his own [Lord]."[57] It is thus by no means the case that "the remains of quasi-sacramental actions increasingly vanished" from the coronation masses during the eighteenth century.[58] Furthermore, the majority of people certainly did not consider the coronation mass "a secular act . . . since the Reformation at the latest."[59] The coronation ritual remained a genuinely ecclesiastic act that culminated in the emperor's fivefold anointing with the symbol of the cross on the part of his hair, his chest, shoulders, right forearm, and right palm by the consecrator.[60] Like the French and English monarchs, the Roman emperors never accepted the papal standards for the consecration of kings, which limited the anointing to the right underarm to signify the difference to Episcopal ordinations. In contrast to the latter, however, catechumenal oil was used for the Roman emperors.[61] Nevertheless, it was precisely the act of anointing that transformed the emperor's status to that of the Lord's Anointed, which is why the coronation mass still represented a *rite de passage*.

Only the anointed emperor could be dressed in the coronation regalia, and only after the anointing could the ecclesiastic electors bestow the insignia of the Empire upon him. The significance of these artifacts distinctly exceeded their alleged provenance from Charlemagne because they signified "the Empire," whose holiness did not derive from its alleged founder but was instead granted by God himself. The accompanying speech acts made it very clear that God was installing the ruler into the office of emperor. They refer to the emperor's dominion *Dei gratia*, his proxy for God on Earth and—in the case of the imperial crown—to his participation in the clerical office.[62] On a contemporary copper engraving (see figure 2.1), the crowning act is performed in front of the altar, above which an oversized eye of God appears. Its design is fueled entirely by the artist's fantasy, making the work an intentional expression of the divine right of the emperor. Already before the crowning, the coronator placed a ring on the emperor's finger as a symbol of his mystical connection to God and his (Catholic) Church. As this element is also encountered in Episcopal ordinations, it could be understood as a sign of investiture into a clerical office. A similar interpretation was possible concerning the dressing in robes of an ecclesiastical pattern[63] as well as the emperor's prostration during the Litany of the Saints.

Until the end of the Empire, the Habsburg kings of the Romans and emperors continued to perform the communion *sub una specie* as they had done from 1486 onward. They only received the ablution chalice during the communion, which some historians have misunderstood as communion *sub utraque specie*.[64] Whereas in the seventeenth century this decisive difference had been made clear by passing only a glass with wine to the emperor, the liturgical procedure changed in the eighteenth century: now the emperor received "Sacram Hostiam and the wine, or preferably the Purification out of the Consecratoris chalice."[65] By using a consecrated vessel, this liturgical act gained symbolic relevance despite the fact that all observers could still see the emperor was not communicating in both species. Frederick III had abandoned the emperor's privilege to communicate *sub utraque* specie in 1468, and by doing so had approved that kings of the Romans would be treated and perceived as equal to lay people, since he intended to dissociate himself and his dynasty from the Hussite movement and its claim to the lay chalice.[66] After the Reformation, the procedure signified an anti-Protestant attitude—which was why the Habsburgs maintained it until 1792 as a key indicator of confessional difference.

The deferment of the enthronement from immediately after the oath, as had been the case until the sixteenth century, until after the end of the mass resulted from an increasing desire to separate genuinely clerical acts from acts with a more secular tendency.⁶⁷ However, the sequence was still linked to several religious interpretative patterns. The accompanying speech act referred to the doctrine of divine right and to the role of the emperor as mediator between the clergy and the people—in comparison to Jesus Christ, who served as mediator between God and humankind. In addition, a suffragan read a passage from the Bible describing the journey of the Three Holy Kings to Bethlehem and their subordination to the newborn king. The observers could easily relate this account to the performance they were witnessing, because the elevators now congratulated the enthroned emperor even though they did not genuflect before him. The subsequent accolade was accompanied by a deafening *Te Deum* resonating throughout the church, and during the last part of the Ambrosian Hymn, the emperor suspended the accolade and kneeled in reference to the Almighty God.⁶⁸

Even the coronation of Francis II, performed on 14 July 1792 in demarcation against the Parisian *Fête de la Fédération* of 1790, was conducted according to the traditional pattern, although the war against France and the dire financial situation of the imperial court would have provided good reason to simplify the procedure. In fact, the councilors of the emperor and the elector of Mainz had recommended several options beforehand, all of which Francis refused for personal reasons or because he was convinced they would not be accepted by the other electors. For example, there were suggestions to move the coronation to Augsburg, Cologne, Regensburg, and, in particular, Mainz—despite the fact that the secular electors would never have agreed to the latter.⁶⁹ Francis similarly implemented the measures drafted by the elector of Mainz and his own councilor Prince Wenzel Anton Kaunitz-Rietberg to reduce the pageantry only in those areas in which they did not directly affect the elevation ritual.⁷⁰ He likewise refused to forego the coronation banquet since this part of the ceremony aimed at the inclusion of broad parts of the population—which he emphatically desired with a view to the revolutionary developments in France.⁷¹ The young monarch had apparently understood the relevance of the coronation act for the acceptance of his dominion far better than his legally educated advisors. While he dispensed with the ceremonial entry, the oath on the electoral capitulation took place in the church as it had before—and not in the emperor's quarters as suggested.⁷²

There are reports on both of the final coronations stating that the imperial family and other princes appeared markedly down-to-earth and avoided excessive pomp. In Schubart's words, "our German princes are gradually unlearning that high demeanor, that looking down from above upon other people, as if Titan had not kneaded them from the same dough."⁷³ Another eyewitness reported: "the emperor and the entire House as well as the king and queen of Naples do not make a lot of fuss, but are very unpretentious and stay out of every person's way."⁷⁴ These statements evidence a different style of rule that cannot be explained exclusively with the goal of preventing revolutionary developments in the Holy Roman Empire. Rather, it points to the development of a fundamentally different concept of rule. The closeness of space in the imperial city of Frankfurt, which imposed strict boundaries on courtly pageantry, was ideally suited to establishing the proximity between the monarch and his subjects that was the declared ideal of rulership at the end of the eighteenth century—in diametric contrast to its early years.

The descriptions of these coronations as well as the associated panegyrics convey a strong emotive tenor not encountered to the same degree during previous elevations.[75] Its goal was to ensure the coronation established an emotional bond between the ruler of the Empire and his subjects that would reinforce the stability of its union even in times of crisis. Hence, publicists depicted Leopold II as the "favorite of hearts" or even as the "adored darling of the nation," and the populace was allegedly completely overwhelmed with happiness and shed hot tears during and after his coronation.[76] The year 1790 also saw the appearance of new visual representations not encountered during previous coronations that allegorically embodied these emotions: One copper engraving (see figure 2.2), for example, shows the emperor, "great through nobleness of the heart," in front of a church portal in full coronation regalia. Kneeling before him, Germania presents the hearts of the German people on a tray, which he graciously accepts.[77] Beside Germania is a putto with a book, a helmet with a laurel wreath, and a palm twig as symbols for erudition, peacefulness, and victoriousness of the new emperor.

Figure 2.2. Allegorical copper engraving for the coronation of Leopold II by J. C. Berndt (Frankfurt am Main, Historisches Museum, Graphische Sammlung, N 42672).

The putto points to a globe on which "*Germanien*" forms the center of the world, while the sun rises behind the public conjoined by scenes of harmony.

The records preserved from the time even contain general discussions of the indispensable need for love between emperor and subjects. The greatness of every ruler, they claim, depends exclusively on the "love that blazes up in the breast of the entire populace, this loudly sounding love is that upon which the true greatness of great men can be defined; only that great man is truly great who places his glory in this love alone."[78] On the one hand, love of the ruler was portrayed as the duty of all obedient subjects, while on the other, the ruler had to earn this love as a universal "pleaser of the people."[79] Thus, the bipolar logic of ascribing certain virtues to the ruler while simultaneously demanding them from him shaped even the panegyrics produced in the context of the final elevations.

Certain differences can be discerned regarding the ideational frames of reference for the coronations of 1790 and 1792 as well, however.[80] For example, Leopold II was glamorized as the new Emperor Frederick III, whose traits—hardly heroic from the contemporary perspective—were now interpreted as expressions of his prudent exercise of rule aimed at securing peace in the Empire.[81] It had been Frederick III, after all, who had initiated the only once interrupted sequence of Habsburgs on the imperial throne that turned the Empire into a quasi-hereditary monarchy. The second dynastic point of reference for the coronation panegyrics was the new emperor's namesake, Leopold I, who had secured the Habsburg emperorship after the low point of the Peace of Westphalia in 1648 and earned its renewed acceptance within the Empire by fending off French expansion attempts—which understandably possessed a particular topicality for Leopold II's contemporaries in 1790.

His successor, Francis II, was aggrandized as the new Maximilian I in 1792; the latter's successful marriage politics had created the preconditions for the territorial expansion of the Habsburgs and thus for the ascent of the dynasty in Europe. In keeping with the ideal of the "last knight," various authors described Emperor Francis II in romanticizing fashion as a youthful hero and handsome prince with golden hair who would lead the Empire back to past greatness. Such notions were enriched with a discourse on virtues referring to the "noble German national character"[82] that used handed-down stereotypes to describe the German population as courageous, honest, and obedient—willing even to devote its own life to the emperor.[83] The preferred symbol for these German virtues was the oak as putative meeting place of the Germanic people since the days of old, and portraits of the emperor correspondingly began to include acorns and oak leaves. In the play "Der Eichenkranz" ("The Oak Wreath") by August Wilhelm Iffland, performed several times in 1792 and allegedly met with great enthusiasm by the audience, the oak served as an allegory for Francis II.[84] Even the exclusion of women from the emperorship could now be interpreted as a "trait of the German national spirit," while Charlemagne—who had previously been exalted as the progenitor of the Empire—was criticized as a "Franconian" tyrant and promotor of the "Pfaffen" (Catholic clerics).[85]

The imperial patriotism already tangible during such events in the sixteenth and seventeenth centuries developed into a patriotism relating to Germany as an imagined cultural *and* state nation—a patriotism that also featured nationalist elements, in particular concerning the anti-French sentiment evident in 1792. The election of 1790 was reinterpreted from an act performed by a small political elite—the electors—into a democratic decision by all German "citizens," which meant that in contrast to France, a revolution in Germany would be unwarranted.[86] Francis II was explicitly addressed as the defender of German "democracy" against French tyranny in 1792.[87] In 1790, Schulin supported his prediction of a Golden Age (see figure 2.2)—a common topos in election and coronation panegyrics—with a reference to Leopold's "felicitous government" in Tuscany, "where an entire part of the world with its peoples of different languages, laws and customs under the leadership of their special regents would constitute just one political society, one family and brotherhood." This vision of political unity in cultural and legal diversity could serve as a benchmark for an Empire characterized by centrifugal tendencies and internal conflicts.

The sacredness of emperorship enacted in the coronation mass now referred to the "German Empire" and, subsumed within it, the German nation as the totality of imperial Estates and subjects. Hommel described the coronation as a holy feast performed at St. Bartholomew and the *Römer* as "sanctums" of the Empire: "Rejoice, Germany! Cheer with joy once more, twice holy be this feast to you, where the Heavens, to please you, have granted you a Leopold."[88] The Catholic liturgy of the coronation mass no longer represented a problem for enlightened coevals anyway, who sometimes attended the services of other confessions without issue as well. What was more, the emperorship—and with it the current office-bearer—represented a supraconfessional institution. For these reasons, too, coronations of emperors would have been conceivable even in a reformed Empire.

The semantic openness of the coronation ritual is also documented in the fact that contemporaries reinterpreted the "amusements of the people," framing the act as a "German national celebration" at the end of the eighteenth century.[89] The hosts of this celebration were the monarch and his court, the electors and princes of the Empire, the imperial city of Frankfurt, and foreign envoys. The multiplicity of illumination, fireworks, balls, processions, theatre plays, and concerts, however, was also initiated in part by the population of the imperial city—including the Jews—and by coronation tourists. These social groups celebrated according to their own agenda.[90] The coronation festivities blended public and private, noble and civic, ruler- and subject-based cultures of celebration, with class barriers being enacted but also intentionally transgressed. They aimed at ideationally connecting the "German" nation with Habsburg emperorship, which was characterized as a "German," not an "Austrian," emperorship.

Conclusions

In premodern Europe, coronations served as common rituals of investiture in most elective and hereditary monarchies. That Emperor Francis II would not even forego this ritual in the precarious situation of 1792 clearly shows the great significance he attached to its legitimizing power and its impact beyond the people gathered in Frankfurt. Precisely at the end of the eighteenth century, when a new concept of rule was developing that declared the emotional bond between monarch and subjects its ideal, coronations had to be considered indispensable since almost all social strata were entitled to participate in the act. With the emperor only appearing rarely in the Empire otherwise, the coronation represented the only occasion where the emperor was able to enact closeness to his imperial subjects. In the early 1790s, populism seemed particularly well suited to avoiding the import of revolutionary ideas and activities to German territories. Only in the course of the coronation—in contrast to the election—was the emperor's physical body indispensable. In the context of the solemn coronation acts, the Empire became tangible as a festive community and, in the age of sensibility, as an imagined community of emotion. By calling into collective memory a thousand-year history, such acts deepened the feeling of cultural belonging in the Empire, which to the majority of contemporaries seemed by no means dilapidated or doomed.

In France—for a long time the rival of the Empire and its Habsburg rulers—coronations no longer took place after 1825. They had survived the first revolution after which Napoleon crowned himself to achieve a symbolical and sacral legitimation of rule that no other elevation ritual would be able to offer. A coronation of the *Roi Citoyen* Louis-Philippe, however, was out of the question in 1830. The British kings and queens retained coronations because they provided an important element of political unity in the far-reaching, multiethnic, and multireligious British Empire and were capable of strengthening the bond between the monarch and his or her mostly distant subjects. It is precisely this purpose that coronation acts could have served in a reformed Empire during the nineteenth century. In contrast to elections, which people linked to the historically obsolescent model of the elective monarchy, the coronation's ritual forms could be reinterpreted as a national celebration of constitution and tradition without significant issue. In addition, the concept of the divine right to rule enacted in the ritual was by no means obsolete after 1800. Neither Leopold II nor Francis II would have claimed to participate in the ministry, but emperorship had already been understood as a secular office as early as the Late Middle Ages. The Reformation and the Enlightenment changed little in this regard.

At the end of the eighteenth century, the sacral body of the emperor enacted in the coronation ritual was not desanctified or secularized—it was modernized by relating it to the idea of a "holy" German nation that seemed to hold promise for the future. As *Pater Patriae*, the emperor stood at the top of an allegedly "democratically" composed imperial nation. Correspondingly, he was revered as the savior of a new era, a notion further supported by the religious messages during the coronation mass. For it was especially the sacral body of the emperor through which his physical body was connected to the institutional body of emperorship. The people understood the sacral dimensions of the ritual no less during the eighteenth century than before—on the contrary, never in the entire history of the Empire had so many people been able to understand so much. And at what other occasion could they have experienced the putative greatness of the nation so intensively with all their senses? During coronations, the Empire as fatherland gained the upper hand among the "multilayered identities"[91] of a politically interested population. It would be wrong to dismiss the sheer number of exuberant sources as mere propaganda.

The oft-cited negative appraisals of coronation acts after 1745 by Wilhelm Ludwig Wekhrlin, Georg Forster, Karl Heinrich Ritter von Lang, or Johann Wolfgang von Goethe distort the perspective onto old and new functions of such rituals in the eighteenth century. The latter two come from the nineteenth century, anyway, and Goethe is often misunderstood. In fact, he (and with him a large percentage of the Empire's population) was fascinated by the coronation ritual. Various sources also prove that the Empire represented in this act was much more than a mere myth, even toward the end of the early modern period, and that the institution of emperorship had by no means been irreparably damaged by the Wittelsbach intermezzo. What Metternich wished to express in his evaluation quoted at the beginning of this chapter was precisely not the view that coronations are nothing more than political theatre. They had an impact that underwent several changes in premodern times in terms of function but not of relevance. Even in the eighteenth century, an uncrowned emperor would have been no emperor at all—regardless of what imperial jurists would have argued. That historical science widely accepted their theory is owed to the fact that the dominion to which the ritual referred ceased to exist—with the decline of the Empire interpreted as necessary and thus foreseeable. But the Empire and its rituals had by no means become obsolete by 1792. Its demise shortly thereafter resulted from a singular concurrence of internal conflicts with the military challenges posed by French expansion—a combination that the Old Empire ultimately could not overcome.

Harriet Rudolph holds the Chair of Early Modern History at the University of Regensburg. Her books include *Das Reich als Ereignis: Formen und Funktionen der Herrschaftsinszenierung bei Kaiserauftritten (1558–1618)* (Cologne, 2011); *Stadt, Reich, Europa: Neue Perspektiven auf den Immerwährenden Reichstag zu Regensburg*, ed. Harriet Rudolph and Astrid von Schlachta (Regensburg, 2015); *The European Wars of Religion: An Interdisciplinary Reassessment of Sources, In-

terpretations, and Myths, ed. Harriet Rudolph, Wolfgang Palaver, and Dietmar Regensburger (Farnham, 2016); *Material Culture in Modern Diplomacy from the 15th to the 20th Century* (European History Yearbook 17), ed. Harriet Rudolph and Gregor Metzig (Berlin, 2016).

Notes

1. Hans Joachim Berbig, "Der Krönungsritus im alten Reich (1648–1806)," *Zeitschrift für Bayerische Landesgeschichte* 38 (1975): 645. See also Berbig, "Zur rechtlichen Relevanz von Ritus und Zeremoniell im römisch-deutschen Imperium," *Zeitschrift für Kirchengeschichte* 92 (1981): 222.
2. Barbara Stollberg-Rilinger, *Maria Theresia: Die Kaiserin in ihrer Zeit. Eine Biographie* (Munich, 2017), 147.
3. Wolfgang Sellert, "Zur rechtshistorischen Bedeutung der Krönung und des Streites um das Krönungsrecht zwischen Mainz und Köln," in *Herrscherweihe und Königskrönung im Frühneuzeitlichen Europa*, ed. Heinz Duchhardt (Wiesbaden, 1983), 30.
4. Matthias Theodor Kloft, "Ideal und Wirklichkeit: Probleme der Umsetzung bei Regel- und Ausnahmegottesdienste in der Königswahlkirche Frankfurt," in *Ritualmacher hinter den Kulissen: Zur Rolle von Experten in historischer Ritualpraxis*, ed. Jörg Gengnagel and Gerald Schwedler (Berlin, 2013), 111.
5. On the history of the early modern Empire, see Karl Otmar von Aretin, *Das Alte Reich 1648–1806*, 4 vols. (Stuttgart, 1993–2000); Georg Schmidt, *Geschichte des Alten Reiches: Staat und Nation in der Frühen Neuzeit 1495–1806* (Munich, 1999); Johannes Burkhardt, *Vollendung und Neuorientierung des frühmodernen Reiches* (Stuttgart, 2006); Hans Ottomeyer, Jutta Götzmann, and Ansgar Reiß, eds., *Altes Reich und neue Staaten 1495–1806*, 2 vols. (Dresden, 2006). In English, see Jason Phillip Coy, Benjamin Marschke, and David Warren Sabean, eds., *The Holy Roman Empire, Reconsidered* (New York, 2010); Richard J. W. Evans, Michael Schaich, and Peter H. Wilson, eds., *The Holy Roman Empire 1495–1806* (Oxford, 2011); Richard J. W. Evans and Peter H. Wilson, eds., *The Holy Roman Empire, 1495–1806: A European Perspective* (Leiden, 2012); Joachim Whaley, *Germany and the Holy Roman Empire*, 2 vols. (Oxford, 2012); Peter H. Wilson, *Heart of Europe: A History of the Holy Roman Empire* (Cambridge, MA, 2016). With the exception of one summarizing chapter, none of these works in English address coronations in detail.
6. Cf. Jinty Nelson, "Carolingian Coronation Rituals: A Model for Europe?" *The Court Historian* 9 (2004): 1–13. For comparative perspectives, see Edward Muir, *Ritual in Early Modern Europe*, 2nd ed. (Cambridge, UK, 2005); Sergio Bertelli, *The King's Body: Sacred Rituals of Power in Medieval and Early Modern Europe* (University Park, 2001); János M. Bak, ed., *Coronations: Medieval and Early Modern Monarchic Ritual* (Los Angeles, 1990); Stefan Weinfurter and Marion Steinicke, eds., *Krönungs- und Investiturrituale: Herrschaftseinsetzungen im kulturellen Vergleich* (Cologne, 2005).
7. For late medieval coronation rituals in the Empire, see Mario Kramp, ed., *Krönungen: Könige in Aachen—Geschichte und Mythos*, 2 vols. (Mainz, 2000); Franz-Rainer Erkens, "Königskrönung und Krönungsordnung im späten Mittelalter," *Zeitschrift des Aachener Geschichtsvereins* 110 (2008): 27–64; recently also Andreas Büttner, *Der Weg zur Krone: Rituale der Herrschererhebung im römisch–deutschen Reich des Spätmittelalters*, 2 vols. (Ost-

fildern, 2012). The sheer amount of literature on earlier coronation rituals is staggering, wherefore further references will be foregone here.

8. This notion was convincingly refuted by Barbara Stollberg-Rilinger: see Barbara Stollberg-Rilinger, "Die zeremonielle Inszenierung des Reiches, oder: Was leistet der kulturalistische Ansatz für die Reichsverfassungsgeschichte?" in *Imperium Romanum—Irregulare Corpus—Teutscher Reichs-Staat: Das Alte Reich im Verständnis der Zeitgenossen und der Historiographie*, ed. Matthias Schnettger (Mainz, 2002), 233–46; Stollberg-Rilinger, *Des Kaisers alte Kleider: Verfassungsgeschichte und Symbolsprache des Alten Reiches* (Munich, 2008); cf. Harriet Rudolph, "Kontinuität und Dynamik—Ritual und Zeremoniell bei Krönungsakten im Alten Reich: Maximilian II., Rudolf II. und Matthias im Vergleich," in *Krönungs- und Investiturrituale: Herrschaftseinsetzungen im kulturellen Vergleich*, ed. Stefan Weinfurter and Marion Steinicke (Cologne, 2005), 377–400; Rudolph, *Das Reich als Ereignis: Formen und Funktionen der Herrschaftsinszenierung bei Kaisereinzügen (1558–1618)* (Cologne, 2011).

9. In addition to the previously mentioned literature on early modern coronations in the Empire, see also Helga Reuter-Pettenberg, *Bedeutungswandel der Römischen Königskrönung in der Neuzeit* (Cologne, 1963); Wilfried Dotzauer, "Die Ausformung der frühneuzeitlichen deutschen Thronerhebung: Stellenwert, Handlung und Zeremoniell unter dem Einfluß von Säkularisation und Reformation," *Archiv für Kulturgeschichte* 68 (1986): 25–80; Bernd Herbert Wanger, *Kaiserwahl und Krönung im Frankfurt des 17. Jahrhunderts: Darstellung anhand der zeitgenössischen Bild- und Schriftquellen und unter besonderer Berücksichtigung der Erhebung des Jahres 1612* (Frankfurt am Main, 1994); Frank-Lothar Kroll and Bernd Heidenreich, eds., *Wahl und Krönung* (Frankfurt am Main, 2006); Evelyn Brockhoff and Michael Matthäus, eds., *Die Kaisermacher: Frankfurt am Main und die Goldene Bulle, 1356–1806*, 2 vols. (Frankfurt am Main, 2006); Ludolf Pelizaeus, ed., *Wahl und Krönung in Zeiten des Umbruchs* (Frankfurt am Main, 2008); despite an upvaluing of the coronation, this perspective also characterizes the portrayal of the coronation of Joseph II in Stollberg-Rilinger, *Des Kaisers alte Kleider*, 229–31. The perception of this event is still heavily influenced by Goethe's description. Cf. Manfred Beetz, "Überlebtes Welttheater: Goethes autobiographische Darstellung der Wahl und Krönung Josephs II. in Frankfurt/Main 1764," in *Zeremoniell als höfische Ästhetik im Spätmittelalter und Früher Neuzeit*, ed. Jörg J. Berns and Thomas Rahn (Tübingen, 1995), 572–99.

10. Ernst H. Kantorowicz, *The King's Two Bodies: A Study in Mediaeval Political Theology* (Princeton, 1957); Bertelli, *The King's Body*. Cf. the concept of the semiotic–sacramental body of the king in Louis Marin, *Le Portrait du Roi* (Paris, 1981), 11. A critical discussion of all these studies cannot be performed in this essay.

11. Cf. in detail Harriet Rudolph, "Manifestationen der Sakralität von Kaisertum und Reich: Die Regensburger Königskrönungen von 1575, 1636 und 1653," in *Gottesdienst in Regensburger Institutionen: Zur Vielfalt liturgischer Traditionen in der Vormoderne*, edited by Harald Buchinger and Sabine Reichert (Regensburg, 2020 [forthcoming]).

12. See Marc Bloch, *The Royal Touch: Monarchy and Miracles in France and England* (New York, 1961), the critical reception of this classic study cannot be discussed here; see also Ronald G. Asch, *Sacral Kingship Between Disenchantment and Re-Enchantment: The French and English Monarchies 1587–1688* (New York, 2014); Stephen Brogan, *The Royal Touch in Early Modern England: Politics, Medicine and Sin* (Woodbridge, 2015).

13. See Stefan Weinfurter, "Wie das Reich heilig wurde," in *Gelebte Ordnung—Gedachte Ordnung: Ausgewählte Beiträge zu König, Kirche und Reich*, ed. Helmuth Kluger, Hubertus Seibert, and Werner Bomm (Stuttgart, 2005), 361–84.

14. Cf. already Johannes Limnaeus, *Ius publicum Imperii Romano-Germanici* (Strasbourg, 1629), vol. 1, 69; for the electoral capitulations, see Wolfgang Burgdorf, ed., *Die Wahlkapitulationen der römisch-deutschen Könige und Kaiser 1519–1792* (Göttingen, 2015). However, some of these authors likewise ascribed to the coronation the effect of increasing the authority and stability of the emperor's rule. On the juridical debate, see Sellert, "Zur rechtshistorischen Bedeutung," 26–31.
15. On this, cf. Rudolph, *Das Reich als Ereignis*, 265–68; see also Albrecht Pius Luttenberger, *Kurfürsten, Kaiser und Reich: politische Führung und Friedenssicherung unter Ferdinand I. und Maximilian II.* (Mainz, 1994), 35.
16. Cf. Gabriele Haug-Moritz, "Die Krise des Reichsverbandes in kaiserlicher Perspektive (1750–1790)," in *Krisenbewusstsein und Krisenbewältigung in der Frühen Neuzeit*, ed. Monika Hagenmaier and Sabine Holtz (Frankfurt am Main, 1992), 73–82. The discussions about constitutional reforms in the final phases of the Old Empire convincingly controvert this negative perspective, however. Cf. Wolfgang Burgdorf, *Reichskonstitution und Nation: Verfassungsreformprojekte für das Heilige Römische Reich Deutscher Nation im politischen Schrifttum von 1648–1806* (Mainz, 1998), 256–384.
17. For general information on this, see Heinz Duchhardt, *Balance of Power und Pentarchie: Internationale Beziehungen 1700–1785* (Paderborn, 1997), 235–383; Paul Kennedy, *The Rise and Fall of the Great Powers: Economic Change and Military Conflict from 1500 to 2000* (New York, 1987), chapter 3; Jeremy Black, *European International Relations 1648–1815* (Basingstoke, 2002), chapters 7–9.
18. The Russo-Austrian war against the Turks (1787–92) only ended for Austria in 1791 with the Peace of Sistova. Leopold II was only able to settle the conflicts with Prussia, which was allied with the Ottoman Empire, by means of the Reichenbach Convention (27 July 1790) shortly before his election in 1790. There was also unrest in Hungary and a revolution in the Austrian Netherlands at the time; in 1792, Austria was at war with France.
19. See Rainer Koch and Patricia Stahl, eds., *Wahl und Krönung in Frankfurt am Main: Kaiser Karl VII. 1742–1745*, Ausstellungskatalog, 2 vols. (Frankfurt am Main, 1986); Dela von Boeselager, *Capella Clementina: Kurfürst Clemens August und die Krönung Kaiser Karls VII.* (Cologne, 2001).
20. See Barbara Stollberg-Rilinger, "'Honores regii': Die Königswürde im zeremoniellen Zeichensystem der Frühen Neuzeit," in *Dreihundert Jahre Preußische Königskrönung: Eine Tagungsdokumentation*, ed. Johannes Kunisch (Berlin, 2002), 1–26.
21. "Vorstellung der Festlichen Krönung Ihro K.K. Majestät Leopoldi II. zum Römischen Kaiser zu Frankfurt den 9. October 1790," copper engraving, Bayerische Staatsbibliothek München, Sammlung Karl von Amira, folder 85, no. II.13. Leopold was only crowned king of Bohemia in 1791, meaning that there were only seven electors in 1790. All spiritual electors were ordained bishops, however, which means that the representations of the robes of Cologne and Trier are incorrect.
22. See Milos Vec, *Zeremonialwissenschaft im Fürstenstaat: Studien zur juristischen und politischen Theorie absolutistischer Herrschaftsrepräsentation* (Frankfurt am Main, 1998).
23. Cf. Stollberg-Rilinger, *Des Kaisers alte Kleider*, 244–45. Both coronations were by no means a "ghostly world theatre" to the majority of contemporaries—and certainly not to the imperial family—as stated by Goethe.
24. Cf. Anna Th. Schwinger, "Der Ornat Kaiser Franz I. Stephan von Lothringen: Barockkopien nach dem Krönungsornat des Heiligen Römischen Reiches," in *Nobiles officinae: Die Königlichen Hofwerkstätten zu Palermo zur Zeit der Normannen und Staufer im 12. und 13.*

Jahrhundert, Ausstellungskatalog, ed. Wilfried Seipel (Vienna, 2004), 137–51. Francis also commissioned a copy of the so-called Sabre of Charlemagne and one of the archducal hat of Rudolf IV for the coronation. Cf. Bernhard A. Macek, *Die Krönung Josephs II. zum Römischen König in Frankfurt am Main: Logistisches Meisterwerk, zeremonielle Glanzleistung und Kulturgüter für die Ewigkeit* (Frankfurt am Main, 2010), 16, 30–32.

25. On the series, cf. Macek, *Die Krönung*, 14–15. The paintings deviate heavily from the sketches made on location by Johann Dallinger von Dalling, correcting the events in terms of the desired imagery. The coronation banquet, for example, shows the moment when emperor and king have taken their seats while the electors are still standing, thus making all the electors' tables empty and not just those of the secular electors, thereby concealing their absence. On the great significance ascribed to her husband's coronation by Maria Theresa, see Thomas Lau, *Maria Theresia: Die Kaiserin* (Cologne, 2016), 98.

26. See Barbara Stollberg-Rilinger, "'Die Puppe Karls des Großen': Das Heilige Römische Reich Deutscher Nation als praktizierter Mythos," in *Mythos als Schicksal: Was konstituiert die Verfassung?*, ed. Otto Depenhauer (Wiesbaden, 2009), 68.

27. Johann Philipp Schulin, *Vollständiges Diarium der Römisch-Königlichen Wahl und Kaiserlichen Krönung Jhro nunmehr allerglorwürdigst regierenden Kaiserlichen Majestät Leopold des Zweiten . . .* , 2 vols. (Frankfurt am Main, 1791), 314–15. Schulin, for the most part, adopts the portrayal in the coronation records of the court of Vienna, since they seemed "more real" and "more reliable" to him than other reports or even his own observations. He even used the procedural draft produced by imperial court officials for his portrayal of the election act, thereby elevating this scheme to a reality: Schulin, *Vollständiges Diarium*, 278.

28. This expression was used with positive connotations by Metternich, in an ambivalent manner by Goethe and Christian Friedrich Daniel Schubart (*Chronik 1790, 2: Halbjahr* [Stuttgart, 1790], 687), and with clearly negative meaning by Wekhrlin. The latter viewed the coronation as a "national drama," with electors and their entourages as actors, envoys and businessmen as "machinists," idlers as the spectators on the floor and—as the lowest category—rip-off merchants, by which he meant Jews, grocers, and footmen: Wilhelm Ludwig Wekhrlin, *Paragrafen* (Nuremberg, 1791), 251–52.

29. Johann Wilhelm Müller, *Beschreibung der Merkwürdigkeiten einer Römischen Kaiserwahl und Krönung, Nebst einer Nachricht von den dazu bestimmten Reichsinsignien und den kurfürstl. Funktionen . . .* (Nuremberg, 1790), Vorrede.

30. Müller, *Beschreibung*.

31. Georg Forster, *Erinnerungen aus dem Jahr 1790 in historischen Gemälden und Bildnissen von D. Chodowiecki, D. Berger, Cl. Kohl, J. F. Bolt und J. S. Ringck* (Berlin, 1793), 78–79.

32. Rudolph Hommel, *Briefe über die Kaiserwahl, während derselben aus Frankfurt geschrieben* (Leipzig, 1791), 169.

33. Symptomatic is the evaluation by Georg Forster: "The eye of the curious, which in Frankfurt had reveled to exhaustion in the barbaric finery and clumsy pageantry of our ancestors, and had finally become weary of the feudal haughtiness and its stiff ceremonies." Georg Forster, "Darstellung der Revolution in Mainz, Fragment," in *Georg Forster: Werke in vier Bänden*, ed. Gerhard Steiner (Frankfurt am Main, 1970), vol. 3: 637.

34. While an extensive coronation diary was still published in 1790, the entirety of the media on the crowning appears far more polyphonic in terms of both form and content than ever before. Johann Philipp Schulin, *Diarium: Vollständige Beschreibung aller Feyerlichkeiten bey den Krönungen und Huldigungen Leopolds II.* (Vienna, 1790); cf. also *Die Krönung*

Leopold II. zum römischen Kaiser: Geschrieben von einem Augenzeugen (Frankfurt am Main, 1790); Hommel, *Briefe*; Johann Christoph Röhling, *Reise eines Marsbewohners auf die Erde: Zur Zeit der Wahl und Krönung Leopold des Zweiten zum teutschen Kaiser* (Frankfurt am Main, 1791); *Frankfurter Staats-Ristretto*, [11] October 1790 (no. 161).

35. The contrast between devaluing the ritual and praising the imperial elites in Wekhrlin is glaring: "But of the German nobility I must impart to you, that one finds it nowhere more sumptuous and ingratiating. From their electors down to the envoys from Nuremberg and Aachen, everything represented itself admirably." According to Wekhrlin, the festivities organized for the coronation represented "masterpieces of greatness, of elegance and of taste" in contrast to the act of coronation itself. Wekhrlin, *Paragrafen*, 252 and 258–59.

36. Compare, for example, Christoph Ludwig Pfeiffer, *Die teutsche Wahl und Crönung des Kaisers und römischen Königs sammt derselben teutschen Staatsgerechtsamen, wie auch herkömmlichen Feierlichkeiten und dabei vorkommenden anderweiten Denkwürdigkeiten* (Frankfurt am Main, 1787); Müller, *Beschreibung*; Julius Wilhelm Hamberger, *Merkwürdigkeiten bey der römischen Königswahl und Kaiserkrönung*, 3rd ed. (Gotha, 1792); *Kurze Beschreibung bei der Wahl und Krönung eines römischen Kaisers* (Frankfurt am Main, 1792); Michael Truckenbrot, *Kurzgefaßter Bericht von den bei der Wahl und Krönung eines römischen Kaisers gewöhnlichen Feierlichkeiten* . . . (Frankfurt am Main, 1790); Christoph Gottlieb von Murr, *Beschreibung der sämtlichen Reichskleinodien und Heiligthümer, welche in des H. R. Reichs freyen Stadt Nürnberg aufbewahret werden* (Nürnberg, 1790); *Ueber Teutschland, Kaisertodesfall, Trauer, Reichsvikarien, Wahltag, Wahlkapitulation, Wahl, Krönung, Gerechsame des teutschen Kaisers* (Kempten, 1790).

37. See Otto Gerhard Oexle, "Die Moderne und ihr Mittelalter: Eine folgenreiche Problemgeschichte," in *Mittelalter und Moderne: Entdeckung und Rekonstruktion der mittelalterlichen Welt*, ed. Peter Segl (Sigmaringen, 1997), 327.

38. Cf. the source edition, still shaped by traditional views, by Erna Berger and Konrad Bund, eds., *Wahl und Krönung Leopolds II. 1790: Brieftagebuch des Feldschers der kursächsischen Schweizergarde* (Frankfurt am Main, 1981); Christian Hattenhauer, *Wahl und Krönung Franz II. AD 1792: Das Heilige Reich krönt seinen letzten Kaiser; das Tagebuch des Reichsquartiermeisters Hieronymus Gottfried von Müller und Anlagen* (Frankfurt am Main, 1995); with greater differentiation, see Rolf Haaser, "Das Zeremoniell der beiden letzten deutsch-römischen Kaiserkrönungen in Frankfurt am Main und seine Rezeption zwischen Spätaufklärung und Frühromantik," in *Zeremoniell als höfische Ästhetik im Spätmittelalter und Früher Neuzeit* ed. Jörg J. Berns and Thomas Rahn (Tübingen, 1995), 600–3; Barbara Dölemeyer, "Wahl und Krönung im Spiegel der Diarien des 18. Jahrhunderts," in *Wahl und Krönung*, ed. Frank-Lothar Kroll and Bernd Heidenreich (Frankfurt am Main, 2006), 80.

39. As early as 1790, the Frankfurt city council prohibited theatre performances containing references to the French Revolution and had the spectators monitored by scouts to prevent a "contagion of the French appreciation for freedom" amongst them: Schulin, *Diarium*, 255–56. Landgrave Wilhelm IX of Hesse-Kassel stationed 8,000 soldiers near Bergen to ensure security: Harriet Rudolph, "Die Herrschererhebung als Fest: Krönungsfeste im Vergleich," in *Festkulturen im Vergleich: Inszenierungen des Religiösen und Politischen*, ed. Michael Maurer (Cologne, 2010), 13–42.

40. See Friedrich W. Becker, *Die Kaiserwahl Leopolds II. 1790: Eine Untersuchung zur Geschichte des alten Reiches und der Nachwirkung des Fürstenbundes* (unpublished doctoral

dissertation, University of Bonn, 1943); Aretin, *Das Altes Reich*, vol. 3: 361–70; Wolfgang Burgdorf, *Protokonstitutionalismus: Die Reichsverfassung in den Wahlkapitulationen der römisch-deutschen Könige und Kaiser* (Göttingen, 2015), 352–84 and 444–50; Whaley, *Germany*, vol. 2: 427–28 and 604–5; as a source publication, see Johann Richard Roth, *Aechtes vollständiges Protocoll des kurfürstl. hohen Wahlkonvents zu Frankfurt im Jahre 1790* . . . (Frankfurt am Main, 1791).

41. There is no current biography of Leopold II. Cf. Adam Wandruszka, *Leopold II.: Erzherzog von Österreich, Grossherzog von Toskana, König von Ungarn und Böhmen, Römischer Kaiser*, 2 vols. (Vienna, 1963–65); Helga Peham, *Leopold II.: Herrscher mit weiser Hand* (Graz, 1987); Lorenz Mikoletzky, "Leopold II.," in *Die Kaiser der Neuzeit 1519–1918: Heiliges Römisches Reich, Österreich, Deutschland*, ed. Anton Schindling and Walter Ziegler (Munich, 1990), 277–87.
42. See in detail and with further literature Rudolph, *Das Reich als Ereignis*, 201–10 and 246–53; in particular for the coronation of 1790, Rudolph, *Die Herrschererhebung*, 34–39.
43. On the limited significance of the Golden Bull of 1356 for coronations, see Rudolph, *Das Reich als Ereignis*, 260–61. The dating of the so-called "ordo of 1309" is called into question by Büttner, *Der Weg zur Krone*, vol. 1: 125–42.
44. Vienna, ÖStA, HHStA, Hausarchiv, Familienakten, 4.19, fol. 1–23. Included is the emperor's speech of thanks to the electors and imperial princes: Vienna, ÖStA, HHStA, Hausarchiv, Familienakten, 4.19, fol. 24. A detailed description of the coronation act, which served as the source for Schulin's coronation diary, can be found in ÖStA, HHStA, OMeA, ÄZA, 93.1, fol. 47–86. It abbreviates the ecclesiastical acts described in the "Directorium" and conveys ceremonial procedures in particular, giving the two texts complementary functions. The minutes by the *Reichserbmundschenk* Count Joseph Althans (ÖStA, HHStA, OMeA, ÄZA, 92 [1790], fol. 71–73) primarily convey the ceremonial circumstances important for the holders of the hereditary imperial offices. See also Schulin, *Diarium*, 314–27; Roth, *Aechtes vollständiges Protocoll*, vol. 2: 431–55.
45. Hommel, *Briefe*, 172.
46. See the densely sensual portrayal by Hommel: "This religious silence [of the communion] was followed by the noisy act of enthronement." Hommel, *Briefe*, 180.
47. For these three dimensions of sacrality, see Franz-Reiner Erkens, *Herrschersakralität im Mittelalter: von den Anfängen bis zum Investiturstreit* (Stuttgart, 2006), 29.
48. The following is based on: ÖStA, HHStA, OMeA, ÄZA 93.1, fol. 47–9; for 1792: ÖStA, HHStA, OMeA, ÄZA 94, fol 37v–53; Nuremberg, StAN, Reichsstadt Nürnberg, Krönungsakten 88, 12v–20; for 1792: Krönungsakten 93, 72–80. For a more detailed description in regard to the political and religious semantics of the liturgy, see Rudolph, "Manifestationen"; see also Dela von Boeselager, "Zur Salbung und Krönung in der Liturgie des Ordo," in *Die Kaisermacher: Frankfurt am Main und die Goldene Bulle, 1356–1806*, ed. Evelyn Brockhoff and Michael Matthäus (Frankfurt am Main, 2006), vol. 2: 338–45.
49. Kloft, "Ideal," 116. Rather, the regalia embodied an element considered indispensable for the proper performance of the ritual, even at the end of the Empire. Kloft's contribution uses printed reports to incorrectly construct a process of decay of the election and coronation liturgy that did not occur in the described form. Kloft, "Ideal," 111, 116. In contrast, Leopold II was impressed by the great age ("das graue Alterthum") of the imperial regalia, and the king of Naples particularly appreciated the blade of Charlemagne's sword. StAN, Reichsstadt Nürnberg, Krönungsakten 88, fol. 9.

50. For the extremely complex dealings with the imperial regalia during the coronation mass, compare the outline of the Nuremberg envoys for 1792 in StAN, Reichsstadt Nürnberg, Krönungsakten 93, 151–58. On the imperial jewelry, see Hans-Jürgen Becker and Karl-Heinz Ruess, eds., *Die Reichskleinodien: Herrschaftszeichen des Heiligen Römischen Reiches* (Göppingen, 1997); Hermann Fillitz, "Die Reichskleinodien: Ein Versuch zur Erklärung ihrer Entstehung und Entwicklung," in *Heilig, römisch, deutsch: Das Reich im mittelalterlichen Europa*, ed. Bernd Schneidmüller and Stefan Weinfurter (Dresden, 2006), 133–61.
51. For Francis II, see StAN, Reichsstadt Nürnberg, Krönungsakten 93, fol. 78.
52. Leopold II knighted seventy-four men, which shows that a large number of noblemen still ascribed considerable significance to this symbolic act. Roth, *Aechtes vollständiges Protocoll*, vol. 2: 462–65. Francis only knighted thirty-six men, which can be explained with the short span of time since the last elevation. *Diarium der römisch-königlichen Wahl und kaiserlichen Krönung Ihro Kaiserlichen Majestät Franz des Zweiten* (Frankfurt am Main, 1798), 171.
53. The music was composed anew for each such act in 1790 by Antonio Salieri. See Arno Paduch, "Festmusiken zu Frankfurter Kaiserwahlen und Krönungen des 17. und 18. Jahrhunderts," *Die Musikforschung* 59, no. 3 (2006): 211–32; Austin Glatthorn, "The Imperial Coronation of Leopold II and Mozart, Frankfurt am Main, 1790," *Eighteenth-Century Music* 14, no. 1 (2017): 89–110, here 98–101 on the coronation acts.
54. Schulin, *Diarium*, 321.
55. Schulin, *Diarium*, 321–22. Schulin even calls for historical examination of this formula.
56. ÖStA, HHStA, OMeA, ÄZA 93.1, fol. 57–58; see also ÖStA, HHStA, Hausarchiv, Familienakten 4–19, fol. 3. Incorrect in Schulin, *Diarium*, 321; likewise incorrect in Kloft, "Ideal," 111, according to which there was only kneeling in the eighteenth century because the sacral significance of the act had allegedly been forgotten. The claim that the preface with its sacral message was eschewed is likewise incorrect: Kloft, "Ideal," 116. For 1792, see ÖStA, HHStA, OMeA, ÄZA 94, fol. 41.
57. Hommel, *Briefe*, 173–74. The crown was taken off and the swords lowered during the supper, while the "emperor humbled himself in deep devotion before the only higher one" on his knees. Hommel, *Briefe*, 179.
58. Kloft, "Ideal," 117.
59. Sellert, "Zur rechtshistorischen Bedeutung," 30.
60. According to Müller, *Beschreibung*, 67, the coronation represented a sacred act due to the anointing performed during it. Cf. Johann Jacob Schmauss, *Compendium iuris publici S.R.I.*, 3rd ed. (Göttingen, 1754), 33.
61. For the French kings, who were anointed only on their chest, "heavenly oil" was taken from the Holy Ampulla and mixed with chrism. On the anointing, cf. Eduard Eichmann, *Die Kaiserkrönung im Abendland: Ein Beitrag zur Geistesgeschichte des Mittelalters. Mit besonderer Berücksichtigung des kirchlichen Rechts, der Liturgie und der Kirchenpolitik*, 2 vols. (Würzburg, 1942), vol. 1: 78–94; Bernd Schneidmüller, "Salburg," in *Handwörterbuch zur Deutschen Rechtsgeschichte* (Berlin, 1990), vol. 4: cols. 1268–73; Rudolph, "Manifestationen."
62. On this, see Eichmann, *Die Kaiserkrönung*, vol. 1: 109, and vol. 2: 75.
63. The phrasing that the emperor was dressed "in Gestalt eines Priesters" (in the guise of a priest) is encountered regularly. He was also likened to a dean or a chaplain. Roth, *Aechtes vollständiges Protocoll*, vol. 2: 411.

64. Cf. the distinct phrasing pointing to the distinguishing character of this act in ÖStA, HHStA, Hausarchiv, Familienakten 4–19, fol. 20v; for 1792, see ÖStA, HHStA, OMeA, ÄZA 94, fol. 49; AZÄ 93, fol. 66.
65. Johann David Jung, *Vollständiges Diarium von der Höchst-erfreulichen Crönung des Allerdurchlauchtigsten, Großmächtigsten und Unüberwindlichsten Fürsten und Herrn, Herrn Franciscus, Erwehlten Römischen Kaysers* . . . (Frankfurt am Main, 1746), 110. This explanation was later omitted in printed diaries.
66. Eichmann, *Die Kaiserkrönung*, vol. 1: 308.
67. Hommel interprets this order as proof that the emperor first had to have "fulfilled the obligations of the Christian before he could attain the rights of majesty." Hommel, *Briefe*, 179.
68. For 1792, compare ÖStA, HHStA, OMeA, ÄZA 94, fol. 51, where the exact verse is specified (*Te ergo quaesumus*) when the emperor left his throne to kneel. See also *Diarium der Römisch-Königlichen Wahl*, 172.
69. Cf. the expert opinion on Mainz as the place of coronation in Hattenhauer, *Wahl und Krönung*, 365–74.
70. ÖStA, HHStA, OMeA, ÄZA 94, fol 4. Cf. the suggestions for cutting costs in Hattenhauer, *Wahl und Krönung*, 380–84 and 401–18. The Electorate of Mainz also suggested foregoing the costly presence of women, which was not met with the emperor's approval, however.
71. Hattenhauer, *Wahl und Krönung*, 379.
72. ÖStA, HHStA, OMeA, ÄZA 94, fol. 18. Not so in Dölemeyer, "Wahl und Krönung," 84; Hattenhauer, *Wahl und Krönung*, 24.
73. Schubart, *Chronik 1790*, 681.
74. Berger and Bund, *Wahl und Krönung*, 68. See also "Wahl und Krönung Joseph des Zweyten zum Römischen Könige," in *Historisches Taschenbuch der Wahl und Krönung der Kaiser aus dem Neu-Österreichischen Hause* (Frankfurt am Main, 1792), vol. 2: 2nd pagination, 71–72, quotations in the following: 72, 128–29.
75. The anonymous author of a coronation report, for example, claimed to be writing about the event "without all grandiosity, only in the language of the heart." *Die Krönung Leopold II.*, 6.
76. Quotations from Schulin, *Diarium*, 286.
77. Historisches Museum Frankfurt am Main, Graphische Sammlung, N 42672, copper engraving by Johann Christian Berndt. The scene cannot be correlated to any part of the coronation ritual. The eulogy on the engraving appeals to the patriotic feelings of all "German brothers." It is iconographically similar to the copper engraving at the beginning of Schulin, *Diarium*, no pagination, which shows the emperor on a throne in an architecture of columns while Germania, who rather resembles Marianne, is handing him the imperial crown.
78. *Historisches Taschenbuch*, vol. 2, 24–25.
79. Schulin, *Diarium*, 310.
80. See also Haaser, *Das Zeremoniell*; and with partially deviating interpretation: Dölemeyer, "Wahl und Krönung."
81. See the sentimental drama by August Wilhelm Iffland, *Friedrich von Österreich: Ein Schauspiel aus der vaterländischen Geschichte in fünf Aufzügen* (Gotha, 1791). During the performance of the play on 8 October 1790, the emperor's family and the rest of the audience allegedly broke out in tears. "Wahl und Krönung Joseph," 2nd pagination, 91; cf. *Journal des Luxus und der Moden* 11 (1790): 614–15.

82. Truckenbrot, *Kurzgefaßter Bericht*, 39.
83. Schulin, *Diarium*, Widmung, no pagination. See also the *Sammlung der Inschriften welche in Wien, als diese Stadt zum Zeichen der der allgemeinen Freude über Franz des II. Glückliche Zurückkunft von der Kaiserkrönung . . . angebracht waren* (Vienna, 1792), no pagination, which reads: "Monarch! We are entirely yours. . . . We give for you body and blood, for all hearts are inclined to you."
84. August Wilhelm Iffland, *Der Eichenkranz: Ein Dialog zur Eröffnung der Frankfurter National-Schaubühne bei der Krönungsfeier Ihro Majestät des Kayser Franz II*. (Frankfurt am Main, 1792).
85. Truckenbrot, *Kurzgefaßter Bericht*, 28–29 and 34.
86. The author of the election and coronation diary, Johann Philipp Schulin, also described himself as a "citizen of Germany." Schulin, *Diarium*, Widmung, no pagination. Quotations in the following: ibid.
87. Various examples in *Sammlung der Inschriften*, no pagination; Schulin, *Diarium*, 310, 322. This theory is a topos frequently repeated in writings on German imperial public law of the seventeenth and eighteenth century. See Harriet Rudolph, "Der Reichstag als Hort der 'deutschen Freiheit': Reichsverfassungsbilder als Medien des Wissenstransfers," in *Stadt, Reich, Europa: Neue Perspektiven auf den Immerwährenden Reichstag zu Regensburg*, ed. Harriet Rudolph and Astrid von Schlachta (Regensburg, 2015), 317.
88. Quotations from Hommel *Briefe*, 4; *Die Krönung Leopold II.*, 7.
89. Schulin, *Diarium*, 346. As a consequence of extensive "coronation tourism," "an unbelievable number of people" came together "from all corners and parts of the Empire" in Frankfurt in 1790. Sixty thousand to eighty thousand visitors are reported for the year 1790; the Frankfurt council even reported the number to be one hundred thousand. "Wahl und Krönung Joseph," 2nd pagination, 57.
90. For 1790, see in detail Rudolph, "Die Herrschererhebung."
91. Wilson, *Heart of Europe*, 252.

Bibliography

Aretin, Karl Otmar von. *Das Alte Reich 1648–1806*. 4 vols. Stuttgart: Klett-Cotta, 1993–2000.

Asch, Ronald G. *Sacral Kingship Between Disenchantment and Re-Enchantment: The French and English Monarchies 1587–1688*. New York: Berghahn Books, 2014.

Bak, János M., ed. *Coronation: Medieval and Early Modern Monarchic Ritual*. Los Angeles: University of California Press, 1990.

Becker, Friedrich W. *Die Kaiserwahl Leopolds II. 1790: Eine Untersuchung zur Geschichte des alten Reiches und der Nachwirkung des Fürstenbundes*. Unpublished doctoral dissertation, University of Bonn, 1943.

Becker, Hans-Jürgen, and Karl-Heinz Ruess, eds. *Die Reichskleinodien: Herrschaftszeichen des Heiligen Römischen Reiches*. Göppingen: Gesellschaft für staufische Geschichte, 1997.

Beetz, Manfred. "Überlebtes Welttheater: Goethes autobiographische Darstellung der Wahl und Krönung Josephs II. in Frankfurt/Main 1764." In *Zeremoniell als höfische Ästhetik im Spätmittelalter und Früher Neuzeit*, edited by Jörg J. Berns and Thomas Rahn, 572–99. Tübingen: Niemeyer, 1995.

Berbig, Hans Joachim. "Der Krönungsritus im alten Reich (1648–1806)." *Zeitschrift für Bayerische Landesgeschichte* 38 (1975): 639–700.

———. "Zur rechtlichen Relevanz von Ritus und Zeremoniell im römisch-deutschen Imperium." *Zeitschrift für Kirchengeschichte* 92 (1981): 204–49.
Berger, Erna, and Konrad Bund, eds. *Wahl und Krönung Leopolds II. 1790: Brieftagebuch des Feldschers der kursächsischen Schweizergarde*. Frankfurt am Main: Waldemar Kramer, 1981.
Bertelli, Sergio. *The King's Body: Sacred Rituals of Power in Medieval and Early Modern Europe*. University Park: Penn State University Press, 2001 (first edition: Florence, 1990).
Black, Jeremy. *European International Relations 1648–1815*. Basingstoke: Palgrave, 2002.
Bloch, Marc. *The Royal Touch: Monarchy and Miracles in France and England*. New York: Dorset Press, 1961 (first edition in French: Strasbourg, 1924).
Boeselager, Dela von. *Capella Clementina: Kurfürst Clemens August und die Krönung Kaiser Karls VII*. Cologne: Kölner Dom Verlag, 2001.
———. "Zur Salbung und Krönung in der Liturgie des Ordo." In *Die Kaisermacher: Frankfurt am Main und die Goldene Bulle, 1356–1806*, edited by Evelyn Brockhoff and Michael Matthäus, vol. 2, 338–45. Frankfurt am Main: Frankfurter Societäts-Druckerei, 2006.
Brockhoff, Evelyn, and Michael Matthäus, eds. *Die Kaisermacher: Frankfurt am Main und die Goldene Bulle, 1356–1806*. 2 vols. Frankfurt am Main: Frankfurter Societäts-Druckerei, 2006.
Brogan, Stephen. *The Royal Touch in Early Modern England: Politics, Medicine and Sin*. Woodbridge: Boydell Press, 2015.
Burgdorf, Wolfgang, ed. *Die Wahlkapitulationen der römisch-deutschen Könige und Kaiser 1519–1792*. Göttingen: Vandenhoeck & Ruprecht, 2015.
———. *Protokonstitutionalismus: Die Reichsverfassung in den Wahlkapitulationen der römisch-deutschen Könige und Kaiser*. Göttingen: Vandenhoeck & Ruprecht, 2015.
———. *Reichskonstitution und Nation: Verfassungsreformprojekte für das Heilige Römische Reich Deutscher Nation im politischen Schrifttum von 1648–1806*. Mainz: Philipp von Zabern, 1998.
Burkhardt, Johannes. *Vollendung und Neuorientierung des frühmodernen Reiches*. Stuttgart: Klett-Cotta, 2006.
Büttner, Andreas. *Der Weg zur Krone: Rituale der Herrschererhebung im römisch–deutschen Reich des Spätmittelalters*. 2 vols. Ostfildern: Jan Thorbecke Verlag, 2012.
Coy, Jason Phillip, Benjamin Marschke, and David Warren Sabean, eds. *The Holy Roman Empire, Reconsidered*. New York: Berghahn Books, 2010.
Diarium der Römisch-Königlichen Wahl und Kaiserlichen Krönung Ihro Kaiserlichen Majestät Franz des Zweiten. Frankfurt am Main: Johann Christian Jäger, 1798.
Die Krönung Leopold II. zum römischen Kaiser: Geschrieben von einem Augenzeugen. Frankfurt am Main: Friedrich Eßlinger, 1790.
Dölemeyer, Barbara. "Wahl und Krönung im Spiegel der Diarien des 18. Jahrhunderts." In *Wahl und Krönung*, edited by Frank-Lothar Kroll and Bernd Heidenreich, 79–98. Frankfurt am Main: Societätsverlag, 2006.
Dotzauer, Wilfried. "Die Ausformung der frühneuzeitlichen deutschen Thronerhebung: Stellenwert, Handlung und Zeremoniell unter dem Einfluß von Säkularisation und Reformation." *Archiv für Kulturgeschichte* 68 (1986): 25–80.
Duchhardt, Heinz. *Balance of Power und Pentarchie: Internationale Beziehungen 1700–1785*. Paderborn: Schöningh, 1997.
Eichmann, Eduard. *Die Kaiserkrönung im Abendland: Ein Beitrag zur Geistesgeschichte des Mittelalters. Mit besonderer Berücksichtigung des kirchlichen Rechts, der Liturgie und der Kirchenpolitik*. 2 vols. Würzburg: Echter, 1942.

Erkens, Franz-Reiner. *Herrschersakralität im Mittelalter: von den Anfängen bis zum Investiturstreit*. Stuttgart: W. Kohlhammer, 2006.

———. "Königskrönung und Krönungsordnung im späten Mittelalter." *Zeitschrift des Aachener Geschichtsvereins* 110 (2008): 27–64.

Evans, Richard J. W., Michael Schaich, and Peter H. Wilson, eds. *The Holy Roman Empire 1495–1806*. Oxford: Oxford University Press, 2011.

Evans, Richard J. W., and Peter H. Wilson, eds. *The Holy Roman Empire, 1495–1806: A European Perspective*. Leiden: Brill, 2012.

Fillitz, Hermann. "Die Reichskleinodien: Ein Versuch zur Erklärung ihrer Entstehung und Entwicklung." In *Heilig, römisch, deutsch: Das Reich im mittelalterlichen Europa*, edited by Bernd Schneidmüller and Stefan Weinfurter, 133–61. Dresden: Sandstein, 2006.

Forster, Georg. "Darstellung der Revolution in Mainz, Fragment." In *Georg Forster: Werke in vier Bänden*, edited by Gerhard Steiner, vol. 3, 629–94. Frankfurt am Main: Insel Verlag, 1970.

———. *Erinnerungen aus dem Jahr 1790 in historischen Gemälden und Bildnissen von D. Chodowiecki, D. Berger, Cl. Kohl, J. F. Bolt und J. S. Ringck*. Berlin: Vossische Buchhandlung, 1793.

Glatthorn, Austin. "The Imperial Coronation of Leopold II and Mozart, Frankfurt am Main, 1790." *Eighteenth-Century Music* 14, no. 1 (2017): 89–110.

Haaser, Rolf. "Das Zeremoniell der beiden letzten deutsch-römischen Kaiserkrönungen in Frankfurt am Main und seine Rezeption zwischen Spätaufklärung und Frühromantik." In *Zeremoniell als höfische Ästhetik im Spätmittelalter und Früher Neuzeit*, edited by Jörg J. Berns and Thomas Rahn, 600–31. Tübingen: Niemeyer, 1995.

Hamberger, Julius Wilhelm. *Merkwürdigkeiten bey der römischen Königswahl und Kaiserkrönung*. 3rd ed. Gotha: Justus Perthes, 1792.

Hattenhauer, Christian. *Wahl und Krönung Franz II. AD 1792: Das Heilige Reich krönt seinen letzten Kaiser; das Tagebuch des Reichsquartiermeisters Hieronymus Gottfried von Müller und Anlagen*. Frankfurt am Main: Peter Lang, 1995.

Haug-Moritz, Gabriele. "Die Krise des Reichsverbandes in kaiserlicher Perspektive (1750–1790)." In *Krisenbewusstsein und Krisenbewältigung in der Frühen Neuzeit*, edited by Monika Hagenmaier and Sabine Holtz, 73–82. Frankfurt am Main: Peter Lang, 1992.

Historisches Taschenbuch der Wahl und Krönung der Kaiser aus dem Neu-Österreichischen Hause. Vol. 2. Frankfurt am Main: Fleischersche Buchhandlung, 1792.

Hommel, Rudolph. *Briefe über die Kaiserwahl, während derselben aus Frankfurt geschrieben*. Leipzig: Georg Joachim Göschen, 1791.

Iffland, August Wilhelm. *Der Eichenkranz: Ein Dialog zur Eröffnung der Frankfurter National-Schaubühne bei der Krönungsfeier Ihro Majestät des Kayser Franz II*. Frankfurt am Main: n.p., 1792.

———. *Friedrich von Österreich: Ein Schauspiel aus der vaterländischen Geschichte in fünf Aufzügen*. Gotha: Karl Wilhelm Ettinger, 1791.

Jung, Johann David. *Vollständiges Diarium Von der Höchst-erfreulichen Crönung des Allerdurchlauchtigsten, Großmächtigsten und Unüberwindlichsten Fürsten und Herrn, Herrn Franciscus, Erwehlten Römischen Kaysers* . . . Frankfurt am Main: Johann David Jung, 1746.

Kantorowicz, Ernst H. *The King's Two Bodies: A Study in Mediaeval Political Theology*. Princeton: Princeton University Press, 1957.

Kennedy, Paul. *The Rise and Fall of the Great Powers: Economic Change and Military Conflict from 1500 to 2000*. New York: Random House, 1987.

Kloft, Matthias Theodor. "Ideal und Wirklichkeit: Probleme der Umsetzung bei Regel- und Ausnahmegottesdienste in der Königswahlkirche Frankfurt." In *Ritualmacher hinter den Kulissen: Zur Rolle von Experten in historischer Ritualpraxis*, edited by Jörg Gengnagel and Gerald Schwedler, 91–120. Berlin: Lit Verlag, 2013.

Koch, Rainer, and Patricia Stahl, eds. *Wahl und Krönung in Frankfurt am Main: Kaiser Karl VII. 1742–1745*. Ausstellungskatalog. 2 vols. Frankfurt am Main: Historisches Museum Frankfurt, 1986.

Kramp, Mario, ed. *Krönungen: Könige in Aachen—Geschichte und Mythos*. 2 vols. Mainz: Philipp von Zabern, 2000.

Kroll, Frank-Lothar, and Bernd Heidenreich, eds. *Wahl und Krönung*. Frankfurt am Main: Frankfurter Societäts-Druckerei, 2006.

Kurze Beschreibung bei der Wahl und Krönung eines römischen Kaisers. Frankfurt am Main: Johann Daniel Knoop, 1792.

Lau, Thomas. *Maria Theresia: Die Kaiserin*. Cologne: Böhlau, 2016.

Limnaeus, Johannes. *Ius publicum Imperii Romano-Germanici*. Vol. 1. Strasbourg: Paul Ledertz, 1629.

Luttenberger, Albrecht Pius. *Kurfürsten, Kaiser und Reich: politische Führung und Friedenssicherung unter Ferdinand I. und Maximilian II*. Mainz: von Zabern, 1994.

Macek, Bernhard A. *Die Krönung Josephs II. zum Römischen König in Frankfurt am Main: Logistisches Meisterwerk, zeremonielle Glanzleistung und Kulturgüter für die Ewigkeit*. Frankfurt am Main: Peter Lang, 2010.

Marin, Louis. *Le Portrait du Roi*. Paris: Les Editions de Minuit, 1981.

Metternich-Winneburg, Klemens Wenzel Nepomuk Lothar Fürst von. *Aus Metternich's nachgelassenen Papieren*. Part 1, vol. 1. Vienna: Wilhelm Braumüller, 1880.

Mikoletzky, Lorenz. "Leopold II." In *Die Kaiser der Neuzeit 1519–1918: Heiliges Römisches Reich, Österreich, Deutschland*, edited by Anton Schindling and Walter Ziegler, 277–87. Munich: C. H. Beck, 1990.

Muir, Edward. *Ritual in Early Modern Europe*. Cambridge, UK: Cambridge University Press, 1997.

Müller, Johann Wilhelm. *Beschreibung der Merkwürdigkeiten einer Römischen Kaiserwahl und Krönung, Nebst einer Nachricht von den dazu bestimmten Reichsinsignien und den kurfürstl. Funktionen . . . .* Nuremberg: Johann Georg Klinger, 1790.

Murr, Christoph Gottlieb von. *Beschreibung der sämtlichen Reichskleinodien und Heiligthümer, welche in des H. R. Reichs freyen Stadt Nürnberg aufbewahret* werden. Nuremberg: Bauer- und Mannische Buchhandlung, 1790.

Nelson, Jinty. "Carolingian Coronation Rituals: A Model for Europe?" *The Court Historian* 9 (2004): 1–13.

Oexle, Otto Gerhard. "Die Moderne und ihr Mittelalter: Eine folgenreiche Problemgeschichte." In *Mittelalter und Moderne: Entdeckung und Rekonstruktion der mittelalterlichen Welt*, edited by Peter Segl, 307–64. Sigmaringen: Jan Thorbecke, 1997.

Ottomeyer, Hans, Jutta Götzmann, and Ansgar Reiß, eds. *Altes Reich und neue Staaten 1495–1806*. 2 vols. Dresden: Sandstein, 2006.

Paduch, Arno. "Festmusiken zu Frankfurter Kaiserwahlen und Krönungen des 17. und 18. Jahrhunderts." *Die Musikforschung* 59, no. 3 (2006): 211–32.

Peham, Helga. *Leopold II.: Herrscher mit weiser Hand*. Graz: Styria, 1987.

Pelizaeus, Ludolf, ed. *Wahl und Krönung in Zeiten des Umbruchs*. Frankfurt am Main: Peter Lang, 2008.

Pfeiffer, Christoph Ludwig. *Die teutsche Wahl und Crönung des Kaisers und römischen Königs sammt derselben teutschen Staatsgerechtsamen, wie auch herkömmlichen Feierlichkeiten und dabei vorkommenden anderweiten Denkwürdigkeiten*. Frankfurt am Main: Jägerische Buchhandlung, 1787.

Reuter-Pettenberg, Helga. *Bedeutungswandel der Römischen Königskrönung in der Neuzeit*. Dissertation, Cologne, 1963.

Röhling, Johann Christoph. *Reise eines Marsbewohners auf die Erde: Zur Zeit der Wahl und Krönung Leopold des Zweiten zum teutschen Kaiser*. Frankfurt am Main: n.p., 1791.

Roth, Johann Richard. *Aechtes vollständiges Protocoll des kurfürstl. hohen Wahlkonvents zu Frankfurt im Jahre 1790*. . . . Frankfurt am Main: n.p., 1791.

Rudolph, Harriet. *Das Reich als Ereignis: Formen und Funktionen der Herrschaftsinszenierung bei Kaisereinzügen (1558–1618)*. Cologne: Böhlau, 2011.

———. "Der Reichstag als Hort der 'deutschen Freiheit': Reichsverfassungsbilder als Medien des Wissenstransfers." In *Stadt, Reich, Europa: Neue Perspektiven auf den Immerwährenden Reichstag zu Regensburg*, edited by Harriet Rudolph and Astrid von Schlachta, 309–38. Regensburg: Schnell & Steiner, 2015.

———. "Die Herrschererhebung als Fest: Krönungsfeste im Vergleich." In *Festkulturen im Vergleich: Inszenierungen des Religiösen und Politischen*, edited by Michael Maurer, 13–42. Cologne: Böhlau, 2010.

———. "Kontinuität und Dynamik—Ritual und Zeremoniell bei Krönungsakten im Alten Reich: Maximilian II., Rudolf II. und Matthias im Vergleich." In *Krönungs- und Investiturrituale: Herrschaftseinsetzungen im kulturellen Vergleich*, edited by Stefan Weinfurter and Marion Steinicke, 377–400 Cologne: Böhlau, 2005.

———. "Manifestationen der Sakralität von Kaisertum und Reich: Die Regensburger Königskrönungen von 1575, 1636 und 1653." In *Gottesdienst in Regensburger Institutionen: Zur Vielfalt liturgischer Traditionen in der Vormoderne*, edited by Harald Buchinger and Sabine Reichert. Regensburg: Schnell & Steiner, 2020 (forthcoming).

Sammlung der Inschriften welche in Wien, als diese Stadt zum Zeichen der der allgemeinen Freude über Franz des II. Glückliche Zurückkunft von der Kaiserkrönung . . . angebracht waren. Vienna: von Baumeister, 1792.

Schmauss, Johann Jacob. *Compendium iuris publici S.R.I.* 3rd ed. Göttingen: Abram Vandenhöcks Wittwe, 1754.

Schmidt, Georg. *Geschichte des Alten Reiches: Staat und Nation in der Frühen Neuzeit 1495–1806*. Munich: C. H. Beck, 1999.

Schneidmüller, Bernd. "Salbung." In *Handwörterbuch zur Deutschen Rechtsgeschichte*. Vol. 4, col. 1268–73. Berlin: Erich Schmidt Verlag, 1990.

Schubart, Christian Friedrich Daniel. *Chronik 1790, 2: Halbjahr*. Stuttgart: Kaiserl. Reichspostamt, 1790.

Schulin, Johann Philipp. *Diarium: Vollständige Beschreibung aller Feyerlichkeiten bey den Krönungen und Huldigungen Leopolds II*. Vienna: Joseph Georg Oehler, 1790.

———. *Vollständiges Diarium der Römisch-Königlichen Wahl und Kaiserlichen Krönung Jhro nunmehr allerglorwürdigst regierenden Kaiserlichen Majestät Leopold des Zweiten* . . . . 2 vols. Frankfurt am Main: Johann Christian Jäger, 1791.

Schwinger, Anna Th. "Der Ornat Kaiser Franz' I. Stephan von Lothringen: Barockkopien nach dem Krönungsornat des Heiligen Römischen Reiches." In *Nobiles officinae: Die Königlichen Hofwerkstätten zu Palermo zur Zeit der Normannen und Staufer im 12. und 13. Jahrhundert*. Ausstellungskatalog, edited by Wilfried Seipel, 137–51. Vienna: Skira, 2004.

Sellert, Wolfgang. "Zur rechtshistorischen Bedeutung der Krönung und des Streites um das Krönungsrecht zwischen Mainz und Köln." In *Herrscherweihe und Königskrönung im Frühneuzeitlichen Europa*, edited by Heinz Duchhardt, 21–32. Wiesbaden: Franz Steiner, 1983.

Stollberg-Rilinger, Barbara. *Des Kaisers alte Kleider: Verfassungsgeschichte und Symbolsprache des Alten Reiches*. Munich: C. H. Beck, 2008.

———. "'Die Puppe Karls des Großen': Das Heilige Römische Reich Deutscher Nation als praktizierter Mythos." In *Mythos als Schicksal: Was konstituiert die Verfassung?*, edited by Otto Depenhauer, 25–69. Wiesbaden: VS Verlag für Sozialwissenschaften, 2009.

———. "Die zeremonielle Inszenierung des Reiches, oder: Was leistet der kulturalistische Ansatz für die Reichsverfassungsgeschichte?" In *Imperium Romanum—Irregulare Corpus—Teutscher Reichs-Staat: Das Alte Reich im Verständnis der Zeitgenossen und der Historiographie*, edited by Matthias Schnettger, 233–46. Mainz: Vandenhoeck & Ruprecht, 2002.

———. "*Honores regii*: Die Königswürde im zeremoniellen Zeichensystem der Frühen Neuzeit." In *Dreihundert Jahre Preußische Königskrönung: Eine Tagungsdokumentation*, edited by Johannes Kunisch, 1–26. Berlin: Duncker & Humblot 2002.

———. *Maria Theresia: Die Kaiserin in ihrer Zeit. Eine Biographie*. Munich: C. H. Beck, 2017.

Truckenbrot, Michael. *Kurzgefaßter Bericht von den bei der Wahl und Krönung eines römischen Kaisers gewöhnlichen Feierlichkeiten . . . .* Frankfurt am Main: Gustav Philipp Jakob Bieling, 1790.

Ueber Teutschland: Kaisertodesfall, Trauer, Reichsvikarien, Wahltag, Wahlkapitulation, Wahl, Krönung, Gerechsame des teutschen Kaisers. Kempten: Joseph Kösel 1790.

Vec, Milos. *Zeremonialwissenschaft im Fürstenstaat: Studien zur juristischen und politischen Theorie absolutistischer Herrschaftsrepräsentation*. Frankfurt am Main: Klostermann, 1998.

"Wahl und Krönung Joseph des Zweyten zum Römischen Könige." In *Historisches Taschenbuch der Wahl und Krönung der Kaiser aus dem Neu-Österreichischen Hause*. Vol. 2. Frankfurt am Main: Fleischersche Buchhandlung, 1792.

Wandruszka, Adam. *Leopold II.: Erzherzog von Österreich, Grossherzog von Toskana, König von Ungarn und Böhmen, Römischer Kaiser*. 2 vols. Vienna: Herold Verlag, 1963–65.

Wanger, Bernd Herbert. *Kaiserwahl und Krönung im Frankfurt des 17. Jahrhunderts: Darstellung anhand der zeitgenössischen Bild- und Schriftquellen und unter besonderer Berücksichtigung der Erhebung des Jahres 1612*. Frankfurt am Main: Verlag Waldemar Kramer, 1994.

Weinfurter, Stefan. "Wie das Reich heilig wurde." In *Gelebte Ordnung—Gedachte Ordnung: Ausgewählte Beiträge zu König, Kirche und Reich*, edited by Helmuth Kluger, Hubertus Seibert, and Werner Bomm, 361–84. Stuttgart: Jan Thorbecke, 2005.

Weinfurter, Stefan, and Marion Steinicke, eds. *Krönungs- und Investiturrituale: Herrschaftseinsetzungen im kulturellen Vergleich*. Cologne: Böhlau, 2005.

Wekhrlin, Wilhelm Ludwig. *Paragrafen*. Nuremberg: Felßeckerische Buchhandlung, 1791.

Whaley, Joachim. *Germany and the Holy Roman Empire*. 2 vols. Oxford: Oxford University Press, 2012.

Wilson, Peter H. *Heart of Europe: A History of the Holy Roman Empire*. Cambridge, MA: Belknap Press of Harvard University Press, 2016.

Chapter 3

THE HUNGARIAN CORONATIONS OF CHARLES VI AND LEOPOLD II AND THE REPRESENTATION OF POLITICAL COMPROMISE

Fanni Hende

The formalities of early modern politics enacted fundamental structures. Among these formalities, symbols and rituals were the most archaic phenomena observable at the imperial diets. Because their appearance, seating, and the way they voted affirmed the constitutional existence of the imperial diets, historian Barbara Stollberg-Rilinger believes that studying these elements is essential when researching the ceremonies. The complex of rituals, symbols, and gestures made the order of the Holy Roman Empire visible *pars pro toto*, and contemporaries grew accustomed to this code system of symbolic forms, imitating its elements in their words and actions. The fundamental concepts were expressed by symbols, though the process of decoding often yielded ambiguous results.[1]

Following Stollberg-Rilinger, I will interpret the ritual of the Hungarian royal coronation and other rites associated with it through the lens of cultural history. I regard these rituals as acts of political communication expressing compromise. Although the sequences and symbols of the Hungarian coronation remained largely unaltered over the centuries, thereby clearly conveying continuity and legitimacy, sporadic minor changes provide evidence of significant shifts in the balance of power between the monarch and the Estates. This confirms that the rite retained political and social significance and represented more than mere spectacle for contemporaries.

In the following sections, I will first describe the location at which the act took place in Pressburg and how the city became the site for Hungarian coronations from the sixteenth century until the end of the eighteenth century. I will subsequently analyze two important elements of the coronations that illustrate the delicate balancing act between ruler and Estates. The first of these was the issuing of the *diploma inaugurale*, which contained the king's promises made before the coronation, as did the analogous *Wahlkapitulationen* of the Roman emperors, but was subsequently codified and became part of the legal system in the course of the king's rule. The other was the election of the palatine, the Hungarian secular elite's highest dignitary (if the office was vacant at the time), since this dignitary had a traditional function in the coronation: it was the palatine who placed the crown of St. Stephen on the king's head together with the archbishop of Esztergom. Palatine Pál Esterházy was alive in 1712, and a new election thus did not take place. There was no palatine in 1790, however, since a royal governor instead of a new palatine had succeeded the previous office holder Lajos Batthyány after his death in 1765. The election of a new palatine to fulfill the important function during the Hungarian coronation of 1790 was therefore necessary. Finally, I will examine the rites of coronation in 1712 and 1790—both of which took place in the wake of anti-Habsburg movements—paying special attention to modifications in the liturgy of the coronation mass. Historians have hitherto not analyzed this part of the rite, instead focusing only on the abolishment of the palatine's question. I argue that these small and, at first glance, seemingly insignificant modifications are indications of tense political negotiations but also show the willingness to achieve a compromise. I will therefore investigate how the bargaining processes between the Habsburgs and the Estates took place in the run-up to the coronations of 1712 and 1790 and what alterations were made to the ritual on each occasion.

In order to be able to fully understand the following analysis, it is important to briefly recall how Hungarian coronations were planned. The first step was a preparatory conference in Vienna attended by the Austrian aulic chancellor, the Hungarian court chancellor, the archbishop of Esztergom, the Hungarian palatine, the president of the Hungarian Chamber (*Kammerpräsident*), the royal equerry (*Oberststallmeister*), and the grand master of the court (*Obersthofmeister*). After hearing the various suggestions and plans, the conference drafted a schedule for the rite. This document was later debated at the assembly of the Hungarian diet. If the Estates had comments regarding any part of the schedule, they could submit them to the monarch and ask for changes. From time to time, such requested modifications were granted.

Historical Background

The Habsburg dynasty governed the Kingdom of Hungary from the beginning of Ferdinand I's reign in 1526. At the same time, however, the Ottoman Empire was expanding northward, occupying Hungarian border regions in 1521 and advancing toward Buda and Vienna. The forces of Sultan Suleiman I defeated the Hungarian army in a decisive battle at Mohács in 1526 and eventually occupied the central territories of the kingdom—including its capital, Buda—in 1541. The Habsburg dynasty thus ascended the throne of a much-diminished kingdom. In 1683, Kara Mustafa Pasha made a second attempt to occupy Vienna, but the army of Emperor Leopold I defeated him in co-operation with Hungarian, Polish, Bavarian, and Saxon forces. This victory marked the beginning of the liberation of Hungary from Ottoman occupation. Buda was recaptured in 1686, and the Ottomans continued to lose ground in the southeastern areas of the former kingdom until 1699. In 1687, Leopold I convened the Hungarian diet, had his son Archduke Joseph crowned king, and forced the Hungarian Estates to accept the principle of hereditary monarchy on account of the Habsburgs' liberation of the kingdom. The diet codified the hereditary succession in the male line, which meant that each king's first-born son would become the next Hungarian king.[2] The next coronation after 1687 took place in 1712, with the heir to be crowned being Joseph's brother, since Joseph had sired no son.

The coronations of Charles VI in 1712 and of Leopold II in 1790 can rightly be regarded as turning points in eighteenth-century Hungarian history. Both events concluded periods burdened by serious conflicts and had a lasting impact on the subsequent decades. Charles VI ascended the throne after the reconquest of Ottoman Hungary and the anti-Habsburg uprising led by Ferenc II Rákóczi (1703–11). One of the reasons for Rákóczi's insurgency had been the tax reform enacted by Emperor Leopold I without the consent or even consultation of the diet, an obvious disregard of Hungarian customs. Leopold died in 1705 and his successor Joseph I tried to make peace, but one of the rebellious assemblies[3] convened by Rákóczi in Ónod (a village in northeastern Hungary) in 1707 dethroned the Habsburg dynasty. Following several unsuccessful efforts to negotiate, Joseph I attempted to counter the Ónod assembly by convening a diet in 1708 but was unable to resolve the domestic crisis. The following year, the king dissolved the diet under the pretext of the plague while the fighting between imperial troops and rebels continued. Rákóczi's resources eventually ran out, however, leaving him unable to continue the war for independence, and peace talks were initiated in 1711. The text of the peace treaty signed in Szatmár county on 29 April 1711 was the result of long negotiations. It returned the prerogative to control taxes to the Estates, and the political elite—including the previously rebellious nobles—was satisfied with this outcome.[4] The fact that Joseph I died prior to the conclusion of the peace talks in 1711 was not communicated to the rebels so as not to impede the ratification of the treaty.[5]

The coronation of Leopold II was likewise preceded by internal conflicts on account of his predecessor's policies. He succeeded Joseph II, whose legitimacy was questioned by a significant part of the Hungarian Estates owing to the lack of a coronation ceremony. Joseph II ruled the Habsburg Monarchy between 1780 and 1790 but refused to be crowned king of Hungary—an unprecedented event in Hungarian history.[6] He attempted to modernize the administration, the tax system, and the military. Among other things, he intended to abolish the tax exemption of noblemen and perform a census to expand the army. He also established districts to replace the existing counties in Hungary and Transylvania, which meant the dissolution of the county assemblies that had often interfered with the execution of royal orders. Owing to this abolishment of the county assemblies and the fact that Joseph II ruled without the Hungarian diet, the Estates felt their rights and prerogatives were infringed. Joseph's transfer of the Hungarian crown from Pressburg to Vienna and the change of the language of administration from Latin to German likewise caused indignation among the Hungarian nobility.[7]

When Leopold II was to succeed his brother, the Hungarian Estates claimed that the earlier line of succession had been interrupted by Joseph II's refusal to be crowned, and as a consequence, demanded Leopold's coronation and a new *diploma inaugurale* in order to accept him as their rightful ruler.[8] They required a new contract and demanded a coronation diet.[9] The Hungarian court chancellor Miklós Pálffy advised the Viennese court to convene the diet in June, a month with symbolic importance: Maria Theresa had issued her *diploma inaugurale* in June 1741, and using a similar date suggested that the court was attempting to link Leopold's reign to that of his mother. This reference to Maria Theresa's legitimate ascension underscored the new king's desire to respect the age-old laws while simultaneously contributing to erasing Joseph II's memory.[10]

Both Charles VI and Leopold II wished to emphasize their legitimacy based on the principle of hereditary monarchy accepted in 1687 and the line of succession defined in the Pragmatic Sanction of 1713, which was adopted in the Kingdom of Hungary in 1723. The mere fact that both heirs to the throne convened coronation diets signaled their intent to co-operate coupled with their respect for the customary laws of the Kingdom of Hungary. The coronations provided excellent opportunities to pacify both sides and help consolidate Habsburg rule in Hungary. Certain small adaptations were however necessary to tailor the traditional ceremony to contemporary circumstances, and corresponding negotiations had to take place between the respective ruler and the Hungarian diet before the coronations could be carried out. With pacification a declared goal, both kings took the traditional customs associated with the crowning into account.[11]

The Location of the Hungarian Coronations

The medieval kings of Hungary were crowned in Székesfehérvár, but the capture of the city by the Ottomans in 1543 necessitated a new setting for the ritual. The choice fell on Pressburg, doubtlessly motivated by its proximity to Vienna and the fact that it had gradually developed into a political center following the loss of the central areas of the kingdom. It housed the Hungarian Chamber from 1531 onward, and mostly the diet as well.[12] The organizers of the first coronation in Pressburg intended to preserve the traditional elements of the Székesfehérvár rites, since they ensured the legitimacy of the Hungarian kings. Continuation of these traditions served to maintain the royal court of Hungary, since the Estates considered the Ottoman occupation and the court's exile to be only temporary.[13] In order to select the proper sites for the various parts of the proceedings in Pressburg, Palatine Tamás Nádasdy wrote a proposal in 1561 that was largely adopted by the Hungarian Council.[14] Besides Nádasdy himself, two other members of the council had already participated in Ferdinand I's coronation in Székesfehérvár in 1527: archbishop Miklós Oláh of Esztergom and János Dessewffy, the grand master.[15] This guaranteed the continuity of the Székesfehérvár coronation traditions at the new location, for which Nádasdy's proposal expressly called.[16] Pressburg would remain the scene of the Hungarian royal coronations until the end of the eighteenth century. Certain parts of the rite took place in St. Martin's Cathedral, others in the Franciscan Church, and some outside the city walls. As part of his administrative reforms, Joseph II moved the Locotenential Council (the central government office in the Kingdom of Hungary from 1722 onward), the Hungarian Chamber, and the diet with the royal archives from Pressburg to Buda in 1784. Since its recapture from the Ottomans a century before, the old capital had witnessed a period of gradual development. The emperor wanted Buda to be a genuine capital once more, as it was located in the middle of the kingdom, which made its administration easier.[17] Despite the fact that the Hungarian diet assembled in Buda (the site of the medieval diets), however, the coronation was still held in Pressburg in 1790. The alleged reason for Leopold's choice was the severe weather,[18] but Pressburg's vicinity to Vienna likely also played a role in his decision, for there was only little time between the Hungarian and imperial coronations. To achieve the desired goal, the court referred to the traditions of the Pressburg coronations as well.[19] The Estates therefore consented to relocating the diet and performing the crowning in Pressburg instead of Buda.[20] The diet opted to move on 21 October so as to be able to hold the coronation on the scheduled date of 15 November.[21] It is characteristic of Leopold II's benevolence and his willingness to respect the wishes of the Estates that he agreed to keep the Holy Crown of St. Stephen in Buda.[22] Although he ordered the crown transferred to Pressburg for the coronation, it was returned to Buda immediately thereafter[23]—which was symbolically important for Buda's aspiration to become

Hungary's capital city again. During the Middle Ages, the crown had been kept in Székesfehérvár until the beginning of the fourteenth century, then in Visegrád, but also sometimes in Buda. A decree issued in 1492 stipulated that two guards of the crown jewels were to safeguard the insignia in Visegrád.[24] They were transferred to Pressburg in 1608, where they were stored until 1790 save for a few short periods.[25]

The Diploma

As indicated by its name, the *diploma inaugurale* was an essential element of the coronation. Issued before the crowning, the document assured that the sovereign would respect the kingdom's laws. Beginning with Ferdinand II (1618), the respective diploma was codified at the beginning of each new king's reign. Its text was subject not just to negotiations, but to intense debates between the Estates and the future king—and the Viennese court therefore preferred to leave little time for squabbling by scheduling the coronation as soon as possible. Diplomas issued before 1687 should effectively be viewed as conditions for election. Leopold I's diploma (1655) contained seventeen points.[26] The basis for the later texts, however, which represented a "fictive permanence" or continuity during the eighteenth century, was Joseph I's diploma comprising only seven points. It included the mode of the crown's guarding, the promise that the king's successors would issue similar diplomas, and the conditions for the Estates to regain the right of free election. The new form gave the Hungarian kings more room to maneuver, since the diploma's wording now reflected the political conditions between unequal parties and primarily served the interests of the court in Vienna.[27]

Prior to Charles VI's coronation in the spring of 1712, the Hungarian Estates took up debate on whether to follow the wording of Leopold I's or Joseph I's *diploma inaugurale*. They had renounced their right to elect the king back in 1687, which amounted to acceptance of the Habsburgs' hereditary succession in the male line. Joseph I's diploma had been designed to reflect this concession. Moreover, it was not only shorter than his predecessor's, but also contained an amendment that made the laws of the kingdom subject to common interpretation between the king and the Estates. This meant that the king was not obliged to accept the Estates' interpretations of their privileges, which severely angered the Hungarian nobles. They had the opportunity to debate the diploma after the convening of the diet, which had to open in the ruler's presence. Knowing this, the court had scheduled Charles' arrival at the diet such that the Estates had only two days prior to the coronation to discuss the diploma—a very short period of time. Aware that the court of Vienna would not return to the Leopoldinian text, the diet voted to use Joseph's diploma—albeit on the condition that the unwelcome amendment of 1687 be omitted. But the diet was only opened on

20 May, and as a result, it did not have enough time to consult with the ruler, leaving the Estates with no alternative but to accept the royal diploma unchanged. Charles showed his goodwill by assuring them that he would not abuse the clause of mutual interpretation. He fulfilled his promise and ultimately codified that promise.[28]

In 1790, with reference to their opinion that the line of succession had been interrupted by Joseph II's refusal to be crowned and the issue of Joseph I's diploma, the Estates intended to finally negotiate a new *diploma inaugurale* that would protect the laws of the kingdom more effectively. In the first days of September, they drafted a document consisting of twenty-five points. Leopold II was unwilling to accept this text, however, and adhered instead to the diploma of Charles VI, which insisted on the hereditary reign laid down in 1687. Leopold argued that the intended alterations suggested that the document was in fact a *Wahlkapitulation* and would break the earlier contracts of inheritance. Nevertheless, he promised that the new points contained in the draft would be codified after his coronation.[29] The diploma was ultimately issued in the Charles VI version without any changes in November 1790, a fact that reflected the political situation in Europe. Prussia had supported the demands of the Hungarian Estates, but only until the signing of the treaty with Leopold II at Reichenbach in July 1790, which no longer guaranteed the Hungarian constitution. At that point, there remained no other option for the Hungarian Estates before Leopold's coronation than to accept a diploma following the wording of Charles VI's from 1712.[30]

The Election of the Palatine

In accordance with old Hungarian tradition, the election of the palatine also took place in the diet until the nomination of the last palatine, István Habsburg, in 1848. From 1608 onward, the palatine was elected at the mixed session of the diet attended by members of both the upper and the lower house. The king nominated two Catholic and two Protestant candidates, and two royal commissioners delivered the sealed envelope containing the nominees' names to the diet. The commissioners were awaited at the staircase of the building of the upper house by a modest delegation that accompanied them to the Council Hall, where the archbishop of Esztergom received the sealed envelope and read out the names of the candidates. Those who were present voted, and the palatine-elect, accompanied by the primate and the Estates, proceeded to the Castle of Pressburg (during the eighteenth century) to take his oath before the sovereign in the Knights' Hall.[31]

Owing to the tasks to be performed by the palatine during the crowning ritual, a new palatine was usually elected prior to a coronation in the eighteenth century. Following the death of Palatine Pál Esterházy in 1713,[32] Miklós Pálffy was elected prior to the coronation of Elisabeth Christine of Brunswick-

Wolfenbüttel, Charles VI's wife, as Hungarian queen in 1714, two years after her husband's crowning. Twenty-seven years later, in 1741, János Pálffy was elected before Maria Theresa's coronation; and after his death in 1751, Lajos Batthyány became palatine. The law of 1608 prescribed that the king had to convene the diet to elect the new palatine within one year of the previous office-holder's death.³³ In the eighteenth century, however, two rulers nominated royal governors instead of new palatines. After the death of palatine Miklós Pálffy in 1732, Charles VI appointed Maria Theresa's fiancé Francis, Duke of Lorraine, as royal governor in disregard of the law. Maria Theresa extended the succession regulation to include royal governors in 1741, which meant that after the death of a governor or palatine, their office was not to be vacant for more than one year. The law did not mention a convening of the diet, however.³⁴ Palatine Lajos Batthyány died in autumn of 1765 immediately after the dissolution of a diet, but the queen did not want to summon the Estates again. With Emperor Joseph II's approval, she nominated her daughter's fiancé Albert of Saxony-Teschen as royal governor. There were important differences between the competencies of the palatine and the royal governor: First of all, the governor's competencies were determined by the king, while the palatine's rights and duties were prescribed by Hungarian law. Secondly, palatines were elected by the diet, while governors were appointed by the kings without hearing the diet's opinion. The office of royal governor thus served the king's interests more than that of the palatine. The two abovementioned appointments of archduchesses' fiancés can also be explained in part by the fact that the respective men required offices worthy of their rank.³⁵

This overall unstable practice meant that it was questionable whether the Hungarian diet—after a twenty-five-year hiatus—would be given the opportunity to elect a palatine in 1790. The court was inclined to appoint a new governor in the person of Archduke Alexander Leopold, Leopold II's fourth-born son. Following the suggestion of the ministerial conference (*Geheime Konferenz*) in Vienna, however, the emperor decided to make the archduke a palatine on the condition that the diet declare him palatine unanimously before the regular election—in other words, before the opening of the envelope with the nominees' names. The conference drew up a list of candidates that included one Catholic and two Protestant candidates whom the Estates would likely not have elected anyway. The idea was that if the other Catholic candidate, the aged Károly Zichy, were to be elected, Leopold Alexander would follow him as royal governor after Zichy's presumably short run of office.³⁶ Formally, the king thus respected the law of the Hungarian kingdom by sending a list containing the names of his candidates, but the acclamation as the mode of election differed from the custom. This procedure served as a compromise between the king and the Estates, since Leopold Alexander as a member of the dynasty served the king's interests on the one hand, while, according to the law, he had obligations toward the Estates as palatine as well, which satisfied their wishes sufficiently.

Before the election, the loyal peerage successfully lobbied in favor of Leopold Alexander among participants of the diet whose intention was ambiguous or who wanted a traditional election. The members of the first group deemed the acclamation illegitimate but were persuaded by reason that the king's son would become palatine and that this would be beneficial for the kingdom.

The election eventually took place on 12 November 1790. At 8:00 a.m., directly before the meeting, the *personalis* József Ürményi,[37] who was chairman of the lower house of the diet, convened the county representatives to gauge their attitude concerning the acclamation of the archduke as palatine. He asked them to express their opinions, whereupon representatives of thirty-seven of the forty-nine counties voiced support for the archduke, while seven stated that they had only been authorized to vote with the majority in the diet. The representatives of five other counties, however, announced that they were only willing to vote for a fellow countryman. Unfortunately, the available sources do not provide any further information on these dissenters. At the end of the engagement, Ürményi asked the representatives not to bring harm to the kingdom under any circumstances. As a consequence, they promised that they would neither approve nor reject the archduke.[38]

Thereafter, the Estates assembled to learn the nominees' names. In his speech, the chief justice—who followed the palatine in hierarchy and substituted for him in case of his absence—called attention to Leopold II's piety, which urged him to respect the laws of the kingdom and hold an election to fill the long-vacant position of palatine. At the end of his address and before opening the sealed letter, he asked the members of the diet to unanimously declare Leopold's son Leopold Alexander the new palatine. He referred to the growing distrust between the Estates and the king, a development that could only be countervailed by the appointment of the archduke. The address achieved its purpose, and the Estates shouted: "Vivat Leopoldus palatinus."[39] The new palatine had to take an oath, the exact wording of which had been subject to prior negotiations between the sovereign and the diet. Its final version was elaborated by the Hungarian Court Chancellery, the court ministry, the archbishop of Esztergom, the chief justice, and the *personalis*, and was sent to Leopold II with the deputation that informed him of the result of the election in the afternoon. Some wished to continue the negotiations on the text of the oath, but the Estates ignored this demand at the request of the chief justice.[40] This process once again testifies to the existence of background negotiations. The importance of the 1790 palatine election is underlined by the fact that Leopold Alexander was the first Habsburg palatine of the Kingdom of Hungary. Members of the dynasty continued to fulfill the function until 1848.

Leopold Alexander's appointment entailed changes in precedence at the coronation banquet. The archdukes preceded the Hungarian ecclesiastical and lay elite according to the so-called Spanish etiquette in use since the Hungarian coronation of Maximilian II in 1563. From the beginning of the seventeenth century, the archbishop of Esztergom occupied a more distinguished place, sitting closer to the ruler.[41] In 1790, however, the palatine preceded the primate by reason of Leopold Alexander's higher rank.[42]

The Coronation and Its Ritual Alterations

Before discussing the alterations made to the rite of coronation, I will briefly touch upon its procedure, which was divided into an ecclesiastical and a secular part. Although the ecclesiastical ritual was based on the Roman Pontifical—the liturgical book containing rites reserved to bishops and made compulsory for the Catholic Church by the Council of Trent (1545–63)—it also contained several elements that were not part of the rite prescribed by the Church. Since the Middle Ages, the secular ceremony took place outside of the mass, although the exact time of its separation is not easy to define. Its elements remained unstable even in the fifteenth century.[43] During the eighteenth century, the ecclesiastical components of the coronation mass for a male monarch were the following: After declaring the candidate to be suitable, the archbishop summarized his duties as king, which included protection of the faith, the Church, orphans, widows, and poor persons as well as the duty to rule for the welfare of his people, not for his personal benefit. The king then took the ecclesiastical oath, which was followed by the consecration (i.e., the anointing with catechumenal oil). The next steps were the monarch's change of royal dress, the placement of the crown on his head, and the handing over of the royal insignia. The archbishop of Esztergom first invested the king with the sword, which the latter pointed in three directions. Next came the *acclamatio*, the question in Hungarian by the palatine to the persons present: Did they want to crown the nominee their king? The three positive answers (*we do*) were followed by the crowning itself, conducted by the archbishop of Esztergom and the palatine: the archbishop held the right side of the crown, the palatine the left.[44] The coronation finished with the passing of the scepter and orb to the new monarch together with the enthronement and a *Te Deum laudamus*. Trumpets and drums sounded and cannons were fired, while the congregation in the cathedral shouted "Vivat rex!" upon a sign by the palatine.[45]

The ensuing secular acts were distributed across several locations in Pressburg. After the coronation mass, the procession headed to the Franciscan Church, where coronation coins were thrown to the onlookers and the king invested several new knights of the Order of the Golden Spur. Besides this knighting, the medieval kings also held plenary court and passed sentences. These symbolic acts marked the beginning of the new monarch's rule; they showed that he was the highest warlord and judge in the kingdom.[46] The names of the candidates for knighthood were read out one by one, whereupon they took a knee in front of the throne and the king touched them three times with the sword of St. Stephen.⁴⁷ This was followed by the coronation oath, which dealt with the maintenance of law and order. From the hill of the oath taking (see figure 3.1), the ruler then rode to the summit of the royal or coronation hill to swing the sword in the four cardinal directions. This act expressed that the ruler was ready to protect the kingdom with his or her blood, no matter from what direction the enemy threatened it. The coronation feast took place in the royal palace in the presence of the upper house aristocracy as well as the representatives of the lower house. The king entered the room wearing the crown and mantle of St. Stephen, and the primate said grace.⁴⁸

Géza Pálffy is of the opinion that the upholding of the Hungarian coronation traditions served the interests not only of the Hungarian Estates, but also of the monarchs. The prestige of the Habsburg Monarchy was enhanced by the fact that it ruled a unique realm able to display its tradition and importance through the extraordinary crowning ritual.⁴⁹ Moreover, the coronation traditions brought to life an independent—albeit virtual—royal court of Hungary, which was of utmost importance to the Hungarian Estates since the real court no longer perma-

Figure 3.1. King Leopold II swearing to uphold the rights and liberties of the Hungarian Estates during his coronation in Pressburg in 1790 (Vienna, Österreichische Nationalbibliothek, Bildarchiv und Graphiksammlung, Pk 400,320).

nently resided within the boundaries of the kingdom. This virtual royal court was the reason why the monarchs continued to appoint Hungarian court dignitaries who had a role only during the coronations. Further symbolism was provided by the Hungarian "flavor" of the coronations and above all by the feasts, where the Hungarian royal court—even if only for a few hours—could affirm its existence. The harsh reality, however, was that the Estates had only limited competence and the final decisions concerning the rite were made at the court in Vienna.[50]

This weak bargaining position of the Estates becomes clear when analyzing the elements that were called into question despite the fact that the liturgy of the coronation continued to follow the *Pontificale Romanum* and most elements and texts were fixed. The envisioned modifications may seem trivial at first glance, but they touch upon structural, political, and legal debates between the court and the Estates. An early modification concerned the *acclamatio*. During the ecclesiastical rite but before the coronation, the palatine asked the Estates three times in Hungarian: "Do you want to crown the nominee your king?" The answer was likewise given three times: "We do!"[51] The scenario of the coronation included the question by the palatine, but the *Pontificale Romanum* did not, so this secular element was not part of the ecclesiastical ritual in the eighteenth century.

This requirement of the expression of agreement can already be found in tenth- and eleventh-century liturgical books. The Romano-Germanic ordo, for example, prescribed the question to be asked by the crowning prelate.[52] A twelfth-century Romano-Germanic pontifical preserved in Cologne also contains the question aimed at the priests and laics, who were to express their agreement three times: "Then the bishop addresses the people saying: Do you want to submit yourself to such a prince and leader, to confirm his royal power through your loyalty and obey his commands . . . ? Then the surrounding clerics and people unanimously say: Let it be done, let it be done, let it be done."[53]

While composing his pontifical in the thirteenth century, however, the French canonist and prelate Guillaume Durand did not take over this element from the Romano-Germanic form.[54] And because the so-called Durandus Ordo was used for the Hungarian coronations during the fourteenth and fifteenth centuries, the liturgy cannot have contained this *acclamatio* at the time. Nevertheless, we know from the account by Lodovico Tubero, a fifteenth- and sixteenth-century historian who wrote about Hungarian history between 1490 and 1522, that the acclamation—which would already have been performed by the palatine—was banned from the coronation for Vladislaus II in 1490 owing to his unpopularity among the nobility.[55] This element of the Romano-Germanic ordo was apparently moved from the ecclesiastical rite to the palatine's competence, where it would remain until its ultimate abolishment in 1712.[56]

In that year, Vienna took measures to do away with the element of the acclamation with reference to the second act accepted by the diet in 1687,[57] which accepted the Habsburgs' hereditary succession in the male line. The Austrian aulic chancellor Count Johann Friedrich von Seilern complained that the question asked by the palatine suggested a free election as opposed to the actual legal situation. The preparatory conference in Vienna eventually omitted the procedure from the ritual in 1712 with palatine Pál Esterházy's consent, and it never appeared again later.[58]

As the case of 1490 shows, this omission was not unprecedented in Hungary.[59] Moreover, it demonstrates that the political interests of the Hungarian Estates influenced their insistence on or objection to the palatine's question as well. The abolition of the *acclamatio* in 1712, however, was in the interest of the Viennese court and the hereditary reign. It is noteworthy that although the court opposed the asking of the palatine's question, it did not disapprove his assistance in the coronation, which symbolized the kingdom's royal election and the consent of the Estates since the Middle Ages.[60]

Reading from the pontifical at the beginning of the liturgy, it was the archbishop of Kalocsa who requested the coronation: "Most Reverend Father, the Holy Mother Church requires that you elevate the glorious knight present into the royal dignity." The primate subsequently asked: "Do you find him worthy and apt for the dignity?"[61] In the spring of 1712, Chancellor Seilern raised objections not only to the acclamation dialogue performed by the palatine, but also to the archbishop's question. He recommended the following formula: "Do you swear enduring loyalty and ceaseless obedience to your hereditary king?"[62] To justify this alteration, Seilern referred to the similar question during the coronation in the Holy Roman Empire,[63] asked by the archbishop of Mainz.[64] The recommended formula was analogous to a question included in the medieval Romano-Germanic ordo and posed by the crowning prelate to both clerics and laymen: Did they want to submit themselves and faithfully obey the future king?[65] In the end, the archbishop of Esztergom, Christian August of Saxe-Zeitz, managed to convince Vienna by arguing that the omission of the prescribed question threatened the validity of the coronation and could thus result in the monarch's suspension by the pope.[66]

A second charge, minor but noteworthy, was made to the prayer recited during the enthronement in 1741, when the Romano-Germanic pontifical's medieval formula replaced the one provided by the *Pontificale Romanum*. The prescribed text in the contemporary ritual book read as follows: "From now stand and keep the place ordered to you by God, from the authority of the almighty God."[67] In all probability, the archbishop repeated these original words at the solemn enthronement of Charles VI,[68] while the prayer at the coronations of Maria Theresa, Leopold II, and Francis II differed slightly: "Sta et retine amodo locum, quem hucusque Paterna successione tenuisti, haereditario iure Tibi a Deo delegatum [From now stand and keep the place eternally ordered to you by God, possessed by you as paternal inheritance until now]."[69] This resembled the wording of the Romano-Germanic ritual used in medieval Hungarian coronations:

"Sta et retine locum amodo quem hucusque paterna successione tenuisti haereditario iure tibi delegatum per auctoritatem Dei omnipotentis."[70] The insertion referred unambiguously to the valid principles of the line of succession (i.e., the hereditary monarchy accepted in 1687 and the Pragmatic Sanction codified in 1723, which enabled succession in the female line).

Apart from the alterations to the liturgy and the issue of the *diploma inaugurale*, other symbolic communication also displayed a willingness to co-operate and observe Hungarian traditions on the part of the ruler. Charles VI entered the coronation church in Hungarian dress and forewent the display of the imperial insignia, which would have been carried by imperial dignitaries during the coronation march.[71] Similarly, Leopold II wore the Hungarian coronation dress during the procession and did not show off the imperial insignia even though he had been crowned emperor earlier.[72] The wooden bridge leading from the coronation church to the Franciscan Church and decked out in the Hungarian colors (i.e., red, white, and green cloth) was also part and parcel of the symbolic communication. Originally, the cloth had been red and gold; it was not until 1608 that it was replaced with a three-colored version.[73]

Conclusions

The formalities of the 1712 and 1790 crowning ceremonies clearly demonstrate that the respective king and the Estates were open to peaceful co-operation and compromise. In both cases, the kings expressed their intent to respect Hungarian customary law, which manifested in the summoning of the Hungarian diet, the issuing of the *diploma inaugurale*—although the king determined the conditions—and the coronation itself. Despite firmly emphasizing the Habsburg dynasty's order of succession and successfully representing the institution of hereditary monarchy, Charles VI and Leopold II made positive symbolic gestures toward the Hungarian Estates—for example, by wearing traditional Hungarian clothes. On the other hand, the Hungarian Estates accepted changes to individual elements of the coronation and indulged the royal intentions that served Viennese court interests but were still in accordance with the kingdom's customary law. Analysis of the modified parts of the liturgy reveals the significance and power of certain political dignitaries. The liturgical change in 1712 demonstrates that the archbishop of Esztergom, whose privilege it was to officiate at the rite, was strong enough to maintain his position. The palatine, on the other hand, relinquished one of his functions during the coronation. Similarly, the next archbishop supported the introduction of certain alterations to the liturgical texts in 1741.

It is apparent, however, that the international political situation heavily influenced the Hungarian Estates' chances of achieving their goal of the issue of a *diploma inaugurale* with new content in 1790; without external support, this ambition was unlikely to be realized. Although both parties made concessions, the compromise was not reached by equals—as was clearly signaled by the timing of both rulers' arrivals in Pressburg. The short period of time between their respective appearance and coronation served the interests of the kings, and suggestions by the Estates were not taken into account. Still, as a result of the compromises reached, the kings convened the Hungarian diet from time to time and respected the customs of the kingdom to a certain degree. This co-operation rendered the coronations magnificent, and the rituals in turn made visible the political unity between the Habsburg dynasty and the Hungarian Estates.

Fanni Hende is a research fellow at the Hungarian Academy of Sciences—National Széchényi Library Res Libraria Hungariae Research Group. She received her PhD in History at Pázmány Péter Catholic University in 2017. Her research has focused on political representation in the Hungarian diet during the first half of the eighteenth century, and she has also explored medieval manuscripts and codices in Hungarian public collections. Her publications include: "A magyar uralkodókoronázás egyházi szertartása a 18. században," in *Egyház és reprezentáció a régi Magyarországon*, ed. Orsolya Báthory and Franciska Kónya (Budapest, 2016) and "Ceremoniálne príchody panovníkov do Bratislavy v 18. storočí," in *Korunovácie a pohreby: Mocenské rituály a ceremónie v ranom novoveku*, ed. Tünde Lengyelova and Géza Pálffy (Békéscsaba, 2016).

Notes

The author is a research fellow of the Hungarian Academy of Sciences—National Széchényi Library Res Libraria Hungariae Research Group. This study was prepared with support from the "Lendület" Holy Crown of Hungary Research Project (2012–17) of the Institute of History, Research Centre for the Humanities, Hungarian Academy of Sciences.

1. Barbara Stollberg-Rilinger, *The Emperor's Old Clothes: Constitutional History and the Symbolic Language of the Holy Roman Empire* (New York, 2015), 1–14.
2. 1687, Act 2–3: *CIH 1657–1740*, 334–36.
3. The rebels held eight assemblies during their uprising. They established a new administration, but their assemblies resembled the diets convened by the Hungarian kings, whereby they intended to emphasize continuity with the Hungarian diet before 1687. Prelates, nobles, delegates of cities, and soldiers faithful to Rákóczi participated in these assemblies, which among other things dealt with grievances, legislation, and justice: Barna Mezey, *A Rákóczi szabadságharc országgyűlései* (Budapest, 1981), 15–73.
4. István M. Szijártó, "The Rákóczi Revolt as a Successful Rebellion," in *Resistance, Rebellion and Revolution in Hungary and Central Europe: Commemorating 1956*, ed. László Péter and Martyn Rady (London, 2008), 67–76.
5. Jean Bérenger and Charles Kecskeméti, *Parlement et vie parlementaire en Hongrie 1608–1918* (Paris, 2005), 141–77.

6. For the connection between a written constitution and Hungarian coronations in the nineteenth century, when the kingdom's legal continuity was questionable, see the contribution by Judit Beke-Martos in this volume.
7. Derek Beales, *Joseph II: Against the World 1780–1790* (Cambridge, UK, 2009), 477–92.
8. Ákos Barcsay, *Herrschaftsantritt im Ungarn des 18. Jahrhunderts: Studien zum Verhältnis zwischen Krongewalt und Ständetum in Zeitalter des Absolutismus* (St. Katherinen, 2002), 45–48.
9. Henrik Marczali, *Az 1790/1—diki országgyűlés*, vol. 1 (Budapest, 1907), 71–72; Barcsay, *Herrschaftsantritt im Ungarn*, 47.
10. Barcsay, *Herrschaftsantritt im Ungarn*, 67–68.
11. Barcsay, *Herrschaftsantritt im Ungarn*, 195.
12. Géza Pálffy, "Návrh uhorských radcov na bratislavský korunovačný ceremoniál z roku 1561: Doteraz neznámy zásadný prameň k uhorským kráľovským korunováciám," *Historický Časopis* 54, no. 2 (2006): 204.
13. Pálffy, *The Kingdom of Hungary and the Habsburg Monarchy in the Sixteenth Century* (New York, 2009), 200.
14. Pálffy, "Nádasdy Tamás nádor a magyar királyok koronázási szertartásáról (1561)," in *Szolgálatomat ajánlom a 60 éves Jankovics Józsefnek*, ed. Tünde Császtvay and Judit Nyerges (Budapest, 2009), 308. Rulers consulted the members of the Hungarian Council, who were prelates and secular nobles holding offices in the kingdom, concerning Hungarian domestic politics. This consultative council had its seat in Pressburg.
15. Pálffy, "Návrh uhorských radcov," 207.
16. Pálffy, "Návrh uhorských radcov," 212.
17. Marczali, *Az 1790/1—diki országgyűlés*, vol. 1: 345; István Nagy, "II. József reformjai Budán," *Tanulmányok Budapest múltjából* 15 (1963): 366–67.
18. Marczali, *Az 1790/1—diki országgyűlés*, vol. 2: 315.
19. Barcsay, *Herrschaftsantritt im Ungarn*, 213.
20. *Naponként-való jegyzései az 1790-dik esztendőben Felséges IIdik Leopold Tsászár, és Magyar Országi Király Által . . . Magyar Országgyűlésének* (Buda, 1791), 168.
21. *Naponként-való . . . Felséges IIdik Leopold*, 180.
22. 1790, Act 6: *CIH 1740–1835*, 154.
23. Marczali, *Az 1790/1—diki országgyűlés*, vol. 2: 332.
24. 1492, Act 3: *CIH 1000–1526*, 482–84.
25. 1608, Act 16: *CIH 1608–57*, 34. The insignia were moved elsewhere in 1663–64 and 1683–87 due to the Ottoman campaign, and in 1619–22 and 1703–12 due to internal conflicts. Joseph II wanted to collect the crowns and regalia of his kingdoms and lands in 1784: Géza Pálffy, "Hazatérés Prágából, 1608," "A korona Bethlen Gábor birtokában, 1619–1622," "A legkevésbé ismert hazatérés: A Szent Korona Bécsben, 1663–1664," and "Menekítés német földre, 1683–1687," *Rubicon* 29, no. 7–8 (2018): 40–49, 50–57, 58–67, and 68–77; Fanni Hende, "Újabb bécsi kitérő: A Szent Korona a Rákóczi-szabadságharc idején, 1703–1712," *Rubicon* 29, no. 7–8 (2018): 78–85, István Soós, "A Szent Korona diadalmenete Bécstől Budáig, 1790," *Rubicon* 29, no. 7–8 (2018): 86–99.
26. István M. Szijártó, *A diéta: A magyar rendek és az országgyűlés 1708–1792* (Keszthely, 2010), 198–99. See also the English summary: Szijártó, "The Diet: The Estates and the Parliament of Hungary, 1708–1792," in *Bündnispartner und Konkurrenten des Landesfürsten? Die Stände in der Habsburgermonarchie*, ed. Gerhard Ammerer, William D.

Godsey Jr., Martin Scheutz, Peter Urbanitsch, and Alfred Stefan Weiß (Vienna, 2007), 151–71. For Leopold I's diploma: 1659, Act 1: *CIH 1657–1740*, 130–38.
27. Szijártó, *A diéta*, 201.
28. András Forgó, "Zu den Möglichkeiten und Grenzen ständisch-politischer Handlungsfähigkeit: Das Beispiel des Herrschaftsantritts Karls VI. im Königreich Ungarn," in *Wiener Archivforschungen: Festschrift für den ungarischen Archivdelegierten in Wien, István Fazekas*, ed. Zsuzsanna Cziráki, Anna Fundárková, Orsolya Manhercz, Zsuzsanna Peres, and Márta Vajnági (Vienna, 2014), 263–68; Szijártó, *A diéta*, 201–5; 1715, Act 3, paragraph 2: *CIH 1657–1740*, 436.
29. Szijártó, *A diéta*, 207–8.
30. Bérenger and Kecskeméti, *Parlement*, 234.
31. Éva Lauter, "'Modus observandus . . .' A 17. századi magyar nádorválasztások rendje," in *Portré és imázs: Politikai propaganda és reprezentáció a kora újkorban*, ed. Nóra G. Etényi and Ildikó Horn (Budapest, 2008), 200–3.
32. Pál Esterházy was elected in 1681 and was palatine until his death in 1713. He placed the crown on the head of Charles VI in 1712.
33. 1608, Act 3: *CIH 1608–57*, 10.
34. 1741, Act 9: *CIH 1740–1835*, 24.
35. Szijártó, *A diéta*, 100; Krisztina Kulcsár, "Ein fremder Adeliger zwischen der Königin und den ungarischen Ständen: Der Lebenslauf von Prinz Albert von Sachsen bis 1765 und seine Ernennung zum Statthalter des Königreichs Ungarn," in *Adel im "langen" 18. Jahrhundert*, ed. Gabriele Haug-Moritz, Hans Peter Hye, and Marlies Raffler (Vienna, 2009), 275–88.
36. Szijártó, *A diéta*, 298–99.
37. The *personalis* represented the king in the royal law court. He judged in the king's name and used the royal seal.
38. Budapest, OSZKK, Fol. Lat. 658/I., fol. 115v–116r.
39. *Naponként-való jegyzései . . Felséges IIdik Leopold*, 211–12.
40. *Naponként-való jegyzései . . Felséges IIdik Leopold*, 215.
41. Pálffy, *The Kingdom of Hungary*, 203.
42. *Naponként-való jegyzései . . Felséges IIdik Leopold*, 240.
43. Erik Fügedi, *Uram, királyom . . . : a XV. századi Magyarország hatalmasai* (Budapest, 1974), 59.
44. Sámuel Decsy, *A' magyar szent koronának és az ahoz tartozó tárgyaknak históriája, mellyet sok régi és újjább írásokból ki jegyzett, rendbe szedett, meg világosított, 's kedves Hazafiainak hasznokra közönségessé tett* (Budapest, 2008), 531.
45. András Forgó, ed., "Acta et observata penes diaetam Hungaricam Posonii celebratam, item coronationem domini Caroli VI ibidem peractam anno 1712. per patrem Engelbertum Hermann professum Velehradensem, qua plenipotentiatum ablegatum reverendissimi domini Floriani abbatis," in *Az 1712. évi pozsonyi diéta egy ciszterci szerzetes szemével* (Pannonhalma, 2013), 204.
46. Erik Fügedi, "A magyar király koronázásának rendje a középkorban," in *Eszmetörténeti tanulmányok a magyar középkorról*, ed. György Székely (Budapest, 1984), 260, 269.
47. Márton György Kovachich, *Solennia inauguralia serenissimorum ac potentissimorum principium utriusque sexus, qui ex augusta stirpe Habspurgo-Austriaca sacra corona apostolica in reges Hungarorum, reginasque periodo tertia redimiti sunt* (Pest, 1790), 151.

48. Forgó, "Acta et observata," 200–7.
49. Pálffy, *The Kingdom of Hungary*, 194.
50. Pálffy, *The Kingdom of Hungary*, 200–4.
51. Budapest, Magyar Nemzeti Levéltár Országos Levéltára, A95, fol. 443r.
52. Emma Bartoniek, *A magyar király-koronázások története* (Budapest, 1987), 26–30; József Gerics, "Az úgynevezett Egbert (Dunstan)-ordo alkalmazásáról a XI. századi Magyarországon (Salamon koronázásának előadása a krónikákban)," in *Eszmetörténeti tanulmányok a magyar középkorról*, ed. György Székely (Budapest, 1984), 243–44.
53. "Deinde dominus metropolitanus affatur populum dicens: Vis tali principi ac rectori subici, ipsiusque regnum firmare, fide stabilire atque iussionibus illius obtemperare . . . regi quasi praecellenti? Tunc ergo a circumstante clero et populo unanimiter dicatur: Fiat. Fiat. Fiat.": Cologne, Dombibliothek, Codex 139, *Pontificale ecclesiae Coloniensis*, fol. 23v.
54. Munich, Bayerische Staatsbibliothek, Clm 10073, fol. 110v–115v.
55. Ludovicus Cervarius Tubero, *Commentaria suorum temporum* (Raguza, 1784), 84–85.
56. Bartoniek, *A magyar király-koronázások*, 30.
57. *CIH 1657–1740*, 335.
58. ÖStA, HHStA, ZA Prot, 7, fol. 86v.
59. Bartoniek, *A magyar király-koronázások*, 43; Tubero, *Commentaria*, 84–85.
60. Fügedi, "A magyar király koronázásának rendje," 271.
61. "Reverendissime Pater, postulat Sancta Mater Ecclesia Catholica, ut praesentem egregium militem ad dignitatem Regiam sublevetis" and "Scitis illum esse dignum et utilem ad hanc dignitatem?": *Pontificale Romanum Clementis VIII. ac Urbani VIII. auctoritate recognitum et ad plurium usum, in commodiorem formam redactum* (Venezia, 1722), 135.
62. "Promittitis haereditario regi vestro constantem fidem et perpetuam obedientiam?": ÖStA, HHStA, ÄZA, 24: *Zeremoniell bei der Krönung Karls VI. in Preßburg, 29.02.1712*, fol. 13r; Barcsay, *Herrschaftsantritt im Ungarn*, 197.
63. Márta Vajnági, "Koronázás a Német-római Birodalomban és Magyarországon a kora újkorban," *Világtörténet* 36, no. 4 (2014): 276–77.
64. Barcsay, *Herrschaftsantritt im Ungarn*, 197; ÖStA, HHStA, ZA Prot, 7, fol. 86v.
65. *Pontificale ecclesiae Coloniensis*, fol. 23v.
66. Barcsay, *Herrschaftsantritt im Ungarn*, 196–99.
67. "Sta et retine amodo locum tibi a Deo delegatum per auctoritatem omnipotentis Dei": *Pontificale Romanum*, 143.
68. Esztergom Primate Archives, Archivum Ecclesiasticum Vetus, 375, no. 5, p. 25. Unfortunately, only the incipits that are identical in both versions are provided by the author of the transcript: "Sta et retine amodo locum tuum [sic]."
69. ÖStA, HHStA, ZA Prot, 18, fol. 287r; Decsy, *A' magyar szent koronának*, 571; *Naponként-való jegyzései az 1792-dik esztendőben Felséges Ferentz . . . király által szab. kir. városába Budára pünkösd havának 20. napjára rendelt . . . .* (Buda, 1792), 65.
70. *Pontificale ecclesiae Coloniensis*, fol. 36v–37r.
71. Barcsay, *Herrschaftsantritt im Ungarn*, 203.
72. *Naponként-való jegyzései . . . Felséges IIdik Leopold*, 235; OSZKK Fol. Lat. 658/I. fol. 425r.
73. Bartoniek, *A magyar király-koronázások*, 139.

Bibliography

Barcsay, Ákos. *Herrschaftsantritt im Ungarn des 18. Jahrhunderts: Studien zum Verhältnis zwischen Krongewalt und Ständetum im Zeitalter des Absolutismus*. St. Katharinen: Scripta Mercaturae Verlag, 2002.

Bartoniek, Emma. *A magyar király-koronázások története*. Budapest: Magyar Történelmi Társulat, Akadémiai Kiadó, Reprint Series, 1987.

Beales, Derek. *Joseph II: Against the World 1780–1790*. Cambridge, UK: Cambridge University Press, 2009.

Bérenger, Jean, and Charles Kecskeméti. *Parlement et vie parlementaire en Hongrie 1608–1918*. Paris: Honoré Champion, 2005.

Decsy, Sámuel. *A' magyar szent koronának és az ahoz tartozó tárgyaknak históriája, mellyet sok régi és újjább írásokból ki jegyzett, rendbe szedett, meg világosított, 's kedves Hazafiainak hasznokra közönségessé tett*. Budapest: Kossuth, 2008.

Forgó, András, ed. "Acta et observata penes diaetam Hungaricam Posonii celebratam, item coronationem domini Caroli VI ibidem peractam anno 1712. per patrem Engelbertum Hermann professum Velehradensem, qua plenipotentiatum ablegatum reverendissimi domini Floriani abbatis." In *Az 1712. évi pozsonyi diéta egy ciszterci szerzetes szemével*, 179–272. Pannonhalma: Pannonhalmi Főapátsági Levéltár, A Magyar Nemzeti Levéltár Veszprém Megyei Levéltára, 2013.

———. "Zu den Möglichkeiten und Grenzen ständisch-politischer Handlungsfähigkeit: Das Beispiel des Herrschaftsantritts Karls VI. im Königreich Ungarn." In *Wiener Archivforschungen: Festschrift für den ungarischen Archivdelegierten in Wien, István Fazekas*, ed. Zsuzsanna Cziráki, Anna Fundárková, Orsolya Manhercz, Zsuzsanna Peres, and Márta Vajnági, 263–69. Vienna: Institut für Ungarische Geschichtsforschung, Balassi Institut—Collegium Hungaricum, and Ungarische Archivdelegation beim Haus-, Hof- und Staatsarchiv, 2014.

Fügedi, Erik. "A magyar király koronázásának rendje a középkorban." In *Eszmetörténeti tanulmányok a magyar középkorról*, ed. György Székely, 255–73. Budapest: Akadémiai, 1984.

———. *Uram, királyom . . . : a XV. századi Magyarország hatalmasai*. Budapest: Gondolat, 1974.

Gerics, József. "Az úgynevezett Egbert (Dunstan)-ordo alkalmazásáról a XI. századi Magyarországon (Salamon koronázásának előadása a krónikákban)." In *Eszmetörténeti tanulmányok a magyar középkorról*, ed. György Székely, 243–54. Budapest: Akadémiai, 1984.

Hende, Fanni. "Újabb bécsi kitérő: A Szent Korona a Rákóczi-szabadságharc idején, 1703–1712." *Rubicon* 29, no. 7–8 (2018): 78–85.

Kovachich, Márton György. *Solennia inauguralia serenissimorum ac potentissimorum principium utriusque sexus, qui ex augusta stirpe Habspurgo-Austriaca sacra corona apostolica in reges Hungarorum, reginasque periodo tertia redimiti sunt*. Pest: Typis Matthiae Trattner, 1790.

Kulcsár, Krisztina. "Ein fremder Adeliger zwischen der Königin und den ungarischen Ständen: Der Lebenslauf von Prinz Albert von Sachsen bis 1765 und seine Ernennung zum Statthalter des Königreichs Ungarn." In *Adel im "langen" 18. Jahrhundert*, ed. Gabriele Haug-Moritz, Hans Peter Hye, and Marlies Raffler, 275–88. Vienna: Österreichische Akademie der Wissenschaften, 2009.

Lauter, Éva. "'Modus observandus . . .' A 17. századi magyar nádorválasztások rendje." In *Portré és imázs: Politikai propaganda és reprezentáció a kora újkorban*, ed. Nóra G. Etényi and Ildikó Horn, 187–206. Budapest: L'Harmattan, 2008.

Marczali, Henrik. *Az 1790/1-diki országgyűlés*. 2 vols. Budapest: Magyar Tudományos Akadémia, 1907.
Mezey, Barna. *A Rákóczi szabadságharc országgyűlései*. Budapest: Eötvös Loránd Tudományegyetem Magyar Állam- és Jogtörténeti Tanszéke, 1981.
Nagy, István. "II. József reformjai Budán." *Tanulmányok Budapest múltjából* 15 (1963): 363–402.
Naponként-való jegyzései az 1792-dik esztendőben Felséges Ferentz . . . király által szab. kir. városába Budára pünkösd havának 20. napjára rendelt . . . . Buda: n.p., 1792.
Naponként-való jegyzései az 1790-dik esztendőben Felséges IIdik Leopold Tsászár, és Magyar Országi Király Által . . . Magyar Országgyűlésének. Buda: n.p., 1791.
Pálffy, Géza. "Hazatérés Prágából, 1608." *Rubicon* 29, no. 7–8 (2018): 40–49.
———. *The Kingdom of Hungary and the Habsburg Monarchy in the Sixteenth Century*. New York: Columbia University Press, 2009.
———. "A korona Bethlen Gábor birtokában, 1619–1622." *Rubicon* 29, no. 7–8 (2018): 50–57.
———. "A legkevésbé ismert hazatérés: A Szent Korona Bécsben, 1663–1664." *Rubicon* 29, no. 7–8 (2018): 58–67.
———. "Menekítés német földre, 1683–1687." *Rubicon* 29, no. 7–8 (2018): 68–77.
———. "Nádasdy Tamás nádor a magyar királyok koronázási szertartásáról (1561)." In *Szolgálatomat ajánlom a 60 éves Jankovics Józsefnek*, ed. Tünde Császtvay and Judit Nyerges, 305–10. Budapest: Balassi Kiadó and Magyar Tudományos Akadémia Irodalomtudományi Intézet, 2009.
———. "Návrh uhorských radcov na bratislavský korunovačný ceremoniál z roku 1561: Doteraz neznámy zásadný prameň k uhorským kráľovským korunováciám." *Historicky Casopis* 54, no. 2 (2006): 201–16.
Pontificale Romanum Clementis VIII. ac Urbani VIII. auctoritate recognitum et ad plurium usum, in commodiorem formam redactum. Venice: n.p., 1722.
Soós, István. "A Szent Korona diadalmenete Bécstől Budáig, 1790." *Rubicon* 29, no. 7–8 (2018): 86–99.
Stollberg-Rilinger, Barbara. *The Emperor's Old Clothes: Constitutional History and the Symbolic Language of the Holy Roman Empire*. New York: Berghahn Books, 2015.
Szijártó, István M. *A diéta: A magyar rendek és az országgyűlés 1708–1792*. Keszthely: Balaton Akadémia, 2010.
———. "The Diet: The Estates and the Parliament of Hungary, 1708–1792." In *Bündnispartner und Konkurrenten des Landesfürsten? Die Stände in der Habsburgermonarchie*, ed. Gerhard Ammerer, William D. Godsey Jr., Martin Scheutz, Peter Urbanitsch, and Alfred Stefan Weiß, 151–71. Vienna: R. Oldenbourg Verlag, 2007.
———. "The Rákóczi Revolt as a Successful Rebellion." In *Resistance, Rebellion and Revolution in Hungary and Central Europe: Commemorating 1956*, ed. László Péter and Martyn Rady, 67–76. London: Hungarian Cultural Centre London, 2008.
Tubero, Ludovicus Cervarius. *Commentaria suorum temporum*. Raguza: n.p., 1784.
Vajnági, Márta. "Koronázás a Német-római Birodalomban és Magyarországon a kora újkorban." *Világtörténet* 36, no. 4 (2014): 267–93.

Chapter 4

Maria Theresa, the Habsburgs, and the Hungarian Coronations in the Light of the Coronation Medals, 1687–1741

Werner Telesko

In her multiple roles as archduchess of Austria, "king"[1] of Hungary, "king" of Bohemia, and wife of Emperor Francis Stephen, Maria Theresa (1717–80) offers a unique point of departure for exploring coronations. She also raises a crucial question: namely, in what ways could the acts of sovereigns and symbolic representations of their rule—especially coronation medals in the context of this chapter[2]—compensate certain deficiencies in their ability to impose the authority and legitimacy of their sovereignty? Maria Theresa became heir to the throne upon the death of her father, Emperor Charles VI, in 1740. Politically, she stood on somewhat shaky ground for two reasons: Firstly, the European powers had been extremely reluctant to recognize the Habsburg Pragmatic Sanction without demanding significant concessions in return (and some of them would eventually renege on it later). Secondly, Frederick II of Prussia had invaded Silesia in the same year. This situation threatened the very existence of the monarchy, and Vienna felt obliged to respond in a wide variety of ways and with all the means at its disposal.

Few other women during the early modern period fulfilled such a remarkable number of overlapping, and in part contradictory, private and political roles (mother, consort, archduchess, "king," queen, and widow) as Maria Theresa. She evidently possessed an exceptional "flexibility of identities,"[3] and her potential for identification and representation cannot be reduced to a limited, programmatic repertoire stage-managed by herself or her "image producers." Instead, her position was more of a shrewd combination of "overlapping subject positions of sovereign, empress, mother, and widow."[4] This circumstance undoubtedly makes the task of accurately defining justification strategies even more difficult. Nevertheless, from an overall perspective, it suggests that the representation of Maria Theresa is perhaps more fruitfully grasped in complementary terms. Different strategies were used at different times, and they form an accurate picture only when viewed in their totality, not individually—especially from our present point of view.[5]

This chapter focuses on Maria Theresa's Hungarian coronation, which took place in Pressburg on 25 June 1741, as seen through the lens of a particular medium: the coronation medals. Since the Habsburgs had been the kings of Hungary for centuries, these medals offer an ideal basis for comparative analysis of statements relating to the dynasty's self-image, implemented across the various artistic genres on the occasion of Maria Theresa's coronation. This comparison forms the central methodological approach of this chapter.

On the one hand, coronation medals can claim a considerable range of distribution; on the other, however, next to nothing is known about the specific intentions of the producers of such medals—in contrast to the activities of the Imperial Coin Cabinet.[6] Surprisingly, virtually no evidence of discussions about the design of pictorial representations and inscriptions of the respective medals can be found in the corresponding archives of the court and the Imperial Mint. This is all the more puzzling since it is the inscriptions on the medals in particular that offer important interpretations and summaries of the coronation scene in the form of concise texts. In addition to the medal minters commissioned by the court, medal makers in the free imperial cities of Augsburg and Nuremberg should also be included in these considerations, since the latter were free entrepreneurs and thus not bound by the directives of the Viennese court. Instead, they were able offer their own inventions on the free market, just like contemporaneous copper engravers in Augsburg and Nuremberg.

This chapter will examine how such coronation medals can provide valuable information about the specific way in which the Habsburgs viewed the role and significance of Maria Theresa's Hungarian coronation in June 1741. As is also the case with other Habsburg coronations, this aspect has not been examined in sufficient depth until now. Yet it is highly relevant, since medals can be considered the artistic medium that presumably reflects the rite of the coronation most directly. This applies to the use of the so-called *Auswurfmünzen* ("thrown" or distributed coronation coins) on the one hand, which were themselves a fixed part of the coronation ceremony. On the other, it also recognizes the fact that the iconography of medals frequently referred to certain acts of the coronation ceremony—in the context of the Hungarian coronation, for example, the famous sword strokes performed in all four cardinal directions by the newly crowned Hungarian ruler on the coronation hill as a visible sign that the country, under the reign of the new king, was prepared to defend itself against all its enemies.[7] While the coronation is symbolically intensified in the context of medals by ingenious combinations of texts and images in the form of emblems, the primary goal of the producers of graphic prints depicting coronation events was a reportage-like rendition of the coronation ceremony in its temporal processes. A different focus is applied to the structure of the reported events in each case, since the intended reproduction of the full sequence of a coronation, as can be observed especially in engravings and etchings, must be viewed in contrast to the emblematic symbolism of the medals. The sheer diversity of the media employed—paintings, frescoes, prints, engravings, and medals—corresponded to an increasingly functional differentiation of the self-image of the rulers in the age of enlightened absolutism. Different genres of art thus had different purposes to fulfill as far as depictions of the broad spectrum of monarchic representation were concerned.

Far too little is known to this day about the creators of medals in terms of their education, relationships, commissioning, and procurement.[8] The surviving distribution lists consigned to the court archives since the coronation of Charles VI[9] provide information about the mid- and high-ranking noble recipients of the distributed coins and medals, which generally came in two different sizes and types of metal embossing (silver and gold). Prince Charles Alexander of Lorraine (1712–80), for example, received twelve medals in gold (six large and six small) and thirty-six in silver (twelve large and twenty-four small) on the occasion of Maria Theresa's Hungarian coronation.[10] The lists also indicate the corresponding quantities and clearly illustrate that a fixed circle of privileged clients were to be quickly provided with a specific and memorable visual interpretation of current events by means of these artifacts.[11] In addition, and unlike the case of virtually any other Habsburg ruler, the era of Maria Theresa also witnessed a carefully orchestrated dissemination of her portraits and currency, with medals playing an important role here as well—according to the accounts in the records of the *Hofkammerzahlamt* (court office of the exchequer), which list the gifts produced by order of the emperor,[12] the preferred artistic genre were precious items decorated with gemstones and often featuring the mottos of the regents. Specifically, these objects included coins and medals, pectoral crosses, *Gnadenpfennige* respectively *-medaillen* ("mercy" medals and chains with portraits), snuffboxes, rings, and receptacles. They were gifted by the court to a remarkable range of recipients, from holders of high court offices and diplomats (above all, Habsburg representatives) to musicians and rectors and even private individuals, for example as a way of marking anniversaries of service. Maria Theresa never handed out these art objects by way of a personal act, but instead symbolically, as it were—with the obvious intended side effect of deepening ties between the giver and the respective recipients.[13]

The medals were generally catalogued, but were also described and interpreted on separate explanatory prints, a circumstance that provides an ideal opportunity to trace the different stages of interpretation and historicization of this medium. Archduchess Maria Anna (1738–89), one of Maria Theresa's daughters with an interest in numismatics, may potentially have been responsible for the publication of *Schau- und Denkmünzen, welche unter der glorwürdigen Regierung der Kaiserinn Maria Theresia gepräget worden sind* (Vienna, 1782). More likely, however, it was the Piarist Adauctus Voigt (1733–87) who took the initiative for this rich compendium ranging from the birth medal to the death medal for Maria Theresa. It has fortunately survived and represents a virtually complete history, including (commentary) text and images, of the empress's rule in the sense that it is an *histoire métallique*—even though the Habsburgs had never verifiably conceived such a history, unlike the efforts undertaken by Louis XIV, the "sun king." When the mintages are perused in their entirety as an iconography of Maria Theresa, one notices that the visual representations gathered in this digest of events during the regency of the ruler cannot be found in other artistic genres. Hence, the medal assumes a special, indeed unique, position in which the specific design of each minting had to meet the challenge of imparting complex content meaningfully in a small format.

Consequently, if the intention is to present certain "images" of coronations with an exceptionally wide range of distribution and high density of content, then we should take medals into consideration first and foremost. At the same time, it should also be emphasized that there was commonly not just a single minting of medals to mark a given historical event. Instead, there were usually several, and they differed considerably from each other in their statements. For the reasons outlined above, such medals can be considered an artistic genre of political iconography par excellence—and this is particularly true for the 1740s, since the diverse strategies relating to the visualization of the claim to preservation of the Habsburg dynasty and its position of power in Europe following the death of Emperor Charles VI (1740) grew significantly in importance. Precisely because of the painful awareness of the difficult defense of Habsburg sovereignty in the War of the Austrian Succession, all resources—including visual ones—had to be tapped to ensure that a serious fault line such as the one existing in 1740 could never appear again. Iconographic flexibility was not only a catchword, but also almost a vital necessity during the eventful years after 1740 in order to politically survive the propaganda battles waged both in texts and in images.

Medals in particular were therefore an important means of conveying Habsburg legitimation strategies,[14] as indicated strikingly by a series minted in 1743 to commemorate Maria Theresa's coronation in Bohemia (see figure 4.1).[15] The inscription on the reverse takes the widespread ancient *topos* of the restoration of public happiness to the extreme (*FELICITATIS PVBL*[ICAE] *REPARATIO*), while the *typus* of a standing figure adapts the large-scale image of a ruler to the purposes of a small-scale medal. The depiction of the Bohemian coronation robe, the St. Wenceslas Crown, and the Austrian archducal hat placed on a pedestal once again tellingly emphasize Maria Theresa's multiple titles as a sovereign ruler.

Under the abovementioned circumstances, the newly acquired sovereignty could be—and had to be—made visible in different formats. Just how crucial the legal acts of the Hungarian and Bohemian coronations (1741 and 1743) were is illustrated by another medal struck in 1743:[16] on its reverse side, below a depiction of the Bohemian St. Wenceslas Crown, is an inscription whose German translation in the numismatic publication *Schau- und Denkmünzen* speaks of the "rightful heir to the Austrian crown," the "providential victor," and the "mother of the fatherland." Pivotal elements of the message to be conveyed, such as *LEGITIMA*, *VICTRIX*, and *MATER*, are deliberately emphasized in large capital letters. It also appeared expedient in this context to draw on the history of salvation to legitimize the Habsburg claim to the Bohemian crown. After all, it was an entirely legitimate claim from the Habsburg point of view. The reverse side of another medal[17] created to mark the Bohemian coronation[18] thus features the radiant triangle of God the Father, and below it the words: *HIER WAR LAENGST BEYGELEGT WAS SIE AUS ERBRECHT TRAEGT* ("Here [by God, W. T.] was long ago predestined what was hers by right of succession")—a characteristic passage intended to underscore the central role of divine providence with regard to the "chosen" Habsburg dynasty.[19]

Figure 4.1. Coronation medal for the Bohemian coronation of Maria Theresa, created by Anton Franz Widemann, reverse, 1743 (Vienna, Kunsthistorisches Museum, Coin Cabinet, inv. no. bß 1937; © Vienna, Kunsthistorisches Museum).

The Coronation of Maria Theresa

When Maria Theresa was crowned "king" of Hungary, great importance was attached to stressing historical continuities in a formal ceremony that was prepared in extensive detail. After all, as a female heir to the throne, she clearly had to demonstrate the legitimacy of her rule to the Hungarian magnates and foreign observers during the War of the Austrian Succession. Regarding the actual procedures of the coronation, Maria Theresa focused strictly on the templates of previous royal coronations—in particular those concerning the formal ceremony, which had applied since Maximilian II. Here, she stipulated that there should be only minimal deviations from the coronation ceremony for her father, Emperor Charles VI (1712).[20] To the Aulic Council's comments and questions regarding the procedures for the ceremony,[21] Maria Theresa replied tersely: "It is nothing new to follow the ceremony of the last coronation."[22] Nevertheless, the "male" crowning of a "female" ruler naturally caused confusion, and it was thus suggested that Maria Theresa should appear at the coronation with an imperial crown (*Hauß Cron*—i.e., the "Rudolphinian crown") on her head, as had been the case at her mother Elisabeth Christine's coronation in 1714. This proposal was rejected by the *Obersthofmeister* (grand master of the court), who argued that things had been handled differently at the coronations of Joseph I and Charles III (Charles VI) and reminded her: "Your royal majesty will be crowned not as queen consort, but as king."[23] In general, the essential difference between the two ceremonies was that Hungarian queens were not crowned with the Holy Crown of Hungary (the *Szent Korona*), which was merely held above their right shoulder during the anointing.[24] Eventually, the Aulic Council agreed to the proposal that Maria Theresa should "wear a finery in the form of a crown" on her way to St. Martin's Cathedral, which would be easy to remove prior to the coronation. Maria Theresa's opinion of this suggestion, however, is evident in her response: "This is easy to say for men, who have no idea of our finery."[25] She ultimately traveled to the coronation ceremony without wearing any headdress at all.

Since 1741 marked the year of Maria Theresa's Hungarian coronation, it can rightly be referred to as the "key year" of symbolic politics. It should be kept in mind, however, that the coronation and the *Reichstag* of 1741 in Pressburg became the subject of intensive debate shortly thereafter, a debate that all but established an imperative for commemoration of these influential events. A panegyric for Maria Theresa, *Der Allerdurchlauchtigst, Großmächtigst, und Unüberwindlichsten Königin, Heldin, und Frauen, Frauen Theresia*, written after 1743 by Friederich Wilhelm Wolßhofer (Friedrich Wilhelm Wolshofer), a priest from Ansbach (Franconia) who primarily had the Hungarians in mind, contained the following lines among others: "You truthful people! You belligerent blood! What your Hungary does this time, everyone will memorize."[26]

This (obviously rapid) consolidation of the events of June and September 1741 (Diet of Pressburg) in Hungarian and Habsburg memory culture also had repercussions on the production of medals. As is the case for many other events during Maria Theresa's reign, medals with different functions and designs also exist in commemoration of her coronation as "king" of Hungary in June 1741. The following pages will briefly present the relevant works, a significant number of which were created after the coronation—mainly in 1745. Their discussion will focus on iconographic and political strategies rather than numismatic aspects.

The so-called *Großer Opferpfennig* ("large offering pfennig")[27], preserved only in copies today since the unique original was "sacrificed" during the coronation festivities, resulted from a custom dating back to the kings of Hungary, who were to donate money at their coronations. On its obverse, it shows the Czech lion with the cross of the Hungarian patriarch and the Austrian striped escutcheon combined with Maria Theresa's motto, *IUSTITITA ET CLEMENTIA* (Justice and Clemency); on the reverse is the St. Stephen's Crown, held by two hovering angels and combined with the specification of the date of the coronation, 25 June 1741 (see figure 4.2).[28] Two smaller versions of this *Opferpfennig* were also minted.[29]

Figure 4.2. Coronation coin for the Hungarian coronation of Maria Theresa, reverse, 1741 (Vienna, Kunsthistorisches Museum, Coin Cabinet, inv. no. bß 1881; © Vienna, Kunsthistorisches Museum).

The front side of a medal created by Matthäus Donner (and Anton Franz Widemann), presumably minted in 1745 and described as an *andere Gedächtnismedaille* ("another commemoration medal") in the abovementioned numismatic work *Schau- und Denkmünzen* (see figure 4.3),[30] depicts a half-length profile portrait of the regent. On its reverse, we see the well-known scene of Maria Theresa's ride onto the coronation hill in Pressburg, where she pointed her sword in all four directions to symbolize the defense of Hungary. The accompanying text below the image refers to the royal anointing on 25 June, and the text at the top to an all-encompassing title of honor: *APOSTOLICI REGNI HONORIFICENTIA*. This is translated as *Ehrenzeichen des apostolischen Reichs* (mark of honor of the apostolic empire) in *Schau- und Denkmünzen*.[31] Earlier, in the third part of Christoph Gottlieb Richter's biography of Maria Theresa (1745), the phrase used is "the Splendor of the Kingdom of Hungary" in an obvious reference to a description

Figure 4.3. Coronation medal for the Hungarian coronation of Maria Theresa created by Anton Franz Widemann, reverse, 1745 (Vienna, Kunsthistorisches Museum, Coin Cabinet, inv. no. bß 1886; © Vienna, Kunsthistorisches Museum).

by the scholar and antiquarian Johann Carl Edler Neuen von Neuenstein (Newen von Newenstein, 1683–1767).[32] Moreover, Richter's biography states that the regent appeared like "an amazon on horseback devoted to God and virtue"[33] during her ride up the coronation hill; there is a clear allusion here to Hungary's well-known role as *antemurale Christianitatis*.[34] The reference to the explanatory print by Johann Carl Edler Neuen von Neuenstein (see figure 4.4)[35] in Richter's description is an instructive example of how plausible interpretations of medals were rapidly disseminated. After all, Neuen von Neuenstein emphasizes—as does Richter in his biography—the "male" virtues of Maria Theresa and praises his sovereign, the amazon on horseback, as a great and wondrous heroine who would defend her paternal heritage like a man.

The term *honorificentia* actually means "tribute" or "homage" as well as "dignity," respectively "fiefdom" (and the dignity it merited), thereby allowing various different interpretations.[36] To this day, it remains unclear whether the glory and honor expressed in the words *APOSTOLICI REGNI HONORIFICENTIA* refer to Hungary, the St. Stephen's Crown, or Maria Theresa. The text also alludes to St. Stephen of Hungary himself, who was awarded the title of Apostolic Majesty by Pope Silvester II in 1001. It was to play a concrete role for Maria Theresa later on as well, since she received the same title of Apostolic Majesty with the pope's consent in 1758.[37] Finally, it also expressed the idea of regarding the Habsburg apostolic king as the true head of the Church of the *regnum Apostolicum*.

And as if this were not enough, it is certainly striking that the term *honorificentia* rarely ever appeared on medals in other contexts. A further specific tradition that likewise implies a Marian dimension of meaning may help to clarify matters here: as part of the *Lob- und Danck-Rede* (speech of laudation and thanks) held by the Jesuit Franciscus Peikhart on 29 June 1741 on the occasion of her Hungarian coronation in Vienna's St. Stephen's Cathedral,[38] Maria Theresa was ultimately presented as a new incarnation of the Old Testament heroine Judith. Among other things, the speech quoted literally from the Book of Judith (15:10), where Judith is praised by her people after accomplishing her heroic deed: *Tu gloria Jerusalem! Tu laetitita Israel! Tu honorificentia populi nostri!*[39] This is no isolated case, as the professed house of the Society of Jesus in Vienna was decorated with the very same Old Testament verse four years later as part of the so-called *Wiennerische Beleuchtungen* celebrating the birth of Archduke Charles.[40] *Tu honorificentia populi nostri* had already become customary as an antiphon sung during the feast of *Maria Immaculata* on 8 December. Maria Theresa's adoration of the Virgin Mary was evidenced *inter alia* when she stopped in front of the Marian column her grandfather Leopold I had had erected on Pressburg's main square before continuing on her way to the Franciscan church as the newly crowned "king" on 25 June 1741.[41]

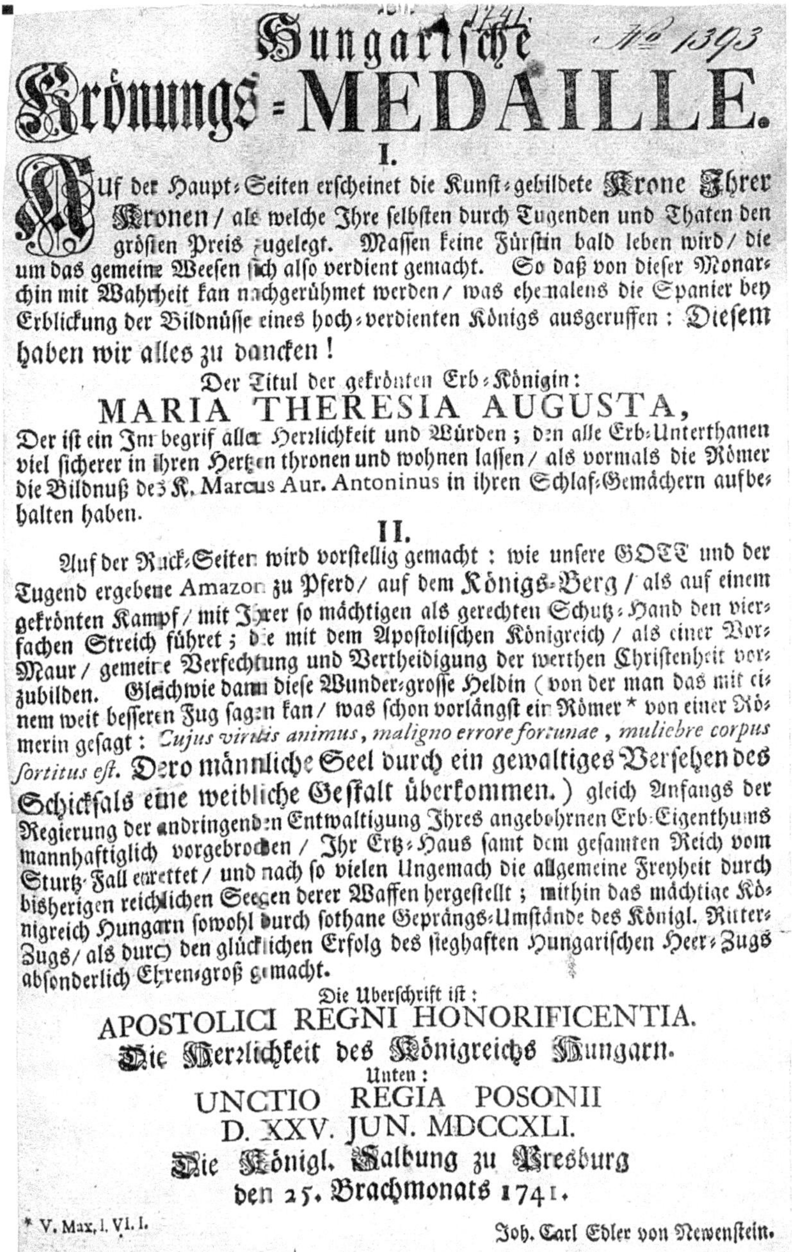

Hungarische Krönungs-MEDAILLE.

I.

Auf der Haupt-Seiten erscheinet die Kunst-gebildete Krone Ihrer Kronen/ als welche Ihre selbsten durch Tugenden und Thaten den grösten Preis zugelegt. Massen keine Fürstin bald leben wird/ die um das gemeine Weesen sich also verdient gemacht. So daß von dieser Monarchin mit Wahrheit kan nachgerühmet werden/ was ehemalens die Spanier bey Erblickung der Bildnüsse eines hoch-verdienten Königs ausgeruffen: Diesem haben wir alles zu dancken!

Der Titul der gekrönten Erb-Königin:

MARIA THERESIA AUGUSTA,

Der ist ein Inbegrif aller Herrlichkeit und Würden; den alle Erb-Unterthanen viel sicherer in ihren Hertzen thronen und wohnen lassen/ als vormals die Römer die Bildnuß des K. Marcus Aur. Antoninus in ihren Schlaf-Gemächern aufbehalten haben.

II.

Auf der Ruck-Seiten wird vorstellig gemacht: wie unsere GOTT und der Tugend ergebene Amazon zu Pferd/ auf dem Königs-Berg / als auf einem gekrönten Kampf/ mit Ihrer so mächtigen als gerechten Schutz-Hand den vierfachen Streich führet; die mit dem Apostolischen Königreich / als einer Vormaur / gemeine Verfechtung und Vertheidigung der werthen Christenheit vorzubilden. Gleichwie dann diese Wunder-grosse Heldin (von der man das mit einem weit besseren Fug sagen kan/ was schon vorlängst ein Römer* von einer Römerin gesagt: *Cujus virilis animus, maligno errore fortunae, muliebre corpus sortitus est.* Dero männliche Seel durch ein gewaltiges Versehen des Schicksals eine weibliche Gestalt überkommen.) gleich Anfangs der Regierung der andringenden Entwaltigung Ihres angebohrnen Erb-Eigenthums mannhaftiglich vorgebrochen / Ihr Ertz-Haus samt dem gesamten Reich vom Sturtz-Fall errettet / und nach so vielen Ungemach die allgemeine Freyheit durch bisherigen reichlichen Seegen derer Waffen hergestellt; mithin das mächtige Königreich Hungarn sowohl durch sothane Gepräng-Umstände des Königl. Ritter-Zugs/ als durch den glücklichen Erfolg des sieghaften Hungarischen Heer-Zugs absonderlich Ehren-groß gemacht.

Die Überschrift ist:

APOSTOLICI REGNI HONORIFICENTIA.

Die Herrlichkeit des Königreichs Hungarn.

Unten:

UNCTIO REGIA POSONII D. XXV. JUN. MDCCXLI.

Die Königl. Salbung zu Presburg den 25. Brachmonats 1741.

* V. Max, l. VI. l.

Joh. Carl Edler von Newenstein.

Figure 4.4. Numismatic explanatory print by Johann Carl Edler Neuen von Neuenstein, 1741 (Vienna, FHKA, Sonderbestände, Sammlungen und Selekte, Hauptmünzamt Wien, Akten, 12, no. 1393; © Vienna, Austrian State Archives).

If this reference to Judith, which ultimately represents a Marian formula of dignity from a typological perspective, deserves to be highlighted in the panegyric, then it also alludes to the tradition of Hungary as a *regnum marianum*, since the childless King Stephan was said to have dedicated his crown and country to the Blessed Virgin Mary. It is for this reason that we encounter Mary as patroness of Hungary on the reverse side of Hungarian thalers and ducats.[42] The design of the medal by Donner thus covered a wide range of arguments and pretensions ranging from the "real" event of the anointing and ride up the coronation hill in Pressburg through specific traditions—vital for Hungary—of the *regnum apostolicum et marianum* all the way to the Marian aspect, with Judith representing the Old Testament model of Mary.

The minting of this medal also continued an important iconographic tradition going back to Emperor Charles VI and his Hungarian coronation as Charles III in 1712.[43] In the image on her medal, the figure of Maria Theresa seems to imitate her father directly in the way she wields the sword on the coronation hill. Yet the corresponding medal struck for Charles VI[44] accentuates the same theme in a different manner: typically for the time, it combines the sword stroke with a quotation taken from Ovid's *Metamorphoses* (XII, 165 et seq.) and refers to the battle between Achilles and the seemingly invulnerable Cygnus. The ancient text reading *ferrumque terebat* and referring to Achilles's "iron" or sword becoming dulled, however, is rendered on the medal as *ferrumque tenebat*, with the replacement verb meaning "to hold." The purpose of this change was to make the holding of the "iron" (meaning the coronation sword) by the emperor the focus of the argument.

Another medal created by Bengt or Benedikt Richter[45] in 1712 to mark the Hungarian coronation of Charles VI also provided an important template for the era of Maria Theresa, since it featured—not unlike the empress's *Opferpfennig* discussed above—the St. Stephen's Crown held by angels as a corresponding motif on its reverse side. Evidently, this distinctive emphasis on the St. Stephen's Crown on medals referred to traditions lying further back in the past, such as the Hungarian coronation of Emperor Ferdinand II (1618).[46] From this we can deduce that some of the most important elements of the iconography of the Hungarian coronation were the insignia themselves, based on a belief in the special dignity of the Holy Crown as a symbol of power. A description of the Hungarian coronation published in 1741, for example, boldly claimed that few other nations worshipped their royal crown with greater respect than the Hungarians. In this context, an excursus may serve to illustrate how the purportedly sacred origin of the St. Stephen's Crown ("as a treasure fallen from the sky")[47] was supposed to symbolize the alleged association of the secular and celestial kingdoms so as to demonstrate the extraordinary nature of the Kingdom of Hungary and the coronation ceremony.

Maria Theresa's sword strokes on the coronation hill also provided the motif for a medal described as a *Schaumünze* (exhibition coin) created by Andreas Vestner from Nuremberg and presumably minted in 1745 (see figure 4.5).[48] The reverse side of this medal depicts the regent pointing her sword while flanked by two putti who appear to be offering a commentary in that the one on the left is holding the Hungarian coat of arms and the one on the right, a palm leaf and olive branch. One might be tempted to think that this merely signifies the continuation of a traditional motif, but a significant new point of emphasis can be found especially in the semantic content of the text at the top: *NEC PRISCIS REGIBVS IMPAR*. This motto, which represents a new invention in linguistic, though not in substantive terms, simply means that Maria Theresa was not dissimilar to her ancestors in her exercise of the royal office. By implication, she was on a par with them or their equal. On the one hand, the aim here was to evoke the notion of Habsburg continuity, as can already be seen in the medals minted under her father Charles VI. On the other hand, it incorporates and appropriately varies one of the most famous mottos of the *histoire métallique*, namely that of King Louis XIV, *NEC PLURIBIS IMPAR*.[49] In both the First and Second Silesian Wars, France supported Prussia, which used the Bourbon motto to celebrate King Frederick II's victorious battle of Roßbach against the French at the beginning of the Seven Years' War (1757).[50] By adapting the famous motto of the "sun king," the Habsburgs introduced a particularly acute political dimension, since the altered motto implied a cer-

Figure 4.5. Coronation medal for the Hungarian coronation of Maria Theresa, created by Andreas Vestner of Nuremberg, reverse, 1745 (Vienna, Kunsthistorisches Museum, Coin Cabinet, inv. no. bß 1889; © Vienna, Kunsthistorisches Museum).

Figure 4.6. Coronation medal for the Hungarian coronation of Emperor Joseph I created by Georg Hautsch and Lazar Gottlieb Lauffer, reverse, 1687 (Vienna, Kunsthistorisches Museum, Coin Cabinet, inv. no. bß 1260; © Vienna, Kunsthistorisches Museum).

tain denigration of their political opponent.⁵¹ Furthermore, the semantic emphasis shifted from *pluribus* to *priscis*; and as a result, the focus was once again placed on incorporating tradition as described above. In this case, the intention was to elevate Maria Theresa to the same lofty status enjoyed by former members of the House of Habsburg in their capacity as kings of Hungary. The adjective *priscus* was specifically selected to convey the sense of "venerable" for good reason: Nuremberg's medal minter Vestner worked for the Habsburgs on the basis of a constantly renewed privilege,⁵² yet ultimately with his own inventions and also for his own account. Although the exact production date of this medal remains unclear (possibly 1745), it seems practically inconceivable that such a subtle strategy in regard to the subject matter could have been pursued without obtaining consent from the Viennese court beforehand.⁵³

The Coronation of Joseph I

Whereas the establishment of the Habsburg tradition was achieved through the use of visual genres and inscriptions on the medals presented above, the example of a medal commemorating the Hungarian coronation of the later emperor Joseph I in Pressburg in 1687 (see figure 4.6)⁵⁴ shows the extent to which such strategies were already deeply rooted in the House of Habsburg some sixty years earlier—despite being realized using different visual media than the ones employed during the era of Maria Theresa. The reverse side of this medal by Georg Hautsch and Lazar Gottlieb Lauffer depicts Joseph's father, Emperor Leopold I, handing the St. Stephen's Crown to his son, who is already holding the imperial orb in his right hand. This act is underscored by the biblical legitimation of the narrative concerning the death of Jacob, in which the dying patriarch says to Joseph (Genesis 48:22): *do tibi partem unam extra fratres tuos quam tuli de manu Amorrei in gladio et arcu meo* ("Moreover I have given to thee one portion above thy brethren, which I took out of the hand of the Amorite with my sword and with my bow").⁵⁵ Here, the biblical quote undergoes a political reinterpretation since the deliberate omissions compared to the Vulgate text shift the thematic emphasis to the assertion that Emperor Leopold I was now passing on the Hungary he had wrested from the Ottomans (*tuli de manu hostis*) to his son Joseph. Against this background of the Bible, the conferral of the crown is clearly portrayed as a process. The reference in this case—as well as in other examples of Habsburg propaganda—was to the biblical theme of the "Egyptian" Joseph, due to the similarity to the name of Archduke Joseph.

The impressive military successes of the Habsburgs over the Ottomans at the time prompted the Estates at the Diet of Pressburg to crown Joseph the first hereditary king of Hungary on 9 December 1687.⁵⁶ Moreover, the Hungarians pledged to henceforth crown the heir during his father's lifetime and at the same time waived their rights to resist and to object. This fundamental change in Hungarian history also serves as a connector to the events of 1741, when the opinion expressed by certain political groups in Hungary was that with the death of King Charles III (Charles VI) without a male heir, Hungary had regained the right to freely elect its king, even though the Hungarian Diet had actually accepted the Habsburg Pragmatic Sanction in 1722–23.[57] But this initiative launched by the (Protestant) delegates from eastern Hungary failed to secure a majority in the diet, as did the somewhat bizarre proposal that the royal throne of Hungary be offered to the Prussian king. Since the Viennese court explicitly insisted in 1741 that the privileges of the Hungarian aristocracy would remain unaffected by a female Habsburg succession, the majority of the members of the Hungarian Diet were quickly prepared to relinquish their right to choose a new Hungarian king in favor of supporting Maria Theresa.

Nevertheless, this did not mark the end of the problematic history of Maria Theresa's coronations. On 21 August 1745, the Aulic Council convened in Vienna to discuss the imperial coronation of Francis Stephen, which had been scheduled for 4 October, and to agree upon the appropriate ceremony and protocol. It was duly noted that a set of imperial regalia would have to be made for Maria Theresa's coronation should she request this. The appearance of such vestments needed to be determined in advance, however, so that the commemorative medals could depict the imperial couple in their proper regalia. At this point in the proceedings, Maria Theresa made the handwritten remark: "I do not want to be crowned."[58] Her decision entailed further problems for the Aulic Council due to her rank as reigning "king" of Hungary and Bohemia: during the procession into Frankfurt, it would be impossible for her to sit next to the emperor in the carriage or to participate in the coronation banquet as his wife, as this would mean assuming a subordinate rank to Francis Stephen. Such a situation would not be feasible, the Aulic Council argued, "the more so as Her Royal Majesty was to be regarded not as the consort of a king of the Romans or emperor but as a crowned king in Hungary and Bohemia." Her role as wife was thus subordinate to her political roles. Moreover, her royal dignity should also be expressed in her regalia. Since she already bore "two king's crowns on her sanctified head,"[59] the Aulic Council recommended that she wear either Bohemian or Hungarian dress while wearing the respective other crown on her head. This was an unconventional proposal, but the Aulic Council nevertheless asked Maria Theresa to announce her choice of dress well ahead of time so that the coronation medals could be minted appropriately. The empress eventually decided not to take part in the festivities at all and remain incognito. Just like Francis Stephen had done in Pressburg in 1741, she too found herself watching the Frankfurt coronation procession from the sidelines—or rather, from a small window next to the *Römersaal*.[60]

Conclusion

This chapter—which should be understood as a case study *in nummis*—provides the first ever comprehensive overview of the design, iconography, and distribution of medals created for the occasion of the coronation of a very prominent Habsburg ruler. Consequently, it sheds light on the intrinsic medial value of this frequently underrated artistic genre and clarifies its role in the politics of dynastic history.

Considerations on the significance of medals commemorating the Hungarian coronation of Maria Theresa (1741) show in what ways the extremely complex range of ceremonial events was implemented in highly memorable types of images: on the one hand, the traditional rite of the four sword strokes by the newly crowned regent plays a central role in this regard; on the other, we note that the use of passages from biblical or mythological texts in works of art—not just on medals—significantly declined during the era of Maria Theresa. This latter circumstance resulted in an increased importance of pictorial representations.

Even so, it would be wrong to interpret the production of medals merely as an illustrative response to the ceremony of the Pressburg coronation in 1741. In their texts and images, these medals formulate clearly independent levels of interpretation of the political scene in Pressburg, even though the authors of the underlying concepts can only rarely be identified. In essence, it seems reasonable to conclude that the various coronation medals had the function of underscoring precisely those significant aspects of the Habsburgs' ideological strategies for domination that would otherwise have been neglected in the media coverage of Maria Theresa's Hungarian coronation. Above all, these aspects include the continuity of the exercise of power following the death of Maria Theresa's father Charles VI in 1740 as well as the emphasis on Habsburg rule in Hungary, which had endured at least since 1526.

In fact there existed no other visual media for the coronation in 1741 representing the same rank and intellectual refinement as the coronation medals. This is the principal difference to the Bohemian coronation of 1743, on the occasion of which lavishly furnished publications like Johann Heinrich Ramhoffsky's *Drei Beschreibungen: erstens des königlichen Einzugs* . . . [of Maria Theresa] appeared.[61]

The medals minted for the crowning of Maria Theresa in Hungary provided an impressive representation—in pointedly iconographic form—of the importance of Hungary for the Habsburgs at the time. In addition, the considerable efforts made for the conception and production of such varied medals emphasize the exceptional significance of the Hungarian coronation. As a result, the specifically political relevance or message conveyed through the medium of medals is primarily and ingeniously expressed in its pronounced support for the Habsburg concept of dynastic and sovereign continuity during a crucial political year—after all, the overall future of the imperial dynasty hung in a precarious balance in 1741.

Werner Telesko is a senior researcher and group leader at the *Institut für die Erfoschung der Habsburgermonarchie und des Balkanraumes* (Institute for Habsburg and Balkan Studies) of the Austrian Academy of Sciences in Vienna. He studied and received his doctorate (1993) and post-doctoral teaching qualification (Habilitation 2000) in art history at the University of Vienna, served as director of the IKM (Institute for History of Art and Musicology) between 2013 and 2017 and as guest curator for the exhibition *Europa in Wien: Der Wiener Kongress 1814/15* [Europe in Vienna: The Congress of Vienna 1814/15] (Belvedere, Vienna 2015), and has written numerous publications on Austrian art history of the early modern period and the nineteenth century. Recent book publications include *Maria Theresia: Ein europäischer Mythos* [*Maria Theresa: A European Legend*] (Vienna, 2012); *Kosmos Barock: Architektur—Ausstattung—Spiritualität. Die Stiftskirche Melk* [*The Universe of the Baroque: Architecture—Furnishing—Spirituality. Melk Abbey*] (Vienna, 2013).

Notes

1. Cf. Eduard Holzmair, "Maria Theresia als Trägerin 'männlicher' Titel: Eine numismatische Studie," *MIÖG* 72 (1964): 126–28. Given that the title of the Hungarian ruler referred to a male, the question whether Maria Theresa should be called *rex* or *regina* was already the subject of contemporary discussions: Carl Andreas Bel, *Vorläufige Antwort auf die von Herrn Johann David Köhler... zu Göttingen wider die Commentationem Historico-Criticam de Maria Hungariae Regina... gemachten Einwürffe* (Leipzig, 1743); *Johann David Köhlers im Jahr 1744 wöchentlich heraus gegebener historischer Münz-Belustigung Sechzehender Theil...* (Nuremberg, 1744), 418–19 (discussions in the context of the coronation coins issued and thrown to the populace from the carriage at the Bohemian coronation in 1743).
2. For a basic introduction to the function and significance of coronation medals, see Eduard Holzmair, "Die offiziellen österreichischen Krönungs- und Huldigungspfennige seit Kaiser Josef I.," *Jahrbuch der kunsthistorischen Sammlungen in Wien* 50 (1953): 199–210; Carolyn A. Edie, "The Public Face of Royal Ritual: Sermons, Medals, and Civic Ceremony in Later Stuart Coronations," *Huntington Library Quarterly* 53, no. 4 (1990): 311–36; for summaries dealing with coronation coins, see Torsten Fried, *Geprägte Macht: Münzen und Medaillen der mecklenburgischen Herzöge als Zeichen fürstlicher Herrschaft* (Cologne, 2015), 102–3, note 62 (bibliography); Heinz Winter, "Auswurfprägungen: Eine Skizze," in *Feste feiern: 125 Jahre, Jubiläumsausstellung*, exhibition catalog Kunsthistorisches Museum Vienna, ed. Sabine Haag and Gudrun Swoboda (Vienna, 2016), 257.
3. Michael Yonan, *Empress Maria Theresa and the Politics of Habsburg Imperial Art* (University Park, 2011), 31.
4. Yonan, *Empress Maria Theresa*, 187.
5. Werner Telesko, *Maria Theresia: Ein europäischer Mythos* (Vienna, 2012); Telesko, "Herrschaftssicherung mittels visueller Repräsentation: Zur Porträtkultur Maria Theresias," in *Höfische Porträtkultur: Die Bildnissammlung der österreichischen Erzherzogin Maria Anna (1738–1789)*, ed. Eva Kernbauer and Aneta Zahradnik (Berlin, 2016), 37–47.

6. For a summary of the history of the Imperial Coin Cabinet during the reign of Maria Theresa, see Elisabeth Hassmann and Heinz Winter, *Numophylacium Imperatoris: Das Wiener Münzkabinett im 18. Jahrhundert* (Vienna, 2016), 41–77.
7. These sword strokes played a special role in the considerations during the Aulic Council meeting on 17 June 1741 to discuss Maria Theresa's coronation ceremony: see ÖStA, HHStA, ZA Prot, 18 (1741–42), fol. 180v; for a detailed discussion of the celebrated symbolism of the four sword strokes performed by the newly crowned king of Hungary, see ÖStA, HHStA, ZA Prot, 18 (1741–42), fol. 299r/v.
8. A lecture given by State Chancellor Kaunitz (to the medal minters Franz and Johann Nepomuk Würth as well as Johann Martin Krafft) on 16 March 1770 offers unusually detailed information about the state's goals and wishes that the minters of coins and medals were required to follow: see ÖStA, HHStA, Staatskanzlei, Vorträge, 105, fol. 40–45.
9. ÖStA, HHStA, Geheimes Kammerzahlamt, Hofkammerzahlamtsakten, 1, fasc. 5, fol. 1–12: coronation coins and medals at the coronation of Charles VI as Roman emperor in Frankfurt in 1711, with a list of the distribution of the corresponding medals by the *Hofkammerpräsident* Count Gundaker Thomas Starhemberg and a payment by the court exchequer on 11 August 1745.
10. ÖStA, FHKA, Sonderbestände, Sammlungen und Selekte, Hauptmünzamt Wien, Akten, 12, no. 1399: coronation coins (distribution list) at Maria Theresa's Hungarian coronation in Pressburg on 25 June 1741.
11. ÖStA, HHStA, Geheimes Kammerzahlamt, Hofkammerzahlamtsakten, 1, fasc. 15, fol. 1–18, here fol. 7–10: distribution of coronation coins on the occasion of the hereditary homage to Maria Theresa by the Lower Austrian Estates on 22 November 1740; fasc. 18, fol. 1–8: distribution of commemorative and coronation coins on the occasion of the hereditary homage to Maria Theresa by the Upper Austrian Estates on 25 June 1743, with a payment by the court exchequer on 22 July 1743. On the latter occasion (fol. 1r), Maria Theresa reportedly received the corresponding coins presented *auf einer Tazza* by the *Obrist-Erbland-Münzmeister* Count Franz Joseph Sprinzenstein during the meal. Similarly, ÖStA, HHStA, ÄZA, 19 (1743–44), fol. 145r. The corresponding ceremony during the homage by the Lower Austrian Estates is related in ÖStA, HHStA, ZA Prot, 17 (1739–40), fol. 335v.
12. Numerous detailed archival records in ÖStA, HHStA, Geheimes Kammerzahlamt, Hofkammerzahlamtsakten, 1, fasc. 15, 18, 19, 25, and 27.
13. See Michael Yonan, "Portable Dynasties: Imperial Gift-Giving at the Court of Vienna in the Eighteenth Century," *The Court Historian* 14, no. 2 (2009): 177–188. Worth mentioning in this context is the fact that coronation medals were also distributed outside the coronation ceremonies themselves, for instance by the majesties among officers at the *Karlstor* in Prague after the Bohemian coronation (1743): see ÖstA, HHStA, ZA Prot, 19 (1743–44), fol. 85v–86r.
14. This fact becomes evident in the archives, especially in view of the coronation coins and medals struck for the election and coronation of Joseph II as king of the Romans, the design of which generated intense discussion in regard to text and image: cf. ÖStA, HHStA, ÄZA, 60 (1762), fasc. 20/VI/1763–31/XII/1763, fol. 1–4, 7–9, 11–24, 76–78, and 82–83 (with drawings); Geheimes Kammerzahlamt, Hofkammerzahlamtsakten, 1, fasc. 26, fol. 1–39.
15. Vienna, Kunsthistorisches Museum, Coin Cabinet, inv. no. bß 1937 (created by Anton Franz Widemann); cf. *Schau- und Denkmünzen, welche unter Kaiserin Maria Theresia ge-*

prägt wurden . . . (Vienna, 1782) [reprinted with an introduction by Günther Probszt-Ohstorff, Graz 1970], 40, no. XXX; Friedrich Polleroß, "Kaiser, König, Landesfürst: Habsburgische 'Dreifaltigkeit' im Porträt," in *Bildnis, Fürst und Territorium*, ed. Andreas Beyer (Munich, 2000), 194, figure 8; for Maria Theresa's Bohemian coronation, see Benita Berning, *'Nach altem löblichen Gebrauch': Die böhmischen Königskrönungen der Frühen Neuzeit (1526–1743)* (Cologne, 2008), 179–87.

16. *Schau- und Denkmünzen* 43, no. XXXIII.
17. Presumably minted in Nuremberg, see *Verzeichniß der raren und fürtreflichen Münzen und Medaillen gesammelt von Hrn. Aug. Polycarp Edlen von Leyser* . . . (Leipzig, 1791), 185, no. 942.
18. *Schau- und Denkmünzen*, 45, no. XXXV.
19. For a basic introduction to the significance of the *Divina Providentia* in the ideology of Habsburg rulers, see Werner Telesko, "Die Kreuzreliquie in der Wiener Hofburg und die Gründung des Sternkreuzordens: Zur Kreuzverehrung der Habsburger in der Frühen Neuzeit," in *Das Kreuz: Darstellung und Verehrung in der Frühen Neuzeit*, ed. Carla Heussler and Sigrid Gensichen (Regensburg, 2013), 194–216.
20. ÖStA, HHStA, ZA Prot. 18 (1741–42), fol. 282r and 300r.
21. ÖStA, HHStA, ZA Prot. 18 (1741–42), fol. 65r–74r and 177v–316r (on Maria Theresa's journey and coronation ceremony); ÖStA, HHStA, ÄZA, 40 (1741), fasc. 14 May to 25 June 1741, fol. 1–10, 79r–85v, and 93–158 (on Maria Theresa's coronation).
22. ÖStA, HHStA, ZA Prot. 18 (1741–42), fol. 180r; cf. Berning, *'Nach altem löblichen Gebrauch,'* 182; Sandra Hertel, "Maria Theresia als 'König von Ungarn' im Krönungszeremoniell in Preßburg (1741)," *Frühneuzeit-Info* 27 (2016): 112.
23. ÖStA, HHStA, ZA Prot. 18 (1741–42), fol. 170r; cf. Hertel, "Maria Theresia," 115.
24. ÖStA, HHStA, ZA Prot. 18 (1741–42), fol. 170r.
25. ÖStA, HHStA, ZA Prot. 18 (1741–42), fol. 180v; cf. Hertel, "Maria Theresia," 115.
26. Friedrich Wilhelm Wolßhofer (Wolshofer), *Der Allerdurchlauchtigst, Großmächtigst, und Unüberwindlichsten Königin, Heldin, und Frauen, Frauen Theresia* (n.p., n.d.), 132, consulted in Klosterneuburg, Monastery Library, Bk III 19 29.
27. Vienna, Kunsthistorisches Museum, Coin Cabinet, inv. no. bß 1880; *Schau- und Denkmünzen*, 28–29, no. XXII. Eduard Fiala, *Katalog der Münzen- und Medaillen-Stempel-Sammlung des k. k. Hauptmünzamtes in Wien* (Vienna, 1902), vol. 2: 244–45, nos. 791–93; W. Engelhardt, 'Der Opferpfennig bei der deutschen Kaiserkrönung, den böhmischen und ungarischen Königskrönungen," *Mitteilungen der Numismatischen Gesellschaft in Wien* 18, New Series 2 (1939): 94; Géza Pálffy, Ferenc Gábor Soltész, and Csaba Tóth, *Coronatus Posonii . . . Bratislavské korunovačné medaily a žetóny (1563–1830)/Coronatus Posonii . . . A pozsonyi magyar uralkodókoronázások érmei (1563–1830)* (Bratislava, 2014), 128, no. 87; Géza Pálffy, Ferenc Gábor Soltész, and Csaba Tóth, *Coronatus in regem Hungariae . . . Medaliile de încoronare ale regilor Ungariei/A magyar uralkodókoronázások érmei* (Cluj-Napoca, 2016), 164–65, nos. 98–100. In summary: Géza Pálffy, Ferenc Gábor Soltész, and Csaba Tóth, *Coronatio Hungarica in nummis: A magyar uralkodók koronázási érmei és zsetonjai (1508–1916)* (Budapest, 2016). The Hungarian coronation medal was minted in gold and weighed 69.73 grams. Only a limited edition was made for the members of the imperial family, see the corresponding directive at the Imperial Mint dated 14 September 1741: ÖStA, FHKA, Sonderbestände, Sammlungen und Selekte, Kammerzahlamtsrechnungen, no. 239 ("Assignationsbuch" 1741), 431; cf. Heinz Winter, *Glanz des Hauses Habsburg: die habsburgische*

Medaille im Münzkabinett des Kunsthistorischen Museums (Vienna, 2009), 86, no. 87, plate 24.

The reverse of this "offering pfennig" corresponds to a copperplate engraving created by the Nuremberg artist and engraver Christoph Melchior Roth after 1744 (Vienna, Wien Museum, inv. no. 84.387). For a summary of the graphic representation of the Habsburgs in their capacity as Hungarian kings, see Friedrich Polleroß, *"Austriacus Hungariae Rex*. Zur Darstellung der Habsburger als ungarische Könige in der frühneuzeitlichen Graphik," in *"Ez világ, mint egy kert . . ." Tanulmányok Galavics Géza tiszteletére*, ed. Orsolya Bubryák (Budapest, 2010), 63–78.
28. Vienna, Kunsthistorisches Museum, Coin Cabinet, inv. no. bß 1881.
29. See Štefan Holčík, Jana Luková, and Zuzana Francová, *Coronation Festivities/Krönungsfeierlichkeiten—Bratislava/Preßburg 1563–1830*, 2nd ed. (Bratislava, 2015), 67–68. Mention of the president of the Royal Hungarian Chamber, Count Georg Erdödy, throwing the corresponding (gold and silver) coins to the populace from the carriage during the procession to the Franciscan Church is made in ÖStA, HHStA, ZA Prot, 18 (1741–42), fol. 292r/v (with the coronation coins referred to as *Die Silber- und goldnen Denck-Müntzen*), in *Ausführliche Beschreibung der den 25. Junii in der Königlichen Ungarischen freyen Reichs-Stadt Preßburg glücklich vollzogenen prächtigen Crönung Ihrer Allerdurchlauchtigsten Majestät Maria Theresiae . . . zur Königin in Ungarn* (Augsburg, 1741), no pagination, and in Christoph Gottlieb Richter, *Geschichte und Thaten der Allerdurchlauchtigsten und Großmächtigsten Fürstin und Frau Maria Theresia . . .* (Scilicet Nuremberg, 1743), vol. 1: 294.
30. Vienna, Kunsthistorisches Museum, Coin Cabinet, inv. no. bß 1886 (Widemann), 1893 (Donner); *Schau- und Denkmünzen*, 30, no. XXIII; *Verzeichnis verkäuflicher Münzen (und Medaillen) aus der fürstlich Montenuovo'schen Münzsammlung* (Frankfurt am Main, 1895), no. 1697; Fiala, *Katalog*, 245–47, nos. 794–96; *Maria Theresia und ihre Zeit. Zur 200. Wiederkehr des Todestages*, exhibition catalog Schloss Schönbrunn (Vienna, 1980), 122, no. 17.08–17.09; *Münzen und Medaillen des österreichischen Heldenzeitalters 1683–1794*, exhibition catalog Europalia 87 (Brussels, 1993), 238, no. 348; *Georg Raphael Donner 1693–1741*, exhibition catalog Österreichische Galerie (Vienna, 1993), 648, no. 204; Winter, *Glanz*, 85–86, no. 86, pl. 24; Pálffy, Soltész, and Tóth, *Coronatus Posonii*, 129–30, 133, nos. 90, 91, 94, and 95; Holčík, Luková, and Francová, *Coronation Festivities*, 79 (figures.); Pálffy, Soltész, and Tóth, *Coronatus in regem*, 165–66, nos. 101–2; 169, nos. 105–6.
31. This translation can also be found in Adauctus Voigt, *Beschreibung der bisher bekannten böhmischen Münzen nach chronologischer Ordnung . . .* (Prague, 1787), vol. 4: 194, no. 23.
32. Christoph Gottlieb Richter, *Geschichte und Thaten der Allerdurchlauchtigsten und Großmächtigsten Fürstin und Frau Maria Theresia . . .* (Scilicet Nuremberg, 1745), vol. 3: 4.
33. Richter, *Geschichte und Thaten*, vol. 3: 3.
34. Richter, *Geschichte und Thaten*, vol. 3: 3.
35. ÖStA, FHKA, Sonderbestände, Sammlungen und Selekte, Hauptmünzamt Wien, Akten, 12, no. 1393 (*Hungarische Krönungs-Medaille*).
36. Ippolito Marracci, *Polyanthae mariana . . .* (Cologne, 1710), 280–81; cf. *Glossarium mediae et infimae Latinitatis conditum a Carolo Dufresne Domino Du Cange cum supplementis integris Monachorum Ordinis S. Benedicti D. P. Carpenterii Adelungii, aliorum, suisque digessit G. A. L. Henschel* (Paris, 1844), vol. 3: 694.

37. ÖStA, HHStA, Obersthofmarschallamt, Akten, 601 (1639–1760), fasc. V/1758: Intimat (notice) by the *Obersthofmeister*'s office to *Obersthofmarschall* Prince Joseph Schwarzenberg (16 October 1758) regarding Pope Clement XIII's awarding of the title of "Apostolic Majesty" to Maria Theresa.
38. Franciscus Peikhart S. J., *Lob- und Danck-Rede Gott dem Allerhöchsten, vor die so glückliche Hohe Crönung Ihro Königlichen Majestät der Allerdurchlauchtigsten Frauen, Frauen Mariae Theresiae . . . zur ungarischen Königin* (Vienna, 1741).
39. Peikhart S. J., *Lob- und Danck-Rede*, 16.
40. *Wiennerische Beleuchtungen, oder Beschreibung aller deren Triumph-und Ehren-Gerüsten . . . welche bey denen wegen der . . . Geburt des zweyten Ertz-Hertzogs von Oesterreich Caroli . . . zu sehen gewesen* (Vienna, 1745), 257.
41. ÖStA, HHStA, ZA Prot. 18 (1741–42), fol. 317r/v; cf. the corresponding depiction in the series of paintings by Franz Messmer and Wenzel Pohl at the Hungarian embassy in Vienna (1768), see *Maria Theresia als Königin von Ungarn*, exhibition catalog Schloß Halbturn (Eisenstadt, 1980), 160, no. 18, pl. 4.
42. See Tassilo Eypeltauer, *Corpus Nummorum Regni Mariae Theresiae: die Münzprägungen der Kaiserin Maria Theresia und ihrer Mitregenten Kaiser Franz I. und Joseph II. 1740–1780* (Basel, 1973), 195–234, nos. 238–317.
43. The coronation was preceded by a session of the Hungarian Diet in Pressburg. Concerning the complex iconography of Charles (VI) as king of Hungary, see Franz Matsche, *Die Kunst im Dienst der Staatsidee Kaiser Karls VI. Ikonographie, Ikonologie und Programmatik des "Kaiserstils"* (Berlin, 1981), passim.
44. Vienna, Kunsthistorisches Museum, Coin Cabinet, inv. no. bß 1541; *Verzeichnis verkäuflicher Münzen*, no. 1387; Maria Theresia Rath, *Kaiser Karl VI. in der Medaille (1685–1740)* (unpublished doctoral dissertation, Katholieke Universiteit Leuven, 1980), vol. 2: 92–93, no. 114; vol. 3: fig. 114; Pálffy, Soltész, and Tóth, *Coronatus Posonii*, 111, no. 65; Holčík, Luková, and Francová, *Coronation Festivities*, 77 (figure); Pálffy, Soltész, and Tóth, *Coronatus in regem*, 145, no. 76.
45. Vienna, Kunsthistorisches Museum, Coin Cabinet, inv. no. 6428 1914/B; *Verzeichnis verkäuflicher Münzen*, no. 1389; Rath, *Kaiser Karl VI.*, vol. 2: 89, no. 108; vol. 3: figure 108; *Münzen und Medaillen des österreichischen*, 233, no. 339; Pálffy, Soltész, and Tóth, *Coronatus Posonii*, 110, no. 64; Pálffy, Soltész, and Tóth, *Coronatus in regem*, 144, no. 75.
46. Note here the corresponding medal by Andreas Sock and Hans Guet; see Holčík, Luková, and Francová, *Coronation Festivities*, 72–73 (figure); Pálffy, Soltész, and Tóth, *Coronatus in regem*, 88–89, nos. 17–20.
47. Cf. *Ausführliche Beschreibung*, no pagination; *Johann David Köhlers im Jahr 1741 wöchentlich herausgegebener historischer Münz-Belustigung Dreyzehender Theil . . .* (Nuremberg, 1741), 313–20 (for details of the coins thrown to the populace during the Hungarian coronation, with an extensive account of the history of the St. Stephen's Crown).
48. Vienna, Kunsthistorisches Museum, Coin Cabinet, inv. no. bß 1889; *Schau- und Denkmünzen*, 31, no. XXIV; *Verzeichnis verkäuflicher Münzen*, no. 1701; Ebba Koch, "Das barocke Reitermonument in Österreich," *Mitteilungen der Österreichischen Galerie* 19/20, no. 63–65 (1975–76): 61; Francisca Bernheimer, *Georg Wilhelm Vestner und Andreas Vestner: Zwei Nürnberger Medailleure* (Munich, 1984), 191, no. 319; Pálffy, Soltész, and Tóth, *Coronatus Posonii*, 131–32, nos. 92, 93; Holčík, Luková, and Francová, *Coronation Festivities*, 78 (figure); Pálffy, Soltész, and Tóth, *Coronatus in regem*, 167–68, nos. 103–04.

49. Cf. Jean Nivet, "Les transepts de la cathédrale Sainte-Croix d'Orléans et la devise de Louis XIV *Nec pluribus impar*," *Bulletin de la Société Archéologique et Historique de l'Orléanais* New Series 14, no. 111 (1996): 17–34; on the adaptation of this motto to *Nunc pluribus impar* in anti-Bourbon propaganda, see Hendrik Ziegler, *Der Sonnenkönig und seine Feinde: Die Bildpropaganda Ludwigs XIV. in der Kritik* (Petersberg, 2010), 38–42. The significance of Louis XIV's motto is also evidenced by the Jesuit Filippo Picinelli's attempt to ascribe it to King Philip II of Spain in 1670. It was rejected by the French Jesuit Claude-François Ménestrier nine years later; see Claudius Sittig, *Kulturelle Konkurrenzen: Studien zu Semiotik und Ästhetik adeligen Wetteifers um 1600* (Berlin, 2010), 81–82; for a basic introduction to sun iconography in Spain, see Víctor Mínguez, *Los reyes solares: Iconografía astral de la Monarquía hispánica* (Castelló de la Plana, 2001).
50. Vienna, Kunsthistorisches Museum, Coin Cabinet, inv. nos. bß 3455 and 3457; Coin Cabinet of the Staatliche Museen zu Berlin, inv. no. 18233493 (diameter: 42 millimeters); cf. *Münzen und Medaillen des österreichischen*, 392, no. 480; Manfred Olding, *Die Medaillen auf Friedrich den Großen von Preußen 1712 bis 1786* (Osnabrück, 2003), 120, no. 629 and 132, no. 652.
51. In his report on the victorious crossing of the Rhine by Prince Charles Alexander of Lorraine (with a high proportion of Hungarian troops), even the author of the 109th part of the *Neue Europäische Fama* 1744, 213–14, wonders about the—in his opinion—peculiar motto *Nec pluribus impar* on the captured French standards.
52. ÖStA, HHStA, Reichshofrat, Akten, Fabriks-, Gewerbe- und Handlungsprivilegien, 11, fol. 147–214: "medal privilege" for Georg Wilhelm Vestner (1728) and Andreas Vestner (as of the year 1748).
53. The situation is clearer in regard to the so-called *Spottmedaillen* ("mockery medals"), which were of a much coarser design. They were commissioned by Maria Theresa's political opponents and therefore, naturally, not included in the Habsburg medal works of 1782, cf. *Schau- und Denkmünzen*, 416. Particularly noteworthy in this regard is a silver-plated medal from the year 1743 (Vienna, Kunsthistorisches Museum, Coin Cabinet, inv. no. bß 1899), which depicts Maria Theresa pouring the contents of a chamber pot over the heads of three kneeling figures (*DAS IST DAS VERITABL UNGARISCH WASSER* ["This is the true Hungarian water"]), cf. *Verzeichnis verkäuflicher Münzen*, no. 1712; *Österreich zur Zeit Kaiser Josephs II. Mitregent Kaiserin Maria Theresias, Kaiser und Landesfürst*, exhibition catalog Stift Melk (Vienna, 1980), 442, no. 561 (with illustration). This is obviously an allusion to the alcohol (or "spirit of wine") obtained from rosemary flowers, a process supposedly invented by Queen Elisabeth of Hungary (1305–1380), and simultaneously refers to the contents of the chamber pot as being a perfume-like "weapon" of Maria Theresa's. On medals mocking the imperial couple, see Gisela Förschner, *Frankfurter Krönungsmedaillen aus den Beständen des Münzkabinetts* (Frankfurt am Main, 1992), 317, no. 291, and 372–78, no. 339–46.
54. Vienna, Kunsthistorisches Museum, Coin Cabinet, inv. no. bß 1260; Pálffy, Soltész, and Tóth, *Coronatus Posonii*, 87, no. 37; Holčík, Luková, and Francová, *Coronation Festivities*, 74–75 (fig.); Pálffy, Soltész, and Tóth, *Coronatus in regem*, 121, no. 48.
55. This passage from Genesis 48:22 was previously already used in a panegyric by the Jesuit Paulus Mezensky entitled *Zodiacus triumphalis Annorum duodecim Josepho Austriaco . . .* (Olomouc, 1690), no pagination. Mezensky's poem lauds Joseph's Roman coronation, and also describes a triumphal arch with the image of Emperor Leopold I; see ÖStA, HHStA, Hausarchiv, Lothringisches Hausarchiv, 191, fasc. III 226, fol. 1–8, here fol. 8v.

56. Peter F. Sugar, Péter Hanák, and Tibor Frank, *A History of Hungary* (Bloomington, 1994), 117; Ákos Barcsay, *Herrschaftsantritt im Ungarn des 18. Jahrhunderts: Studien zum Verhältnis zwischen Krongewalt und Ständetum im Zeitalter des Absolutismus* (St. Katharinen, 2002).
57. Sugar, Hanák, and Frank, *History of Hungary*, 144–45; Wolfgang Kessler, "Stände und Herrschaft in Ungarn und seinen Nebenländern im 18. und frühen 19. Jahrhundert," in *Stände und Landesherrschaft in Ostmitteleuropa in der Frühen Neuzeit*, ed. Hugo Weczerka (Marburg, 1995), 178.
58. ÖStA, HHStA, ÄZA, 44 (1745), fasc. 5, fol. 40v.
59. ÖStA, HHStA, ÄZA, 44 (1745), fasc. 5, fol. 304v–5v.
60. ÖStA, HHStA, Zeremonialakten, special series, 14 (*Die Röm. Kay. Crönung zu Franckfurth und derselben Beschreibung de Anno 1745 betreffend*), fol. 83v.
61. Johann Heinrich Ramhoffsky, *Drey Beschreibungen: erstens, des königlichen Einzugs, welchen Ihro Königliche Majestät . . . Maria Theresia, in Hungarn und Böheim Königin . . . in dero königliche drey Prager-Städte gehalten: andertens, der Erb-Huldigung, welche Ihro Königlichen Majestät, als Königin zu Böheim die gesammte treu-gehorsamste Stände des Königreichs Böheim, Praeaters, Herren, Rittern und Burger-Stand alerunterthänigst abgeleget: drittens, allerhöchst ernannte Ihro Königlichen Majestät Königlich-Böhmischen Cronung; so alles auf Ihro Königlichen Majestät Allergnädigsten Befehl mit allen Umständen ausführlich und gründlich beschrieben worden . . .* (Prague, 1743).

Bibliography

Ausführliche Beschreibung der den 25. Junii in der Königlichen Ungarischen freyen Reichs-Stadt Preßburg glücklich vollzogenen prächtigen Crönung Ihrer Allerdurchlauchtigsten Majestät Maria Theresiae . . . zur Königin in Ungarn. Augsburg: Bernhardus Homodeus Mayer, 1741.

Barcsay, Ákos. *Herrschaftsantritt im Ungarn des 18. Jahrhunderts: Studien zum Verhältnis zwischen Krongewalt und Ständetum im Zeitalter des Absolutismus.* St. Katharinen: Scripta Mercaturae Verlag, 2002.

Bel, Carl Andreas. *Vorläufige Antwort auf die von Herrn Johann David Köhler . . . zu Göttingen wider die Commentationem Historico-Criticam de Maria Hungariae Regina . . . gemachten Einwürffe.* Leipzig: n.p., 1743.

Bernheimer, Francisca. *Georg Wilhelm Vestner und Andreas Vestner: Zwei Nürnberger Medailleure.* Munich: Uni-Druck, 1984.

Berning, Benita. *'Nach alltem löblichen Gebrauch': Die böhmischen Königskrönungen der Frühen Neuzeit (1526–1743).* Cologne: Böhlau Verlag, 2008.

Edie, Carolyn A. "The Public Face of Royal Ritual: Sermons, Medals, and Civic Ceremony in Later Stuart Coronations." *Huntington Library Quarterly* 53, no. 4 (1990): 311–36.

Engelhardt, W. "Der Opferpfennig bei der deutschen Kaiserkrönung, den böhmischen und ungarischen Königskrönungen." *Mitteilungen der Numismatischen Gesellschaft in Wien* 18, New Series 2 (1939): 93–95.

Eypeltauer, Tassilo. *Corpus Nummorum Regni Mariae Theresiae: die Münzprägungen der Kaiserin Maria Theresia und ihrer Mitregenten Kaiser Franz I. und Joseph II. 1740–1780.* Basel: Münzen und Medaillen AG, 1973.

Fiala, Eduard. *Katalog der Münzen- und Medaillen-Stempel-Sammlung des k. k. Hauptmünzamtes in Wien.* Vol. 2. Vienna: Kaiserlich-königliche Hof- und Staatsdruckerei, 1902.

Förschner, Gisela. *Frankfurter Krönungsmedaillen aus den Beständen des Münzkabinetts*. Frankfurt am Main: Historisches Museum, 1992.

Fried, Torsten. *Geprägte Macht: Münzen und Medaillen der mecklenburgischen Herzöge als Zeichen fürstlicher Herrschaft*. Cologne: Böhlau 2015.

Georg Raphael Donner 1693–1741, exhibition catalog Österreichische Galerie. Vienna: Österreichische Galerie Belvedere, 1993.

Glossarium mediae et infimae Latinitatis conditum a Carolo Dufresne Domino Du Cange cum supplementis integris Monachorum Ordinis S. Benedicti D. P. Carpenterii Adelungii, aliorum, suisque digessit G. A. L. Henschel. Vol. 3. Paris: Firmin Didot, 1844.

Hassmann, Elisabeth, and Heinz Winter. *Numophylacium Imperatoris: Das Wiener Münzkabinett im 18. Jahrhundert*. Vienna: Kunsthistorisches Museum, 2016.

Hertel, Sandra. "Maria Theresia als 'König von Ungarn' im Krönungszeremoniell in Preßburg (1741)." *Frühneuzeit-Info* 27 (2016): 110–23.

Holčík, Štefan, Jana Luková, and Zuzana Francová. *Coronation Festivities/Krönungsfeierlichkeiten—Bratislava/Preßburg 1563–1830*. 2nd ed. Bratislava: Múzeum mesta Bratislavy, 2015.

Holzmair, Eduard. "Die offiziellen österreichischen Krönungs- und Huldigungspfennige seit Kaiser Josef I." *Jahrbuch der kunsthistorischen Sammlungen in Wien* 50 (1953): 199–210.

———. "Maria Theresia als Trägerin 'männlicher' Titel: Eine numismatische Studie." *MIÖG* 72 (1964): 122–34.

Johann David Köhlers im Jahr 1741 wöchentlich heraus gegebener historischer Münz-Belustigung Dreyzehender Theil. . . . Nuremberg: Christoph Weigel, 1741.

Johann David Köhlers im Jahr 1744 wöchentlich heraus gegebener historischer Münz-Belustigung Sechzehender Theil. . . . Nuremberg: Christoph Weigel, 1744.

Kessler, Wolfgang. "Stände und Herrschaft in Ungarn und seinen Nebenländern im 18. und frühen 19. Jahrhundert." In *Stände und Landesherrschaft in Ostmitteleuropa in der Frühen Neuzeit*, edited by H. Weczerka, 171–91. Marburg: Herder-Institut, 1995.

Koch, Ebba. "Das barocke Reitermonument in Österreich." *Mitteilungen der Österreichischen Galerie* 19/20, no. 63–65 (1975–76): 32–80.

Maria Theresia als Königin von Ungarn, exhibition catalog Schloß Halbturn. Eisenstadt: Amt der Burgenländischen Landesregierung, 1980.

Maria Theresia und ihre Zeit. Zur 200. Wiederkehr des Todestages, exhibition catalog Schloss Schönbrunn. Vienna: Residenz, 1980.

Marracci, Ippolito. *Polyanthae mariana . . . .* Cologne: Franciscus Metternich, 1710.

Matsche, Franz. *Die Kunst im Dienst der Staatsidee Kaiser Karls VI. Ikonographie, Ikonologie und Programmatik des "Kaiserstils."* 2 vols. Berlin: Walter de Gruyter, 1981.

Mezensky, Paulus. *Zodiacus triumphalis Annorum duodecim Josepho Austriaco . . . .* Olomouc: n.p., 1690.

Mínguez, Víctor. *Los reyes solares: Iconografía astral de la Monarquía hispánica*. Castelló de la Plana: Publicacions de la Universitat Jaume, 2001.

Münzen und Medaillen des österreichischen Heldenzeitalters 1683–1794, exhibition catalog Europalia 87. Brussels: Nationale Bank van België, 1993.

Nivet, J. "Les transepts de la cathédrale Sainte-Croix d'Orléans et la devise de Louis XIV *Nec pluribus impar*." *Bulletin de la Société Archéologique et Historique de l'Orléanais* New Series 14, no. 111 (1996): 17–34.

Olding, Manfred. *Die Medaillen auf Friedrich den Großen von Preußen 1712 bis 1786*. Osnabrück: Gietl, 2003.

Österreich zur Zeit Kaiser Josephs II. Mitregent Kaiserin Maria Theresias, Kaiser und Landesfürst, exhibition catalog Stift Melk. Vienna: Amt der Niederösterreichischen Landesregierung, 1980.

Pálffy, Géza, Ferenc Gábor Soltész, and Csaba Tóth. *Coronatio Hungarica in nummis: A magyar uralkodók koronázási érmei és zsetonjai (1508–1916)*. Budapest: MTA Bölcsészettudományi Kutatóközpont, 2016.

———. *Coronatus in regem Hungariae . . . Medaliile de încoronare ale regilor Ungariei/A magyar uralkodókoronázások érmei*. Cluj-Napoca: Erdélyi Nemzeti Történet. Múzeum, Magyar Nemzeti Múzeum, 2016.

———. *Coronatus Posonii . . . Bratislavské korunovačné medaily a žetóny (1563–1830)/Coronatus Posonii . . . A pozsonyi magyar uralkodókoronázások érmei (1563–1830)*. Bratislava: Slovenské národné múzeum, 2014.

Peikhart S. J., Franciscus. *Lob- und Danck-Rede Gott dem Allerhöchsten, vor die so glückliche Hohe Crönung Ihro Königlichen Majestät der Allerdurchlauchtigsten Frauen, Frauen Mariae Theresiae . . . zur ungarischen Königin*. Vienna: n.p., 1741.

Polleroß, Friedrich. "*Austriacus Hungariae Rex*. Zur Darstellung der Habsburger als ungarische Könige in der frühneuzeitlichen Graphik." In *"Ez világ, mint egy kert . . ." Tanulmányok Galavics Géza tiszteletére*, edited by Orsolya Bubryák, 63–78. Budapest: MTA Müveszettörténeti Kutatóintézet/Gondolat Kiadó, 2010.

———. "Kaiser, König, Landesfürst: Habsburgische 'Dreifaltigkeit' im Porträt." In *Bildnis, Fürst und Territorium*, edited by A. Beyer, 189–218. Munich: Deutscher Kunstverlag, 2000.

Ramhoffsky, Johann Heinrich *Drey Beschreibungen: erstens, des königlichen Einzugs, welchen Ihro Königliche Majestät . . . Maria Theresia, in Hungarn und Böheim Königin . . . in dero königliche drey Prager-Städte gehalten: andertens, der Erb-Huldigung, welche Ihro Königlichen Majestät, als Königin zu Böheim die gesammte treu-gehorsamste Stände des Königreichs Böheim, Praelaten, Herren, Rittern und Burger-Stand alerunterthänigst abgeleget: drittens, allerhöchst ernannt Ihro Königlichen Majestät Königlich-Böhmischen Cronung; so alles auf Ihro Königlichen Majestät Allergnädigsten Befehl mit allen Umständen ausführlich und gründlich beschrieben worden . . . .* Prague: Carl Franz Rosenmüller, 1743.

Rath, Maria Theresia. *Kaiser Karl VI. in der Medaille (1685–1740)*. 3 vols. Unpublished doctoral dissertation, Katholieke Universiteit Leuven, 1980.

Richter, Christoph Gottlieb. *Geschichte und Thaten der Allerdurchlauchtigsten und Großmächtigsten Fürstin und Frau Maria Theresia . . . .* Vol. 1. Scilicet Nuremberg: n.p., 1743.

———. *Geschichte und Thaten der Allerdurchlauchtigsten und Großmächtigsten Fürstin und Frau Maria Theresia . . . .* Vol. 3. Scilicet Nuremberg: n.p., 1745.

Schau- und Denkmünzen, welche unter Kaiserin Maria Theresia geprägt wurden . . . . Vienna: Johann Paul Krauß, 1782 [reprinted with an introduction by Günther Probszt-Ohstorff, Graz: Adeva, 1970].

Sittig, Claudius. *Kulturelle Konkurrenzen: Studien zu Semiotik und Ästhetik adeligen Wetteifers um 1600*. Berlin: De Gruyter, 2010.

Sugar, Peter F., Péter Hanák, and Tibor Frank. *A History of Hungary*. Bloomington: Indiana University Press, 1994.

Telesko, Werner. "Die Kreuzreliquie in der Wiener Hofburg und die Gründung des Sternkreuzordens: Zur Kreuzverehrung der Habsburger in der Frühen Neuzeit." In *Das Kreuz: Darstellung und Verehrung in der Frühen Neuzeit*, edited by Carla Heussler and Sigrid Gensichen, 194–216. Regensburg: Schnell und Steiner, 2013.

———. "Herrschaftssicherung mittels visueller Repräsentation: Zur Porträtkultur Maria Theresias." In *Höfische Porträtkultur: Die Bildnissammlung der österreichischen Erzherzogin*

Maria Anna (1738–1789), edited by Eva Kernbauer and Aneta Zahradnik, 37–47. Berlin: De Gruyter, 2016.

———. *Maria Theresia: Ein europäischer Mythos*. Vienna: Böhlau Verlag, 2012.

Verzeichnis verkäuflicher Münzen (und Medaillen) aus der fürstlich Montenuovo'schen Münzsammlung. Frankfurt am Main: n.p., 1895 [Reprint Frankfurt am Main: Schulten, 1977].

Verzeichniß der raren und fürtreflichen Münzen und Medaillen gesammelt von Hrn. Aug. Polycarp Edlen von Leyser . . . . Leipzig: Wolf Gottlob Pezold, 1791.

Voigt, Adauctus. *Beschreibung der bisher bekannten böhmischen Münzen nach chronologischer Ordnung* . . . . 4 vols. Prague: Gerl, 1771–87.

Wiennerische Beleuchtungen, oder Beschreibung aller deren Triumph-und Ehren-Gerüsten . . . welche bey denen wegen der . . . Geburt des zweyten Ertz-Hertzogs von Oesterreich Caroli . . . zu sehen gewesen. Vienna: Ghelen, 1745.

Winter, Heinz. "Auswurfprägungen: Eine Skizze." In *Feste feiern: 125 Jahre, Jubiläumsausstellung*, exhibition catalog Kunsthistorisches Museum Vienna, edited by Sabine Haag and Gudrun Swoboda, 256–57. Vienna: Kunsthistorisches Museum, 2016.

———. *Glanz des Hauses Habsburg: die habsburgische Medaille im Münzkabinett des Kunsthistorischen Museums*. Vienna: Kunsthistorisches Museum, 2009.

Wolshofer, Friedrich Wilhelm. *Der Allerdurchlauchtigst, Großmächtigst, und Unüberwindlichsten Königin, Heldin, und Frauen, Frauen Theresia*. N.p.: n.p., n.d.

Yonan, Michael. *Empress Maria Theresa and the Politics of Habsburg Imperial Art*. University Park: Penn State University Press, 2011.

———. "Portable Dynasties: Imperial Gift-Giving at the Court of Vienna in the Eighteenth Century." *The Court Historian* 14, no. 2 (2009): 177–88.

Ziegler, Hendrik. *Der Sonnenkönig und seine Feinde: Die Bildpropaganda Ludwigs XIV. in der Kritik*. Petersberg: Imhof, 2010.

Chapter 5

THE BOHEMIAN CORONATION OF CHARLES VI AND ITS HIDDEN MESSAGE

Petra Vokáčová

In memory of Zdeněk Vokáč †, my selfless and beloved father-in-law

In contrast to the early establishment of Charles VI as Roman emperor, his crowning as king of Bohemia was delayed. The ceremony eventually took place twelve years later, but it remained shrouded in mystery for a considerable time. The actual reasons leading to its arrangement were long unknown; and even today, many questions remain unanswered. But paradoxically, the pomposity and medial reach of the Bohemian festivities far surpassed those of the politically more important coronations in the Holy Roman Empire (1711) and Hungary (1712, Elisabeth Christine 1714). Even Charles's election as king of the Romans occurred in his absence by way of commissioned deputies, and the coronation itself after his arrival in the Empire was enacted rather hastily: he spent less than two months in Frankfurt. By contrast, the complexity, expense, and even the duration of Charles's public staging of power during his stay in the Bohemian lands (1723), where he spent no less than five months, would remain unmatched during his reign.

Was there a "hidden message" in Charles's Bohemian coronation? In 2004–09, an interdisciplinary team of researchers focused on this question in detail and came to a new interpretation of the crowning in 1723. Four experts from the fields of history, art history, and musicology produced a number of documented findings on the topic that permitted them to correct older theses and develop a fresh reading of the events. The authors innovatively interpreted Charles's coronation in Prague in the indispensable context of the contemporary international situation, particularly with regard to political symbols reflected in the fine arts, literature, and dramatic and musical productions on the occasion of the festivity. The outcome was an extensive publication in Czech quoting relevant sources and literature and publishing an array of pictorial documents, many of which were previously unknown.

This chapter seeks to elucidate the key results of this project.[1] Its main argument is that the Bohemian coronation was not primarily linked to Charles VI's ascension to power in Bohemia, Moravia, and Silesia—the major lands of the so-called Bohemian Crown—but instead was a vehicle for broadcasting important political messages to the international community when his succession seemed uncertain. The imperial couple had not produced a male heir, and Charles sought international backing for the Pragmatic Sanction that was to warrant the preservation of the Habsburg Monarchy against territorial claims by rivaling princes. In this context, the crowning in 1723 proved the ideal opportunity to respond to the threats and propagate Vienna's point of view in the public sphere.

The Road to Power and the Prague Coronation

There is very little information to be read in history textbooks about Emperor Charles VI. The father of the far better known Maria Theresa is nowadays linked only to a notion of the largest territorial expansion of the Austrian Habsburgs in history and to the dynastic crisis that the Pragmatic Sanction attempted to avert.[2] More in-depth knowledge on how this ruler, the last member of his dynasty who aspired to preserve a global empire, governed his hereditary lands is still missing.[3] This is all the more surprising given that he was the head of the Habsburg Monarchy for a respectable period of twenty-nine years.

Charles's accession to the throne was quite nonstandard. He assumed government as a consequence of the early and unexpected death of his elder brother Joseph I in 1711. At the time, Charles had been residing on the Iberian Peninsula—where his father Leopold had sent him after the death of the last Spanish Habsburg king Charles II and the igniting of the international struggle for the Spanish European and colonial dominion—for seven years.[4] With British and Dutch military and financial help as well as with the support of his father and brother, Charles attempted to gain control over the Spanish territories on the Iberian Peninsula as Charles III against his Bourbon rival Philip of Anjou, the grandson of the French king Louis XIV. He did so with mixed fortunes, however. In Barcelona, his city of residence for most of his stay in Spain, he also wed Elisabeth Christine, princess of Brunswick-Wolfenbüttel, in 1708.

Three years later, the news of his brother's death would take Charles by surprise, and he was not immediately prepared to leave Spain. In fact, he only agreed to return to Vienna after a great deal of persuasion by the dowager empress and regent Eleonor Magdalene of Neuburg and her cabinet members.[5] Considering that he had already lobbied for the imperial dignity in the past, the prospect of the imperial crown may have attracted him, even though the idea of resigning from Spain must still have seemed undesirable.[6] In reality, Charles never entirely gave up his Spanish dream—as indicated in some segments of his coat of arms and the ornamentation on his sarcophagus in the Capuchin Crypt in Vienna, where the Castilian crown is clearly present. He even used the Spanish royal titles until his death despite the fact that his dominion was restricted to the former European domains of the Spanish Crown outside of the Iberian Peninsula after the War of the Spanish Succession.

Nevertheless, on 27 September 1711, he left Barcelona and sailed to Italy. By November, he had already met the inner circle of ministers at a conference in Innsbruck and designated the first officers of his new court.[7] Following the imperial election in October, he was crowned as Emperor Charles VI in Frankfurt on 22 December 1711.[8] Even taking into account all the journeys he undertook for other coronations or homages by various Estates in the subsequent years, he never left the territory of the Habsburg Monarchy again.[9]

Scattered references to Charles's future Bohemian crowning appear in the minutes of the Viennese court only in 1721.[10] The first court conference to discuss concrete organizational questions regarding the coronation took place in December 1722.[11] On 25 February 1723, Charles officially communicated to the vicegerency in Bohemia his intention to be crowned in Prague along with his spouse.[12] The following months were dedicated entirely to preparing this great event, both from the Viennese and the Bohemian side. All sorts of regulations, instructions, reports, and requests related not only to the coronation ceremony itself, but also to the scheduling of the other festivities during the sojourn of the court in Bohemia and, last but not least, to the arrangement of a number of purely practical matters such as transport, accommodation, logistics, cleaning, and fire-prevention measures were exchanged.[13]

Finally, on 19 June 1723, after many wagoners had transferred the courtiers' baggage to Prague, Emperor Charles and Empress Elisabeth Christine left Vienna with their daughters Maria Theresa and Maria Anna and their cortege and traveled to Bohemia via Lower Austria and Moravia.[14] The journey took twelve days and included a number of "excursions": visits, greetings, parties, masses, and hunting trips. It was a planned ride of prestige about which the public not only at home, but also throughout the entire continent had to be informed. On 30 June, the imperial court triumphantly entered Prague, where the councilors, clerics, and other citizens of the New Town, Old Town, Lesser Town, and Hradčany in turn saluted their ruler. There followed a reception by the supreme land officers and the archbishop of Prague directly within the premises of Prague Castle, which would become the main residence of the imperial family and the prominent dignitaries and servants of its court for the next few months.[15]

During their stay in Prague, the members of the imperial family and their courtiers participated in various formal events, theater performances, recreational outings, and casual visits to the demesnes of Bohemian aristocrats.[16] Masses and solemn processions for the adoration of relevant saints also constituted an important part of the court festivities, which corresponded to the program-propagated devotion of the House of Habsburg—the *Pietas Austriaca*.[17] Several *gala days* took place during the sojourn as well; Maria Theresa celebrated her name day, and both of her parents feted as well. The birthday feast for the empress held on 28 August was particularly splendid. On this occasion, the premiere of the court opera *Costanza e Fortezza* was staged in the open air at the Summer Riding School near the royal residence in Prague, which undoubtedly constituted the climax of the common court festivities in baroque Bohemia.[18]

But the formal events in Prague naturally culminated on Saturday, 4 September 1723, when the Bohemian Estates assembled in the diet hall of Prague Castle to render homage to their sovereign and swear the oath of fealty. On 5 September, Charles was crowned king of Bohemia at St. Vitus Cathedral, and Elisabeth Christine was crowned queen in the same place three days later.[19] During the respective ceremonies, the archbishop of Prague, Ferdinand of Khuenburg, placed on the head of the king—and the abbess of St. George's Monastery, Isidora Constantie Roudnická of Březnice, on the head of the queen—the so-called St. Wenceslas Crown, a Bohemian medieval royal diadem crafted in 1346 under Charles IV of Luxembourg and consecrated to the Bohemian prince-martyr Wenceslas I of Přemyslid.

Both rituals were followed by a ceremonial procession across the castle courtyard, where bread, coins, and wine from a fountain were distributed among the onlookers, and then by a banquet, where the king dined in the presence of the supreme land officers and the queen in the company of eminent noble ladies in the late gothic Great (today Vladislav) Hall of the Old Royal Palace.[20] The imperial couple left Prague on 6 November 1723 and set forth on their return journey to Vienna, this time taking a total of sixteen days.

Reported Reasons for the Delay

It is important to remember that Charles acceded to the throne of the Bohemian lands twelve years before being crowned. Moreover, his coronation in Prague in 1723 was the first in Bohemia since the crowning of Leopold I in 1656. Two essential questions arise in this context: Why did it take so long before the coronation took place? And why did it take place precisely in 1723?

Older historiography offers the following reasons for the deferment. In the first place, at the time of Charles's assumption of power in the Habsburg Monarchy, the War of the Spanish Succession was still underway. After it ended, the Habsburgs reengaged in armed conflicts with the Turks and in Italy. Furthermore, although the Austrian and Bohemian lands were no longer under direct attack and "only" experiencing an outflow of war recruits and money (and eventually had to sustain troops over winter), a heavy plague epidemic affected both countries at the turn of 1713 to 1714. This may explain why the coronation could not take place immediately after the beginning of Charles's reign. One reason provided in existing historiography for the choice of 1723 for the coronation is that Charles's Bohemian crowning was primarily a recompense for the loyalty of the Bohemian Estates and their acceptance without opposition in 1720 of a new principle stipulating the indivisibility of the hereditary lands and governing the Habsburg succession both in the male and female line: the so-called Pragmatic Sanction.[21] Nowadays, we assume the existence of different motives for Charles being crowned when he was, although the Pragmatic Sanction—proclaimed in 1713 and accepted by the lands of the monarchy between 1720 and 1725—surely played an important role in the Prague coronation.

Moreover, it seems pertinent to mention a personal incentive for the emperor and empress to travel to Bohemia following the death of their only son Leopold Johann in 1716, as they still hoped to bring a male successor into the world. A Bohemian fable related to this topic may have provided additional persuasion, namely that no Bohemian royal couple could produce a male descendant before being crowned.[22] Although this motivation was likely not of key importance, its existence is documented. As we know from ministerial records and the private correspondence of courtiers, there was a common hope that Elisabeth Christine would quickly conceive a child—whether in Prague or with the help of a therapeutic cure in the famed Western Bohemian springs of Karlsbad. It is noteworthy that the coronation journey was eventually much shorter than originally intended for the simple reason that personal physicians confirmed the empress's pregnancy during her stay in Bohemia.[23]

Actual Reasons for the Delay

In reality, it was no longer necessary during Charles's time for a Bohemian ruler to be formally crowned in order to take control of the government. The *Obnovené zřízení zemské* (*Verneuerte Landesordnung*, a mandatory land constitution) had proclaimed the Bohemian throne hereditary for the Habsburg dynasty in 1627.[24] Even the local political situation at the beginning of the eighteenth century—in contrast to Hungary, for example—did not require the personal presence of the sovereign. Joseph I was never crowned in Bohemia despite ruling as its king for seven years. As far as we know, the Estates committee officially addressed Charles VI regarding the coronation for the first time upon his return from Frankfurt in early 1712.²⁵ When the question of the Bohemian crowning was reopened one decade later, however, the initiative came not from the Estates, but from the court of Vienna. Why was this so?

The main reason was foreign policy. From approximately the early 1720s, several European powers began to profit ostentatiously from the succession complications within the House of Habsburg. Above all, the electors of Saxony and Bavaria—two immediate neighbors of the Habsburg Monarchy who were well aware of the lack of a male descendant in the extended family of Charles VI—did not hesitate to reestablish dynastic alliances with the Habsburgs so as to increase their chances of acquiring at least parts of the heritage. They seized the opportunity to initiate a risky power play, a strategy not unusual in the history of the Saxon Wettins and the Bavarian Wittelsbachs. The Bavarian electors in particular could build on a considerable tradition in this respect.

Looking back in time, there had already been connections between the Wittelsbachs and the Habsburgs during the Middle Ages. Then in 1600, Archduke Ferdinand of Inner Austria, the later emperor Ferdinand II, married Maria Anna of Bavaria. Their daughter Maria Anna was espoused to her own uncle, the elector Maximilian I, brother of Maria Anna of Bavaria. The next successor in the order of the Bavarian dukes and electors, Maximilian II Emanuel, followed the same dynastic marriage policy by wedding a daughter of Emperor Leopold I from the latter's first matrimony with Margaret Theresa of Spain. Moreover, he also matched his son Charles Albrecht with Archduchess Maria Amalia, second daughter of the deceased emperor Joseph I and a niece of Charles VI, in 1722. The Bavarian elector thus did exactly what the Saxon elector and Polish king, August II the Strong, had done three years earlier in 1719 when he married his son Frederick August to Maria Amalia's older sister, Maria Josepha.

Before entering into such marriages, both the Wettins and the Wittelsbachs had to officially renounce their claims to the Habsburg heritage.²⁶ In addition, the Pragmatic Sanction had already disadvantaged both archduchesses in favor of the daughters of Charles VI in the order of the Habsburg succession. Nevertheless, these dynastic alliances became the foundation for ambitious propaganda programs by both Saxony and Bavaria that showed their tremendous interest in the Habsburg inheritance and the imperial title.²⁷ They did so implicitly, half-covertly by way of subtle allusions, but publicly nonetheless. The Pragmatic Sanction both powers had accepted to secure their princes' marriages did not have to be disputed explicitly. Instead, the political rivalry of the Wettins and the Wittelsbachs with the Habsburgs, still stigmatized by the scars from the recent struggles to do with the Spanish succession, now extended to the level of the arts and print media.

Saxon and Bavarian Propaganda

The festive decoration, ephemeral architecture, and illumination of both of the electoral residences as well as the production of commemorative medals and panegyric poetry for the occasions of the abovementioned weddings in 1719 and 1722 offered suitable platforms for the medial strategy of the Wettins and Wittelsbachs.[28] Panegyric prints published both in Dresden and Munich featured on their frontispieces epic engravings defining the new matrimonies as reciprocal bonds not just between the respective dynasties, but also between the countries they ruled. Coats of arms depicting the alliance and symbols of the marital union of the two families appeared along with the traditional allegorical figures of the imperial Jupiter, the double eagle, the Bavarian Hercules, and the lion. A crancelin of common rue, the heraldic plant of the Saxon coat of arms, encircled the Austrian laurel bush. Two palm trees with the coats of arms of the Habsburgs and Wittelsbachs were shown repeatedly bound together as the sign of frequent intermarriages throughout history. It is also possible that the work *Immergrünender Lorber-Baum*, whose author Johann Joseph Pock claimed the matrimony of Charles Albrecht and Maria Amalia to be the reunification of two stems of a single original dynasty, was created by order of the Bavarian court.[29]

But the power aspirations of the Wettins and Wittelsbachs were probably best mirrored in the two representational operas staged on the occasions of the espousals: *Teofane* by composer Antonio Lotti and librettist Stefano Benedetto Pallavicino in Dresden, and *Adelaide* by composer Pietro Torri and librettist Antonio Salvi in Munich.[30] It is surely no coincidence that the action of both operas was temporally situated within the reign of Otto I, who was descended from the Ottonian, originally Saxon, dynasty and had been the first head of the Holy Roman Empire. As a matter of fact, some minor differences in the storyline notwithstanding, both pieces shared an identical plot: the struggle between the two lead male characters for territory, a crown, and an honorable bride—and eventually her inheritance.

These symbolic jibes by the two electoral courts directed at the Habsburgs devolved to all but open provocation after Maria Josepha gave birth to three baby princes in 1720, 1721, and 1722. The firstborn prince, Frederick August (who would die before his first birthday), was welcomed euphorically in Dresden as "an Austrian seed replanted into the Saxon land" in the words of court poet Johann Ulrich König within a panegyric poem.[31] Casual mintage utilized emblems in the same spirit—for example, a scene depicting the imperial and Polish eagles jointly holding a coronal in their claws. In a particularly striking example, the obverse of a medal produced by court medalist Oluf Wif based on a design by Johann Jacob Haake de Bopsingen in 1720 portrays the figure of Providence with a cornucopia and a small boy on her lap, while the reverse features the audacious motif of a dying tree with only one new stolon and the following circumscription: SAXONIAE DE STIRPE RENASCITUR AUSTRIA CEDRUS ("From the Saxon trunk the Austrian cedar grows again").

Similar symbols of vegetation pervaded the congratulatory poetry and commemorative medals created after the births of Maria Josepha's two younger sons, Joseph August and Frederick Christian. A motif from Virgil's *Aeneid* is encountered, for example: an oak tree consecrated to the goddess Proserpina, which regrew a single golden bough after it was broken off. Another metaphor employed was that of a young cane planted into the trunk of a different tree. Likewise worthy of note is a scene from the obverse side of a silver medal produced by Oluf Wif following a design by Johann Christoph Weingolt in commemoration of the birth of Prince Joseph August in 1721. It depicts a sun rising from behind the sphere of the earth above the inscription EL[ectoratus] SAX[oniae], thereby indirectly alluding to the universal claims of the Wettin dynasty.

By contrast, Charles VI was still waiting in vain for a son, and the chilling prescience of the Pragmatic Sanction seemed to be proving true when, after the death of Archduke Leopold Johann, the imperial couple gave birth only to two daughters: Maria Theresa in 1717 and Maria Anna in 1718. This situation in which Saxony and Bavaria were vehemently stylizing themselves as the rightful closest relatives urged Charles VI to react, and it is for this reason that the succession and the Pragmatic Sanction were among the most important themes of the Prague coronation.

The Counter-Propaganda of the Bohemian Coronation

Under these circumstances, the coronation in Prague can be understood as Charles's determined answer to the Saxon and Bavarian challenges.[32] In reality, a highly sophisticated program formulated in symbolic language was hidden under the guise of an official coronation feast with the intent—as we will soon see—of demonstrating the stability of Habsburg power in holding several thrones at once. Therefore, most of the numerous emblems, engaged rhetoric, panegyric, and dramatic production came directly from the imperial court. Although the Bohemian Estates and the cities of Prague largely participated in the preparation of the crowning, everything was organized in co-operation with the central administration, and the office that made the ultimate decision was the Bohemian Court Chancellery in Vienna.[33] Even some of the domestic themes used in the festivities thus depended iconographically upon Viennese models.

It should be noted that Charles VI was the first ruler in Bohemian history to be crowned king of Bohemia after his imperial coronation. He therefore had to be regarded simultaneously as the Bohemian king, the head of the Habsburg Monarchy, and the emperor—and he did not refrain from performing all of these identities during the ritual in the St. Vitus Cathedral. As a result, the combining of the Bohemian, Austrian, and imperial symbols in the program of the Prague coronation closely and purposely reflected Charles's power position in Europe. The emperor was the most important monarch of the western Christian world, and the Bohemian king was an acknowledged *primus* among the princes of the empire (i.e., the electors of the king of the Romans, the designated emperor). The Golden Bull of Emperor Charles IV had first legalized this status in 1356, and the so-called readmission of the Bohemian electoral vote had reaffirmed it in 1708. This was why it was so important for Charles VI to emphasize the hereditary character of the Bohemian throne in connection with the Habsburg dynasty during his crowning in Prague.[34]

This naturally influenced the iconography as well as the titles, the ceremonial exchanging of coronation insignias—even of several crowns, one after the other—and the "transformations" of vestures during the ritual in the cathedral.[35] Three crowns were used in the course of both the king's and queen's coronations in Prague in 1723, all of which were brought from their permanent repository in the imperial treasury of the Viennese Hofburg. The first of these was the St. Wenceslas Crown, the authentic gothic crown of the Bohemian kings; the second was the so-called "private" royal crown, supposedly part of the Habsburg family treasure; and the third was the dynastic crown (*Hauskrone*) crafted during the rule of Rudolf II as a private insignia for the Habsburgs. After the abolishment of the Holy Roman Empire, this latter crown would become the highest regal symbol of the new Austrian Empire.

The ceremonial court commission resolved the sequence of the exchanging of the crowns down to the minutest details, for it was desirable to let the ruler metaphorically transform from one "territorial sovereignty" to another before the spectators' eyes at specific moments.[36] Charles was not a common *prince*, as the claimant to the Bohemian throne was designated in the original coronation order. Nor was he a mere *Royal Majesty* either, as other monarchs from the Habsburg dynasty were ordinarily called prior to their Bohemian crowning.[37] In this complicated position, he accordingly wore a hat with a red imperial feather while receiving the Estates' homage in the castle or marching in the inaugural coronation procession, thereby expressing that he was not yet the crowned Bohemian king, but already emperor. Later, after entering the St. Wenceslas Chapel in the cathedral, he exchanged the hat for the private royal crown with assistance from the grand master of the court (*Obersthofmeister*), the grand chamberlain of the court (*Obersthofkämmerer*), and the grand territorial chamberlain (*Oberstlandkämmerer*), and would leave it on his head until he took the royal oath and chrism at the main rite in the church presbytery.[38] During the coronation with the Bohemian crown, he simultaneously received other royal regalia: the St. Wenceslas Sword, the ring, the scepter, and the orb, nowadays stored together in Prague as parts of the royal treasure.[39] Thereafter, the king, with the St. Wenceslas Crown on his head, left the cathedral for the public banquet in the Great Hall. After the meal, he handed the crown over to the grand territorial chamberlain.

The ritual changing of dress by the ruler in the St. Wenceslas Chapel carried similar symbolism. Here, Charles not only swapped the hat for the crown, but also the so-called *gala* vesture for the coronation robe.[40] The neutral, mostly black dress decorated with laces and bands and used on the occasion of court festivities was replaced in the sacral space with a royal vestment made from luxurious silk tissue of carmine color.[41] It is documented that the very same set of textiles consisting of a satin maniple, a stole, a belt, and a brocade overcoat with ermine trim and a sweep was also worn by Maria Theresa at her coronation in 1743, as well as by her successors to the Bohemian throne.[42]

For a change, Charles wore the *Hauskrone* three days later during the crowning of his spouse Elisabeth Christine.[43] Within this ceremony, six heralds accentuated the majesty and multiple thrones of the ruler: one Austrian, one Spanish, one Hungarian, one Bohemian, and two from the Empire. The superimposition of royal, dynastic, and imperial elements was similarly visible in the embellishment of the Great Hall, with tapestries picturing the campaign of Charles V in Tunisia, as well as in the symbols of decorative confetti—celebratory sweets displayed as sugary works of art on the tables during both coronation banquets.[44] They were topped with allegorical figurines representing Constantia and Fortitudo in reference to Charles VI's personal device: the former was to symbolically protect the Kingdom of Bohemia against enemies, while the second was to provide a trustworthy government within it. Other figures included Jupiter, who represented both the emperorship and the emperor himself, and Juno, who stood for the hope of a hereditary succession. The presence of Mercury and Fame personified the guarantee of a golden age and the good reputation of Habsburg government.

Similar symbolism appeared on the silver commemorative medals designed by Carl Gustav Heraeus, a native Swedish scholar, numismatist, and poet, and the main ideological creator of the "imperial style" at the court of Charles VI. As the author of the concepts for three prestigious mintages for the Prague coronation, Heraeus combined traditional Bohemian legends with historical events, which he cleverly reinterpreted as though the prophecies stemming from the mythical founders of the Bohemian polity, princess Libuše and Přemysl the Plowman, had come true. These predictions related to a future acquisition of the imperial crown, a forthcoming glory of the ruling dynasty, and its continuation in female succession. In doing so, Heraeus proved his familiarity with fundamental contemporary works of Bohemian historiography—for instance, the popular *Bohemian Chronicle* of Václav Hájek of Libočany, published for the first time in print in 1541. This knowledge is clearly visible in the selection of motifs for the design of the coronation medals, which included the founding millennium of Prague, the accentuation of continuity with previous ruling dynasties in Bohemia (i.e., with the Přemyslids and the Luxembourgs), and most importantly the often emphasized legitimacy of Habsburg succession to the Bohemian throne not only in the male, but also in the female line.[45] These themes were all inseparably connected to attributes of a felicitous government and underlined the enormous expanse of Charles VI's composite realm, by far the largest in the entire history of the Habsburg Monarchy. Aside from the obligatory symbols of the St. Wenceslas Crown and the Bohemian lion, the heraldic emblems of the eagle, the two-ply cross and the tower appear on the reverse of Heraeus's medals as acknowledgments of the three other crown domains governed (though some of them only in name) by Charles: the Holy Roman Empire and the kingdoms of Hungary and Spain (see figure 5.1).

Analogical symbols referring to Charles's world supremacy (the globe) and, in a later stage, even to the pregnancy of Elisabeth Christine (the figure of the "Bohemian" prince), can be found on other contemporary mintages as well, for example on the golden oblatory coins by Antonio Maria Gennaro and on the allegorical medals by Georg Wilhelm Vestner, both made for the Bohemian coronation.[46]

Conrad Adolph von Albrecht, another inventor, scientist, and numismatist to the emperor, and the author of the allegorical sheet printed for the occasion of the crowning, worked with similar images (see figure 5.2).[47] His graphics feature illustrations of the Bohemian coronation jewels and of many objects emblematizing the golden age of Charles's reign. The well-being of society is symbolized by cornucopias; peace and prosperity by the staff of Mercury; happiness and felicity by the rudder wrapped with laurel. Furthermore, the heraldic figure of the Bohemian lion holds Fortune's Wheel in its paws, and the Moravian and

Figure 5.1. Silver commemorative medal for the Bohemian coronation of Charles VI and Elisabeth Christine and the founding millennium of Prague, designed by Carl Gustav Heraeus and created by Benedikt Richter and Daniel Warou, obverse and reverse, 1723 (© Prague, Národní muzeum, inv. č. H5-69ARVIIIa17).

Figure 5.2. Allegorical copper engraving for the Bohemian coronation of Charles VI and Elisabeth Christine by Conrad Adolph von Albrecht, 1723 (© Prague, Národní galerie v Praze, inv. č. R 95 685).

Silesian eagles stand on the mythical threshold (also depicted on the reverse of the figure 5.1) that refers to Prague's imaginary millennium and reportedly gave the city its name—in the interpretation of Václav Hájek of Libočany, *Praha* is derived from the Czech word *práh*, meaning "threshold."[48] Even the plow of the legendary forefather of the Přemyslid dynasty, Přemysl the Plowman, is present. The design for a further commemorative medal that was never produced features the busts of the emperor and empress as Hercules and Hebe on the obverse. On the reverse, against the background of an antique temple, is a picture of the imperial couple accompanied by the figure of kneeling Czechia laying the royal crown at their feet. The Latin inscriptions CORONIS CONSTANTER FIRMANDIS FORTITTER UNITIS and BEATITUDO PUBLICA SALUS PROVINCIARUM proclaim the common felicity and salvation of the provinces of the monarchy on the basis of the consistent and persistent connection of Charles's crowns. They especially stress the unwavering solidarity of the Bohemian lands within the Habsburg realm.

Conrad Adolph von Albrecht conceived yet another document in the same spirit, namely the encomiastical print *Herculi Musagetae* published in the summer of 1723 and dedicated to Charles VI as an art-loving Hercules and master of the muses.[49] In this panegyric, which was evidently designed to impress both the learned and lay public immediately before the Bohemian coronation, the allegorical figure of Czechia similarly offers the royal diadem to the Habsburg lion. The multiplicity of the Habsburg crowns plays a fundamental role here as well, for example in the Latin inscription CAROLUS VI. GERM[anicus] HISP[anicus] HUNG[aricus] BOH[emicus] AUST[riacus] P[ater] P[atriae] S[ecuritatis] P[ublicae] P[ropagator] ("Charles VI, the father of the fatherland and guarantor of common security in Germany, Spain, Hungary, Bohemia, and Austria"). In fact, the scene with Czechia is situated next to a grouping of allegorical figures of the emperor's providence, the hope of the dynasty, and selected provinces, all of which together personify the Hungarian diet. The Bohemian and Hungarian motifs correspond to parallel pictures of the St. Wenceslas and St. Stephen's Crowns at the top of the illustration. Their connection, expressed visually in this work, was symbolic as well. The topic of the Hungarian Diet was appropriate because the Estates had accepted the Pragmatic Sanction in Pressburg in 1722. The following two ceremonies (i.e., the hereditary homage by the Estates and the royal coronation arranged a year later in Bohemia) symbolized the culmination of the "magnificent task of successorship" in the unified Habsburg Monarchy.[50]

The most spectacular public festivity in Prague in 1723 aside from the crownings of the king and queen was the performance of *Costanza e Fortezza*.[51] This opus, sometimes incorrectly referred to as the "coronation opera" and utilizing the emperor's personal motto in its title, was originally conceived as a standard *festa teatrale per musica*. Thanks to its dimensions and mission, however, it actually far exceeded the framework of normal *Augustinian* performances that generally accompanied the celebrations for the empress's birthday. For this unique *Gesamtkunstwerk*, composed by court chapel-master Johann Joseph Fux using the libretto by court poet Pietro Pariati, a special open-air theater designed by court architect Giuseppe Galli-Bibiena was built at the Summer Riding School at Prague Castle in 1723. Unfortunately, it was only used for the premiere and a single reprise. The storyline of the opera, situated in the epoch of early Roman history, is based on the second book of Titus Livius's *History of Rome*, which depicts the expulsion of the Etruscan royal dynasty of the Tarquinians from the town and the constitution of the republic represented by the senate and consuls. A suitable implied meaning was afforded by Livius's interpretation of the events, in which Titus Tarquinius had attempted to go back to the city and reestablish his power by force with the help of his ally King Porsenna.

Porsenna's siege of Rome constitutes the central scene of the first act, in which the Romans are requested to surrender. After the chorus of the river gods halts the Etruscan soldiers in their attack on the town, Porsenna decides to negotiate with Consul Publius Valerius about the enthronement of King Tarquinius in Rome. The consul's two children, Erminio and Valeria, play key roles in these proceedings. Despite becoming captives of the Etruscans, they demonstrate loyalty to their homeland. In the second act, the spectators witness a dramatic scene in which the Roman Muzio, Valeria's fiancé, infiltrates the Etruscan camp and attempts to assassinate Porsenna. His plan fails, however, and he is put on trial by the king. As proof of his determination to defend the liberty of Rome, Muzio holds his hand into the oblatory fire in view of all who are present, and in doing so, he wins Porsenna's admiration: the king grants him freedom. At that moment, Consul Publius Valerius arrives at the camp to negotiate with the Etruscans. These negotiations continue in the third act, which takes place in the gardens on the Janiculum, and eventually cause the besiegers to realize that the citizens of Rome would rather voluntarily continue the war than accept peace under the Etruscans' terms. Ashamed, Porsenna finally acknowledges the admirable constancy and force of his rivals; he ends the war and declares himself a friend of the Romans. The licenza aria, which traditionally served as a congratulatory addendum to such a musical drama, ends the opera with the chorus singing of the gods headed by the Genius of Rome and a dance by allegorical figures representing the love of peace and the common good.

Upon reading the text of the libretto, several noteworthy parallels to actual circumstances and the environment from which the opus arose are apparent.[52] Even the presence of two enemies of Rome, the figures of Tarquinius and Porsenna, can be considered symbolic. Given the international tensions at the turn of the 1720s, they may represent the Saxon and Bavarian rivals of the Habsburgs. The first Roman consul Publius Valerius precisely personifies the monarchical ideal Charles VI proclaimed himself to be—despite the consul not being a sovereign, but an elected delegate of the Senate and the public. He is a wise and virtuous statesman whose utmost concern is the preservation of peace; while at the same time, he is not opposed to waging war if the freedom of the people and his personal credit are at risk. The dismissal by the two noble Roman women Valeria and Clelia of the marriage proposals by Tarquinius and Porsenna is symbolic as well, partly because of their fidelity and their existing engagements to Romans, and partly because of their pride that prevents them from offering their native land as a dowry to foreign rulers. This may mirror the fate of Charles VI's two daughters. Finally, the honored Elisabeth Christine herself, equated in the opera to the ancient Roman goddess Vesta as the patroness of the family and protectress of the dynasty, is explicitly revered as the queen of a new Rome, which is equated to Prague.

It is surprising that historians and musicologists did not fully comprehend this connection for many years, even though it was common to reflect on the current political situation by way of seemingly unrelated themes in baroque musical drama. With the Kingdom of Bohemia symbolized by antique Latium— and Prague by ancient Rome—in *Costanza e Fortezza*, the conflict between the legitimate and the usurped government thus becomes a metaphor discrediting the hereditary claims of the Habsburgs' rivals. Together with the allegorical and encomiastic insertions, the plot of the opera exhibits a striking correspondence to the dynastic and external situation around 1723. Indeed, it clarifies Charles VI's attitude toward the power plans of Saxony and Bavaria with its frequent use of scenic parables. In addition, certain passages of the opus demonstrably respond to the political ambitions made public in the operas *Teofane* and *Adelaide* staged in Dresden and Munich. Hence, the key message of *Costanza e Fortezza*, addressed to the inhabitants of the Habsburg Monarchy as well as to its possible infighters, is a victory without a single drop of blood, along with the fact that it is precisely the extolled freedom that will guarantee future prosperity and peace for the loyal populace of the hereditary lands.

Conclusion

At the time of Charles VI's Bohemian coronation, much had changed since his return from Spain to assume the imperial crown and take control of the Habsburg Monarchy. The outcome of the War of the Spanish Succession, even though it was not unfavorable for the Habsburgs, transformed almost the entire political map of Europe. In truth, Great Britain had already resolved the fierce fight for hegemony in 1711 when it made a secret pact with the Estates General of the Dutch Republic and, unbeknownst to its Austrian ally, proceeded to make an arrangement with France as well. Great Britain and France had even signed a preliminary peace agreement prior to Charles's arrival in Central Europe.[53] The two states reached a compromise because they feared the eventuality that Charles could simultaneously govern the vast territories of the Holy Roman Empire, the Habsburg Monarchy, and Spain with its extensive colonies—a possibility that seemed imminent after the sudden death of his elder brother Joseph I in April 1711. Philip of Anjou definitively became the king of Spain as Philip V, and in return, Great Britain reinforced its position against France on the North American continent and acquired Menorca and Gibraltar in Europe. On the other hand, peace conferences adjudged the Spanish (southern) Netherlands, Milan, Mantua, the Stato dei Presidi, Naples, and Sardinia to the Habsburgs.

It is against the background of these geopolitical changes and challenges that the coronation in 1723 must be interpreted. The librettos and panegyrics, the iconography of the artworks, and the dramaturgy of the ceremonies expressed the idealized Habsburg world domination along with Charles's pretensions toward Spain and its overseas possessions. These messages were transmitted to the participants and audiences of the ritual spectacles, the theater performances, the orations, and all churchly and secular celebrations. Many of them were also published in printed sheets, books, periodicals, and newspapers like *Nova litteraria eruditorum*, *Pražské Posstowské Nowiny*, *Wienerisches Diarium*, and *Die Europäische*

Fama, thereby disseminating them beyond the circle of the immediate attendees. The events in Bohemia became the subject of secret diplomatic dispatches as well, as evidenced in reports by the envoys Girolamo Grimaldi, Francesco Donado, Jakob Heinrich Flemming, and Franz Hannibal Mörmann to the pope, the Senate of Venice, and the Saxon and Bavarian courts respectively.[54] The images of the celebratory mintages, partly created immediately on site in Prague, were also printed. During the coronation festivities, the imperial couple presented the oblatory coins, medals, and tokens to the archbishop and the high-ranking guests and courtiers as well as to the masses of the people.[55]

Given the impending dynastic crisis, the intensity of the media resonance to the public announcement of the empress's pregnancy precisely on her birthday is understandable. This surprising and joyful news suddenly and significantly modified the result not only of the performance of the opera *Costanza e Fortezza*, but also of both coronation festivities. Large numbers of spontaneous congratulations were transmitted along with predications, poems, medals, engravings, and, of course, the mandatory blessings, all hoping for the long-expected male successor to the throne.[56] Unfortunately for Charles and Elisabeth Christine, as today we know what the congratulators at the time could only suspect, the imperial couple would deliver another daughter, Maria Amalia, instead of the long-desired prince. Under the circumstances, the emperor's search for future bridegrooms appears supremely provident. It is the reason why the European sovereigns closely monitored the visit of Francis Stephen of Lorraine to Bohemia as well as Maria Josepha of Saxony's stay in Prague during the sojourn of the imperial court, both of which were related to the diplomatic competition for the potential bride: the young Maria Theresa.[57]

As a consequence, the capital of Bohemia became the focus of attention for the leading powers of Europe in 1723. The coronation of Charles VI, the grandest secular festivity in the Bohemian lands during the entirety of the baroque era, transformed Prague into the prestigious arena of Charles's contest for international acceptance of the Pragmatic Sanction upon which the future existence of the Habsburg Monarchy as a whole seemed to depend.

Petra Vokáčová is an archivist at the Prague City Archives. She studied history, museology, and Germanics in Brno, Heidelberg, and Vienna and received her PhD at Masaryk University in Brno in 2008. Her research focuses on the personality and reign of Emperor Charles VI as well as on the court and the political careers of the nobility in the Bohemian lands and the Habsburg Monarchy in the seventeenth and eighteenth centuries. She has published several articles and books, including "Karel VI." in *Čeští králové*, ed. Marie Ryantová and Petr Vorel (Prague, 2008); *Karel VI. & Alžběta Kristýna: Česká korunovace 1723* (with Štěpán Vácha, Irena Veselá, and Vít Vlnas, Prague, 2009); *Příběhy o hrdé pokoře:*

Aristokracie českých zemí v době baroka (Prague, 2014); and some chapters in *Habsburkové: Země Koruny české ve středoevropské monarchii 1526–1740*, ed. Václav Bůžek and Rostislav Smíšek (Prague, 2017).

Notes

1. In its fundamental parts, this chapter is based upon the research results published in Štěpán Vácha, Irena Veselá, Vít Vlnas, and Petra Vokáčová, *Karel VI. & Alžběta Kristýna: Česká korunovace 1723* (Prague, 2009). I thank my co-authors for kindly permitting me to conceive and publish this text and Emily Bullock Protopapas and Stephan Stockinger for their linguistic revision and corrections. A German summary of the mentioned book can be found in Štěpán Vácha, Irena Veselá, Vít Vlnas, and Petra Vokáčová, "Karl VI. & Elisabeth Christine: Die böhmische Krönung 1723," *Frühneuzeit-Info* 21, no. 1+2 (2010): 226–31. See also Petra Luniaczková, "Der Aufenthalt des Wiener Hofes Kaiser Karls VI. in Böhmen und Mähren anläßlich der königlichen Krönung im Jahre 1723," *Frühneuzeit-Info* 13, no. 1+2 (2002): 25–32.
2. Most historians regard the Pragmatic Sanction as "the birth certificate" of the Habsburg-Lorraine Monarchy: Gustav Turba, *Geschichte des Thronfolgerechtes in allen habsburgischen Ländern bis zur pragmatischen Sanktion Kaiser Karls VI. 1156 bis 1732* (Vienna, 1903), 398–99; Turba, ed., *Die Pragmatische Sanktion: Authentische Texte samt Erläuterungen und Übersetzungen* (Vienna, 1913), xi; Irmgard Pangerl, "Die Pragmatische Sanktion und ihre Folgen: Das Regelwerk der Erbfolge auf dem Prüfstand," in *Maria Theresia 1717–1780: Strategin—Mutter—Reformerin*, ed. Elfride Iby, Martin Mutschlechner, Werner Telesko, and Karl Vocelka (Vienna, 2017), 57–63; Valentin Urfus, *19. 4. 1713 Pragmatická sankce: Rodný list podunajské monarchie* (Prague, 2002), especially 87–91 and 101—see, for example, the appellative of the Pragmatic Sanction as "the omnipresent spine of the Habsburg dynastic state," but also the polemic about its suitability for the development of this multinational monarchy. On the other hand, Charles Ingrao, "Pragmatic Sanction and the Theresian Succession: a Reevaluation," *Études danubienses* 9, no. 1 (1999): 71–87, considers this document merely by virtue of necessity, claiming that the real foundations of the modern Danubian Monarchy in Central Europe were laid by Maria Theresa.
3. The work of Bernd Rill, *Karl VI.: Habsburg als barocke Großmacht* (Graz, 1992), remains the only modern but still very general political biography of Charles VI. The volume Stefan Seitschek, Herbert Hutterer, and Gerald Theimer, eds., *300 Jahre Karls VI. (1711–1740): Spuren der Herrschaft des "letzten" Habsburgers* (Vienna, 2011), provides the newest summary on his reign in a wider familial, political, economical, and cultural context. For a reflection on the emperor as a maecenas and supporter of contemporary art, see the seminal book by Franz Matsche, *Die Kunst im Dienst der Staatsidee Kaiser Karls VI.: Ikonographie, Ikonologie und Programmatik des "Kaiserstils,"* 2 vols. (Berlin, 1981). Currently, an edition of Charles's diaries is prepared by Stefan Seitschek.
4. Marcus Landau, *Geschichte Kaiser Karls VI. als König von Spanien* (Stuttgart, 1889); William O'Reilly, "Lost Chances of the House of Habsburg," *Austrian History Yearbook* 40 (2009): 53–70; similarly, O'Reilly, "A Life in Exile: Charles VI (1685–1740) between Spain and Austria," in *Monarchy and Exile: The Politics of Legitimacy from Marie de Médicis to Wilhelm II*, ed. Philip Mansel and Torsten Riotte (Basingstoke, 2011), 66–90, with numerous references to further literature.

5. Alfred von Arneth, ed., *Eigenhändige Correspondenz des Königs Karl III. von Spanien (nachmals Kaiser Karl VI.) mit dem Obersten Kanzler des Königreiches Böhmen, Grafen Johann Wenzel Wratislaw* (Vienna, 1856), 148–49 and 189.
6. Anna Hedwig Benna, "Ein römischer Königswahlplan Karls III. von Spanien (1708–10)," *MÖStA* 14 (1961): 1–17; see also O'Reilly, "Lost Chances," 53: "The echo of Spain and Spanish government was always there . . . ," then in detail 64–70.
7. *Diario Del Viaggio fatto Dalla Maestà Di Carlo III. Da Barcelona à Milano, ed à Francfort* (Naples, 1712).
8. *Ausfuehrliche Beschreibung Der Croenung Ihr. Roem. Kaeyserl. Majest. Caroli VI. So den 22. Decembr. 1711. in . . . Franckfurt am Mayn . . . paßiret, Nach dem zu Wien gedruckten Original* (Leipzig, 1712).
9. Hanns Leo Mikoletzky, "Hofreisen unter Kaiser Karl VI.," *MIÖG* 60 (1952): 265–85; Wilhelm Rausch, *Die Hofreisen Kaiser Karl VI.* (unpublished doctoral dissertation, University of Vienna, 1949).
10. *Protocollum aulicum*, 5 April 1721, Vienna, ÖStA, HHStA, ZA Prot., 11, fol. 23v; *Protokol hraběte Leopolda Šlika, nejvyššího kancléře Království českého, o říšských konferencích*, 1721, Zámrsk (Czech Republic), Státní oblastní archiv in Zámrsk, Rodinný archiv Šliků, 174 (III.36), carton 18; Rausch, *Die Hofreisen*, 59; Ottocar Weber, "Eine Kaiserreise nach Böhmen im Jahre 1723," *Mittheilungen des Vereines für Geschichte der Deutschen in Böhmen* 36, no. 2 (1897): 138, footnote 1.
11. Weber, "Eine Kaiserreise," 140.
12. Prague, NA, SM, 1580 (K 1/75/1).
13. NA, ČDK, 558, carton 7–10.
14. See the representational manuscript by Johann Adam von Heintz, *Ausführliche Beschreibung der Anno 1723 . . . Nacher Prag in Böhäim verrichteten Reiß, . . . Erb-Huldigung, . . . Zwey-fachen Königl. Crönungen, u. . . . Zuruck-Reyße nacher Wienn*, ÖStA, HHStA, Handschriften, 525 (Handschriften Weiss, Cod. Böhm, 1043).
15. Gottfried Joseph Martin, *Außfuehrlich und Gruendliche Vier Beschreibungen . . .* (Prague, n.d.), chapter 1.
16. For this paragraph, see the detailed *Diarium* in Vácha et al., *Karel VI. & Alžběta Kristýna*, 468–76. Ibid., 213–30 and 239–50, the dramatic and musical opuses are analysed.
17. Anna Coreth, *Pietas Austriaca: Ursprung und Entwicklung barocker Frömmigkeit in Österreich* (Vienna, 1959); Anna Coreth, *Pietas Austriaca: Österreichische Frömmigkeit im Barock* (Vienna, 1982).
18. The contemporary engravings by Anton Birckhardt, Johann II. van der Bruggen, Johann Heinrich Martin, Jakob Wilhelm Heckenauer, Johann Jacob Lidl, Franz Ambroz, and Christoph Dietel, created based on patterns by Giuseppe Galli-Bibiena and portraying the design of particular acts of the opera, were repeatedly published, for instance in Jiří Hilmera, *Perspektivní scéna 17. a 18. století v Čechách* (Prague, 1965). See also the image catalog in Vácha et al., *Karel VI. & Alžběta Kristýna*, 441–49.
19. Martin, *Außfuehrlich und Gruendliche Vier Beschreibungen . . .* (n.d.), chapter 2–4.
20. Prague, APH, Dvorní stavební úřad, 1983, carton 103, fasc. 23, among others fol. 24.
21. For example, Jan Muk, *Po stopách národního vědomí české šlechty pobělohorské* (Prague, 1931), 158–59; Josef Svátek, *Dějiny Čech a Moravy nové doby. Kniha čtvrtá: Panování císaře Josefa I. a Karla VI.* (Prague, 1896), 219–33.
22. Franz Martin Pelzel, *Geschichte der Boehmen, von den aeltesten bis auf die neuesten Zeiten: Aus den besten Geschichtsschreibern, Kroniken und gleichzeitigen Handschriften zusammen*

getragen. Zweyter Theil (Prague, 1782), 849–50. The Venetian ambassador to Vienna, Francesco Donado, who was present in Prague in 1723, also mentioned this fable: Weber, "Eine Kaiserreise," 139, footnote 1.
23. Mikoletzky, *"Hofreisen,"* 269–70. See the following passage from the letter of Count Rudolf Josef Kořenský of Terešov written to Count František Josef Černín of Chudenice, 24 March 1723, Jindřichův Hradec (Czech Republic), Státní oblastní archiv in Třeboň, outpost in Jindřichův Hradec, Rodinný archiv Černínů z Chudenic, carton 338, fol. 39 (originally in German): "One does not yet know how long the emperor will stay, because this depends on whether the empress becomes pregnant, and when. If this does not occur before autumn, then she might take the baths in Karlsbad together with the emperor and stay in Bohemia the entire winter. If she is pregnant sooner, then we will be here [in Vienna] sooner for the delivery."
24. Hermenegild Jireček, ed., *Obnovené Právo a Zřízení Zemské dědičného království Českého—Verneuerte Landes-Ordnung des Erb-Königreichs Böhmen 1627* (Prague, 1888); Karel Malý, Jiří Šouša, and Klára Kučerová, eds., "Deklaratoria a Novely Obnoveného zřízení zemského," in *Vývoj české ústavnosti v letech 1618–1918*, ed. Karel Malý and Ladislav Soukup (Prague, 2006), 793–873.
25. Svátek, *Dějiny Čech a Moravy*, 115–16 and 234.
26. Turba, *Die Pragmatische Sanktion*, 54–87; Peter Claus Hartmann, *Karl Albrecht—Karl VII.: Glücklicher Kurfürst, unglücklicher Kaiser* (Regensburg, 1985), 43–44.
27. Cf. two letters by Maximilian II Emanuel of Bavaria to his son Charles Albrecht in 1725, also designated as the elector's political testament: Karl Theodor Heigel, *Quellen und Abhandlungen zur neueren Geschichte Bayerns* (Munich, 1884), 261–72.
28. For the specification including the reproductions of images and links to sources, see Vácha et al., *Karel VI. & Alžběta Kristýna*, 34–49.
29. Johann Joseph Pock, *Immergrünender Lorber-Baum* . . . (Munich, 1722).
30. Antonio Lotti, *La Teofane: Drama per musica in occassione Delle felicissime Nozze de Serenissimi Principi Federigo Augusto . . . e Maria Gioseffa . . . nell' anno 1719 in Dresda*, SLUB, Mus 2159-F-7; Stefano Benedetto Pallavicino, *Teofane: Opera rappresentata alla Regia Elletoral Corte di Dresda Anno 1719*, SLUB, MT 2558 Rara; Antonio Salvi, *Adelaide: Primo Drama Per Musica Da Rappresentarsi Alle Augustissime Nozze De Serenissimi Sposi Carlo Alberto Principe Elettorale Di Baviera etc. etc. e Maria Amalia Arciduchessa D'Austria etc. etc. L'Anno MDCCXXII* (Munich, 1722). See Rainer Kleinertz, "Thronfolge als Problem: Zur Bedeutung der Pragmatischen Sanktion von 1713 für das Dramma per musica," in *Maria Theresias Kulturwelt: Geschichte, Religiosität, Literatur, Oper, Balettkultur, Architektur, Malerei, Kunsttischlerei, Porzellan und Zuckerbäckerei im Zeitalter Maria Theresias*, ed. Pierre Béhar, Marie-Thérèse Mourey, and Herbert Schneider (Hildesheim, 2011), 77–90.
31. Johann Ulrich König, *Die Hohe Geburth eines Chur-Sächsischen Printzen* . . . (Dresden, 1720), E/b.
32. Andreas Gugler was probably the first who pointed out the noteworthy cohesion between the representational strategies in Dresden, Munich, and Prague. In his analysis of the allegorical decorations at the coronation banquets of Charles VI and Elisabeth Christine from 1723, he interpreted a series of these parallels as an intended reaction to the Saxon and Bavarian festivities on the part of the imperial court: Andreas Gugler, "Constantia et Fortitudine (Bankette und Schauessen im Zusammenhang der Krönungsfeierlichkeiten in Prag 1723)," in *Život na dvorech barokní šlechty (1600–1750)*, ed. Václav Bůžek (České Budějovice, 1996), 282–83 and 285–87. This idea contradicts the interpretation of "two

loyal allies" of Charles VI and of the emperor's "happy prospect of territorial expansion through the addition of the dominions of the archduchess' husband" by Ingrao, "Pragmatic Sanction," 78–79.

33. Prague, Archiv hlavního města Prahy, Sbírka rukopisů, 167, 175, 205, 273, 338, 339, 1000, and 7953. On the arrangements in Prague in particular, see Petra Vokáčová, "Korunovační hostina na Pražském hradě v roce 1723," in *Dobrou chuť, velkoměsto*, ed. Olga Fejtová, Václav Ledvinka, and Jiří Pešek (Prague, 2007), 265–79.

34. Similarly, he received additional Estates' homages in person in Inner (1728) and Upper Austria (1732), although the Pragmatic Sanction had already been accepted there in 1720: Stefan Seitschek, "Die Erbhuldigung 1728 in Kärnten, ihre Organisation und Durchführung anhand ausgewählter Quellen," *Carinthia: Zeitschrift für geschichtliche Landeskunde von Kärnten* 202 (2012): 125–78; Gustav Otruba, "Die Erbhuldigungen der oberösterreichischen Stände 1732-1741-1743: Eine Studie zur Geschichte des Treueverhaltens von Klerus, Adel und Bürgertum gegenüber Karl VI., Karl Albert und Maria Theresia," *Mitteilungen des Oberösterreichischen Landesarchivs* 16 (1990): 135–301.

35. Štěpán Vácha, "'Mutatio vestis' v korunovačním ceremoniálu českých králů z rodu Habsburků v 16. až 18. století," *Folia Historica Bohemica* 22 (2006): 259–62. Moreover, some new offices of the Bohemian royal court based on the imperial model were created in 1723 (*Schatzmeisteramt, Banneramt*).

36. Vácha, "'Mutatio vestis'," 252.

37. Jiří Hrbek, *České barokní korunovace* (Prague, 2010), 84.

38. Heintz, *Ausführliche Beschreibung*..., ÖStA, HHStA, Handschriften, 525, fol. 126v and 146v.

39. Matěj Kovář, "Korunovace císaře Karla VI. na krále českého dne 5. září 1723," *Sborník historického kroužku* 4, no. 3 (1903): 141–43; Ivana Kyzourová and Vít Vlnas, eds., *Žezlo a koruna: Karel IV. a české královské korunovace—The Sceptre and the Crown: Charles IV and Bohemian Royal Coronations* (Prague, 2016).

40. See the notation of the court conference on 13 April 1723, ÖStA, HHStA, Ältere Zeremonialakten, 1721–23, carton 30, fasc. K 18, fol. 91; similarly in *Protocollum aulicum*, 1723–24, ÖStA, HHStA, ZA Prot., 12, fol. 142r.

41. The royal vestment is described in more detail in *Protocollum aulicum*, 1723–24, ÖStA, HHStA, ZA Prot., 12, fol. 230v–231r, and also in Heintz, *Ausführliche Beschreibung*..., ÖStA, HHStA, Handschriften, 525, fol. 146.

42. This set of garments, apparently made for Ferdinand IV of Habsburg in 1653, has been preserved as part of the coronation insignia to this day. See in detail Štěpán Vácha, "Repräsentations- oder Krönungsornat? Zum Ursprung und zur Funktion des Zeremonialgewands Ferdinands IV. aus dem Jahre 1653," *Umění* 54, no. 3 (2006): 229–39.

43. *Protocollum aulicum*, 1723–24, ÖStA, HHStA, ZA Prot., 12, fol. 292v–293r; likewise Matěj Kovář, "Korunovace císařovny Alžběty, choti Karla VI., na královnu českou dne 8. září 1723," *Sborník historického kroužku* 5, no. 1 (1904): 39.

44. The tapestries had been made for Charles VI at the workshop of Judocus de Vos in Brussels between 1712 and 1721 and were brought to Prague in 1723 explicitly for the purpose of the coronation: Gugler, "Constantia et Fortitudine," 280–82.

45. The medals are described in the print Carl Gustav Heraeus, *Explicatio Numismatum Publica Vulgatorum Inter Solennia Inaugurationis Regiae Bohemicae, Quae Conditae Urbis Pragae Saeculum Milliarium Auspicato Aeternae Memoriae Commendat* (n.p., 1723), ÖStA, HHStA, Hausarchiv, Familienakten, carton 4, fasc. 4–16.

46. For images of all the medals, see Vácha et al., *Karel VI. & Alžběta Kristýna*, 192–93 (X), 216, and 452–54.
47. This sheet was published as an appendix to a later edition of Gottfried Joseph Martin, *Außfuehrlich- und Gruenätiche Beschreibungen* . . . (Strasbourg, 1724); it can also be found separately in the collections of the National Gallery of Prague, R 95 685. For more details, see Štěpán Vácha, "Tři alegorie k pražské korunovaci roku 1723: K politické motivaci 'císařského' stylu Karla VI.," in *Pictura verba cupit: Sborník příspěvků pro Lubomíra Konečného—Essays for Lubomír Konečný*, ed. Beket Bukovinská and Lubomír Slavíček (Prague, 2006), 260.
48. Jan Linka, ed., *Václav Hájek z Libočan, Kronika česká* (Prague, 2013), 57–8.
49. Conradus Adolphus ab Albrecht, *Herculi Musagetae, Priscam Monumentis Majestatem, Novum Antiquis Splendorem, Antiquam Novis Gratiam Restituenti* . . . (Prague, 1723), ÖStA, HHStA, Hausarchiv, Kartensammlung, Ke 3-1/2. Compare with the hand-drawn version in *Codex Albrecht* [Conrad Adolph von Albrecht, *Verschiedene Erfindungen Hieroglyphisch-Historisch- und Poëtischer Gedancken* . . . , 1736), Vienna, Österreichische Nationalbibliothek, Handschriften, Cod. ser. nov. 7853, fol. 14r. In detail, see Vácha, "Tři alegorie," 261–63.
50. "Das grosse Werck der Erbfolge": Frantz Christoph Khevenhüller, *Annales Ferdinandei IX.* (Leipzig, 1724), b2 (recto). This can be compared to the circumscription on the medal by the Nuremberg medalist Andreas Vestner, minted in memory of the Bohemian coronation but without commission by the Viennese court: CORONATIS AUGUSTIS SUCCESSIONE FIRMATA MDCCXXIII ("For the crowned emperor and empress after the confirmation of their succession").
51. Johann Joseph Fux, *Costanza e Fortezza: Festa Teatrale Per Musica, Da Rappresentarsi Nel Reale Castello Di Praga* . . . *1723*, Vienna, Österreichische Nationalbibliothek, Musiksammlung, Mus. Hs. 17 266 Mus.; Pietro Pariati, *Costanza e Fortezza: Festa Teatrale Per Musica, Da Rappresentarsi Nel Reale Castello Di Praga Per Il Felicissimo Giorno Natalizio Della Sac. Ces. e Catt. Reale Maestà Di Elisabetta Cristina Imperadrice Regnante, Per Commando Della Sac. Ces. e Catt. Reale Maestà Di Carlo VI. Imperadore De' Romani Sempre Augusto. L'Anno MDCCXXIII* . . . (Vienna, n.d.); Pariati, *Die Staercke und Bestaendigkeit: Theatral-Fest, An dem Glorwuerdigsten Geburts-Tag Der Roemisch-Kaiserlich- wie auch Koeniglich-Spanisch-Catholischen Majestaet Elisabethae Christinae* . . . (Vienna, n.d.). For the analysis of the opus, see Vácha et al., *Karel VI. & Alžběta Kristýna*, 133–72, with an extensive bibliography.
52. Irena Veselá, "Venga quel dì felice! Dynastisch-politische Botschaften in musikalischen Huldigungswerken für Karl VI. und Elisabeth Christine (1723)," in *Representing the Habsburg-Lorraine Dynasty in Music, Visual Media and Architecture 1618–1918*, ed. Werner Telesko (Vienna, 2017), 139–42.
53. Oswald Redlich, *Das Werden einer Grossmacht: Österreich von 1700 bis 1740* (Brno, 1942), 107–8; Rill, *Karl VI.*, 90; Vít Vlnas, *Princ Evžen Savojský: Život a sláva barokního válečníka* (Prague, 2001), 395–96, 418–19.
54. Vatican City, Archivio Segreto Vaticano, Segretaria di Stato, Germania, 229, fol. 249; 279, fols. 456–636; Venice, Archivio di Stato di Venezia, Senato, Dispacci ambasciatori, Germania, 216, no. 13, fols. 106–37; Dresden, Sächsisches Hauptstaatsarchiv Dresden, Geheimes Kabinett, 696/7, fols. 55r–58v, 61r–62r, 63r–72r, 102v–3r, and 118r–19r; 763/9, fols. 150, 155v–56r, 161r–62v, 165r–68v, and 190r–92v; Munich, Bayerisches Hauptstaatsarchiv München, Kasten Schwarz, 360; 363, fol. 20 e. s., 80 e. s. I am grateful

to Jana Spáčilová and Štěpán Vácha for providing me with the copies and excerpts of these documents.
55. Heintz, *Ausführliche Beschreibung . . .* , ÖStA, HHStA, Handschriften, 525, fol. 178r; Kovář, "Korunovace císaře Karla VI.," 227; Mikoletzky, "Hofreisen," 283, footnote 103; Weber, "Eine Kaiserreise," 186, footnote 1.
56. Similarly, three dramatic and musical opuses, the serenate *Il Giorno felice, La Concordia de' Pianeti*, and *Il bel Genio dell'Austria ed il Fato*, glorified Elisabeth Christine as mother of a new Austrian sun and of a future Roman king and emperor: Vácha et al., *Karel VI. & Alžběta Kristýna*, 213–50; Veselá, "Venga," 142–47.
57. Vácha et al., *Karel VI. & Alžběta Kristýna*, 115–32; Renate Zedinger, *Hochzeit im Brennpunkt der Mächte: Franz Stephan von Lothringen und Erzherzogin Maria Theresia* (Vienna, 1994).

Bibliography

Albrecht, Conradus Adolphus ab. *Herculi Musagetae, Priscam Monumentis Majestatem, Novum Antiquis Splendorem, Antiquam Novis Gratiam Restituenti.* Prague: n.p., 1723.

Arneth, Alfred, ed. *Eigenhändige Correspondenz des Königs Karl III. von Spanien (nachmals Kaiser Karl VI.) mit dem Obersten Kanzler des Königreiches Böhmen, Grafen Johann Wenzel Wratislaw.* Vienna: Kaiserlich-königliche Staatsdruckerei zu Wien, 1856.

Ausfuehrliche Beschreibung Der Croenung Ihr. Roem. Kaeyserl. Majest. Caroli VI. So den 22. Decembr. 1711. in . . . Franckfurt am Mayn . . . paßiret, Nach dem zu Wien gedruckten Original. Leipzig: Johann Theodor Boetius, 1712.

Benna, Anna Hedwig. "Ein römischer Königswahlplan Karls III. von Spanien (1708–10)." *MÖStA* 14 (1961): 1–17.

Coreth, Anna. *Pietas Austriaca: Österreichische Frömmigkeit im Barock.* Vienna: Verlag für Geschichte und Politik, 1982.

———. *Pietas Austriaca: Ursprung und Entwicklung barocker Frömmigkeit in Österreich.* Vienna: Verlag für Geschichte und Politik, 1959.

Diario Del Viaggio fatto Dalla Maestà Di Carlo III. Da Barcelona à Milano, ed à Francfort. Naples: Michele Luigi Muzio, 1712.

Gugler, Andreas. "Constantia et Fortitudine (Bankette und Schauessen im Zusammenhang der Krönungsfeierlichkeiten in Prag 1723)." In *Život na dvorech barokní šlechty (1600–1750)*, edited by Václav Bůžek, 267–92. České Budějovice: Editio Universitatis Bohemiae Meridionalis, 1996.

Hartmann, Peter Claus. *Karl Albrecht—Karl VII.: Glücklicher Kurfürst, unglücklicher Kaiser.* Regensburg: Verlag Friedrich Pustet, 1985.

Heigel, Karl Theodor. *Quellen und Abhandlungen zur neueren Geschichte Bayerns.* Munich: M. Rieger'sche Universitäts-Buchhandlung Gustav Himmer, 1884.

Heraeus, Carl Gustav. *Explicatio Numismatum Auctoritate Publica Vulgatorum Inter Solennia Inaugurationis Regiae Bohemicae, Quae Conditae Urbis Pragae Saeculum Milliarium Auspicato Aeternae Memoriae Commendat.* N.p.: n.p., 1723.

Hilmera, Jiří. *Perspektivní scéna 17. a 18. století v Čechách.* Prague: Scénografický ústav, 1965.

Hrbek, Jiří. *České barokní korunovace.* Prague: Nakladatelství Lidové noviny, 2010.

Ingrao, Charles. "Pragmatic Sanction and the Theresian Succession: a Reevaluation." *Études danubienses* 9, no. 1 (1999): 71–87.

Jireček, Hermenegild, ed. *Obnovené Právo a Zřízení Zemské dědičného království Českého— Verneuerte Landes-Ordnung des Erb-Königreichs Böhmen 1627*. Prague: F. Tempský, 1888.
Katzi von Ludwigstorff, Aemilianus. *Dem Allerdurchleuchtigsten ... Carl dem VI. ... dieses mein in Teutsche Reimb gebundenes goldenes ABC ....* N.p.: n.p., 1723.
Khevenhüller, Frantz Christoph. *Annales Ferdinandei IX*. Leipzig: Moritz Georg Weidmann, 1724.
Kleinertz, Rainer. "Thronfolge als Problem: Zur Bedeutung der Pragmatischen Sanktion von 1713 für das Dramma per musica." In *Maria Theresias Kulturwelt: Geschichte, Religiosität, Literatur, Oper, Balettkultur, Architektur, Malerei, Kunsttischlerei, Porzellan und Zuckerbäckerei im Zeitalter Maria Theresias*, edited by Pierre Béhar, Marie-Thérèse Mourey, and Herbert Schneider, 77–90. Hildesheim: Georg Olms Verlag, 2011.
König, Johann Ulrich. *Das Gedoppelte Boehmische Kroenungs-Fest ....* Prague: Johann Wentzl Helm, 1723.
———. *Die Hohe Geburth eines Chur-Sächsischen Printzen ....* Dresden: Johann Conrad Stößel, 1720.
Kovář, Matěj. "Korunovace císaře Karla VI. na krále českého dne 5. září 1723." *Sborník historického kroužku* 4, no. 3 (1903): 129–44; no. 4 (1903): 221–36.
———. "Korunovace císařovny Alžběty, choti Karla VI., na královnu českou dne 8. září 1723." *Sborník historického kroužku* 5, no. 1 (1904): 36–41.
Kyzourová, Ivana, and Vít Vlnas, eds. *Žezlo a koruna: Karel IV. a české královské korunovace— The Sceptre and the Crown: Charles IV and Bohemian Royal Coronations*. Prague: Správa Pražského hradu, 2016.
Landau, Marcus. *Geschichte Kaiser Karls VI. als König von Spanien*. Stuttgart: J. G. Cotta, 1889.
Linka, Jan, ed. *Václav Hájek z Libočan, Kronika česká*. Prague: Academia, 2013.
Luniaczková, Petra. "Der Aufenthalt des Wiener Hofes Kaiser Karls VI. in Böhmen und Mähren anläßlich der königlichen Krönung im Jahre 1723." *Frühneuzeit-Info* 13, no. 1+2 (2002): 25–32.
Malý, Karel, Jiří Šouša, and Klára Kučerová, eds. "Deklaratoria a Novely Obnoveného zřízení zemského." In *Vývoj české ústavnosti v letech 1618–1918*, edited by Karel Malý and Ladislav Soukup, 793–873. Prague: Univerzita Karlova, Karolinum, 2006.
Martin, Gottfried Joseph. *Außführlich- und Gruendliche Beschreibungen, Erstens: Des Einzugs, Welchen Beyde Roem. Kayserl. und Koenigl. Majestaeten Carolus VI. Mit Dero Allerdurchlauchtigsten Frauen Gemahlin Elisabetha Christina, In die Koenigliche drey Prager Staedte gehalten. Andertens: Der Ihro Maj. dem Kays. als Koenig zu Boeheim Von denen gesammten Boeheimischen Staendten abgelegten Allgemeinen Erb-Huldigung. Drittens: Mehr Allerhoechst besagt Ihro Majestaet deß Kaeysers den 5. Sept. Und Vierdtens: Ihrer Majestaet der Kaeyserin den 8. Sept. Anno 1723. vorbeygegangenen Koeniglichen Boehmischen Croenungen*. Strasbourg: Dieterich Lerse, 1724.
———. *Außfuehrlich und Gruendliche Vier Beschreibungen, Erstens: Deß Einzugs, Welchen Beyde Roemische Kayser- und Koenigliche Majestaeten Carolus Der Sechste, Mit Dero Allerdurchlauchtigsten Frauen Gemahlin Elisabetha Christina, In die Koenigliche drey Prager-Staette gehalten. Andertens: Der Ihro Majestaet dem Kayser als Koenig zu Boeheim Von denen gesammten Boehmischen Staenden abgelegten Allgemeinen Erb-Huldigung. Drittens: Mehr Allerhoechst besagt Ihro Majestaet deß Kaysers Und Viertens: Ihrer Majestaet der Kaeyserin Anno 1723. vorbeygegangenen Koeniglichen Boehmischen Croenungen*. Prague: Wolffgang Wickhart, n.d.
Matsche, Franz. *Die Kunst im Dienst der Staatsidee Kaiser Karls VI.: Ikonographie, Ikonologie und Programmatik des "Kaiserstils."* 2 vols. Berlin: Walter de Gruyter, 1981.

Mikoletzky, Hanns Leo. "Hofreisen unter Kaiser Karl VI." *MIÖG* 60 (1952): 265–85.
Muk, Jan. *Po stopách národního vědomí české šlechty pobělohorské*. Prague: Politický klub Československé národní demokracie, 1931.
O'Reilly, William. "A Life in Exile: Charles VI (1685–1740) between Spain and Austria." In *Monarchy and Exile: The Politics of Legitimacy from Marie de Médicis to Wilhelm II*, edited by Philip Mansel and Torsten Riotte, 66–90. Basingstoke: Palgrave Macmillan, 2011.
———. "Lost Chances of the House of Habsburg." *Austrian History Yearbook* 40 (2009): 53–70.
Otruba, Gustav. "Die Erbhuldigungen der oberösterreichischen Stände 1732–1741–1743: Eine Studie zur Geschichte des Treueverhaltens von Klerus, Adel und Bürgertum gegenüber Karl VI., Karl Albert und Maria Theresia." *Mitteilungen des Oberösterreichischen Landesarchivs* 16 (1990): 135–301.
Pangerl, Irmgard. "Die Pragmatische Sanktion und ihre Folgen: Das Regelwerk der Erbfolge auf dem Prüfstand." In *Maria Theresia 1717–1780: Strategin—Mutter—Reformerin*, edited by Elfride Iby, Martin Mutschlechner, Werner Telesko, and Karl Vocelka, 57–63. Vienna: Amalthea Signum Verlag, 2017.
Pariati, Pietro. *Costanza e Fortezza: Festa Teatrale Per Musica, Da Rappresentarsi Nel Reale Castello Di Praga Per Il Felicissimo Giorno Natalizio Della Sac. Ces. e Catt. Reale Maestà Di Elisabetta Cristina Imperadrice Regnante, Per Commando Della Sac. Ces. e Catt. Reale Maestà Di Carlo VI. Imperadore De' Romani Sempre Augusto. L'Anno MDCCXXIII* . . . . Vienna: Giovanni Pietro Van Ghelen, n.d.
———. *Die Staercke und Bestaendigkeit: Theatral-Fest, An dem Glorwuerdigsten Geburts-Tag Der Roemisch-Kaiserlich- wie auch Koeniglich-Spanisch-Catholischen Majestaet Elisabethae Christinae* . . . . Vienna: Johann Peter Van Ghelen, n.d.
Pelzel, Franz Martin. *Geschichte der Boehmen, von den aeltesten bis auf die neuesten Zeiten: Aus den besten Geschichtschreibern, Kroniken und gleichzeitigen Handschriften zusammen getragen. Zweyter Theil*. Prague: Johann Ferdinand Edler von Schönfeld, 1782.
Pock, Johann Joseph. *Immergrünender Lorber-Baum* . . . . Munich: Maria Magdalena Riedlin Wittib, 1722.
Rausch, Wilhelm. *Die Hofreisen Kaiser Karl VI.* Unpublished doctoral dissertation, University of Vienna, 1949.
Redlich, Oswald. *Das Werden einer Grossmacht: Österreich von 1700 bis 1740*. Brno: Rudolf M. Rohrer, 1942.
Rill, Bernd. *Karl VI.: Habsburg als barocke Großmacht*. Graz: Verlag Styria, 1992.
Salvi, Antonio. *Adelaide: Primo Drama Per Musica Da Rappresentarsi Alle Augustissime Nozze De Serenissimi Sposi Carlo Alberto Principe Elettorale Di Baviera etc. etc. e Maria Amalia Arciduchessa D'Austria etc. etc. L'Anno MDCCXXII*. Munich: Enrico Teodoro di Côllen, 1722.
Seitschek, Stefan. "Die Erbhuldigung 1728 in Kärnten, ihre Organisation und Durchführung anhand ausgewählter Quellen." *Carinthia: Zeitschrift für geschichtliche Landeskunde von Kärnten* 202 (2012): 125–78.
———. *Die Tagebücher Kaiser Karls VI.: Zwischen Arbeitseifer und Melancholie*. Horn: Verlag Berger, 2018.
Seitschek, Stefan, Herbert Hutterer, and Gerald Theimer, eds. *300 Jahre Karls VI. (1711–1740): Spuren der Herrschaft des "letzten" Habsburgers*. Vienna: Österreichisches Staatsarchiv, 2011.
Svátek, Josef. *Dějiny Čech a Moravy nové doby. Kniha čtvrtá: Panování císaře Josefa I. a Karla VI.* Prague: I. L. Kober, 1896.

Turba, Gustav, ed. *Die Pragmatische Sanktion: Authentische Texte samt Erläuterungen und Übersetzungen.* Vienna: Kaiserlich-königlicher Schulbücher-Verlag, 1913.

———. *Geschichte des Thronfolgerechtes in allen habsburgischen Ländern bis zur pragmatischen Sanktion Kaiser Karls VI. 1156 bis 1732.* Vienna: Verlag der kaiserlichen und königlichen Hof-Buchdruckerei und Hof-Verlags-Buchhandlung Carl Fromme, 1903.

Urfus, Valentin. *19. 4. 1713 Pragmatická sankce: Rodný list podunajské monarchie.* Prague: Havran, 2002.

Vácha, Štěpán. "'Mutatio vestis' v korunovačním ceremoniálu českých králů z rodu Habsburků v 16. až 18. století." *Folia Historica Bohemica* 22 (2006): 251–66.

———. "Repräsentations- oder Krönungsornat? Zum Ursprung und zur Funktion des Zeremonialgewands Ferdinands IV. aus dem Jahre 1653." *Umění* 54, no. 3 (2006): 229–39.

———. "Tři alegorie k pražské korunovaci roku 1723: K politické motivaci 'císařského' stylu Karla VI." In *Pictura verba cupit: Sborník příspěvků pro Lubomíra Konečného—Essays for Lubomír Konečný,* edited by Beket Bukovinská and Lubomír Slavíček, 257–69. Prague: Artefactum, 2006.

Vácha, Štěpán, Irena Veselá, Vít Vlnas, and Petra Vokáčová. *Karel VI. & Alžběta Kristýna: Česká korunovace 1723.* Prague: Paseka, Národní galerie v Praze, 2009.

———. "Karl VI. & Elisabeth Christine: Die böhmische Krönung 1723." *Frühneuzeit-Info* 21, no. 1+2 (2010): 226–31.

Veselá, Irena. "Die Serenata 'La concordia de' pianeti' für Kaiserin Elisabeth Christine und ihre Aufführung in Znaim im Jahre 1723." *Frühneuzeit-Info* 27 (2016): 80–96.

———. "Venga quel dì felice! Dynastisch-politische Botschaften in musikalischen Huldigungswerken für Karl VI. und Elisabeth Christine (1723)." In *Representing the Habsburg-Lorraine Dynasty in Music, Visual Media and Architecture 1618–1918,* edited by Werner Telesko, 135–57. Vienna: Böhlau Verlag, 2017.

Vlnas, Vít. *Princ Evžen Savojský: Život a sláva barokního válečníka.* Prague: Paseka, Národní galerie v Praze, 2001.

Vokáčová, Petra. "Korunovační hostina na Pražském hradě v roce 1723." In *Dobrou chuť, velkoměsto,* edited by Olga Fejtová, Václav Ledvinka, and Jiří Pešek, 265–79. Prague: Archiv hlavního města Prahy, Scriptorium, 2007.

Weber, Ottocar. "Eine Kaiserreise nach Böhmen im Jahre 1723." *Mittheilungen des Vereines für Geschichte der Deutschen in Böhmen* 36, no. 2 (1897): 137–204.

Zedinger, Renate. *Hochzeit im Brennpunkt der Mächte: Franz Stephan von Lothringen und Erzherzogin Maria Theresia.* Vienna: Böhlau Verlag, 1994.

Chapter 6

INAUGURATIONS IN THE AUSTRIAN NETHERLANDS
Flexible Formats at the Interface between Constitution, Political Negotiation, and Representation

Klaas Van Gelder

In memory of Thomas Goossens (1983–2017), great lover of the Austrian Netherlands

Between 1703 and 1794, forty-five inaugurations of Habsburg rulers took place in the Austrian Netherlands (see appendix, table 6.1).[1] Although contemporaries considered these lands *une masse indivisible*, each of the territories or principalities comprising this conglomerate retained its autonomy and distinctive constitutional character until the end of the Austrian regime. As a result, every new prince had to be invested separately in each territory.[2] Contrary to what historians have long assumed, I argue that these inaugurations remained hugely important in constitutional, political, and social terms.[3] Through them, individuals and corporations defended various interests and pursued a myriad of sometimes contradictory goals that can be identified by looking at both the negotiations preceding the inaugurations and the rituals themselves. As I will explain throughout this chapter, there were several reasons why organizing the inaugurations remained indispensable in the Netherlands. First, there was a strong tradition of inaugural ceremonies, which were often the focal point of hard bargaining between the prince and the powerful Estates. Second, the traditional format was adaptable to contemporary circumstances. Third, the Netherlands were remote from the center of the monarchy, and as a result, the prince was usually absent.

The first part of this chapter is a brief outline of the constitutional and political relevance of the inaugurations, while the subsequent sections contain analyses of their organization and how they actually took place. Finally, in the conclusion, I briefly explain how princely inaugurations served as an inverse model for ritually deposing Joseph II during the revolution in the Austrian Netherlands. Once again, this demonstrates the adaptability and recognizability of their format. In Belgium, the pictorial language of these inaugurations even survived until the mid-nineteenth century, albeit in a completely different constitutional framework.

My emphasis is on the Duchy of Brabant and the County of Flanders, since these were the most important principalities—not only population-wise, but also with respect to their fiscal contributions, commercial and industrial activities, and political leverage *vis-à-vis* the prince.[4] Furthermore, Brussels, one of the three capital cities of Brabant, was the seat of the majority of the central government institutions and home to the governor-general—usually a member of the dynasty—and his or her household. Indeed, even the inaugurations reflected the predominance of Brabant and Flanders. Usually, these were the only regions in which the governor-general personally performed the reciprocal swearing of oaths. Elsewhere, aristocrats, high functionaries, or military governors performed this duty in his stead. However, my emphasis on the inaugurations in Brussels (for Brabant) and Ghent (for Flanders) does not exclude brief observations on their counterparts elsewhere. It is possible that, in certain respects, the other inaugurations underwent different evolutions, but more research is needed to come to conclusions on this issue. Nevertheless, the official correspondence between Vienna and Brussels makes it clear that Vienna attached the greatest importance to what happened in Brussels and Ghent, and that the Habsburgs valued Brabantine and Flemish consent with the investitures more highly than that of other territories.

Inaugurations in the Habsburg Netherlands: An Introduction

Whichever regional variations existed, the core of these inaugurations was always the same: the prince swore to uphold the laws and privileges of the principality and protect its inhabitants, and the Estates as representatives of their region subsequently swore obedience and loyalty to the prince. The only exception to this rule was the small district of the Retroceded Lands. Louis XIV of France had conquered these territories in the south of Flanders in the seventeenth century, and under his rule, the district lost its representation by means of an Estates' assembly.

The Austrians maintained this situation after their return in 1719, and as a result, the Retroceded Lands were the only region where the Habsburgs could freely impose taxes without the consent of their subjects. Another consequence was that inaugurations had a different character here: the representatives of towns and countryside swore an oath to the prince, but not the other way around. Wherever they took place, inaugurations always began with a joyous entry by the representative of the prince in the host city. On his route, he passed by a string of highly symbolic ecclesiastic and secular spaces. These buildings, squares, or monuments highlighted the privileges, power, or wealth of the different Estates in society and specific regional and urban corporations. At other stages of the ceremony, sung masses and *Te Deums* pled for heavenly support for the new sovereign.

Additionally, artillery salvos resounded and illuminations and fireworks turned the city into a spectacular festive scene. Sometimes the organizers also gave commemorative medals to the privileged invitees and threw commemorative coins over the assembled crowd. The prince or his representative pardoned a selection of delinquents, banquets and balls welcomed the distinguished guests, and popular festivities filled the streets. The wide array of celebrations thus encompassed both commoners and the privileged classes. The inaugurations themselves took place on elevated stages in the open, which underlines their public character (see figure 6.1).[5]

Figure 6.1. Stage on the Friday Market in Ghent for the inauguration of Joseph II as count of Flanders, 1781. Watercolor presumably by P. J. Goetghebuer based on a painting by Engelbert Lieven van Siclers (Ghent, Stadsarchief Gent, Oud archief, Atlas Goetghebuer, Lade 125, no. 117).

Charles VI, Maria Theresa, Joseph II, Leopold II, and Francis II successively ruled the Austrian Netherlands, and they were at the heart of the respective inaugurations. Nevertheless, it is important to keep in mind that during the entire eighteenth century, only one ruler attended in person (see table 6.1): on 23 April 1794, Francis II participated in the joint Brabant-Limburg inauguration and personally swore to safeguard the constitutions of these regions. On all other occasions, the governor-general, the minister plenipotentiary, aristocrats, or high officials represented the prince.[6] By the eighteenth century, the nomination of proxies for the inaugurations was a long-standing tradition. In fact, since the second half of the sixteenth century, the southern Netherlands were used to being governed by an absent prince and by governors-general, preferably of royal blood. After the definitive departure of Philip II in 1559, Albert and Isabella were the only rulers who, from 1598 to 1621, actually resided in the Netherlands, and after 1621, no sovereign visited this region again until Joseph II in 1781. As a result, the Estates and the subjects in the eighteenth century did not consider princely absence to be a problem, nor a sign of disrespect. Legal proxies from the higher ranks of society represented the prince in the same way that diplomats did in foreign courts. Furthermore, during the inaugurations, portraits of the prince were on display, usually under a canopy and hung above a throne, as if the prince were present.[7] Nevertheless, precisely because of the fact that the sovereign was usually absent, his attendance at the inauguration of 1794 was a strong signal, especially after five years of extreme political turmoil, as we will see further on.

In the sources, *huldinghe* or *huldiging* (Dutch) and *inauguration* (French) appear as the common terms for the combined ritual. The terms *Blijde Inkomst* or *Joyeuse Entrée* refer to the unique constitutional situation of the Duchy of Brabant. Since the mid-fourteenth century, Brabant had a charter that contained the basic privileges of its subjects: the so-called *Blijde Inkomst/Joyeuse Entrée*. Unlike the other regions, in Brabant, the prince had to swear to guarantee each of its clauses before being invested. This considerably strengthened Brabant's political leverage and turned out to be crucial in legitimizing the revolution against Joseph II.[8] On the contrary, the constitutions of other regions consisted of a vague set of ancient traditions, customs, statutes, and privileges that the prince swore to uphold in general terms.

Eighteenth-century inaugurations drew on a long-standing tradition of princely investitures in the Netherlands—rites that had often been caught up in the rivalry between the prince and the powerful cities. The wealth of medieval Flanders and Brabant was grounded on frenzied commercial and industrial activities in a network of comparatively large and very self-confident cities, linked with a densely populated hinterland. By the late Middle Ages, the main cities in both principalities had also gained a powerful position in the respective Estates' assemblies, which they retained until the eighteenth century. This clearly set these territories apart from the rest of the Habsburg Monarchy. Ghent, Bruges, and

Ieper held a virtual monopoly in Flanders: the only other actors who had a vote were the Franc of Bruges (since 1385) and the clergy (since 1596). When Ieper lost its seat after its annexation by France in 1678, Bruges and Ghent still had half of the votes.[9] Clergy, nobility, and cities (since 1629 only Leuven, Brussels, and Antwerp) all had a seat in the Estates' assembly in Brabant. This may not seem as impressive as their Flemish colleagues, but given the unanimity rule in the Brabant Estates, one city, and even one of the bodies comprising the city council, could stop any unfriendly resolution. They did not hesitate to threaten to use, and indeed actually use, this political weapon, which was as frustrating for the Austrian Habsburgs as it was for their predecessors.[10]

Since the twelfth century, the Low Countries had developed a tradition of urban revolt. The powerful burghers did not hesitate to rebel when the prince acted against their interests, or when he jeopardized their cherished autonomy and their hold on the surrounding countryside.[11] From the Burgundian era onward, both the prince and the cities increasingly used joyous entries—with or without constitutional oath swearing—as a platform for the ceremonial voicing of discontent or, conversely, as a means of reconciliation. The historian Hugo Soly correctly pointed out that princes pursued contradictory goals during these joyous entries: they wanted to create goodwill and spur loyalty among the citizens as well as demonstrate their power. The urban authorities tried to find a similar balance between glorifying the prince, emphasizing the opulence, power, and prestige of their city, and convincing their fellow citizens of the righteousness of their policy. In times of tension, the evermore sophisticated iconographic messages on stages and triumphal arches that adorned the streets and squares along the processional route served as mirrors of princes. They allegorically emphasized the duties of the new duke or count.[12] After the deposition of Philip II in 1581, some joyous entries and inaugurations even went one step further, visualizing the claims of pretenders to the throne and their supporters.[13] In sum, it is beyond doubt that, for centuries, joyous entries and inaugurations in the Low Countries were at the heart of a number of entangled bargaining processes between the prince and the subjects, as well as between groups of subjects. They were no mere end of political negotiations, but also constituted a tool in the game of give and take of the prince and the privileged classes.

During the seventeenth century, inaugurations in the Habsburg Netherlands underwent a lasting transformation. The prince no longer swore an oath in every major city. Instead, joyous entries and inaugurations were restricted to the capital of every principality.[14] In the County of Artois in 1600, for example, the other Artesian cities sent delegates to Arras. Nevertheless, this seems to have been the exception among the acts of homage for Albert and Isabella. In that same year, the city of Douai successfully resisted a unified inauguration for Walloon Flanders in Lille.[15] The inaugurations for Philip III of Spain in 1616 seem to have been a turning point. They took place during the sovereign rule of Albert and Isabella. Representatives of the fourteen territories swore on four different occasions in Mariemont and in Brussels. This was also the last time a ruling monarch in the Habsburg Netherlands had his successor sworn in during his reign, as Charles V had done for the future Philip II in 1549.[16] As a corollary of the transition to one act of homage for every separate territory, the Estates took the place of the city councils as the main interlocutors of the prince and his government in preparation of the investiture. Delegates of the Estates swore the oaths instead of the aldermen of the city.[17] It is within this changed institutional framework that, henceforth, the negotiations that preceded the inauguration as well as the inaugurations themselves took place. Moreover, when comparing sixteenth-century and eighteenth-century inaugurations, the bargaining process that preceded the actual homages seems to have gained in importance, although more research on the seventeenth-century is needed to verify and explain this transition. Nevertheless, the relationship between the prince and his privileged subjects always remained at the heart of these investitures.

Inaugurations and the Negotiations between Prince and Estates

The inaugurations remained a cornerstone of the constitutions in the Austrian Netherlands, and both prince and subjects were indispensable for their occurrence. As a result, every inauguration was preceded by negotiations, which for Brabant and Flanders—regions with a lot of political leverage as they paid on average 73.57 percent of all taxes—could last for months.[18] Moreover, during the start of the Austrian regime, the new ruler was facing very self-confident Estates. Decades of weakening central authority and a virtual collapse of central government during the War of the Spanish Succession had given them a strong institutional continuity. In 1715–16, at the beginning of the Austrian regime, the government was in dire need of resources. The militant Estates exploited this situation and issued their demands, cowing Emperor Charles VI by making use of their right to consent to—or decline—princely monetary demands. As a result, the negotiations preceding Charles's inaugurations proved a hard nut to crack and lasted almost two years. This close entanglement of organizing inaugurations and bargaining over princely taxes seems to be unique in the eighteenth-century Habsburg Monarchy. It certainly helps to explain the regular assiduousness of the Estates in wresting concessions before accepting to co-organize an investiture.

The first major thorn in their side was the Barrier Treaty. This international agreement, signed in November 1715, had paved the way for the Austrian takeover in the southern Netherlands. However, it did so at a high price. The treaty stipulated the positioning of Dutch soldiers in eight garrison towns in the southern Netherlands, a huge annual payment to the Dutch Republic, and border changes resulting in loss of Flemish territory among other things. Both Brabant and Flanders reacted vehemently. They sent delegates to Vienna to plead for changes. They also decided to postpone its implementation and threatened to stop paying the government in Brussels. Charles VI yielded and decided to renegotiate the agreement. This pleased the Estates and paved the way for the princely investitures of October 1717.[19]

The Barrier Treaty was not the only international treaty impeding the organization of inaugurations. In 1789, during the revolution in the Austrian Netherlands—the so-called "Brabant Revolution"—a modest patriot army succeeded in expelling the Austrian troops. Shortly after this, and based on Brabant's constitutional charter, the Estates' assemblies of the different regions—with the exception of Luxembourg—divested Joseph II. This led to the brief appearance of the independent *Verenigde Nederlandse Staten/Etats belgiques unis* (United Netherlandish States), which disappeared again after less than a year. Joseph's successor, Leopold II, started the military recapture of the Netherlands in the autumn of 1790. As a condition, his allies—Great Britain, Prussia, and the Dutch Republic—forced him to sign the Convention of The Hague (which he did on 10 December 1790), to respect the constitutions of the southern Netherlands, and to issue a general pardon. The Brussels's government then considered a quick organization of the inaugurations as the best means to suppress rebellious feelings and boost pro-Austrian sentiments in a country where loyalty was divided. As a sign of deference, Governor-General Albert of Saxony-Teschen personally represented Emperor Leopold II in every region; usually, the governor-general took part only in Brabant and Flanders. Moreover, the government recommended the emperor to design the ceremony according to the example of the 1744 inauguration of Maria Theresa instead of the 1781 inauguration for the despised Joseph II. Leopold's inaugurations thus clearly served the government's policy of seeking compromise.[20]

Nevertheless, the Convention of The Hague caused turmoil in Brabant. Several members of the Estates feared that the treaty would not sufficiently protect Brabant's constitution. They argued that the convention did not exclude future changes of the composition of the Estates. Moreover, it did not restore all the previous rights of the University of Leuven. The convention was also contradictory: its first article took the constitutional order at the time of the inaugurations of Charles VI and Maria Theresa as points of reference, whereas other articles stipulated the restoration of the situation at the end of Maria Theresa's reign. These articles thus sanctioned several of her reforms that the Estates regarded as unconstitutional. As a result, various bodies—among others, the deans of the Antwerp craft guilds—only wanted to give permission for the inauguration after obtaining the explicit confirmation that the ratification of the convention did not hurt Brabant's constitution as initially accepted by Maria Theresa. Furthermore, the Antwerp city council asked the emperor to undo his reforms of the personnel structure of the Council of Brabant, reduce the number of princely prosecutors in the duchy, and cease violations to the *Blijde Inkomst*, such as illegal military arrests.[21] Although the government required the Estates' unconditional consent, and certainly did not want to give a written "appeasement" (as the craft guilds demanded), in the end, just as in 1717, concessions were made. Some prisoners were released, and the government issued a decree stating that the ratification of the convention did not in any way harm the Brabant constitution.[22]

The Estates of Flanders and certainly Brabant were a force that Vienna and Brussels could not neglect. Their financial strength and Brabant's constitutional charter were powerful instruments that made them a force to be reckoned with. But lesser regions also put forward their demands when the government invited them to coorganize inaugurations. In 1791, several members of the Estates of the tiny Duchy of Limburg, which paid a mere 3.27 percent of the consented taxes to the government, wanted a capital vote instead of a vote per estate. The latter system was beneficial to the clergy and nobility and detrimental to the third estate. Emperor Leopold II allowed the reform. The members also demanded more representatives of the third estate within the general assembly and requested the prince to reestablish a separate princely court of justice in Limburg—such a court had shortly been set up in 1789 and released the region from a centuries-old subordination to the Council of Brabant. To these requests, however, Leopold refused to consent.[23] At the same time, the representatives of the Retroceded Lands lobbied heavily to have their own Estates' assembly—they were the only land in which the prince did not need the approval of the Estates in order to levy taxes—but this request also remained unfulfilled.[24]

These examples show that inaugurations remained important and delicate political events used by the Estates or their members to promote their interests. Nevertheless, in the late eighteenth century, the precise meaning of these inaugurations became a matter of debate. The Council of Brabant, traditionally an ardent defender of regional privileges, explicitly denounced the aforementioned objections of the Antwerp craft guilds and assured the government that it should not take their grievances into account. The council stated that the permission of the Estates was not necessary for the inauguration nor for legitimizing the reign of the new prince.[25] The government adopted a similar stance, which is much less surprising, and stated that sovereignty in Brabant was hereditary and that, therefore, the new duke did not need the approval of the Estates. The Council of Brabant had the right to approve or disapprove the powers of attorney of the sovereign's representative and could control the terms of the oaths that were to be sworn, but the investiture itself did not depend on its consent.[26] Two years later, in May 1793, Emperor Francis II even affirmed that Brabant first had to pay its outstanding taxes before he would even consider being inaugurated. In doing so, he wanted to deprive the Estates of their arguments that they only owed tax money after the prince's inauguration as duke of Brabant. Several months later, he added that its organization should be slowed down due to the conduct of the

Estates, which he clearly condemned. He even believed that the inauguration did not add any right or duty to his sovereignty.[27]

This question whether or not the prince could levy taxes before being inaugurated was not new. The Estates also seem to have threatened to withhold taxes during the preparations for the inaugurations of Charles VI and Leopold II, and it may also have been an argument for the quick Luxembourg inauguration in 1717.[28] In reality, however, stating that the prince was a full natural prince only after being sworn in—from this perspective the inauguration constituted the end point of a period that can be considered an interregnum—was mere bluff. For Charles VI, Maria Theresa, and Francis II, it took years before they were inaugurated in all of their Netherlandish territories, yet this did not prevent the Estates from granting taxes nor these monarchs from collecting them.[29] On the other hand, the Habsburgs never seriously considered abandoning these inaugurations, in contrast with territories such as Moravia, Tyrol, Styria, and others.[30] The reason is that the inaugurations yielded benefits for the prince as much as for the other participants.

Inaugurations, Order of Precedence, and the Public Sphere

Not only the preparations of the inaugurations were politically important. In several respects, the rites themselves were highly meaningful, not in the least in the field of representation. The performance of the oath swearing and the other rituals allowed both government members and privileged orders to publicly stage their social and political position. Every new ruler promulgated that the inauguration had to be an exact copy of his predecessor's, without departing from the adopted ranking order. However, old arguments about ranking regularly arose, and new ones emerged. This was apparent in the 1744 inauguration of Maria Theresa in Flanders. Several subaltern cities and castellanies—rural districts with important fiscal, administrative, and to a lesser degree judicial authority—quarreled over their position in the inauguration and the accompanying entry procession. Moreover, two rivaling noblemen debated which of them should carry the Flemish standard in the parade. And the two aldermen's benches of Ghent bickered over which of them would welcome the governor-general in the city.[31]

The investiture of Joseph II in 1781 led to even more discussions. In 1754, the government succeeded in drastically altering the composition of the Flemish Estates due to a financial scandal and the ensuing political crisis in the County of Flanders. Before that year, only the clergy, the cities of Ghent and Bruges, and the rural district Franc of Bruges had a vote in this body. From 1754 onward, several towns and castellanies also obtained a seat and a vote.[32] As a result, in the next inauguration of 1781, some new members, among others the castellanies of Oudenaarde and Kortrijk, advocated a new ranking order and wished their new status to be ceremonially reflected. Aalst and Dendermonde, on the other hand, defended the status quo that gave them some priority. The other members of the Estates were divided. In the end, the emperor ordered the different administrations to follow the exact same order as in 1744.[33]

The privilege of being represented, and if so, at a high rank in the order, was not the only matter of debate. The precise number of delegates was another issue that roused the emotions. For example, whether the Land of Bornem could send one or two delegates to the Flemish inauguration was a point of discussion in 1717, 1744, and 1781.[34] Similar discussions took place in Brabant. In 1794, Wolfgang Guillaume d'Ursel, Duke of Hoboken, successfully argued that the ceremonial function of hereditary marshal of Brabant belonged to him and that only he and not the government had the right to appoint a replacement during the inauguration.[35]

As Barbara Stollberg-Rilinger argues in her book *Des Kaisers alte Kleider*, ritual-symbolic actions were of primary importance in premodern societies. Due to their material tangibility, performative rites such as coronations and inaugurations transformed the institutional order they embodied into an objective reality. However, different actors could ascribe different and sometimes incompatible meanings to these rites. This occurred frequently and gave way to adaptations and transformations. As a result of the importance of visual ritual-symbolic actions, the order of precedence to speak, sit, stand, or walk was anything but trivial. Furthermore, ranking order was not only the expression of a certain social or political position. The converse was true as well: its visual demonstration was indispensable for upholding status.[36] Therefore, the fact that matters of ranking caused so much debate need not surprise us—they were the order of the day until the end of the *Ancien Régime*, even though their importance slowly diminished through the emergence of an alternative and more egalitarian public sphere. Moreover, Stollberg-Rilinger's observation that conflicts often remained unresolved and were ritually kept alive also applies to the inaugurations in the Austrian Netherlands. At every single Brabant inauguration, Leuven lobbied to host the event, based on the argument of ancient tradition. From the seventeenth century onward, however, the central government preferred Brussels, but over and over again granted Leuven *lettres de non-préjudice*.[37] By doing so, competing legal claims were ceremonially solved and the stability of the body politic preserved.[38]

The inaugurations were useful not only for evoking and visualizing the hierarchies in early modern society. They also allowed the prince to display his authority for hundreds, perhaps even thousands of spectators that were a cross section of society. This was crucial in composite monarchies where princes were often absent in the individual lands of their dynastic conglomerate. The Habsburg Monarchy was no exception to this rule. We can even state that the Austrian Habsburgs ruled the composite monarchy *par excellence*. As Petr Maťa points out in Chapter 1, respecting the privileges of its different lands and legitimizing power through participation in manifold acts of homage were an essential part of the Habsburg conception of rule. Moreover, these investitures, both coronations and inaugurations, often constituted the culmination of strongly mediatized travels of the prince and his court. These travels contributed to the dissemination of the image of the ruler and helped overcome the disadvantages of princely absence.

In his long-term analysis of joyous entries and inaugurations in the Habsburg Netherlands, Hugo Soly remarked that the number of these rituals rose significantly at the beginning of the sixteenth century, when the Netherlands became part of the Spanish composite monarchy and experienced the increased absence of their prince.[39] The tradition of rulers not being present did not change in the eighteenth century; the Austrian Netherlands enjoyed a princely visit only twice, with Joseph II in 1781 and Francis II in 1794. Governors-general, usually members of the dynasty with a proper court in Brussels, compensated for the distant sovereign.

The fact that the prince was absent did not pose problems in the Netherlands, as long as a proxy of royal blood with full power replaced him or her. However, during the first decade of the Austrian rule, there was no governor-general of royal blood in Brussels. Hence, a series of recurrent dynastic rites and ceremonies, including *Te Deums* and masses of thanksgiving on the emperor and empress's birthdays and on the days of their patron saints or on more exceptional occasions, had to enhance royalist feelings and bring the dynasty closer to the subjects.[40] Among the less regular events, the inaugurations were undoubtedly the most important, given their scale and splendor and their vital role in the contractual relationship between the prince and the still powerful Estates. Taken together, this series of ceremonies and rites centered on the dynasty was crucial for maintaining loyalty to the princely authority and the Habsburgs in general, thereby helping to make their rule in the faraway Netherlands easier. It can therefore be argued that the eccentric location of the Netherlands, aside from the long-standing tradition of inaugurations and their constitutional and political significance, was among the key arguments for the prince not to neglect the inaugurations in these territories. Urban revolts such as Brussels's in 1718, or the revolution of 1787–89, reminded Vienna that loyalty in these regions was not self-evident. The subsequent inaugurations helped Leopold II reconstruct the damaged relationship of his subjects with their lord. However, Leopold II soon died, French troops briefly occupied the country in 1792–93, and the public sphere was divided along ideological lines. In this tense context, and with a new invasion of French troops looming, Francis II decided to travel to the Netherlands to help fan royalist feelings and military fervor. Personally participating in the Brabant inauguration was the clearest message of reconciliation and a desire to co-operate the prince could give.[41]

The above discussion indicates that the older historiographical viewpoints, which state that early modern joyous entries and inaugurations developed from ceremonial communication and negotiation into a mere spectacle for passive audiences, are inaccurate.⁴² Nevertheless, the ways in which the subjects—or at least the representatives of the privileged classes—participated, changed. In the late Middle Ages and the sixteenth and seventeenth centuries, both prince and subjects sent messages through the iconographic programs adorning the stages and triumphal arches built for the entries and inaugurations. Up until the sixteenth century, townspeople often made use of *tableaux vivants*—theatrical and originally mute performances of a certain scene, a stage with living statues—to express expectations toward the new prince.⁴³ Hugo Soly has shown that during the sixteenth century, these iconographic messages aligned with elite culture and became more elaborate. Classical allegories replaced biblical scenery. At the same time, the host cities and later the Estates as main organizers ordered the printing of books with detailed accounts of the inauguration. Quite often, these volumes contained woodcuts depicting the ephemeral architecture and its decorative program.⁴⁴ Text and image informed an elite group of readers about the precise meaning of the iconography, the specific order of the events, and the exact ranking order at every stage in the rite. This tradition continued in the eighteenth century (see table 6.2).⁴⁵

In the eighteenth century, however, the significance of sophisticated iconographic programs, laden with allegorical messages, waned. The stage for the inauguration of Charles VI in Brussels contained six large paintings picturing his major military successes, thus emphasizing his ability to protect the then wartorn Netherlands. Moreover, a series of portraits of twenty-two previous dukes of Brabant placed him in a long line of rulers.⁴⁶ In Flanders, the stage for both Charles VI and Maria Theresa contained a large allegorical painting depicting the homage of the Estates to the new count.⁴⁷ However, during the other inaugurations in Brabant and Flanders, the inauguration books merely mention that the theaters and triumphal arches were nicely decorated, and usually do not give any further information. The only paintings that were still there were the obligatory representative portraits of the prince.⁴⁸

The construction plans, prints, and engravings from the inaugurations in Flanders and Brabant that are still at our disposal confirm this image. Nevertheless, there were some exceptions to this rule in the smaller regions. A triumphal arch in Namur for the inauguration of Maria Theresa referred to Austria's military successes during the War of the Austrian Succession and expressed the prosperity Namur's inhabitants expected from their new countess. The stage for the inauguration of Joseph II in Hainaut in 1781 showed, among other things, cornucopias and the coats of arms of all members of the Estates. The inauguration books explain this iconography in detail.⁴⁹ Even more elaborate was the iconographic program for Leopold II's inauguration in Gelderland in 1791, with several triumphal arches adorned with emblems and inscriptions expressing the hope for a bright future after several years of political instability.⁵⁰ Nevertheless, it is fair to say in general that the Estates no longer participated primarily through iconography. Rather, they expressed their ambitions throughout the preceding negotiations and through the order of precedence, which was all the more crucial since the books printed on the occasion of the inaugurations painstakingly recorded every seat and every position at every stage of the investiture.

Conclusion

Inaugurations in the Habsburg Netherlands remained important for the ruler, the Estates, and the host cities throughout the eighteenth century for several reasons. They retained their constitutional function, gave rise to political negotiations between prince and Estates, and continued to be a welcome stage for different groups to express hierarchy. They were an important opportunity to simulate the faraway ruler's presence in the Netherlands and stage the relationship between prince and subjects. At the same time, the ceremonial discussions gave the ruler the opportunity to take the role of arbiter, albeit mainly via the governor-general, who interacted with local administrations. The inaugurations thus strengthened the authority of the new prince and the existing channels of decision-making; and at the same time, they fortified the social system and body politic. These investitures thus helped stabilize the Austrian regime. However, this does not mean that the inaugurations stayed the same throughout history. On the contrary, they were perfectly adaptable to new circumstances and actual occurrences. In the 1790s, they caused and were the subject of constitutional debates. In doing so, they (modestly) integrated modern discourses—first and foremost, the desire to have a written constitutional charter.[51] Moreover, archival sources reveal that several persons and bodies raised questions about the juridical importance of the inaugurations. Francis II and his entourage constitute the most notable example in this respect. Nevertheless, he still authorized the inauguration; he even participated personally when the survival of Habsburg rule in the Netherlands was at stake.

Since the organizers of the inaugurations had the ability to adapt them, they did so and thus these rites remained relevant to the point that they even served as a model for a ritual staging the exact opposite: the deposition of the prince. In 1789, a widespread rebellion against Joseph II's reforms broke out, and in December 1789 and January 1790, the southern Netherlands' principalities declared independence. The Estates' assemblies except Luxembourg assumed sovereignty from the dethroned prince, Joseph II. In every region, this happened with at least some kind of ritual performance. In Ghent, there was a remarkable celebration that mirrored the inaugurations by incorporating artillery salvos, a procession through the city, and a public ritual on the Friday Market. On a stage resembling the inauguration theaters, the manifesto containing the juridical arguments legitimizing the dethronement of Joseph II and Flanders's independence was read aloud. Moreover, by granting the nobility a vote in the Estates and assuming sovereignty, the Estates established a new constitutional order—or, in their view, reconstituted a broken order. Finally, a *Te Deum* was sung in the cathedral. The organizers even minted commemorative medals.[52] Thus, in many respects, this deposition was fashioned after the inaugurations. This is perhaps the best evidence that inaugurations continued to be powerful instruments to visualize power relations for large audiences, even in the age of revolutions and burgeoning democratic ideologies. This also proves how much these investitures bore constitutional meaning in a society that lacked the modern conception of written constitutions; in addition to the legal manifestoes, some sort of ritual was necessary to undo the contractual bond between prince and Estates.

The end of Austrian rule did not signify the end of the imagery associated with the inaugurations: the format of open-air stages proved useful in the nineteenth century as well. The inaugurations of William I, king of the United Kingdom of the Netherlands, in 1815 and of Leopold, first king of the Belgians, in 1831 took place on Brussels's *Koningsplein/Place Royale*, exactly where the eighteenth-century Brabant swearing of the oaths had been staged. For both inaugurations, a columnar theater was erected, reminiscent of the eighteenth-century investiture theaters.[53] In May 1815, the constituent assembly discussed the oath swearing by William I, and the members eventually agreed on a public, open-air inauguration. Jan Jozef Raepsaet, one of the assembly members, stated: "We have to observe tradition as much as possible, and it [the swearing of the oaths] took place that way in Brabant, Friesland and elsewhere."[54] In 1856, Belgium celebrated the twenty-fifth anniversary of the reign of Leopold I. Several impressive triumphal arches adorned the *Koningsplein/Place Royale* in Brussels and other squares in the old city center. However, the main celebrations took place outside the old city walls, without a link with previous inaugurations. The situation was different in Ghent, where the city solemnly welcomed the king in a joyous-entry-like procession. On the Friday Market, on the exact same spot where the inauguration stages had been built, a pavilion once again resembled these, albeit in a more modest size.[55] Although these appear to have been the last festivities to recycle visual elements of the inaugurations of the Austrian Habsburgs, they testify to the enduring power of their pictorial language half a century after the last traditional investiture had taken place.

Klaas Van Gelder is a postdoctoral researcher at the State Archives in Ghent and at Ghent University, Belgium. Until August 2020, he was a postdoctoral fellow of the Research Foundation—Flanders (FWO). From November 2016 until October 2018, he was a Lise Meitner-Fellow of the Austrian *Wissenschaftsfonds* (FWF) at the *Institut für Österreichische Geschichtsforschung* (Institute for Austrian

Historical Research) at the University of Vienna. His research interests include early modern political culture, elites and nobilities, the Habsburg Monarchy and its links to the Austrian Netherlands, and dynastic ritual and ceremony. He is the author of *Regime Change at a Distance: Austria and the Southern Netherlands Following the War of the Spanish Succession (1716–1725)* (Leuven, 2016) as well as articles in several peer-reviewed journals, including *Zeitschrift für historische Forschung*, *European Review of History/Revue européenne d'Histoire*, *Revue d'Histoire moderne et contemporaine*, and *Tijdschrift voor Geschiedenis*.

Appendices: Tables

Table 6.1. List of inaugurations in the Austrian Netherlands

	Date	Ruler	Territory	Place	Performed by
1	6 Dec. 1703[56]	Charles III (VI)	Limburg	Unknown	Count Sinzendorf, minister plenipotentiary of Charles III (VI)
2	21 Feb. 1717[57]	Charles VI	Luxembourg	Luxembourg	Count Gronsfeld, governor of Luxembourg
3	11 Oct. 1717	Charles VI	Brabant and Limburg	Brussels	Marquis of Prié, minister plenipotentiary
4	18 Oct. 1717	Charles VI	Flanders	Ghent	Marquis of Prié, minister plenipotentiary
5	18 Oct. 1717	Charles VI	Namur	Namur	Count de Lannoy de Clervaux, administrator of Namur
6	18 Oct. 1717	Charles VI	Hainaut	Mons	Prince of Rubempré, councilor of state
7	18 Oct. 1717	Charles VI	Mechelen	Mechelen	de Baillet, president of the Great Council of Malines
8	6 Dec. 1719	Charles VI	Gelderland	Roermond	Hemselrode, vice-chancellor of Gelderland
9	12 and 24 Feb. 1720	Charles VI	Retroceded Lands	Ieper and Menin	Prince de Ligne, councilor of state, general
10	29 Feb. 1720	Charles VI	Tournai/Tournaisis	Tournai	Prince de Ligne, councilor of state, general
11	20 Apr. 1744	Maria Theresa	Brabant and Limburg	Brussels	Charles Alexander of Lorraine, governor-general
12	27 Apr. 1744	Maria Theresa	Flanders	Ghent	Charles Alexander of Lorraine, governor-general

Table 6.1. continued

	Date	Ruler	Territory	Place	Performed by
13	4 May 1744	Maria Theresa	Luxembourg	Luxembourg	Count Neipperg, field marshal, colonel, provisional commander of the city and province of Luxembourg
14	4 May 1744	Maria Theresa	Hainaut	Mons	Prince of Arenberg
15	4 May 1744	Maria Theresa	Namur	Namur	Prince of Gavere, governor of Namur
16	4 May 1744	Maria Theresa	Mechelen	Mechelen	d'Olmen, Baron of Poederlé, president of the Great Council of Malines
17	18 May 1744	Maria Theresa	Gelderland	Roermond	Count de Baillet, chancellor of Gelderland
18	18 May 1744	Maria Theresa	Tournai/Tournaisis	Tournai	Prince de Ligne, councilor of state, general
19	1 Oct. 1749	Maria Theresa	Retroceded Lands	Ieper	Prince de Ligne, councilor of state, general
20	17 July 1781	Joseph II	Brabant and Limburg	Brussels	Albert of Saxony-Teschen, governor-general
21	31 July 1781	Joseph II	Flanders	Ghent	Albert of Saxony-Teschen, governor-general
22	20 Aug. 1781	Joseph II	Luxembourg	Luxembourg	Prince de Ligne, lieutenant-general and colonel of an infantry regiment, governor of the city of Mons
23	20 Aug. 1781	Joseph II	Gelderland	Roermond	Luytgens, chancellor of Gelderland
24	20 Aug. 1781	Joseph II	Tournai/Tournaisis	Tournai	d'Ursel, Duke of Hoboken, commander of the infantry regiment de Ligne
25	20 Aug. 1781	Joseph II	Mechelen	Mechelen	Fierlant, president of the Great Council of Malines
26	27 Aug. 1781	Joseph II	Hainaut	Mons	Duke of Arenberg, high bailiff of Hainaut
27	27 Aug. 1781	Joseph II	Namur	Namur	Prince of Gavere, governor of Namur
28	27 Aug. 1781	Joseph II	Retroceded Lands	Ieper	d'Ursel, Duke of Hoboken, commander of the infantry regiment de Ligne

(continued)

Table 6.1. continued

	Date	Ruler	Territory	Place	Performed by
29	30 June 1791	Leopold II	Brabant and Limburg	Brussels	Albert of Saxony-Teschen, governor-general
30	6 July 1791	Leopold II	Flanders	Ghent	Albert of Saxony-Teschen, governor-general
31	12 July 1791	Leopold II	Hainaut	Mons	Albert of Saxony-Teschen, governor-general
32	28 July 1791	Leopold II	Mechelen	Mechelen	Albert of Saxony-Teschen, governor-general
33	8 Aug. 1791	Leopold II	Retroceded Lands	Ieper	Albert of Saxony-Teschen, governor-general
34	10 Aug. 1791	Leopold II	Tournai/ Tournaisis	Tournai	Albert of Saxony-Teschen, governor-general
35	22 Aug. 1791	Leopold II	Namur	Namur	Albert of Saxony-Teschen, governor-general
36	25 Aug. 1791	Leopold II	Luxembourg	Luxembourg	Albert of Saxony-Teschen, governor-general
37	22 Sep. 1791	Leopold II	Gelderland	Roermond	Albert of Saxony-Teschen, governor-general
38	11 June 1792	Francis II	Hainaut	Mons	Prince de Ligne, colonel
39	11 June 1792	Francis II	Namur	Namur	Prince of Gavere, sovereign-bailiff and administrator-general of Namur
40	3 July 1792	Francis II	Luxembourg	Luxembourg	Marshal Bender, governor of the city and province of Luxembourg
41	31 July 1792	Francis II	Flanders	Ghent	Albert of Saxony-Teschen, governor-general
42	13 Aug. 1792	Francis II	Mechelen	Mechelen	de Fierlant, president of the Great Council of Malines
43	13 Aug. 1792	Francis II	Gelderland	Roermond	Luytgens, chancellor of Gelderland
44	13 Aug. 1792	Francis II	Tournai/ Tournaisis	Tournai	Prince of Gavere, sovereign-bailiff and administrator-general of Namur
45	23 Apr. 1794	Francis II	Brabant and Limburg	Brussels	Francis II, Roman emperor

(continued)

Note: In the autumn of 1793, there were preparations for Francis II's inauguration in the Retroceded Lands. Due to French incursions in this region, however, it could not take place.
Sources: Klaas Van Gelder, "The Investiture of Emperor Charles VI in Brabant and Flanders: A Test Case for the Authority of the New Austrian Government," *European Review of History/Revue européene d'histoire* 18, no. 4 (2011): 443–63; Klaas Van Gelder, "Revolution, Krieg und Stände. Die Reise von Kaiser Franz II. in die Österreichischen Niederlande 1794," *Frühneuzeit-Info* 28 (2017): 155–70; Eric Wychlacz, "Habsburgische Rechtspolitik im Herzogtum Luxemburg und den Herrschaftswechsel in den Südlichen Niederlanden von 1714–1725," *Hémecht. Zeitschrift für Luxemburger Geschichte* 63, no. 1 (2011): 288–93; Guy van Dievoet, "L'empereur Joseph II et la Joyeuse Entrée de Brabant: Les dernières années de la constitution brabançonne," *Anciens Pays et Assemblées d'États/Standen en Landen* 16 (1958): 90–102; Reginald De Schryver, "De Oostenrijkse aanspraken op de Spaans-Habsburgse erfenis. De Zuidelijke Nederlanden tijdens de Spaanse Successieoorlog, 1700–1716," in *Oostenrijks België 1713–1794: De Zuidelijke Nederlanden onder de Oostenrijkse Habsburgers*, ed. Hervé Hasquin (Brussels, 1987), 16; Heinrich Ritter von Zeissberg, *Belgien unter der Generalstatthalterschaft Erzherzog Carls (1793, 1794): II. Theil* (Vienna, 1794), 24; Louis-Prosper Gachard, *Histoire de la Belgique au commencement du XVIIIe siecle* (Brussels, 1880), 441–43 and 496–99; inauguration books in the appendix; AR–AGR, GR/CP, 10A, 10B, 11A, 11B, 12, 13A, 13B, 14, 15, 16A, and 16B Stadsarchief Mechelen, Stad Mechelen (ancien regime), vorstelijke inhuldigingen, 124, 125, and 126.

Table 6.2. Printed inauguration books in the Austrian Netherlands

	Territory	Ruler	Book Title	Location
1	Brabant-Limburg	Charles VI	*Relation des cérémonies et des réjouissances publiques, faites en la ville de cour de Bruxelles le 11. d'Octobre 1717, jour de la Joyeuse Entrée & Inauguration de Sa Sacrée Majesté impériale et catholique Charles VI*. Brussels: Joseph t'Serstevens, 1717.	UB Gent
2	Brabant-Limburg	Maria Theresa	*Relation de l'inauguration solemnelle de Sa Majesté Marie Thérèse, Reine de Hongrie et de Bohème, en qualité de Duchesse de Lothier, de Brabant, de Limbourg et de Marquise du St. Empire Romain, celebrée en la ville de Brusselles, le 20. Avril 1744*. Brussels: François Claudinot, n.d.[58]	UB Gent
3	Brabant-Limburg	Joseph II	*Relation des cérémonies observées à l'inauguration de Sa Majesté l'empereur Joseph II, qui a eu lieu à Bruxelles le 17 juillet 1781*. Brussels: J. Vanden Berghen, 1781.	AR–AGR, HF/FH, 250/2
4	Flanders	Charles VI	*Relation de l'inauguration solemnelle de Sa Sacrée Majesté impériale et catholique, Charles VI, Empereur des Romains . . . comme Comte de Flandres, celebrée à Gand, ville capitale de la Province, le XVIII. Octobre 1717*. Ghent: Augustin Graet, 1719.	UB Gent

(continued)

Table 6.2. continued

	Territory	Ruler	Book Title	Location
5	Flanders	Maria Theresa	*Relation de l'inauguration solemnelle de Sa Sacrée Majesté Marie Thérèse . . . comme Comtesse de Flandres, célébrée à Gand, ville capitale de la province, le XXVII. avril 1744.* Ghent: La Veuve Pierre de Goesin, 1744.	UB Gent
6	Flanders	Joseph II	*Inauguration en Flandre, Gand.* Ghent: Pierre de Gousin, n.d.	UB Gent
7	Flanders	Leopold II	*Relation de l'inauguration solemnelle de sa Sacrée Majesté Léopold II, Empereur des Romains . . . comme Comte de Flandres, célébrée à Gand, ville capitale de la Province, le VI juillet 1791.* Ghent: Adrien Colier, 1792.	UB Gent
8	Hainaut	Joseph II	*Relation de l'inauguration de S. M. l'Empereur et Roi Joseph II, en qualité de Comte de Hainau, solemnisée le 27 Août 1781, en la Ville de Mons.* Mons: Henri Hoyois, 1781.	UB Gent
9	Hainaut	Leopold II	*Précis de la solemnité de l'inauguration de Sa Majesté l'Empereur et Roi Léopold II, comme comte de Hainau, fixé au 12 juillet 1791.* Mons: N. J. Bocquet, n.d.	UB Gent
10	Namur	Maria Theresa	*Relation des ceremonies de l'inauguration solemnelle de Sa Majesté Marie Thérèse Reine de Hongrie et de Bohème, en qualité de Comtesse de Namur, celebrée a Namur le quatrième de may 1744.* Namur: Jean François Lafontaine, 1744.	AR–AGR, GR/CP, 15
11	Luxembourg	Leopold II	*Inauguration de Sa Majesté l'Empereur et Roi Leopold II Glorieusement Regnant en qualités de Duc de Luxembourg & de Comte de Chiny, célébrée à Luxembourg le 25 août 1791.* Luxembourg: De l'Imprimerie des Héritiers de François Perle, n.d.	BNL
12	Luxembourg	Leopold II	*Beschreibung der am 25 August 1791 zu Luxemburg feyerlichst gehaltenen Huldigungs=Zeremonie, nebst einigen Nebenumständen. Zusammengetragen und verfasset von einem Augenzeugen.* Luxembourg: In der Perlschen Buchdruckerey, 1791.	BNL
13	Gelderland	Leopold II	*Description de la solemnité inaugurale de Sa Majesté l'Empereur et Roi, Léopold II comme Duc de Gueldres célébrée à Ruremonde le 22 septembre 1791.* Roermond: G. Gruyters, n.d.	AR–AGR, HF/FH, 286

(continued)

Note: Not included in this list are short printed leaflets containing directions for the proceedings of the rites, sometimes called "short instruction," "order of the ceremonies," or "report of the formalities to be observed." Several of these can be found in the aforementioned "Heraldisch Fonds/Fonds héraldique," registers 250/2 and 286, and in the library of Ghent University. The German eyewitness account of the inauguration of Leopold II in Luxembourg in 1791 is probably the only item in the above list that was not printed in order of an Estates' assembly.

Notes

I wish to express my sincere gratitude to Jonas Roelens and Luc Duerloo for their comments on an earlier draft of this chapter. Moreover, Luc Duerloo gave me the valuable advice to consult the much-ignored *Heraldisch Fonds*. This text also benefited greatly from the vivid discussion following my talk on dynastic ritual in the "Research Seminar Europe 1000–1800" series at the University of Leiden on 23 March 2018. I am very grateful to Jeroen Duindam for giving me this chance.

1. In the autumn of 1715, Austrian troops gradually occupied the southern Netherlands, but Charles VI officially assumed power in the bulk of these territories in February 1716. Up until the summer of 1794, the Habsburgs administered these regions, with the exception of large sections of this territory taken by the French between 1744 and 1749. The Duchy of Limburg, however, was in Habsburg hands since 1703, and Luxembourg remained Austrian until 1795: Klaas Van Gelder, *Regime Change at a Distance: Austria and the Southern Netherlands following the War of the Spanish Succession, 1716–1725* (Leuven, 2016), 94 and 113–44.
2. In the sources, these territories are usually called "provinces," but they do not correspond to current Belgian provinces, either geographically or in terms of powers and competences. Following Edmond Poullet, ten regions can be discerned: the Duchies of Brabant, Luxembourg, Limburg, and Gelderland; the Counties of Flanders, Hainaut, and Namur; the city of Tournai and its immediate surroundings; the region called *le Tournaisis*; and finally the city of Malines and its small district. On top of that, there was one district without Estates—the so-called "Retroceded Lands" or "Western Flanders": Edmond Poullet, *Les constitutions nationales belges de l'ancien régime à l'époque de l'invasion française de 1794* (Brussels, 1875), 2–3.
3. Hugo Soly argued that, from the seventeenth century onward, inaugurations and joyous entries evolved into pure spectacle, top-down events directed to passive audiences: Hugo Soly, "Plechtige intochten in de steden van de Zuidelijke Nederlanden tijdens de overgang van Middeleeuwen naar Nieuwe Tijd: communicatie, propaganda, spektakel," *Tijdschrift voor Geschiedenis* 97 (1984): 341–60. For a similar argument on the southern German and Swiss area, see André Holenstein, "Huldigung und Herrschaftszeremoniell im Zeitalter des Absolutismus und der Aufklärung," in *Zum Wandel von Zeremoniell und Gesellschaftsritualen in der Zeit der Aufklärung*, ed. Klaus Gerteis (Hamburg, 1992), 21–46.
4. The Estates of Brabant and Limburg usually held a joint inauguration in Brussels, even though these bodies negotiated with the prince separately.
5. In Brussels, the *Baliënplein/Place des Bailles* and later the *Koningsplein/Place Royale* was the place for the swearing of the oaths. In Ghent, the oath swearing took place at the Friday Market (*Vrijdagmarkt*); in Malines, on the central market square (*Grote Markt*). In Namur, the St. Aubain Cathedral hosted the rite, but at least in 1744, portraits of Maria

Theresa and Francis Stephen were on display under a canopy before the city hall and a triumphal arch with allegorical messages adorned Namur's city center. This public character is in contrast with many Central-European lands of the Habsburg Monarchy, where the acts of homage occurred behind closed doors.

6. Although many of the eighteenth-century inaugurations have never been studied, around a dozen journal articles and chapters have been dedicated to them. For Charles VI, see Klaas Van Gelder, "The Investiture of Emperor Charles VI in Brabant and Flanders: A Test Case for the Authority of the New Austrian Government," *European Review of History/ Revue européenne d'histoire* 18, no. 4 (2011): 443–63; Luc Duerloo, "Discourse of Conquest, Discourse of Contract: Competing Visions on the Nature of the Habsburg Rule in the Netherlands," in *Bündnispartner und Konkurrenten der Landesfürsten? Die Stände in der Habsburgermonarchie*, ed. Gerhard Ammerer, William D. Godsey Jr., Martin Scheutz, Peter Urbanitsch, and Alfred Stefan Weiß (Vienna, 2007), 463–78; Eric Wychlacz, "Habsburgische Rechtspolitik im Herzogtum Luxemburg und den Herrschaftswechsel in den Südlichen Niederlanden von 1714–1725," *Hémecht: Zeitschrift für Luxemburger Geschichte* 63, no. 1 (2011): 288–93; W. L. Braekman, "De inhuldiging van keizer Karel VI te Gent in oktober 1717," *Van mensen en dingen: tijdschrift voor volkscultuur in Vlaanderen* 1, no. 3 (2003): 268–77; Louis Lebeer, "Les estampes relatives aux inaugurations de Philippe V et de Charles VI à Bruxelles," *Anciens Pays et Assemblées d'États/Standen en Landen* 16 (1958): 35–63. For Maria Theresa, see Klaas Van Gelder and Bert Van Cauter, "Een publieke ceremonie in een turbulent tijdvak: De inauguratie van Maria Theresia als gravin van Vlaanderen (1744)," *Handelingen der Maatschappij voor Geschiedenis en Oudheidkunde te Gent* 67 (2013): 101–30; see also Thomas Cambrelin's chapter in this volume. For Joseph II, see Guy van Dievoet, "L'empereur Joseph II et la Joyeuse Entrée de Brabant: Les dernières années de la constitution brabançonne," *Anciens Pays et Assemblées d'États/ Standen en Landen* 16 (1958): 90–102; Walter Ravez, *Tournai et le Tournaisis pendant la révolution brabançonne: Essai d'histoire politique, sociale et économique* (Tournai, 1937), 12–19; Alex Carmes, "L'entrée du Prince de Ligne à Luxembourg en 1781 à l'occasion de l'inauguration de l'empereur Joseph II comme duc de Luxembourg et comte de Chiny," *Hémecht: Revue d'Histoire luxembourgeoise* 45, no. 4 (1993): 441–89. For Leopold II, see A. Viaene, "De laatste keizerlijke inauguratie te Ieper, 8 augustus 1791," *Biekorf* 61, no. 11 (1960): 389–97. For Francis II, see Klaas Van Gelder, "Revolution, Krieg und Stände: Die Reise von Kaiser Franz II. in die Österreichischen Niederlande 1794," *Frühneuzeit-Info* 28 (2017): 155–70; A. Viaene, "Frans II, Keizer der Romeinen, als laatste Graaf van Vlaanderen," *Biekorf* 76, no. 1–2 (1975–76): 5–14. Micheline Soenen published a very informative article on festivities in early modern Brussels that includes princely inaugurations: Micheline Soenen, "Fêtes et cérémonies publiques à Bruxelles aux Temps Modernes," *Bijdragen tot de Geschiedenis* 68 (1985): 47–101. Brigitte d'Hainaut-Zveny focused on the entries and inaugurations performed by Governor-General Charles Alexander of Lorraine: Brigitte d'Hainaut-Zveny, "Feesten en vermakelijkheden onder de regering van Karel van Lotharingen," in *Karel Alexander van Lotharingen: Gouverneur-generaal van de Oostenrijkse Nederlanden* (Brussels, 1987), 115–36.

7. On the power of portraits, see Philipp Zitzlsperger, "Distanz und Präsenz: Das Porträt in der Frühneuzeit zwischen Repräsentation und Realpräsenz," in *Abwesenheit beobachten: Zu Kommunikation auf Distanz in der Frühen Neuzeit*, ed. Mark Hengerer (Münster, 2013), 41–78, which, however, largely neglects the eighteenth century; Friedrich Pol-

leroß, "Des abwesenden Prinzen Porträt: Zeremonielldarstellung im Bildnis und Bildnisgebrauch im Zeremoriell," in *Zeremoniell als höfische Ästhetik in Spätmittelalter und Früher Neuzeit*, ed. Jörg Jochen Berns and Thomas Rahn (Tübingen, 1995), 382–409. It remains to be examined how these beliefs developed in the early modern Low Countries.

8. On the Brabant *Blijde Inkomst*, see Van Dievoet, "L'empereur Joseph II," 87–140; van Dievoet, "De Blijde Inkomst: De geschreven grondwet van Brabant (1356–1794)," in *De gewestelijke en lokale overheidsinstellingen in Brabant en Mechelen tot 1795*, ed. Raymond Van Uytven, Claude Bruneel, Herman Coppens, and Beatrijs Augustyn (Brussels, 2000), vol. 1: 19–31. Very recently, a monograph came out that thoroughly investigates the medieval origins and fifteenth-century adaptations of Brabant's constitutional charter: Valerie Vrancken, *De Blijde Inkomsten van de Brabantse hertogen: Macht, opstand en privileges in de vijftiende eeuw* (Brussels, 2018).

9. Michel Nuyttens and Antoine Zoete, "De vier Leden en de Staten van Vlaanderen (1127–1795)," in *De gewestelijke en lokale overheidsinstellingen in Vlaanderen tot 1795*, ed. Walter Prevenier and Beatrijs Augustyn (Brussels, 1997), 67–78.

10. Beatrijs Augustyn, "Staten van Brabant (14de eeuw–1795)," in *De gewestelijke en lokale overheidsinstellingen in Brabant en Mechelen tot 1795*, ed. Raymond Van Uytven, Claude Bruneel, Herman Coppens, and Beatrijs Augustyn (Brussels, 2000), vol. 1: 97–132; Herman Coppens, *Het institutioneel kader van de centrale overheidsfinanciën in de Spaanse en Oostenrijkse Nederlanden tijdens het late Ancien Régime (c. 1680–1788)* (Brussels, 1993), 148–52.

11. Marc Boone and Maarten Prak, "Rulers, Patricians and Burghers: The Great and the Little Traditions of Urban Revolt in the Low Countries," in *A Miracle Mirrored: The Dutch Republic in European Perspective*, ed. Karel Davids and Jan Lucassen (Cambridge, UK, 1995), 99–134.

12. Offering many examples: Soly, "Plechtige intochten."

13. A small selection from the many recent publications on inaugurations and the accompanying ritual and artistic messages as gauges of the relationship between prince and subjects: Peter Arnade, "The Emperor and the City: The Cultural Politics of the Joyous Entry in Early Sixteenth-Century Ghent and Flanders," *Handelingen van het Genootschap voor Geschiedenis en Oudheidkunde te Gent* 54 (2000): 65–92; Anne-Laure Van Bruaene, "Spectacle and Spin for a Spurned Prince: Civic Strategies in the Entry Ceremonies of the Duke of Anjou in Antwerp, Bruges and Ghent (1582)," *Journal of Early Modern History* 11, no. 4–5 (2007): 263–84; Margit Thøfner, *A Common Art: Urban Ceremonial in Brussels and Antwerp during and after the Dutch Revolt* (Zwolle, 2007).

14. The Duchy of Gelderland seems to constitute an exception. Both in 1666 for Charles II and in 1702 for Philip V, representatives of the lordship and town of Weert swore an oath of obedience to the new ruler as Duke of Gelderland several days or weeks after the Estates had done so. Weert was not formally part of Upper-Gelderland and was thus not represented in Gelderland's Estates. Interestingly, the representative of the duke did not swear an oath during Weert's investitures. In 1716, upon the Austrian take-over of the duchy, all the free lordships attached to Gelderland swore loyalty to the new ruler, Charles VI, a couple of days after the Estates of Gelderland. It is unclear whether this habit continued throughout the eighteenth century: A. M. J. A. Berkvens, *Plakkatenlijst Overkwartier 1665–1794. Deel I: Spaans Gelre. Instellingen, territorium, wetgeving (1580–)1665–1702* (Nijmegen, 1990), 109–12.

15. François Zanatta, "Pour une relecture du serment public entre le prince et les communautés d'habitants: l'exemple des joyeuses entrées des Archiducs," *Revue du Nord*, no. 377 (2008): 738 and 742–43.
16. Luc Duerloo, *Dynasty and Piety: Archduke Albert (1598–1621) and Habsburg Political Culture in an Age of Religious Wars* (Farnham, 2012), 398–412.
17. Luc Duerloo, "Verbeelde gewesten: Zelfbeeld en zelfrepresentatie in de Zuidelijke Nederlanden," *De Zeventiende Eeuw* 16, no. 2 (2000): 3–13.
18. This calculation is based on figures for the years 1715–45 and 1749–88, in which the percentage of Flemish and Brabant taxes oscillated between 65.55 and 76.91 percent of all regional taxes transferred to the government: Herman Coppens, *Basisstatistieken voor de reconstructie van de centrale staatsrekening der Spaanse en Oostenrijkse Nederlanden ca. 1680–1788* (Brussels, 1993), 136–41.
19. Van Gelder, "The Investiture"; Klaas Van Gelder, "The Estates of Flanders Manning the Barricades for Territorial Integrity: The Protest against the Barrier Treaty of 1715," in *Intermediate Institutions in the County of Flanders in the Late Middle Ages and the Early Modern Era*, ed. Georges Martyn, René Vermeir, and Chantal Vancoppenolle (Brussels, 2012), 115–37.
20. Heinrich Ritter von Zeissberg, *Zwei Jahre belgischer Geschichte (1791, 1792). I. Theil: Von der Convention im Haag bis zum Tode Kaiser Leopolds II.* (Vienna, 1891), 105–16. It is possible that this context of restoration and appeasement also explains the large number of books commemorating Leopold II's inaugurations in the southern Netherlands (see table 6.2).
21. Count Mercy-Argenteau to (presumably) the Estates of Brabant, 13 April 1791: AR–AGR, GR/CP, 8B: fol. 170r–73v; resolutions of the members of the Antwerp city council, May and June 1791: AR–AGR, GR/CP, 8A: fol. 127r–133v; advisory note to the archdukes, 9 January 1792: AR–AGR, GR/CP, 8A: fol. 304r–17r.
22. Excerpt from the protocols, 13 April and 13 August 1791, and sketch of a resolution: AR–AGR, GR/CP, 8B: fol. 174r, 175r–76v, and 177r–78r; Count Mercy-Argenteau to the Estates of Brabant, 13 April 1791, with appendices: AR–AGR, GR/CP, 8B: fol. 184–201. See also Zeissberg, *Zwei Jahre*, 60–74 and 105–16.
23. Between 1715–45 and 1749–88, Limburg's share in the taxes fluctuated between 2.47 and 4.87 percent: Coppens, *Basisstatistieken*, 136–41; Bruno Dumont, "Les Etats de Limbourg et la fin de l'ancien régime," in *Het einde van het Ancien Régime in België: Colloquium van zaterdag 3 december 1988 te Brussel*, ed. Piet Lenders (Coutray-Heule, 1991), 81–139.
24. E. Defoort, "De Staten van West-Vlaanderen, 1787–1791," *Handelingen van het Genootschap voor Geschiedenis "Société d'Emulation" te Brugge* 102 (1965): 98–104.
25. Council of Brabant to Maria Christina and Albert of Saxony-Teschen, 30 November 1791: AR–AGR, GR/CP, 8A: fol. 79r–89v.
26. Zeissberg, *Zwei Jahre*, 108; Poullet, *Les constitutions*, 61–77.
27. Francis II to Archduke Charles, 18 May and 21 December 1793, and 4 March 1794: ÖStA, HHStA, Belgien-Depeschen, 58.
28. Zeissberg, *Zwei Jahre*, 73; Van Gelder, "The Investiture," 448; Wychlacz, "Habsburgische Rechtspolitik," 293.
29. Poullet, *Les constitutions*, 66–68. The request to be inaugurated was not the prince's first juridical act, as Poullet rightly pointed out. As a rule, the new prince first reinstalled the personnel of his predecessor.

30. These monarchs issued requests to be inaugurated quickly after ascending the throne. Charles VI formally assumed power in the Netherlands on 4 February 1716. He invited the Estates to coorganize the inaugurations on 23 February: AR–AGR, DN/DPB, 316: fol. 175r–76r. Two days after Charles's death, on 22 October 1740, Maria Theresa signed a dispatch confirming all the officials of her father and ordering them to provide information on the inaugurations, thus setting their preparation in motion: ÖStA, HHStA, Belgien–Depeschen, 18. Upon his recovery of the rebellious Netherlands at the end of 1790, Leopold II dispatched orders for his inauguration on 14 February 1791. However, he died already on 1 March 1792; his son and heir to the throne Francis II signed dispatches for the inaugurations on 3 March: ÖStA, HHStA, Belgien–Depeschen, 58. Joseph II seems to have been the only ruler not to take this step personally. Maria Theresa died on 29 November 1780. Only when documents regarding previous inaugurations came in from Brussels did Joseph dispatch orders to start the preparations on 22 February 1781: ÖStA, HHStA, Belgien–Depeschen, 56.
31. Van Gelder and Van Cauter, "Een publieke ceremonie," 117–18 and 122–23.
32. For a detailed account, see Piet Lenders, *De politieke crisis in Vlaanderen omstreeks het midden der achttiende eeuw: Bijdrage tot de geschiedenis van de Aufklaerung in België* (Brussels, 1956).
33. Documents concerning the order of precedence during the Flemish inauguration in 1781: AR–AGR, GR/CP, 10A: fol. 22r–63v, fol. 239r–40v, and fol. 253r–54v.
34. Excerpt from the resolutions of the Privy Council, 19 July 1781, and decree to the Land of Bornem, 23 July 1781: AR–AGR, GR/CP, 10A: fol. 317r.
35. Documents concerning this discussion can be found in: AR–AGR, GR/CP, 8A: fol. 42r–48v. See also resolutions of the Ministerial Conference in Brussels, 3 and 17 May 1794: AR–AGR, Ministerconferentie/Conférence ministérielle, 19: fol. 59r–60v and 239r–40v; Duke of Hoboken to Trauttmansdorff, court chancellor for the Netherlands, 20 April 1794: ÖStA, AVA, Familienarchiv Trauttmansdorff, 291. The honorary title of marshal of Brabant was attached to the Baronetcy of Wezemaal, owned by the Schetz and d'Ursel families from the fifteenth to the eighteenth centuries: Hamoir, *Qualité princière et dignités nobiliaires: Essai comparatif sur les distinctions de dignités au sein du second ordre dans divers pays* (Brussels, 1974), 59.
36. Barbara Stollberg-Rilinger, *Des Kaisers alte Kleider: Verfassungsgeschichte und Symbolsprache des alten Reiches* (Munich, 2013), 9–21.
37. See Van Gelder, "The Investiture," 449–50; Poullet, *Les constitutions*, 11–12; unknown sender to Privy Council, 6 March 1781: AR–AGR, GR/CP, 6: fol. 465r–65v.
38. Stollberg-Rilinger, *Des Kaisers alte Kleider*, 79–84 and passim.
39. Soly, "Plechtige intochten," 346–48.
40. Van Gelder, *Regime Change*, 296–98 and 303–6.
41. Van Gelder, "Revolution."
42. Soly, "Plechtige intochten," passim.
43. Gradually, banderoles, facial expression, gestures, and declamation were added to their communicative capacities: Stijn Bussels and Bram van Oostveldt, "De traditie van de tableaux vivants bij de plechtige intochten in de Zuidelijke Nederlanden (1496–1635)," *Tijdschrift voor Geschiedenis* 115, no. 2 (2002): 166–80.
44. Soly, "Plechtige intochten," passim.
45. John Landwehr's inventory of printed ceremony books is anything but complete, at least as far as the Austrian Netherlands are concerned: John Landwehr, *Splendid Ceremonies:*

State Entries and Royal Funerals in the Low Countries, 1515–1791. A Bibliography (Nieuwkoop, 1971). I have found thirteen different printed inauguration books, a list of which can be found in table 6.2.

46. Van Gelder, *Regime Change*, 167; Van Gelder, "The Investiture," 453–54; Duerloo, "Discourse," 474–76; J. P. van Baurscheit, *Description abregée du grand amphitheatre de l'inauguration dressé dans les Bailles de la Cour Ducale de Bruxelles le 11. Octobre 1717* (Brussels, n.d.). A copy can be found in the AR–AGR, HF/FH, 250/2. In the autumn of 2017, this collection was moved from the archives of the Belgian Department of Foreign Affairs, where I consulted it, to the National Archives of Belgium (AR–AGR) in Brussels.

47. The engravings can be found, among others, in Stadsarchief Gent, Atlas Goetgheheur, Lade 125, no. 102 and Lade 125, no. 112. For a reproduction of the latter, see Van Gelder and Van Cauter, "Een publieke ceremonie," 105.

48. An exception in this respect was the dessert table for the governors-general in 1744 in Flanders, which consisted of fifty-nine sugar figures and scenes depicting the virtues and talents of the new monarch in an allegorical fashion: *Beschryvinge van het laetste taefelgeregt (ofte) dessert, dienende op de Solemnele Huldinge van Haere Konniglyke Majesteyt Maria Theresia Koninginne van Hongarien, en Bohemen, &c. &c. &c. als gravinne van Vlaenderen, gedaen binnen Ghendt, den 27. April 1744* (Ghent, 1744). A copy can be found in AR–AGR, GR/CP, 9B.

49. *Relation des ceremonies de l'inauguration solemnelle de Sa Majesté Marie Thérèse Reine de Hongrie et de Bohème, en qualité de Comtesse de Namur, celebrée a Namur le quatrième de may 1744* (Namur, 1744), 9–10; *Relation de l'inauguration de S.M. l'Empereur et Roi Joseph II, en qualité de Comte de Hainau, solemnisée le 27 Août 1781, en la Ville de Mons* (Mons, 1781), 35–42.

50. *Description de la solemnité inaugurale de Sa Majesté l'Empereur et Roi, Léopold II comme Duc de Gueldres célébrée à Ruremonde le 22 septembre 1791* (Roermond, n.d.).

51. Klaas Van Gelder, "The Convention of The Hague and the Constitutional Debates in the Estates of Flanders and Brabant, 1790–1794," *Early Modern Low Countries* 1, no. 1 (2017): 156–76, https://www.emlc-journal.org/articles/10.18352/emlc.6/.

52. This section is based on archival documents in Stadsarchief Gent, Oud Archief—reeks 107, 35: fol. 11v–39v. A brief examination of the manifesto can be found in Georges Martyn and Luk Burgelman, "Les États de Flandres et l'absolutisme de l'Empereur Joseph II: à propos de la déclaration d'indépendance du 4 janvier 1790," in *L'absolutisme éclairée: Actes des journées internationales tenues à Versailles du 1er au 4 juin 2000*, ed. Serge Dauchy and Catherine Lecomte (Lille, 2002), 137–50.

53. For more information on the pictorial continuities in state festivities in Brussels up until the mid-nineteenth century, with illustrations, see Micheline Soenen, "La place, scène théâtro-politique," in *Le Quartier Royal*, ed. Arlette Smolar-Meynart and André Vanrie (Brussels, 1998), 217–37.

54. H. T. Colenbrander, ed., *Ontstaan der grondwet: Bronnenverzameling* (The Hague, 1909), vol. 2: 98–107, quotation 104.

55. André H. C. Van Hasselt, *Cérémonies et fêtes qui ont lieu à Bruxelles, du 21 au 23 juillet 1856 à l'occasion du XXVe anniversaire de l'inauguration de Sa Majesté le Roi Léopold Ier* (Brussels, 1856), 17–21 and plates; Jean-Baptiste Lammens, *Herinnering aen de feesten te Gent. 31^{en} van oogst- en 1^{en} van herfstmaend 1856* (Ghent, 1857), 21.

56. This act led to discussion in 1717. In spite of it, a joint Brabant-Limburg inauguration took place in October of that year (no. 3 in table 6.1).

57. Minister Plenipotentiary Prié ratified this hastily organized inauguration on 20 May 1718.
58. A pocket version was printed in Flanders. It is unclear who gave the instructions to print it: *Relation de la ceremonie de l'inauguration de Sa Majesté la Reine d'Hongrie et de Boheme comme Duchesse de Lothier, de Brabant, du Limbourg & Marquise du S. Empire, faite à Bruxelles le 20. Avril 1744* (Ghent, n.d.), consulted in AR–AGR, HF/FH, 250/2.

Bibliography

Arnade, Peter. "The Emperor and the City: The Cultural Politics of the Joyous Entry in Early Sixteenth-Century Ghent and Flanders." *Handelingen van het Genootschap voor Geschiedenis en Oudheidkunde te Gent* 54 (2000): 65–92.
Augustyn, Beatrijs. "Staten van Brabant (14de eeuw–1795)." In *De gewestelijke en lokale overheidsinstellingen in Brabant en Mechelen tot 1795*. Vol. 1, edited by Raymond Van Uytven, Claude Bruneel, Herman Coppens, and Beatrijs Augustyn, 97–132. Brussels: Algemeen Rijksarchief, 2000.
Berkvens, A. M. J. A. *Plakkatenlijst Overkwartier 1665–1794. Deel I: Spaans Gelre. Instellingen, territorium, wetgeving (1580–) 1665–1702*. Nijmegen: Gerard Noodt Instituut, 1990.
Beschreibung der am 25 August 1791 zu Luxemburg feyerlichst gehaltenen Huldigungs=Zeremonie, nebst einigen Nebenumständen: Zusammengetragen und verfasset von einem Augenzeugen. Luxembourg: In der Perlschen Buchdruckerey, 1791.
Beschryvinge van het laetste taefel-geregt (ofte) dessert, dienende op de Solemnele Huldinge van Haere Konniglyke Majesteyt Maria Theresia Koninginne van Hongarien, en Bohemen, &c. &c. &c. als gravinne van Vlaenderen, gedaen binnen Ghendt, den 27. April 1744. Ghent: Weduwe van Petrus de Goesin, 1744.
Boone, Marc, and Maarten Prak. "Rulers, Patricians and Burghers: The Great and the Little Traditions of Urban Revolt in the Low Countries." In *A Miracle Mirrored: The Dutch Republic in European Perspective*, edited by Karel Davids and Jan Lucassen, 99–134. Cambridge, UK: Cambridge University Press, 1995.
Braekman, W. L. "De inhuldiging van keizer Karel VI te Gent in oktober 1717." *Van mensen en dingen: tijdschrift voor volkscultuur in Vlaanderen* 1, no. 3 (2003): 268–77.
Bussels, Stijn, and Bram van Oostveldt. "De traditie van de tableaux vivants bij de plechtige intochten in de Zuidelijke Nederlanden (1496–1635)." *Tijdschrift voor Geschiedenis* 115, no. 2 (2002): 166–80.
Carmes, Alex. "L'entrée du Prince de Ligne à Luxembourg en 1781 à l'occasion de l'inauguration de l'empereur Joseph II comme duc de Luxembourg et comte de Chiny." *Hémecht: Revue d'Histoire luxembourgeoise* 45, no. 4 (1993): 441–89.
Colenbrander, H. T., ed. *Ontstaan der grondwet: Bronnenverzameling*. Vol. 2. The Hague: Nijhoff, 1909.
Coppens, Herman. *Basisstatistieken voor de reconstructie van de centrale staatsrekening der Spaanse en Oostenrijkse Nederlanden ca. 1680–1788*. Brussels: Algemeen Rijksarchief, 1993.
———. *Het institutioneel kader van de centrale overheidsfinanciën in de Spaanse en Oostenrijkse Nederlanden tijdens het late Ancien Régime (c. 1680–1788)*. Brussels: Algemeen Rijksarchief, 1993.
Defoort, E. "De Staten van West-Vlaanderen, 1787–1791." *Handelingen van het Genootschap voor Geschiedenis "Société d'Emulation" te Brugge* 102 (1965): 69–105.

De Schryver, Reginald. "De Oostenrijkse aanspraken op de Spaans-Habsburgse erfenis: De Zuidelijke Nederlanden tijdens de Spaanse Successieoorlog, 1700–1716." In *Oostenrijks België 1713–1794: De Zuidelijke Nederlanden onder de Oostenrijkse Habsburgers*, edited by Hervé Hasquin, 11–36. Brussels: Gemeentekrediet van België, 1987.

Description de la solemnité inaugurale de Sa Majesté l'Empereur et Roi, Léopold II comme Duc de Gueldres célébrée à Ruremonde le 22 septembre 1791. Roermond: G. Gruyters, n.d.

d'Hainaut-Zveny, Brigitte. "Feesten en vermakelijkheden onder de regering van Karel van Lotharingen." In *Karel Alexander van Lotharingen: Gouverneur-generaal van de Oostenrijkse Nederlanden*, 115–36. Brussels: Generale Bankmaatschappij, 1987.

Duerloo, Luc. "Discourse of Conquest, Discourse of Contract: Competing Visions on the Nature of the Habsburg Rule in the Netherlands." In *Bündnispartner und Konkurrenten Der Landesfürsten? Die Stände in der Habsburgermonarchie*, edited by Gerhard Ammerer, William D. Godsey Jr., Martin Scheutz, Peter Urbanitsch, and Alfred Stefan Weiß, 463–78. Vienna: R. Oldenbourg Verlag, 2007.

———. *Dynasty and Piety: Archduke Albert (1598–1621) and Habsburg Political Culture in an Age of Religious Wars*. Farnham: Ashgate, 2012.

———. "Verbeelde gewesten: Zelfbeeld en zelfrepresentatie in de Zuidelijke Nederlanden." *De Zeventiende Eeuw* 16, no. 2 (2000): 3–13.

Dumont, Bruno. "Les Etats de Limbourg et la fin de l'ancien régime." In *Het einde van het Ancien Régime in België: Colloquium van zaterdag 3 december 1988 te Brussel*, edited by Piet Lenders, 81–139. Courtray-Heule: UGA, 1991.

Gachard, Louis-Prosper. *Histoire de la Belgique au commencement du XVIIIe siècle*. Brussels: Muquardt, 1880.

Hamoir. *Qualité princière et dignités nobiliaires: Essai comparatif sur les distinctions de dignités au sein du second ordre dans divers pays*. Brussels: Les éditions de la Librairie encyclopédique, 1974.

Holenstein, André. "Huldigung und Herrschaftszeremoniell im Zeitalter des Absolutismus und der Aufklärung." In *Zum Wandel von Zeremoniell und Gesellschaftsritualen in der Zeit der Aufklärung*, edited by Klaus Gerteis, 21–46. Hamburg: Felix Meiner Verlag, 1992.

Inauguration de Sa Majesté l'Empereur et Roi Leopold II Glorieusement Regnant en qualités de Duc de Luxembourg & de Comte de Chiny, célébrée à Luxembourg le 25 août 1791. Luxembourg: De l'Imprimerie des Héritiers de François Perle, n.d.

Inauguration en Flandre, Gand. Ghent: Pierre de Gousin, n.d.

Lammens, Jean-Baptiste. *Herinnering aen de feesten te Gent. 31^{en} van oogst- en 1^{en} van herfstmaend 1856*. Ghent: Van Doosselaere, 1857.

Landwehr, John. *Splendid Ceremonies: State Entries and Royal Funerals in the Low Countries, 1515–1791. A Bibliography*. Nieuwkoop: De Graaf, 1971.

Lebeer, Louis. "Les estampes relatives aux inaugurations de Philippe V et de Charles VI à Bruxelles." *Anciens Pays et Assemblées d'États/Standen en Landen* 16 (1958): 35–63.

Lenders, Piet. *De politieke crisis in Vlaanderen omstreeks het midden der achttiende eeuw: Bijdrage tot de geschiedenis van de Aufklaerung in België*. Brussels: Paleis der Academiën, 1956.

Martyn, Georges, and Luk Burgelman. "Les États de Flandres et l'absolutisme de l'Empereur Joseph II: à propos de la déclaration d'indépendance du 4 janvier 1790." In *L'absolutisme éclairée: Actes des journées internationales tenues à Versailles du 1er au 4 juin 2000*, edited by Serge Dauchy and Catherine Lecomte, 137–50. Lille: Centre d'Histoire judiciaire, 2002.

Nuyttens, Michel, and Antoine Zoete. "De vier Leden en de Staten van Vlaanderen (1127–1795)." In *De gewestelijke en lokale overheidsinstellingen in Vlaanderen tot 1795*, edited by Walter Prevenier and Beatrijs Augustyn, 67–78. Brussels: Algemeen Rijksarchief, 1997.

Polleroß, Friedrich. "Des abwesenden Prinzen Porträt: Zeremonielldarstellung im Bildnis und Bildnisgebrauch im Zeremoniell." In *Zeremoniell als höfische Ästhetik in Spätmittelalter und Früher Neuzeit*, edited by Jörg Jochen Berns and Thomas Rahn, 382–409. Tübingen: Niemeyer, 1995.

Poullet, Edmond. *Les constitutions nationales belges de l'ancien régime à l'époque de l'invasion française de 1794*. Brussels: F. Hayez, 1875.

Précis de la solemnité de l'inauguration de Sa Majesté l'Empereur et Roi Léopold II, comme comte de Hainau, fixé au 12 juillet 1791. Mons: N. J. Bocquet, n.d.

Ravez, Walter. *Tournai et le Tournaisis pendant la révolution brabançonne: Essai d'histoire politique, sociale et économique*. Tournai: Imprimerie des Etablissements Casterman, 1937.

Relation de la ceremonie de l'inauguration de Sa Majesté la Reine d'Hongrie et de Boheme comme Duchesse de Lothier, de Brabant, du Limbourg & Marquise du S. Empire, faite à Bruxelles le 20. Avril 1744. Ghent: Jean Meyer, n.d.

Relation de l'inauguration de S. M. l'Empereur et Roi Joseph II, en qualité de Comte de Hainau, solemnisée le 27 Août 1781, en la Ville de Mons. Mons: Hoyois, 1781.

Relation de l'inauguration solemnelle de Sa Majesté Marie Thérèse, Reine de Hongrie et de Bohème, en qualité de Duchesse de Lothier, de Brabant, de Limbourg et de Marquise du St. Empire Romain, celebrée en la ville de Brusselles, le 20. Avril 1744. Brussels: François Claudinot, n.d.

Relation de l'inauguration solemnelle de Sa Sacrée Majesté impériale et catholique, Charles VI, Empereur des Romains . . . comme Comte de Flandres, célébrée à Gand, ville capitale de la Province, le XVIII. Octobre 1717. Ghent: Augustin Graet, 1719.

Relation de l'inauguration solemnelle de sa Sacrée Majesté Léopold II, Empereur des Romains . . . comme Comte de Flandres, célébrée à Gand, ville capitale de la Province, le VI juillet 1791. Ghent: Adrien Colier, 1792.

Relation de l'inauguration solemnelle de Sa Sacrée Majesté Marie Thérèse . . . comme Comtesse de Flandres, célébrée à Gand, ville capitale de la province, le XXVII. avril 1744. Ghent: Veuve Pierre de Goesin, 1744.

Relation des ceremonies de l'inauguration solemnelle de Sa Majesté Marie Thérèse Reine de Hongrie et de Bohème, en qualité de Comtesse de Namur, celebrée a Namur le quatrième de may 1744. Namur: Jean François Lafontaine, 1744.

Relation des cérémonies et des réjouissances publiques, faites en la ville de cour de Bruxelles le 11. d'Octobre 1717, jour de la Joyeuse Entrée & Inauguration de Sa Sacrée Majesté impériale et catholique Charles VI. Brussels: Joseph t'Serstevens, 1717.

Relation des cérémonies observées à l'inauguration de Sa Majesté l'empereur Joseph II, qui a eu lieu à Bruxelles le 17 juillet 1781. Brussels: J. Vanden Berghen, 1781.

Soenen, Micheline. "Fêtes et cérémonies publiques à Bruxelles aux Temps Modernes." *Bijdragen tot de Geschiedenis* 68 (1985): 47–101.

———. "La place, scène théâtro-politique." In *Le Quartier Royal*, edited by Arlette Smolar-Meynart and André Vanrie, 217–37. Brussels: CFC-Éditions, 1998.

Soly, Hugo. "Plechtige intochten in de steden van de Zuidelijke Nederlanden tijdens de overgang van Middeleeuwen naar Nieuwe Tijd: communicatie, propaganda, spektakel." *Tijdschrift voor Geschiedenis* 97 (1984): 341–60.

Stollberg-Rilinger, Barbara. *Des Kaisers alte Kleider: Verfassungsgeschichte und Symbolsprache des Alten Reiches.* Munich: C. H. Beck, 2008 (2nd ed. 2013).

Thøfner, Margit. *A Common Art: Urban Ceremonial in Brussels and Antwerp during and after the Dutch Revolt.* Zwolle: Waanders Publishers, 2007.

van Baurscheit, J. P. *Description abregée du grand amphitheatre de l'inauguration dressé dans les Bailles de la Cour Ducale de Bruxelles le 11. Octobre 1717.* Brussels: Simon t'Serstevens, n.d.

Van Bruaene, Anne-Laure. "Spectacle and Spin for a Spurned Prince: Civic Strategies in the Entry Ceremonies of the Duke of Anjou in Antwerp, Bruges and Ghent (1582)." *Journal of Early Modern History* 11, no. 4–5 (2007): 263–84.

van Dievoet, Guido [Guy]. "De Blijde Inkomst: De geschreven grondwet van Brabant (1356–1794)." In *De gewestelijke en lokale overheidsinstellingen in Brabant en Mechelen tot 1795.* Vol. 1, edited by Raymond Van Uytven, Claude Bruneel, Herman Coppens, and Beatrijs Augustyn, 19–31. Brussels: Algemeen Rijksarchief, 2000.

———. "L'empereur Joseph II et la Joyeuse Entrée de Brabant: Les dernières années de la constitution brabançonne." *Anciens Pays et Assemblées d'États/Standen en Landen* 16 (1958): 87–140.

Van Gelder, Klaas. "The Convention of The Hague and the Constitutional Debates in the Estates of Flanders and Brabant, 1790–1794." *Early Modern Low Countries* 1, no. 1 (2017): 156–76. https://www.emlc-journal.org/articles/10.18352/emlc.6/. Accessed 23 August 2018.

———. "The Estates of Flanders Manning the Barricades for Territorial Integrity: The Protest against the Barrier Treaty of 1715." In *Intermediate Institutions in the County of Flanders in the Late Middle Ages and the Early Modern Era*, edited by Georges Martyn, René Vermeir, and Chantal Vancoppenolle, 115–37. Brussels: Algemeen Rijksarchief, 2012.

———. "The Investiture of Emperor Charles VI in Brabant and Flanders: A Test Case for Authority of the New Austrian Government." *European Review of History/Revue européenne d'histoire* 18, no. 4 (2011): 443–63.

———. *Regime Change at a Distance: Austria and the Southern Netherlands following the War of the Spanish Succession, 1716–1725.* Leuven: Peeters Publishers/KVAB Press, 2016.

———. "Revolution, Krieg und Stände: Die Reise von Kaiser Franz II. in die Österreichischen Niederlande 1794." *Frühneuzeit-Info* 28 (2017): 155–70.

Van Gelder, Klaas, and Bert Van Cauter. "Een publieke ceremonie in een turbulent tijdvak: De inauguratie van Maria Theresia als gravin van Vlaanderen (1744)." *Handelingen der Maatschappij voor Geschiedenis en Oudheidkunde te Gent* 67 (2013): 101–30.

Van Hasselt, André H. C. *Cérémonies et fêtes qui ont lieu à Bruxelles, du 21 au 23 juillet 1856 à l'occasion du XXVe anniversaire de l'inauguration de Sa Majesté le Roi Léopold Ier.* Brussels: Géruset, 1856.

Viaene, A. "De laatste keizerlijke inauguratie te Ieper, 8 augustus 1791." *Biekorf* 61, no. 11 (1960): 389–97.

———. "Frans II, Keizer der Romeinen, als laatste Graaf van Vlaanderen." *Biekorf* 76, no. 1–2 (1975–76): 5–14.

Vrancken, Valerie. *De Blijde Inkomsten van de Brabantse hertogen: Macht, opstand en privileges in de vijftiende eeuw.* Brussels: Academic and Scientific Publishers, 2018.

Wychlacz, Eric. "Habsburgische Rechtspolitik im Herzogtum Luxemburg und den Herrschaftswechsel in den Südlichen Niederlanden von 1714–1725." *Hémecht: Zeitschrift für Luxemburger Geschichte* 63, no. 1 (2011): 281–314.

Zanatta, François. "Pour une relecture du serment public entre le prince et les communautés d'habitants: l'exemple des joyeuses entrées des Archiducs." *Revue du Nord* 377 (2008): 729–45.

Zeissberg, Heinrich Ritter von. *Belgien unter der Generalstatthalterschaft Erzherzog Carls (1793, 1794). II. Theil*. Vienna: Tempsky, 1794.

———. *Zwei Jahre belgischer Geschichte (1791, 1792). I. Theil: Von der Convention im Haag bis zum Tode Kaiser Leopolds II*. Vienna: Tempsky, 1891.

Zitzlsperger, Philipp. "Distanz und Präsenz: Das Porträt in der Frühneuzeit zwischen Repräsentation und Realpräsenz." In *Abwesenheit beobachten: Zu Kommunikation auf Distanz in der Frühen Neuzeit*, edited by Mark Hengerer, 41–78. Münster: LIT, 2013.

Chapter 7

CONDITIONING SOVEREIGNTY IN THE AUSTRIAN NETHERLANDS

The Joyous Entry Charter and
the Inauguration of Maria Theresa in Brabant

Thomas Cambrelin

On 20 April 1744, three and a half years after her accession to the throne, the official Brabantine inauguration of Maria Theresa was finally held in Brussels. On the *Place des Bailles*, at the foot of the burnt Coudenberg Palace, the emblematic place of government power in the Austrian Netherlands, stood the ephemeral theatre built for the inauguration. The following quotation describes the most important moment of the inauguration: the exchange of oaths between the members of the Estates of Brabant and the representative of the sovereign, the governor-general of the Netherlands, which followed the reading of the text of the *Joyous Entry* (in French: *Joyeuse Entrée*; in Dutch: *Blijde Inkomst*), the Duchy of Brabant's secular constitutional charter. Taken from the *Relation de l'inauguration solennelle de Marie-Thérèse*, this passage, written in theatrical rhetoric, clearly outlines the implications of the sovereign's inauguration in the Duchy of Brabant:

> In this day of joy and allegiance, the Estates of the Duchies of Brabant and Limburg had the honor to appear before Her, to receive from her lips the sacred assurances, the inviolable promises and the most precious pledge of benignity, of the love and maternal affection of H. M. their legitimate Sovereign.

H. M. following the example of her Glorious Predecessors, was to conclude with her people a Perpetual Covenant, which, by assuring them the enjoyment of their Privileges, their Rights, their customs and their liberties, assures the Sovereign Obedience and the most unalterable Fidelity.[1]

After reading this excerpt, one might conclude that all had been said at this stage—or at least all that is essential. Throughout the very descriptive account, the exchange of oaths is encountered as "simple formalities of use."[2] Upon closer examination, however, nothing could be less certain.

The source of the (translated) passage is a book containing the program of all the rituals and symbolic messages of the inauguration and thus fitting into the category of "inauguration books" that became a true literary genre in the sixteenth century.[3] The accounts of inaugural ceremonies in the principalities of the Habsburg Netherlands form part of a narrative tradition of political communication—with roots dating back at least to the Middle Ages—that blossomed in the modern era thanks to printing.[4] These written documents accompanied and contributed to the rise of princely power. But if we analyze the chronology of the events described in the account, everything indicates that the reality was far more complex than it may seem at first glance. Why did it take nearly four years for Maria Theresa to be inaugurated in Brabant, and how should we interpret the inauguration ceremony? To answer these questions, we must consider the specific context and procedures that directly influenced the preparations for the inauguration of the young Duchess of Brabant. In my opinion, the entire episode constitutes an act of ritual communication of shared exercise of power with highly symbolic content. As we will discover in the following pages, the question of respect for the "constitutions"[5] of the various principalities in the Netherlands—and especially for the Joyous Entry—posed enormous problems for the Austrian authorities.

Historiography and Actors

From a historiographical point of view, the studies dedicated to inaugural festivities at the time of the Dukes of Burgundy are relatively numerous in contrast to the near absence of similar research for the early modern era.[6] Micheline Soenen's study on the festivities in Brussels barely sketches out the true implications of the inaugurations in the city.[7] At best, it paved the way for the consultation of archives, thereby drawing attention to the conspicuous lack of archival material in Brussels compared to other cities such as Ghent and Bruges. Recently, Élodie Lecuppre-Desjardin showed that innovative interpretations of the inaugural ceremonies are in fact possible.[8] For the French historian, these ceremonies—far from being mere entertainment—are to be seen as acts of political communication in which power is staged.⁹ She examines ceremonies organized in the cities of the Burgundian Netherlands, clearly demonstrating that each of these ceremonies, including the inaugurations, represented an instrument of symbolic communication essential to the exercise of power. She also points out that ceremonials accompany rather than form the basis of state building, drawing attention to the importance of propaganda and negotiation in the different principalities of the Burgundian Netherlands.

What, then, can be said about the early modern era? Until recently, historiographical interest in the subject of inaugurations relating to the eighteenth century was limited. It is only the studies by Luc Duerloo and Klaas Van Gelder that provide new insights into the issues at stake in the respective ceremonies: their research clearly demonstrates that the true nature of the exercise of power in the Netherlands was contractual and based on a consensus developed between the provincial Estates and the central government in Brussels.¹⁰

The topic of ceremonial acts and procedures is more common in studies on the Holy Roman Empire. We owe a great deal to Barbara Stollberg-Rilinger for her crossover approach to rituals incorporating a perfect assimilation of the theories of communication. She explains that the solemn ritual of royal investiture allowed the emperor to establish the legitimacy of his power in the absence of a formal constitution.¹¹ Inaugurations in the Netherlands appear to have been acts of political communication equivalent to the imperial coronation in Frankfurt that were still effective in the mid-eighteenth century.

Before addressing the points related to the historical context and the form that the exercise of power assumed in the Netherlands, I will briefly mention the actors of this affair and present the proponents of the Joyous Entry of Brabant. During the ceremony, the Brabantine people, with whom the prince was obligated to conclude a form of covenant conditioning his or her accession to the throne, were represented—in the sense of a delegation, as Michel Hébert points out¹²—by the Estates. The hosting city of Brussels was not only one of the main cities of the Duchy of Brabant, but also assumed the role of capital of the southern Netherlands.¹³ This part of the Habsburg composite monarchy was an autonomous territorial unit composed of around ten independent principalities conjoined in a personal union. The territory corresponded roughly to modern Belgium and the Grand Duchy of Luxembourg, with the exception of the Prince-Bishopric of Liège.

The provincial Estates of the Duchies of Brabant and Limburg acted as intermediaries toward the young sovereign.¹⁴ Maria Theresa herself was not present at the ceremony, nor did she ever set foot in the Netherlands. In fact, this outlying region of the Habsburg Monarchy had been governed by delegation since the sixteenth century; and beginning with the reign of Charles V, the sovereign was represented by a governor-general who was usually a prince or princess of royal blood.¹⁵ Two of these governors-general played a role in the Brabant inauguration of Maria Theresa. Her aunt, Archduchess Maria Elisabeth, initiated the preparations for the celebration; and after Maria Elisabeth's death, it was Maria Theresa's brother-in-law, Prince Charles Alexander of Lorraine, who represented her at the ceremony.

As for the specific relationship between the prince and the people, it was materialized in the oaths exchanged between the sovereign and his or her Brabantine and Limburg subjects following the reading of the Joyous Entry, which bound the sovereign to the subjects in a very concise manner. But the term "Joyous Entry" has a second meaning as well: as pointed out by François Zanatta, it also refers to a ceremony belonging to an "ancient tradition" (i.e., the inauguration or ceremonial reception itself), and "territorial princes in the ancient Netherlands have followed this procedure since the Middle Ages."[16] For reasons of clarity, however, it is more appropriate in the case of Brabant to speak of the inauguration when referring to the ceremony, and of the Joyous Entry when we mean the charter.

Historical Context

The southern Netherlands had been part of the Habsburg Monarchy for only about thirty years[17] when Emperor Charles VI died in Vienna on 20 October 1740.[18] The great European powers soon began to threaten the monarchy and almost had it dissolved.[19] A few years earlier, however, the emperor had succeeded in getting his patrimonial lands to accept the Pragmatic Sanction so that they would remain within the House of Habsburg. After 1725, he was able to secure recognition of the Pragmatic Sanction by the great European powers as well.[20] Because Charles had no male heir, his edict enabled his daughters to become universal legatees and succeed him in his patrimonial domains. These were the conditions (summarized very broadly) that enabled Charles VI's eldest daughter, Maria Theresa, to inherit her father's rule in 1740.

Nevertheless, when Emperor Charles VI died, the Pragmatic Sanction was quickly challenged from all sides. The Bavarian Elector contested Maria Theresa's legitimacy and soon secured the support of France for his claims. Frederick II of Prussia also had his eye on the young queen's patrimony. The Habsburg Monarchy found itself isolated on the international stage and engaged in a race against time to stabilize its power and respond to the forces that threatened it. Aged twenty-three, Maria Theresa was a young mother with three daughters and expecting a fourth child when the dispute over Charles's succession began. Following the disasters of the War of the Polish Succession (1733–33) and the war against the Ottomans (1737–39), the state coffers were empty and the army hopelessly disorganized.[21] The War of the Austrian Succession would begin in earnest in December 1740 with King Frederick II of Prussia's invasion of the province of Silesia.[22]

Archduchess Maria Elisabeth, the late emperor's sister, had been governor-general of the Netherlands since 1725.[23] The region had benefitted from a high degree of autonomy due in part to the distance between Brussels and Vienna and in part to the authoritarian personality of Maria Elisabeth, to whom Charles had willingly granted significant freedom in the administration of the territory.[24] When Maria Theresa inherited the Netherlands, she initially kept her aunt as governor-general, hoping Maria Elisabeth would continue to perform her duties for many years to come.[25] The young queen did not wish to offend her aunt in any way, as she was determined to ultimately regain supreme control over these outlying regions whose links to the center of the monarchy had grown progressively weaker.[26] But Maria Elisabeth's health declined, forcing the government to consider the possibility of her replacement. In her correspondence with Vienna, the governor-general suggested that she would not be able to continue "such a painful" task forever.[27] Charles of Lorraine was eventually appointed as deputy governor-general alongside Maria Elisabeth on 17 April 1741, but would not arrive in the Netherlands until 1744.[28]

Maria Elisabeth effectively delegated her authority to her grand master of the court (*grand maître de la cour/Obersthofmeister*), Count Friedrich Harrach. The grand master was responsible for monitoring and advising the governor.[29] Like the archduchess, Harrach had an authoritarian personality, and he frequently clashed with the commander-in-chief of the troops in the Netherlands, the powerful Duke of Arenberg. This inevitably led to a deterioration of the political climate in the Netherlands.[30] Nevertheless, Harrach was appointed governor-general *ad interim* after Maria Elisabeth's death, pending the arrival of Prince Charles of Lorraine. The latter's mission would be to reestablish the links between Brussels and Vienna, restore order to the central government in Brussels, and eventually replace Maria Elisabeth. Above all else, he would have to respect the Estates' sensitivities so as to obtain from them the subsidies necessary for the upkeep of the armies.[31]

The question of finances was a constant concern for the Habsburg Monarchy, which faced a "frequent imbalance between its expenses and its receipts."[32] The situation of the government in Brussels was hardly any better.[33] Indeed, at the time of Maria Theresa's accession, the Austrian authorities in the Netherlands were faced with the discontent of the Brabantine Estates, who had decided to suspend payment of the subsidies—as the money transfers from the Estates to the central government were called—for the current year. This embarrassing situation for the government impeded payment of the salaries of the administration and the army. To maintain Austrian authority in this remote region of the monarchy, it was therefore vital to restore order and ensure the fastest possible transition of power. The context of the change of reign, along with Maria Theresa's desire to win the favor of the provincial Estates, would considerably aggravate an already tense situation in the Netherlands.

The young monarch attempted to appease the Estates to secure their vote for the taxes necessary for the war effort. The High Council of the Netherlands in Vienna, the advisory institution in charge of matters relating to the southern Netherlands, had advised caution—no doubt inspired by the letters of warning written by the Duke of Arenberg.[34] Maria Theresa respected the High Council's opinion and suspended several ordinances that had angered the Estates of Brabant. Vienna was pursuing the objective of taking control of the Netherlands, and any means were acceptable to further that plan.

Analysis of the various advisory notes and reports by the High Council sheds light on the strategy that Maria Theresa and the ministers in Vienna employed to handle the situation. Between December 1740 and February 1741, Vienna propelled the figure of the Duke of Arenberg to the forefront, since Maria Theresa knew she could count on him to reconcile the provincial Estates. In his correspondence, the duke did not fail to point out the dysfunctions in the government, even though his opinion and remarks were clearly colored by his hostility toward Count Harrach.[35]

Seeking allies who could help her establish her legitimacy in the Netherlands, Maria Theresa wrote to the Duke of Arenberg and placed her trust in him.[36] As a consequence, the various provincial assemblies (in particular the Estates of Flanders and Brabant) were persuaded to vote in favor of the subsidies.[37] Later, when Charles of Lorraine was appointed governor-general of the Austrian Netherlands, the monarch did not hesitate to ask the duke to offer Charles his help and advice.[38] At the time of Charles VI's death in 1740, however, it was still Maria Elisabeth who was in charge—and the confrontation between Count Harrach and the Duke of Arenberg was raging. It was in this tense atmosphere that preparations for the Brabantine inauguration began.

A First Inauguration Project (1740–41)

On 20 October 1740, the ministerial conference (*Geheime Konferenz*), the central advisory body in Vienna that primarily dealt with foreign policy issues, met to process the death of Emperor Charles VI and proclaim Maria Theresa sovereign.[39] From this point on, Vienna worked frenetically to establish the legitimacy of the young princess and have her recognized in her various hereditary territories. The question of the diverse inauguration ceremonies would thus be of central importance during the years to come. At the end of October, the governorate-general of the Netherlands received the dispatch announcing the emperor's death. Without waiting for instructions from Vienna—and following Maria Elisabeth's impulse—Brussels took measures to prepare the mourning of Charles VI and the inauguration of the new monarch.[40]

Shortly thereafter, another disaster struck the monarchy: Frederick II invaded Silesia on 16 December 1740, but not without first having attempted to secure this rich province in exchange for Prussian support for the election of Maria Theresa's spouse, Francis Stephen of Lorraine, to the imperial throne.[41] The Austrian authorities were now faced with the risk of a conflict on two fronts, as Harrach had revealed in his private correspondence his fears that France, an ally of the elector of Bavaria (the main opponent of Maria Theresa's rule and candidate for the imperial throne), would invade the Netherlands.[42]

The Estates in the Netherlands were in the process of applying financial pressure when the alarming news of the change of reign was received: despite its agreement to grant a subsidy, for example, Flanders had reduced its aid by nearly four hundred thousand guilders.[43] And as mentioned before, Brabant had withheld its subsidy in 1740 as well. The war chest in the Netherlands was in a precarious state and desperately needed replenishment, and it was under these circumstances that the government in Brussels set about preparing Maria Theresa's inauguration.

The preparations were to be delayed by several major obstacles, however. First of all, the authorities in Brussels had fallen victim to a "loss of memory" following the destruction of a substantial part of the archives of the Collateral Councils[44] in a fire at Coudenberg Palace in 1731.[45] The administration was thus forced to painstakingly collect all the documents relevant to the inauguration procedure anew—a mammoth task. Meanwhile, the ministerial conference in Vienna was distracted by a huge new problem when Maria Theresa announced her intent to promote her husband to coregent of all her dominions.

On 19 November 1740, Maria Elisabeth instructed the Privy Council, the second of the three Collateral Councils with particular responsibility for legislative matters, to examine the question of the inauguration preferentially and provide her with any relevant information.[46] The Privy Council then asked Count Harrach to entrust this task to a specially created committee.[47] The *Jointe pour les recherches pour l'inauguration* was later renamed *Jointe pour les affaires de l'Inauguration de Marie-Thérèse*. On 23 November, Charles of Lorraine—who was not yet officially a deputy to the government—asked the privy councilors Pycke and Robiano along with the council's chief president Steenhault to carry out the research into the inauguration.[48] The committee received the onerous task of collecting and presenting everything it considered necessary for the queen's inauguration in all the principalities of the Netherlands,[49] and the papers it compiled reveal the minutia of all aspects of the preparations for the event. They also elucidate the difficulties that the government in Brussels and the authorities in Vienna faced during this short period of time.

The first inauguration project submitted by the *Jointe* was a response to Maria Theresa's desire to organize an inauguration ceremony at the lowest possible cost.[50] The authorities' intentions were twofold: limiting expenses and protecting the governor-general's deteriorating health. The proposed solution was to organize a single inauguration ceremony in Brussels (either in the town hall or in the palace), to which the various provinces of the Netherlands were to send deputies to represent them.[51] A richly decorated and public stage for the ceremony, as was customary in the Netherlands, was not budgeted. This unique solution, which the authorities would have preferred, was envisaged at no other occasion during the seventeenth and eighteenth centuries.

Another point of discussion concerned the so-called letters of full power that the governor-general in the Netherlands received from the sovereign.[52] These letters supported the exercise of power by the governor-general and had to be presented to the various ordinary assemblies of the provincial Estates in the Netherlands. They were produced by the *Jointe* and submitted to Vienna to be amended, validated, and subsequently returned to Brussels. The documents took into account the customs and privileges of the different principalities and explained how the sovereign wished to be recognized and inaugurated. After reviewing whether the letters of full power had been drawn up in due form, the Estates would allow the inauguration to be prepared. The entire process caused much ink to flow between December 1740 and February 1741.

The ministerial conference and the High Council of the Netherlands quickly notified Maria Theresa that it was paramount for the very survival of the House of Habsburg that the Pragmatic Sanction be respected.[53] She therefore had to be inaugurated as the sole sovereign of her territories despite her decision to promote her husband, Francis Stephen, to the status of coregent. The Viennese authorities had already found a way to ensure that Maria Theresa would be recognized as sovereign without the act of coregency posing any problem: the latter would simply not be published until after the inauguration.

But the functionaries in Brussels thought otherwise. Maria Theresa was married and, according to the laws and constitutions of the Netherlands, a woman could do nothing without her spouse's consent. In other words, a husband was considered his wife's lord and guardian. The members of the *Jointe* and the Privy Council raised this very clear point of law, and the only solution in their opinion would be a coinauguration of Maria Theresa with Francis Stephen as coregent.[54] In her report written on 13 December 1740, Maria Elisabeth transmitted the various plans for the full powers to Vienna.[55] The report was not well received. How could the Netherlanders refuse to recognize Maria Theresa as sovereign ruler without Francis Stephen as coregent, while she had been recognized that way in her other hereditary territories?

Jealous of their privileges, the provincial Estates of the southern Netherlands blocked the full powers and considered them null and void.[56] To the members of the ministerial conference, this situation was unacceptable in light of the agreement by the various Estates' assemblies at the time of their acceptance of the Pragmatic Sanction. They saw it as a danger that could open the door to possible claims by foreign powers.

The government in Brussels scrutinized precedents dating back to the times of Albert and Isabella, which to the knowledge of those responsible was the only recent case where such an adaptation had been made to the full powers. A similar solution was out of the question as far as Vienna was concerned, however. The vice-president of the High Council, Count Königsegg-Erps, deemed it better at this point to not proceed with the inauguration at all.[57] Viscount Patin, a native of the Netherlands and councilor-regent at the High Council in Vienna, explained that the act of coregency should not be changed for the Netherlands, while simultaneously adding that the provincial Estates would certainly object on the grounds that the provisions were against the law and contrary to customs.[58] He pointed out that tradition in the Habsburg Netherlands provided for genuine coregency, coenjoyment of property, and coadministration by which the husband stood on the same power level as his spouse, a sovereign princess. The viscount then proposed two solutions: one was to allow a coinauguration; the other was to force the provincial Estates to accept coregency on an equal footing with the other hereditary states.

The *Jointe* for the inauguration insisted that the acts of full power were to be communicated to the provincial Estates of the various principalities by way of authentic copies.[59] In Brabant, the documents had to be presented by the chancellor with a letter of credence. Apart from these procedural considerations, however, the members of the *Jointe* also deemed it necessary—to solve the problem of the coinauguration—to insert a clause stipulating that Maria Theresa remained the sole and universal heir and reigning princess as much by right of blood as by virtue of the Pragmatic Sanction. This argument was intended to countervail the idea that the husband was his wife's lord and guardian. Eventually, the ministerial conference decided on the question of coregency and suggested in a report to Maria Theresa on 26 January 1741 that she suspend its declaration until after the inauguration, since the projects submitted by the *Jointe* were not adaptable to the situation and violated the Pragmatic Sanction.[60] In reality, the government in Brussels feared that the provincial Estates would otherwise block the measure for not respecting local customs. To justify respect for these customs, the members of the *Jointe de Cabinet* (an advisory institution assembling councilors to discuss politics on an *ad hoc* basis and to support the governor-general) mentioned the examples of the inaugurations of Archduke Maximilian of Austria and Mary of Burgundy as well as of Albert and Isabella. These arguments were rejected by the ministerial conference, however, which maintained that the princesses were not queens in either example and were thus not subject to international treaties.[61]

Subsequently, Vienna ultimately sent an act of full power expressing Maria Theresa's desire to be inaugurated alone. The Viennese court attempted to convince the provincial Estates by reminding them that the sovereign had been recognized in the same way in all of her other hereditary states.

But a new obstacle now arose. The members of the *Jointe de Cabinet* in Brussels noticed that the Viennese authorities had not mentioned the Joyous Entry of Brabant and the privileges that were the main object of the oath, binding the sovereign to his or her subjects.[62] The *Jointe* for the organization of the inauguration was charged by Count Harrach with examining previous acts to clarify whether or not the Joyous Entry and the privileges of the other principalities of the Austrian Netherlands had been mentioned in the past. It discovered that the full powers given to the Marquis of Prié during the reign of Charles VI did not mention the Joyous Entry either. The High Council in Vienna, after considering the corresponding report by the *Jointe de Cabinet*, advised the queen not to change her full powers act.[63] On 5 April 1741, in a letter to Maria Elisabeth, Maria Theresa reiterated her wish to be inaugurated alone and included a copy of the full powers she had sent on 15 February.[64] It was not until May 1741 that these original full powers were accepted by the two most prominent members of the Brabant Estates: the nobility and the clergy.[65]

Second Inauguration Project (1742–44)

Archduchess Maria Elisabeth died in her hunting castle in Mariemont on 26 August 1741, having outlived her brother by less than a year. Vienna had been forced to wait until the death of the distinguished princess, who was ardent about her prerogatives, to finally have free rein in the Netherlands. Now that the governor-general was dead, however, the act of full power had to be reviewed and renewed, and the preparations for the inauguration were once again delayed by this new setback. The path was now clear for Charles of Lorraine; but despite being designated governor-general of the Netherlands, he was hindered by the ongoing war. While waiting for her brother-in-law to take possession of the Netherlands, Maria Theresa appointed Count Harrach as interim governor-general.[66]

In the eyes of the provincial Estates, Maria Elisabeth's infirmity could now no longer serve as an excuse to justify an inauguration by deputation in Brussels. Inaugurations attended by the representative of the sovereign in Brabant and Flanders, and by commissioners in the other principalities, were to become the norm again as they had been in 1717[67]—and an appropriate new act of full powers had to be presented to the Estates.

Harrach wrote to Maria Theresa on 21 October:

> I do not see how it [the inauguration] can be forgone separately in the accustomed manner in each province, that is, that this Serene Prince should go there successively in person, which would be most useful, both to become acquainted with the consistency of each province, and with the disposition of which the different bodies are composed, in order to win their hearts by graceful and popular means, which are so natural to this Great Prince, and which are so indispensably necessary in a country of such republican spirit as this.[68]

In the same letter, Harrach mentioned a further issue being taken by the Estates of Brabant in regard to procedural matters relating to the inauguration.[69] The new point of friction between the Brabant representative assembly and the government pertained to the role of the signing secretary in Brabant. According to the Joyous Entry Charter, an official signature was necessary for the act of full power to be valid. But the counter-signature affixed by Her Majesty's secretary Dirix—a native of Brabant who had provisionally exercised the function of signing secretary of the duchy since the resignation of the *audiencier*[70] Count Cuvelier—now apparently posed a problem for the Estates, who were no longer satisfied with Dirix. Without a signing secretary in Brabant, the inauguration could not be organized. Moreover, without an official secretary, neither petitions for subsidies nor letters from the government could be addressed to the Estates of Brabant. This created a major obstacle, particularly since it was a constitutional question in the eyes of the Brabant assembly. The Estates maintained vis-à-vis the government that it was essential for the signing secretary to be a native of the duchy and to have a secretary's license with the great seal of Brabant. There was still the first official of the *Audience*, Charles Henri Cosqui, who had replaced Cuvelier after 1736, but he did not truly exercise the function of *audiencier*. Cosqui was permitted to sign dispatches only thanks to a special authorization he had requested and received from Maria Elisabeth.[71] The problem of the *audiencier* and his signature in Brabant was not actually new; in fact, it dated back to the beginning of the Austrian regime.[72] It was most urgent for the government to find a solution.

The High Council in Vienna, wishing to uphold Charles VI's decision to remove the *audiencier* Cuvelier without forcing Maria Theresa to intervene by means of a decree, found an expedient to circumvent the objection voiced by the Estates:[73] it decided to issue a license with the great seal of Brabant to the secretary of the Privy Council, Neny—a naturalized Brabanter.

Meanwhile, in 1742, relations between Vienna and Brussels had reached an all-time low. The conflict between interim governor-general Harrach and the Duke of Arenberg, head of the armies in the Netherlands, was turning sour,[74] and the extent to which the government had allowed itself to be manipulated by the provincial Estates was becoming increasingly apparent. Exploiting the power vacuum in Brussels's central government, the assemblies were progressively resisting their requests: they now "demanded the *ad hoc* repayment of the loans contracted by Vienna and threatened to use up the proceeds of the annual subsidies in the event of default."[75] The loans in question had been raised in the Netherlands in 1739 after negotiations with Charles VI to help finance his campaign against the Ottomans, but their repayment had ceased when the War of Succession started.[76]

As a result of all these obstacles, it was only from 1743 onward that all the questions relating to the inauguration were finally resolved and the actual preparations for the ceremony could begin. Charles of Lorraine would be present in Brussels for the Duchy of Brabant, and in Ghent for the County of Flanders.[77] The High Council in Vienna, hostile toward Harrach, thought Harrach had imprudently consulted too many members of the *Jointe* for the inauguration, thereby delaying the organization of the ceremony even further. Maria Theresa consequently appointed Count Königsegg-Erps as minister plenipotentiary in the absence of Charles of Lorraine on 13 February 1743.[78] Harrach was recalled.

Königsegg-Erps revisited the entire business of Maria Theresa's inauguration from the beginning. In a *Jointe de Cabinet* on 11 June 1743, he assembled only a handful of government members around the table and invited the chancellor of Brabant to reexamine the file of previous acts relating to the inauguration.[79] Among other things, the new *Jointe* scrutinized the delicate question of how to communicate the circumstances of Francis Stephen's coregency. Königsegg-Erps was surprised to learn that Maria Theresa's spouse, universally recognized elsewhere throughout the monarchy, was not acknowledged in the Netherlands. He deemed it essential to communicate the coregency to the various principalities of the Netherlands before the inauguration so as to avoid giving rise to new grievances on the part of the Estates. At the chancellor's demand, however, it was necessary this time not to forgo presenting the Estates with the originals of the acts of full power on behalf of the queen and her husband so that both documents could be examined in the general assembly.[80] On 13 June 1743, the assembly issued a decree to the *Jointe* for the inauguration, ordering it to undertake all preparations relating to the inauguration and to communicate the specifics of Francis Stephen's coregency to the Estates.[81] The request to the various assemblies was to be made by late August or early September. On 11 August, in two separate letters, Maria Theresa gave her assent to the communication of the coregency and the inauguration.[82] On 25 August, Königsegg-Erps informed the *Jointe* that the monarch had decided to assemble the Estates in mid-September to announce the act of coregency and propose the inauguration. The impending arrival of Charles of Lorraine undoubtedly softened the Estates' stance.

In October 1743, the Estates of the Duchy of Limburg gave their consent to the inauguration and to the ordinary subsidy for 1744.[83] The Estates of Brabant, however, still conditioned their agreement to the subsidy on the arrival of the new governor-general Charles of Lorraine. Other representations came from the city of Leuven, which—until the announcement in February or March 1744 of Charles's imminent arrival in the Netherlands—had refused its consent on the pretext that it was the historic capital of the duchies of Brabant and Limburg and should therefore be allowed to host the inauguration.[84] It was only under threat that Leuven finally gave way by accepting a letter of no prejudice.

Conclusion

The Estates finally granted their additional financial support after the arrival of Charles of Lorraine in the Netherlands on 26 March 1744.[85] On 20 April 1744, according to the *Brussels Gazette*, the festivities accompanying the inauguration were celebrated with joy and happiness,[86] with Charles of Lorraine representing the queen. In most other principalities, eminent members of the nobility replaced the governor-general.

The inauguration of Maria Theresa and the difficulties caused by the Estates of Brabant brandishing the Joyous Entry go beyond a simple chronological account of the various setbacks with which the Viennese authorities had to deal. The pertinent question of the content of the acts of full power linked to Francis Stephen's coregency highlights the deeper meaning of Maria Theresa's inauguration and the constitutional practices of the premodern period in the Netherlands. In fact, through this inauguration, we witness issues of consensus and representation that were intimately linked to the exercise of sovereignty in the Habsburg Monarchy. The ceremony was a memorable moment during which the key structures of the society of the *Ancien Régime* were put on display. In this particular case, the political society was that of the Duchy of Brabant—represented by its Estates, who cited the duchy's laws, customs, and constitutions (among them the Joyous Entry) as prerequisites to be respected. In order to acknowledge and respond to these traditions, protracted and binding processes had to be observed. It was all a question of procedure, and the procedure respecting the Joyous Entry of Brabant constituted the very foundation and condition of sovereignty. In the case of Brabant, it is perfectly admissible to speak of "constitution" in its old meaning, or of "constitutional" culture.

Brabant may represent an exceptional case in regard to its written constitutional charter. Nevertheless, I firmly believe that we can speak of constitution and constitutionalism for the entirety of the Austrian Netherlands even though the other principalities did not have a "written Joyous Entry charter" like Brabant.[87] If we view a constitution as a fundamental law or set of principles that determines the organization of a state and preserves the common good (in this case, the laws, customs, and privileges of Brabant), and then cast in a set of constitutional rules (declaring war, meting out justice, etc.), we can effectively use these words in relation to the obligations that the Joyous Entry of Brabant imposed on rulers before the fall of the *Ancien Régime*.[88]

The negotiations between the government and the Estates constituted opportunities for the latter, through their petitions and grievances, to recall and display that they were the "depositaries of authority"—to use Wim Blockmans's words concerning the deposition of Philip II by the Estates in 1581.[89] Even if this idea is not clearly expressed in this case, it is nevertheless how the mindset of the Brabant Estates should be interpreted when they requested that certain procedures should be respected and remained meticulous in their examination of the letters of full power. The imperatives of the War of the Austrian Succession required the government to treat the Estates with care.

Of course, like everywhere else in the monarchy, the inauguration served the prince's propaganda. The political celebration took the form of "a theatrical performance in which designated actors play specific roles, even according to agreed texts, in several consecutive acts."[90] However, the moment in which the exchange of oaths between the ruler (or her representative) and the Estates—the embodiment of the Brabant community—took place restored the prince to her contractual obligations. The inauguration and the oath of respect to the Joyous Entry charter of the Duchy of Brabant were the keys to truly recognizing the sovereign as the legitimate prince. On the other hand, the oath imposed on the prince made it possible to limit her power and to protect the people from tyranny. That is what was at stake.

The inauguration and the oath on the Joyous Entry were nothing less than a "constitution *in actu*." What occurred in the inauguration theatre was a reminder of the place and role of the various protagonists and the ultimate respect for the political contract that governed the exercise of power in the Netherlands. During the inauguration, the mechanisms that "found the legitimacy of power and make it acceptable and efficient"[91]—to use Jean-Philippe Genêt's words—were activated; it thus formed the highly symbolic moment "when the agreement between power and political society is established."[92] As François Zanatta suggests, the various types of ceremonies all served the same purpose of declaring the respective ruler truly legitimate and thus of providing "constitutional continuity."[93] The four years of Maria Theresa's reign preceding the swearing of the oaths must therefore be seen as a time of consensus-seeking on the exercise of power in the Netherlands.

Two ideologies of power clashed and dialogued at the same time: on the one hand, a princely absolutism that did not understand that it could be opposed by rights and customs differing from the rules adopted within the hereditary territories of the monarchy; and on the other hand, the discourse of respect for the law, customs, privileges, and freedoms hammered out by the Estates' assemblies. The Brabant case shows the extent to which the government was obliged to respect the Estates' privileges under penalty of complete blockage of the system. Maria Theresa's rule in Brabant had been negotiated and conditioned by respect for the constitutions and freedoms of her subjects.

As has been pointed out, Harrach did not hesitate to speak of a "republican spirit" for all the principalities of the Netherlands. But what meaning was attached to the minister's words? Undoubtedly, we must interpret this allusion to the "republican spirit" as an evocation of a political virtuality that appeared in the second half of the fifteenth century in the first texts written to "constitutionally regulate" political exchanges, as François Foronda writes: the Republic, which was understood as a resistance "to tyranny, that is, to the absolutization of sovereign power." In my opinion, Maria Theresa's inauguration in Brabant demonstrates that this was still relevant in the middle of the eighteenth century.[94]

Thomas Cambrelin is a teaching assistant and PhD candidate in early modern history at the Faculty of Philosophy and Social Sciences at the Université libre de Bruxelles (ULB). His doctoral research focuses in particular on the role of the provincial Estates in the construction of the modern state during the eighteenth century. He examines the power relations between the Estates of the Duchy of Brabant and the central state apparatus in the Austrian Netherlands. The objective of this study is also to shed light on the specific political culture in these outlying regions of the composite Habsburg Monarchy. He is currently preparing an article on the role of the high nobility in the state apparatus in the Austrian Netherlands.

Notes

1. Extract from *Relation de l'inauguration solemnelle de Sa Majesté Marie Thérèse reine de Hongrie et de Bohème, en qualité de Duchesse de Lothier, de Brabant, de Limbourg, et de Marquise du St. Empire Romain, célébrée en la ville de Brusselles, le 20. Avril 1744* (Brussels, n.d.), 8: Brussels, AR–AGR, SEG/SSO, 1495. The Duchy of Limburg had been united with the Duchy of Brabant since the second half of the thirteenth century (1288) while retaining its own institutions. For more information about the landmark event of the Battle of Worringen and the Limburg-Brabant dynastic union, see Ulrich Lehnart, *Die Schlacht von Worringen 1288. Kriegsführung im Mittelalter: Der Limburger Erbfolgekrieg unter besonderer Berücksichtigung der Schlacht von Worringen, 5.6.1288* (Frankfurt am Main, 1994).
2. Élodie Lecuppre-Desjardin, "Parcours festifs et enjeux de pouvoirs dans les villes des anciens Pays-Bas bourguignons au xve siècle," *Histoire Urbaine* 9, no. 1 (2004): 29–30.
3. Stéphane Demeter and Cécilia Paredes, "Quand la marche raconte la ville: quelques itinéraires de la cour à Bruxelles (xvie–xviie siècles)," *CLARA Architecture/Recherche* 1 (2013): 81–101.
4. Helen Watanabe-O'Kelly, "The Early Modern Festival Book: Function and Form," in *Europa Triumphans: Court and Civic Festivals in Early Modern Europe*, ed. J. R. Mulryne, Helen Watanabe-O'Kelly, and Margaret Shewring, 2 vols. (Aldershot, 2004), vol. 1: 3–17.
5. Edmond Poullet, *Les constitutions nationales belges de l'ancien régime à l'époque de l'invasion française de 1794* (Brussels, 1875).
6. For an exhaustive list of works devoted to the Burgundian inaugurations, see Élodie Lecuppre-Desjardin, *La ville des cérémonies: essai sur la communication politique dans les anciens Pays-Bas bourguignons* (Turnhout, 2004). For an inventory of the works on the Duchy of Brabant, see Erik Aerts, "Het historisch onderzoek naar de instellingen van het hertogdom Brabant tijdens het Ancien Régime: een stand van zaken," in *Het gebruik van Brabantse archieven voor de instellingengeschiedenis: Symposium georganiseerd te Brussel*

op 21 april 2000, ed. Raymond Van Uytven, Claude Bruneel, Herman Coppens, and Beatrijs Augustyn (Brussels, 2001), 13–59; Aerts, "L'histoire institutionnelle du duché de Brabant pendant l'Ancien Régime: état de la recherche," *Revue Belge de Philologie et d'histoire/Belgisch Tijdschrift voor Filologie en Geschiedenis* 80, no. 2 (2002): 457–90.
7. Micheline Soenen, "Fêtes et cérémonies publiques à Bruxelles aux Temps Modernes," *Bijdragen tot de Geschiedenis* 68 (1985): 47–101.
8. Lecuppre-Desjardin, *La ville des cérémonies*; Lecuppre-Desjardin, "Parcours festifs."
9. Lecuppre-Desjardin, "Parcours festifs," 30. See also Barbara Stollberg-Rilinger, "Verfassung und Fest: Überlegungen zur festlichen Inszenierung vormoderner und moderner Verfassungen," in *Interdependenzen zwischen Verfassung und Kultur*, ed. Hans-Jürgen Becker (Berlin, 2003), 7–37; Stollberg-Rilinger, "La communication symbolique à l'époque prémoderne: Concepts, thèses, perspectives de recherche," *Trivium: Revue franco-allemande de sciences humaines et sociales/Deutsch-französische Zeitschrift für Geistes-und Sozialwissenschaften* 2 (2008). http://trivium.revues.org/1152.
10. Luc Duerloo, "Discourse of Conquest, Discourse of Contract: Competing Visions on the Nature of the Habsburg Rule in the Netherlands," in *Bündnispartner und Konkurrenten der Landesfürsten? Die Stände in der Habsburgermonarchie*, ed. Gerhard Ammerer, William D. Godsey Jr., Martin Scheutz, Peter Urbanitsch, and Alfred Stefan Weiß (Vienna, 2007), 463–78 Klaas Van Gelder, "The Investiture of Emperor Charles VI in Brabant and Flanders: A Test Case for the Authority of the New Austrian Government," *European Review of History/Revue européenne d'histoire* 18, no. 4 (2011): 443–63; Klaas Van Gelder and Bert Van Cauter, "Een publieke ceremonie in een turbulent tijdvak: De inauguratie van Maria Theresia als gravin van Vlaanderen (1744)," *Handelingen der Maatschappij voor Geschiedenis & Oudheidkunde te Gent* 67 (2013): 101–30.
11. Stollberg-Rilinger, "Verfassung und Fest"; Stollberg-Rilinger, "The Impact of Communication Theory on the Analysis of the Early Modern Statebuilding Processes," in *Empowering Interactions: Political Cultures and the Emergence of the State in Europe 1300–1900*, ed. Wim Blockmans, André Holenstein, and Jon Mathieu (Farnham, 2009), 313–18; Stollberg-Rilinger, "Le rituel de l'investiture dans le Saint-Empire de l'époque moderne: histoire institutionnelle et pratiques symboliques," *Revue d'Histoire Moderne et Contemporaine* 56, no. 2 (2009): 7–29; Stollberg-Rilinger, "La communication symbolique"; Stollberg-Rilinger, "State and Political History in a Culturalist Perspective," in *Structures on the Move: Technologies of Governance in Transcultural Encounter*, ed. Antje Flüchter and Susan Richter (Berlin, 2012), 43–58; Stollberg-Rilinger, *The Emperor's Old Clothes: Constitutional History and the Symbolic Language of the Holy Roman Empire* (New York, 2015); Joachim Stieber, "Ritual and Ceremonial in Early Modern European Politics as a Dimension of a Cultural History of Representative Institutions and Constitutional Government: An Introduction to the Scholarship of Barbara Stollberg-Rilinger on Representative Institutions in Early Modern Germany with its Inclusion of Symbolic-Expressive Communication through Ritual and Ceremonial in a Cultural History of Politics," *Parliaments, Estates and Representation* 32, no. 2 (2012): 171–87.
12. Michel Hébert, "Consensus et représentation en Europe occidentale, XIIIe–XVIIe siècle: Une introduction," in *Consensus et représentation: Actes du colloque organisé en 2013 à Dijon par SAS; avec la collaboration du centre Georges-Chevrier de l'Université de Dijon*, ed. Jean-Philippe Genêt, Dominique Le Page, and Olivier Mattéoni (Paris, 2017), 18.
13. Raymond Van Uytven, "La prééminence du duché de Brabant et de la ville de Bruxelles dans les Pays-Bas espagnols et autrichiens," in *Gouvernance et administration dans les Prov-*

inces belgiques (XVIe–XVIIIe siècles): Ouvrage publié en hommage au professeur Claude Bruneel, ed. Claude de Moreau de Gerbehaye, Sébastien Dubois, and Jean-Marie Yante, 2 vols. (Brussels, 2013), vol. 1: 203–25.

14. For a brief overview on the Estates of Brabant and their links to the prince, see Beatrijs Augustyn, "Staten van Brabant (14de eeuw–1795)," in *De gewestelijke en lokale overheidsinstellingen in Brabant en Mechelen tot 1795*, ed. Raymond Van Uytven, Claude Bruneel, Herman Coppens, and Beatrijs Augustyn, 2 vols. (Brussels, 2000), vol. 1: 97–132; Erik Aerts et al., eds., *De hertog en de staten, de kanselier en de Raad, de Rekenkamer, het leenhof, de Algemene ontvangerij, de drossaard en de woudmeester, het notariaat en het landgraafschap Brabant* (Brussels, 2011).

15. Michèle Galand, *Charles de Lorraine, gouverneur général des Pays-Bas autrichiens (1744–1780)* (Brussels, 1993); Galand, "Les gouverneurs généraux, souverains des Pays-Bas?," in *Gouvernance et Administration dans les Provinces belgiques (XVIe–XVIIIe siècles): Ouvrage publié en hommage au Professeur Claude Bruneel*, ed. Claude de Moreau de Gerbehaye, Sébastien Dubois, and Jean-Marie Yante, 2 vols. (Brussels, 2013), vol. 1: 109–29; René Vermeir, "Les gouverneurs-généraux aux Pays-Bas habsbourgeois," in *À la place du roi: Vice-rois, gouverneurs et ambassadeurs dans les monarchies françaises et espagnoles (XVIe–XVIIIe siècles)*, ed. Daniel Aznar, Guillaume Hanotin, and Niels F. May (Madrid, 2014), 17–33; Sandra Hertel, *Maria Elisabeth: Österreichische Erzherzogin und Statthalterin in Brüssel (1725–1741)* (Vienna, 2014).

16. François Zanatta, "Pour une relecture du serment public entre le prince et les communautés d'habitants: l'exemple des joyeuses entrées des Archiducs," *Revue du Nord* 377 (2008): 729; Guido Van Dievoet, "De Blijde Inkomst: De geschreven grondwet van Brabant (1356–1794)," in *De gewestelijke en lokale overheidsinstellingen in Brabant en Mechelen tot 1795*, ed. Raymond Van Uytven, Claude Bruneel, Herman Coppens, and Beatrijs Augustyn, 2 vols. (Brussels, 2000), vol. 1: 19–31.

17. For a general overview of the history of the Austrian Netherlands, see Hervé Hasquin, ed., *La Belgique autrichienne, 1713–1794: Les Pays-Bas méridionaux sous les Habsbourg d'Autriche* (Brussels, 1987). On the War of the Spanish Succession and the beginnings of the Austrian regime in the Netherlands, see Klaas Van Gelder, *Regime Change at a Distance: Austria and the Southern Netherlands following the War of the Spanish Succession, 1716–1725* (Leuven, 2016).

18. Victor-Lucien Tapié, *L'Europe de Marie-Thérèse du Baroque aux Lumières* (Paris, 1998), 1.

19. Jean Bérenger, *Les Habsbourg et l'argent: De la Renaissance aux Lumières* (Paris, 2014), 14–15; Élisabeth Badinter, *Le pouvoir au féminin: Marie-Thérèse d'Autriche, 1717–1780: l'impératrice reine* (Paris, 2016), 96–97.

20. Wilhelm Brauneder, "Die Pragmatische Sanktion—das Grundgesetz der Monarchia Austriaca," in *Prinz Eugen und das Barocke Österreich*, ed. Karl Gutkas (Salzburg, 1985), 141–50; Charles Ingrao, "Pragmatic Sanction and the Theresian Succession: A Reevaluation," *Études danubiennes* 9, no. 1 (1993): 71–87.

21. Michael Hochedlinger, *Austria's Wars of Emergence: War, State and Society in the Habsburg Monarchy 1683–1797* (London, 2003), 208–18; Franz A. Szabo, *Kaunitz and Enlightened Absolutism, 1753–1780* (Cambridge, UK, 1994), 2–3.

22. Tapié, *L'Europe de Marie-Thérèse*, 47–49; Hochedlinger, *Austria's Wars of Emergence*, 247.

23. Ghislaine De Boom, "L'archiduchesse Marie-Elisabeth et les Grands Maîtres de la Cour," *Revue Belge de Philologie et d'Histoire/Belgisch Tijdschrift voor Filologie en Geschiedenis* 5, no. 2 (1926): 493–506; Hertel, *Maria Elisabeth*.

24. De Boom, "L'archiduchesse Marie-Elisabeth"; Galand, *Charles de Lorraine*, 47.
25. AR-AGR, DN/DPB, 362: report by Maria Elisabeth to Maria Theresa, 3 November 1740.
26. Galand, *Charles de Lorraine*, 47.
27. AR-AGR, DN/DPB, 362: report by Maria Elisabeth to Maria Theresa, 3 November 1740.
28. Galand, *Charles de Lorraine*, 45–56.
29. De Boom, "L'archiduchesse Marie-Elisabeth," 499–501; Piet Lenders, "Les conceptions politiques et la personnalité du Grand Maître de la cour Frédéric de Harrach (1733–1743): Leur reflet dans la correspondance des premières années de l'exercice de ses fonctions à Bruxelles," *Bulletin de la Commission royale d'histoire* 160, no. 1 (1994): 87–141.
30. AR-AGR, DN/DPB, 113: Leopold Philip of Arenberg to Count Savalla (Viscount Roccaberti), fol. 206–315; De Boom, "L'archiduchesse Marie-Elisabeth," 504–5.
31. Galand, *Charles de Lorraine*, 47–48.
32. Bérenger, *Les Habsbourg et l'argent*, 383.
33. Hervé Hasquin, "Les difficultés financières du gouvernement des Pays-Bas autrichiens au début du XVIIIe siècle (1717–1740)," *Revue Internationale d'Histoire de la Banque* 6 (1976): 99–133.
34. See note 30 for the correspondence between the Duke of Arenberg and Count Savalla (Viscount Roccaberti).
35. AR–AGR, DN/DPB, 113 fol. 231r–234r: Leopold Philip of Arenberg to Count Savalla (Viscount Roccaberti), 16 February 1740.
36. Enghien/Edingen, ACA, Corr. L-P., 40–18, 6: Maria Theresa to Leopold Philip, 22 October 1740.
37. ACA, Corr. L-P., 40–18, 6 Maria Theresa to Leopold Philip, 7 September 1741.
38. ACA, Corr. L-P., 40–18, 6 Maria Theresa to Leopold Philip, 11 January 1742.
39. AR–AGR, DN/DPB, 560: minutes of the ministerial conference, 20 October 1740.
40. AR–AGR, DN/DPB, 362: counsel by the High Council to Maria Theresa, 23 November 1740.
41. Charles W. Ingrao, *The Habsburg Monarchy, 1618–1815* (Cambridge, UK, 1994), 152–53; Hochedlinger, *Austria's Wars of Emergence*, 248–49.
42. ÖStA, AVA, Familienarchiv Harrach, 76: Friedrich August to Aloys Thomas Raymund, 13 January 1741.
43. Herman Coppens, *Basisstatistieken voor de reconstructie van de centrale staatsrekening der Spaanse en Oostenrijkse Nederlanden ca. 1680–1788* (Brussels, 1993), 138.
44. The Council of State, Privy Council, and Council of Finance were the three so-called "Collateral Councils" that advised the prince with respect to governing the Habsburg Netherlands since the early sixteenth century: Erik Aerts et al., eds., *Les institutions du gouvernement central des Pays-Bas habsbourgeois (1482–1795)* (Brussels, 1995), 2 vols.
45. Laetitia Cnockaert, "Le grand incendie de 1731," in *Le palais du Coudenberg à Bruxelles: Du château médiéval au site archéologique*, ed. Vincent Heymans (Brussels, 2014), 124–25.
46. AR–AGR, GR/CP, 6: folder A, fol. 34r: decree by Maria Elisabeth, 19 November 1740.
47. AR–AGR, GR/CP, 6: folder A, fol. 34r; Chief President Neny to Harrach, November 1740: AR–AGR, GR/CP, 6: folder A, fol. 35r and fol. 36r.
48. AR–AGR, GR/CP, 6, fol. 36r: decree by Charles of Lorraine, 23 November 1740. This seems to suggest that Charles of Lorraine was already dealing with Netherlands affairs before 1741.

49. AR–AGR, GR/CP, 6, fol. 39: decree by Charles of Lorraine to the Jointe pour les recherches pour l'inauguration, 28 November 1740.
50. Van Gelder and Van Cauter, "Een publieke ceremonie," 112.
51. Van Gelder and Van Cauter, "Een publieke ceremonie," 112; AR–AGR, DN/DPB, 560: opinion of the Duke of Arenberg concerning the inauguration as communicated to Maria Elisabeth, 9 December 1740, discussed in Vienna and presented as written advice to Maria Theresa on 17 January 1741.
52. AR–AGR, GR/CP, 6: collection of acts concerning the inauguration of Her Majesty in the provinces of the Netherlands, 1740.
53. AR–AGR, DN/DPB, 560: report by the ministerial conference, 22 January 1741.
54. AR–AGR, DN/DPB, 560: counsel by the Privy Council, 3 January 1741, attached to the report by Maria Elisabeth to Maria Theresa, 13 January 1741.
55. AR–AGR, DN/DPB, 560: report by Maria Elisabeth to Maria Theresa, 13 December 1740.
56. AR–AGR, DN/DPB, 560: report by Maria Elisabeth to Maria Theresa, 16 December 1740.
57. AR–AGR, DN/DPB, 560: memorandum by Count Königsegg-Erps on the report by Maria Elisabeth of 16 December 1740, presumably January 1741.
58. AR–AGR, DN/DPB, 560: reflections by councilor-regent Viscount Patin on the inauguration of Maria Theresa and the admission of the coregency, attached to the counsel by the High Council of 17 January 1741.
59. AR–AGR, DN/DPB, 560: counsel by the Jointe pour les recherches pour l'inauguration, 3 December 1740 (with two projects of full powers), received with the report of 16 December 1740. Counsel was given to Maria Theresa, probably by the High Council, on the basis of these documents on 17 January 1741. The ministerial conference discussed the matter on January 22.
60. AR–AGR, DN/DPB, 560: report by the ministerial conference, 26 January 1741.
61. AR–AGR, DN/DPB, 560: report by the ministerial conference, 26 January 1741.
62. AR–AGR, DN/DPB, 560: resolution by the Jointe de Cabinet on 27 February 1741, attached to Maria Elisabeth's report to Maria Theresa on 7 March 1741.
63. AR–AGR, DN/DPB, 363: counsel by the High Council to Maria Theresa, 20 March 1741.
64. AR–AGR, DN/DPB, 363: Maria Elisabeth to Maria Theresa, 28 April 1741.
65. AR–AGR, DN/DPB, 363: Maria Elisabeth to Maria Theresa, 12 May 1741.
66. Galand, *Charles de Lorraine*, 48–49.
67. Van Gelder and Van Cauter, "Een publieke ceremonie," 115.
68. AR–AGR, DN/DPB, 363: Harrach to Maria Theresa, 21 October 1741.
69. AR–AGR, DN/DPB, 363: Harrach to Maria Theresa, 21 October 1741.
70. The audiencier, who played a major role in the sealing ceremony within the princely chancellery, was the first secretary of the Netherlands. See Catherine Henin, *La charge d'audiencier dans les anciens Pays-Bas (1413–1744)* (Brussels, 2001).
71. Henin, *La charge d'audiencier*, 184.
72. Henin, *La charge d'audiencier*, 171.
73. AR–AGR, DN/DPB, 363: counsel by the High Council to Maria Theresa, 9 November 1741.
74. Galand, *Charles de Lorraine*, 49.

75. Galand, *Charles de Lorraine*, 49.
76. Ghislaine De Boom, *Les ministres plénipotentiaires dans les Pays-Bas autrichiens, principalement Cobenzl* (Brussels, 1932), 37.
77. Van Gelder and Van Cauter, "Een publieke ceremonie," 115.
78. Galand, *Charles de Lorraine*, 49.
79. AR–AGR, GR/CP, 6, fol. 155–161: resolution by the Jointe de Cabinet, 11 June 1743.
80. AR–AGR, GR/CP, 6, fol. 154r/v: decree by Königsegg-Erps to the Jointe for the inauguration, 13 June 1743.
81. AR–AGR, DN/DPB, 561 Maria Theresa to Königsegg-Erps, 11 August 1743.
82. AR–AGR, GR/CP, 6, fol. 188r: Königsegg-Erps to the Jointe for the inauguration, 25 August 1743.
83. AR–AGR, DN/DPB, 373: report by Königsegg-Erps to Maria Theresa, 9 October 1743.
84. On 31 March 1744, Charles of Lorraine finally fixed the date of the inauguration in Brabant for 20 April 1744; AR–AGR, GR/CP, 6, fol. 213r/v, fol. 216r: decree by Charles of Lorraine, 31 March 1744. The protests by the city of Leuven were not new: in 1717, the city had disputed Brussels's privilege of hosting the inauguration for the Duchy of Brabant. Indeed, Leuven had been the capital of the duchy until 1599, after which the inauguration became a Brussels affair. See Van Gelder, "The Investiture," 449.
85. Van Gelder and Van Cauter, "Een publieke ceremonie," 120.
86. AR–AGR, GR/CP, 7A, fol. 209r: *Suplement a la Gazette de Bruxelles. No XXXIII. Du vendredi 24 avril 1744*.
87. Klaas Van Gelder recently demonstrated that Flanders had envisaged drafting a "Joyous Entry" along the same lines as the Brabantine charter in the late eighteenth century. See Klaas Van Gelder, "The Convention of The Hague and the Constitutional Debates in the Estates of Flanders and Brabant, 1790–1794," *Early Modern Low Countries* 1, no. 1 (2017): 156–76 https://www.emlc-journal.org/articles/10.18352/emlc.6/.
88. We can likewise apply these words to the other provinces without a constitutional charter. On the charging meanings of the concept of "constitution," see Wolfgang Schmale, "Constitution, Constitutionnel," in *Handbuch politisch-sozialer Grundbegriffe in Frankreich, 1680–1820*, ed. Rolf Reichardt and Hans-Jürgen Lüsebrink (Munich, 1992), 31–63; Gerald Stourzh, "Constitution: Changing Meanings of the Term from the Early Seventeenth to the Late Eighteenth Century," in *Conceptual Change and the Constitution*, ed. Terence Ball and John G. A. Pocock (Lawrence, 1988), 35–54; Wyger R. E. Velema, "Revolutie, Republiek en Constitutie: De ideologische context van de eerste Nederlandse Grondwet," in *De eeuw van de grondwet: Grondwet en politiek in Nederland, 1798–1917*, ed. Niek C. F. van Sas and Henk te Velde (Deventer, 1998), 20–44; Jean-Philippe Genêt, "Les Constitutions avant le Constitutionnalisme," and Diego Quaglioni, "Constitution et Constitutionnalisme (XVIe–XVIIe Siècle)," in *Des Chartes aux Constitutions: Autour de l'idée constitutionnelle en Europe (XIIe–XVIIe Siècle)*, ed. François Foronda and Jean-Philippe Genêt (Paris, 2019), 11–30 and 441–50.
89. Wim Blockmans, "Du contrat féodal à la souveraineté du peuple: Les précédents de la déchéance de Philippe II dans les Pays-Bas (1581)," in *Assemblee di stati e istituzioni rappresentative nella storia del pensiero politico moderno (secoli XV–XX): Atti del convegno internazionale tenuto a Perugia dal 16 al 18 settembre 1982* (Rimini, 1983), 135–50. See also Jonas Braekevelt, "Constitutions, State and Estates: Interactions between Princely Restrictions and Reforms, Privileges of the Governed and the Control of Absolute Power

in the Burgundian Low Countries," in *Des chartes aux Constitutions: Autour de l'idée constitutionnelle en Europe (XIIe–XVIIe Siècle)*, ed. François Foronda and Jean-Philippe Genêt (Paris, 2019), 233–51.
90. Michel Hébert, "Consensus et représentation," 19.
91. Jean-Philippe Genêt, "Pouvoir symbolique, légitimation et genèse de l'État moderne," in *La légitimité implicite: Actes des conférences organisées à Rome en 2010 et en 2011 par SAS en collaboration avec l'École française de Rome*, ed. Jean-Philippe Genêt (Paris, 2015), vol.1: 9.
92. Genêt, "Pouvoir symbolique," 1: 9. Concerning the question of the "political contract," see François Foronda, "Du contrat ou de la structure proprement politique des sociétés politiques," in *Avant le contrat social: Le contrat politique dans l'Occident médiéval XIIIe–XVe Siècle*, ed. François Foronda (Paris, 2011), 5–13. We can also speak of respect for "ritual-symbolic actions," as Barbara Stollberg Rillinger describes it. See Stollberg-Rilinger, *The Emperor's Old Clothes*.
93. Zanatta, "Pour une relecture," 732.
94. Foronda, "Du contrat," 12–13.

Bibliography

Aerts, Erik. "Het historisch onderzoek naar de instellingen van het hertogdom Brabant tijdens het Ancien Régime: een stand van zaken." In *Het gebruik van brabantse archieven voor de instellingengeschiedenis: Symposium georganiseerd te Brussel op 21 april 2000*, edited by Raymond Van Uytven, Claude Bruneel, Herman Coppens, and Beatrijs Augustyn, 13–59. Brussels: Algemeen Rijksarchief, 2001.

———. "L'histoire institutionnelle du duché de Brabant pendant l'Ancien Régime: état de la recherche." *Revue Belge de Philologie et d'Histoire/Belgisch Tijdschrift voor Filologie en Geschiedenis* 80, no. 2 (2002): 457–90.

Aerts, Erik, Michel Baelde, Herman Coppens, Hugo de Schepper, Hugo Soly, Alfons K. L. Thijs, and Karin Van Honacker, eds. *Les institutions du gouvernement central des Pays-Bas habsbourgeois (1482–1795)*. 2 vols. Brussels: Archives générales du Royaume, 1995.

Aerts, Erik, Paul De Win, Jaak Ockeley, Eddy Put, Fernand Vanhemelryck, Raymond Van Uytven, and Frans Van Droogenbroeck, eds. *De hertog en de staten, de kanselier en de Raad, de Rekenkamer, het leenhof, de Algemene ontvangerij, de drossaard en de woudmeester, het notariaat en het landgraafschap Brabant*. Brussels: Algemeen Rijksarchief, 2011.

Augustyn, Beatrijs. "Staten van Brabant (14de eeuw–1795)." In *De gewestelijke en lokale overheidsinstellingen in Brabant en Mechelen tot 1795*. Vol. 1, edited by Raymond Van Uytven, Claude Bruneel, Herman Coppens, and Beatrijs Augustyn, 97–132. Brussels: Algemeen Rijksarchief, 2000.

Badinter, Élisabeth. *Le pouvoir au feminine: Marie-Thérèse d'Autriche, 1717–1780: l'impératrice reine*. Paris: Flammarion, 2016.

Bérenger, Jean. *Les Habsbourg et l'argent: De la Renaissance aux Lumières*. Collection du Centre Roland Mousnier. Paris: Presses de l'Université Paris-Sorbonne, 2014.

Blockmans, Wim. "Du contrat féodal à la souveraineté du peuple: Les précédents de la déchéance de Philippe II dans les Pays-Bas (1581)." In *Assemblee di stati e istituzioni rappresentative nella storia del pensiero politico moderno (secoli XV–XX): Atti del convegno inter-*

nazionale tenuto a Perugia dal 16 al 18 settembre 1982, 135–50. Rimini: Maggioli Editore, 1983.

Braekevelt, Jonas. "Constitutions, State and Estates: Interactions between Princely Restrictions and Reforms, Privileges of the Governed and the Control of Absolute Power in the Burgundian Low Countries." In *Des Chartes aux Constitutions: Autour de l'idée constitutionnelle en Europe (XIIe–XVIIe Siècle)*, edited by François Foronda and Jean-Philippe Genêt, 233–51. Paris: Éditions de la Sorbonne, 2019.

Brauneder, Wilhelm. "Die Pragmatische Sanktion—das Grundgesetz der Monarchia Austriaca." In *Prinz Eugen und das Barocke Österreich*, edited by Karl Gutkas, 141–50. Salzburg: Residenz Verlag, 1985.

Cnockaert, Laetitia "Le grand incendie de 1731." In *Le palais du Coudenberg à Bruxelles: Du château médiéval au site archéologique*, edited by Vincent Heymans, 124–25. Brussels: Mardaga, 2014.

Coppens, Herman. *Basisstatistieken voor de reconstructie van de centrale staatsrekening der Spaanse en Oostenrijkse Nederlanden ca. 1680–1788*. Brussels: Algemeen Rijksarchief, 1993.

De Boom, Ghislaine. "L'archiduchesse Marie-Elisabeth et les grands maîtres de la Cour." *Revue Belge de Philologie et d'Histoire/Belgisch Tijdschrift voor Filologie en Geschiedenis* 5, no. 2 (1926): 493–506.

———. *Les ministres plénipotentiaires dans les Pays-Bas autrichiens, principalement Cobenzl*. Brussels: Lamertin, 1932.

Demeter, Stéphane, and Cécilia Paredes. "Quand la marche raconte la ville: quelques itinéraires de la cour à Bruxelles (XVIe–XVIIe siècles)." *CLARA Architecture/Recherche* 1 (2013): 81–101.

Duerloo, Luc. "Discourse of Conquest, Discourse of Contract: Competing Visions on the Nature of the Habsburg Rule in the Netherlands." In *Bündnispartner und Konkurrenten der Landesfürsten? Die Stände in der Habsburgermonarchie*, edited by Gerhard Ammerer, William D. Godsey Jr., Martin Scheutz, Peter Urbanitsch, and Alfred Stefan Weiß, 463–78. Vienna: R. Oldenbourg Verlag, 2007.

Foronda, François. 'Du contrat ou de la structure proprement politique des sociétés politiques." In *Avant le contrat social: Le contrat politique dans l'Occident médiéval XIIIe–XVe Siècle*, edited by François Foronda, 5–13. Paris: Publications de la Sorbonne, 2011.

Galand, Michèle. *Charles de Lorraine, gouverneur général des Pays-Bas autrichiens (1744–1780)*. Brussels: Éditions de l'Université de Bruxelles, 1993.

———. "Les gouverneurs généraux, souverains des Pays-Bas?" In *Gouvernance et Administration dans les Provinces belgiques (XVIe–XVIIIe siècles): Ouvrage publié en hommage au Professeur Claude Bruneel*. Vol. 1, edited by Claude de Moreau de Gerbehaye, Sébastien Dubois, and Jean-Marie Yante, 109–29. Brussels: Archives et bibliothèques de Belgique, 2013 [Special Issue *Archives et bibliothèques de Belgique* 99 (2013)].

Genêt, Jean-Philippe "Les Constitutions avant le Constitutionnalisme." In *Des Chartes aux Constitutions: Autour de l'idée constitutionnelle en Europe (XIIe–XVIIe Siècle)*, edited by François Foronda and Jean-Philippe Genêt, 11–30. Paris: Éditions de la Sorbonne, 2019.

———. "Pouvoir symbolique, légitimation et genèse de l'État moderne." In *La légitimité implicite: Actes des conférences organisées à Rome en 2010 et en 2011 par SAS en collaboration avec l'École française de Rome*. Vol. 1, edited by Jean-Philippe Genêt, 9–47. Paris: Publication de la Sorbonne/École française de Rome, 2015.

Hasquin, Hervé, ed. *La Belgique autrichienne, 1713–1794: Les Pays-Bas méridionaux sous les Habsbourg d'Autriche*. Brussels: Crédit communal de Belgique, 1987.

———. "Les difficultés financières du gouvernement des Pays-Bas autrichiens au début du xviiie siècle (1717–1740)." *Revue Internationale d'Histoire de la Banque* 6 (1976): 99–133.

Hébert, Michel. "Consensus et représentation en Europe occidentale, XIIIe–XVIIe siècle: Une introduction." In *Consensus et représentation: Actes du colloque organisé en 2013 à Dijon par SAS; avec la collaboration du centre Georges-Chevrier de l'Université de Dijon*, edited by Jean-Philippe Genêt, Dominique Le Page, and Olivier Mattéoni, 11–40. Paris: Publication de la Sorbonne/École française de Rome, 2017.

Henin, Catherine. *La charge d'audiencier dans les anciens Pays-Bas (1413–1744)*. Brussels: Éditions de l'Université de Bruxelles, 2001.

Hertel, Sandra. *Maria Elisabeth: Österreichische Erzherzogin und Statthalterin in Brüssel (1725–1741)*. Vienna: Böhlau, 2014.

Hochedlinger, Michael. *Austria's Wars of Emergence: War, State and Society in the Habsburg Monarchy 1683–1797*. London: Longman, 2003.

Ingrao, Charles. *The Habsburg Monarchy, 1618–1815*. Cambridge, UK: Cambridge University Press, 1994.

———. "Pragmatic Sanction and the Theresian Succession: A Reevaluation." *Études danubiennes* 9, no. 1 (1999): 71–87.

Lecuppre-Desjardin, Élodie. *La ville des cérémonies: essai sur la communication politique dans les anciens Pays-Bas bourguignons*. Turnhout: Brepols, 2004.

———. "Parcours festifs et enjeux de pouvoirs dans les villes des anciens Pays-Bas bourguignons au xve siècle." *Histoire urbaine* 9, no. 1 (2004): 29–45.

Lehnart, Ulrich. *Die Schlacht von Worringen 1288. Kriegsführung im Mittelalter: Der Limburger Erbfolgekrieg unter besonderer Berücksichtigung der Schlacht von Worringen, 5.6.1288*. Frankfurt am Main: AFRA-Verlag, 1994.

Lenders, Piet. "Les conceptions politiques et la personnalité du Grand Maître de la cour Frédéric de Harrach (1733–1743): Leur reflet dans la correspondance des premières années de l'exercice de ses fonctions à Bruxelles." *Bulletin de la Commission royale d'histoire* 160, no. 1 (1994): 87–141.

Poullet, Edmond. *Les constitutions nationales belges de l'ancien régime à l'époque de l'invasion française de 1794*. Brussels: F. Hayez, 1875.

Quaglioni, Diego. "Constitution et Constitutionnalisme (XVIe–XVIIe Siècle)." In *Des Chartes aux Constitutions: Autour de l'idée constitutionnelle en Europe (XIIe–XVIIe Siècle)*, edited by François Foronda and Jean-Philippe Genêt, 441–50. Paris: Éditions de la Sorbonne, 2019.

Relation de l'inauguration solennelle de Sa Majesté Marie Thérèse, Reine de Hongrie et de Bohème, en qualité de Duchesse de Lothier, de Brabant, de Limbourg et de Marquise du St. Empire Romain, celebrée en la ville de Brusselles, le 20. Avril 1744. Brussels: François Claudinot, n.d.

Schmale, Wolfgang. "Constitution, Constitutionnel." In *Handbuch politisch-sozialer Grundbegriffe in Frankreich, 1680–1820*, edited by Rolf Reichardt and Hans-Jürgen Lüsebrink, 31–63. Munich: De Gruyter Oldenburg, 1992.

Soenen, Micheline. "Fêtes et cérémonies publiques à Bruxelles aux Temps Modernes." *Bijdragen tot de Geschiedenis* 68 (1985): 47–101.

Stieber, Joachim. "Ritual and Ceremonial in Early Modern European Politics as a Dimension of a Cultural History of Representative Institutions and Constitutional Government: An Introduction to the Scholarship of Barbara Stollberg-Rilinger on Representative Institutions in Early Modern Germany with its Inclusion of Symbolic-Expressive Communication through Ritual and Ceremonial in a Cultural History of Politics." *Parliaments, Estates and Representation* 32, no. 2 (2012): 171–87.

Stollberg-Rilinger, Barbara. *The Emperor's Old Cloths: Constitutional History and the Symbolic Language of the Holy Roman Empire.* New York: Berghahn Books, 2015.

———. "The Impact of Communication Theory on the Analysis of the Early Modern Statebuilding Processes." In *Empowering Interactions: Political Cultures and the Emergence of the State in Europe 1300–1900,* edited by Wim Blockmans, André Holenstein, and Jon Mathieu, 313–18. Farnham: Ashgate, 2009.

———. "La communication symbolique à l'époque pré-moderne: Concepts, thèses, perspectives de recherche." *Trivium: Revue franco-allemande de sciences humaines et sociales/Deutsch-französische Zeitschrift für Geistes-und Sozialwissenschaften* 2 (2008). https://journals.opendition.org/trivium/1152. Accessed 17 March 2017.

———. "Le rituel de l'investiture dans le Saint-Empire de l'époque moderne: histoire institutionnelle et pratiques symboliques." *Revue d'Histoire Moderne et Contemporaine* 56, no. 2 (2009): 7–29.

———. "State and Political History in a Culturalist Perspective." In *Structures on the Move: Technologies of Governance in Transcultural Encounter,* edited by Antje Flüchter and Susan Richter, 43–58. Berlin: Springer, 2012.

———. "Verfassung und Fest: Überlegungen zur festlichen Inszenierung vormoderner und moderner Verfassungen." In *Interdependenzen zwischen Verfassung und Kultur,* edited by Hans-Jürgen Becker, 7–37. Berlin: Duncker & Humblot, 2003.

Stourzh, Gerald. "Constitution: Changing Meanings of the Term from the Early Seventeenth to the Late Eighteenth Century." In *Conceptual Change and the Constitution,* edited by Terence Ball and John G. A. Pocock, 35–54. Lawrence: University Press of Kansas, 1988.

Szabo, Franz A. J. *Kaunitz and Enlightened Absolutism, 1753–1780.* Cambridge, UK: Cambridge University Press, 1994.

Tapié, Victor-Lucien. *L'Europe de Marie-Thérèse du Baroque aux Lumières.* Paris: Fayard, 1998.

van Dievoet, Guido [Guy]. "De Blijde Inkomst: De geschreven grondwet van Brabant (1356–1794)." In *De gewestelijke en lokale overheidsinstellingen in Brabant en Mechelen tot 1795.* Vol. 1, edited by Raymond Van Uytven, Claude Bruneel, Herman Coppens, and Beatrijs Augustyn, 19–31. Brussels: Algemeen Rijksarchief, 2000.

Van Gelder, Klaas. "The Convention of The Hague and the Constitutional Debates in the Estates of Flanders and Brabant, 1790–1794." *Early Modern Low Countries* 1, no. 1 (2017): 156–76. https://www.emlc-journal.org/articles/10.18352/emlc.6/. Accessed 23 August 2018.

———. "The Investiture of Emperor Charles VI in Brabant and Flanders: A Test Case for Authority of the New Austrian Government." *European Review of History/Revue européenne d'histoire* 18, no. 4 (2011): 443–63.

———. *Regime Change at a Distance: Austria and the Southern Netherlands following the War of the Spanish Succession, 1716–1725.* Leuven: Peeters Publishers/KVAB Press, 2016.

Van Gelder, Klaas, and Bert Van Cauter. "Een publieke ceremonie in een turbulent tijdvak: De inauguratie van Maria Theresia als gravin van Vlaanderen (1744)." *Handelingen der Maatschappij voor Geschiedenis en Oudheidkunde te Gent* 67 (2013): 101–30.

Van Uytven, Raymond. "La prééminence du duché de Brabant et de la ville de Bruxelles dans les Pays-Bas espagnols et autrichiens." In *Gouvernance et Administration dans les Provinces belgiques (XVIe–XVIIIe siècles): Ouvrage publié en hommage au Professeur Claude Bruneel.* Vol. 1, edited by Claude de Moreau de Gerbehaye, Sébastien Dubois, and Jean-Marie Yante, 203–25. Brussels: Archives et bibliothèques de Belgique, 2013. [Special issue *Archives et bibliothèques de Belgique* 99 (2013)].

Velema, Wyger R. E. "Revolutie, Republiek en Constitutie: De ideologische context van de eerste Nederlandse Grondwet." In *De eeuw van de grondwet: Grondwet en politiek in Nederland, 1798–1917*, edited by Niek C. F. van Sas and Henk te Velde, 20–44. Deventer: Kluwer, 1998.

Vermeir, René. "Les gouverneurs-généraux aux Pays-Bas habsbourgeois." In *À la place du roi: Vice-rois, gouverneurs et ambassadeurs dans les monarchies françaises et espagnoles (XVIe–XVIIIe siècles)*, edited by Daniel Aznar, Guillaume Hanotin, and Niels F. May, 17–33. Madrid: Casa de Velázquez, 2014.

Watanabe-O'Kelly, Helen. "The Early Modern Festival Book: Function and Form." In *Europa Triumphans: Court and Civic Festivals in Early Modern Europe*. Vol. 1, edited by J. R. Mulryne, Helen Watanabe-O'Kelly, and Margaret Shewring, 3–17. Aldershot: Ashgate, 2004.

Zanatta, François. "Pour une relecture du serment public entre le prince et les communautés d'habitants: l'exemple des joyeuses entrées des Archiducs." *Revue du Nord* 377 (2008): 729–45.

Chapter 8

SHAPING A NEW HABSBURG TERRITORY
The 1773 Lemberg Act of Homage
and the Galician Polish Nobility

Miloš Řezník

When Russia, Prussia, and Austria acquired large swathes of Polish territory through the First Partition of Poland in 1772, they faced the task of securing the loyalty of the population—especially that of the upper echelons of society. This task was particularly challenging for Prussia and the Habsburg Monarchy, since the annexation itself and the administrative and legal reforms in the new territories were to be carried out in consideration of enlightened civilization discourse. This ideology, as formulated on the political, cultural, social, and to a degree on the ecclesiastical level, tended to be highly critical of Poland and its nobility. The new administration ordained the abolishment of the nobility's participation in state affairs and implemented government interference in landlord–peasantry relations that had previously been under the sole sway of the nobility.

In a political, legal, and ethical sense, the subjects' loyalty to their new ruler had to be established, conveyed, and legitimized in a homage-paying ceremony. Through this ceremony, the subjects would be released from their previous allegiance and subordinated to the new one—and the treaty between the Habsburg Monarchy and the Polish-Lithuanian Commonwealth, ratified by the Warsaw diet (*Sejm*) in 1773, provided for the procedure explicitly.

With this in mind, the 1773 Galician act of homage might be regarded as a mere routine ritual; especially since *hereditary* changes of rulers in the Habsburg lands were a common occurrence during the early modern period. But paying homage after a change of sovereignty in a country without regard for its own traditions of homage and without any representation of its Estates was rather more unusual. The act was conditioned by the specific circumstances under which the change of sovereignty in Galicia had taken place, and a great many political and legal issues had to be duly considered and clarified in preparation of the ceremony. Not least of these was the fact that the annexation of Galicia was Austria's first major territorial acquisition in more than fifty years. Apart from the territories of the *Innviertel* (1779) and Bukovina (1775), which was later incorporated into Galicia, it was also the only territorial acquisition during the entire Theresian-Josephine era. In contrast to the territorial gains in southeastern Europe (e.g., the Banat and the new parts of the Military Frontier) at the turn of the seventeenth to the eighteenth century and Bukovina between 1775 and 1784, no military administration was established in Galicia. Instead, provisions were made from the start to set up a civil administration. This naturally had an impact on the way in which the country was incorporated into the monarchy as well.[1]

In general terms, the Austrian government succeeded in establishing an entirely new act of inauguration that deeply contradicted the traditional Polish "republican" understanding of the relationship between the ruler and the "nation" as well as of the acts that had been accompanying the transition to a new ruler since the sixteenth century: there was, of course, no election and consequently no *pacta conventa*, oaths, or any other form of assurance on the part of the Habsburg ruler. Both legally and symbolically, the inauguration functioned as a transition between rulers, states, and political systems—with the latter being of at least equal importance in the case of Galicia. Despite the many contradictions to Polish tradition, the act referred to identical or similar symbolic forms of completing the change of ruler by way of its visualization as a solemn transfer ritual. However, one could also consider the Galician inauguration a test case for new forms of homage in which the obligations of the ruler were treated subordinately or disappeared entirely (see the Introduction to this volume by Klaas Van Gelder). Against this background, the Galician act of 1773 successfully fulfilled a further trial function: it verified the minimal potential of resistance against the regime change among the Polish nobility immediately after the annexation, thereby allowing the government to view its control over the country as relatively stable for the time being. Since a crowning as King/Queen of Galicia never even seems to have been considered in Vienna, the act of homage became the most important among the symbolic rituals linked to the transfer of power, followed almost ten years later by the acts accompanying the introduction of the Galician Estates and diet.

The objective of this chapter is to conduct an analysis of the Galician act of homage, which was specially conceived for the occasion. The text will focus less on the ceremony itself and more on the preparations leading up to it, during which various problems related to organizing the homage had to be tackled. Contemporary debates on difficulties and dilemmas will be discussed in order to determine what purposes and intrinsic meanings were assigned to the act of homage by the late Central European estates-based society. These debates mirror the specific circumstances prevailing in Galicia after the First Partition of Poland, which were shaped by enlightened absolutism and the beginnings of modern state-building processes in the Habsburg Monarchy. As the first Galician act of homage to take place in Lemberg (Polish Lwów, Ukrainian L'viv), the new capital of the hereditary territory, the ceremony on 29 December 1773 laid the foundations for a new tradition that would continue until the early nineteenth century. How this tradition developed and was carried forth represents a field of research that is currently unexplored and worthy of examination. Primarily symbolizing the transfer of power, like in the other Habsburg territories, the act of homage gained additional significance in Galicia due to the lack of corresponding state ceremonies. In particular, a coronation never took place despite the fact that the region had been declared a hereditary kingdom of the Habsburgs in 1772.

The transfer of power and the late estates-based society form the context for the question of the connections existing between the specifics of the act of homage, the concepts of an estates-based constitution, and the Habsburg policies relating to the nobility in Galicia. First and foremost, these policies were conceived at the court in Vienna and by Galicia's first governor, Johann Anton von Pergen. The Galician nobility itself, however, used the period preceding the act of homage to discuss the outlines of its own precepts and demands for the first time, albeit rather incoherently. They will be discussed later in this chapter.

Preconditions

The specific contexts and political options that affected the planning and execution of the Galician investiture and had to be taken into consideration by the contemporary decision-makers included the fact that the Kingdom of Galicia-Lodomeria had been created from the Polish territories annexed by Austria as a new political entity with no direct connection to any previous body politic. Within this new entity, institutions and regulations had to be conceived and imposed on society from scratch. Many basic questions remained open during the first months of Habsburg rule; it was unclear, for example, whether there would be a representative body of the Galician Estates or not.

As the transfer of power over Galicia was not determined by the outcome of a war nor based on a treaty with Poland-Lithuania, according to Vienna, it was not tied to any preconditions or obligations to be assumed by the government. The Austrians therefore regarded Galicia as a clean slate: there was no need for the ruler to take into account any prerogatives, privileges, dignified customs, or freedoms. As a result, the new ruler would be the sole arbiter for the establishment of the country's laws and politics, and any notion that the investiture would have to be combined with a reinstatement of erstwhile privileges was rendered redundant.

This was simultaneously the historical context in which the penchant for reforming policies displayed by the Austrian court—and by Emperor Joseph II in particular—came to the fore. Galicia was considered an experimental ground for the reforms that had already been conceived in the capital. Yet the experiment was not undertaken for its own sake: established structures and laws would need to be taken into account to a much lesser degree than in the other parts of the monarchy—or so the decision makers in Vienna reasoned. They also believed that the conditions in Galicia demanded thorough restructuring in any case. The territory would thus be an ideal test bed for the introduction of reforms that were to be implemented in other parts of the monarchy as well.[2] The Galician constitution based on estates was among the array of issues to be tackled, with the act of homage representing just one aspect of it.

The transfer of rule in Galicia was equivalent to a change of ruler and of political system. The political constitution was replaced at once with the prince, the ruling dynasty, and the state affiliation of territory and population. The "Noble Republic" of Poland-Lithuania had been characterized by the strong influence of clientele-oriented groups headed by the magnates as well as by parochial, highly decentralized politics. By comparison, the Habsburg Monarchy was an absolute monarchy that was governed in an increasingly centralistic fashion. Striving to build a more unified and homogeneous body politic, its enlightened elites relied heavily on measures conceived in and imposed by the central government. They believed that these measures would entail a mental reeducation of the aristocracy, the landed nobility, and the other groups of society in Galicia.

The developments in Galicia were influenced to a high degree by the discourse of the enlightened elites and the imperial court as well as by the despotic style of reform as imposed by the emperor. This discourse was critical of the hierarchical division of society into estates, and it assailed the nobility in particular. But although a critical stance toward elite recruitment according to ancestry and the estates-based system in general was very much in vogue at the time, Maria Theresa and Joseph II established in their new hereditary territory a constitution based on estates and featuring a new *Ständegemeinde* (literally a "community of estates") consisting of a diet, the indigenate (membership in the country Estates), the matricula of the nobility, the Galician *Landtafel* (literally "land table," a register of hereditary noble landholdings) and the *Erzämter* ("arch offices") of the crown land. All of these followed the models established in the other hereditary lands, especially that of Bohemia.[3] The estate-building process entered its critical phase two years after Joseph became sole ruler of the country, when the first Galician diet (*Landtag*) was convened. A new estate system ostensibly conforming to early modern traditions was therefore put in place under Maria Theresa's and Joseph's rule in the 1770s and 1780s. This may appear to be a paradoxical development at first, but it must be viewed in the context of two important aspects. First, the rights and privileges of the Galician Estates did not generally conflict with the absolutistic and centralistic approach to governance taken by the Viennese court. The Estates and their legal and political institutions were in part governmentalized, integrated into the state administration, and designed to support the state authorities. These bodies were thus a hybrid of estate and princely institutions. One of their purposes was to serve "as an ornament, relief and benefit to the government," as State Chancellor Prince Wenzel Anton Kaunitz put it at the beginning of Austrian rule over Galicia.[4] Representation of the Estates was intended to legitimize Habsburg rule as well as the new style of governance. Second, from the very beginning, the government sought to integrate the new hereditary territory into the administrative and political structures of the monarchy as a whole as quickly as possible. In a way, this purpose was ill-aligned with using Galicia as an experimental ground, since the Kingdom of Galicia-Lodomeria was to be considered a land no different from the other kingdoms and principalities of the monarchy.

Considerations and Preparations

The homage and other political events, such as the first Galician diet convened in September 1782, resulted from the changes, policies, and factors outlined above. At the same time, however, the latter were made visible and could be influenced by the former. The act of homage irrevocably established the loyalty of the subjects to their new ruler. It was a procedure without historical precedent and undetermined by any existing routine, and the ceremonial details and timing therefore had to be negotiated and agreed upon first.

In previous years, the Habsburg government had had the opportunity to examine some issues of organization and legislature when it had, under the pretext of a *cordon sanitaire*, occupied and annexed areas in southern Poland along the Hungarian border. This occupation preceded the transfer of territories in the ensuing First Partition of Poland. Following the annexation of Spiš (Zips in German, Szepés in Hungarian, Spisz in Polish), Habsburg troops marched into the *starostwa*[5] of Nowy Targ, Sącz (Sandez in German), and Czorsztyn.[6] As early as January 1772, an act of homage to Maria Theresa as queen of Hungary was staged in the Sącz *starostwo*.[7]

This was the context in which the competent departments of the Austrian court along with Maria Theresa, her son Joseph II, and Governor Pergen pondered—as of September 1772—the possibility of an act of homage for the whole of Galicia. From the outset, the project was fraught with numerous problems of ritual and timing, but the decision to stage an act of homage was nevertheless made early on—and most of the following year was spent planning and preparing the event. In their correspondence, Maria Theresa, Joseph II, State Chancellor Kaunitz, and Pergen discussed whether it should take place immediately or at a later point in time. They soon came to the conclusion that it should be postponed until the organizational preparations for the act were finalized and legal conditions were more conducive to the ceremony. Among these conditions were the conclusion of a defensive treaty with Poland regarding the territorial cessions and the new borders as well as the rescindment of the Galicians' fealty to the king of Poland. In the overall discussion, political and legal arguments were equally important to questions of practicality.[8]

When Pergen was sent to his new position in Lemberg in September 1772, the arrangements for the act of homage were high on his list of priorities. He would soon notice that certain local exigencies collided with the principles of Vienna's policy toward the Estates and the nobility, and the homage thus became one of the first fields of contention in which the inner discrepancies of Austrian policies came to the fore. For example, the government was adamant that all institutional vestiges of the Polish-Lithuanian Noble Republic were to be abrogated immediately—meaning that no assembly of the nobility would be tolerated, let alone organized. But as soon as Pergen became aware of just how important the position of the nobility within the Polish body politic was, he found it very difficult to ignore it entirely as a sociopolitical institution the way he was expected to. Considering the large percentage of the overall population constituted by the nobility (up to 6 percent), it proved impossible to organize the act of homage in a way that made it clear that all nobles were obliged to participate. There was also no way to ensure that all the noble families of Galicia would actually send their representatives to the act; even in the following decades, the Austrian administration did not have a comprehensive and definitive register of the Galician nobility at its disposal.

The only way to proceed with the ceremony was to let mandatories pay homage on behalf of the nobility. Yet this constituted a twofold contradiction of the principle of not acknowledging the nobility as a legal body: first, if the nobility was to be represented by elected deputies, this implied that the nobility constituted an estate in the legal sense; second, it would be necessary to organize the nobility into territorial groups, each of which would then be represented.

Pergen conveyed these considerations to State Chancellor Kaunitz in November 1772.[9] He considered it problematic to insist on the act of homage by representatives, and he also warned against a lengthy postponement. In Pergen's opinion, the act was of supreme importance on the symbolic as well as the legal level, since it was supposed to finalize the incorporation of Galicia into the monarchy. He pointed out that there were many among the local inhabitants who strongly doubted the perpetuity of Habsburg rule over Galicia and therefore did not dare declare their fealty to Maria Theresa, fearing the repercussions should their country return to Poland.¹⁰

Pergen thus urged for a prompt performance of the homage ceremony. The purpose, he argued, was no longer only to secure and legitimize the transfer of power—instead, the act would calm the widespread political commotion among the nobility. Pergen also wished to countervail the rumors of a quick return to Poland that were being spread from the Polish side of the border. Last, the investiture was to rein in the nobles and make it clear beyond any doubt that they would no longer enjoy their former liberties. Hence, the act of homage appeared to be a legal, political, and tactical exigency.

On the other hand, Pergen conceded that it would be necessary to acknowledge the nobility as a legal body to allow a rapid and smooth organization of the inauguration. For this purpose, he thought it mandatory to divide the subjects into "classes"—denoting Estates in a general sense—and organize the act along the lines of that division. In his opinion, this was absolutely essential because otherwise, "in a word, there will not be a stable monarchic rule." He recommended that the classes retain their privileges so long as they did not conflict with the prerogatives of the ruler.¹¹

It had soon become clear that a full prohibition of corporations of the Estates could not be enforced, and this was one of the first and most important modifications of the court's policies initiated by Pergen. Meanwhile, the decision-makers in Vienna were becoming aware of the fact that their original approach to the act of homage was hardly feasible. Maria Theresa therefore proposed to establish the new Galician Estates according to rural districts (*Landkreise*). In a letter to Pergen, she wrote: "If you should find this raw idea unobjectionable or useful, you will bring it into a better and more accomplished form. . . . In this way, at least the commotion among the entire noble Estate may be somewhat eased, and also . . . the act of homage could be carried out more easily if prior to it this could be put in place and made public."¹²

Given the circumstances, the Viennese court realized that the inauguration and the pledge of fealty to the House of Habsburg, consequential as they were as a political symbol and for the purpose of legitimation, would have to be postponed even further. Constructing the Galician estate system from scratch by replacing the traditional Polish Estates with new classes established by Maria Theresa was viewed as a viable loophole: in this way, the newly formed Estates and their homage would represent a complete rescindment of Polish traditions. On a symbolic level, reestablishing the Estates provided an even better solution than their mere abolishment.¹³

Pergen duly integrated Maria Theresa's proposals into his own conceptions of how the Estates should be established and represented.¹⁴ These conceptions would only come to fruition in 1775 and 1782,¹⁵ but some of the relevant issues had to be tackled immediately. Particular attention was paid to the administrative division of the territory as a means of organizing the nobility. In obvious agreement with Maria Theresa's suggestions, Pergen recommended grouping the nobility according to rural districts headed by a palatine or *voivode*. This would allow the heads of the Estates and the palatines to pay homage on behalf of the Estates of their districts while every nobleman could confirm the oath by signature and seal. And yet, as Pergen pointed out, nearly every single district was inhabited by more noblemen than Upper and Lower Austria combined, and all issues concerning the organization of the nobility therefore had to be looked into even more thoroughly regarding the new administrative division into districts and counties.[16]

When preparations for the act of homage were underway in 1772 and 1773, the Austrian authorities had not yet decided how the Estates should be constituted, and it remained a permanent matter of discussion. Yet what the authorities came up with amounted more to makeshift measures than to a long-term policy concerning the Estates and the nobility. New challenges arising during the first months and years of Austrian rule led to increasing modification of the principle of not acknowledging the nobility as a legal body. How the Estates were to be systematically organized in a hereditary country ruled by an absolute monarch would continue to be negotiated and eventually decided upon much later.

The Act of Homage

The investiture was finally scheduled for 29 December 1773, and the letters patent describing the organization of the nobility went into elaborate detail regarding the legitimacy of the transfer of rule. They focused on the rescindment of the new subjects' former fealty by quoting the Austrian-Polish cessation treaty at great length.[17] This was intended to dispel any doubts as to the lawfulness and validity of the Austrian rulership. Governor Pergen was authorized to accept the oath of fealty in Lemberg on behalf of both Maria Theresa and Joseph II. Three classes of the population were to pay homage: the nobility, the clergy, and the urban and rural municipalities. From the perspective of Vienna, the thorny question of the homage by the nobility had been satisfactorily resolved by way of representation: before 3 December, the district gatherings of the nobility convened to elect six deputies each. Six days later, these deputies met at the respective county authority, where they in turn appointed six representatives who were to swear the oath of fealty in Lemberg on behalf of the entire county. The Habsburg government thus made a different decision than the Prussian authorities—for in the Prussian territories annexed from Poland, the act of homage had taken place as early as September 1772 (i.e., without even waiting until the cession agreement with Poland was complete). Moreover, the oath was taken by the nobles in person, or by their own plenipotentiaries if they chose to do so.[18] In Galicia, the representatives of the dioceses and archdioceses, chapters, monastic orders, and monasteries, as well as other prelates—in contrast to the nobility—were obliged to show up in person. Urban and rural municipalities as well as Jewish communities likewise had to send their respective heads.

The ceremony began in front of the governor's residence in Lubomirski Palace on the Lemberg market place. From there, an imposing procession headed off toward the former church of the Jesuit order, which had been abrogated shortly before.[19] A herald at the head was followed by a military outfit, behind which walked the "liveried servants of all persons present" along with the officials of the Galician governorate institutions. Next came the monastic priests, Lemberg's municipal authorities, the county deputies, the secular priests, the chamberlains, and other court officials, then Governorate Counselor (*Gubernialrat*) Count Wratislaw Mitrowitz, specially appointed as *Huldigungskanzler* (literally "homage chancellor") for the occasion, and Governor Pergen accompanied by Commanding General Count Andreas Hadik and Lieutenant Field Marshal Count Almásy. The governorate counselors and members of the law courts formed the next group, followed by "other personalities of the nobility present," and a further army unit brought up the rear. The procession also included people not participating in the act of homage itself.

After the procession had arrived at its destination, Pergen took his seat beneath an empty throne symbolizing the absent ruler. Count Wratislaw then proceeded to read out the oath, which was repeated by the participants. The oath pledged loyalty to Maria Theresa "as from now on our most gracious King [sic]" and to Joseph as coregent and to all their heirs "of both sexes."[20] In doing so, the adjuration explicitly referred to the Pragmatic Sanction. The entire ceremony was accompanied by cannon and artillery salvos and bell ringing. Maintaining its previous order, the procession then walked from the former Jesuit church to the Cathedral of the Assumption, which had been refurbished in late baroque style not long before, for a mass before returning to the governor's residence. The subsequent celebrations opened with an audience while "three roasted oxen as well as several roasts and bread [were given out] to the common folk. . . . Also at many places beer, mead and spirits were flowing in large amounts."[21] The festivities ended with a masked ball in the governor's residence for the nobility and in the building of the redoubt for the rest of the participants, and an illumination of the city.

For the participants in the act of homage, the representatives of the monarchs, and the populace, the accompanying festivities were an integral part of the investiture itself. This was presumably the very first occasion at which the new Galician symbolism could be publicly manifested and the country's new political status as a Habsburg hereditary land be conveyed performatively. Galicia's coat of arms was installed at prominent locations, and a commemorative coin with the portraits of Maria Theresa and Joseph II was printed at the government's order.

Alongside the coat of arms, this medal depicted Austria and Galicia represented by allegorical female figures, the latter "kneeling in front of the former, holding her right hand on her chest." It also quoted the historical and legal formula legitimizing the annexation by the Habsburgs: *Antiqua Jura Vindicata, Galicia Lodomiria in Fidem receptis MDCCLXXIII*.[22]

In the current state of research, little to nothing is known about attempts to avoid participation in the act of homage. By mid-January 1774, persons obliged to pay homage who had not been present at the official act were prompted to report to the respective authorities in person within three months to pledge their fealty. Absentee nobles who failed to do so were threatened with forfeiture of their landholdings.[23] A well-known case is that of Jan Kicki, a high-ranking Polish dignitary who had ostentatiously distanced himself from the new government after the Austrian troops had entered the country. He also refused to take part in any festivities or church services devoted to the Habsburg rulers and did not pay homage to Maria Theresa, contending that he did not feel released from his allegiance to the king of Poland.[24] Through this refusal, Kicki would become somewhat of a legend in Polish history—but this very fact illustrates that he was an exception among the Polish nobility. His stance was not typical, nor did the vast majority of Polish noblemen see it as an example to be followed. Kicki would remain one of the most prominent figures in Polish politics, however: among other offices, he became a member of the Permanent Council, a central government board in Warsaw, in 1775.

Noble Desiderata on the Occasion of the Investiture

While the preparations for the act of homage were underway, the relations between Vienna, the newly established authorities in Galicia, and the Polish nobility were put to the test for the first time. The problems caused by the organization of the festivities made it clear to the Viennese court that it had to come up with a political strategy concerning the Polish nobility. The new subjects had to be legally bound to loyalty and the acquisition of the territory safeguarded, but it was also necessary to ensure legal certainty, and the local elites were to be given the chance to publicly embrace the new political situation. In a memorandum written in July 1773, governor Pergen voiced his hopes for a positive development: "In general, there is no doubt that as soon as the act of homage has passed, some of the foremost [magnates] will find their way to Vienna in order to plead for the highest protection and graciousness."[25]

While the act of homage, as explained above, required submitting the Galician nobility to a new organizational framework, basic outlines of a constitution based on the Estates were also being drafted by the rulers and central institutions in Vienna. The Polish noblemen thus received a first opportunity to voice their political wishes and expectations.

The members of the government in Lemberg who were not native to the country, on the one hand, and the Polish nobility—which was still finding it difficult to digest the transfer of rule and the ensuing political changes—on the other, held diametrically opposed positions in some of the matters at hand. The historical sources at our disposal make it difficult to describe this situation more precisely, but they seem to suggest that the initial confrontation was soon assuaged by a range of compromises, emerging political options, and the divergence between conceptual approaches and their implementation. Iryna Vushko has correctly pointed out the fact that the impersonal dichotomy between administrators and citizens soon vanished;[26] this process was neither automatic nor unavoidable, and initially had its limitations—but it began contemporaneously with the Austrian rule.

Prior to the act of homage, the Austrian administration found no way to prevent the Polish nobility from holding its traditional conventions. This meant the nobles had a limited, yet (given the circumstances) real opportunity to communicate among themselves as a group and formulate their political desiderata. The homage as a constitutional act literally stipulated a listing of the "desiderata of the country" (*Landeswünsche*) The Galician nobility was not allowed to convene as a corporate body for the entire country, however—they met at the district level, but a summary of all resulting desiderata was not produced. Instead, each part of the country had to come up with a document of its own.

These desiderata were based in part on earlier deliberations among the nobility. There is still much research to be done on these programmatic ideas, as very few of them are known for the period between May 1772 and autumn 1773. Among the most important, and almost certainly brought to the attention of the Viennese court, was a project conceived by the nobleman Andrzej Wiesiołowski in January 1773.[27]

During the entire period between the First and Third Partitions of Poland and Lithuania, the assurances of fealty and loyalty pervading these programs barely veiled a harsh criticism of the Habsburg style of governance and the direction it was taking. Nevertheless, the very fact that projects and demands were formulated, initiated, and received demonstrated the existence of a will to compromise and cooperate on both sides. While the desiderata directed at the authorities of Galicia-Lodomeria conveyed an underlying sense of conflicting interests, their authors in principle assured their loyalty—or at least expressed their wish to be given a suitable incentive to remain loyal to the new rulers.

In 1773, the Habsburg government was certainly not willing to provide an official platform for the wishes of the Polish nobles, let alone encourage the establishment of a noble corporation that would have given their desiderata an institutional framework from which to voice their political ambitions. On the other hand, it was in the government's own interest to familiarize itself with the nobility's suggestions and accommodate its wishes as long as they did not collide with the principles of absolutist rule. By signaling a genuine interest in the opinions of the elites and a willingness to compromise, the government also hoped to calm the political commotion running rampant among the nobility. Pergen was a proponent of this approach, and Kaunitz's opinions as well as the intentions of Maria Theresia and her coruler obviously ran along similar lines. In the first year of Austrian rule, Pergen managed to prevent the nobility from taking an openly hostile stance toward the new rulership by following an accommodating approach.[28] Besides exercising great restraint in many instances, he also showed a certain openness toward encouraging the nobles to articulate their wishes at other times. The governor also took initiative to let the nobility voice their desires in the run-up to the first act of homage.

The Austrian government could only afford to take this considerate stance if its control over Galicia was solid and permanent. In 1773, the demarcation of the new borders was yet to be finalized—and most importantly, in September 1773, the Polish-Lithuanian diet ratified the cession of territories of the previous year and approved them by concluding a treaty with Austria. This treaty stipulated that Poland's Galician subjects were released from their obligation of loyalty toward the Commonwealth, and many nobles in Galicia consequently felt they had been abandoned by their native country and forced to accept Austrian rule.[29] Nevertheless, a very significant legal and ethical obstacle that had given Vienna severe headaches and prompted the government to postpone the act of homage had been overcome. There was no longer a reason for Kaunitz to ponder whether a speedy investiture was "in agreement with justice and conscience," as he had written in a letter to Pergen in December 1772.[30]

All seemed well in Galicia at this point, and the mood among the nobility appeared calm. Eighteen months after the occupation, there were no inner disturbances, and no imminent danger threatened Austrian rule. The nobility no longer appeared to be a political liability; on the contrary, many Polish magnates were willing to cooperate, even if they possessed landholdings on the Polish side of the border and were members of the Warsaw diet. In the autumn of 1772, a decree ordered all Galician landlords to return to Austria;[31] but it was largely ignored, with the nobles staying at their manors in Poland or Lithuania. Most of them did seek special permission to do so, however, and their absence was looked upon by the Habsburg government "with equitable forbearance."[32] When elections for the Warsaw diet were held in 1773, these *sujets mixtes* elected representatives who were willing to support the Polish-Austrian treaty of cession.[33]

During the autumn and winter of 1773, the Galician governorate took a rather nonchalant stance concerning the nobility's desiderata that were being penned. When the nobles were called upon to take part in the act of homage, all previous considerations that this would raise undue hopes apparently disappeared.³⁴ The desiderata did not have any real political impact; instead, they were of a primarily symbolic nature. Nevertheless, when meeting to discuss them, the nobles made certain to assure the new government of their loyalty, going far beyond what was common and expected in such a situation. In a speech occasioned by the imminent investiture, for example, Ignacy Golejewski—who would eventually be a member of the Polish-Lithuanian Great *Sejm* from 1788 to 1792—voiced the nobility's ill feelings about its liberties being taken away, as well as the hope that Maria Theresa would reinstate them. On the other hand, he also harshly criticized the "Golden Freedom" of the Commonwealth, a criticism that was very much in line with the opinions of the enlightened decision-makers in Vienna.³⁵

The nobility attempted to legitimize its privileges in various areas, but also exercised considerable restraint when it came to openly displaying any form of Polish patriotism. It can be assumed that this was because the nobles did not wish to endanger their core interests, among which was the wish to retain a say in the administration of the country. At the same time, it was an obvious success for the government that the Polish nobility referred to the newly established Kingdom of Galicia and Lodomeria as a whole in its desiderata, which implied acceptance of or at least passive subordination to the new territorial and political framework, and may have been more than a mere outward pretense.

All in all, the nobles were primarily focused on safeguarding their privileges, but there were also more specific requests by individual noblemen. One important question that resurfaced time and again during the following years was the justification of their manorial power over the subjects. The nobles legitimized this power by underlining the role their forefathers had played in the defense of the country; it was thus derived from the warrior tradition of medieval knighthood, which the nobles claimed to be their ancestry.³⁶

While most of the requests formulated by the noble conventions at the district and county levels used rather general terms, those produced in the County of Stanisławów were much more urgent and politically controversial, since they were worded as preconditions for the act of homage. It was no coincidence that the authorities in Vienna paid special attention to the "Instruction" penned by the Stanisławów nobles, which they scathed as "republican."³⁷ All the other instructions pleading for the preservation of privileges in more general terms were viewed with a kind of gratification, however. Freiherr von Gabler, member of the State Council in Vienna, even opined that the desiderata showed "devotion and subordination" on the part of the Galician nobility.³⁸

During the final phase prior to the act of homage, most noble representatives exercised particular restraint by declaring that the desiderata were not intended as prerequisites for the act, but as requests to be forwarded to the monarchs thereafter. The majority of the counties thus did not deem the stance taken by the Stanisławów nobles to be valid, and it was presumably due to Pergen's personal intervention that the Galician noble representatives made this decision. After taking the oath, thirteen of them no longer considered it necessary to forward their desiderata to Vienna at all. They maintained that the oath had been taken without any preconditions, making any further requests superfluous.[39]

While most representatives continued to labor over a petition to the throne, they were unable to agree upon a common document. Consequently, they gave Governor Pergen two separate petitions: in the first, a majority of twenty representatives had signed a more restrained presentation and wording, while the second petition contained fourteen very comprehensive postulates but was signed by only nine noblemen, with the rest of the deputies having found the text too offensive and radical. The two documents actually differed very little in regard to their contents, since both of them were geared to the presentation and retention of the same interests, privileges, and rights.

The nobility felt entitled to certain privileges that it believed should be valid in the new kingdom as well. But by demanding them, it also resigned itself—albeit grudgingly—to the new political reality. To request respect for the historical traditions and constitutional peculiarities of the specific country was common for any given historical entity that was part of a Central European monarchy. In this respect, there was no difference between the Noble Republic of Poland-Lithuania and the enlightened absolutism of the Habsburg Monarchy—with Lithuania and Royal Prussia, respectively Hungary, Transylvania, and the German hereditary territories including Bohemia, being the prime examples. The signatories of both petitions linked their demands to maintain the autonomy and the exceptional position of Galicia to the reinstatement of noble privilege. Apparently, as had been the case throughout the early modern period, the rights of the country were practically identified with the prerogatives of the Estates.[40] As the speaker of the Galician nobility contended, the two were not only linked, but in fact conditioned each other. Furthermore, both were connected to Catholicism as a state religion. And while this connection did not necessarily establish a new line of conflict with the ruling dynasty and the Habsburg elites, it certainly contradicted the Josephinist church policies that culminated in Joseph II's Patent of Toleration of 1781.[41]

Despite their generalizing character, the desiderata of 1773 still comprised a number of more specific demands and subjects that would remain at the center of Galician Estate policies throughout the following decades. Equivalents of many of these were to be found in the political programs of other Habsburg hereditary territories as well, among them the idea that the Estates of the country were entitled to report directly to the ruler (*Immediatrecht*), submitting their requests to the monarch under circumvention of the governor and the court authorities, which usually had to be addressed first in the Habsburg Monarchy. Furthermore, each county was to be allowed to delegate two deputies to the Country Governorate (*Landesgubernium*). It is difficult to tell if this measure was in some way intended to replace the country diet, as suggested by Wacław Tokarz.[42] If this were the case, these delegations would more likely have replaced the previous dietines (*sejmiki*) at the district and voivodship level in Poland. At these gatherings, the local nobles elected their representatives for the higher levels (i.e., for the voivodship in the district dietines and for the Warsaw *Sejm* in the voivodship dietines). They also discussed problems concerning the respective region as well as the entire country. Following the Polish model as proposed for Galicia by the representatives, the nobility would have been able to act and be represented as a corporate body. The nobles from all regions of the country would have had the possibility of presenting their interests directly to the *Landesgubernium* according to the same principle as was suggested for direct communication at the country level (i.e., between the Galician Estates as a whole and the ruler).

The political programs of the nobility intended, among other things, to provide sinecures for its members. They postulated exceptionless observance of the indigenate, which meant that all offices in the country were to be reserved for the landed gentry and the noble landowners of Galicia who were members of the Galician Estates. However, the desiderata showed some restraint in demanding that only Poles should be admitted to government positions.[43] The Galician indigenate was intended to secure the noble entitlements. It was to be a precondition for acquiring a noble landholding (*Dominikalgut*), thus reserving an exclusive right to landownership for the Galician nobility from which foreign nobles—even if they came from other Habsburg territories—and nonnobles in general were excluded.

Some of the instructions at the county level were more forthright regarding the traditions of the Polish nobility and the demands for reinstatement of its privileges, such as the organization of the dietines. By contrast, however, the desiderata as formulated for the occasion of the act of homage opted for a less provoking wording, avoiding direct allusions to the "Golden Age" of Polish nobility. Instead, they offered a compromise with Vienna, seeking to connect Habsburg and Polish noble interests in a twofold manner. First, the desiderata pointed out the link—if not equivalence—between nobles' interests and those of the country; second, the demand for the indigenate and the ways in which it was to be enforced and applied largely adopted the constitutional model found in other hereditary territories of the Habsburg Monarchy. These desiderata thus reflected Galicia's sociopolitical alignment with and integration into the Habsburg composite state.

In effect, the noble representatives displayed a high degree of political flexibility and pragmatism as well as considerable knowledge of the political and legal system of the Habsburg Monarchy. Their flexibility concerning the economic interests of the landed nobility was much less pronounced, however, and in this respect, the desiderata were simply unacceptable to the Habsburg government. There was no way to reconcile them with the absolutist and economic principles upheld by Vienna (e.g., elements of participation, direct communication between the Estates and the ruler). Moreover, they also partially contradicted measures that had already been taken. For example, the nobility wished to see no alteration to its disposal of royal demesnes (such as *starostwa*, etc., that were possessed by the rich nobles)—even though a patent issued in late January 1773 had already decided otherwise.[44] Whereas the lands that nominally belonged to the kings of Poland (or the Polish Crown, respectively) were allocated to the influential nobles (a procedure that allowed the king to form his own royal party) and returned to the king only to be assigned once more (with some of them even being passed down informally within noble families), the Viennese government ordered a gradual conveyance of these demesnes "back" into the state property administrated by the *Kammer*. Wacław Tokarz maintains that it was these unrealistic hopes of retaining possession of the royal lands that caused the Polish nobility to soften their demands.[45] Somewhat more realistic may have been the request for a preemptive right whenever royal demesnes (*Kameralgüter*) were offered for sale. It goes without saying that this would have been the only option had the nobility's demand for a Galician indigenate been met. At any rate, most of the desiderata were a far cry from the political reality and the cameralistic policy imposed by Vienna. This was also true for the landlords' wish to maintain control over the production of salt despite the state salt monopoly, or their hope to leave the relation between manorial lords and their subjects unchanged. The most the nobles were willing to concede was a rental reform that would conform entirely to their interests.

The Viennese authorities, foremost the Galician Court Chancellery (*Hofkanzlei*) and the State Council, rejected most of the demands in their replies to the aforementioned noble instructions in 1774. This was unsurprising since state cameralism and absolute monarchy simply could not be reconciled with what the Polish nobility wished and intended. As for the *Immediatrecht*, Vienna considered it an unfounded privilege for Galicia; it was denied, arguing that all the other hereditary territories had to communicate their requests via their respective governorates as well. And since the reservation of state posts for Galician nobles would have limited the monarch's prerogative to decide on the awarding of any such positions, the indigenate was likewise refused despite the fact that similar regulations—at least on a legal level—existed in other parts of the monarchy.[46]

On the other hand, the court was not entirely dissatisfied with the demands, since they were ultimately much less radical than expected. Horst Glassl characterizes the program of 1773 as follows: "[the nobility] wished for participation in the government of the country while at the same time rejecting the assumption of any responsibility."[47] The postulates devised by the noble conventions when they elected their representatives for the act of homage generally combined an insistence on noble privilege and assertiveness with compliance, restraint, and moderation. As the Polish legal historian Stanisław Grodziski aptly states, the nobility treated the county conventions of December 1773 like traditional *sejmiki*, formulating their demands as "instructions" to the representatives.[48] The answers to these instructions from Vienna were respectful and accommodating in tone, but simultaneously vague, evasive, or negative in content. Furthermore, they were conveyed in an informal and unofficial manner via the new governor, General Andreas Hadik, by being addressed to individual noblemen as private persons.[49] The Viennese government thus returned to its basic principle of not acknowledging the nobility as a corporate body and not providing any pretext that the noble assemblies had constituted representative bodies. After all, their sole purpose had been to elect the delegates to the act of homage, not to compose the desiderata. Seen from this perspective, Habsburg policy in Galicia remained unchanged: the nobility was to be won over and brought into a mood more accepting of the new rulership, but no concessions were to be made that would be more than symbolic gestures. This strategy was not devoid of inner contradictions, but all in all, it yielded positive results. After all, Habsburg rule over Galicia was in its very early stages, and Vienna did not know whether the nobility was hiding its true disposition while participating in the act of homage. Or, as Maria Theresa drily commented to Joseph: this "oath of fealty is no more than a ritual, since it will always be forced upon these poor people."[50]

The Galician Investiture as Experience and Model

The concepts and strategies employed by the authorities and displayed in the nobles' desiderata provided new experiences for all participants. The Habsburg Monarchy had not faced the challenge of taking over an important part of a foreign state and incorporating it into the monarchy since the early eighteenth century. Similarly, the Polish nobility had no experience with being transferred to another rule and having to transform their part of the Commonwealth politically and constitutionally. In this regard, the years 1772 to 1774 provided a test bed or model of sorts for the later Austrian annexations of Polish territories or of Bukovina, incorporated from the Ottoman Empire and united with Galicia after nine years of Austrian military administration (1775–84). In the Bukovinian case, specific social structures, Moldovan political and legal traditions, and the differing background of the annexation had to be taken into account for the organization of the investiture on 12 September 1777 in Czernowitz (Černivci in Ukrainian, Cernăuți in Romanian). The organization of this act has hitherto been insufficiently studied, however, and would need to be analyzed more profoundly before becoming an object of systematic comparison with other inaugurations in the region.[51]

As far as the Prussian annexation of West (formerly Royal) Prussia is concerned, it is a well-known fact that it constituted a model for the integration of

Polish territories after the Second and Third Partitions.[52] For the case of Western Galicia (i.e., the Polish territories acquired by the Habsburg Monarchy through the Third Partition in 1795), connections to the processes discussed in this chapter remain a desideratum for research. So far, the findings seem to support the hypothesis of the Galician model case,[53] especially considering the debates over whether the previous regulations in Galicia should be expanded to incorporate the newly acquired territories. The same holds true for the West-Galician act of homage in 1796.[54]

In the "old" Galicia (i.e., the kingdom as established in 1772), the first investiture was considered valid for Maria Theresa's successors as well: as hereditary rulers, the Habsburgs could remind their subjects of the act of 1773–74 and oblige them to loyalty without organizing another special ceremony.[55] This was the case after the deaths of Maria Theresa (1780), Joseph II (1790), and Leopold II (1792). Only in the Galician territories of the County of Tarnopol (Ternopil in Ukrainian), ceded to Russia during the Napoleonic wars and recovered by the Habsburg Empire after the Congress of Vienna, was the relation of fealty restored by a new act of homage that also completed the release of the inhabitants from their obedience to the czar. The same was true for the surroundings of Podgórze and Wieliczka, small territories lost to the Duchy of Warsaw after the War of 1809. But the inaugurations taking place there on 9 September 1816 likewise "only" renewed the original Galician oath. For this reason, their organization mirrored quite precisely (and with explicit reference) that of the acts of December 1773 and January 1774.[56] The first Galician act of homage not only established a new tradition but also remained in force for the future rulers and subjects, and was only renewed in cases where its effectiveness was formally voided by a change of sovereignty.

Miloš Řezník, historian, has been director of the German Historical Institute Warsaw since 2014. He studied history at Charles University in Prague (1989–94), obtained his PhD there in 2001 with a thesis on territorial patriotism in Polish Prussia during the eighteenth century, and completed his habilitation at the University of Olomouc in 2007. He served as specialist adviser for Poland at the Ministry of Foreign Affairs of the Czech Republic in 1995–96 and as researcher at Charles University in 1998–2001. In 2001–02, he worked at the Leibniz Institute for the History and Culture of Eastern Europe (GWZO) in Leipzig. Following a junior professorship in 2002–08, he has been Professor of European regional history at the University of Chemnitz, Germany, since 2009 (2009–14 as vice-dean of the Faculty of Arts). He has also cochaired the Czech-German Historians' Commission since 2009. Fields of research consist of Polish history, the Habsburg Monarchy, nation building, collective identities, historical memory, and elites during the late eighteenth to the early twentieth century. His publications include *Neuorientierung einer Elite: Aristokratie, Ständewesen und Loyalität in Galizien 1772–1795* (Frankfurt am Main, 2016) and *Za vaši a naši svobodu: Století polských povstání 1794–1864* (Prague, 2010).

Notes

Translated from the German by Andreas R. Hofmann. Some sections of this chapter are derived from Miloš Řezník, *Neuorientierung Einer Elite: Aristokratie, Staendewesen Und Loyalitaet in Galizien (1772–1795)* (Frankfurt am Main, 2016).

1. For the most recent literature, see Iryna Vushko, *The Politics of Cultural Retreat: Imperial Bureaucracy in Austrian Galicia, 1772–1867* (New Haven, 2015), 51.
2. See, for example, Horst Glassl, *Das österreichische Einrichtungswerk in Galizien (1772–1790)* (Wiesbaden, 1975), 12; more recently, see Hans-Jürgen Bömelburg, "Inklusion und Exklusion nach der Ersten Teilung Polen-Litauens: Die österreichische, preußische und russländische Regierungspraxis in Galizien, Westpreußen und den weißrussischen Gouvernements Polack und Mahilëŭ im Vergleich (1772–1806/7)," in *Die Teilungen Polen-Litauens: Inklusion- und Exklusionsmechanismen—Traditionsbildung—Vergleichsebenen*, ed. Hans-Jürgen Bömelburg, Andreas Gestrich, and Helga Schnabel-Schüle (Osnabrück, 2013), 182; Daniela Druschel, "Die Einführung des habsburgischen Rechts in Galizien: Herrschaftswechsel als Reformmotor für die Straf- und Zivilrechtskodifikation in der Habsburgermonarchie?" in *Die Teilungen Polen-Litauens*, 293, 304–6, and 315; Hans-Christian Maner, *Galizien: Eine Region im Kalkül der Donaumonarchie im 18. und 19. Jahrhundert* (Munich, 2007); Klemens Kaps, "Kulturelle Differenzen des Ökonomischen: Galizische Entwicklungsdiskurse im Spannungsfeld räumlicher Funktionalisierung und sozialer Bruchlinien (1772–1848)," *Historyka: Studia metodologiczne* 42 (2012): 104.
3. Glassl, *Das österreichische Einrichtungswerk*, e.g., 58–59.
4. ÖStA, AVA, Hofkanzlei, carton 229, 163 ex September 1772, fol. 12.
5. *Starostwa* were administrative territorial units in Poland-Lithuania connected to the crown lands and generally possessed by magnates and wealthy nobles.
6. Stanisław Grodziski, *Studia galicyjskie: Rozprawy i przyczynki do historii ustroju Galicji* (Cracow, 2007), 59–60.
7. Ludwig Albrecht Gebhardi, *Geschichte der Königreiche Galizien, Lodomirien und Rothreussen* (Pest, 1804), 122; cf. Johann Jacob Herz, *Geschichtliche Darstellung der Gesetze und Gewohnheiten welche in Galizien und Lodomerien vor dessen Einverleibung mit Österreich Kraft hatten* (Vienna, 1835), 49.
8. As late as four weeks before the act of homage, Pergen proposed to the chancellor to further postpone it by five days, suggesting that many representatives would be inclined to spend Christmas with their families instead of attending (the scheduled date was 26 December). Pergen obviously had no such reservations concerning New Year's Eve and New Year's Day. He was convinced that many nobles would honestly regret their absence later on. In his opinion, the nobles regarded the act as a social event giving them an opportunity to show off, prove their loyalty to Maria Theresa, and distinguish themselves. Pergen also hinted at the presumably more important fact that the administration was having difficulties translating all the necessary documents into Latin and Polish in time

for the event. Pergen to Kaunitz, 11 November 1773: Wrocław, Zakład Narodowy im. Ossolińskich, Manuscript 9747/III, 29–30.
9. ÖStA, HHStA, Staatskanzlei, Provinzen—Galizien, carton 5, Pergen to Kaunitz, Lemberg, 16 November 1772.
10. ÖStA, HHStA, Staatskanzlei, Provinzen—Galizien, carton 5, Pergen to Kaunitz, Lemberg, 16 November 1772.
11. ÖStA, HHStA, Staatskanzlei, Provinzen—Galizien, carton 5, Pergen to Kaunitz, Lemberg, 16 November 1772.
12. L'viv, Centralnyj deržavnyj istoryčnyj archiv Ukrajiny, 146—Halyc'ke namistnyctvo 1772–1921, op. 1—Besondere Akten, spr. 4, fol. 57–58.
13. L'viv, Centralnyj deržavnyj istoryčnyj archiv Ukrajiny, 146—Halyc'ke namistnyctvo 1772–1921, op. 1—Besondere Akten, spr. 4, fol. 57–58.
14. L'viv, Centralnyj deržavnyj istoryčnyj archiv Ukrajiny, 146—Halyc'ke namistnyctvo 1772–1921, op. 1—Besondere Akten, spr. 4, fol. 316.
15. Miloš Řezník, *Neuorientierung einer Elite: Aristokratie, Ständewesen und Loyalität in Galizien (1772–1795)* (Frankfurt am Main, 2016), 247–94.
16. L'viv, Centralnyj deržavnyj istoryčnyj archiv Ukrajiny, 146—Halyc'ke namistnyctvo 1772–1921, op. 1—Besondere Akten, spr. 4, fol. 57–58, 329, 332.
17. Patent of 15 November 1773, printed in Latin and Polish in *Continuatio Edictorum et mandatorum universalium in Regnis Galiciae et Lodomeriae a die 1. Mensis Januar: Anno 1773 emanatorum* (L'viv, 1774), 14–37. The official German version was printed in *Kurtz-Gefaßte Historische Nachrichten zum Behuf der Neuern Europäischen Begebenheiten auf das Jahr 1774* (Regensburg, 1774), 101–7.
18. Max Bär, *Westpreußen unter Friedrich dem Großen* (Leipzig, 1909), vol. 1: 38–39.
19. For a description of the ceremony to which this chapter refers, see the contemporary description in the Regensburg newspaper: *Kurtz-Gefaßte Historische Nachrichten*, 74–75 and 81–84.
20. "als Unser[n] nunmehrigen allergnädigsten König," *Kurtz-Gefaßte Historische Nachrichten*, 83. The full text of the oath is also quoted by Ignaz de Luca, *Geographisches Handbuch von dem östreichischen Staate*, vol. 5, part 1: *Galicien, und Lodomerien, nebst der Bucowine* (Vienna, 1791), 17–18.
21. *Kurtz-Gefaßte Historische Nachrichten*, 82.
22. *Kurtz-Gefaßte Historische Nachrichten*, 84.
23. *Continuatio Edictorum*, 45.
24. Władysław A. Serczyk, "Kicki Jan h. Gozdawa," in *Polski Słownik Biograficzny* (Wrocław, 1966), vol. 12: 388.
25. L'viv, Centralnyj deržavnyj istoryčnyj archiv Ukrajiny, 146—Halyc'ke namistnyctvo 1772–1921, op. 1—Besondere Akten, spr. 4, 311–12.
26. Vushko, *The Politics*, 1–17.
27. ÖStA, AVA, Hofkanzlei, Neue Provinzen, Staatsverwaltung, carton 229. For more details, see Řezník, *Neuorientierung*, 233–36.
28. Glassl, *Das österreichische Einrichtungswerk*, 61–62.
29. Wacław Tokarz, "Pierwsze dezyderaty szlachty galicyjskiej (1773)," in *Studya historyczne wydane ku czci prof. Wincentego Zakrzewskiego* (Cracow, 1908), 360, referring to Ignotus [= Kazimierz Chłędowski], "Zajęcie Galicyi," *Ateneum* 13, no. 1 (1880): 48.
30. Kaunitz to Pergen, Vienna, 18 December 1772: Wrocław, Zakład Narodowy im. Ossolińskich, Manuscript 12026/III, 9–22, here 9.

31. *Edicta et mandata universalia Regnis Galiciae et Lodomeriae a die 11. Septembr. 1772 initiae possessionis promulgata* (L'viv, 1773), 3–5.
32. A "Resolution" dated 26 August 1772: ÖStA, AVA, Hofkanzlei, carton. 229, 163 ex September 1772.
33. Glassl, *Das österreichische Einrichtungswerk*, 97.
34. Kaunitz to Pergen, Vienna, 18 December 1772: Wrocław, Zakład Narodowy im. Ossolińskich, Manuscript 12026/III, 9–22, here 9–10: "Since it can, speaking by the by, certainly be predicted that of the hitherto existing privileges, especially of the clergy and the nobility, very little or nothing at all is advisable to be reinstated. Her Majesty considers it to be questionable to provoke all classes of Her subjects to submit the entirety of their rights and freedoms so as to raise new hopes with them, only to finally abolish nearly all of these freedoms."
35. Wrocław, Zakład Narodowy im. Ossolińskich, Manuscript 12026/III, 147–50, especially 148.
36. Stanisław Grodziski, *Historia ustroju społeczno-politycznego Galicji 1772–1848* (Wrocław, 1971), 267.
37. Tokarz, "Pierwsze dezyderaty," 361. It is quite remarkable that this short article by Wacław Tokarz, published in a *festschrift* more than one hundred years ago, remains the most comprehensive study of the Galician desiderata of 1773 to this day.
38. Vortrag der gallitzischen Hofdeputation vom 22. Februar 1774: ÖStA, HHStA, Staatsrat-Akten, 1774, no. 469, quoted in Tokarz, "Pierwsze dezyderaty," 361–62.
39. Tokarz, "Pierwsze dezyderaty," 362.
40. See Kersten Krüger, *Die landständische Verfassung* (Munich, 2003), passim; Barbara Stollberg-Rilinger, *Vormünder des Volkes? Konzepte landständischer Repräsentation in der Spätphase des alten Reiches* (Berlin, 1999).
41. See Tokarz, "Pierwsze dezyderaty," 363.
42. Tokarz, "Pierwsze dezyderaty," 364.
43. Vortrag der gallitzischen Hofdeputation vom 22. Februar 1774: HHStA, Staatsrat-Akten, 1774, No. 469; quoted in Tokarz, "Pierwsze dezyderaty," 361–62.
44. *Edicta et mandata*, 34–37.
45. Tokarz, "Pierwsze dezyderaty," 365.
46. Tokarz, "Pierwsze dezyderaty," 365.
47. Glassl, *Das österreichische Einrichtungswerk*, 103.
48. Grodziski, *Studia galicyjskie*, 88–89; cf. Tokarz, "Pierwsze dezyderaty," 360.
49. Tokarz, "Pierwsze dezyderaty," 367–69.
50. ". . . serment de fidélité . . . n'est qu'une cérémonie, car il sera toujour forcé et arraché à ces pauvres gens": Maria Theresa to Joseph II, Schönbrunn, 20 June 1773. The letter is quoted extensively in Alfred von Arneth, *Geschichte Maria Theresia's* (Vienna, 1877), vol. 8: 409–11; the original version is printed in Alfred von Arneth, ed., *Maria Theresia und Joseph II.: Ihre Correspondenz sammt Briefen Joseph's an seinen Bruder Leopold*, (Vienna, 1867), vol. 2: 9–11, quoted passage on p. 10. See Boris Olschewski, "Zwangsinklusion durch Herrschaftswechsel—Besitzergreifungspatent und Erbhuldigungseid im Kontext der ersten Teilung Polens und Litauens," in *Fremde Herrscher—fremdes Volk: Inklusions- und Exklusionsfiguren bei Herrschaftswechseln in Europa*, ed. Helga Schnabel-Schüle and Andreas Gestrich (Frankfurt am Main, 2006), 360–1; Druschel, "Die Einführung," 297.
51. Johann Polek, "Die Huldigung der Bukowina am 12. Oktober 1777," *Jahrbuch des Bukowiner Landesmuseums* 10 (1902), 3–36. See also Mircea Pahomi, "'Jurământul Bucovinei':

Față de Austria în Anul 1777," *Analele Bucovinei* 8 (2001): 319–29, and Kurt Scharr, *Die Landschaft Bukowina: Das Werden einer Region an der Peripherie* (Vienna, 2010), 143.
52. Hans-Jürgen Bömelburg, *Zwischen polnischer Ständegesellschaft und preußischem Obrigkeitsstaat: Vom Königlichen Preußen zu Westpreußen (1756–1806)* (Munich, 1995), 462–65. In South Prussia, on the other hand, references were primarily to the annexation of Silesia: see Jan Wąsicki, *Ziemie polskie pod zaborem pruskim: Prusy Południowe 1793–1806. Studium historycznoprawne* (Wrocław, 1957), 24–25.
53. Tadeusz Mencel, *Galicja Zachodnia 1795–1809: Studium z dziejów ziem polskich zaboru austriackiego po III rozbiorze* (Lublin, 1976), e.g., 33–46; see Bömelburg, Gestrich, and Schnabel-Schüle, eds., *Die Teilungen Polen-Litauens* (Osnabrück, 2013), passim.
54. Mencel, *Galicja Zachodnia*, 56–57; with regard to the demands and desiderata of the Polish nobility in this context, see Stanisław Grodziski, "Postulaty szlachty Galicji Zachodniej z okazji hołdu 1796 roku," *Czasopismo Prawno-Historyczne* 20, no. 2 (1968): 81–93, and Tadeusz Mencel, "Magnateria polska Galicji w polityce władz austriackich w latach 1795–1809," in *Ziemiaństwo polskie 1795–1945: Zbiór prac o dziejach warstwy i ludzi*, ed. Janina Leskiewiczowa (Warsaw, 1985), 44–51.
55. Joseph Winiwarter, *Handbuch der politischen und Justiz-Gesetzkunde für die Königreiche Galizien und Lodomerien*. vol. 1: *Darstellung der Organisation der Landes und der Verwaltung* (Lviv, 1826), § 12, 18–19.
56. Winiwarter, *Handbuch der politischen*.

Bibliography

Arneth, Alfred von. *Geschichte Maria Theresia's*. Vol. 8. Vienna: Wilhelm Braumüller, 1877.

———, ed. *Maria Theresia und Joseph II.: Ihre Correspondenz sammt Briefen Joseph's an seinen Bruder Leopold*. Vol. 2. Vienna: Carl Gerold's Sohn, 1867.

Bär, Max. *Westpreußen unter Friedrich dem Großen*. Vol. 1. Leipzig: S. Hirzel, 1909.

Bömelburg, Hans-Jürgen. "Inklusion und Exklusion nach der Ersten Teilung Polen-Litauens: Die österreichische, preußische und russländische Regierungspraxis in Galizien, Westpreußen und den weißrussischen Gouvernements Polack und Mahilëŭ im Vergleich (1772–1806/7)." In *Die Teilungen Polen-Litauens: Inklusion- und Exklusionsmechanismen—Traditionsbildung—Vergleichsebenen*, edited by Hans-Jürgen Bömelburg, Andreas Gestrich, and Helga Schnabel-Schüle, 171–200. Osnabrück: Fibre, 2013.

———. *Zwischen polnischer Ständegesellschaft und preußischem Obrigkeitsstaat: Vom Königlichen Preußen zu Westpreußen (1756–1806)*. Munich: Oldenbourg, 1995.

Bömelburg, Hans-Jürgen, Andreas Gestrich, and Helga Schnabel-Schüle, eds. *Die Teilungen Polen-Litauens: Inklusion- und Exklusionsmechanismen—Traditionsbildung—Vergleichsebenen*. Osnabrück: Fibre, 2013.

Continuatio Edictorum et mandatorum universalium in Regnis Galiciae et Lodomeriae a die 1. Mensis Januar: Anno 1773 emanatorum. L'viv: Piller, 1774.

de Luca, Ignaz. *Geographisches Handbuch von dem östreichischen Staate*. Vol. 5, part 1: *Galicien, und Lodomerien, nebst der Bucowine*. Vienna: Joseph V. Degen, 1791.

Druschel, Daniela. "Die Einführung des habsburgischen Rechts in Galizien: Herrschaftswechsel als Reformmotor für die Straf- und Zivilrechtskodifikation in der Habsburgermonarchie?" In *Die Teilungen Polen-Litauens: Inklusion- und Exklusionsmechanismen—Tradi-

tionsbildung—Vergleichsebenen, edited by Hans-Jürgen Bömelburg, Andreas Gestrich, and Helga Schnabel-Schüle, 291–320. Osnabrück: Fibre, 2013.

Edicta et mandata universalia Regnis Galiciae et Lodomeriae a die 11. Septembr. 1772 initiae possessionis promulgata. Lviv: Piller, 1773.

Gebhardi, Ludwig Albrecht. *Geschichte der Königreiche Galizien, Lodomirien und Rothreusse*. Pest: Leyer, 1804.

Glassl, Horst. *Das österreichische Einrichtungswerk in Galizien (1772–1790)*. Wiesbaden: Harrassowitz, 1975.

Grodziski, Stanisław. *Historia ustroju społeczno-politycznego Galicji 1772–1848*. Wrocław: Zakład Narodowy im. Ossolińskich, 1971.

———. "Postulaty szlachty Galicji Zachodniej z okazji hołdu 1796 roku." *Czasopismo Prawno-Historyczne* 20, no. 2 (1968): 81–93.

———. *Studia galicyjskie: Rozprawy i przyczynki do historii ustroju Galicji*. Cracow: Księgarnia Akademicka, 2007.

Herz, Johann Jacob. *Geschichtliche Darstellung der Gesetze und Gewohnheiten welche in Galizien und Lodomerien vor dessen Einverleibung mit Österreich Kraft hatten*. Vienna: v. Hirschfeld'scher Bücherverlag, 1835.

Ignotus [= Kazimierz Chłędowski]. "Zajęcie Galicyi." *Ateneum* 13, no. 1 (1880): 48.

Kaps, Klemens. "Kulturelle Differenzen des Ökonomischen: Galizische Entwicklungsdiskurse im Spannungsfeld räumlicher Funktionalisierung und sozialer Bruchlinien (1772–1848)." *Historyka: Studia metodologiczne* 42 (2012): 97–116.

Krüger, Kersten. *Die landständische Verfassung*. Munich: Oldenbourg, 2003.

Kurtz-Gefaßte Historische Nachrichten zum Behuf der Neuern Europäischen Begebenheiten auf das Jahr 1774. Regensburg: Seiffart, 1774.

Maner, Hans-Christian. *Galizien: Eine Region im Kalkül der Donaumonarchie im 18. und 19. Jahrhundert*. Munich: IKGS Verlag, 2007.

Mencel, Tadeusz. *Galicja Zachodnia 1795–1809: Studium z dziejów ziem polskich zaboru austriackiego po III rozbiorze*. Lublin: Wydawnictwo Lubelskie, 1976.

———. "Magnateria polska Galicji w polityce władz austriackich w latach 1795–1809." In *Ziemiaństwo polskie 1795–1945: Zbiór prac o dziejach warstwy i ludzi*, edited by Janina Leskiewiczowa, 27–84. Warsaw: Państwowe Wydawnictwo Naukowe, 1985.

Olschewski, Boris. "Zwangsinklusion durch Herrschaftswechsel—Besitzergreifungspatent und Erbhuldigungseid im Kontext der ersten Teilung Polens und Litauens." In *Fremde Herrscher—fremdes Volk: Inklusions- und Exklusionsfiguren bei Herrschaftswechseln in Europa*, edited by Helga Schnabel-Schüle and Andreas Gestrich, 359–84. Frankfurt am Main: Peter Lang, 2006.

Pahomi, Mircea. "'Jurământul Bucovinei': Față de Austria în Anul 1777." *Analele Bucovinei* 8 (2001): 319–29.

Polek, Johann. "Die Huldigung der Bukowina am 12. Oktober 1777." *Jahrbuch des Bukowiner Landesmuseums* 10 (1902): 3–36 [separately printed as Johann Polek, *Die Huldigung der Bukowina Am 12. Oktober 1777* (Černovcy, 1902), and reprinted in *Pro Bucovina. Repere istorice și naționale*, edited by Mihai-Bogdan Atanasiu and Mircea-Cristian Ghenghea (Bucharest: Biblioteca Națională A României/Editura Mitropolit Iacov Putneanul, 2010), 351–56].

Řezník, Miloš. *Neuorientierung einer Elite: Aristokratie, Ständewesen und Loyalität in Galizien (1772–1795)*. Frankfurt am Main: Peter Lang, 2016.

Scharr, Kurt. *Die Landschaft Bukowina: Das Werden einer Region an der Peripherie.* Vienna: Böhlau, 2010.

Serczyk, Władysław A. "Kicki Jan h. Gozdawa." In *Polski Słownik Biograficzny.* Vol. 12: 388. Wrocław: Zakład Narodowy im. Ossolińskich, 1966.

Stollberg-Rilinger, Barbara. *Vormünder des Volkes? Konzepte landständischer Repräsentation in der Spätphase des alten Reiches.* Berlin: Duncker & Humblot, 1999.

Tokarz, Wacław. "Pierwsze dezyderaty szlachty galicyjskiej (1773)." In *Studya historyczne wydane ku czci prof. Wincentego Zakrzewskiego*, 357–69. Cracow: Drukarnia Uniwersytetu Jagiellońskiego, 1908.

Vushko, Iryna. *The Politics of Cultural Retreat: Imperial Bureaucracy in Austrian Galicia, 1772–1867.* New Haven: Yale University Press, 2015.

Wąsicki, Jan. *Ziemie polskie pod zaborem pruskim: Prusy Południowe 1793–1806. Studium historycznoprawne.* Wrocław: Zakład Narodowy im. Ossolińskich, 1957.

Winiwarter, Joseph. *Handbuch der politischen und Justiz-Gesetzkunde für die Königreiche Galizien und Lodomerien.* Vol. 1: *Darstellung der Organisation der Landes und der Verwaltung.* L'viv: Kuhn und Millikowski, 1826.

Chapter 9

PAGEANTRY IN THE REVOLUTIONARY AGE
Inaugural Rites in the Habsburg Monarchy, 1790–1848

William D. Godsey

The onset of the revolutionary age had little discernable impact on the incidence of inaugural rites across Europe and beyond. In the decades following the French revolution of 1789, acts of homage and coronations took place from Moscow to Berlin to London to Rio de Janeiro. Those crowned ranged from new dynasts such as Napoleon in France (1804) and his former marshal Bernadotte in Sweden and Norway (1818) to rulers from established houses such as the Russian emperor Alexander I (1801) and the British king George IV (1821). In 1822, the first emperor of Brazil introduced a coronation ritual to that country. The grand show put on by Napoleon in the cathedral of Notre Dame hardly a decade after Louis XVI's bloody end in Paris has fascinated succeeding generations. The historian Ambrogio Caiani has now subjected Napoleon's less known coronation as king of Italy in Milan in 1805 to brilliant analysis.[1] The notorious *sacre* in 1825 of the French king Charles X, a brother of Louis XVI, has likewise drawn attention.[2] Modern studies that take revolutionary-age ritual into account exist for other countries.[3] That monarchy remained the prevalent form of government in Europe underscores the continuing relevance of pageant as well.[4] Ritual and (invented) tradition retained significance in times of rapid change. Inaugural rites in all of their rich variety proved as compatible with modern forms of despotic or constitutional monarchy as with older forms of political order.

Yet perhaps the most remarkable concentration of such rites under one government has largely escaped notice. In the half-century after 1790, Habsburg rulers and their consorts personally absolved more than two dozen inaugural rites—from the solemn act of homage (*Erbhuldigung*) rendered to Leopold II as Austrian archduke in 1790 to the coronation of Ferdinand I as king of Lombardy-Venetia in 1838 (see table 9.1).[5] With the possible exception of the celebrations surrounding the Congress of Vienna, these ceremonies surely constituted the outstanding displays of imperial and royal pomp across three reigns: Leopold II (1790–92); Francis II, later Francis I (1792–1835); and Ferdinand I (1835–48). Of the twenty-six rites under consideration, fifteen were coronations and eleven were acts of homage. A total of twenty-four spectacles involved hereditary or newly (re-)acquired dynastic lands, while two concerned the coronation of an elected Roman emperor. There were six coronations of queen consorts, strikingly including a Bohemian one near the beginning of every reign. The coronation of a fourth Bohemian queen (the third wife of Francis I) did not get beyond the planning stage.[6] Three of Francis' four wives were crowned queen of Hungary. By contrast, those ceremonies that did not transpire in the ruler's personal presence do not appear in the table, though they too belong in the broader picture, especially when a member of the dynasty deputized for an absent monarch. For example, in 1790, the archduchess Maria Elisabeth stood in for Leopold II in Tyrol; in 1815, the archduke John, for the emperor Francis in Lombardy-Venetia; and in 1837, the archduke Ferdinand, for the emperor of the same name in Transylvania.[7]

Following a brief historical introduction, this chapter will explore the meaning and implications of Habsburg inaugural pageantry between 1790 and 1848 on the basis of a discussion of four specific cases: (1) Leopold II's Lower Austrian inauguration of 1790 in Vienna; (2) the coronation of Maria Ludovica of Austria-Este, the third wife of the emperor Francis, as queen of Hungary in 1808 in Pressburg; (3) Francis I's Tyrolian inauguration of 1816 in Innsbruck; and (4) Ferdinand I's Lombardo-Venetian coronation of 1838 in Milan. The evidence in connection with these events shows how Habsburg rulers rose to the challenges of the revolutionary age in ways that were not merely backward looking. Though Austria—like Great Britain and Russia—did not undergo political upheaval in its core lands, the French revolution also forced its rulers "continuously to make certain of their legitimacy and where necessary to develop strategies to adapt to social change."[8] It will be argued here that the arrangements in connection with these rites illustrate how the Habsburg government was endeavoring to expand its political base from the older, status-based Estates to the broader propertied interest in an agriculture-based monarchy; to rally popular-patriotic sentiment in a new key, also to meet foreign challenges; to manage regional diversity in a large composite state in a feasible way; and to lend legitimacy to novel, written forms of constitutional order. The search for stability in the revolutionary age involved adjustment to the times rather than the mere preservation or even resurrection of

Table 9.1. Inaugural rites personally undergone by Habsburg rulers or their consorts, 1790–1848

	Date	Ruler or Consort	Territory	Rite	Place
1	6 Apr. 1790	Leopold II	Lower Austria	act of homage (archduke)	Vienna
2	9 Oct. 1790	Leopold II	Holy Roman Empire	coronation (emperor)	Frankfurt am Main
3	15 Nov. 1790	Leopold II	Hungary	coronation (king)	Pressburg
4	4 Sept. 1791	Leopold II	Bohemia	act of homage (king)	Prague
5	6 Sept. 1791	Leopold II	Bohemia	coronation (king)	Prague
6	12 Sept. 1791	Marie Louise of Spain	Bohemia	coronation (queen)	Prague
7	25 Apr. 1792	Francis II	Lower Austria	act of homage (archduke)	Vienna
8	6 June 1792	Francis II (I)	Hungary	coronation (king)	Buda
9	10 June 1792	Maria Theresa of the Two Sicilies	Hungary	coronation (queen)	Buda
10	14 July 1792	Francis II	Holy Roman Empire	coronation (emperor)	Frankfurt am Main
11	7 Aug. 1792	Francis II (I)	Bohemia	act of homage (king)	Prague
12	9 Aug. 1792	Francis II (I)	Bohemia	coronation (king)	Prague
13	11 Aug. 1792	Maria Theresa of the Two Sicilies	Bohemia	coronation (queen)	Prague
14	23 May 1794	Francis II	Brabant/Limburg	act of homage (duke)	Brussels
15	7 Sept. 1808	Maria Ludovica of Austria-Este	Hungary	coronation (queen)	Pressburg
16	30 May 1816	Francis I	Tyrol, Vorarlberg	act of homage	Innsbruck
17	12 June 1816	Francis I	Salzburg, Inn- und Hausruckviertel	act of homage	Salzburg
18	25 Sept. 1825	Caroline Augusta of Bavaria	Hungary	coronation (queen)	Pressburg
19	28 Sept. 1830	Ferdinand I (V)	Hungary	coronation (king)	Pressburg
20	14 June 1835	Ferdinand I	Lower Austria	act of homage (archduke)	Vienna
21	3 Sept. 1836	Ferdinand I (V)	Bohemia	act of homage (king)	Prague
22	7 Sept. 1836	Ferdinand I (V)	Bohemia	coronation (king)	Prague
23	12 Sept. 1836	Maria Anna of Savoy	Bohemia	coronation (queen)	Prague
24	12 Aug. 1838	Ferdinand I	Tyrol, Vorarlberg	act of homage	Innsbruck
25	3 Sept. 1838	Ferdinand I	Lombardy-Venetia	act of homage	Milan
26	6 Sept. 1838	Ferdinand I	Lombardy-Venetia	coronation (king)	Milan

the past.⁹ To the extent possible, the perspectives of participants and spectators other than the rulers will be taken into consideration.

The inauguration of Leopold II in 1790 in Lower Austria was the first such ceremony to have taken place in the Habsburg lands since the 1740s, when Maria Theresa personally underwent four rites in all. At that time, their political significance derived from the exceptional circumstance of a woman assuming power following the extinction of the dynasty's male line. Her reign's first rite—the Lower Austrian inauguration—was staged comparatively quickly. One of Maria Theresa's first acts was to schedule it. Within a month, it followed.¹⁰ Similarly, her government employed inaugural ritual to consolidate control after lands that had fallen under foreign rule were retaken. The coronation in Prague and inauguration in Linz, both in 1743, were cases in point.¹¹ The acquisition of territories later in the reign also entailed inaugural rites, if not in the empress's personal presence. In 1777, the local clergy and nobility (and possibly other landowners) assembled at Czernowitz for an act of homage as a consequence of the annexation of Bukovina from the Ottoman Empire a few years earlier.¹²

Until not long ago, the influence of enlightened forms of rationalism was thought to have robbed what was already mere "baroque" show of whatever meaning it might have preserved after the triumph of "absolutism."¹³ In the French context, this thesis perhaps retains some plausibility. Louis XVI's coronation did not reverse the ongoing desacralization of the monarchy in France.¹⁴ The course of action—or inaction—of Maria Theresa's son, co-ruler, and heir, the emperor Joseph II, would seem to confirm the thesis as well. Famously, he failed to submit to inaugural rites except for his coronation as king of the Romans in 1764.¹⁵ In the Habsburg case, it seems nonetheless safe to assume that inaugural rites had not become anachronistic, even if Joseph personally found them outlandish. He was clearly aware of the meaning they retained for large numbers of his subjects. We might recall that he was already fantasizing soon after the Seven Years' War about despotic power for the purpose of carrying out sweeping reform.¹⁶ Such power gainsaid the guarantee of legal order that inaugural rites in an estates-based society entailed. Ceremonial customs and forms gave that order visible expression. Joseph's disregard was an attempt "to break the symbolic spine" of that order.¹⁷ He was aiming for greater freedom of political maneuver from the start of his personal rule.

In the event, Joseph's rejection of coronations and inaugurations in his patrimonial lands only heightened their appeal.¹⁸ His successor, Leopold II, was furthermore a principled opponent of despotic rule. Leopold underwent a series of inaugural rites that followed the pattern apparent in outline earlier in the century; it was the one to which his two successors would also adhere. Each would be invested in the central territory of each of the three core groups of Habsburg lands: (1) the Lower Austrian act of homage in Vienna; (2) the Bohemian act of homage/coronation in Prague; and (3) the Hungarian coronation whose location varied over time. Francis II experienced all of these rites as well as the imperial coronation within less than four months. His father's comparatively recent submission to precisely those same rites and the financial constraints imposed by the wars since the late 1780s together put a premium on cost-savings in their staging.[19] Later, Francis was additionally inaugurated as duke of Brabant and Limburg; as count of Tyrol and ruler of Vorarlberg; and as duke of Salzburg and ruler of the Inn- and Hausruck districts. The events of the revolutionary period explain all of these latter rituals.

The revival and then survival of a diverse palette of inaugural rites across the revolutionary era might suggest political stasis or even reaction or dilapidation, all labels that have been applied with relish to the Habsburg Monarchy at this time. Yet a closer look reveals how Habsburg political culture was adapting to changing circumstances. The historian David Cannadine has called attention to the fact that the sense of ritual derives in the first place from the historical setting rather than from any possibly unchanging nature of that ritual:

> So, in order to rediscover the "meaning" of royal ritual during the modern period, it is necessary to relate it to the specific social, political, economic, and cultural milieu within which it was actually performed. . . . For clearly, even if the text of a repeated ritual like a coronation remains unaltered over time, its "meaning" may change profoundly depending on the nature of the context.[20]

Indeed the ritual itself was hardly immutable. The Habsburg court staged rites of longer historical standing, such as the Lower Austrian act of homage or the Hungarian coronation, which changed over time. It also mounted ceremonial performances, such as the inauguration in Tyrol in 1816, that are best regarded in the light of Eric Hobsbawm's celebrated notion of "invented tradition."[21] The government also created novel ceremonies that were not meant to conjure up the past—the most impressive of which was the coronation in Lombardy-Venetia.

If we take into consideration the entirety of the rites performed over the half-century after 1790, we can of course detect "recurring" semiotic messages. The holy oil that was a part of every coronation rite undergone by a Habsburg conveyed the dynasty's continuing Roman Catholic commitment. At the same time, the Habsburgs had never employed inaugural rites to arrogate unto themselves a sacred aura, as the Bourbons of France had done. There was no discernable attempt to do so after 1790 in the manner of "reaction." The consistent adherence to the rite of unction even so set Habsburg rulers apart from Protestant ones and also distinguished them from Napoleon, the heir to the French revolution who himself was increasingly at odds with the pope and Roman hierarchy. In 1701, the first Prussian king was crowned and anointed in ceremonies that were spatially and temporally distinct. The unction possessed "an absolutely secondary significance."[22] Napoleon, citing the holy oil he had received at the coronation in Paris, declined it at Milan in 1805.[23]

Like the English coronation, Habsburg inaugural rites highlighted the issue of political order, most particularly the relationship between monarch and (privileged) subjects. Here, the practice differed from the French or Prussian one as well.[24] The councils of power in Vienna attached immanent importance to the supposedly consensual nature of dominion, a political maxim in the realms over which the dynasty presided, including the Holy Roman Empire.[25] An effort was accordingly made to display consensus at every inaugural rite. This required that the territory concerned be "represented" on the occasion in question. Ruler and ruled were juxtaposed. Though scholars long accepted the idea of an enduring policy of "absolutist" rollback toward the Estates in the Habsburg lands, the inaugural practices betrayed consistent heedfulness that the local elites appear in an organized, corporate way, one that elevated them as well. For the coronation in 1808, the emperor Francis directed that the Hungarian Estates receive appropriate seating on the revealing reasoning that the rites "properly concerned them."[26] The leading representative of those elites—the palatine in Hungary or the grand burgrave in Bohemia—assisted in the actual act of crowning. This custom too had no equivalent in Prussia or France. Frederick I and Napoleon set the crowns on their own heads.[27]

Still, each inaugural rite performed between 1790 and 1838 must be examined in its own time. Even "recurring" messages may acquire a new tenor. The historian Christopher Clark has helpfully referred to the Prussian coronation of 1701 as a "politico-cultural artefact designed to convey a specific set of meanings" embedded in time and place.[28] The same label may usefully be applied to each rite that took place in the Habsburg Monarchy between 1790 and 1838. We also should keep in mind that the significance of ritual depended upon perspective, and hence was "inherently ambiguous."[29] Concrete political content—as opposed to simplified truths—was difficult for those in power to convey, while participants and witnesses might impute their own meanings to what they had experienced. As the scholar David I. Kertzer has argued, it was less the intellectual than the emotional appeal of exercises that made "symbols salient and promote[d] attachment to them."[30] In the inaugural rites under consideration here, rulers and ruled found themselves face-to-face for the first time—an often dramatic moment.

Let us turn first to the Lower Austrian inauguration. From his predecessor Joseph II, Leopold II had inherited a monarchy in "crisis in west and east."[31] In alliance with Russia, Austria was mired in the third year of a grueling Balkan war with the Ottoman Empire. In the Austrian Netherlands, Joseph's policies had triggered an armed revolt that put an end to Habsburg rule. This disaster occurred with the connivance of Prussia, a power that was trying to capitalize on Habsburg troubles to secure gains in Poland. Those troubles included the internal unrest caused by reform activity in other parts of the monarchy, including Tyrol and Hungary. Even in those lands where the concurrence of interests between government and elites was traditionally strongest, as in Lower Austria, protests by the Estates marked the final months of Joseph's reign.³² Only in his last weeks did the beleaguered emperor attempt to pacify the situation by sacrificing portions of his reform program.³³ It would fall to his brother and successor, however, to restore the regime's internal footing and foreign balance.

The Lower Austrian act of homage on 6 April 1790 was Leopold's first great symbolic gesture to achieve those closely interrelated goals. As a classical exponent of what the historian Michael Broers has called the "conservative enlightenment," Leopold sought progress primarily within existing structures.³⁴ He stood for the consensual form of rule that his immediate predecessor had abandoned. Leopold accepted the territorial Estates as a key element of the political order—he had been dismayed by Joseph's assault on them—even as he advocated the idea that they should reflect changing socioeconomic conditions and physiocratic ideas of good governance.³⁵ After Joseph's death, Leopold began sending out conciliatory signals to the politically discontented—the landed interest that was his monarchy's political backbone. As he traveled north to his new capital from Florence, where he had been an enlightened grand duke with a European reputation, he met with delegations of the Estates of the lands through which he passed. He also let it be known that he would be crowned king of Hungary. Four days after his arrival in Vienna on 12 March 1790, he received a deputation of the Lower Austrian Estates, the financially potent intermediary corps of the monarchy's central province. Though Joseph's highly unpopular tax and labor services reform was the meeting's pretext Leopold told the Estates that he considered the "suspension" of their "constitution" to be "a greater, more damaging ill."³⁶ He invited them to compile a list of their grievances. Traditionally, the right of remonstration was exercised in connection with the inauguration.

Leopold's claims to the inheritance were not in question, but the speed with which the investiture took place nonetheless pointed up the high importance attributed to it. Indeed, it was staged even more quickly than in Maria Theresa's day if we recall that he did not arrive in his new capital until the second week of March and the inauguration occurred in the first week of April. Seen another way, nearly a month passed in 1740 between official notification that the rite would occur and the event itself, whereas in 1790, only two weeks elapsed.³⁷ A committee consisting of high-ranking representatives from the government and Estates worked out the ritual that was to underlie the solemnities.³⁸ The inaugurations of Charles VI and Maria Theresa offered the main precedents. Though a host of specific issues were discussed, the meeting's ultimate significance derived from the ceremonial consensus achieved. The organization was agreed among the parties involved rather than imposed from above. In the meanwhile, the Estates had begun compiling their grievances.

The act of homage was embedded in a series of carefully staged rites. The day itself began with a public procession by the Estates from the Landhaus to the Hofburg, followed by a procession of Leopold, his court, and the Estates to St. Stephen's Cathedral for a mass of the Holy Spirit. After returning to the palace in the same order, Leopold soon appeared on a dais in the "great hall," the Estates arrayed before him. Following an address by Grand Aulic Chancellor Kolowrat, *Landmarschall* Pergen as head of the Estates spoke of the "trust" that Leopold had already secured from the "peoples over whom he was in future to rule," a statement that was remarkable both on account of the fact that he was already ruling and the inference that the monarch needed his subjects' confidence.[39] The king himself, as Leopold was called before his election to the imperial dignity, then guaranteed the "privileges, freedoms, usages, rights, and immunities" of the Estates.[40] As the church bells across the city pealed, the Estates in their turn swore the oath of fealty.[41] In keeping with custom, Leopold spoke the guarantee before the Estates made their pledge. After the oath, the grand aulic chancellor handed over a written version of the guarantee signed by Leopold as archduke. The participants then attended a service of thanksgiving (*Te Deum*) in the Hofburg Chapel. A banquet concluded the festivities.

The following day, another highly emblematic gesture emphasized the distance that Leopold II placed between himself and his predecessor's methods of government. The jewel-encrusted, ermine-lined "archducal hat" (*Erzherzogshut*), which was always present as a symbol at the investiture though it was not worn like a crown, was returned to the abbey of Klosterneuburg, where it had customarily been kept. In 1784, Joseph II had famously had the hat as well as the crowns of Bohemia and Hungary removed from their historic places of safekeeping and deposited in his treasury in Vienna. The signal was clear: any pretense that he would undergo inaugural rites ceased.[42] Scholars have shown that inaugural ritual at a time before the advent of written fundamental laws signified a kind of unwritten constitution.[43] The performance of ritual "enacted" the overriding legal order both as a set of existing sociopolitical arrangements and as an ideal. Ritual referred to and derived its meaning from that order. Hence, constitutional order, social hierarchy, and ceremonial practice were not clearly distinguishable. Joseph's rejection of the latter signified a rejection of the others, though his actual policy proved less radical in the archduchy than in Hungary, for example. For financial reasons, he was forced to convoke the Lower Austrian diet annually, whereas he never called the Hungarian one and for a time suspended the noble county assemblies in that kingdom as well. As long as the ritualized assemblies in Lower Austria took place, the Estates, however browbeaten, still existed in the understanding of the day.[44]

Leopold II's inauguration in Vienna revitalized an unwritten legal order embodied by the ceremonial hierarchy on display. In their official history of the occurrence, the Estates characterized the meaning as follows: "The current celebration of the act of homage ... betokens the revival of the estates-based constitution, which is inseparable from the weal of a monarchical state."[45] In this sense, the rite not only "demonstrated" consensus;⁴⁶ its preparation and performance were meant to "restore" consensus following the conflict of Joseph's reign. Still, the precise outlines of the reestablished order remained ambiguous, the expectations of the participants diverse. Some historians have highlighted the circumstance that political ritual invariably takes place within a social context of "disharmony" or dissent. To quote Edward Muir, "States exist precisely because people do not seem to be able to get along among themselves without them."⁴⁷ From this point of view, ritual papers over difference, creates the impression of harmony, and legitimates hegemony through an appeal to emotion.⁴⁸

In 1790, tears of joy and rapture are invariably recorded as accompanying Leopold's contacts and exchanges with the Estates.⁴⁹ For the moment, these emotions concealed the grievances that remained unresolved at the time of the inauguration. The main compilation would not be handed over until after the event. In time, one key demand of the Estates—the restoration of their right to privileged jurisdiction in criminal matters—would be rejected by both Leopold and his successor. A number of dispositions in connection with the investiture reveal that a constitutional order was being recreated without simply putting the clock back. The bishop of St. Pölten, a Josephian creation, assumed the ceremonial place formerly reserved to the bishop of Wiener Neustadt.⁵⁰ Following the pledge of fealty on 6 April, the bishop intoned the *Te Deum* in the Hofburg Chapel. Hence, Joseph's sweeping reform of the Church was given symbolic expression in the act of constitutional renewal. The changing times were apparent in other ways. Leopold increased the number of representatives that the city of Vienna could send to the inauguration on the revealing grounds "that the current constitution is very different to the previous one."⁵¹ He was attempting to reconcile the rising importance of urban areas to the still-dominant rural and manorial world that the other Estates embodied.

Whatever the actual ingredients of the "unwritten constitution," its swift enactment by a monarch well known for his enlightened attachment to consensus and representation sent a signal far beyond the archduchy's borders. Geographically and financially, Lower Austria was a vital Habsburg possession, and its capital, Vienna, was the imperial residence and political nerve center. In contemporary parlance, Lower Austria figured as the monarchy's "motherland."⁵² The investiture occasioned the expression of broader forms of Austrian patriotism that appear to have overshadowed specifically territorial loyalties.⁵³ Vienna was a cosmopolitan city filled with people from across the monarchy, many of whom witnessed the celebrations. One Austro-Bohemian countess later recorded the impressions she gained from events witnessed first from a window along the processional route and later from the gallery reserved to ladies in the Hofburg's great hall.⁵⁴ On the day after the inauguration, one of the Austrian Netherlands' leading noblemen, the celebrated Prince de Ligne, reported from Vienna that there "has never been a finer start to a Reign. Every day is marked by a new benefaction or by the righting of an injustice."⁵⁵ As the news radiated outward, another magnate from the Austrian Netherlands, the duke of Arenberg, rallied from his place of exile in revolutionary Paris to "the moderate government on offer by Leopold II."⁵⁶ The Whiggish duke had participated in the uprising in the Netherlands against Joseph II.

Where inaugural rites in the Habsburg context are typically interpreted as a form of territorial particularism, the scholar David I. Kertzer's work on ritual suggests how we might understand them in a different way—without negating other possible meanings. According to Kertzer, all large-scale structures face the problem of how "to integrate local activity into the higher organizational level."⁵⁷ The Habsburg composite polity continually had to meet that very challenge. Perhaps paradoxically, the staging of the surviving inaugural rites offered ways of symbolically anchoring the territorial-particular into the monarchical whole. The commemorative coins minted on the occasion of the act of homage of 1790, closely modeled on those of earlier reigns, carried an iconographic message that located Austria within the wider Habsburg context. On the obverse side, the Bohemian lion grasps the Hungarian cross in one paw, the Austrian heraldic shield in the other. On the reverse, the archducal hat is depicted with the inscription: "Leopoldo II Hungariae, Bohemiae, Galic[iae], Lodom[eriae] Etc. Regi Archiduci Austriae Homagium praest[itum] Viennae 6 Apr[il] 1790" (see figure 9.1).⁵⁸ If the inaugural rites demonstrated that the archduchy retained a specific identity, the circumstances also revealed that it had become an irrevocable part of the larger Austrian Monarchy.

The constellation of persons present by right or invitation manifested the idea in a different way. The Estates received the written confirmation of their privileges out of the hands of Grand Aulic Chancellor Kolowrat, a Bohemian grandee

Figure 9.1. Silver commemorative coin from the Lower Austrian act of homage of Leopold II, 1790 (Vienna, Kunsthistorisches Museum, Coin Cabinet, inv. no. 000484ab).

who headed the principal ministry for domestic affairs (*Vereinigte Hofstelle*) that was itself an institutional product of the amalgamating reforms of the previous generation. There was no longer a specifically Austrian chancellery. Similarly, the holders of the grand cross of the Order of St. Stephen, a Hungarian honor, and the knights of the Golden Fleece, a dynastic order whose bearers (including the Prince de Ligne) came from all over the monarchy, had assigned places in the solemnities.[59] The nobility of the Lower Austrian Estates possessed myriad ties of blood and friendship across borders, ones clearly apparent during the inaugural rites. The young Count Rudolph Czernin, the heir to one of Bohemia's great lineages, stood in as acting "hereditary grand territorial steward" (*Oberstersblandtruchseß*) for his father-in-law, Count Eugen Erwein Schönborn-Buchheim, a member of the Estates and himself the scion of a transterritorial house. Czernin bore the orb during the proceedings. As grand chamberlain, he would be one of the planners of the Lombardo-Venetian coronation almost a half-century later.

The coronation of the empress Maria Ludovica as queen of Hungary in September 1808 took place against a domestic and foreign background much different to eighteen years earlier. In the west, a new hegemonic power in the guise of Napoleonic France now appeared to threaten the Habsburg Monarchy, whose contours had mutated strikingly as a consequence of the wars since the 1790s. At the Battle of Austerlitz in 1805, Napoleon had displayed not only his own genius but also his regime's stunning military-administrative capacities. The following year, he almost annihilated Prussia on the battlefield. At the famous encounter at Tilsit in 1807, the Russian czar acknowledged Napoleon as a "pan-European superpower."[60] Through an economic blockade of Britain, Napoleon aimed to control the continent's entire coastline. But it would be his attempted subjugation of Spain and dethronement of the Spanish royal house in 1808 that convinced the Habsburgs that the Corsican was bent on their destruction. In response, the government in Vienna launched a concerted effort to harness popular patriotism across the monarchy and other parts of central Europe outside the Habsburg realms in the aid of the planned renewal of war.[61] It was an operation commensurate with the monarchy's composite structure and thoroughly in the spirit of the times.

The strategy employed in Hungary paralleled the one used in the dynasty's other lands; the kingdom was not left "out of the reckoning," as is sometimes thought.[62] To be sure, skepticism had met the idea of calling the occasionally intractable Hungarian diet at such a critical juncture.[63] Only the previous year, it had balked at most official demands. Yet the archduke-palatine, the king's representative in the Hungarian capital of Buda, argued that a coronation diet staged around Francis's consort offered a chance to muster the kingdom for the contest with Napoleon.[64] Francis himself had been crowned in Buda in 1792 in one of several inaugural rites to which he submitted to cover his domestic base following revolutionary France's declaration of war.[65] In January 1808, Maria Ludovica, who belonged to a conveniently anti-Napoleonic family driven out of its Italian homeland by the French occupation, became his third wife. Though she played no discernable part in planning her coronation in Hungary, she was hardly a marionette. In the course of the same year, she was to become a leading exponent of the "war party" at the court of Vienna.[66]

A queen-consort's coronation had specific political advantages.[67] It raised fewer tricky legal issues than crowning a king. She was not the country's ruler under the laws of succession. There was no need for an inaugural diploma whose negotiation might result in new limits on royal power. The rite nonetheless spectacularly evoked the very legal and social order perceived as under threat by Napoleon. In times of past peril, the coronation of a consort had drawn king and country together. In the 1620s, the coronation of the elder Eleonora of Mantua had sealed the compromise achieved between her husband, Ferdinand II, and the Hungarian Estates following the suppression of an uprising led by Gabriel Bethlen.[68] The plan for Maria Ludovica's installation laid consensual groundwork ahead of the diet. In 1808, the office of the grand master of Francis's court carefully worked with the principal local authority—the Hungarian Chancellery—in planning the event. *Obersthofmeister* Trauttmansdorff met personally with Chancellor Erdődy to discuss matters ranging from how the bishop of Veszprém was to crown the queen to whether she would wear a crown during the coronation banquet. When the two parties disagreed, the matter went to Francis personally. In the question of who would bear the sword of state at the diet's opening, he opted for the dignitary known as the *agazonum regalium magister* (master of the horse) over the grand marshal because "the [Hungarian] nation attaches special importance to it."[69] The precedents consulted for the festivities included the diet of 1802 and the coronations of 1790, 1714, and 1655.[70] Leaving nothing to chance, the government strove to ensure the election to the diet of well-disposed deputies.[71]

The coronation was integrated into a series of events that marked the diet's opening in the presence of the king, itself a ceremonial happening of the first rank.[72] The transfer on 26 August of the St. Stephen's Crown to Pressburg from its place of safekeeping at Buda constituted one rite that had a compelling tie to the coronation. The Estates gathered for the first time on the 28th. On 1 September at Schloss Hof, a baroque hunting lodge erected for Prince Eugene almost within sight of Pressburg on the Lower Austrian side of the border, Francis and Maria Ludovica received a deputation of the Estates. The next day, the pair encountered the Estates collectively just outside Pressburg. A solemn entry into the city and *Te Deum* in the Trinitarian Church followed the meeting. The royal couple took up residence in the Grassalkovich Palace, a sumptuous rococo edifice situated just outside the old town. On 3 September, the singing of the *Veni Sancte Spiritus* in the chapel of the Hungarian primate's palace preceded the opening of the diet in the great hall of the same building. In an address to the assembly, Francis strongly appealed to his listeners' patriotism, adeptly linking its Hungarian and dynastic aspects. Only in alliance with the House of Austria, he proclaimed, could Hungary expect to maintain its laws and privileges. The Estates well understood the allusion to the Napoleonic menace: "Your constitution comprises your fame and your happiness. I am no less proud to call myself your king. Strive to remain Hungarians and to uphold your admirable national qualities. Direct your efforts at ensuring the perpetuation of the fatherland for all time."[73] The impact was almost immediate. A few hours later, they reassembled before the throne with the promise to do all in their power to ensure the country's safety and defense.

The coronation itself ensued on 7 September. For the procession to St. Martin's Cathedral, Francis appeared in a field marshal's uniform adjusted in the Hungarian manner, his wife in Hungarian costume and headdress.[74] Upon arrival, he put on the St. Stephen's Crown and Mantle, while she assumed a diadem (not clearly identified in the sources) because the "house crown" was "too heavy."[75] This was the first of three crowns in use during the ceremony.[76] There had been uncertainty at the planning stage about which crown to employ for the actual coronation. Hungarian queen-consorts of this period were notably not crowned with the St. Stephen's Crown, but rather with the most magnificent dynastic diadem, the so-called "house crown" (also known as the Crown of Rudolf II). Yet after assuming the Austrian imperial dignity in 1804, Francis had designated that crown as the "Austrian imperial crown." Neither he nor his wife had admittedly ever been crowned with it. In the event, it would now be used to crown Maria Ludovica as queen of Hungary.

Once the royal pair had moved in state toward the high altar and the service was underway, Francis formally demanded of the Hungarian primate—his wife's older brother Charles of Austria-Este, archbishop of Esztergom—that Maria Ludovica be crowned. At this point, the queen's *Oberthofmeister*, Count Franz Althann, removed from her head the diadem that she had assumed upon entering the church, while the crown of St. Stephen was transferred from Francis's head to the high altar. Charles then applied the holy oil to his sister's right arm and between the shoulder blades. Thus anointed, she was prepared for investiture with the regalia and enthronement. The prelate who possessed the historic right to crown the queen of Hungary, the bishop of Veszprém, placed the "house crown" on her head. The archduke-palatine—a younger brother of Francis—then handed the crown of St. Stephen to the primate. The greatest peculiarity of the Hungarian ritual followed: the kingdom's highest-ranking ecclesiastical and secular dignitaries, the primate and the palatine, together rested the crown briefly on the queen's right shoulder in accordance with tradition. With the assistance of the court official known as the *magister curiae*, the palatine then returned the relic to the king's head. Carrying the scepter and the orb, the queen proceeded in state to her throne amid the sound of trumpets and kettledrums and cries of "vivat." The concluding *Te Deum* had a personal touch as Francis had requested that the music composed by *Vizehofkapellmeister* Eybler for his marriage to Maria Ludovica be performed on this occasion as well.[77]

At the coronation banquet attended by hundreds of guests, the king and queen circulated among the tables, a highly unusual gesture of esteem. They halted where the "barons and magnates" were seated to toast first the health of the Estates and then the "fame of the Hungarian nation."[78] Later in the day, the celebrations shifted into Pressburg's streets and open spaces with a shooting competition, an illumination, and fireworks.[79] While the many allusions to the Hungarian "nation" might tempt us to view this coronation through the lens of territorial particularism, it in fact constituted a contemporary patriotic festival staged as part of the wider campaign across the Habsburg monarchy and elsewhere in central Europe. The powerful mix of patriotisms in other places underlay, as we know, the famous revolt in Bavarian-occupied Tyrol and the establishment of a new provincial militia (*Landwehr*) in the Bohemian and Austrian lands.[80] In Hungary, the fusion of dynastic and national feeling apparent at the coronation produced a comparable outcome. The wider monarchy beyond Hungary was in evidence in Pressburg much as it had been at the Lower Austrian inauguration in 1790. The knights of the Golden Fleece and the Military-Maria-Theresa-Order, whose holders were officers of the standing army, marched in the procession within the cathedral. The head of the empress-queen's household, Count Althann, an aristocrat of Austrian background, attended her throughout the ceremony. He led her to her throne after she had been crowned.

One of the leading exponents of popular-patriotic mobilization for war, Foreign Minister Stadion, who had been doubtful about the success of the exercise, was also present in Pressburg.[81] By all accounts, the diet proved a brilliant political coup, demonstrating how seemingly unchanging territorial ritual could be adapted to present challenges and the broader Habsburg cause. The diet took the occasion of the newly crowned queen's name day to concede the government's demands, going beyond them, in fact, to grant unprecedented three-year powers in respect of the territorial militia, the so-called "insurrection." Twenty thousand recruits for the Hungarian regiments of the Habsburg standing army were also approved.[82] In this way, the use of emotionally charged ritual contributed to integrating local (Hungarian) activity into the higher organizational level (of the monarchy). The close alliance of dynasty and nation manifest in 1808 would survive the battlefield defeat of 1809. The Hungarians turned a deaf ear to Napoleon's attempt to play them against the rest of the Habsburg patrimony.[83]

Where the Hungarian coronation transpired in the run-up to the war of 1809, the Tyrolian inauguration of 1816 was ultimately a consequence. One of the House of Austria's oldest possessions, the Alpine county of Tyrol had passed to France's ally Bavaria by the peace of Pressburg following the shattering defeat at Austerlitz in 1805. In the following years, Bavaria attempted to integrate Tyrol into its new unitary state being built under French influence. The old order was abolished. The result was the counter-revolutionary uprising that would be the most conspicuous expression of the potent mixture of Habsburg-dynastic and provincial loyalties in 1809. Because its suppression required his assistance, Napoleon took the Italian-speaking parts of Tyrol away from Bavaria and attached them to his own kingdom of Italy.[84] As the conqueror's own defeat began to take shape in the fall of 1813, Bavaria bought its way into the ranks of his enemies by promising to restore Tyrol and other lands to Austria once peace returned.[85] Habsburg troops would occupy the Italian parts of Tyrol while the war was still on.

The deep hatred the Napoleonic-style states had engendered in Tyrol, as well as outrage because the occupying Austrians did not immediately dismantle them, inspired recurrent petitions and protests by the local elites in favor of a return to the former "constitution." Just before the Congress of Vienna met, emperor Francis received a group of deputies from Tyrol and Vorarlberg who had come to make their wishes known. Though he avoided making specific promises, he did proudly reply: "the devotion of Tyrol to My House has become the model of popular loyalty in Europe."[86] At the congress itself, a consensus prevailed among the leading participants, both liberal and conservative—including Austria—that the peace settlement must provide for constitutions in places where they did not obtain. In addition to staving off a renewal of revolutionary upheaval, the authorities felt themselves to be in line with broader sentiment. The result was what a recent scholar has labeled "one of the greatest waves of constitutional establishments in European history."[87] Over the following century, "monarchical constitutionalism" would be the most widely practiced form of government in Europe.[88] Even as the congress was still in session, the new kingdom of Lombardy-Venetia received the first of what would be four constitutional patents issued in Habsburg-ruled lands. Tyrol followed in 1316, Galicia in 1817, and Carniola in 1818.

In the opening line of the one promulgated for Tyrol on 24 March 1816, some two months before the inauguration at the end of May, the emperor cited the "manifold merits and the generous patriotic sentiments of the honest inhabitants" in his decision to "establish" the estates-based constitution that had been abrogated by the Bavarians.[89] Yet the very same passage reveals that he was not reviving the old regime.[90] The Congress of Vienna had been concerned with ensuring legal order between and within viable states for the purpose of containing France. The use of the word "establish" rather than "reestablish" in reference to the new Tyrolian constitution was itself illuminating. While based on historic "privileges" and "liberties," that constitution contained in its own words "those improvements which the changed conditions and the needs of the time" demanded. The form itself indicated that no older order was undergoing simple revival. As a *written* document, this new basic law recalled the charter famously issued by Louis XVIII under his own authority upon his return to France in 1814. In the closing section of the patent, Francis promised to submit to a solemn act of homage once the deputies to the planned assembly had been elected. Here again we detect the central role reserved to the relationship between ruler and local elites in Habsburg inaugural rites.

Coming from Italy, the emperor arrived in Innsbruck on 27 May 1816. The investiture—the first for Francis in Tyrol—took place three days later. Charles VI was the last ruler to have been personally inaugurated there (1711). Because of the changed constitutional parameters, the ceremony of 1816 possessed a quality fundamentally different to previous ones or to the rites that survived in lands such as Lower Austria or Hungary that had not been revolutionized. These retained their unwritten constitutions. The sources indicate, to be sure, that Francis's Tyrolian inauguration bore outward similarities to earlier usages.[91] Yet there were key differences in planning and detail. The Estates were not involved in organizing the event, which the court's master of ceremonies, Count Heinrich Wurmbrand, undertook in conjunction with the governor of Tyrol. To ensure greater public visibility of the spectacle, the celebratory mass preceding the act of homage took place in the parish church of St. Jacob rather than the more traditional *Hofkirche*, a circumstance that required a longer processional route through urban space.[92] Most importantly, the ceremony did not "enact" a legal order in the former sense. The new, written constitution already provided for that order; hence, it did not have to be called ceremonially into being.[93] In his address to the representatives of the Estates assembled for the inauguration, Francis referred to the promulgation that had already taken place: "I have restored to the land of Tyrol a constitution appropriate to its needs and the conditions of the times."[94] He did not formally promise to uphold provincial privileges, nor did he utter an oath. For their part, the deputies swore fidelity to the "emperor of Austria" rather than the "count of Tyrol"—an act impossible before the creation of the imperial dignity in 1804.[95]

The seemingly time-honored forms as well as the general elation helped obscure how the present differed from the past. Again, inaugural ritual created ambiguity as well as clarity. After the dislocations of the Napoleonic era, all major participants appear to have collaborated in what was in effect a sleight of hand. In the very first line of the program drawn up for the inaugural fete, the authorities evoked the precedent of Charles VI.[96] Francis himself spoke of the "renewal of the tie that for hundreds of years had bound this people to My House," as if that tie had not undergone irrevocable transformation.[97] The inauguration of 1816 was a classic case of the "invention of tradition," a phenomenon perhaps most common when rapid change has destroyed the patterns for which older traditions had been designed.[98] Francis's investiture created the comforting illusion that the past had been recaptured. It was what the scholar Kertzer referred to in another context as a "re-elaboration of old symbols to meet changing political reality."[99]

In the eighteenth century, enlightened commentators had pointed up the potential inherent in public festivities for national–patriotic purposes. The idea quickly translated to the public ceremonial that was an inherent aspect of monarchy. The problem of inaugural rites and legitimacy had already occupied the practitioners of the ceremonial sciences. In the revolutionary age, popularly staged festivals offered a new font of ideological validity to monarchy.[100] It was Francis's reign that appears to have marked a turning point in the Habsburg use of inaugural ritual for purposes of wider (popular) legitimacy. As early as 1792, a "people's celebration" was planned as part of his coronation as king of Bohemia, whereas this had not been the case only the previous year at Leopold II's coronation in Prague.[101] The outbreak of the war with revolutionary France noticeably separated the two events. The popular–patriotic mobilization of the Stadion years inspired, as we have seen, the Hungarian coronation of 1808.

The Tyrolian rite of 1816 lifted the practice to a new level. Ultimately, that rite responded to a genuine popular uprising in favor of the dynasty. Though later commentators have sometimes dismissed the estates-based constitutions implemented in Austria after 1815 as a sham, the Tyrolian one allowed for the comparatively broad representation of the rural world. It entailed the free election of deputies to the principal provincial assembly known as the *Großer Ausschuß*—thirteen from each of the four individual Estates of prelates, nobles, burghers, and peasants, for fifty-two in total.[102] At the decisive moment, the inaugural spotlight shone precisely on these deputies, who took the oath to the emperor in the great hall of the Innsbruck Hofburg on behalf of the county of Tyrol.[103] The concern with a sufficiently broad social base was apparent a short time later at Francis's inauguration in Salzburg to which not only the nobility but also all owners of demesne land (*Dominikal=Gutsbesitzer*) were summoned.[104] The responsibilities reserved by the new-old constitution to the Tyrolian Estates—including the imposition, repartition, and collection of taxes and other charges, as well as the administration of public debt—were politically sensitive ones and served to ground the regime in the localities. This in turn facilitated the effective organization of regional-political diversity in a large, agrarian monarchy.

The inauguration in Innsbruck was the first thoroughly modern Habsburg inaugural ceremony: it was a popular–patriotic celebration of the return to Habsburg rule and legal order as embodied in the new constitution. The festal activities that followed the rite accentuated this circumstance. The emperor Francis took the salute of locally recruited military units, including a regiment of rangers that bore his name: an episode that produced a powerful engraved image of him among banner-carrying Tyrolians and common people. The mountains that had proven such a trap for the Franco-Bavarians rise in the background (see figure 9.2). The following day, he appeared at a shooting competition carefully designed at his express wish to be "as generally inclusive as possible."[105] Francis and his grand aulic chancellor opened the event with four shots each.[106] The local newspaper characterized this "national festival" as "unique in the history of the land."[107]

Figure 9.2. Emperor Francis being hailed in Innsbruck by local people following the Tyrolian act of homage, 1816. Lithograph by Johann Nepomuk Hoechle, 1835 (Vienna, Österreichische Nationalbibliothek, Bildarchiv und Graphiksammlung, Pk 187,16).

The coronation of Ferdinand I in 1838 in Milan was the most spectacular inaugural festival in the new key in the Habsburg monarchy before 1848. Francis I had provided that his successors in Lombardy-Venetia be crowned, declining to undergo the rite himself on account of his conquest of the region in the late Napoleonic period. Unlike Ferdinand's coronations in Hungary (1830) and Bohemia (1836), the performance of the rite in Lombardy-Venetia—like that in Tyrol—did not symbolically "enact" an unwritten constitutional order. The constitutional charter that Francis had issued for the kingdom in 1815 remained in force in 1838. The Lombardo-Venetian coronation was instead at the heart of an unprecedented, full-blown public relations campaign aimed at the hearts of the monarchy's north Italian subjects. Historians continue to dismiss the coronation as "phony ritual" or even "artifice."[108] The emperor's many ailments certainly rendered him incapable of ruling, a grave deficit in a composite polity such as the Habsburg one where the institution of the monarchy was the lynchpin of the system. Yet the regime was not reducible to Ferdinand. And disregarding a pageant produced on such a scale. and at such expense, risks, as the historian David Cannadine has suggested in another connection, that we forget those who took the trouble to stage it, those who participated in it, those at whom it was directed, or those who in some way responded to it. If the ceremony did not effectuate legal order in the previous sense, it was "integral" to "power and politics themselves."[109]

The Habsburg monarchy emerged from the Napoleonic period as the new hegemon in Italy. Composed of territories that at one time or another had been folded into various French revolutionary and Napoleonic states, the new kingdom of Lombardy-Venetia was ruled from Vienna and anchored Habsburg power firmly on the peninsula. The kingdom's entire area had belonged to Napoleon's "inner empire" and consequently been subject to his highly invasive administrative model.[110] After taking control, the Austrians did not revive the old regime, which in any event would have been unfeasible in view of the circumstances. Key features of French-induced modernization were retained and combined with Habsburg practices. This state of affairs together with the charter of 1815 made Lombardy-Venetia a distinct political space within the wider Habsburg composite polity, comparable to the Austrian or Bohemian lands. Because the Habsburgs would remain at peace in the decades after 1815, their rule "proved far less burdensome and oppressive" than Napoleon's had been.[111] It also showed greater sensitivity to local needs. The scholarship of recent decades has debunked the tenacious myth of inveterate Austrian reaction and oppression. As David Laven has shown, comparative stability and good government characterized Austrian rule in the area during the 1820s and 1830s.[112] Neither domestic upheaval nor serious foreign threats disturbed its tranquility. The widespread resentment that did exist arose not from the obstruction of an allegedly inevitable Italian national state—as posited by Risorgimento historiography—but rather from the preservation of much of the hated Napoleonic administrative legacy. That resentment alienated in particular the very propertied classes that were meant to constitute the social basis of Habsburg authority.[113]

It was against this calm if hardly satisfactory backdrop that the splendid appeal to local sensibilities in the form of the Lombardo-Venetian coronation transpired. The occasion had to be planned from scratch, as "no earlier example" existed.[114] The last Habsburg to have worn the Lombard iron crown, the ancient diadem chosen for use, had been the emperor Charles V at his coronation as king of Italy in Bologna.[115] Because that occasion lay more than three hundred years in the past, Habsburg officials anxious for a pageant in keeping with the times did not see it as a model to be emulated. It was seriously considered only in one respect, when the Lombardo-Venetian governor, Count Hartig, recommended that Ferdinand not be anointed on the supposed precedent of Charles V.[116] Hartig was mistaken on this point, and he oddly appears to have been unaware that Napoleon had refused unction in Milan. Napoleon's coronation in the same city a generation earlier was indeed the proverbial elephant in the room. For Austria, it had been an occasion "rich in menacing symbolism."[117] Among other offensive aspects, a replica of Charlemagne's crown was on display there at a time when the real one was still resting on Francis II's head.[118] Hartig himself objected to a design for Ferdinand's robe that he thought was too close to the one worn by Napoleon.[119] Any too striking similarity generally risked arousing among local people unwelcome associations.

Some resemblance could not be helped on account of the setting, centered on the *duomo* in Milan. Yet because of the range of inaugural rites that still existed across the lands over which it ruled, the Habsburg court drew on an unusually rich ceremonial heritage to imbue events with meaning.[120] Unlike at Innsbruck, in 1816, rites—not traditions—were being invented. For the coronation itself the Roman Pontifical, as enriched by the indigenous Ambrosian ritual, furnished the order of service—even as Grand Aulic Chancellor Mittrowsky (the interior minister) took care to change wording that suggested that power came from the Church rather than God.[121] Mittrowsky formulated the simple oath that Ferdinand would swear to rule with justice and uphold the Catholic religion. The emperor would also receive the holy oil because it was, in the words of the grand master of the court, "an essential element of a royal coronation."[122] The implication was that Napoleon's rite had been a fraud.

A series of distinct ceremonial events that stretched over more than a week (the solemn entry into Milan; the transfer to Milan of the iron crown from its place of safekeeping in the treasury of the Cathedral of Monza; the act of homage; and a visit to the Basilica of Sant'Ambrogio) framed the coronation itself. The inaugural customs in the other Habsburg lands offered essential guidance in fashioning them. The entry into Milan was patterned on the processional order observed at the inauguration in Vienna because of the presence of burghers in both places.[123] In a few ways, the Hungarian coronation was seen as exemplary. Most often, the organizers mined the Bohemian rites for inspiration, which should not surprise us given that the grand master of the court, the grand chamberlain, the grand aulic chancellor, and the governor were all Austro-Bohemian aristocrats.[124] Most strikingly, the performance of a discrete act of homage a few days before the coronation replicated the tradition in Prague.[125] But notably, the empress would not be crowned in Milan as she had been in the Bohemian capital.

The authorities did not simply impose outside usages on Lombardy-Venetia, as might be imagined. Prince Colloredo-Mannsfeld summed up the prevailing approach as follows: "The existing observances in the other lands of the monarchy should be kept in mind unless the special circumstances of the Lombardo-Venetian kingdom recommend against it."[126] The consultative practices so ingrained into Habsburg government operated here as well. A "coronation committee" met under the chairmanship of the governor in Milan. Its key member was the Lombardo-Venetian master of ceremonies, Count Luigi Settala, a noble of an old Milanese family who as early as the autumn of 1836 was drafting plans for the pageant.[127] In general, the coronation provided an ideal opportunity to cater to the sensibilities of the local elites, whose support was ultimately essential to the success of Austrian rule. The more liberal admission rules to the archduke-viceroy's court remained in effect for the stricter imperial court, which was to be in residence in Milan.[128] In this way, the different traditions and revolutionary-era experiences of the north Italian nobility were taken into account. The decision-makers in Vienna ignored another piece of ill-conceived advice from Governor Hartig by providing that the local nobility should escort the emperor on his solemn entry into Milan, a signal mark of distinction visible to the wider public.

In the attempt to foster local opinion, the Lombardo-Venetian coronation resembled the Italian one of 1805, as analyzed by the historian Ambrogio Caiani.[129] Yet the premises of the two episodes differed profoundly. Whereas Napoleon wanted to win over the Italians as the "subordinate partners" in a larger imperial enterprise that was clearly based on France, the Habsburgs were cultivating provincial elites in the classic fashion of composite monarchy, as defined by J. H. Elliott.[130] In the Habsburg case, we can detect neither the concern for a specifically *imperial* hierarchy nor the arrogant cultural imperialism that marked the French expansion in Europe. Lombardy-Venetia was a kingdom within a wider composite polity that lacked a dominant constituent part, such as France was to the Napoleonic empire or even England to the United Kingdom. The records for the Lombardo-Venetian rite demonstrate the pains taken not only to ensure that Lombardy and Venetia were symbolically present in equal measure at the coronation—the cardinal-archbishop of Milan and the cardinal-patriarch of Venice together crowned Ferdinand[131]—but also that the arrangements neither favored nor disadvantaged Lombardy-Venetia unduly in relation to the other Habsburg lands.[132]

In another crucial if related way, the rituals of 1838 contrasted to both the Napoleonic ones and other nineteenth-century coronations that bore an anticonstitutional or reactionary-religious imprint.[133] It was an age-old "precept" (*Grundsatz*) of Habsburg ceremonial that the "difference" (*Gegensatz*) between "court" (*Hof*) and "territory" (*Land*) always be visible (*in steter Evidenz gehalten*).[134] In practice, this meant that the territory in question had to be "represented" during the solemnities. In the case of Lombardy-Venetia, this obligation caused the planners a good deal of cogitation. The local estates-based constitutions had long ceased to exist; the form of representation familiar to Colloredo-Mannsfeld and the others in Bohemia or Hungary was therefore lacking. The grand master rejected the idea of skirting the problem by having a few high-ranking administrators play the role of "representatives" in what would have been little more than exaltation of the monarchy.[135] Finally, it was decided that the so-called "central and provincial congregations" would assume the role in question. Created in the wake of the Congress of Vienna, these bodies had been inspired by comparatively recent physiocratic and Romantic conceptions of representation for socioeconomic interests (wealth). Emperor Francis had provided for a relatively generous, two-tier form of the congregations throughout the kingdom.[136] Their purpose had been to root the regime in the propertied classes by involving their elected deputies in local government. At the act of homage in 1838, these deputies (a total of 176 in all) were the people who stood facing the throne.[137] If they owed their position neither to the older status-based form of representation nor to the newer democratic one, they did embody in an organized way the very elements of the population to whom the celebrations were most designed to appeal. Their presence also gave the display of Austrian rule on offer a consensual finish that would otherwise have been lacking.

The emperor's personal incapacity was particularly unfortunate in view of the stamina he showed during an arduous program by any standards. Immediately before coming to Lombardy-Venetia, he had been inaugurated in Tyrol.[138] The sojourn in Milan lasted for two weeks. There, he not only had the separate rites of homage and coronation to undergo but many other engagements and public appearances. On 2 September, he went to the Scala to hear music by Rossini; on the 4th, he presided over a court ball for four thousand people; other days were occupied with tours of exhibitions of fine arts and industrial products, or visits to public establishments and military installations.[139] On the day of the coronation itself, the "festa popolare" that was now an obligatory ingredient of Habsburg inaugural rites took place. After Milan, a royal progress took the newly crowned king and his consort to Bergamo, Brescia, Cremona, Mantua, Verona, Vicenza, and Padua, among other places. A further highpoint involved a solemn entry into Venice followed by another round of observances and duties.

Though the press censorship of the day and the lack of opinion polls make any conclusive judgment hazardous, the evidence suggests that the events made a favorable impact, at least among those elements of the public that the Habsburg regime had a realistic chance of reaching. Giuseppe Mazzini expressed bitterness at what he perceived as the coronation's success, but he and his adherents were an insignificant minority. Optimism and enthusiasm appear in fact to have surrounded the visit.[140] The imperial couple was everywhere received not only without incident but also with good will. In some places, jubilant crowds filled the streets. Foreign diplomats testified favorably. After the event, the British minister, who had been on the scene, relayed his impressions in these terms: "The Emperor & his Italian subjects have parted in mutual good humour with each other. The Italians have heart that their interests & feelings are attended to, while the Gov't. not only feels the advantage but sees the possibility of attaching them by these ties instead of relying upon force."[141] The representative of Savoy reported to Turin in a similar vein.[142] Still, once the court had disappeared back over the Alps, the structural problem remained: it was not rule by Vienna, per se, but rather rule in the tradition of Napoleon. The coronation's success created a window of opportunity for the government to address this source of dissatisfaction. Whether it would be exploited was another matter.

Let us conclude with the coronation that famously never happened—that of the emperor of Austria. Under the pressure of Napoleon's plan to assume an imperial distinction and amid fears that the Roman one would pass out of his hands, Emperor Francis had in 1804 taken the Austrian imperial title. Until 1806, he was both Roman emperor and emperor of Austria. Why was the new dignity not given the luster of a coronation? After all, Francis had received the older imperial crown in Frankfurt in 1792. In 1804, there was in fact some discussion of a coronation. At one level, the makeshift character of the new title and the circumstances of the years around 1804—international tension and financial disarray—were not conducive to the performance of such a ceremony, one that moreover might have seemed a poor imitation of French imperial rites. A coronation was expensive, while the head of Europe's time-honored imperial house could hardly be seen to be aping Napoleon.

Still, an explanation for the lack of an Austrian coronation lies at a more fundamental level. The "Austrian Empire," as the Habsburg inheritance came increasingly to be called after 1804, remained a "composite monarchy": a union of discrete political units bound in indissoluble union by the Pragmatic Sanction of 1713. This circumstance accounts for the survival or creation of the multifarious inaugural rites discussed above just as the monarchy's increasing integration explained why inaugural rites in the lesser lands had become obsolete. The patent of 1804 provided explicitly for the preservation of the "constitutions" of all the Habsburg lands inside and outside the still-extant Holy Roman Empire.[143] Though it opened up new possibilities, the Austrian imperial title did not change the monarchy's fundamentally composite nature. The proclamation did not provide for a written constitution in all or even some of those lands; and there was no unwritten legal order apart from the Pragmatic Sanction encompassing all of them. Thus, an Austrian coronation could at best have been a modern patriotic celebration without legal consequences, though one that would have raised tricky constitutional issues given the lack of the common representation that was traditionally considered imperative to Habsburg inaugural ritual. The unwritten constitutions of the individual lands remained in force.

To my knowledge, there was only one occasion in this period—and perhaps in modern Habsburg history—in which a ruler faced an assembly composed of representatives of all of his lands. Upon his triumphal return to Vienna following the defeat of Napoleon, Emperor Francis granted a collective audience to deputations from the monarchy's various constituent parts. The places where the customary unwritten legal orders remained in force, in some cases in connection with the performance of inaugural rites, as in Lower Austria, Hungary, and Bohemia, sent formal delegations of their Estates. The areas newly annexed or retaken sent informal groups, given that the older unwritten legal orders with their representative bodies had disappeared and written constitutional statutes providing for new ones had yet to be promulgated. The deputations had come to offer the emperor what was called "the homage of their good wishes" (*die Huldigung ihrer Glückwünsche*) on the successful conclusion of the war against France. Surrounded by his officers of state and captains of the guards, Francis received them jointly in the ceremonial hall of the Hofburg on 21 June 1814.[144] The use of the term *Huldigung* on an occasion when practically the entire monarchy stood incarnate in its variety before the emperor is certainly suggestive. The inaugural rites exemplified that variety, even as their performance manifested in diverse ways the integration of the parts into the composite whole.

William D. Godsey is a Senior Research Associate at the Institute for Habsburg and Balkan Studies at the Austrian Academy of Sciences. His fields of research are the Habsburg Monarchy (seventeenth through twentieth centuries) and the early modern Holy Roman Empire. His latest book is entitled *The Sinews of Habsburg Power: Lower Austria in a Fiscal-Military State 1650–1820* (Oxford, 2018). He is a Fellow of the Royal Historical Society.

Notes

The author gratefully acknowledges the generous help of Michael Alram (Vienna), Ambrogio Caiani (Canterbury), Katrin Keller (Vienna), and Géza Pálffy (Budapest) in preparing this chapter.

1. Ambrogio A. Caiani, "Ornamentalism in a European Context? Napoleon's Italian Coronation, 26 May 1805," *English Historical Review* 132, no. 554 (2017): 41–72. As Napoleon's regime was threatening to come unraveled after the defeat in Russia, he toyed with the idea of crowning his second wife (Archduchess Marie Louise) and infant son, the king of Rome: reports by the Austrian chargé Floret to Foreign Minister Metternich, Paris, 16 and 29 January 1813, ÖStA, HHStA, Staatskanzlei, Berichte, Frankreich, 217.
2. Richard A. Jackson, *Vive le Roi! A History of the French Coronation from Charles V to Charles X: Vivat Rex* (Chapel Hill, 1984); Matthias Schnettger, "'Il Viaggio a Reims' oder die Restauration auf der Opernbühne," *Majestas* 12 (2004): 161–94.
3. Roy Strong, *Coronation from the 8th to the 21st Century* (London, 2005); Sabine Heym, "Prachtvolle Kroninsignien für Bayern—aber keine Krönung," in *Bayerns Krone 1805: 200 Jahre Königreich Bayern*, ed. Johannes Erichsen and Katharina Heinemann (Munich, 2006), 36–47; Matthias Schwengelbeck, *Die Politik des Zeremoniells: Huldigungsfeiern im langen 19. Jahrhundert* (Frankfurt, 2007); David E. Barclay, "Ritual, Ceremonial, and the 'Invention' of a Monarchical Tradition in Nineteenth-Century Prussia," in *European Monarchy: Its Evolution and Practice from Roman Antiquity to Modern Times*, ed. Heinz Duchhardt, Richard A. Jackson, and David Sturdy (Stuttgart, 1992); Johannes Kunisch, ed., *Dreihundert Jahre Preußische Königskrönung: Eine Tagungsdokumentation* (Berlin, 2002).

4. Volker Sellin, *Gewalt und Legitimität: Die europäische Monarchie im Zeitalter der Revolutionen* (Munich, 2011); Dieter Langewiesche, *Die Monarchie im Jahrhundert Europas: Selbstbehauptung durch Wandel im 19. Jahrhundert* (Heidelberg, 2013); Andrzej Olechnowicz, ed., *The Monarchy and the British Nation, 1780 to the Present* (Cambridge, UK, 2007); Philip Mansel, *The Eagle in Splendour: Inside the Court of Napoleon*, 2nd ed. (London, 2015); James Loughlin, *The British Monarchy and Ireland: 1800 to the Present* (Cambridge, UK, 2007).
5. The focus has typically been on the individual lands: Hugh LeCaine Agnew, "Ambiguities of Ritual: Dynastic Loyalty, Territorial Patriotism and Nationalism in the Last Three Royal Coronations in Bohemia, 1791–1836," *Bohemia* 41 (2000): 3–22; William D. Godsey, "Herrschaft und politische Kultur im Habsburgerreich: Die niederösterreichische Erbhuldigung (ca. 1648–1848)," in *Aufbrüche in die Moderne: Frühparlamentarismus zwischen altständischer Ordnung und monarchischem Konstitutionalismus 1750–1850. Schlesien—Deutschland—Mitteleuropa*, ed. Roland Gehrke (Cologne, 2005), 141–77.
6. "Vorläufige Anfangen der Krönungsfeyerlichkeit Ihrer Majestät der Königin von Böhmen," [1808], ÖStA, HHStA, ZA Prot 42, fol. 183v–185r.
7. In 1790 and 1792, nondynastic commissioners had represented the ruler at the acts of homage in Transylvania. Joseph Kropatschek, *Oestreichs Staatsverfassung* (Vienna, 1794), vol. 1: 72–74.
8. Quotation from Sellin, *Gewalt und Legitimität*, 5.
9. On this point see the highly perceptive reflections by Ambrogio A. Caiani, "Re-inventing the *Ancien Régime* in Post-Napoleonic Europe," *European History Quarterly* 47 (2017): 437–60, especially 439.
10. Godsey, "Herrschaft und politische Kultur," 152.
11. Gustav Otruba, "Die Erbhuldigungen der oberösterreichischen Stände 1732–1741–1743: Eine Studie zur Geschichte des Treueverhaltens von Klerus, Adel und Bürgertum gegenüber Karl VI., Karl Albert und Maria Theresia," *Mitteilungen des Oberösterreichischen Landesarchivs* 16 (1990): 135–301. For Maria Theresa's Hungarian coronation in 1741 as well as her refusal to be crowned Roman empress, see Barbara Stollberg-Rilinger, *Maria Theresia: Die Kaiserin in ihrer Zeit. Eine Biographie* (Munich, 2017), 84–89, 146–50. See also Sandra Hertel, "Maria Theresia als 'König von Ungarn' im Krönungszeremoniell in Preßburg (1741)," *Frühneuzeit-Info* 27 (2016): 110–23.
12. Johann Polek, "Die Huldigung der Bukowina am 12. Oktober 1777," *Jahrbuch des Bukowiner Landesmuseums* 10 (1902): 5 and 7.
13. For this view, see André Holenstein, "Huldigung und Herrschaftszeremoniell im Zeitalter des Absolutismus und der Aufklärung," in *Zum Wandel von Zeremoniell und Gesellschaftsritualen in der Zeit der Aufklärung*, ed. Klaus Gerteis (Hamburg, 1992), 22.
14. Chantal Grell, "The *sacre* of Louis XVI: The End of a Myth," in *Monarchy and Religion: The Transformation of Royal Culture in Eighteenth-Century Europe*, ed. Michael Schaich (London, 2007), 345–66.
15. For that coronation, see Barbara Stollberg-Rilinger, *Des Kaisers alte Kleider: Verfassungsgeschichte und Symbolsprache des Alten Reiches* (Munich, 2008), 227–46. For Joseph and inaugural rites generally, see Derek Beales, *Joseph II* (Cambridge, UK, 1987/2009), vol. 1: 110–16; vol. 2: 63–64 and 159–63. After the start of his personal rule, Joseph allowed inaugurations to go forward in the Austrian Netherlands, Transylvania, Milan, and Mantua, where oaths were sworn by his representatives. Elke Josupeit-Neitzel, *Die Reformen Josephs II. in Siebenbürgen* (Munich, 1986), 77–80.

16. Derek Beales, "Joseph II's Rêveries," in *Enlightenment and Reform in Eighteenth-Century Europe*, ed. Derek Beales (London, 2005), 164–65.
17. Quotation from Stollberg-Rilinger, *Maria Theresia*, 529; Beales, *Joseph II*, vol. 2: 163.
18. Grete Klingenstein, "The Meanings of 'Austria' and 'Austrian' in the Eighteenth Century," in *Royal and Republican Sovereignty in Early Modern Europe*, ed. Robert Oresko, G. C. Gibbs, and H. M. Scott (Cambridge, UK, 1997), 467. See also Stollberg-Rilinger, *Des Kaisers alte Kleider*, 297.
19. The court's desire to keep down the costs associated with the rites is mentioned repeatedly in the reports of the British minister at Vienna. Sir Robert Murray Keith to Lord Grenville, Vienna, 10 and 31 March 1792, The National Archives (Kew), Foreign Office 7/29; Keith to Grenville, Vienna, 9 June 1792, The National Archives (Kew), Foreign Office 7/30.
20. David Cannadine, "The Context, Performance and Meaning of Ritual: The British Monarchy and the 'Invention of Tradition,' c. 1820–1977," in *The Invention of Tradition*, ed. Eric Hobsbawm and Terence Ranger (Cambridge, UK, 1983), 105.
21. Eric Hobsbawm, "Inventing Traditions," in *The Invention of Tradition*, ed. Eric Hobsbawm and Terence Ranger (Cambridge, UK, 1983), 1–14.
22. Heinz Duchhardt, "Die preussische Königskrönung von 1701: Ein europäisches Modell?," in *Herrscherweihe und Königskrönung im frühneuzeitlichen Europa*, ed. Heinz Duchhardt (Wiesbaden, 1983), 85 and 90 (quotation).
23. Caiani, "Ornamentalism," 53, has pointed out the overlooked significance of this.
24. Edward Muir, *Ritual in Early Modern Europe* (Cambridge, UK, 1997), 249; Duchhardt, "Die preussische Königskrönung," 94.
25. Peter H. Wilson, *Heart of Europe: A History of the Holy Roman Empire* (Cambridge, MA, 2016), 43. See also Agnew, "Ambiguities of Ritual," 4.
26. "Relation über den im Jahre 1808 zu Preßburg abgehaltenen Krönungslandtag," ÖStA, HHStA, ZA Prot 42, fol. 225.
27. Elizabeth I of Russia did the same, setting a precedent that would be followed by her successors. Francine-Dominique Liechtenhan, *Élisabeth Ire de Russie* (Paris, 2007), 113; Sellin, *Gewalt und Legitimität*, 100.
28. Christopher Clark, "When Culture Meets Power: The Prussian Coronation of 1701," in *Cultures of Power in Europe during the Long Eighteenth Century*, ed. Hamish Scott and Brendan Simms (Cambridge, UK, 2007), 17.
29. Muir, *Ritual in Early Modern Europe*, 6.
30. David I. Kertzer, *Ritual, Politics, and Power* (New Haven, 1988), 40.
31. Paul W. Schroeder, *The Transformation of European Politics 1763–1848* (Oxford, 1994), 61.
32. William D. Godsey, *The Sinews of Habsburg Power: Lower Austria in a Fiscal-Military State 1650–1820* (Oxford, 2018), 317–19.
33. Beales, *Joseph II*, vol. 2: 624–25 and 628–30.
34. Michael Broers, *Europe under Napoleon*, 2nd ed. (London, 2015), 113; Schroeder, *The Transformation*, 64.
35. Adam Wandruszka, *Leopold II.: Erzherzog von Österreich, Grossherzog von Toskana, König von Ungarn und Böhmen, Römischer Kaiser* (Vienna, 1963), vol. 1: 387–88; Pietro Leopoldo d'Asburgo Lorena, *Relazione sullo stato della monarchia (1784)*, ed. Derek Beales and Renato Pasta (Rome, 2013), 74; Godsey, *The Sinews of Habsburg Power*, 350–52.

36. As reported two days later at the Estates by Floridus Leeb, provost of Klosterneuburg, who had been present at the meeting. Minutes of the Lower Austrian diet, 18 March 1790, NÖLA, Ständische Bücher, 279, fol. 81r.
37. Godsey, "Herrschaft und politische Kultur," 152.
38. "Protokoll über die dem 24. März 1790 abgehaltenen Ceremoniel Conferenz zur Erbhuldigung S: Maj: des Königs Leopold des 2t:," NÖLA, Neue Ständische Registratur 1782–92, carton 183.
39. The speech is reproduced in *Wiener Zeitung*, 7 April 1790, 881.
40. Franz Freiherr von Prancau, "Ausführliche Beschreibung der Erbhuldigung welche dem Allerdurchlauchtigsten Großmächtigsten Herrn Herrn Leopold dem Zweyten König in Ungarn, Böhmen, Gallizien, und Lodomerien Erzherzoge zu Oesterreich von den vier Ständen des Erzherzogthums Oesterreich unter der Ens den 6ten April 1790 geleistet ward," NÖLA, Handschriften, 52, fol. 72r.
41. *Wiener Zeitung*, 7 April 1790, 881–82.
42. Beales, *Joseph II*, vol. 2: 365–66. Prandau, "Ausführliche Beschreibung," NÖLA, Handschriften, 52, fol. 26v.
43. Muir, *Ritual in Early Modern Europe*, 230; Barbara Stollberg-Rilinger, "On the Function of Rituals in the Holy Roman Empire," in *The Holy Roman Empire 1495–1806*, ed. R. J. W. Evans, Michael Schaich, and Peter H. Wilson (London, 2011), 359–73; Stollberg-Rilinger, "Verfassung und Fest: Überlegungen zur festlichen Inszenierung vormoderner und moderner Verfassungen," in *Interdependenzen zwischen Verfassung und Kultur*, ed. Hans Jürgen Becker (Berlin, 2003), 7–37.
44. Godsey, *The Sinews of Habsburg Power*, chapter 8.
45. Prandau, "Ausführliche Beschreibung," NÖLA, Handschriften, 52, fol. 4r.
46. Barbara Stollberg-Rilinger, "Herstellung und Darstellung politischer Einheit: Instrumentelle und symbolische Dimensionen politischer Repräsentation im 18. Jahrhundert," in *Die Sinnlichkeit der Macht. Herrschaft und Repräsentation seit der Frühen Neuzeit*, ed. Jan Andres, Alexa Geisthövel, and Matthias Schwengelbeck (Frankfurt, 2005), 73–92.
47. Muir, *Ritual in Early Modern Europe*, 230.
48. Kertzer, *Ritual, Politics, and Power*, 40.
49. *Wiener Zeitung*, 7 April 1790, 881; Prandau, "Ausführliche Beschreibung," NÖLA, Handschriften, 52, fol. 21r.
50. Prandau, "Ausführliche Beschreibung," NÖLA, Handschriften, 52, fol. 76v.
51. Aulic decree to *Landmarschall* Pergen, 29 March 1790, NÖLA, Neue Ständische Registratur 1782–92, carton 183.
52. Martin P. Schennach, "Die 'österreichische Gesamtstaatsidee': Das Verhältnis zwischen 'Gesamtstaat' und Ländern als Gegenstand rechtshistorischer Forschung," in *Rechtshistorische Aspekte des österreichischen Föderalismus*, ed. Martin P. Schennach (Vienna, 2015), 22.
53. Godsey, "Herrschaft und politische Kultur," 150–51.
54. Diary of Countess Marie Sidonie Chotek, née Clary-Aldringen, Státní oblastní archiv v Litoměřicích pobočka Děčín (Czech Republic), Rodinný archiv Clary-Aldringenů, carton 110, vol. for January–May 1790, 6 April 1790, 121–26.
55. Philip Mansel, *Prince of Europe: The Life of Charles-Joseph de Ligne 1735–1814* (London, 2003), 130.
56. Janet L. Polasky, *Revolution in Brussels 1787–1793* (Brussels, 1982), 176–77.
57. Kertzer, *Ritual, Politics, and Power*, 21.

58. *Wiener Zeitung*, 7 April 1790, 883. For the comparable coins under Maria Theresa, see Sabine Haag, ed., *Zuhanden Ihrer Majestät: Medaillen Maria Theresias* (Vienna, 2017), 56.
59. *Wiener Zeitung*, 7 April 1790, 879.
60. Broers, *Europe under Napoleon*, 46.
61. Schroeder, *The Transformation of European Politics*, 351–53.
62. C. A. Macartney, *The Habsburg Empire 1790–1918* (New York, 1969), 186–87.
63. Hellmuth Rössler, *Graf Johann Philipp Stadion: Napoleons deutscher Gegenspieler* (Vienna, 1966), vol. 1: 296.
64. Eduard Wertheimer, "Der ungarische Krönungsreichstag von 1808," in *Geschichte Oesterreichs und Ungarns im ersten Jahrzehnt des 19. Jahrhunderts* (Leipzig, 1884), vol. 2: 286–88. This account is based on unpublished sources.
65. Macartney, *The Habsburg Empire*, 154.
66. Eduard Wertheimer, *Die drei ersten Frauen des Kaisers Franz* (Leipzig, 1893), 87–88.
67. On the phenomenon of the queen consort generally, see Clarissa Campbell Orr, ed., *Queenship in Europe 1660–1815: The Role of the Consort* (Cambridge, UK, 2004).
68. Géza Pálffy, "Crisis in the Habsburg Monarchy and Hungary, 1619–1622: The Hungarian Estates and Gábor Bethlen," *Hungarian Historical Review* 2 (2013): 751–54.
69. "Relation über den im Jahre 1808 zu Preßburg abgehaltenen Krönungslandtag," ÖStA, HHStA, ZA Prot 42, fol. 233v–34r.
70. "Relation über den im Jahre 1808 zu Preßburg abgehaltenen Krönungslandtag," ÖStA, HHStA, ZA Prot 42, fol. 207, 223v, 229, and 233v–34r.
71. Wertheimer, "Der ungarische Krönungsreichstag," 289–90; Macartney, *The Habsburg Empire*, 186.
72. The following is drawn from "Relation über den im Jahre 1808 zu Preßburg abgehaltenen Krönungslandtag," ÖStA, HHStA, ZA Prot 42, fol. 238r–99r.
73. Wertheimer, "Der ungarische Krönungsreichstag," 290–91. See also Macartney, *The Habsburg Empire*, 153.
74. As appropriate, the empress was also known to don "Teutonic fashion": Macartney, *The Habsburg Empire*, 185. At her coronation in 1741, Maria Theresa had worn "magnificent Hungarian costume": Stollberg-Rilinger, *Maria Theresia*, 86. For the British royal family in Scottish dress, see Philip Mansel, *Dressed to Rule: Royal and Court Costume from Louis XIV to Elizabeth II* (New Haven, 2005), 45–49.
75. "Relation über den im Jahre 1808 zu Preßburg abgehaltenen Krönungslandtag," ÖStA, HHStA, ZA Prot 42, fol. 282r. In 1838, Ferdinand I wore an imitation of the "house crown" (the crown of Rudolf II) at the Lombardo-Venetian coronation because of the original's weight: ÖStA, HHStA, ZA, Prot 57, fol. 64v. In earlier coronations of Hungarian queen-consorts, kings had worn "house crowns" rather than the crown of St. Stephen: see Géza Pálffy, "An 'Old Empire' on the Periphery of the Old Empire: The Kingdom of Hungary and the Holy Roman Empire in the Sixteenth and Seventeenth Centuries," in *The Holy Roman Empire, 1495–1806: A European Perspective*, ed. R. J. W. Evans and Peter H. Wilson (Leiden, 2012), 279.
76. For the question of the crowns used in the ceremony, see "Relation über den im Jahre 1808 zu Preßburg abgehaltenen Krönungslandtag," ÖStA, HHStA, ZA Prot 42, fols. 198v–99v, 282r, 285v, and 286v. Cf. "Ordo Coronationis," ÖStA, HHStA, Ungarische Akten, Specialia, 269, fols. 265v, 266v, 267r, and 269v.
77. "Relation über den im Jahre 1808 zu Preßburg abgehaltenen Krönungslandtag," ÖStA, HHStA, ZA Prot 42, fol. 212r.

78. "Relation über den im Jahre 1808 zu Preßburg abgehaltenen Krönungslandtag," ÖStA, HHStA, ZA Prot 42, fol. 297v.
79. Wertheimer, "Der ungarische Krönungsreichstag," 291–92; Štefan Holčík, *Krönungsfeierlichkeiten in Preßburg/Bratislava 1563–1830* (Bratislava, 1992), 50.
80. For the "synchronicity" of the various forms of patriotism in the early nineteenth century, see Brian E. Vick, *The Congress of Vienna: Power and Politics after Napoleon* (Cambridge, MA, 2014), 41. For the problem of Austrian "national" feeling, see André Robert, *L'Idée nationale autrichienne et les guerres de Napoléon: L'Apostolat du baron de Hormayr et le salon de Caroline Pichler* (Paris, 1933).
81. Wertheimer, "Der ungarische Krönungsreichstag," 294; Rössler, *Graf Johann Philipp Stadion*, vol. 1: 296–97.
82. Wertheimer, "Der ungarische Krönungsreichstag," 294–95; Adolf Beer, *Zehn Jahre österreichischer Politik 1801–1810* (Leipzig, 1877), 315.
83. László Péter, "Die Verfassungsentwicklung in Ungarn,' in *Die Habsburgermonarchie 1848–1918*, vol. 7/1: *Verfassung und Parlamentarismus*, ed. Helmut Rumpler and Peter Urbanitsch (Vienna, 2000), 274. See also Orsolya Szakály, "Opportunity or Threat? Napoleon and the Hungarian Estates," in *Collaboration and Resistance in Napoleonic Europe: State-Formation in an Age of Upheaval, c. 1800–1815*, ed. Michael Rowe (Basingstoke, 2003), 153–68.
84. Schroeder, *The Transformation of European Politics*, 400; Broers, *Europe under Napoleon*, 167.
85. Schroeder, *The Transformation of European Politics*, 480–81.
86. *Der Bote von Tyrol*, 7 September 1814, 152. See Albert Jäger, *Tirols Rückkehr unter Oesterreich und seine Bemühungen zur Wiedererlangung der alten Landesrechte von 1813 bis 1816* (Vienna, 1871).
87. Vick, *The Congress of Vienna*, 233, also 248–55. See also Enno E. Kraehe, *Metternich's German Policy*, vol. 2: *The Congress of Vienna 1814–1815* (Princeton, 1983), 395; Wolfram Siemann, *Metternich: Stratege und Visionär* (Munich, 2016), 505 and 519.
88. Sellin, *Gewalt und Legitimität*, 182.
89. The constitution is reproduced in *Sr. k. k. Majestät Franz des Ersten politische Gesetze und Verordnungen für die Oesterreichischen, Böhmischen und Galizischen Erbländer* (Vienna, 1818), vol. 24: 127–34.
90. On this point generally, see Caiani, "Re-inventing the *Ancien Régime*," 443.
91. The ceremonial records preserved in Vienna are slim on this event, reporting only that "the act of homage proceeded according to the program": ÖStA, HHStA, ZA Prot 48, fol. 98v–99r. A copy of that program, dated Innsbruck 26 May 1816, has survived in ÖStA, HHStA, Kaiser Franz Akten, carton 41, folder Miscellanea. See also *Der Bote von Tyrol*, 1 June 1816, 353–57.
92. Julian Lahner, 'Repräsentation und Herrschaftswechsel in Tirol und Salzburg, 1806–1816," *Mitteilungen des Instituts für Österreichische Geschichtsforschung* 126 (2018): 286–92.
93. On this point, see Matthias Schwengelbeck, "Monarchische Herrschaftsrepräsentationen zwischen Konsens und Konflikt: Zum Wandel des Huldigungs- und Inthronisationszeremoniells im 19. Jahrhundert," in *Die Sinnlichkeit der Macht: Herrschaft und Repräsentation seit der Frühen Neuzeit*, ed. Jan Andres, Alexa Geisthövel, and Matthias Schwengelbeck (Frankfurt, 2005), 129–30.
94. *Der Bote von Tyrol*, 1 June 1816, 355.

95. The oaths sworn at the inaugurations of 1790 (in which the archduchess Maria Elisabeth deputized for her brother, Leopold II) and 1816 are reproduced in Lahner, "Repräsentation und Herrschaftswechsel," 298.
96. "Programm," Innsbruck, 26 May 1816, ÖStA, HHStA, Kaiser Franz Akten, carton 41, folder Miscellanea.
97. *Der Bote von Tyrol*, 1 June 1816, 354.
98. Hobsbawm, "Inventing Traditions," 4.
99. Kertzer, *Ritual, Politics, and Power*, 175.
100. Schwengelbeck, *Die Politik des Zeremoniells*, 108–10.
101. Agnew, "Ambiguities of Ritual," 17 and 19.
102. §§ 1 and 11 of the patent of 24 March 1816, in *Sr. k. k. Majestät Franz des Ersten politische Gesetze und Verordnungen*, 128 and 130. Macartney, *The Habsburg Empire*, 207, averred that there "was naturally no place [in Francis's system] for any kind of representative institutions," but at the same time reported that the Tyrolian Estates "were now more democratic in form." Cf. Robin Okey, *The Habsburg Monarchy: From Enlightenment to Eclipse* (New York, 2001), 76.
103. Lahner, "Repräsentation und Herrschaftswechsel," 298, unaccountably reported that the government "rejected" the Estates' participation in the ceremony and that the Estates were "absent" from it.
104. Aulic decree, 28 May 1816, ÖStA, HHStA, ZA Prot 48, fol. 100v.
105. *Der Bote von Tyrol*, 1 May 1816, 273.
106. ÖStA, HHStA, ZA Prot 48, fol. 99.
107. *Der Bote von Tyrol*, 8 June 1816, 369. The term *Volksfest* also occurs in this context: *Der Bote von Tyrol*, 1 May 1816, 273.
108. Brigitte Mazohl-Wallnig, *Österreichischer Verwaltungsstaat und administrative Eliten im Königreich Lombardo-Venetien 1815–1859* (Mainz, 1993), 312; John Deak, *Forging a Multinational State: State Making in Imperial Austria from the Enlightenment to the First World War* (Stanford, 2015), 37. Cf. A. J. P. Taylor, *The Habsburg Monarchy 1809–1918* (Chicago, 1948), 49.
109. David Cannadine, "Introduction: Divine Rites of Kings," in *Rituals of Royalty: Power and Ceremonial in Traditional Societies*, ed. David Cannadine and Simon Price (Cambridge, UK, 1987), 6.
110. Broers, *Europe under Napoleon*, 242–45.
111. David Laven, *Venice and Venetia under the Habsburgs 1815–1835* (Oxford, 2002), 214.
112. Laven, *Venice and Venetia*, 213.
113. Schroeder, *The Transformation of European Politics*, 718–20; Alan Sked, *The Decline and Fall of the Habsburg Empire 1815–1918* (London, 1989), 32–33; Marco Meriggi, "State and Society in Post-Napoleonic Italy," in *Napoleon's Legacy: Problems of Government in Restoration Europe*, ed. David Laven and Lucy Riall (Oxford, 2000), 49–63.
114. Count Rudolph Czernin (grand chamberlain) to Prince Rudolph Colloredo-Mannsfeld (grand master of the court), 5 January 1838, ÖStA, HHStA, OKäA, Reihe B, Akten 1838, r. 28, folder 4.
115. Wilson, *Heart of Europe*, 183.
116. Prince Colloredo-Mannsfeld to Emperor Ferdinand, 15 March 1837, ÖStA, HHStA, NZA, Gruppe II, carton 3a.
117. Schroeder, *The Transformation of European Politics*, 268; See also Caiani, "Ornamentalism," 56 (footnote 90).

118. Caiani, "Ornamentalism," 54–55. See also Michael Broers, *Napoleon*, vol. 1: *Soldier of Destiny, 1769–1805* (London, 2014), 416–17 and 497.
119. Archduke Rainer (viceroy of Lombardy-Venetia) to Grand Chamberlain Czernin, Venice, 5 March 1838, ÖStA, HHStA, OKäA, Reihe B, Akten 1838, r. 28, folder 1.
120. Scholars have called attention to the large canon of rituals across Europe that could be drawn on in designing inaugural ceremony. Hobsbawm, "Inventing Traditions," 6; Clark, "When Culture Meets Power," 35; Caiani, "Re-inventing the *Ancien Régime*," 440. Stollberg-Rilinger, "Verfassung und Fest," 34–35, points out that the same rituals tend to turn up again and again.
121. Count Anton Friedrich Mittrowsky to Prince Colloredo-Mannsfeld, 1 June 1838, ÖStA, HHStA, NZA, Gruppe II, carton 5. A generation before, Leopold II had recited the traditional wording. See Agnew, "Ambiguities of Ritual," 14.
122. Prince Colloredo-Mannsfeld to Emperor Ferdinand I, 15 March 1837, ÖStA, HHStA, NZA, Gruppe II, carton 3a.
123. Prince Colloredo-Mannsfeld to Emperor Ferdinand, 10 June 1838, ÖStA, HHStA, NZA, Gruppe II, carton 5.
124. For the Bohemians at the highest levels of Austrian service, see R. J. W. Evans, *Austria, Hungary, and the Habsburgs: Essays on Central Europe, c. 1683–1867* (Oxford, 2006), 94–96.
125. Prince Colloredo-Mannsfeld to Emperor Ferdinand, 22 May 1838, ÖStA, HHStA, NZA, Gruppe II, carton 5.
126. Prince Colloredo-Mannsfeld to Emperor Ferdinand, 10 June 1838, ÖStA, HHStA, NZA, Gruppe II, carton 5.
127. Because of Settala's "exact knowledge" of "provincial and local conditions," the court of Vienna foresaw his participation in all rites that specifically concerned Lombardy-Venetia. Prince Colloredo-Mannsfeld to Emperor Ferdinand I, 8 April 1838, ÖStA, HHStA, NZA, Gruppe II, carton 5. For Settala, see Marco Meriggi, *Il Regno Lombardo-Veneto* (Turin, 1987), 128.
128. The more liberal admissions practice in Milan is referred to in the communication from Grand Aulic Chancellor Mittrowsky to Prince Colloredo-Mannsfeld, 21 March 1838, ÖStA, HHStA, NZA, Gruppe II, carton 5.
129. Caiani, "Ornamentalism."
130. J. H. Elliott, "A Europe of Composite Monarchies," *Past and Present* 137 (1992): 48–71. For the quotation, see Caiani, "Ornamentalism," 54.
131. ÖStA, HHStA, ZA Prot 57, fol. 353r.
132. The grand master of the court rejected the idea of allowing the knights of the Iron Crown to appear at the festivities in the order's costume because other provinces did not have associated orders. Colloredo-Mannsfeld to Emperor Ferdinand, 15 March 1837, ÖStA, HHStA, NZA, Gruppe II, carton 3a.
133. For the Prussian and Russian coronations, see Sellin, *Gewalt und Legitimität*, 96 and 99–101.
134. Prince Colloredo-Mannsfeld to Emperor Ferdinand, 8 April 1838, ÖStA, HHStA, NZA, Gruppe II, carton 5.
135. Colloredo-Mannsfeld to Emperor Ferdinand, 8 April 1838, ÖStA, HHStA, NZA, Gruppe II, carton 5.
136. Andreas Gottsmann and Stefan Malfèr, "Die Vertretungskörperschaften und die Verwaltung in Lombardo-Venetien," in *Die Habsburgermonarchie 1848–1918*, vol. 7/2: *Die*

regionalen Repräsentativkörperschaften, ed. Helmut Rumpler and Peter Urbanitsch (Vienna, 2000), 1594–98.
137. A chart showing the placement of the various participants is attached to the document entitled "Ceremoniale del Solenne Omaggio in Milano," ASMi, Atti di Governo, Potenze Sovrana, 247. I am deeply grateful to Ambrogio Caiani for supplying copies of this document and others from these archives.
138. See Leo Andergassen, ed., *Eduard Gurk: Der Griff nach der Krone. Die Krönungsreisen Kaiser Ferdinands I. nach Prag, Tirol und Mailand* (Schloss Tirol, 2013).
139. "Prospetto delle feste, cerimonie ecc. che avranno luego nei giorni della dinora in Milano delle LL. MM. II. e RR. per l'incoronazione," ASMi, Atti di Governo, Potenze Sovrana, 247. See Henrike Mraz, "Das Königreich Lombardo-Venetien im Vormärz," in *Kaisertum Österreich 1804–1848: Ausstellung Schallaburg 27. April bis 27. Oktober 1996*, ed. Gottfried Mraz, Henrike Mraz, and Gottfried Stangler (Bad Vöslau, 1996), 74–79.
140. A clipping to this effect from a French newspaper unfavorable to the Habsburg cause (*Le Courier français* from 11 August 1838) is preserved in ÖStA, HHStA, Staatskanzlei, Provinzen, Lombardei-Venetien, carton 31, folder Krönung in Mailand, fol. 18v. See also Mraz, "Das Königreich Lombardo-Venetien," 75.
141. Sir Frederick Lamb to the Foreign Office, Venice, 25 October 1838, The National Archives (Kew), Foreign Office 120/169.
142. Heinrich Ritter von Srbik, *Metternich: Der Staatsmann und der Mensch*, 2nd ed. (Munich, 1957), vol. 2: 30.
143. Patent of 11 August 1804, reproduced in Edmund Bernatzik, ed., *Die österreichischen Verfassungsgesetze mit Erläuterungen* (Vienna, 1911), 49–52. This key provision tends to be played down in traditional interpretations. See Wilhelm Brauneder, "Kaiserwürde durch Verwaltungsakt: Der österreichische Kaisertitel von 1804," in *Wahl und Krönung in Zeiten des Umbruchs*, ed. Ludolf Pelizaeus (Frankfurt am Main, 2008), 206, 209.
144. ÖStA, HHStA, ZA Prot 47, fol. 158r–60r.

Bibliography

Agnew, Hugh LeCaine. "Ambiguities of Ritual: Dynastic Loyalty, Territorial Patriotism and Nationalism in the Last Three Royal Coronations in Bohemia, 1791–1836." *Bohemia* 41 (2000): 3–22.

Andergassen, Leo, ed. *Eduard Gurk: Der Griff nach der Krone. Die Krönungsreisen Kaiser Ferdinands I. nach Prag, Tirol und Mailand*. Schloss Tirol: Landesmuseum, 2013.

Barclay, David E. "Ritual, Ceremonial, and the 'Invention' of a Monarchical Tradition in Nineteenth-Century Prussia." In *European Monarchy: Its Evolution and Practice from Roman Antiquity to Modern Times*, edited by Heinz Duchhardt, Richard A. Jackson, and David Sturdy, 207–20. Stuttgart: Steiner, 1992.

Beales, Derek. *Joseph II*. 2 vols. Cambridge, UK: Cambridge University Press, 1987/2009.

———. "Joseph II's Rêveries." In *Enlightenment and Reform in Eighteenth-Century Europe*, edited by Derek Beales, 157–81. London: Tauris, 2005.

Beer, Adolf. *Zehn Jahre österreichischer Politik 1801–1810*. Leipzig: Brockhaus, 1877.

Bernatzik, Edmund, ed. *Die österreichischen Verfassungsgesetze mit Erläuterungen*. Vienna: Manz, 1911.

Brauneder, Wilhelm. "Kaiserwürde durch Verwaltungsakt: Der österreichische Kaisertitel von 1804." In *Wahl und Krönung in Zeiten des Umbruchs*, edited by Ludolf Pelizaeus, 199–213. Frankfurt am Main: Lang, 2008.

Broers, Michael. *Europe under Napoleon*. 2nd ed. London: Tauris, 2015.

———. *Napoleon*. Vol. 1: *Soldier of Destiny, 1769–1805*. London: Faber & Faber, 2014.

Caiani, Ambrogio A. "Ornamentalism in a European Context? Napoleon's Italian Coronation, 26 May 1805." *English Historical Review* 132, no. 554 (2017): 41–72.

———. "Re-inventing the *Ancien Régime* in Post-Napoleonic Europe." *European History Quarterly* 47 (2017): 437–60.

Campbell Orr, Clarissa, ed. *Queenship in Europe 1660–1815: The Role of the Consort*. Cambridge, UK: Cambridge University Press, 2004.

Cannadine, David. "The Context, Performance and Meaning of Ritual: The British Monarchy and the 'Invention of Tradition,' c. 1820–1977." In *The Invention of Tradition*, edited by Eric Hobsbawm and Terence Ranger, 101–64. Cambridge, UK: Cambridge University Press, 1983.

———. "Introduction: Divine Rites of Kings." In *Rituals of Royalty: Power and Ceremonial in Traditional Societies*, edited by David Cannadine and Simon Price, 1–19. Cambridge, UK: Cambridge University Press, 1987.

Clark, Christopher. "When Culture Meets Power: The Prussian Coronation of 1701." In *Cultures of Power in Europe during the Long Eighteenth Century*, edited by Hamish Scott and Brendan Simms, 14–35. Cambridge, UK: Cambridge University Press, 2007.

d'Asburgo Lorena, Pietro Leopoldo. *Relazione sullo stato della monarchia (1784)*, edited by Derek Beales and Renato Pasta. Rome: Edizioni di Storia e Letteratura, 2013.

Deak, John. *Forging a Multinational State: State Making in Imperial Austria from the Enlightenment to the First World War*. Stanford: Stanford University Press, 2015.

Duchhardt, Heinz. "Die preussische Königskrönung von 1701: Ein europäisches Modell?" In *Herrscherweihe und Königskrönung im frühneuzeitlichen Europa*, edited by Heinz Duchhardt, 82–95. Wiesbaden: Steiner, 1983.

Elliott, J. H. "A Europe of Composite Monarchies." *Past and Present* 137 (1992): 48–71.

Evans, R. J. W. *Austria, Hungary, and the Habsburgs: Essays on Central Europe, c. 1683–1867*. Oxford: Oxford University Press, 2006.

Godsey, William D. "Herrschaft und politische Kultur im Habsburgerreich: Die niederösterreichische Erbhuldigung (ca. 1648–1848)." In *Aufbrüche in die Moderne: Frühparlamentarismus zwischen altständischer Ordnung und monarchischem Konstitutionalismus 1750–1850. Schlesien—Deutschland—Mitteleuropa*, edited by Roland Gehrke, 141–77. Cologne: Böhlau Verlag, 2005.

———. *The Sinews of Habsburg Power: Lower Austria in a Fiscal-Military State 1650–1820*. Oxford: Oxford University Press, 2018.

Gottsmann, Andreas, and Stefan Malfèr. "Die Vertretungskörperschaften und die Verwaltung in Lombardo-Venetien." In *Die Habsburgermonarchie 1848–1918*. Vol. 7/2: *Die regionalen Repräsentativkörperschaften*, edited by Helmut Rumpler and Peter Urbanitsch, 1593–632. Vienna: Verlag der Österreichischen Akademie der Wissenschaften, 2000.

Grell, Chantal. "The *sacre* of Louis XVI: The End of a Myth." In *Monarchy and Religion: The Transformation of Royal Culture in Eighteenth-Century Europe*, edited by Michael Schaich, 345–66. London: German Historical Institute/Oxford University Press, 2007.

Haag, Sabine, ed. *Zuhanden Ihrer Majestät: Medaillen Maria Theresias*. Vienna: Kunsthistorisches Museum, 2017.

Hertel, Sandra. "Maria Theresia als 'König von Ungarn' im Krönungszeremoniell in Preßburg (1741)." *Frühneuzeit-Info* 27 (2016): 110–23.
Heym, Sabine. "Prachtvolle Kroninsignien für Bayern—aber keine Krönung." In *Bayerns Krone 1805: 200 Jahre Königreich Bayern*, edited by Johannes Erichsen and Katharina Heinemann, 36–47. Munich: Residenz, 2006.
Hobsbawm, Eric. "Inventing Traditions." In *The Invention of Tradition*, edited by Eric Hobsbawm and Terence Ranger, 1–14. Cambridge, UK: Cambridge University Press, 1983.
Holčík, Štefan. *Krönungsfeierlichkeiten in Preßburg/Bratislava 1563–1830*. Bratislava: Tatran, 1992.
Holenstein, André. "Huldigung und Herrschaftszeremoniell im Zeitalter des Absolutismus und der Aufklärung." In *Zum Wandel von Zeremoniell und Gesellschaftsritualen in der Zeit der Aufklärung*, edited by Klaus Gerteis, 21–46. Hamburg: Felix Meiner Verlag, 1992.
Jackson, Richard A. *Vive le roi! A History of the French Coronation from Charles V to Charles X: Vivat Rex*. Chapel Hill: University of North Carolina Press, 1984.
Jäger, Albert. *Tirols Rückkehr unter Oesterreich und seine Bemühungen zur Wiedererlangung der alten Landesrechte von 1813 bis 1816*. Vienna: Sartori, 1871.
Josupeit-Neitzel, Elke. *Die Reformen Josephs II. in Siebenbürgen*. Munich: Trofenik, 1986.
Kertzer, David I. *Ritual, Politics, and Power*. New Haven: Yale University Press, 1988.
Klingenstein, Grete. "The Meanings of 'Austria' and 'Austrian' in the Eighteenth Century." In *Royal and Republican Sovereignty in Early Modern Europe*, edited by Robert Oresko, G. C. Gibbs, and H. M. Scott. Cambridge, UK: Cambridge University Press, 1997.
Kraehe, Enno E. *Metternich's German Policy*. Vol. 2: *The Congress of Vienna 1814–1815*. Princeton: Princeton University Press, 1983.
Kropatschek, Joseph. *Oestreichs Staatsverfassung*. Vol. 1. Vienna: Mößle, 1794.
Kunisch, Johannes, ed. *Dreihundert Jahre Preußische Königskrönung: Eine Tagungsdokumentation*. Berlin: Duncker & Humblot, 2002.
Lahner, Julian. "Repräsentation und Herrschaftswechsel in Tirol und Salzburg, 1806–1816." *Mitteilungen des Instituts für Österreichische Geschichtsforschung* 126 (2018): 286–92.
Langewiesche, Dieter. *Die Monarchie im Jahrhundert Europas: Selbstbehauptung durch Wandel im 19. Jahrhundert*. Heidelberg: Winter, 2013.
Laven, David. *Venice and Venetia under the Habsburgs 1815–1835*. Oxford: Oxford University Press, 2002.
Liechtenhan, Francine-Dominique. *Élisabeth Ire de Russie*. Paris: Fayard, 2007.
Loughlin, James. *The British Monarchy and Ireland: 1800 to the Present*. Cambridge, UK: Cambridge University Press, 2007.
Macartney, C. A. *The Habsburg Empire 1790–1918*. New York: Macmillan, 1969.
Mansel, Philip. *Dressed to Rule: Royal and Court Costume from Louis XIV to Elizabeth II*. New Haven: Yale University Press, 2005.
———. *The Eagle in Splendour: Inside the Court of Napoleon*. 2nd ed. London: Tauris, 2015.
———. *Prince of Europe: The Life of Charles-Joseph de Ligne 1735–1814*. London: Weidenfeld & Nicolson, 2003.
Mazohl-Wallnig, Brigitte. *Österreichischer Verwaltungsstaat und administrative Eliten im Königreich Lombardo-Venetien 1815–1859*. Mainz: Zabern, 1993.
Meriggi, Marco. *Il Regno Lombardo-Veneto*. Turin: UTET, 1987.
———. "State and Society in Post-Napoleonic Italy." In *Napoleon's Legacy: Problems of Government in Restoration Europe*, edited by David Laven and Lucy Riall, 49–63. Oxford: Berg, 2000.

Mraz, Henrike. "Das Königreich Lombardo-Venetien im Vormärz." In *Kaisertum Österreich 1804–1848: Ausstellung Schallaburg 27. April bis 27. Oktober 1996*, edited by Gottfried Mraz, Henrike Mraz, and Gottfried Stangler, 67–79. Bad Vöslau: Niederösterreichisches Landesmuseum, 1996.

Muir, Edward. *Ritual in Early Modern Europe*. Cambridge, UK: Cambridge University Press, 1997.

Okey, Robin. *The Habsburg Monarchy: From Enlightenment to Eclipse*. New York: St. Martin's Press, 2001.

Olechnowicz, Andrzej, ed. *The Monarchy and the British Nation, 1780 to the Present*. Cambridge, UK: Cambridge University Press, 2007.

Otruba, Gustav. "Die Erbhuldigungen der oberösterreichischen Stände 1732–1741–1743: Eine Studie zur Geschichte des Treueverhaltens von Klerus, Adel und Bürgertum gegenüber Karl VI., Karl Albert und Maria Theresia." *Mitteilungen des Oberösterreichischen Landesarchivs* 16 (1990): 135–301.

Pálffy, Géza. "An 'Old Empire' on the Periphery of the Old Empire: The Kingdom of Hungary and the Holy Roman Empire in the Sixteenth and Seventeenth Centuries." In *The Holy Roman Empire, 1495–1806: A European Perspective*, edited by R. J. W. Evans and Peter H. Wilson, 259–79. Leiden: Bell, 2012.

———. "Crisis in the Habsburg Monarchy and Hungary, 1619–1622: The Hungarian Estates and Gábor Bethlen." *Hungarian Historical Review* 2 (2013): 733–60.

Péter, László. "Die Verfassungsentwicklung in Ungarn." In *Die Habsburgermonarchie 1848–1918*. Vol. 7/1: *Verfassung und Parlamentarismus*, edited by Helmut Rumpler and Peter Urbanitsch, 239–540. Vienna: Verlag der Österreichischen Akademie der Wissenschaften, 2000.

Polasky, Janet L. *Revolution in Brussels 1787–1793*. Brussels: Palais des Académies, 1982.

Polek, Johann. "Die Huldigung der Bukowina am 12. Oktober 1777." *Jahrbuch des Bukowiner Landesmuseums* 10 (1902): 3–36.

Robert, André. *L'Idée nationale autrichienne et les guerres de Napoléon: L'Apostolat du baron de Hormayr et le salon de Caroline Pichler*. Paris: Alcan, 1933.

Rössler, Hellmuth. *Graf Johann Philipp Stadion: Napoleons deutscher Gegenspieler*. 2 vols. Vienna: Herold, 1956.

Schennach, Martin P. "Die 'österreichische Gesamtstaatsidee': Das Verhältnis zwischen 'Gesamtstaat' und Ländern als Gegenstand rechtshistorischer Forschung." In *Rechtshistorische Aspekte des österreichischen Föderalismus*, edited by Martin P. Schennach, 1–29. Vienna: Verlag Österreich, 2015.

Schnettger, Matthias. "'Il Viaggio a Reims' oder die Restauration auf der Opernbühne." *Majestas* 12 (2004): 161–94.

Schroeder, Paul W. *The Transformation of European Politics 1763–1848*. Oxford: Clarendon, 1994.

Schwengelbeck, Matthias. *Die Politik des Zeremoniells: Huldigungsfeiern im langen 19. Jahrhundert*. Frankfurt: Campus, 2007.

———. "Monarchische Herrschaftsrepräsentationen zwischen Konsens und Konflikt: Zum Wandel des Huldigungs- und Inthronisationszeremoniells im 19. Jahrhundert." In *Die Sinnlichkeit der Macht: Herrschaft und Repräsentation seit der Frühen Neuzeit*, edited by Jan Andres, Alexa Geisthövel, and Matthias Schwengelbeck, 123–62. Frankfurt: Campus, 2005.

Sellin, Volker. *Gewalt und Legitimität: Die europäische Monarchie im Zeitalter der Revolutionen*. Munich: Oldenbourg, 2011.

Siemann, Wolfram. *Metternich: Stratege und Visionär*. Munich: Beck, 2016.
Sked, Alan. *The Decline and Fall of the Habsburg Empire 1815–1918*. London: Longman, 1989.
Sr. k. k. *Majestät Franz des Ersten politische Gesetze und Verordnungen für die Oesterreichischen, Böhmischen und Galizischen Erbländer*. Vol. 24. Vienna: Kurzbeck, 1818.
Srbik, Heinrich Ritter von. *Metternich: Der Staatsmann und der Mensch*. 2nd ed. Vol. 2. Munich: Bruckmann, 1957.
Stollberg-Rilinger, Barbara. *Des Kaisers alte Kleider: Verfassungsgeschichte und Symbolsprache des Alten Reiches*. Munich: C. H. Beck, 2008.

———. "Herstellung und Darstellung politischer Einheit: Instrumentelle und symbolische Dimensionen politischer Repräsentation im 18. Jahrhundert." In *Die Sinnlichkeit der Macht: Herrschaft und Repräsentation seit der Frühen Neuzeit*, edited by Jan Andres, Alexa Geisthövel, and Matthias Schwengelbeck, 73–92. Frankfurt: Campus, 2005.

———. *Maria Theresia: Die Kaiserin in ihrer Zeit. Eine Biographie*. Munich: C. H. Beck, 2017.

———. "On the Function of Rituals in the Holy Roman Empire." In *The Holy Roman Empire 1495–1806*, edited by R. J. W. Evans, Michael Schaich, and Peter H. Wilson, 359–73. London: Oxford University Press, 2011.

———. "Verfassung und Fest: Überlegungen zur festlichen Inszenierung vormoderner und moderner Verfassungen." In *Interdependenzen zwischen Verfassung und Kultur*, edited by Hans-Jürgen Becker, 7–37. Berlin: Duncker & Humblot, 2003.

Strong, Roy. *Coronation from the 8th to the 21st Century*. London: Harper Perennial, 2005.
Szakály, Orsolya. "Opportunity or Threat? Napoleon and the Hungarian Estates." In *Collaboration and Resistance in Napoleonic Europe: State-Formation in an Age of Upheaval, c. 1800–1815*, edited by Michael Rowe, 153–68. Basingstoke: Palgrave Macmillan, 2003.
Taylor, A. J. P. *The Habsburg Monarchy 1809–1918*. Chicago: University of Chicago Press, 1948.
Vick, Brian E. *The Congress of Vienna: Power and Politics after Napoleon*. Cambridge, MA: Harvard University Press, 2014.
Wandruszka Adam. *Leopold II.: Erzherzog von Österreich, Grossherzog von Toskana, König von Ungarn und Böhmen, Römischer Kaiser*. 2 vols. Vienna: Herold Verlag, 1963/65.
Wertheimer, Eduard. "Der ungarische Krönungsreichstag von 1808." In *Geschichte Oesterreichs und Ungarns im ersten Jahrzehnt des 19. Jahrhunderts*. Vol. 2: 286–97. Leipzig: Duncker & Humblot, 1884.

———. *Die drei ersten Frauen des Kaisers Franz*. Leipzig: Duncker & Humblot, 1893.

Wilson, Peter H. *Heart of Europe: A History of the Holy Roman Empire*. Cambridge, MA: The Belknap Press of Harvard University Press, 2016.

Chapter 10

AFTER 1848

The Heightened Constitutional Importance of the Habsburg Coronation in Hungary

Judit Beke-Martos

> ... the Hungarian coronation is not a simple ceremony,
> it is a public legal fact containing the complete acceptance of the constitution
> —Henrik Marczali

Introduction

Coronation ceremonies were necessary elements of a monarch's ceremonial legitimization process to bestow upon him the entirety of his power, and this circumstance alone sufficed to make them more than mere spectacle.[1] While the role and importance of such coronations varied depending on the time period as well as on the geographical area within the Habsburg-ruled territories, their legal relevance cannot be denied. One could argue that coronations lacked written rules—with the exception of the religious *ordines*—and were mostly governed by tradition, which is why their importance slowly diminished with the appearance of written constitutions. However, legal tradition survived and maintained its importance (and sometimes even its binding force) through repetition and practice—as well as through its observance by the people, who continued to abide by it. This adherence to the tradition and practice of coronations did not cease in the territories of the Hungarian crown as long as the head of state was a monarch, not even when written constitutional frameworks began to appear, thereby proving that these ceremonial events also remained legally relevant. In order to avoid unnecessarily broad statements and observations, this chapter will focus only on developments in Hungary with emphasis on the mid-nineteenth century.

Following the dissolution of the estates-based social structure in 1848, the crowning of the Habsburg king on the Hungarian throne became even more important. The coronation of 1867 ended a nearly two-decade-long constitutional crisis in Hungary and reinstated the Hungarian constitutional order. It provides the perfect example—in line with the general theme of this volume—of the Habsburg coronations remaining an integral part of the Habsburg conception of rule while strengthening the contractual nature of its administration. It also proves that even in the nineteenth century, coronations could retain or even increase their constitutional, political, and social significance.

What Was a Hungarian Coronation by the Middle of the Nineteenth Century?

Though Hungary was a monarchy from its foundation in 1000 until 1946,[2] not all of its monarchs were crowned: the most famous exception was Joseph II, who reigned between 1780 and 1790 and refused a Hungarian coronation altogether.[3] The nearly twenty years following the unilateral abdication of King Ferdinand V[4] on 2 December 1848 were likewise a period of a noncrowned—that is to say a *de facto*, but not *de jure*—king. The kings and queens who were crowned, however, were inducted into their inherited or elected offices through a variety of ceremonies, among them the coronation ceremony involving the archbishop of Esztergom,[5] Székesfehérvár Basilica,[6] and the Holy Crown of St. Stephen.[7] During the first three centuries of Hungary's history, the House of Árpád was the ruling dynasty, and occasional disagreements on who was to inherit the Hungarian crown notwithstanding, the coronation ceremonies were mainly religious occasions.[8] Although some scholars claim that the very first Hungarian coronation was already a product of public legal development,[9] the early coronations were mainly considered a form of "this peculiar office-transferring procedure from the Middle Ages."[10]

The religious aspect of the coronation derives from the God-given nature of the monarch's power. In fact, there is a reciprocity to be observed between the king and the Church: the king, as the possessor of the God-given authority, was entitled to order the Church to perform the coronation mass, since his position was higher than that of the representatives of the Church.[11] In reality, however, the king required a Church representative to perform the coronation mass and crown him to be accepted as the one "above" the Church. Accordingly, there was a mutual give and take during coronation masses. Yet the co-operation or mutual acceptance of king and Church did not stop there; in fact, the monarch and the representative of the Church exchanged promises during the coronation. The Church bestowed upon the king the God-given authority and personal sanctity by blessing and anointing him with sacred oil. The Church did this in exchange for protection, symbolized during the coronation mass by the king pulling his sword from its sheath and swinging it through the air toward those present. The promises expressed through the participants' words and actions in the ceremony can be considered a contract with bilateral obligations for both parties. By swearing the religious oath, the *iuramentum iustitiae et pacis*, the king provided security for the performance of this contract on his part.

The Hungarian king's coronation was not solely a religious ceremony, however; it had legal relevance as well, which constantly increased over the centuries. At what time this legal relevance can first be observed is still being debated; and while some claim that the very first coronation already had legal implications,[12] most scholars link this aspect to the appearance of the secular oath taken by the king upon his induction into office, which connected the religious and legal roles of the coronation.[13] It is unclear when the secular oath became a part of the ceremony. There are sources claiming that as early as 1205, Andrew II[14] swore an oath to "maintain the kingdom's rights and the crown's solemnity."[15] It is safe to conclude that the first secular oath took place during the first half of the thirteenth century. In addition to his swearing of a secular oath, the importance of Andrew II lies in his issuance of the Golden Bull in 1222, thereby providing and guaranteeing rights and privileges to certain Estates. The origin of the feudal—and later the feudal-representative—monarchy in Hungary dates back to this document— the first milestone in the historical constitution of the country. It is all the more important to note that the secular oath became a part of the power-transferring ceremony at approximately the same time that the first Estates began to gain some form of political power.[16]

With the establishment of the secular oath, the coronation ceremony started to expand. In addition to the aforementioned contractual relationship between the king and the Church, another relationship can be identified between the monarch and the Estates. While it would be too early to call this exchange between the Estates and the king a social contract as described by Rousseau,[17] it is undeniable that a certain exchange of promises occurred: the king pledged to protect the country and the crown, and the Estates agreed to assist the monarch in this endeavor. Such an exchange of promises is, in essence, a contract. Accepting this premise, the secular oath can be considered a security to ensure the performance of this contract.[18] A Hungarian scholar of the early twentieth century, Ákos Timon, explained how the initially religious event of the royal coronation was continuously expanded with new and legally, or even constitutionally, relevant elements. Since this ceremony was not regulated by written laws but instead based on old customary law, it became a "conviction living within the nation."[19] This explains why and how the observed and practiced legal traditions survived the test of time despite the constitutional and military challenges facing Hungary.

During the first three hundred years of Hungary's history, the hereditary rule of the Árpáds, some kings already not only swore their secular oaths in addition to the coronation mass, but were also prepared to put their promise into writing by issuing a so-called *diploma inaugurale*. As with the appearance of the secular oath, scholars dispute the exact time this *diploma* originated. Some date it to St. Stephen's documents at the beginning of the eleventh century, while others claim that the abovementioned Andrew II issued the first such writing. Many authors seem to agree, however, that Andrew III,[20] the last monarch of the Árpád dynasty, provided the first written promise.[21] Act no. 1 of 1453[22] was the first law to contain the text of the king's oath in the form of a legislative act.[23] Issuing the *diploma inaugurale* and putting the royal promise into writing was voluntary for a long time. The significance of this procedure grew as the hereditary monarchy turned into an elective monarchy following the death of Andrew III in 1301: the Estates had earned political rights through representation in the feudal assembly and claimed the right to elect their king. These elections were neither democratic nor balanced; in fact, they were heavily disputed, and their results favored the wishes of the wealthiest and politically most powerful. Thus, between 1301 and the beginning of the Turkish occupation in 1526, the Hungarian Estates elected their monarch, in the majority of cases, from one of the neighboring countries' royal dynasties. Throughout this period, the coronation ceremony and its constitutive elements, its traditions and actors, and the issuance of the *diploma inaugurale* as well as the monarch's oath as additional security became increasingly important.

One key element of the coronation that gained in significance was the crown itself. It was during this period of elective monarchy that the St. Stephen's Crown became the Holy Crown of Hungary, embodying and objectifying Hungarian sovereignty.[24] Though there is debate as to when the crown currently on display in the Hungarian parliament in Budapest was made and delivered to Hungary, sources seem to agree that by the beginning of the fourteenth century, it was this very crown, which was also known as the Holy Crown of St. Stephen.[25] In the period of the elective monarchy, the crown sealed the agreement regarding the person chosen as king. Whoever ended up being crowned, preferably by the archbishop of Esztergom at Székesfehérvár Basilica with the Holy Crown, was considered to be king of Hungary, even if only a minority of the Estates supported that king's candidacy for the Hungarian throne. The coronation as an act became a constitutive event with the crown representing the population—or at least those parts that had some form of representation. The Estates understood the Hungarian Holy Crown to represent Hungarian sovereignty, and by placing it on someone's head, the sovereignty was transferred to that person. The crowned head of state thus acquired the obligation to always serve Hungary's interests, for in the event that he failed to do so, the Estates retained the right—derived from the Golden Bull—to resist the actions and the rule of the elected and crowned monarch.[26] The theories surrounding the Holy Crown, as well as numerous others (like the organic state theory, which claims that the nation constitutes a body that has received its head—the king—by way of the coronation) appeared in nineteenth-century Hungarian scholarship and continue to be an important focal point of reinterpretations of early Hungarian history to this very day.[27]

The year 1526 marked the beginning of the Ottoman occupation in Hungary;[28] and even though the country officially remained an elective monarchy until 1687, the Habsburgs practically inherited the Hungarian crown during this time. The territories of the Hungarian Kingdom only encompassed the western parts of Hungary, while the Ottoman Empire occupied the central parts, and Transylvania became domestically independent as a principality in the east. As an act of gratitude for the assistance of the Habsburg troops in liberating Hungary from the Ottoman occupation, the feudal assembly of 1687 put the Habsburg's hereditary right to the Hungarian throne into writing.[29]

The very scarce statutory regulation of the coronation, primarily Acts nos. 1, 2, and 3 of 1687, was only supplemented with two further acts throughout the remaining years of Habsburg rule in Hungary. First, as part of the Pragmatic Sanction, which was enacted by law in Hungary in 1723, Act no. 2 of 1723 extended the hereditary nature of the Hungarian crown to female descendants of the Habsburg dynasty in the event that there was no male heir anywhere in the line of succession.[30] The second and last regulatory change was made as a reaction to Joseph II's refusal to be crowned in Hungary: Act no. 3 of 1790–91 stipulated a maximum delay of six months for the heir apparent to participate in a coronation ceremony and thereby complete the constitutional transfer of power.[31] It is to be noted that the regulation did not define any sanctions in the event that an heir apparent missed this deadline. Some scholars therefore argue that if an heir was not crowned within the given six months, the governed would no longer be obliged to comply with that ruler's decisions, as all of his (or her) actions would be unconstitutional.[32]

In addition to the written regulations—and by the time the Habsburgs became the hereditary rulers in Hungary—the issuance of the *diploma inaugurale*, the swearing of the secular oath, and the coronation of the monarch with the Holy Crown of St. Stephen became, through practice, the legally relevant elements of the coronation. In the hereditary monarchy of the Habsburgs, in comparison to the elective monarchy preceding it, the practical relevance of the coronation may have decreased inasmuch as it no longer served as the finalizing act following a long debate. Its symbolic relevance, on the other hand, only *increased*—especially since the Habsburg monarchs were still considered by many Hungarians to be foreigners on the Hungarian throne.[33] Every time a new king or queen agreed to uphold the constitutional order of the Hungarian territories in the *diploma inaugurale* and swore an oath upon it, the historical constitution was reinforced and guaranteed for the duration of the new monarch's reign.

Accordingly, by the mid-nineteenth century, a Hungarian coronation was a symbolic constitutional act of ceremonial legitimization sealing two parallel contractual relationships: that between the king and the Church as well as that between the king and the Estates. This somewhat simplified summary of what a Hungarian coronation meant by the middle of the nineteenth century would be difficult to understand without an introduction to the Hungarian constitutional development leading up to that time.

The Effect of the Hungarian Constitutional Development on the Coronation

Hungary had no written constitution in the modern sense until the middle of the nineteenth century.[34] Before that time, the historical constitution—a set of fundamental legal documents, laws, and declarations—formed the legal basis of the Hungarian Kingdom, and it was this constitutional order that the new monarch promised to uphold and protect during his or her reign. Due to this system functioning as well as it did, there were practically no attempts to create a written constitution for Hungary prior to the nineteenth century.

In 1848, when the revolutionary wave swept through Western Europe and brought constitutional changes in its wake, Hungary successfully completed a constitutional revolution by enacting the so-called "Laws of April."[35] This set of thirty-two separate acts (called articles)[36] could easily be assessed collectively as a constitution, since it provided the basic framework of a constitutional monarchy. This revolutionary success, however, was very short-lived: in September 1848, the Hungarian War of Independence erupted, in which Austrian troops, as well as the military units of the various nationalities living on the territories of the Hungarian crown, faced the Hungarians on the battlefield. The Habsburg court in Vienna wanted to crush the Hungarians' attempts at independence in this military conflict, and even thought it could revoke Hungary's constitutional changes (i.e., the "Laws of April") by replacing its king, Ferdinand V, who had signed those changes into law.

Hence, Ferdinand V abdicated as Austrian emperor and king of Hungary on 2 December 1848.[37] With his younger brother forfeiting his right to the throne, Ferdinand's nephew Francis Joseph became Austrian emperor.[38] Francis Joseph, however, did not *de jure* become king of Hungary on the same day—in fact, it would not be until 8 June 1867 that he, as part of the Compromise of 1867 (which also established the Austro-Hungarian Monarchy), agreed to issue a *diploma inaugurale*, swore the secular oath upon it, and was ultimately crowned with the Holy Crown in the cities of Buda and Pest, the capital cities of the Hungarian crown's territories that would later be joined.

Two questions arose as a result of the events of 2 December 1848: first, the question of the abdication, and second, the potential accession of a new heir to the throne. Independent of the legality of Ferdinand's unilateral abdication, the new heir—assuming he or she was within the line of succession—would have had to issue the *diploma inaugurale*, take the secular oath, and be crowned Hungarian king in order to obtain the full power of head of state in Hungary.[39] Since Francis Joseph apparently had no intention to fulfill any of these requirements at the time he became emperor of Austria, this already created a rupture in the Hungarian constitutional order. Yet the problem could still have been remedied through acceptance of the abdication by the Hungarian parliament and the coronation of Francis Joseph as the new monarch. Neither of these happened in 1848, however, thereby deepening the constitutional crisis of the country and ultimately leading to the suspension of Hungary's constitutional order.

The news of Ferdinand's abdication reached the Hungarian capital on 5 December 1848. At the session of parliament the next day, there were initial suggestions in favor of accepting the abdication, but many—primarily those harboring republican, antiroyalist sentiments—opposed this, seeing an opportunity to get rid of the Habsburgs and the monarchy altogether. In light of the ongoing fighting, those opposing the acceptance of the abdication were in the majority. From a legal perspective, however, both the Habsburgs and the Hungarian parliament were mistaken. For if one accepts the contractual nature of the coronation as an act establishing a bilateral contractual relationship between the monarch and the governed, then neither the monarch nor the governed could terminate this contractual relationship unilaterally. Accordingly, Ferdinand's abdication could not terminate his rule without Hungary's consent. Yet it is also clear that by refusing to accept Ferdinand's abdication, the Hungarian parliament could not extend his rule beyond his abdication. Hungary thus found itself in a constitutional deadlock in which the *de jure* king refused to govern the country while the country refused to accept the *de facto* king. Francis Joseph as the *de facto* king claimed to assume all the rights and obligations of the Hungarian throne and considered his accession to be complete based exclusively on the fact that he was next in the line of succession.

Due to the Hungarian parliament's refusal to accept the abdication, the second question concerning the potential accession of a new heir to the throne became moot as well. Even if Francis Joseph had wished to have himself crowned, as required by the laws and customs of Hungary, he would have had to initiate negotiations with parliament to establish his "contract" with the governed. Yet at the turn of 1848–49, neither the Hungarians nor Francis Joseph were willing to engage in the necessary negotiations.[40]

The unresolved rupture between the head of state and the country led to the complete suspension of Hungary's constitutional order on 4 March 1849, when Francis Joseph, in his capacity as the Austrian emperor, issued the Imposed March Constitution (*Oktroyierte Märzverfassung*) for all Habsburg-ruled territories, including Hungary. This document dissolved the Hungarian parliament and included the territories of the Hungarian crown in those of the Austrian Empire. As for the ceremonial, the March Constitution only required the coronation of the Austrian emperor, who swore an oath on the Austrian constitution.[41] The question whether a noncrowned monarch could issue a constitution is justified. Since heirs who had not yet been crowned were not even permitted to sign laws into force, it is safe to assume that Francis Joseph could not legally issue a new constitution.[42] Yet under Hungarian law at the time, if a legal heir to the throne did something within the first six months of his or her rule (which was the period of time in which he or she had to be crowned) that he or she was not yet authorized to do, there was no sanction, as the heir to the throne was inviolable. Accordingly, one could only hold responsible the minister who signed off on the royal act, if there was in fact such a minister.[43] Since the March Constitution suspended the Hungarian constitutional order, it also rendered all Hungarian laws ineffective, and the question of what the Hungarian laws provided for such or similar situations became legally irrelevant. The political reality created an unconstitutional situation from Hungary's perspective that persisted until the Compromise of 1867.

Though the reinstatement of the Hungarian constitutional order was completed only with the coronation in 1867, the situation did change somewhat between 1849 and 1867. Francis Joseph issued three constitutional documents during this period: the New Year's Eve Patent of 31 December 1851, the October Diploma of 20 October 1860, and the February Patent of 26 February 1861. None of these documents changed Hungary's public legal status, however, as all of them treated the country as an integral part of the Habsburg-ruled Austrian territories.[44]

The unresolved constitutional situation served neither the Austrian Empire nor Hungary during the mid-nineteenth century, but it was clear that the initiative for negotiations had to come from the king. Having suffered military losses in the west, primarily in the battle of Solferino in 1859, as a result of which the Austrian Empire had to give up some of its northern Italian territories, and faced with the diminishing chances of a united German state under Habsburg leadership, Francis Joseph seemed more and more open to the idea of somehow settling his disagreement with the Hungarians. He initiated talks concerning a possible Hungarian coronation in 1860, having understood that if the Austrian Empire lost territories in the west, it could not survive the independence of the territories of the Hungarian crown, including all of the nationalities that lived there.[45] The Hungarian leadership was increasingly aware of the toll the existing situation had been taking on the country. Passive resistance against all that was Austrian or Habsburg did not serve to advance the country. The king eventually convened a session of the Hungarian parliament for April 1861 with the explicit wish to be crowned—as noted in a letter addressed to the session and dated 21 July 1861.[46] The response to this royal letter on behalf of parliament was very significant, as its author, Ferenc Deák—the driving force behind the success of the Compromise—addressed Francis Joseph as "His Royal Highness," thereby acknowledging the emperor's *de facto* succession to the Hungarian throne.[47] Neither the Hungarians nor Francis Joseph were quite ready to make the necessary concessions at the parliamentary session in 1861, however. The monarch wished to return to the way the relationship had been prior to 1848 and the "Laws of April," while the Hungarians wished to reclaim all the benefits they had temporarily enjoyed after the bloodless revolution. The positions were too distant from each other and too rigid, and the monarch therefore dissolved the session as early as November. Another four years would pass before the next session of the Hungarian parliament was convened.

By 1865, both parties understood the importance of resolving the constitutional situation. The Habsburg Monarchy continued to lose ground toward its western neighbors (the Italian and German areas), shrinking not just in terms of territory but also in significance, while Hungary stagnated in its economic and cultural development. Throughout the correspondence between the king and Deák, it became clear that Francis Joseph wished to become the crowned king of Hungary and thereby reinstate the Hungarian constitutional order, while Hungary wished to regain its constitutional independence along with a crowned head of state.[48] From the perspective of the monarch, who was experiencing difficulties with other neighbors and former allies as well as the diminishing and failing of the empire's military strength, it was logical to fear that he could only maintain the unresolved situation concerning the territories of the Hungarian crown temporarily. The Hungarians, very generally speaking, were not necessarily in favor of a Habsburg ruler on the Hungarian throne, but they were certainly opposed to the existing situation, as it was highly insecure for a country not to know who its head of state was. They accordingly feared unforeseeable consequences. Francis Joseph even admitted that the suspension of the Hungarian constitutional order had not been right, proving that he understood the constitutional, legal, and at this point undeniable political significance of the Hungarian coronation. With the necessary will now present on both sides, the consolidation process began in practice with the appointment of the Hungarian government on 17 February 1867.[49]

The Restoration of the Hungarian Constitutional Order and the Political Reality of 1867

The preparations for the coronation occurred in parallel to the drafting of the Austrian-Hungarian Compromise. Acts nos. 1–4 provided the legal basis for the rule of the new Hungarian king, while most of the remaining acts of 1867 laid the foundation for the new and unique dual state: the Austro-Hungarian Monarchy.[50] Parliament was in session, and the newly appointed Hungarian government took the initiative to supervise both the legislative process for the Compromise and the ceremonial preparations for the coronation. Based on a proposal made by the Hungarian prime minister, Count Gyula Andrássy, in parliament on 25 May 1867, a committee for the drafting of the *diploma inaugurale* and the secular oath was appointed. The twenty-four-man committee commenced work on 27 May and presented the final drafts on 3 June 1867.[51] In the meantime, parliament prepared all other legislative drafts, including the one accepting Ferdinand's abdication from the Hungarian throne.[52] For the first time in history, the ceremony was to take place in the cities of Buda and Pest instead of in Pressburg, where the previous Hungarian coronations since the Ottoman occupation had been staged. Francis Joseph arrived in Buda on 8 May 1867, a month before the festivities. Once all documents were ready in their final versions, they were taken to the king by a delegation of sixty members of both houses of the Hungarian parliament. Francis Joseph received the delegation on 4 June 1867 at 5:00 p.m., and read and agreed to the content of all legislation.[53] The texts were then returned by the delegation to the various parliamentary committees, which saw to their codification to prepare them for the king's signature on 12 June 1867, after his coronation and prior to his departure from the country.[54]

The Hungarian government put the deputy grand master, Count Antal Szapáry, in charge of the ceremonial preparations on 10 April 1867.[55] Szapáry supervised the delivery of the soil from the country's seventy-two counties,[56] which was dumped onto a designated area on the Pest side of the Chain Bridge on 5 June 1867 to create the coronation hill that the king was to ascend on his horse, swinging his sword to all four points of the compass as a representation of his promise to protect the country from attacks coming from any direction.[57] Also as part of the ceremonial preparations, the sealed casket containing the royal regalia was brought to the king on 6 June 1867 and opened in his presence. The two guards of the crown jewels appointed by Francis Joseph, Count György Károlyi and Baron Miklós Vay, whose duty was regulated by Act no. 6 of 1867, escorted the jewels from the royal palace to the coronation church and stayed with them until the coronation took place on 8 June, as well as during the days that they were on public display thereafter. The crown, the scepter, the orb, and St. Stephen's robe and sword were returned to the king's quarters on 11 June, where they were registered and the casket sealed once more to safeguard the regalia until the next—and final—Hungarian coronation in 1916.[58]

The day of the coronation, 8 June 1867, had a schedule very similar to all previous Hungarian coronation days: the procession to the coronation church, the coronation mass followed by the conferral of the Order of the Golden Spur upon selected soldiers, the procession leading to the secular part of the event, the secular oath taking and the ride onto the coronation hill to swing the sword in all four points of the compass, and finally the procession leading back to the Royal Castle, where a lunch concluded the day's events. Both Francis Joseph and his wife Elisabeth wore Hungarian attire, a very important symbolic gesture.[59] The bicameral parliament held a brief special session in the morning. Both Hungarian archbishops of the time—from Esztergom and Kalocsa—were present, but it was the archbishop of Esztergom who performed the coronation mass. During this mass, the king swore the religious oath, the *iuramentum iustitiae et pacis*, was anointed with sacred oil and clothed with the robe of St. Stephen, and was seated to observe the holy mass. Later on, he was girded with the sword, which he pulled from its sheath and swung toward those present to signal his will to protect the Church and the people from any kind of attack. Francis Joseph then knelt, and the Holy Crown of St. Stephen was placed on his head. The scepter was placed in his right hand and the orb in his left. In full regalia, he was then led to and seated upon the throne, thereby completing the coronation act. His wife Elisabeth was likewise crowned, and the royal couple left the coronation church following the sacrament.[60]

During the coronation mass, there was a traditional role assigned to the palatine,[61] who acted as a deputy of sorts to the king, thus making him the highest-ranking nonreligious participant in the coronation. In 1867, however, there was no palatine, and parliament therefore decided to assign this role to the prime minister. Maintaining the role of the palatine is an excellent example of continuity expressed through the ceremony (i.e., of Hungarian tradition being observed and maintained). Traditionally, the palatine had two tasks. The first was to conduct the questioning of the crowd in the church prior to the religious oath, asking whether the attendees wished to have the monarch crowned as their king. This was the earlier form of the *acclamatio*, the popular election of the ruler by the people present. As Fanni Hende points out (see Chapter 3), this act seems to have disappeared from the coronation mass in 1712. In the time that followed, popular support for the crowning of the king was ascertained through the session of parliament, where the representatives of the people drafted the *diploma inaugurale*, forming the basis of the agreement between the ruler and his subjects. Sources are silent on whether or not the prime minister conducted the traditional question and answer routine in 1867, and it therefore seems likely that he did not.[62] The second task of the palatine, duly performed by Count Andrássy in 1867 together with the archbishop, was to place the crown on the king's head. This element of the ceremony, which had been performed in the same way for centuries, once again shows the dual nature of the coronation: the symbolic legitimizing act of elevating the head of state to his role through the Church as well as through the people.

Following the religious part of the coronation, the newly crowned king conferred the Order of the Golden Spur upon some of his soldiers while still on the castle hill. The procession then led to the parish church on the Pest side of the Danube. There, Francis Joseph swore the secular oath, whose text he had agreed to in advance when the parliamentary delegation delivered the draft to him. During this act, the text was handed from the prime minister to the archbishop, who administered the oath to the king. This happened outdoors in the presence of significant crowds to witness the king's promise.[63] A little further to the north, where the coronation hill had been built from soil sent from all parts of Hungary, the king performed the symbolic act of promising to protect his country. The procession eventually returned to the Buda side and to the castle for a lunch with a select few invited guests. Festivities were limited for the remainder of the day, as the royal family was still mourning the death of Matilda, the eighteen-year-old daughter of Archduke Albert, Duke of Teschen. Franz Liszt's coronation mass composed for the occasion was premiered, but the National Theater did not hold its traditional performance in the evening. Oxen were roasted for the people in a public park on the Buda side of the Danube.

The coronation day thus concluded the months-long process of drafting the Compromise and restored the Hungarian constitutional order. It was a constitutional and a political event as well as a legitimizing act by means of ceremony. By crowning the *de facto* head of state, the necessary bridge between 1848 and 1867 was established—and by ensuring legal continuity, Hungary could regain its former public legal status. In addition, with the formation of Austria-Hungary, a dual state in which the two constituting parts (the Cisleithanian territories and the Kingdom of Hungary) became equal partners, Hungary could no longer be considered a part of Austria. In fact, the country acquired a significant role on the nineteenth century's international stage.

The coronation of 1867 proved highly challenging in that it strove to bridge divides and focused on continuity. By organizing a celebration that introduced the new state of the Austro-Hungarian Monarchy to Europe, it had political relevance beyond the domestic. The ceremony itself aimed to abide by the centuries-old traditions of earlier Hungarian coronations and follow their examples, despite the new location and the fact that almost twenty years had passed since Francis Joseph had effectively assumed power.

The coronation on 8 June 1867, as the finalizing and public event of a long and arduous process, was a constitutional act of immense political importance.[64] It is quite possible that without Francis Joseph's crowning as Hungarian king, the Austro-Hungarian Monarchy would not have been established. Restoring the Hungarian constitutional order through the coronation was a fundamental condition put forth by the Hungarians during the negotiations, and one that Francis Joseph had to meet in order to strike a deal with Austria's eastern neighbors. Had Austria-Hungary not been established, both countries could have easily disappeared from the European map by the end of the nineteenth century. Through the coronation and its elaborate preparation process, a new and significant political force was born in Europe.

Concluding Remarks

Coronations elevate the designated person to the office of the crowned head of state and bestow upon him or her the totality of power. In the case of Hungary, however, coronations meant even more throughout the country's monarchical history. Given that Hungary had no written constitution until 1949, the actual coronation of the monarch was a renewed enforcement of the historical constitution as well as—through the *diploma inaugurale* and the swearing of the secular oath—a guarantee for the maintaining of the Hungarian constitutional order. It was this constitutional order that, through legal continuity abridging potential pauses and ruptures, upheld Hungary's sovereignty from its foundation in 1000 all the way to the enactment of the written constitution. Accordingly, coronations—though highly symbolic—were not mere spectacles but legally relevant constituting elements of the affirmation of the country's basic order, establishing the monarchs' reign and laying the foundation for the relationships between the king, the Church, and the governed.

By the mid-nineteenth century, Hungary had a (albeit somewhat limited) legal framework regulating the coronation of the monarch. In the dichotomy of written regulation and unwritten customs, most elements were still based on tradition, and the symbolism of these elements was so deeply rooted that, in theory, no alterations to them were acceptable. Nevertheless, both the written and unwritten regulatory frameworks allowed for adjustments and adaptations to occur as necessitated by ongoing political developments. The coronation was an essential constitutional element in the peaceful transfer of power, which is why Francis Joseph *had* to be crowned Hungarian king regardless of the legal assessment of Ferdinand's abdication in 1848. The political situation between the Austrian Empire and the Kingdom of Hungary (also taking into consideration the Austrian Empire's other international relations at the time) changed over the nearly two decades between 1849 and 1867, during which the Hungarian constitutional order was suspended by the Imposed March Constitution and the lack of a coronation of the acting head of state.

The heightened importance of the coronation is therefore prominently displayed in the Hungary of 1867, especially due to the lack of a written constitution that could have changed the legal significance of the coronation.[65] Despite the advancement of legal thought in the nineteenth century and the increasingly widespread demand for codification and written constitutions, it was essential that Francis Joseph be crowned in accordance with the largely customary rules stemming from Hungarian traditions developed over many centuries. Neither the Austrians nor the Hungarians questioned the fact that the Hungarians' agreement to the Compromise was contingent upon the king's coronation. The Hungarians might not have had sufficient bargaining power vis-à-vis the Habsburg ruler leading up to the Compromise, but they still insisted on the basic requirement of the coronation, which at the same time reinstated the Hungarian constitutional order—the fundamental result the Hungarians wished for. Their ultimate goal was to secure the achievement they briefly enjoyed following the promulgation of the "Laws of April": a constitutional monarchy. Instead, Hungary became one part of a dual state with a neoabsolutistic ruler who had little affection for, understanding of, or interest in the developments in Hungary and the country's nationalist aims. The coronation was thus not only symbolic, but also legally and politically essential for the survival of Hungary as a separate political entity in the tumults of the nineteenth century.

Judit Beke-Martos is a postdoc researcher in the MTA-ELTE Legal History Research Group, as well as the managing director of the Center for International Affairs at the Legal Faculty of the Ruhr University in Bochum, Germany, where she also teaches courses on American law. She earned her JD and PhD in Law at Eötvös Loránd University in Budapest, Hungary, and her LLM in US and Global Business Law at Suffolk University Law School (SULS) in Boston, USA. She spent a year in residence as a visiting scholar at SULS in 2008–09 and three months as a foreign legal researcher at the Legal History Institute of Ghent University in Belgium in 2015. She has published a book and several scholarly articles in English, German, and Hungarian with an emphasis on the power-transferring procedures of monarchs and presidents. Her current research focuses on comparative constitutional and legal history, including legal tradition, custom, and culture.

Notes

1. In the opening quote, Marczali is referring to Francis Joseph's royal letter to the Hungarian parliament on 21 July 1861: Henrik Marczali, "A koronázás történeti előzményei," in *Koronázási emlékkönyv*, ed. Dénes Kovács and János Sziklay (Budapest, 1892), 20.
2. There were so-called democratic attempts during the Hungarian Revolution and War of Independence in 1848–49 as well as after World War I in 1918–19, but the monarchy was reinstated as the official form of state after both of them.
3. Most sources praising the importance of the 1867 coronation do not fail to mention the complete lack of such a ceremony in 1780. The ten-year reign of Joseph II was considered a "pause in the functioning of the Hungarian constitution," which was ultimately reinstated with the coronation of the following king, Leopold II: Imre Halász, "A koronázáskor," *Vasárnapi Újság* Special edition (5 June 1892): 4. Joseph II refused

to be crowned because he did not want to swear an oath to maintain the constitutional order of the country. In light of the fact that this oath formed an element of the ceremonial legitimization, his refusal once again proves the importance and legal relevance of coronations.

4. Ferdinand V was king of Hungary between 1835 and 1848, when he abdicated—even though this unilateral action was not acknowledged by the Hungarian parliament. Hence Ferdinand was considered the *de jure* Hungarian king until 1867.
5. The archbishop of Esztergom was the head of the Hungarian Roman Catholic Church.
6. Székesfehérvár Basilica was the setting for all coronations prior to the Ottoman occupation in 1526.
7. For details on the role and relevance of these three elements, which also constitute the so-called general theory as to which elements were necessary for a legal and complete Hungarian coronation, see Judit Beke-Martos, *Elevating the Monarch to the Throne: The Legal Relevance of the Coronation* (Budapest, 2013), 9–10.
8. While János Király claimed—based on the crown being a *res sacra*—that the coronation was a religious act, most sources refer to a much more complex role being assigned to the ceremony: János Király, *A király-koronázás eredete, egyházi kifejlődés és ordóbeli kialakulása* (Budapest, 1918), 4.
9. Mihály Latkóczy, *Korona és koronázás* (Eperjes, 1892), 10. János Lutter called the first Hungarian coronation "the overture of the Hungarian constitutional development": János Lutter, *A szent koronával való koronázás alkotmányjogi jelentősége* (Nagyvárad, 1917), 5.
10. Emma Bartoniek, *A magyar király-koronázások története* (Budapest, 1987), 6.
11. The royal title "King of Hungary," which Stephen received from the pope in Rome, allowed him to establish and develop the Hungarian Church, which was why the king was considered to stand above the Church in Hungary at the time. On the request for a crown, see Ákos Mihályfi, *A magyar királykoronázás jelentősége* (Budapest, 1917), 4–5.
12. See note 8.
13. See, for example, Gyula Szende, *Királylyá avatás Magyarországon a egyes korszakban 1301–1526—Doktori értekezés* (Budapest, 1893), 33; or Ákos Timon, *A szent korona elmélete és a koronázás* (Budapest, 1920), 5.
14. Andrew II was king of Hungary between 1205 and 1235.
15. Ferenc Eckhart, *Magyar Alkotmány- és Jogtörténet* (Budapest, 2000), 80; or Lutter, *A szent koronával*, 7.
16. By the beginning of the thirteenth century, the king was no longer the largest landowner in Hungary, which is why the various landlords, nobles, and those providing military assistance to the king gained access to politics and a shift from patrimonial to feudal monarchy occurred: Barna Mezey, *Alkotmánytörténet* (Budapest, 2002), 40–54.
17. The most well-known work on the so-called social contract is Rousseau's book written in 1762. It was and still is a highly controversial piece of scholarship, however: Jean-Jacques Rousseau, *On the Social Contract* (Mineola, NY, 2003).
18. Szende, *Királylyá avatás*, 32.
19. Timon, *A szent korona elmélete*, 31.
20. Andrew III was king of Hungary from 1290 to 1301.
21. Latkóczy refers to the document St. Stephen issued after the assembly for the coronation, which only contained the decisions made during that assembly. The king nevertheless signed and sealed the document: Latkóczy, *Korona*, 10. Others claim that the *diploma*

inaugurale dates back to a time before the coronation of the first king. Falk relates the document to the Golden Bull and the reign of Andrew II: Miksa Falk, "A koronázás közjogi jelentősége," in *Koronázási emlékkönyv*, ed. Dénes Kovács and János Sziklay (Budapest, 1892), 31. Linking it to Andrew III, for example, see Lutter, *A szent koronával*, 7; Eckhart, *Magyar Alkotmány- és Jogtörténet*, 80.

22. Throughout Hungarian history, there were three main sources of law: written law, customary law, and, as a subsidiary, Roman law. Written law during the early centuries of the monarchy were the king's decrees, which were put into writing, enacted, and announced. They were drafted as so-called *articles* of law. As soon as the Estates claimed and received participation in the legislative process through feudal and feudal-representative assemblies, these bodies also enacted written laws in the form of articles of law. The articles resulting from the assemblies were in reality individual acts, which are also called statutes today. Only in the twentieth century did the Hungarian terminology change these articles into acts, which is why many scholars use the term "act" for all of these early pieces of legislation enacted by the assemblies, and later by parliament. An act is therefore a statute, a written law by a legislative body. These acts serve as the primary sources of law together with the king's decrees, orders, patents, and so on. They are to be distinguished from unwritten customary law, which was frequently used in adjudication and often had regional character and validity. All of the acts referenced in this chapter with number and year are written laws from the specified session of the assembly or parliament, providing the regulations everyone had to abide by.

23. Act no. 1. of 1453: "First, the king shall swear an oath that he maintains his Hungary, together with its people, in the freedom and laws, as well as acknowledged customs, universally and individually, undisturbed, in which his forebears, like his grandfather, the emperor Sigmund, and his father Albert maintained and protected this country and its inhabitants. / 1. § And that he will not alienate the borders of Hungary, but to the best of his ability will protect them and reclaim those alienated." See https://1000ev.hu/ (last accessed 10 September 2017). See also Szende, *Királylyá avatás*, 35–36.

24. Ferenc Eckhart, *The Holy Crown of Hungary* (Budapest, 1941).

25. Kálmán Benda and Erik Fügedi, *A magyar korona regénye* (Budapest, 1979); Iván Bertényi, *A magyar korona története, harmadik bővített kiadás* (Budapest, 1986); Béla Czobor, "A koronázási jelvények," in *Koronázási emlékkönyv*, ed. Dénes Kovács and János Sziklay (Budapest, 1892), 42–49; János Pauer, *Székes-Fehérvárott koronázott királynők—Történelmi értekezés* (Székesfehérvár, 1872), 34.

26. Act no. 31 of 1222. The second paragraph stipulates the so-called *ius resistendi*, the right of those addressed and privileged in and by the Golden Bull to disrespect and disregard both their obligations toward the king and the king himself should the latter fail to comply with his obligations arising from the acts of 1222. https://1000ev.hu/ (last accessed 10 September 2017).

27. The primary source for the Holy Crown is still Eckhardt, *The Holy Crown*; but see also Endre Tóth and Károly Szelényi, *A magyar szent korona: királyok és koronázások* (Budapest, 1999); Timon, *A szent korona elmélete*, 6; Mihályfi, *A magyar királykoronázás*, 20; Szende, *Királylyá avatás*, 32.

28. When the Hungarians were defeated in the battle of Mohács in 1526 and their childless king Louis lost his life on the battlefield, the country was divided into two parts. Following the loss of Buda in 1541, Hungary was divided into the Hungarian Kingdom, the territories under Ottoman control, and the Transylvanian Principality. Buda was liberated

in 1686; but due to the ensuing internal fights, Hungary's complete liberation including the signing of the necessary peace treaties and partial reunification would take another thirty years.
29. Act no. 2 of 1687 elevated the Habsburg heir apparent (in the male line of succession) to the throne. Act no. 3 of 1687 regulated the further line of succession in case there was no male heir apparent within the then-living Habsburg dynasty. This act was later modified by accepting Charles VI's (Charles III in the line of Hungarian kings) Pragmatic Sanction, allowing the female line of inheritance in Act no. 2 of 1723. https://1000ev.hu/ (last accessed 10 September 2017).
30. Act no. 2 of 1723 allowed the female heirs of this Habsburg dynasty to inherit the Hungarian crown, but only if there was no male heir. As a consequence, Maria Theresa was "king" of Hungary between 1740 and 1780. https://1000ev.hu/ (last accessed 10 September 2017).
31. Act no. 3 of 1790–91. https://1000ev.hu/ (last accessed 10 September 2017).
32. Lutter, *A szent koronával*, 17–18.
33. Lutter, *A szent koronával*, 14.
34. The "Laws of April" issued in 1848 are not to be considered Hungary's first written constitution, since they are a collection of thirty-two articles rather than a single document. They did, however, provide the basis for the peaceful transition from absolute to constitutional monarchy, and were the foundation of the state-formation process following the bloodless revolution. Yet these reforms were short-lived, since Francis Joseph's neoabsolutistic monarchy discarded them. The "Laws of April," along with their content, meaning, and subsequent implementation, could therefore only be kept and maintained as another landmark of the historical constitution.
35. Mezey, *Alkotmánytörténet*, 208–10.
36. See note 22.
37. The Habsburgs considered the abdication an internal affair. The exchange took place behind closed doors at the archbishop's castle in Olomouc, based on the rules of the Habsburg family, and little is accordingly known about the details. Apparently, the regalia of the Austrian emperor—the crown of Emperor Rudolf II and the scepter—were on display but were not used for any purpose during the exchange: Imre Gonda and Emil Niederhauser, *A Habsburgok* (Budapest, 1977), 186.
38. German-language sources call the act a "Thronwechsel," to be translated as "change on the throne:" Hellmut Andics, *Das österreichische Jahrhundert—Die Donaumonarchie 1804–1918* (Vienna, 1986), 109.
39. A crowned head of state in a hereditary monarchy had the royal prerogatives connected to his person as soon as his predecessor died. Yet the monarch only received those royal prerogatives, which were connected to governance and not immediately necessary for the continued functioning of the state, by having himself crowned. For more on the individual prerogatives as well as theories on the division of royal power, see Beke-Martos, *Elevating the Monarch*, 18–20.
40. Zsolt László Kocsis, *A magyar államfő jogállása, hatásköre és helyettesítése 1000–1944 között* (n.p., 2004), 152.
41. Kocsis, *A magyar államfő*, 153.
42. Ákos Timon, *A szent korona és a koronázás közjogi jelentősége* (Budapest, 1907), 10.
43. Lutter, *A szent koronával*, 17.
44. Mezey, *Alkotmánytörténet*, 218–20.

45. Francis Joseph wrote a letter to his chancellor, Baron Miklós Vay, dated 20 October 1860, in which he mentioned for the first time that he wished to resolve his constitutional relationship with Hungary—meaning having himself crowned. Referenced in Marczali, "A koronázás történeti," 19.
46. Marczali, "A koronázás történeti," 20.
47. Kocsis, *A magyar államfő*, 160.
48. Deák authored the lead article of the *Pesti Napló*, the number one newspaper of the time, on 16 April 1865 (also known as the "Easter Article"), in which he expressed the nation's wish to consolidate the situation for a stable and secure future. In a letter dated 14 December 1865, Francis Joseph expressed his wish to be crowned as soon as possible, to which Deák responded on 8 February 1866 with the claim that the Hungarian people already wished to crown Francis Joseph with St. Stephen's Crown. This was a constitutionally necessary act in any event. Marczali, "A koronázás történeti," 21–22.
49. Latkóczy, *Korona*, 31.
50. Acts of 1867: https://1000ev.hu/ (last accessed 10 September 2017).
51. The following members of parliament were selected as members of the drafting committee: Sámuel Bónis, Ferencz Deák, Frigyes Podmaniczky, Pál Nyáry, Kálmán Tisza, Kálmán Ghyczy, Pál Somssich, Antal Csengery, Baron István Kemény, Pál Trifunácz, László Bezerédj, György Joannovics, Imre Szabó, Emil Trauschenfels, Lajos Vadnay, Ede Zsedényi, Count György Apponyi, Elek Dósa, Károly Szász, György Bartal, József Hosszu, István Bittó, József Justh, and Ferencz Pulszky: Dénes Kovács and János Sziklay, "A koronázás története: Az előkészületek," in *Koronázási emlékkönyv*, ed. Dénes Kovács and János Sziklay (Budapest, 1892), 52–54.
52. Latkóczy, *Korona*, 31.
53. Péter Simon, *Király és korona—Pillantás a múltra és jelenre* (Budapest, 1892), 312. Other sources date this audience to 6 June: Kovács and Sziklay, "A koronázás története: Az előkészületek," 58.
54. Latkóczy, *Korona*, 36.
55. Budapest, MOL, K 27 (Minisztertanácsi ülések): 1. cs., 25 April 1867. 8. np. and 7 May 1867, 3. np.
56. Bartoniek, *A magyar király-koronázások története*, 167.
57. Latkóczy, *Korona*, 32.
58. Kovács and Sziklay, "A koronázás története: Az előkészületek," 58–60 and 72. For Act no. 6 of 1867, see https://1000ev.hu/ (last accessed 10 September 2017).
59. The exact order of the procession is documented in Simon, *Király*, 315–17 and Latkóczy, *Korona*, 33.
60. Lutter, *A szent koronával*, 28–31 and Latkóczy, *Korona*, 34–35.
61. The palatine was the second-highest-ranking person at court, a general deputy of the king. He took over the king's duties whenever the monarch was away or otherwise incapable of exercising his office. The role of the palatine changed over the centuries and was first regulated in 1485. According to these rules, the palatine convened the assembly that chose the king, was the legal guardian of the minor monarch, led the court in the king's absence, and was the highest judge of the country after the king. Despite being the king's deputy and sworn to loyalty to the former, the palatine also became the representative of the Estates' interests. During the Ottoman occupation, the Habsburgs wished to diminish the importance of the palatine, but the office was reconfirmed in 1608 in a decree satisfy-

ing the Hungarian interests. In practice, however, the Habsburgs continued to nominate the palatine, thereby securing his unconditional loyalty to the Viennese court. The last palatine was in office until 1848, and the position remained vacant until 1867, when the prime minister took over the majority of the tasks: Mezey, *Alkotmánytörténet*, 129–30.
62. Falk, "A koronázás közjogi jelentősége," 26; Kovács and Sziklay, "A koronázás története: Az előkészületek," 63–65.
63. Simon, *Király*, 323.
64. In her seminal book, Barbara Stollberg-Rilinger criticized the traditional approach to symbolic acts and ceremonies as lacking political character. In her opinion, early modern state rituals were political acts in and of themselves: Barbara Stollberg-Rilinger, *Des Kaisers alte Kleider: Verfassungsgeschichte und Symbolsprache des Alten Reiches* (Munich, 2008), 15.
65. Hungary must therefore at least be considered different from those territories for which Matthias Schwengelbeck examines nineteenth-century investiture rituals: Matthias Schwengelbeck, *Die Politik des Zeremoniells: Huldigungsfeiern im langen 19. Jahrhundert* (Frankfurt, 2007), 155–56.

Bibliography

Andics, Hellmut. *Das österreichische Jahrhundert—Die Donaumonarchie 1804–1918*. Vienna: Kremayr & Scheriau, 1986.
Bartoniek, Emma. *A magyar király-koronázások története*. Budapest: Magyar Történelmi Társulat, Akadémiai Kiadó, Reprint Series, 1987.
Beke-Martos, Judit. *Elevating the Monarch to the Throne: The Legal Relevance of the Coronation*. Budapest: Eötvös Loránd University, 2013.
Benda, Kálmán, and Erik Fügedi. *A magyar korona regénye*. Budapest: Magvető Könyvkiadó, 1979.
Bertényi, Iván. *A magyar korona története, harmadik bővített kiadás*. Budapest: Kossuth Könyvkiadó, 1986.
Czobor, Béla. "A koronázási jelvenyek." In *Koronázási emlékkönyv*, edited by Dénes Kovács and János Sziklay, 42–49. Budapest: Könyves Kálmán magyar irodalmi és könyvkereskedési részvénytársaság kiadása, 1892.
Eckhart, Ferenc. *The Holy Crown of Hungary*. Budapest: Athenaeum, 1941.
———. *Magyar Alkotmány- és Jogtörténet*. Budapest: Osiris Kiadó, 2000.
Falk, Miksa. "A koronázás közjogi jelentősége." In *Koronázási emlékkönyv*, edited by Dénes Kovács and János Sziklay, 24–41. Budapest: Könyves Kálmán magyar irodalmi és könyvkereskedési részvénytársaság kiadása, 1892.
Gonda, Imre, and Emil Niederhauser. *A Habsburgok*. Budapest: Gondolat, 1977.
Halász, Imre. "A koronázáskor." *Vasárnapi Újság* Special edition (5 June 1892): 4–6.
Király, János. *A király-koronázás eredete, egyházi kifejlődés és ordóbeli kialakulása*. Budapest: Stephaneum Nyomda, Rt., 1918.
Kocsis, Zsolt László. *A magyar államfő jogállása, hatásköre és helyettesítése 1000–1944 között*. N.p.: Graf-X Media Consulting gondozásában kiadja Dr. Kocsis Zsolt László, 2004.
Kovács, Dénes, and János Sziklay. "A koronázás története: Az előkészületek." In *Koronázási emlékkönyv*, edited by Dénes Kovács and János Sziklay, 50–73. Budapest: Könyves Kálmán magyar irodalmi és könyvkereskedési részvénytársaság kiadása, 1892.

Latkóczy, Mihály. *Korona és koronázás*. Eperjes: Divald Károly Fiai, 1892.
Lutter, János. *A szent koronával való koronázás alkotmányjogi jelentősége*. Nagyvárad: Szent-László-Nyomda Részvénytársaság, 1917.
Marczali, Henrik. "A koronázás történeti előzményei." In *Koronázási emlékkönyv*, edited by Dénes Kovács and János Sziklay, 17–23. Budapest: Könyves Kálmán magyar irodalmi és könyvkereskedési részvénytársaság kiadása, 1892.
Mezey, Barna. *Alkotmánytörténet*. Budapest: Osiris Kiadó, 2002.
Mihályfi, Ákos. *A magyar királykoronázás jelentősége*. Budapest: M. Kir. Tudományegyetem nyomda, 1917.
Pauer, János. *Székes-Fehérvárott koronázott királynők—Történelmi értekezés*. Székesfehérvár: Klökner Péter Könyvkereskedő, 1872.
Rousseau, Jean-Jacques. *On the Social Contract*. Mineola, NY: Dover Publications, 2003.
Schwengelbeck, Matthias. *Die Politik des Zeremoniells: Huldigungsfeiern im langen 19. Jahrhundert*. Frankfurt: Campus, 2007.
Simon, Péter. *Király és korona—Pillantás a múltra és jelenre*. Budapest: Kormos Műintézet Nyomása, 1892.
Stollberg-Rilinger, Barbara. *Des Kaisers alte Kleider: Verfassungsgeschichte und Symbolsprache des Alten Reiches*. Munich: C. H. Beck, 2008.
Szende, Gyula. *Királylyá avatás Magyarországon a vegyes korszakban 1301–1526—Doktori értekezés*. Budapest: Fried S. Nyomda, 1893.
Timon, Ákos: *A szent korona elmélete és a koronázás*. Budapest: Stephaneum Nyomda, 1920.
———. *A szent korona és a koronázás közjogi jelentősége*. Budapest: Rákosi Jenő Budapesti Hírlap Újságvállalata, 1907.
Tóth, Endre, and Károly Szelényi. *A magyar szent korona: királyok és koronázások*, Budapest: Kossuth Könyvkiadó, 1999.

Afterword

THE LAST HABSBURG CORONATION AND WHAT IT MEANS TO BE ANOINTED

Helen Watanabe-O'Kelly

The inaugurations and coronations of the Habsburgs that this volume discusses are both centrally concerned, as Petr Mat'a says in Chapter 1, with "the authorization and legitimation of a new sovereign to exercise full princely jurisdiction over a particular political unit." I should like to argue, however, that there are essential differences between the two types of ceremony, and that only by understanding the differences can we grasp why the last Habsburg emperor and king did not, indeed could not, abdicate in 1918.

Inaugurations—*Huldigungen* or acclamations—are secular ceremonies establishing or confirming a contract between ruler and ruled. Coronations in the Catholic, and also in the British Anglican, understanding are performative religious ceremonies in which, by virtue not so much of the crowning but of the anointing, the ruler is transformed into God's representative on earth. The English term "coronation," like the German *Krönung*, places exclusive emphasis on the crown. The French *sacre*, like the German *Salbung*, is more helpful in understanding the consecration of the ruler by anointing him or her with holy oil or chrism. It is the anointing, the unction, that is the source of what Klaas Van Gelder in his Introduction calls *Gottesgnadentum*: the divine mandate given by God himself to his representative on earth. The ceremonial employed at a Catholic coronation is not merely symbolic. Like the sacraments, it is understood as being in a very real sense transformative. During the coronation mass, as Harriet

Rudolph shows in Chapter 2, the last two Roman emperors—Leopold II and Francis II—prostrated themselves in the shape of a cross before the altar like priests about to be ordained. Francis II's anointing resembled that of a bishop, comments Christian Hattenhauer in his edition of a contemporary account of the 1792 coronation.[1] The Roman emperor, after all, as part of the ceremony was admitted as a canon of the Marienstift in Aachen and was allowed to vote in the chapter.

William Godsey mentions in Chapter 9 how many coronations there were in the first half of the nineteenth century, among them the coronation of Napoleon I in Paris in 1804. What is striking about them is that they all included anointing as part of the ceremony. Napoleon insisted on being crowned not, as was first mooted, on the Champ de Mars, but in the Cathedral of Notre Dame. At the coronation mass, in the presence of the archbishops of Paris and Milan and twenty-four other bishops, as well as supporting clergy, he famously crowned himself; but he was anointed by Pope Pius VII whom he had brought from Rome especially for the occasion. At this coronation mass, the confessed unbeliever, who did not take communion as the ceremonial demanded, submitted himself to an elaborate ecclesiastical ritual, allowing the pope to anoint him and pronounce him emperor and to bless the insignia that had been so carefully designed as symbols of his power. Napoleon entered Notre Dame garbed as an emperor to indicate that it was the people who had chosen him, and he swore a constitutional oath at the other end of Notre Dame as the final act of the coronation; but the religious ceremony presented him to the people as God's representative on earth, a divinely sanctioned being to whom loyalty and obedience were due because of his divine mandate. God had chosen him as emperor, was the message, not merely the two and a half million citizens who had voted for his new dignity.

Charles XIV, king of Sweden and Norway, in 1818; George IV, king of Great Britain and Ireland, in 1821; Pedro I, emperor of Brazil, and Agustín I, emperor of Mexico, in 1822; Charles X, king of France, in 1825; Victoria, queen of Great Britain and Ireland, in 1838; and Pedro II, emperor of Brazil, in 1841 were all both crowned and anointed, just as Francis Joseph in 1867 and Charles I as Charles IV in 1916 were crowned and anointed in Hungary. Even if not all these monarchs were themselves personally pious—Napoleon I certainly was not—the point is that their subjects frequently were. They needed to know that God had given them this man or woman as their ruler whom they were to love and obey as they did God. A coronation was, of course, a contract between prince and people, and the emperor or king usually had to swear an oath to uphold certain freedoms or abide by certain laws or even, if there was one, by the constitution. The fact remains, however, that it was the holy oil that drew God's power down onto the ruler and that gave him or her the authority to rule.

We see the difference between a monarch who has been inaugurated and a monarch who has been anointed and crowned if we examine the events of November 1918. On 11 November 1918, the Armistice that signaled the end of World War I was signed in Compiègne in France. In the same month, two great European imperial regimes came to an end. One, the Austrian Empire led by a Habsburg, had come into being in 1804, the other, the German Empire led by a Hohenzollern, in 1871. Their holders in both cases were also kings, so it might be expected that this would also spell the end of the two kingdoms of Hungary and Prussia respectively. This did happen in the case of Prussia, whereas the Kingdom of Hungary continued to exist until 1946, with an intermission of some fifteen and a half months between November 1918 and the end of February 1920.

The two documents that ended the rule of the two king-emperors are very different. On 9 November 1918, the Federal German Chancellor Prinz Max von Baden (1867–1929) had declared the abdication of William II, German emperor and king of Prussia (1859–1941). Some weeks later, on 28 November 1918, from his refuge at Amerongen in the Netherlands, William signed the so-called "Abdankungsurkunde" or Document of Abdication. In the original, the full text reads as follows:

> I hereby renounce for all time to come ("für alle Zukunft") [my] rights in the crown of Prussia and the rights in the German imperial crown connected to them. I simultaneously release from the oath of allegiance which they have sworn to me as their emperor, king and supreme commander of the armed forces all civil servants of the German Empire and of Prussia, as well as all officers, non-commissioned officers and troops of the navy, the Prussian army and Federal troops. I expect of them that, until there is a new order for the German Empire, they will assist those who actually hold power in Germany to protect the German people against the imminent dangers of anarchy, famine and foreign domination.[2]

Contrast this comprehensive abdication "for all time to come" with the "Verzichtserklärung" or Declaration of Renunciation signed on 11 November by Charles I, emperor of Austria, Charles IV, king of Hungary (1887–1922), of which this is the relevant passage:

> The people's representatives have taken over the government. I renounce any participation in state affairs. I simultaneously release My Austrian government from office.[3]

Charles does not abdicate in this document and indeed refused to do so, and, unlike William II, he does not release his civil servants or military personnel from their oath of allegiance. Two days later, in the Habsburg hunting lodge of Eckartsau to the east of Vienna, where he and his family had taken refuge, he signed a very similar declaration with respect to Hungary, agreeing not to take part in the affairs of state in the kingdom but again without abdicating. These two very different renunciations of a throne illustrate the difference between the Habsburg and the Hohenzollern tradition, between Catholic and Protestant coronation ritual, and, in a volume about inaugurations and coronations, the difference between these two sorts of ceremonies. Charles cannot abdicate because he is the anointed king of Hungary.

William II and the Prussian Tradition

William II ascended the Prussian throne on 15 June 1888 by virtue of dynastic succession in the famous "Year of the Three Emperors," in which his father Frederick III succeeded his grandfather William I and ruled for ninety-nine days before dying of throat cancer. William II's beloved grandfather, William I, whom he sought to turn into a cult figure by naming him William the Great, had been crowned king of Prussia in Königsberg (modern-day Kaliningrad) in 1861. He was the first Hohenzollern to be crowned since the kingdom was inaugurated in 1701, when Frederick III, elector of Brandenburg, traveled to Königsberg to become "king in Prussia."[4]

This first coronation is described in detail by the "Ceremonienmeister" or Lord High Chamberlain Johann von Besser (1674–1729), who was responsible for the arrangements.[5] The title of his account tells the reader that the king accepted the royal dignity, which he himself had created, but that through the unction, he and his consort were consecrated king and queen ("Durch die Salbung als König und Königin einweihen lassen"). He describes how the elector, a Calvinist ruling over a largely Lutheran population, first crowned himself in a secular ceremony in the Castle on 15 January 1701, and then, on 17 January, went to church for the ceremony of anointing.[6] We can agree with Heinz Duchhardt that the anointing was secondary to the coronation because when Frederick I went to church to be anointed, he was robed as a king and wore his crown. However, if the anointing had meant nothing, Frederick could simply have left it out. A recognized authority on ceremonial, Besser admits that in 1701, the coronation and the anointing happened the wrong way round and then goes on to describe the latter in great detail over eighteen folio pages of his account.[7] Frederick asked both the Calvinist and the Lutheran Senior Court Preachers to play the role of bishops in the anointing ceremony, and he had the chrism (the "Salb-Oel") poured into a precious ampoule of jade and placed on a golden plate. The officiating minister then poured oil over his own fingers and made a circle surrounding two crosses on the king's forehead and on each of his wrists. The minister asks the king to accept the anointing

> as a divine symbol through which God formerly, through his priests and prophets, confirmed to the kings that it was He Himself, God in the Highest, who had made, named and ordained them kings; and may the Lord our God hereby also anoint Your Royal Majesty with the Holy Ghost! So that You, as an Anointed of the Lord, may rule and govern Your people and kingdom with a cheerful, courageous and willing heart.[8]

In 1861, William I also crowned himself in Königsberg, but this time, there was no anointing. The official account explains that this was because it would only have been a repetition of the anointing undergone by Frederick I in 1701 on behalf of all Prussian kings.[9] Ten years later, after the three so-called wars of unification, William was proclaimed German emperor in the Hall of Mirrors in Versailles on 18 January 1871, the 170th anniversary of Frederick I's coronation as king in Prussia. The ceremony in Versailles was rather rushed and improvised, since Paris was still under siege and everyone present was in military uniform. This made William II's only inaugural ceremony, the formal opening of the Reichstag—the German Federal Parliament—in the White Hall of the Berlin Palace on 25 June 1888, a unique and important event. The German empire was now seventeen years old and all the ruling German princes of the Empire, led by Albert, king of Saxony, and Luitpold, prince regent of Bavaria, were present to acclaim the new young emperor, the head of their confederation, for the first time in the imperial capital. Also present were politicians—Prussian and Federal ministers and members of the Reichstag and of the Prussian parliament—courtiers, and army officers. William II planned a coronation as king of Prussia in 1889 and even had a new crown made for it, the so-called Hohenzollern crown, but this never took place. The only inauguration ceremony that he had, therefore, was that first opening of the Reichstag, a ceremony that was repeated each year thereafter. William II firmly believed in his own God-given right to rule, but his royal authority did not stem from a quasi-sacramental act as part of a church service, mediated by an ordained minister. When forced to step down by force of circumstance, he could and did do so, though of course unwillingly.

The Coronation of Charles I, Emperor of Austria, as Charles IV, King of Hungary

In contrast to the Prussian tradition, all of Charles's forebears were both crowned and anointed at some stage during their reigns. The Roman emperors, including the last of them, Francis II, were crowned and anointed. Francis was also crowned and anointed as king of Bohemia and king of Hungary. His son, Ferdinand I, was crowned and anointed as king of Bohemia, king of Hungary, and king of Lombardy-Venetia, as discussed by William Godsey in his chapter. Francis Joseph and Charles I were both crowned and anointed as kings of Hungary: the former nearly twenty years into his reign, as described by Judit Beke-Martos in Chapter 10, the latter in a great hurry on 30 December 1916, about five weeks after the death of his predecessor Francis Joseph on 21 November.[10]

The rationale for Charles's hurried coronation as king of Hungary in the third year of World War I was that, according to Hungarian law, royal assent was needed in order to pass the annual budget before the end of the calendar year 1916, and for this, Charles needed to be crowned. All the politicians and the important members of the Hungarian court had gone to Vienna for the old emperor's funeral, in which Charles, his wife Zita, Princess of Bourbon-Parma (1892–1989), and their six-year-old son Otto had walked behind the coffin through the streets of Vienna to the Habsburg burial vault in the Kapuzinerkirche. Hardly had the functionaries returned to Budapest than the coronation had to be arranged in a great hurry, while at the same time following the time-honored ceremonial in order to insure its legitimacy, using the traditional insignia of crown, scepter, and coronation mantle. Count Miklós Bánffy (1873–1950) has left a vivid account of Charles's coronation in the first part of his memoirs.[11] Patrick Thursfield characterizes Bánffy as "Hungarian magnate, politician, writer, designer, Transylvanian landowner, director of the state theatres from 1913 to 1918, and foreign minister from 1921 to 1922."[12] He was also the son of György Bánffy (1845–1929), who played an important ceremonial role at the coronation, while he himself was heavily involved in designing the decoration of the church. Bánffy describes the bringing out of the cloak of St. Stephen and of the coronation insignia, last used almost fifty years before, and their beauty and workmanship—the crown with its glowing enamelwork and hundreds of pearls, the scepter with its big crystal ball. He describes how everyone took their traditional Hungarian court dress and their jewels out of store, how the Coronation Church was decorated, with seamstresses working until the last minute, the officiating clergy in their vestments, the standard bearers, and the keepers of the regalia. He describes the appearance of Princess Zita, "both womanly and regal" in her long veil of white lace, and he relates how, when the king had been anointed and had returned from the altar wearing the mantle of St. Stephen, "a shaft of light shone through the window above the altar, a pale wintry ray but sunlight nevertheless, transforming the scene into a magical shining picture" at the very moment when Charles was crowned.[13] He goes on to evoke the glowing chandeliers "metamorphosing the multiplicity of ritual hieratic garments, the all-white brocades of the clergy's pluviales, the gold-embroidered mitres, the *infulaes* [sic], into one translucent, crystalline, unreal, angelic mist." He describes how Charles dubbed fifty veterans, many of them old, wounded, and ill, knights of the Golden Spur, before going out, wearing his crown and mantle, to swear the coronation oath in the open air in front of the people and then to ride up the coronation hill to slash with his sword to the four points of the compass. After the ceremony and the state banquet, those of sufficient rank and importance were presented to the emperor and empress in a rushed procedure caused by the fact that Charles and Zita wanted to catch the six o'clock train back to Vienna, where Charles felt that he was needed because of the war. Everything fell flat after that. The aristocrats and courtiers were exhausted from wearing their heavy garments and the even heavier diadems and tiaras all day, "every vestige of beauty and pageantry drained away," and it began to snow.[14] As can be deduced from the above, Bánffy was not only a man with a keen sense of theatre, he was also a novelist with a gift for vivid description. Charles was king of Hungary for not quite two years before he had to renounce the throne and go into exile in Switzerland. He made two attempts in 1921 to return to Hungary and reclaim the throne but was unsuccessful and was finally sent with his family to the Portuguese island of Madeira, where he died of pneumonia on 1 April 1922, still, in his own understanding and that of his wife, emperor of Austria and king of Hungary.

Pietas Austriaca

What has to be borne in mind when thinking about the Habsburgs is the overt and visible religious devotion known as the *pietas austriaca* that was part of the dynasty's self-definition.[15] This was particularly fervent during the almost seventy-year reign of Emperor Francis Joseph from 1848 to 1916, who had been brought up a strict Catholic by his mother, Sophia of Bavaria, and who was himself devout. Habsburg piety was visible in the public participation by the imperial family and the court in the major religious ceremonies of the Catholic church, such as Maundy Thursday and Corpus Christi. Charles and Zita were personally genuinely pious and fully aligned with Habsburg religious practices. The ceremony of anointing in Budapest will therefore have had for them a real religious force, above and beyond its political significance and emotional impact. As Godsey says in his chapter, "the holy oil that was a part of every coronation rite undergone by a Habsburg conveyed the dynasty's continuing Roman Catholic commitment," and "the consistent adherence to the rite of unction . . . set Habsburg rulers apart from Protestant ones." A Catholic priest who has been anointed at his ordination is anointed forever. He may be defrocked and forbidden to say Mass, but he is still in Holy Orders, for an anointing cannot be undone or negated. The same applies to anointed sovereigns, and we may speculate that this is the difference in our own day between British monarchs and those in the Netherlands or in Spain. The former are anointed and cannot abdicate or go into retirement (the only British king who did, Edward VIII, had not yet been crowned), the latter are inaugurated and so may stand down. As historians working in a secular age, we always have to remind ourselves that, in the periods we are investigating and in many territories, belief was the bedrock on which kingly authority, and therefore the relationship between monarchs and their subjects, was built.

Helen Watanabe-O'Kelly is Professor of German Literature at the University of Oxford and Emeritus Fellow of Exeter College, Oxford. Among her books are *Triumphal Shews: Tournaments at German-Speaking Courts in their European Context 1560–1730* (Gebrüder Mann Verlag, 1992) and *Court Culture in Dresden from Re-*

naissance to Baroque (Palgrave Macmillan, 2002). She has edited *The Cambridge History of German Literature* (Cambridge University Press, 1997), *Spectaculum Europaeum: Theatre and Spectacle in Europe (1580–1750)* with Pierre Béhar (Harrassowitz, 1999) and *Europa Triumphans: Court and Civic Festivals in Early Modern Europe* with J.R. Mulryne and Margaret Shewring (Ashgate, 2004). Her most recent books are *Beauty or Beast? The Woman Warrior in the German Imagination from the Renaissance to the Present* (Oxford University Press, 2010) and *Queens Consort, Cultural Transfer and European Politics 1550–1750* with Adam Morton (Routledge, 2016). From 2013 to 2016 she was the leader of the HERA-funded project: Marrying Cultures: Queens Consort and European Identities 1500–1800.

Notes

1. Christian Hattenhauer, *Das Heilige Reich krönt seinen letzten Kaiser. Das Tagebuch des Reichsquartiermeisters Hieronymus Gottfried von Müller und Anlagen* (Frankfurt, 1995), 185.
2. Wilhelm II's Document of Abdication: Wilhelm II.: Abdankungsurkunde als Deutscher Kaiser und König von Preußen," https://www.wilhelm-der-zweite.de/dokumente/abdankungsurkunde.php.
3. Charles I's Declaration of Renunciation: "Category: Karl I of Austria," Wikimedia Commons, https://commons.wikimedia.org/wiki/Category:Karl_I_of_Austria?uselang=de#/media/File:Verzichtserkl%C3%A4rung_Karl_I._11.11.1918.jpg.
4. Johann von Besser, *Preußische Krönungs-Geschichte, Oder Verlauf der Ceremonien, Mit welchen Der Allerdurchlauchtigste, Großmächtigste Fürst und Herr, Hr. Friderich der Dritte, Marggraf und Churfürst zu Brandenburg, Die Königliche Würde Des von Ihm gestiffteten Königreichs Preussen angenommen, Und Sich und Seine Gemahlin Die Allerdurchlauchtigste Fürstin und Frau, Fr. Sophie Charlotte, Aus dem Chur-Hause Braunschweig, Den 18. Januarii des 1701. Jahres Durch die Salbung als König und Königin einweihen lassen: Nebst allem was sich auf Jhrer Majestäten Preußischen Hin- und Her-Reise bis zu Jhrer Wiederkunfft und Einzuge in Berlin, und dem darauf erfolgtem Danck- Buß- und Beth-Tage zugetragen; Aufs sorgfältigste beschrieben, und im Jahre 1702. das erstemahl gedruckt* (Cölln an der Spree, 1702).
5. Heinz Duchhardt, "Die preussische Königskrönung von 1701: Ein europäisches Modell?," in *Herrscherweihe und Königskrönung im frühneuzeitlichen Europa*, ed. Heinz Duchhardt (Wiesbaden, 1983), 82–95. Strangely, Besser himself and his account are not mentioned at all by Duchhardt.
6. Karin Friedrich and Sara Smart, eds., *The Cultivation of Monarchy and the Rise of Berlin: Brandenburg-Prussia, 1700* (Farnham, 2010); Sara Smart, "Johann von Besser and the Court of Friedrich III/I," in *The Ideal Image: Studies in Writing for the German Court 1616–1706*, ed. Sara Smart (Amsterdam, 2005), 277–312.
7. Besser, *Preußische Krönungs-Geschichte*, 25–42.
8. Besser, *Preußische Krönungs-Geschichte*, 39.
9. Rudolph Graf von Stillfried-Alcantara and Rudolph Graf von Stillfried-Rattonitz, *Die Krönung Ihrer Majestäten des Königs Wilhelm und der Königin Auguste von Preußen am 18. October 1861* (Berlin, 1873), 105. This second edition was printed after Wilhelm I had been chosen as German emperor in 1871.

10. Hermann Meynert, *Das königliche Krönungszeremoniell in Ungarn* (Vienna, 1867); Arthur Graf Polzer-Hoditz, *Kaiser Karl—Aus der Geheimmappe seines Kabinettchefs* (Zurich, 1929); Christopher Brennan, *Reforming Austria-Hungary: Beyond His Control or beyond His Capacity? The Domestic Politics of Emperor Karl I November 1916–May 1917* (Unpublished doctoral dissertation, London School of Economics, 2012): http://etheses.lse.ac.uk/529/.
11. Miklós Bánffy, *The Phoenix Land: The Memoirs of Count Miklós Bánffy, Including Emlékeimböl—from My Memories and Huszonöt Ev (1945)—Twenty-Five Years (1945)* (London, 2003); Graham Gendall Norton, "The Budapest Habsburg Coronation of 1916," *The Court Historian* 9 (2004): 61–68.
12. Patrick Thursfield, "The Last Habsburg Coronation: Budapest—1916," *Contemporary Review* 268 (1996): 41.
13. Bánffy, *The Phoenix Land*, 43.
14. Bánffy, *The Phoenix Land*, 46.
15. Karl Vocelka and Lynne Heller, eds., *Die Lebenswelt der Habsburger: Kultur- und Mentalitätsgeschichte einer Familie* (Graz, 1997), 13–38.

Bibliography

Bánffy, Miklós. *The Phoenix Land: The Memoirs of Count Miklós Bánffy, Including Emlékeimböl—from My Memories and Huszonöt Ev (1945)—Twenty-Five Years (1945)*. London: Arcadia, 2003.

Besser, Johann von. *Preußische Krönungs-Geschichte, Oder Verlauf der Ceremonien, Mit welchen Der Allerdurchlauchtigste, Großmächtigste Fürst und Herr, Hr. Friderich der Dritte, Marggraf und Churfürst zu Brandenburg, Die Königliche Würde Des von Ihm gestiffteten Königreichs Preussen angenommen, Und Sich und Seine Gemahlin Die Allerdurchlauchtigste Fürstin und Frau, Fr. Sophie Charlotte, Aus dem Chur-Hause Braunschweig, Den 18. Januarii des 1701. Jahres Durch die Salbung als König und Königin einweihen lassen: Nebst allem was sich auf Jhrer Majestäten Preußischen Hin- und Her-Reise bis zu Jhrer Wiederkunfft und Einzuge in Berlin, und dem darauf erfolgtem Danck- Buß- und Beth-Tage zugetragen; Aufs sorgfältigste beschrieben, und im Jahre 1702. das erstemahl gedrucket*. Cölln an der Spree: Liebpert, 1702. Accessed 14 February 2020. https://digital.slub-dresden.de/werkansicht/dlf/81845/1/.

Brennan, Christopher. *Reforming Austria-Hungary: Beyond His Control or beyond His Capacity? The Domestic Politics of Emperor Karl I November 1916–May 1917*. Unpublished doctoral dissertation, London School of Economics, 2012. Accessed 14 February 2020. http://etheses.lse.ac.uk/529/.

"Category: Karl I of Austria." Wikimedia Commons. Accessed 14 February 2020. https://commons.wikimedia.org/wiki/Category:Karl_I_of_Austria?uselang=de#/media/File:Verzichtserkl percentC3 percentA4rung_Karl_I._11.11.1918.jpg

Duchhardt, Heinz. "Die preussische Königskrönung von 1701: Ein europäisches Modell?" In *Herrscherweihe und Königskrönung im frühneuzeitlichen Europa*, edited by Heinz Duchhardt, 82–95. Wiesbaden: Steiner, 1983.

Friedrich, Karin, and Sarah Smart, eds. *The Cultivation of Monarchy and the Rise of Berlin: Brandenburg-Prussia, 1700*. Farnham: Ashgate, 2010.

Gendall Norton, Graham. "The Budapest Habsburg Coronation of 1916." *The Court Historian* 9 (2004): 61–68.

Hattenhauer, Christian. *Das Heilige Reich krönt seinen letzten Kaiser: Das Tagebuch des Reichsquartiermeisters Hieronymus Gottfried von Müller und Anlagen*. Frankfurt: Peter Lang, 1995.

Meynert, Hermann. *Das königliche Krönungszeremoniell in Ungarn*. Vienna: Beck, 1867.

Polzer-Hoditz, Arthur Graf. *Kaiser Karl—Aus der Geheimmappe seines Kabinettchefs*. Zurich: Amalthea Verlag, 1929.

Smart, Sara. "Johann von Besser and the Court of Friedrich III/I." In *The Ideal Image: Studies in Writing for the German Court 1616–1706*, edited by Sara Smart, 277–312. Amsterdam: Weidler, 2005.

Stillfried-Alcantara, Rudolph Graf von, and Rudolph Graf von Stillfried-Rattonitz. *Die Krönung Ihrer Majestäten des Königs Wilhelm und der Königin Auguste von Preußen am 18. October 1861*. Berlin: Decker, 1873.

Thursfield, Patrick. "The Last Habsburg Coronation: Budapest—1916." *Contemporary Review* 268 (1996): 41–46.

Vocelka, Karl, and Lynne Heller, eds. *Die Lebenswelt der Habsburger: Kultur- und Mentalitätsgeschichte einer Familie*. Graz: Styria, 1997.

"Wilhelm II.: Abdankungsurkunde als Deutscher Kaiser und König von Preußen." Wilhelm II. Accessed 14 February 2020. https://www.wilhelm-der-zweite.de/dokumente/abdankungsurkunde.php.

INDEX

Aachen, 12
acclamatio, in Hungarian coronations, 106–8, 110, 293
acts of homage. *See* inaugurations
Albert and Isabella (archdukes), 171–73, 206
Albert of Saxony-Teschen (governor-general of the southern Netherlands), 174
Albrecht, Conrad Adolph von, 153–55
Alexander III (czar), 8
Althann, Franz (count), 259–60
Andrássy, Gyula (count), 292–93
Andrew II (king of Hungary), 285–86
Andrew III (king of Hungary), 286
anointing, coronation and, 68, 77–78, 252, 285, 304; healing powers and, 7–8. *See also* holy oil
Apostolic king (Hungary), 126, 128
Aragon, 40
Arenberg, Leopold Philip (duke), 202–3, 208
Armistice, World War I, 305
Árpád dynasty, 286
August II the Strong (elector of Saxony, king of Poland, grand duke of Lithuania), 148
Aulic Chamber (Vienna), 45
Aulic Council (Vienna), 12, 124, 131
Austria, 248; Archduchy of, 34; Galicia and, 225–27, 232–34; Lombardo-Venetia and, 265–66; against Napoleonic France, 16; Polish territory and, 223–24, 239. *See also* Lower Austria
Austria-Hungary, 16, 288, 291–92, 294

Austrian constitution, 290
Austrian emperor(ship), 15, 17, 288, 290
Austrian Empire, 151, 269, 290, 295, 305
Austrian hereditary provinces, 34, 41, 44–45
Austrian-Hungarian Compromise, 16, 290–92, 294, 296
Austrian imperial coronation, 269
Austrian imperial crown, 151, 259
Austrian Netherlands (Habsburg Netherlands,'southern Netherlands), 4, 180, 200, 206; Barrier Treaty and, 173–74; Brabant Revolution in, 174; Charles VI, 173, 176; constitutions of, 174, 199, 210–11; Estates and, 10–11, 173, 204–5, 207, 209–10; in Habsburg Monarchy, 201; Habsburg Monarchy on finances of, 202; iconography of, 179–80; inauguration books in, 179, 185–87; Joseph II in, 169, 171–72, 174, 178, 180–81; Leopold II and, 174–75, 178, 255–56; political communication in, 199; Pragmatic Sanction in, 201, 205; recurrent rites and ceremonies in, 178; Retroceded Lands in, 11, 169–70, 175. *See also* Brabant; Flanders; Gelderland; Hainaut; Limburg; Luxembourg; Retroceded Lands
Austrian Netherlands, inaugurations in, 32, 49, 168–81, 198; Estates and, 173–76, 178–81; first project of Maria Theresa's Brabant inauguration, 1740-1741, 203–7; Habsburg inaugural rites, 32, 176–78; Habsburg investitures, 177–80;

Habsburg Netherlands, 169–81; historical context of, 201–3; Leuven, Brabant and, 177; list of, 182–85; Maria Theresa, 174, 176, 198–201, 204, 207–12; order of precedence, public sphere and, 176–80; second project of Maria Theresa's Brabant inauguration, 1742-1744, 207–9
Austro-Hungarian Monarchy. *See* Austria-Hungary
Auswurfmünzen ("thrown" or distributed coronation coins), 120

Baden, Max von (prince), 305
Bánffy, Miklós (count), 308–9
Barcelona, 40
Barrier Treaty, 10, 173–74
Batthyány, Lajos, 100, 106
Bavaria, 9, 71, 148–50, 201, 260–61
Belgian kings, 24n60
Belgium, 15, 169, 181
Berndt, Johann Christian, 80, 92n77
Besser, Johann von, 306
Bohemia: Charles VI as king of, 150–51, 153; crown of, 30, 32–33; Ferdinand I and, 35; Ferdinand III, 41; Habsburgs and, 9, 123, 150–52; Hungary and, 32–33, 35–36, 131; Joseph I and, 44, 147–48; Maximilian II, Rudolf II and, 35; queens of, 248
Bohemian coronations, 4–6, 12, 49, 143, 145–46, 266; Charles VI, 7–10, 14, 141, 143–58; coronation medals for Charles VI, 153–54; coronation medals for Maria Theresa, 122–23, 132; *Costanza e Fortezza* in, 155–58; Habsburg counter-propaganda and, 150–57; Habsburg inaugural rites and, 44; Joseph I and, 44–45; Leopold I, 42, 146; Maria Theresa, 48, 122–23, 152; personal investitures, early modern, 46; Saxon and Bavarian propaganda and, 149–50; at St. Vitus Cathedral in Prague, 32; St. Wenceslas Crown in, 122–23
Bohemian Estates, 4–5, 10; Charles VI and, 147–48; Czech "awakeners" and, 15–16; Ferdinand I and, 35; Leopold II and, 49; succession and, 36

Bohemian lion, 153–54
Bourbons, 251
Brabant: Council of Brabant, 174–75; Duchy of, 12, 198–200, 209–11; Flanders and, 169, 173–75, 177, 179, 204, 207, 209; Francis II and, 251; hereditary sovereignty in, 175, 177; Joseph II and, 171; Joyous Entry of, 199–201, 206–8, 210–11; Leuven and, 177, 209; nobility and clergy of, 207; taxation of, 175–76
Brabant Estates, 10, 172, 174–75, 198, 209–11; Maria Theresa and, 202, 207–8, 210–11
Brabantine inaugurations, 177, 179, 181, 203; Maria Theresa, 198–201, 204–5, 207–12
Brabant-Limburg inauguration, 171
Brabant Revolution, 174
Bratislava. *See* Pressburg
Breslau, 37–38, 42
British Empire, 83
British Isles, kingdoms in, 38
Broers, Michael, 253
Bruges, 171–72, 176, 199
Brussels, 12, 174–75, 177–78; Estates and, 200; Vienna and, 169, 175, 178, 202–6, 208
Buda, 101, 103–4, 257, 288–89, 292, 294
Bukovina, 49, 224, 250
Burgundian Netherlands, 200
Burgundy, Dukes of, 199

Calvinists, 306
Cannadine, David, 14, 21n26, 251
Carinthia, 10; Ferdinand I and, 34–35; inaugural rites in, 32, 44
Carniola, 34
Carolingians, 68
Castile, 39–40
Catholic Church, 37, 108, 284–85, 293, 309
Catholic coronation liturgy (in imperial coronations), 70, 73–74, 82
Catholicism, 236, 251, 266
ceremonial science (*Zeremonialwissenschaft*), 9

Index | 315

ceremonies: enthronements, political relevance and, 37; Joseph II and, 7, 15, 17, 250, 254; Maria Theresa on, 123–24; public, celebrations and, 12–14, 262–63; renaissance of, 16; rituals and, 9–11, 13
Charlemagne, 78, 81–82, 266
Charles Albrecht/Charles VII (Bavarian elector, Roman emperor), 71–72, 148–49
Charles Alexander of Lorraine (prince), 121, 201, 202–4, 207, 209–10
Charles I (emperor of Austria), 304–5, 307–9
Charles I (king of England), 38
Charles II (king of England), 38
Charles III (Charles VI), 124, 128, 131, 144
Charles IV (king of Hungary), 305, 307–9. *See also* Charles I (emperor of Austria)
Charles IX (king of France), 38, 40
Charles of Austria-Este (archbishop of Esztergom), 259
Charles V (king of France), 2
Charles V (Roman emperor), 34, 70, 173, 265
Charles VI, 48, 70, 137n1, 207. Barrier Treaty of 1715 and, 10; Bohemian coronation of, 7–10, 14, 141, 143–58; Bohemian Estates and, 147–48; as Charles III, 124, 128, 131, 144; coronation medals and, 121–22, 128–29, 153–54; *diploma inaugurale* of, 104–5; election as king of Romans, 143; Elisabeth Christine and, 105–5, 152–53, 158; Estates and, 173–74; Frankfurt coronation, 143, 145; Habsburg Netherlands inauguration of, 173–74, 176, 179; Habsburg succession and, 148; heritage of, 9; Hungarian coronation, 46, 101–2, 104–5, 111–12, 128; inaugural ceremonies for, 35, 46–47; *Kaiserstil* during reign of, 14; Leopold II and, 11, 45, 101–2, 112, 176; Maria Theresa and, 119, 124, 128, 132, 144, 150, 158, 174, 179, 191n30, 201–3, 208, 253; personal investitures, 46–47; Pragmatic Sanction and, 150, 158; Prague coronations of, 145, 147, 150–51, 155; Spain and, 144–45, 157; Styrian inauguration of, 47–48; Tyrolean homage of, 46; Tyrolean inauguration of, 262
Charles VII. *See* Charles Albrecht
Charles X (king of France), 2, 247
Christian August of Saxe-Zeitz, 111
Church of St. Bartholomew (Frankfurt), 76–77, 82
Clark, Christopher, 8, 252
Collateral Councils (Brussels), 204
Colloredo-Mannsfeld, Rudolph (prince), 266–67
Cologne, archbishop of, 12
composite monarchy: coronations in, 29; Habsburg, 177–78, 200, 256, 267, 269; inaugural rites and, 29, 34; Spanish, 39–40, 178
Congress of Vienna, 240, 248, 261, 267–68
consecrations, 6–7, 75, 77–78
constitutional monarchy, 247, 261, 296, 299n34
constitutions: Austrian, 290; in Austrian (southern/Habsburg) Netherlands, 174, 199, 210–11; eighteenth-century inaugurations and, 49; Estates and, 261, 263, 267; Hungarian constitutional order, 284, 287–96; Hungarian coronations and, 283–91, 295; imperial coronation and, 73; Tyrol, 261, 263; written, 16–17, 181, 261, 283–84, 295
Convention of The Hague, 174
coregency of Francis Stephen, 205–6, 209
The Coronation (documentary film), 1
coronation ceremonies: coronation medals and, 120–21; Habsburg, 284; investitures in, 30
coronation mass, 75–79, 82, 100, 108, 293, 303–4
coronation medals and coins, 149–50; for Bohemian coronation of Maria Theresa, 122–23, 132; ceremonial acts and, 120–21; Charles VI and, 121–22, 128–29, 153–54; in Hungarian coronation of Maria Theresa, 124–26, 128–30, 132; for Lower Austrian inauguration of Leopold II, 256; Maria Theresa and, 14, 120–26, 128–30, 132; as political iconography, 122

coronation regalia, Habsburg dynasty, 72–73
coronations, 1–2, 12; Alexander III, 8; anointments and, 68, 77–78, 285, 304; Austrian, 269, 307–9; ceremonies, 30, 71–72, 120–21, 123–24, 284–86, 292; Charles V, 70; Charles VI, Leopold II and, 11; Charles VII, 71–72; in composite monarchies, 29; elections and, Roman kings and emperors, 69–72, 75, 143; elections versus early modern, 68–69; English, 38, 69, 252; in Enlightenment, 73; Francis II, 20n22, 79; Francis Joseph, in 1867, 16; Francis Stephen, 131; French, 15, 38, 69, 250; George IV, 8; Goethe on, 84; in Holy Roman Empire, 5, 9, 12, 45–46, 67–84, 111, 143, 303–4; homages and, 30–33, 46, 248; images of, 122; insignias, 151; Joseph II, 45–46, 67, 71; Leopold I, 42; Leopold II, 14, 71–72; Lombardo-Venetian, 4, 257; Medieval, Holy Roman Empire and, 70–74; Milan, 264, 267; Muir on, 2; as political spectacles, 73; Prussian, 6–8, 252, 306–7. *See also* Bohemian coronations; Frankfurt coronations; Habsburg inaugural rites; Hungarian coronations
coronations and inaugurations, 1–3, 7, 303; consecrations and, 6–7; Habsburg Monarchy, 2–3, 5–6, 8, 11, 177–78; Joseph II against, 250; in Prussia, 6–8; regional variations on, 6; revival of, 4; social status and, 13; societal changes and, 16–17
corporations, 12, 229, 233–34
Cortes, 39–40
Cosqui, Charles Henri, 208
Costanza e Fortezza, in Bohemian coronation of Charles VI, 155–58
Council of Brabant, 174–75
Council of Trent, 108
court culture, public sphere and, 14
Cranmer, Thomas, 7
Croatia, 35–36
crowning. *See* coronations
Crown of Aragon, 40
Cuvelier, François Gaston (count), 208

Czech "awakeners," 15–16
Czernin, Rudolph (count), 257

Deák, Ferenc, 291
Dessewffy, János, 103
Diego Félix (prince of Asturias and Portugal), 39
Diet of Pressburg, 124, 130
Dietzler, Johann Josef, 5
diploma inaugurale, 11, 100, 104–5, 112–13, 286–89, 292, 295
Diploma Leopoldinum, 49
Donner, Matthäus, 125
Duchy of Brabant, 12, 198–200, 209–11
Duchy of Lower and Upper Silesia, 37
Duchy of Styria, 48
Duerloo, Luc, 200
Durand, Guillaume, 110
Dutch Republic, 10, 173

Edward VIII (king of the United Kingdom), 309
elections: coronations and, Roman kings and emperors, 69–72, 75, 143; early modern coronations versus, 68–69; *Kaiserwahl*, 69; of Leopold II, 75; of palatines, in Hungarian coronations, 105–8
elective monarchy, 5, 83, 286–87
elector of Mainz, 69, 79
electors, in Holy Roman Empire, 69–72, 79
Eleonora of Mantua (queen of Hungary, Roman empress), 258
Eleonor Magdalene of Neuburg (Roman empress), 145
Elisabeth Christine (Roman empress), 105–6, 124, 144–45, 152–54, 158
Elizabeth II (queen of the United Kingdom), 1
emperorship, 15, 17, 69, 72–74, 81–82
English coronations, 38, 69, 252
English kings, 38, 69, 77
Enlightenment, 14, 73–74
enthronements, 17, 33, 41; ceremonies, political relevance of, 37; Habsburg practices as unique, 38; personal, of Leopold II, 48–49; social status and, 12–13. *See also* coronations; inaugurations
Erasmus, 7

Erbfürstentümer, 37–38
Erbhuldigung (homage), 30, 42–43, 248
Erblande, 36
Estates, 3–4, 8–9; Austrian Netherlands and, 10–11, 173, 200–207, 209–10; Austrian Netherlands inaugurations, princes and, 169–76, 178–81; Bohemian coronation of Charles VI and, 141; Charles VI and, 173–74; constitutions and, 261, 263, 267; corporations of, 229; Ferdinand I and, 34–36; Habsburg coronations and, 100, 145; Habsburg inaugural rites and, 12, 15, 34–37, 40, 47, 224, 248, 250, 252; Hungarian coronation and, 103–6, 109–13, 286–88; Hungarian monarch and, 285–86; Joseph II and, 174, 252–53; Leopold II and, 253–55; Maria Theresa and, 202–3, 205, 229–30; Pergen on, 229; Pragmatic Sanction and, 155, 205; taxation and, 175–76. *See also specific Estates*
estates-based society, 16–17, 284
Estates of Croatia, 35
Esterházy, Pál, 100, 105–6, 111
Esztergom, archbishop of, 100, 105, 107–8, 111–12. *See also* Charles of Austria-Este

Ferdinand I (Austrian emperor, king of Lombardy-Venetia), 248, 265–66; Milan coronation of, 264, 267. *See also* Ferdinand V
Ferdinand I (Roman emperor), 50, 307; Estates and, 34–36; investitures of, 34–35; as Roman emperor, 70
Ferdinand II (Roman emperor): Habsburg inaugural rites and, 41; Hungarian coronation of, 128; investitures of, 35–36; Maria Anna and, 148
Ferdinand III (Roman emperor), 41–42
Ferdinand III/IV (king of Sicily, king of Naples), 75
Ferdinand IV (Roman emperor), 42
Ferdinand V (king of Hungary), 284, 288–89, 292, 295. *See also* Ferdinand I (Austrian emperor)
Fête de la Fédération, of 1790, 79
First and Second Silesian Wars, 129

First Partition of Poland, 1772, 223, 225, 228, 233
Flanders, 11, 171–72; Brabant and, 169, 173–75, 177, 179, 204, 207, 209; Estates of, 10, 173–75; independence, 180–81; Maria Theresa's inauguration in, 1744, 174, 176, 179
Flemish inaugurations, 13, 170, 174, 176–77, 179
Foronda, Francois, 211–12
Forster, Georg, 73, 88n33
France, 16; Bourbons of, 251; Congress of Vienna and, 261; Germany and, 82; Habsburg Monarchy and, 30, 83; inaugural rituals in, 38, 43–44; Prussia and, 129–30
Francis I/Francis Stephen (Roman emperor), 15, 77, 119, 131, 205, 209–10, 248, 257–64, 268–69; Habsburg inaugural rites and, 263; Hungarian coronation, 258–60; in Hungary, 257–59; Joseph II and, 72
Francis II (Roman emperor), 4, 14–15, 46, 49, 266, 268, 304, 307; as Austrian Emperor, 15; Brabant-Limburg inauguration of, 171; Brabant taxation by, 175–76; coronation in 1792, 20n22, 79; Germany and, 81–82; Habsburg inaugural rites and, 251; Leopold II and, 83; as Maximilian I, 81
Francis Joseph (Austrian emperor), 16, 288–96, 307, 309
Francis Stephen. *See* Francis I
Frankfurt, 21n37, 33
Frankfurt coronations, 12, 80; of Charles VI, 143, 145; of Leopold I, 42; of Leopold II, 1790, 14, 71–72; Maria Theresa and, 131
Frederick August II (elector of Saxony, king of Poland, grand duke of Lithuania), 148–49
Frederick Christian of Saxony, 150
Frederick I (king in Prussia), 6–7, 252, 307. *See also* Frederick III (elector of Brandenburg)
Frederick II (king in/of Prussia), 6, 8; Silesian invasion, 119, 201, 204

Frederick III (elector of Brandenburg), 306. *See also* Frederick I
Frederick III (Roman emperor), 78, 81
French coronations, 15, 38, 69, 250
French kings, 6–7, 38–40, 43–44, 69, 77
French Revolution, 4, 74–75, 79, 89n39, 247–48
Freyenfels, Johann Johann Christoph von, 47, 58n83

Gabler, Freiherr von, 235
Gabriel Bethlen, 258
Galicia, 11, 49; Austria and, 225–27, 232–34; Habsburgs and, 223–25, 227–29, 232, 236, 239–40; inaugurations/homages in, 4, 223–24, 227–35, 239–40; Joseph II and, 226; Maria Theresa and, 226–32, 234–35, 239–40; Ottomans and, 239; Pergen in, 228–32, 234–36; Poland and, 228–29, 234, 237; Polish nobility and, 224, 232–35, 237–39; Vienna on, 225–27, 229, 234–35, 237–39
Galician Diet, 227
Galician Estates, 224–25, 227, 229, 236–37
Galician inaugurations, 4, 223–25, 227–40
Galician nobility, 225, 228, 233, 235–37
Gelderland, 179, 189n14
Genêt, Jean-Philippe, 211
Gennaro, Antonio Maria, 153
George III (king of Great Britain), 8
George IV (king of Great Britain), 8
German Empire, 82, 305, 307
Germany, 16, 33, 41, 81–82, 290
Gestrich, Andreas, 11
Ghent, 169–72, 176, 199, 209
Glassl, Horst, 238
Godsey, William D., 4–5, 10, 43
Goetghebuer, P. J., 170
Goethe, Johann Wolfgang von, 84
Golden Bull of 1222 (Hungary), 285, 287
Golden Bull of 1356 (Holy Roman Empire), 12
Golejewski, Ignacy, 235
Gorizia, 34, 37, 43
Gottesgnadentum, 14, 303
Gottlob von Justi, Johann Heinrich, 6
Graz, 43, 47–48

Grodziski, Stanisław, 238–39
Großer Opferpfennig (large offering pfennig), 125

Habsburg, István (archduke, palatine of Hungary), 105
Habsburg coronations: ceremonies, monarchy and, 284; coronation medals and, 120–21; Estates and, 100, 145; homages and, 30–33; inaugurations and, 2–3, 5–6, 8, 11, 177–78; regalia, 72–73. *See also* Bohemian coronations; Hungarian coronations; *specific topics*
Habsburg dynasty: Bohemian throne and, 147; coronation regalia, 72–73; *Gottesgnadentum* of, 14; Holy Roman Empire and, 71, 81; Hungary and, 101, 107, 113; Prague coronation of Charles VI and, 150–51; Roman Catholicism of, 251
Habsburg emperorship: coronation regalia, 72–73; German nation and, 82
Habsburg inaugural rites, 15, 30, 34–36, 44; Austrian coronation, 269; in Austrian Netherlands, 32, 176–80; Bohemian coronation and, 44; Central European provinces, 32, 39–40; coronations, homages and, 248; Estates and, 12, 15, 34–37, 40, 47, 248, 250, 252; estates-based society and, 17; European parallels to, 38–40; as facultative, 41–43; Ferdinand I and, 34–35; Ferdinand II and, 41; Ferdinand III and, 41–42; Francis I and, 263; Francis II and, 251; Habsburg Monarchy and, 30, 41, 251–52, 263–65, 269–70; holy oil in, 251; Hungarian coronation, 24n61, 257–58, 263; Hungarian Estates and, 252, 257–58; in Innsbruck, 263; investitures, eighteenth-century, 45–50; Joseph II on, 16–17, 250; in legitimacy, 47–48; Leopold I avoiding, 42–46; Leopold II and, 250–51; in Lombardo-Venetian coronation, 264–68; Lower Austrian, 5–6, 35, 41, 44–45; Maria Theresa and, 250; in Milan, 266–68; in Moravia, 41–42, 47; numbers of, 1526-1800, 33–34;

Index | 319

pageantry, between 1790 and 1848, 248–50; process, 34–38, 41; reciprocity in, 11–12, 46; in revolutionary era, 15–16, 248, 263; rulers or consorts personally undergoing, 249; rules discontinuing, 41; in Silesia, 37; succession and, 36, 45; Tyrolean inauguration, 261–63; *vivente praedecessore*, 45, 173; wars, costs and, 44

Habsburg-Lorraine, 33

Habsburg Monarchy: on Austrian Netherlands finances, 202; Bohemia, Charles VI and, 150–51, 153; as composite, 177–78, 200, 256, 267, 269; consecrations in, 6; *Costanza e Fortezza* and, 157; First Partition of Poland and, 225; France and, 30, 83; Habsburg inaugural rites and, 30, 41, 251–52, 263–65, 269–70; hereditary territories and, 236–37, 287; Holy Roman Empire and, 15; Hungarian coronations and, 109; Hungarian territories and, 287–88, 291; Joseph II, Hungary and, 102; Joseph II's anticeremonial stance and, 15; lands of, 2, 4, 30, 71; Ottoman Empire and, 79, 81; Poland-Lithuania and, 223, 226, 236; Polish territories and, 239–40; the Pragmatic Sanction and, 45–46, 144, 147, 158; southern Netherlands in, 201; succession crises, 45, 47–48; Vienna, 5–6, 9–11, 119, 144; War of the Spanish Succession, 147

Habsburg Netherlands. *See* Austrian Netherlands

Habsburgs: Austrian, 46, 49, 144, 177–78; Bohemia and, 9, 123, 150–52; on Bohemian crown, 123; coronations medals, Maria Theresa and, 120; counter-propaganda of, 150–57; focus on hereditary lands, 68; Galicia and, 223–25, 227–29, 232, 236, 239–40; *histoire métallique* of, 122; Hohenzollerns and, 305–6; Holy Roman Empire and, 15, 71, 78, 81, 252, 269; Hungarian coronations and, 100–102, 104–5, 107–10, 120–21, 129, 284; Hungary and, 100–102, 107, 113, 120, 132, 287–91, 305–6; *Königreiche und Länder*, 34; in Lombardy-Venetia, 265; Napoleon and, 257, 260, 265, 267–69; Ottoman Empire and, 130, 252; *pietas austriaca*, 309; Polish nobility and, 233–34; propaganda of, 130; reciprocity in inaugural rites, 11; Spain and, 144; Wittelsbachs and, 148–49

Habsburg succession: Bohemian throne, 36, 152–53; Charles VI and, 148; crises, of monarchy, 45, 47–48; hereditary, 104, 110, 223–24; inaugural rites and, 36, 45; Maria Theresa and, 45, 47–48, 201

Hadik, Andreas, 239

Hainaut, 179

Harrach, Friedrich (count), 202–3, 207–8, 211

Hartig, Franz (count), 265–67

Hautsch, Georg, 129–30

healing and supernatural powers, coronation rituals and, 7–8

Heraeus, Carl Gustav, 152–53

hereditary lands: Bohemian, 144, 147, 226; Habsburg emperors on, 68

hereditary monarchy, 81, 83, 101–2, 112, 286–87, 299n39; in Brabant, sovereignty and, 175, 177

hereditary provinces, Austrian, 34, 41, 44–45

hereditary succession, 36; of Habsburgs, 104, 110, 223–24

hereditary territories, 203, 205, 211, 225–27, 236–37, 257, 287

High Council of the Netherlands in Vienna, 203, 205–7, 209

histoire métallique, 122, 129

Hobsbawm, Eric, 251

Hoechle, Johann Nepomuk, 264

Hohenzollerns, 305–6

Holy Crown of Hungary/Holy Crown of St. Stephen, 1, 16, 103–4, 124–26, 128, 155, 259, 284, 286–89, 293, 308

holy oil, 251, 259, 266, 285, 304. *See also* anointing

Holy Roman Empire, 5, 9, 12, 35, 99, 151, 200; anointment and coronation in, 68, 77–78; Catholic coronation liturgy, 70, 73–74, 82; Charlemagne and, 81–82; communion, Habsburg kings performing,

78; coronation mass, 75–79, 82, 303–4; coronations in, 67–84, 111, 143, 303–4; decline of, 68; elections and coronations, 69–72, 75; electors in, 69–72, 79; Francis II and, 81; Habsburgs and, 15, 71, 78, 81, 252, 269; investiture of Roman king in, 67, 69, 83; Joseph I crowned in, 43; Joseph II's coronation, 45, 67, 71; Leopold I and, 81; Leopold II and, 80–82; love between emperor and subjects, 80–81; loyalty oaths in, 33; Napoleon and, 251; Roman emperors and kings, 67–84, 100, 143, 269, 303–4

homage of good wishes, 270

homages. *See* inaugurations

Hommel, Rudolph, 73, 82

Huldigung. *See* inaugurations

Hungarian Chamber, 103

Hungarian constitutional order, 284, 287–96

Hungarian coronations, 15, 24n61, 35, 41, 123–24, 143, 266, 285–86, 292; *acclamatio* in, 106–8, 110, 293; anointments in, 285, 304; archbishop of Esztergom in, 100, 105, 107–8, 111–12; banquet, 13; Catholic Church and, 284–85, 293; Charles I, 307–9; Charles IV, 307–9; Charles VI, 46, 101–2, 104–5, 111–12, 128; Charles VI, Maria Theresa and, 128; constitutional development and, 288–91; constitutional order and, 284, 287–96; constitution and, 283–91, 295; coronation church in, 112, 292–93; coronation hill, 125–26, 129, 292; coronation mass in, 100, 108, 293; coronation medals in, 124–26, 128–30, 132; *diploma inaugurale* in, 100, 104–5, 112–13, 286–89, 292, 295; ecclesiastical ritual in, 108, 110; election of the palatine in, 105–8; Estates and, 103–6, 109–13, 286–88; Ferdinand I, 35; Ferdinand II, 128; formal ceremony of, 123–24; Francis I and, 258–60; Francis Joseph, 289–96; Habsburg coronations, coronation medals and, 120–21; Habsburgs and, 100–102, 104–5, 107–10, 120–21, 129, 284; Holy Crown of St. Stephen in, 103–4; Joseph I, 130–31; Leopold Alexander and, 106–8; Leopold II, 101–2, 105, 112; locations of, 32–33, 103–4; Maria Ludovica, 257–60; Maria Theresa, 48, 120–21, 123–32; Maximilian II, 107–8; mid-nineteenth century, 284–88; palatines in, 100, 103, 105–8, 110–11, 293, 300n61; personal investitures, early modern, 46; Pressburg and, 100, 103, 105, 120, 132, 260; of queen-consort, 257–60; ritual alterations of, 108–12; Romano-Germanic ordo in, 110–12; sword of St. Stephen in, 108–9; symbols in, 99–100, 108; in Székesfehérvár, 103–4

Hungarian Council, 103

Hungarian Court Chancellery, 107

Hungarian Diet, 11, 100–106, 113, 131, 155, 257

Hungarian Estates, 10–11; Ferdinand I and, 35; Hungarian coronations and, 109–10, 112–13, 257–58, 286; Leopold I and, 101; Leopold II and, 101–2, 105, 109; Prussia and, 105; succession and, 36

Hungarian parliament, 289–91

Hungarian territories, 287–88, 291

Hungarian War of Independence, 288

Hungary, 1, 5–6, 9, 248; Árpád dynasty in, 286; Austrian-Hungarian Compromise, 16, 290–92, 294, 296; Bohemia and, 32–33, 35–36, 131; constitutional crisis, 289–90; constitution and, 16; crown of, 30, 32–33; Ferdinand I and, 35; Ferdinand V's abdication from throne, 284, 288–89, 292, 295; Francis I in, 257–59; Habsburgs and, 100–102, 107, 113, 120, 132, 287–91, 305–6; Holy Crown of Hungary, 124, 286–89; Imposed March Constitution, 289–90, 295; Joseph I crowned in, 43; Joseph II and, 102, 254, 284, 296n3; law in, 286, 298n22; Laws of April, 288, 291, 296; Leopold I and, 42, 101, 130; Leopold II and, 253; Maria Ludovica in, 257–59; monarchy of, 284–86; Ottoman Empire and, 101, 103, 287, 292; St. Stephen's Crown, 1, 16, 125–26, 128, 155, 259, 284, 286, 293, 308

Iberian Peninsula, 144–45
Ieper, 171–72
Imperial Coin Cabinet, 120
imperial crowns, 1, 30, 78, 259
imperial diets, 99
Imposed March Constitution, 289–90, 295
inauguration books, 13, 179, 185–87, 199
inaugurations (acclamations/acts of homage/homages/Huldigungen), 8, 15–16, 30–35, 42–44, 50, 303; Brabantine, 177, 179, 181, 198–201, 203–5, 207–12; in Carinthia, 10, 32, 44; of Charles VI, 46–47; composite monarchy and, 29, 34; constitutions and, eighteenth century, 49; coronations and, 30–33; of Ferdinand I, 34–35; of Ferdinand II, 35–36; Flemish, 13, 170, 174, 176–77, 179; of Francis I, in Tyrol, 261–62; of French kings, 38, 43–44; in Galicia, 4, 32, 49, 223–24, 227–40; Joseph II, in Hainaut, 179; Leopold II, 48–49, 248, 253–54; in Lower Austria, 5–6, 30–32, 42–44, 248, 253–54, 256; in Moravia, 30, 32, 48; negotiations between princes and Estates, 173–76; number of, 1526-1800, 33–34; in revolutionary era, 247–48; in Spain, 39; in Styria, 42–43; symbolic communication in Burgundian Netherlands, 200; Tyrolean, 4, 15, 46, 48–49, 251, 260–64, 268; in Upper Austria, 42. *See also* Austrian Netherlands, inaugurations in; coronations and inaugurations; Habsburg inaugural rites; *specific topics*
Inner Austrian provinces, 41–43, 47
Innsbruck, 262–63, 266
Innviertel, 224
Italy, 8–9, 262, 265–67

Jackson, Richard A., 2, 38
James VI/I (king of England and Scotland), 38
Jesuits, 231
Jointe pour les affaires de l'Inauguration de Marie-Thérèse, 204–7
Joseph August of Saxony, 150

Joseph I, 31, 77, 144; archduke, 101; Bohemia and, 44, 147–48; *diploma inaugurale* of, 104; Hungarian coronation medals for, 129–30; Hungarian coronation of, 130–31; Hungarian Estates and, 101–2; investitures avoided by, 43–45
Joseph II, 4–5, 7, 9, 106; anticeremonial stance of, 15, 17, 250, 254; Austrian Netherlands and, 169, 171–72, 174, 178, 180–81; coronation, as king of the Romans, 45, 67, 71; against coronations and inaugurations, 250; Estates and, 174, 252–53; Flemish inauguration of, 170, 176–77; Francis I and, 72; on Habsburg inaugural rites, 16–17, 250; Hungary and, 102, 254, 284, 296n3; inauguration in Hainaut, 179; Leopold II and, 9, 49, 75, 250, 252–55; Lower Austria and, 252–55; Maria Theresa and, 226–28, 230–31, 250; Patent of Toleration of 1781, 236; personal investitures avoided by, 46
Joyous Entry of Brabant, 199–201, 206–8, 210–11
juramentos, 39–40

Kaiserhuldigungen, 33
Kaiserstil, 14
Kantorowicz, Ernst H., 68–69
Kaunitz, Maximilian Ulrich von (count), 47
Kaunitz-Rietberg, Wenzel Anton (count/prince, state chancellor), 20n22, 79, 227–28, 234
Kertzer, David I., 252, 256, 262
Kicki, Jan, 232
Kingdom of Bohemia, 9, 16, 152, 156–57
Kingdom of Galicia-Lodomeria, 225, 227, 235
Kingdom of Hungary, 101–2, 128, 287, 295, 305
Klagenfurt, 10, 32
König, Johann Ulrich, 149
Königsberg coronation, of William I, 16, 306–7
Königsegg-Erps, Karl Ferdinand (count), 206, 209

Lauffer, Lazar Gottlieb, 129–30
Laws of April, Hungary, 288, 291, 296
LeCaine Agnew, Hugh, 15
Lecuppre-Desjardin, Élodie, 199
Lemberg, 228, 230–31, 233
Leopold Alexander (archduke, palatine of Hungary), 13, 106–8
Leopold I (king of the Belgians), 181
Leopold I (Roman emperor), 35, 126; Bohemian coronation of, 42, 146; Habsburg inaugural rites and, 42–46; Holy Roman Empire and, 81; Hungary and, 42, 101, 130; Margaret Theresa and, 148; Moravia and, 41–43, 45
Leopold II (Roman emperor), 4, 11, 45, 101–2, 112, 176; Austrian Netherlands and, 255–56; Buda and, 103–4; coronation mass of, 76–77; *diploma inaugurale* of, 105; election of, 75; Estates and, 253–55; Francis II and, 83; Frankfurt coronation in 1790, 14, 71–72; Frederick III and, 81; Habsburg inaugural rites and, 250–51; Holy Roman Empire and, 80–82; homages, 48–49, 248, 253–54; Hungarian Estates and, 101–2, 105, 109; Hungary and, 253; inaugurations in Gelderland, 1791, 179; inaugurations in Lower Austria, 250, 252, 254–55; inaugurations in the Habsburg Netherlands, 174–75, 178; Joseph II and, 9, 49, 75, 250, 252–55; Leopold Alexander and, 107; Maria Theresa and, 250, 253; Moravia and, 49; personal enthronements of, 48–49; Prague coronation of, 263
Leopold Johann (archduke), 147, 150
Leuven, 177, 209
Limburg, 175, 209
lit de justice, 29, 38, 43–44
Lobkowitz (prince), 12
Lokalhuldigungen, 33
Lombardo-Venetian coronation, 4, 257, 264–68
Lombardy-Venetia, 248, 251, 261, 265–68
London Tower, 1
Louis-Philippe (king of France), 83
Louis XIII (king of France), 38–39
Louis XIV (king of France), 39, 122, 144, 169
Louis XVI (king of France), 7, 75, 250
Louis XVIII (king of France), 261
Low Countries, 172
Lower Austria: Joseph II and, 252–55; Vienna and, 31–32, 254–55
Lower Austrian Estates, 10, 31, 253, 256–57
Lower Austrian inauguration, 5–6, 30–32, 35, 41–45, 47, 253–54, 260; of Leopold II, 250, 252, 254–55
Luebke, David M., 13
Lutherans, 306
Luxembourg inauguration in 1717, 176
L'viv. *See* Lemberg
Lwów. *See* Lemberg

Mainz: archbishop of, 12, 111; elector of, 69, 79
March Constitution, Hungary, 289–90, 295
Margaret Theresa (Roman empress), 148
Maria Amalia (archduchess, electress of Bavaria), 148–49, 158
Maria Anna (archduchess consort), 148
Maria Anna (archduchess, daughter of Charles VI), 145, 150
Maria Anna (archduchess, daughter of Maria Theresa), 122
Maria Anna (archduchess, electress of Bavaria), 148
Maria Carolina (archduchess, queen of Naples and Sicily), 75
Maria Elisabeth (archduchess, daughter of Leopold I), 201–3, 205, 207
Maria Elisabeth (archduchess, daughter of Maria Theresa), 48–49
Maria Josepha (archduchess, electress of Saxony, queen consort of Poland), 148–50
Maria Ludovica (queen of Hungary), 257–60
Maria Theresa, 5, 9, 14, 20n25, 75, 106; Aulic Council and, 131; Bohemian coronation of, 48, 122–23, 132, 152; Brabant Estates and, 202, 207–8, 210–11; Brabantine inauguration of, 198–201, 204–5, 207–12; on ceremony

procedures, 123–24; Charles VI and, 119, 124, 128, 132, 144, 150, 158, 174, 179, 191n30, 201–3, 208, 253; at coronation hill, 125–26, 129; coronation medals and coins of, 14, 120–26, 128–30, 132; coronation paintings of, 73; crowned as "king" of Hungary, 123–24; Duke of Arenberg and, 203; Estates and, 202–3, 205, 229–30; Flanders inauguration, 1744, 174, 176, 179; flexibility of identities, 119–20; Francis Stephen and, 205, 209–10; Frankfurt coronation of, 131; Galicia and, 226–32, 234–35, 239–40; Habsburg inaugural rites and, 250; Habsburg Netherlands inaugurations, 174, 176; Harrach and, 207–8; Hungarian coronation, 48, 120–21, 123–32; Hungary, Bohemia and, 33; Inner Austrian lands and, 47; *Jointe pour les affaires de l'Inauguration de Marie-Thérèse*, 204–7; Joseph II and, 226–28, 230–31, 250; Leopold II and, 250, 253; Maria Elisabeth and, 201–3, 205, 207; Moravian *Huldigung* for, 48–49; name day of, 146; Old Testament figures and, 126, 128; personal investitures and, 47–48; Pragmatic Sanction and, 205–6, 231; provincial Estates and, 202–3, 206–7; Silesian inauguration and, 49; succession of, 45, 47–48, 201
Marquis of Condorcet, 6–7
Matthias (Roman emperor), 35
Maximilian I (Roman emperor), 81
Maximilian II (Roman emperor), 35, 37, 107–8, 123–24
Mazzini, Giuseppe, 268
Medici, Catherine de' (queen of France), 38
Metternich-Winneburg, Klemens Wenzel Nepomuk Lothar (prince), 67, 84, 88n28
Meytens, Martin van, 73
Milan, 8–9, 39, 264, 266–68
Military Frontier, 11
Mittrowsky (grand aulic chancellor), 266
monarchy: Austro-Hungarian, 16, 291–92, 294; authority, in Austrian rule, 14; constitutional, 247, 261, 296, 299n34; elective, 5, 83, 286–87; French, royal entries into cities, 38; hereditary, 81, 83, 101–2, 112, 175, 177, 286–87, 299n39; Hungary, 284–86; parliamentary, 15–16; public ceremonials and, 262–63; in revolutionary era, 15–16; Spanish, 39–40, 178. *See also* composite monarchy; Habsburg Monarchy
Moravia: Ferdinand III's inauguration in, 41; Habsburg inaugural rites canceled, 41–42, 47; homage ceremonies in, 30, 32; *Huldigung* for Maria Theresa, 48–49; Leopold I and, 41–43, 45; Leopold II and, 49; personal investiture in, 37
Moravian Estates, 35, 41, 49–50
Muir, Edward, 2, 17, 255
Mustafa Pasha, Kara, 101

Nádasdy, Tamás, 103
Napoleon, 15–16, 251; coronations of, 8–9, 265–67, 304; Habsburgs and, 257, 260, 265, 267–69; Maria Ludovica and, 257–58; self-crowning, 83, 252
Napoleonic Wars, 4
national identity, 14–15
nationalism, 17, 35, 82
Navarre, 40
The Netherlands, 15
Neuen von Neuenstein, Johann Carl Edler, 125–27
Nicholas II (czar), 2

Oláh of Esztergom, Miklós, 103
Opferpfennig, 125, 128
Order of St. Wenceslas, 15–16
Order of the Golden Spur, 108, 292–94
Otto I (Roman emperor), 149
Ottoman Empire, 11, 201, 208, 250; Galicia and, 239; Habsburgs and, 130, 252; Holy Roman Empire and, 69, 71; Hungary and, 101, 103, 287, 292
Ovid, 128

the Palatinate, 71
Pálffy, Géza, 2, 109
Pálffy, János, 106
Pálffy, Miklós, 105–6
parliamentary monarchies, 15–16

Patent of Toleration of 1781, 236
Patin, Charles Philippe de (viscount), 206
patriotism, 15–16, 82
Peace of Augsburg, 1555, 70
Peace of Westphalia, 1648, 81
Pergen, Johann Anton von (governor of Galicia), 228–32, 234–36
Pest, Buda and, 288–89, 292, 294
Peter the Great (czar), 2
Philip II (king of Spain), 39–40, 171–73, 210
Philip III (king of Spain), 39–40, 172
Philip of Anjou/Philip V (king of Spain), 40, 144, 157
pietas austriaca, 309
Pius VII (pope), 304
Poland, 252; First Partition of, 223, 225, 228, 233; Galicia and, 228–29, 234, 237; Kicki and, 232; Prussian territories and, 230; Third Partition of, 233
Poland-Lithuania (Polish-Lithuanian Commonwealth), 225–26, 228, 234–36
Polish Estates, 229
Polish-Lithuanian Diet, 234
Polish nobility, 224, 232–35, 237–39
Polish territory, 223–24, 239–40
political communication, 199–200
Pontificale Romanum, 110–11
popular sovereignty, 14
Portugal, 39
Pragmatic Sanction, 47, 102, 112, 119, 131, 148; Charles VI and, 150, 158; composite monarchy and, 269; Estates and, 155, 205; Habsburg Monarchy and, 45–46, 144, 147, 158; Maria Theresa and, 205–6, 231; in southern Netherlands, 201, 205
Prague Castle, 145–46
Prague coronations, 15–16, 32; of Charles VI, 145, 147, 150–51, 155; of Leopold II, 263; road to power and, 144–46
Pressburg (Bratislava): Buda and, 103–4; Hungarian coronations and, 100, 103, 105, 120, 132, 260; Reichstag of 1741 in, 124
Privy Council in Brussels, 204–5, 208
propaganda, 9, 14, 84, 130, 149–57, 211

Protestant Estates, 37, 41
Protestant secular electors, 69–70
Prussia: Bavaria and, 9; France and, 129–30; Frederick I and Frederick II in, 6–8; Habsburg Monarchy and, 223; Hungarian Estates and, 105; Hungary and, 305; parliament, 307; Polish territories and, 239–40; William II and, 305–7
Prussian coronations, 6–8, 252, 306–7
Prussian territories, Poland and, 230
public sphere, 14–15, 176–80

Raepsaet, Jan Jozef, 181
Rákóczi, Ferenc II, 101
reciprocity, in Habsburg inaugural rites, 11–12, 46
the Reformation, 74, 77–78
regnum Apostolicum. See apostolic king
Reichstag, 124, 307
Rentz, Michael Heinrich, 5
Retroceded Lands, 11, 169–70, 175
revolutionary era, 15–16, 247–48, 263
Richter, Benedikt, 128
Richter, Christoph Gottlieb, 125–26
rituals: coronation, 1–2, 7–8, 68, 71–74, 82, 84, 108–12; dynastic, 9, 16; ecclesiastical, 108, 110; historical settings of, 251; Leopold II and, 9; medieval, 32, 70–74; Muir on, 17; newspapers on, 16; as performative acts, 73, 254; propaganda and, 9, 14; *sacre*, 6–7, 247, 303; society and, 12–14, 16–17; symbols, Holy Roman Empire and, 99
Roman emperors and kings, 67–84, 100, 143, 269, 303–4. See also specific topics
Roman Empire. See Holy Roman Empire
Romano-Germanic ordo, 110–12
Roman Pontifical, 108, 266
Römerplatz (Frankfurt), 21n37
Rudolf II (Roman emperor), 35–37, 151

sacral body, of Roman emperor/king, 68–69, 83–84
sacre, 6–7, 247, 303
sacredness: anointments, coronations and, 68, 77–78, 285, 304; consecrations, 6–7,

75, 77–78; of emperorship, 82; holy oil and, 251, 259, 266, 285, 304
Sagan, 35
Salzburg inauguration, of Francis I, 263
Saxony, Bavaria and, 148–50
Schatzkammer, 1, 49
Schau- und Denkmünzen, 122–23, 125
Schierl von Schierendorff, Christian Julius, 45
Schönborn-Buchheim, Eugen Erwein (count), 257
Schulin, Philipp Johann, 77, 82, 88n27
Schwarzenberg (prince), 12
Schweidnitz-Jauer, 35
Schwengelbeck, Matthias, 2–3, 16
Scotland, James VI/I and, 38
Seilern, Johann Friedrich von, 110–11
self-coronation, 11; cf Frederick II, 8; of Napoleon, 83, 252
Settala, Luigi (count), 266–67
Seven Years' War, 49, 71, 129, 230
Silesia, 8, 32, 35, 37–38, 49; Ferdinand III and, 41–42; First and Second Wars, 129; Frederick II invading, 119, 221, 234; Joseph I and, 44
Silvester II (pope), 126
social contract, 14, 285
Soenen, Micheline, 199
Soly, Hugo, 178–79, 187n3
southern Netherlands. *See* Austrian Netherlands
Spain: Charles VI and, 144–45, 157; inaugural rites in, 39
Spanish Habsburgs, 144
Spanish monarchy, 39–40, 178
St. Edward's Crown, 3
Stollberg-Rilinger, Barbara, 12, 99, 177, 200
Strohmeyer, Arno, 37
Strong, Roy, 2
St. Stephen's Crown. *See* Holy Crown of Hungary
St. Vitus Cathedral (Prague), 32, 146, 150–51
St. Wenceslas Crown, 15–16, 122–23, 151–53, 155
Styria, 34, 42–44
Styrian Estates, 47–48

succession. *See* Habsburg succession
Suleiman I (Ottoman sultan), 101
sword of St. Stephen, in Hungarian coronations, 108–9
symbols, 99–100, 108, 177
Szapáry, Antal (count), 292
Székesfehérvár, Hungarian coronations in, 103–4

Third Partition of Poland, 233
Thirty Years' War, 37, 74
"thrown" or distributed coronation coins (*Auswurfmünzen*), 120
Thursfield, Patrick, 308
Timon, Ákos, 285
Tokarz, Wacław, 236–38
tourism, public ceremonies and, 13–14
Transylvania, 46, 49, 102
Trieste, 43
Turgot, Anne Robert Jacques, 6–7
Tyrol: Bavaria and, 260–61; homage for Charles VI in, 46; homage to Francis I, 261–64; homage to Leopold II, 48–49
Tyrolean inauguration, 4, 15, 251, 260–64, 268

Unction. *See* anointing
Union of Crowns (England and Scotland), 38
United Kingdom of the Netherlands, 181
Upper Austrian inauguration, 35, 41
Ürményi, József, 107

Versailles, 307
Vestner, Andreas, 129–30
Vestner, Georg Wilhelm, 153
Vienna, 1; Brussels and, 169, 175, 178, 202–6, 208; Buda and, 101; Congress of Vienna, 240, 248, 261, 267–68; on Galicia, 225–27, 229, 234–35, 237–39; as Habsburg Monarchy capital, 5–6, 9–11, 119, 144; High Council of the Netherlands in, 203, 205–7, 209; *Kapuzinergruft* in, 48; Lower Austria and, 31–32, 254–55; Maria Theresa and, 203–6; Pressburg and, 103
Voigt, Adauctus, 122

Voltaire, 7
Vushko, Iryna, 233

Wahlkapitulationen, 12, 70, 100, 105
Wandruszka, Adam, 9
War of the Austrian Succession, 74, 122–23, 179, 201, 211
War of the Polish Succession, 201
War of the Spanish Succession, 70–71, 145, 147, 173
Warsaw Diet, 223, 234
Wettins, Wittelsbachs and, 148–49
Widemann, Anton Franz, 123, 125
Wiener Neustadt, 255
Wiesiołowski, Andrzej, 233
Wif, Oluf, 149–50
William I (king of Prussia, German emperor), 16, 306–7
William I (king of the United Kingdom of the Netherlands), 181
William II (German emperor), 305–7
Wittelsbachs, 73, 84, 148–49
Wolshofer, Friedrich Wilhelm, 124
World War I, 305, 307–8
Wortman, Richard, 2, 8
Wratislaw Mitrowitz (count), 231
written constitutions, 16–17, 181, 261, 283–84, 295
Wrocław. *See* Breslau

Zaragoza, 40
Zeremonialwissenschaft (ceremonial science), 9
Zichy, Károly, 106
Zita of Bourbon-Parma (empress of Austria), 307–9

www.ingramcontent.com/pod-product-compliance
Lightning Source LLC
Chambersburg PA
CBHW071148070526
44584CB00019B/2711